Medical Negligence

AUSTRALIA
The Law Book Company
Sydney

CANADA
The Carswell Company
Toronto, Ontario

INDIA
N.M. Tripathi (Private) Ltd.
Bombay

Eastern Law House (Private) Ltd.
Calcutta

MPP House
Bangalore

Universal Book Traders
Delhi

ISRAEL
Steimatzky's Agency Ltd.
Tel Aviv

PAKISTAN
Pakistan Law House
Karachi

Medical Negligence

by

Michael A. Jones

B.A., L.L.M., Solicitor of the Supreme Court
Senior Lecturer in Law, University of
Liverpool

London
Sweet & Maxwell
1991

Published in 1991 by
Sweet & Maxwell Limited of
South Quay Plaza
183 Marsh Wall
London E14 9FT
Computerset by LBJ Enterprises Ltd.
of Aldermaston and Chilcompton
and printed by Butler and Tanner Ltd.,
Frome

ISBN 0–421–37680 5

A catalogue record for this book is available
from the British Library

For Annie

PREFACE

It is now widely accepted that the number of claims for medical negligence has increased markedly over the last 10 years or so, although there is less agreement on the causes of this phenomenon. The impact on the medical profession, particularly in terms of the increase in subscription rates to the defence organisations and allegations about the practice of "defensive medicine," has been widely canvassed. The impact on the legal profession has, perhaps, been less apparent. In the early 1980s there were few lawyers acting for plaintiffs with extensive experience of medical malpractice litigation. Defendants' work, on the other hand, was channelled through the defence organisations and health authorities to a small number of solicitors' firms who had the appropriate expertise. This imbalance between plaintiffs and defendants has, to some extent at least, been redressed, with the emergence of specialist firms acting for plaintiffs, and the establishment of Action for the Victims of Medical Accidents, which provides a support service for plaintiffs' lawyers and undertakes an important educational role.

This book is directed primarily at legal practitioners, though I would hope that it would also make the law of medical negligence accessible to non-lawyers. Medical negligence is an all-encompassing term. The major focus of the text is on the professional liability of doctors and other health care professionals, and on the organisations providing facilities for health care. On the whole, I have not distinguished between the liability of doctors and other health professionals such as dentists, nurses, or pharmacists (for an extensive definition of "health professional" see the Access to Health Records Act 1990, s.2). The legal principles applicable to their liability for negligence are essentially the same. Differences, such as they are, arise from the different roles of the professionals concerned and, where relevant, these are indicated in the text. *Medical Negligence* is principally concerned with the tort of negligence applied in the specific context of the provision of health care, but I have sought to deal with all aspects of professional liability which may arise out of medical treatment, and accordingly I have included discussion of contractual liability, the duty of confidentiality, consent to treatment, product liability, damages for personal injury and death, and some aspects of procedure.

I have concentrated on the law of England and Wales, though I have made frequent reference to Commonwealth caselaw, wherever appropriate, on the basis that as a general rule Commonwealth jurisdictions apply much the same common law principles to the question of medical negligence. The cases provide concrete illustrations of the relevant principles, and where there are differences they are indicated in the text (*e.g.* in relation to the Canadian law on "informed consent"). Canadian caselaw tends to dominate the Commonwealth material, but this is simply due to the fact that there is far more of it. There are also occasional references to American caselaw.

It is inevitable that lawyers specialising in this area of the law will tend to come across some of the worst aspects of medical practice. It is worth pausing, however, to reflect that by far the greater part of medical treatment is provided by highly skilled, competent and dedicated professionals. The lawyer's perspective can become distorted through the filter of aggrieved patients. It is also understandable that, as more patients have sued their doctors, an element of hostility towards the legal profession has become apparent within the ranks of the medical profession. This too may be the product of a particular perspective, which does not take into account the lawyer's corresponding duty to represent the interests and rights of the client/patient with skill, competence and dedication. That the professional skills of doctor and lawyer may sometimes lead to conflict is a matter for regret, but it should not diminish the high mutual respect and esteem that the two professions have long shared.

The team at Sweet and Maxwell has been patient and supportive throughout. I am extremely grateful for all their encouragement and hard work. Special thanks are due to my colleague Anne Morris, who kindly read the manuscript, prepared the index, and helped to compile the glossary of medical terms. Her assistance has been invaluable. I would also like to thank Bernadette Walsh, who cheerfully explained the intricacies of the Children Act 1989 to me, insofar as it affects consent to medical treatment of children. Any remaining errors, of course, are my sole responsibility. The task of writing a book puts a strain, not merely on the author, but on family, friends and colleagues. My thanks are due to all who endured the process with such fortitude, tact and charm.

The law is stated as at the end of July 1991.

MICHAEL A. JONES
Liverpool
October 1991

CONTENTS

ABBREVIATIONS

A.B.P.I. = Association of the British Pharmaceutical Industry
A.C. = Appeal Cases (Law Reports)
A.L.J. = Australian Law Journal
A.L.J.R. = Australian Law Journal Reports
A.L.R. = Australian Law Reports
A.R. = Alberta Reports 1977–
A.V.M.A. = Action for the Victims of Medical Accidents
aff'd = affirmed
All E.R. = All England Law Reports
Alta. Q.B. = Alberta Queen's Bench
Alta. C.A. = Alberta Court of Appeal
Am. J. Comp. Law = American Journal of Comparative Law
Anglo-American L.R. = Anglo-American Law Review

B.C.C.A. = British Columbia Court of Appeal
B.C.L.R. = British Columbia Law Reports
B.C.S.C. = British Columbia Supreme Court
B.M.A. = British Medical Association
B.M.J. = British Medical Journal
B.N.F. = British National Formulary
Build.L.R. = Building Law Reports

C.C.L.T. = Canadian cases on the Law of Torts 1976–
C.J.Q. = Civil Justice Quarterly
C.L. = Current Law
C.L.B. = Commonwealth Law Bulletin
C.L.J. or Camb.L.J. = Cambridge Law Journal
C.L.R. = Commonwealth Law Reports
C.L.Y. = Current Law Year Book
C.M.L.R. = Common Market Law Reports
C.R.M. = Committee on the Review of Medicines
C.S.M. = Committee on the Safety of Medicines
Cal. L. Rev. = California Law Review
Can. Bar Rev. = Canadian Bar Review
Ch. = Chancery (Law Reports)
Com.Cas = Commercial Cases
Com.L.R. = Commercial Law Reports
Conv.(N.S.) (*or* Conv. *or* Conveyancer) = Conveyancer and Property
   Lawyer (New Series)
Cr.App.R. = Criminal Appeal Reports
Crim.L.J. = Criminal Law Journal
Crim.L.R. = Criminal Law Review
Crim.R. = Criminal Reports

D.C. = Divisional Court
D.L.R. = Dominion Law Reports

E.A.T. = Employment Appeal Tribunal
E.E.C. = European Economic Community
E.G. = Estates Gazette

F.C.R. = Family Court Reporter
F.H.S.C. = Family Health Services Committee
F.L.R. = Family Law Reports
Fam. = Family Division (Law Reports)
Fam.Law = Family Law

G.M.C. = General Medical Council

H.C. of Aus. = High Court of Australia
H.L.R. = Housing Law Reports
Har.L.R. *or* Harvard L.R. = Harvard Law Review

I.C.L.Q. = International and Comparative Law Quarterly
I.C.R. = Industrial Case Reports
I.L.J. = Industrial Law Journal
I.L.T. *or* Ir.L.T. = Irish Law Times
I.L.T.R. = Irish Law Times Reports
I.R. *or* Ir.R. = Irish Reports (Eire)
I.R.L.R. = Industrial Relations Law Reports
Ir.Jur = Irish Jurist
Ir.Jur.(N.S.) = Irish Jurist (New Series)

J. *and* JJ. = Justice, Justices
J.P. = Justice of the Peace Reports
J.P.L. = Journal of Planning and Environmental Law
J.P.N. = Justice of the Peace Journal
J.R. = Juridical Review
J.S.P.T.L. = Journal of the Society of Public Teachers of Law.
J.S.W.L. = Journal of Social Welfare Law.
J. of Law and Soc. = Journal of Law and Society
J. of the M.D.U. = Journal of the Medical Defence Union

K.B. = King's Bench (Law Reports)
K.I.L.R. = Knight's Industrial Law Reports
K.I.R. = Knight's Industrial Reports

L.J. = Law Journal Newspaper
L.J.R. = Law Journal Reports
L.Q.R. = Law Quarterly Review
L.R. = Law Reports
L.S. = Legal Studies
L.S.Gaz. = Law Society's Gazette
L.T. = Law Times
L.T.J. = Law Times Journal
L.T.R. = Law Times Reports

Ll.L.Rep. = Lloyd's List Reports (before 1951)
Lit. = Litigation
Lloyd's Rep. = Lloyd's List Reports (1951 onwards)

M.D.U. = Medical Defence Union
M.L.R. = Modern Law Review
M.P.S. = Medical Protection Society
M.R.C. = Medical Research Council
McGill L.J. = McGill Law Journal
Man. C.A. = Manitoba Court of Appeal
Man. Q.B. = Manitoba Queen's Bench
Med. L.R. = Medical Law Reports
Med.Sci. & Law = Medicine, Science and the Law
Melbourne Univ. L.R. = Melbourne University Law Review
M.I.M. = Monthly Index of Medical Specialists
Monash Univ. L.R. = Monash University Law Review

N.B.C.A. = New Brunswick Court of Appeal
N.B.Q.B. = New Brunswick Queen's Bench
N.B.R. = New Brunswick Reports
N.H.S. = National Health Service
N.I. = Northern Ireland; Northern Ireland Reports
N.I.J.B. = Northern Ireland Judgment Bulletin
N.I.L.Q. = Northern Ireland Legal Quarterly
N.I.L.R. = Northern Ireland Law Reports
N.S.S.C. = Nova Scotia Supreme Court
N.S.W.C.A. = New South Wales Court of Appeal
N.S.W.L.R. = New South Wales Law Reports
N.Z.C.A. = New Zealand Court of Appeal
N.Z.L.R. = New Zealand Law Reports
N.Z.U.L.R. = New Zealand Universities Law Review
New L.J. = New Law Journal
Newfd. C.A. = Newfoundland Court of Appeal
Newfd. S.C. = Newfoundland Supreme Court

O.J. = Official Journal (European Community)
O.J.L.S. = Oxford Journal of Legal Studies
O.R. = Ontario Reports
Ont. C.A. = Ontario Court of Appeal
Ont. H.C. = Ontario High Court
Osgoode Hall L.J. = Osgoode Hall Law Journal

P. = Probate, Divorce and Admiralty (Law Reports)
P.L. = Public Law
P.M.I.L.L. = Personal and Medical Injuries Law Letter
P.N. = Professional Negligence

Q.B. = Queen's Bench (Law Reports)
Q.L.R. = Queensland Law Reporter
Qd.R. = Queensland Reports
Q.S. = Quarter Sessions
Q.S.R. = Queensland State Reports

R.S.C. = Rules of Supreme Court
R.T.R. = Road Traffic Reports
revd. = reversed

S.A.S.R. = South Australian State Reports
S.C. = Session Cases
S.C.C. = Supreme Court of Canada
S.C. of S. Aus. = Supreme Court of South Australia
S.J. = Solicitor's Journal
S.L.T. = Scots Law Times
S.L.T.(Notes) = Scots Law Times Notes of Recent Decisions
S.L.T (Sh. Ct.) = Scots Law Times Sheriff Court Reports
S.N. = Session Notes
Sask. C.A. = Saskatchewan Court of Appeal
Sask. K.B. = Saskatchewan King's Bench
Sask. Q.B. = Saskatchewan Queen's Bench
Stat.L.R. = Statute Law Review
Sydney L.R. = Sydney Law Review

Tas.S.R. = Tasmanian State Reports
Tulane L.R. = Tulane Law Review

U.T.L.J. = University of Toronto Law Journal

V.L.R. = Victorian Law Reports
V.R. = Victorian Reports

W.A.L.R. = West Australian Law Reports
W.L.R. = Weekly Law Reports
W.N. = Weekly Notes (Law Reports)
W.W.R. = Western Weekly Reports
Washington L.Q. = Washington Law Quarterly

Yale L.J. = Yale Law Journal

TABLE OF CASES

TABLE OF STATUTES

xliii

TABLE OF STATUTORY INSTRUMENTS

TABLE OF RULES OF THE SUPREME COURT

CHAPTER 1

MEDICAL NEGLIGENCE IN CONTEXT

Medical negligence is an emotive term: emotive for both doctors and **1.01**
patients. Lawyers, however, have to take a more dispassionate view
about the rights and wrongs of medical accidents. The tort of negligence applies an objective standard as a measure of professional
conduct, and although it is known as "fault liability," there is no
necessary correlation between a finding that a doctor was negligent in
law and a judgment that his conduct was morally blameworthy.
Mistakes are made in all areas of professional life. Some are negligent,
some are not; some cause harm, most probably do not. When Lord
Denning insisted that in order to reach the conclusion that a doctor
was negligent his conduct should be deserving of censure or inexcusable,[1] he clearly took the view that it should be more difficult to prove
negligence against a doctor. The converse of this proposition,
however, is that whenever a doctor is held liable in negligence his
conduct deserves censure. This has probably made it more difficult to
view negligence in the context of medical practice in terms of the
inadvertent slip, the error which almost anyone could have (and
probably has) made, and which though careless does not say anything
about the defendant's general competence in the practice of medicine.
On another occasion Lord Denning sought to characterise such mistakes as errors of clinical judgment and, accordingly, not negligent.
This view was categorically rejected by the House of Lords on the
ground that to state that the defendant made an error of judgment,
whether clinical or otherwise, tells one nothing about whether the
error was negligent or not.[2] One consequence, perhaps, of judicial
attitudes such as that of Lord Denning is that a claim for compensation
by an injured patient is often perceived by doctors to be accompanied
by denigration of the defendant's professional competence. This may
partly explain why the medical profession, of all the professions, is
most sensitive to allegations of negligence.

The process of identifying individual fault through the tort of **1.02**
negligence tends to overlook the wider issues involved in dealing with
medical accidents. While on the one hand it may be acknowledged that

---

[1] *Hucks* v. *Cole* (1968) 112 S.J. 483, 484; *Hatcher* v. *Black, The Times,* July 2, 1954.
[2] The disagreement occurred in *Whitehouse* v. *Jordan* [1980] 1 All E.R. 650, C.A.;
[1981] 1 All E.R. 267, H.L.; see § 3.51.

some accidents are inevitable, and indeed that some accidents through carelessness will always occur, on the other hand the tort action is not well-suited to identifying those accidents attributable to "organisational errors," or methods of delivering health care which equate cost-cutting with efficiency, and result in overworked staff, inadequate safety measures, and an emphasis on the quantity at the expense of the quality of health care provision. An action for medical negligence must focus on the particular accident. One of the strengths of the forensic process is the ability to dissect events in fine detail, although this cannot always achieve that elusive goal "the truth." But by focussing on the particular, tort cannot hope to address the broader question of how accidents might be prevented, apart from the notion that the threat of an action for negligence has some value in deterring careless conduct.

1.03 On the other hand, to concentrate simply on the general question of medical accidents obscures the significance of medical negligence as an ethical or moral issue. Doctors are familiar with the principle of non-maleficence ("do no harm") as an element of medical ethics. Normally the problem in applying this principle lies in identifying what is harmful and how it should be avoided, but these difficulties do not apply to negligence. Other things being equal, it is *always* better to be careful than to be careless if the consequences of carelessness are personal injury to a patient. Negligence is also a moral issue in that it is concerned with attributing responsibility and, in some instances, blame. To say that accidents are inevitable and that mistakes will always be made, though perfectly true, misses the significance that an injured patient may attach to having an explanation and apology for his injuries, and the satisfaction of knowing that steps have been taken to prevent a recurrence of the error. The evidence from organisations representing patients' interests, such as Action for the Victims of Medical Accidents, is that the absence of an adequate explanation is frequently the spur to litigation.[3] Information and accountability are seen as central to the needs of medical accident victims, and they are at least as important as compensation.[4]

1.04 A book on the law of medical negligence is not the place to enter what, in recent years, has become a somewhat heated debate about the problems surrounding medical malpractice litigation. It may be helpful, however, to identify the main themes of that debate to enable practitioners, whether lawyers or doctors, to see the wider context within which the law operates. There are three linked strands: (i) the suggestion that there is a "malpractice crisis"; (ii) the argument that doctors practise defensive medicine in response to this crisis; and (iii) the proposal that a system of no-fault compensation specifically for the victims of medical accidents would both solve these problems and

---

[3] " . . . the vast majority of the victims of medical accidents do not initially seek financial compensation but want an explanation for what went wrong, sympathetic treatment and, if appropriate, an apology": Simanowitz, "Medical Accidents: The Problem and the Challenge" in P. Byrne (Ed.) *Medicine in Contemporary Society: Kings College Studies 1986–7.*

[4] These concerns are also apparent in the New Zealand *Report of the Inquiry into the Treatment of Cervical Cancer*, 1988: see McGregor Vennell "Medical Misfortune in a No Fault Society" in Mann and Havard, *No Fault Compensation in Medicine*, 1989, p. 40.

provide a fairer and more efficient method of compensating injured patients.

1. A malpractice crisis?

It is not presently possible to identify the number of medical **1.05** accidents that occur each year or the number which result from negligence, because this information has not been systematically collected.[5] It is clear, however, that over the last 10 years or so the number of claims for medical negligence has increased. Between 1983 and 1987 alone the number of claims doubled, and this was accompanied by a substantial increase in the value of damages awards.[6] This was reflected in a marked increase in doctors' annual subscription rates to the medical defence organisations.[7] Whatever the reasons for this increase in medical malpractice litigation,[8] it provoked an outcry from the medical profession against lawyers, patients, the Legal Aid system, and the courts.[9] It was claimed that there was a "malpractice crisis" and that doctors were practising defensive medicine.[10] There were calls for the introduction of a scheme of no-fault compensation for the victims of medical accidents.[11] The response of government was first to reimburse two-thirds of defence organisation subscription fees for National Health Service hospital doctors (general practitioners had always been permitted to deduct subscription fees as a practice expense under the contract with the family practitioner committee), and then to take over the whole cost of hospital medical accidents (which is where most accidents occur) under arrangements for N.H.S. indemnity.[12] In the absence of any reliable information about how many injuries occur each year as a result of medical negligence it is

---

[5] This will change under the arrangements for N.H.S. indemnity in respect of accidents in N.H.S. hospitals by virtue of H.C. (89) 34, Annex B, which requires health authorities to supply annual returns to the Department of Health about the number and cost of claims for medical negligence, starting at May 31, 1990.

[6] Ham, Dingwall, Fenn, Harris, *Medical Negligence: Compensation and Accountability* (1988) King's Fund Institute, p. 11. This phenomenon is not new. In the 1950s Lord Nathan commented that the post-war years had seen a very substantial increase in the volume of medical negligence actions: Nathan, *Medical Negligence*, Butterworths 1957, p. 5. This was attributed to the introduction of the N.H.S., which had created a subtle change in the relationship between doctor and patient, to the introduction of the Legal Aid system which enabled impecunious patients to litigate, and finally to changes in the law on the liability of hospitals (on which see §§ 7.03–7.08).

[7] In 1977 the cost of subscription to a medical defence organisation (the Medical Defence Union or the Medical Protection Society) was £40. By 1988 this had reached £1,080.

[8] For discussion of possible reasons see Ham, Dingwall, Fenn and Harris, *Medical Negligence: Compensation and Accountability*, 1988, p. 15.

[9] See Jones (1987) 3 P.N. 43.

[10] Comparisons with the position in the U.S.A. were often drawn, implying that the U.K. would follow a similar path. The analogy is unhelpful, however, for many reasons: see Quam, Fenn and Dingwall (1987) 294 B.M.J. 1529 and 1597; Ham, Dingwall, Fenn and Harris, *Medical Negligence: Compensation and Accountability*, 1988, pp. 19–20. There is considerable dispute as to the causes of the American medical malpractice "crises": see Terry (1986) 2 P.N. 145; and the evidence now suggests that claim rates in the U.S.A. have been falling since 1985: Fenn, Dingwall and Quam (1990) 301 B.M.J. 949.

[11] See Jones (1987) 3 P.N. 83.

[12] See §§ 7.38–7.39.

impossible to identify what the appropriate level of litigation should be. It seems likely, however, that there are far more patients who suffer medical injury as a result of negligence who do not sue their doctors, than patients with spurious claims who do.[13] From the patients' perspective it could be argued that the malpractice "crisis" arises from too few patients being able to litigate, rather than too many doctors becoming defendants. In this arena perceptions are everything. It remains to be seen whether the new financial arrangements for funding medical negligence claims will change doctors' perceptions about a malpractice crisis.

2. Defensive medicine

1.06   Defensive medicine has to be viewed in terms of a reaction by doctors to the perceived threat of litigation. In *Whitehouse* v. *Jordan* Lawton L.J. said that defensive medicine consists of "adopting procedures which are not for the benefit of the patient but safeguards against the possibility of the patient making a claim for negligence."[14] This has two aspects: positive defensive medicine, which involves undertaking additional procedures, such as diagnostic tests and X-rays, which in the doctor's professional judgment are unnecessary; and negative defensive medicine, which involves avoiding procedures, which in the doctor's professional judgment are necessary in the patient's best interests, because of the risk of something going wrong. Positive defensive medicine, it is said, is wasteful of time and resources and possibly increases the risk to patients of medical intervention, and negative defensive medicine deprives patients of potentially beneficial treatment. It is important to appreciate that the term "defensive medicine" is used in a perjorative sense, to indicate that the risk of liability induces doctors to adopt practices which are not medically required or justified. The charge is that the law dictates medical practice, indeed, dictates bad medical practice.

1.07   The difficulty with the argument about defensive medicine is that as a legal concept defensive medicine does not make sense. The standard of care required by the *Bolam* test[15] is that of a reasonably competent medical practitioner exercising and professing to have that skill. This is essentially a medical test requiring medical evidence as to proper professional practice. If a defendant's fellow professionals agree that a specific procedure was unnecessary and wasteful, a doctor cannot be held negligent for omitting to carry it out. On this basis it is difficult to see how a doctor can *protect* himself from a claim in negligence by

---

[13] A California study in 1974 estimated that of 140,000 medical injuries, 24,000 were the result of negligence, but there were only 4,000 claims of which only 2,000 were successful: cited in Smith (1986) 293 B.M.J. 461. This suggests that the vast majority of negligence victims do not sue, even in the U.S.A. More recently the Report of the Harvard Medical Practice Study to the State of New York found that while 1 per cent. of patients suffered injury as a result of negligence, over 90 per cent. of these patients went uncompensated: *Patients, Doctors and Lawyers: Medical Injury, Malpractice Litigation and Patient Compensation in New York*, 1990.

[14] [1980] 1 All ER 650, 659.

[15] *Bolam* v. *Friern Hospital Management Committee* [1957] 2 All E.R. 118; see §§ 3.07 *et seq.*

carrying out an unnecessary test or procedure. If he could not be held liable for failing to do something, he could not protect himself from liability by doing it. Indeed, to the extent that the procedure carries additional risk to the patient a doctor increases the risk of a claim if something goes wrong precisely *because* the procedure was unnecessary. Moreover, under the *Bolam* test it does not matter that some doctors do regard the procedure as essential provided that there is a responsible body of medical opinion that takes a contrary view. The same argument applies to negative defensive medicine. If the procedure would have been performed by a responsible body of professional opinion, the doctor cannot be negligent for performing it (even where a responsible body of opinion would not have undertaken the procedure), and so he cannot "protect" himself by declining to undertake it, and he may increase the risk of a finding of negligence on the basis that he has failed to perform a procedure which responsible medical opinion considers to have been necessary.

Although the existence of defensive medicine as a sociological fact **1.08** appears to have achieved some acceptance in the English courts,[16] there is very little empirical, as opposed to anecdotal, evidence to support the theory that doctors do practise defensively.[17] Doctors may *say* that they practise defensively, but there is considerable scope for confusion as to what, precisely, "defensive" means and, indeed, whether it is detrimental to patients.[18] Some doctors use the term "defensive" simply to mean treating patients conservatively or even "more carefully." What to one doctor may seem defensive may to another doctor be good practice. Moreover, from the point of view of the individual patient, defensive practice, such as over-testing, may be positively beneficial if it discovers something previously unsuspected or even if it simply sets the patient's mind at rest, although it is arguably prejudicial to the N.H.S. because of the extra costs involved.

In any event, defensive medicine can only be relevant to certain **1.09** types of medical negligence. There is a difference between, on the one hand, the negligence involved in leaving a swab in a patient or removing the wrong kidney or prescribing the wrong dosage of a drug and, on the other hand, the conscious assessment of risk as between alternative procedures or the risk in not doing certain things. Inadvertent errors (which probably constitute the bulk of medical accidents) cannot be the subject of defensive medicine in its pejorative sense, since the doctor has not made a conscious decision to do or avoid something due to the risk of liability. Indeed, if he had thought about it he would have avoided the error. Moreover, insofar as the threat of

---

[16] See § 3.91. It was also assumed both to exist and to be detrimental to the consumers of N.H.S. care in the National Health Service (Compensation) Bill 1991, Sched. 2, para. 4.

[17] A commonly cited example of defensive practice is an increased rate of Caesarian section deliveries as a consequence of obstetricians fearing that claims in respect of birth injuries could arise from forceps deliveries or allowing a difficult labour to progress too long. Caesarian section rates have been increasing, however, in many developed countries with very different systems of health care provision and different patterns of litigation, and may be explained by factors which have very little to do with litigation: Ham, Dingwall, Fenn and Harris, *Medical Negligence: Compensation and Accountability*, 1988, p. 14.

[18] Jones and Morris (1989) 5 J. of the M.D.U. 40; Tribe and Korgaonkar (1991) 7 P.N. 2.

litigation may lead to the introduction of procedures which are specifically designed to avoid inadvertent errors, the law serves an important function in promoting good practice and preventing accidents. By definition, defensive medicine implies that doctors respond to liability rules, *i.e.* they modify their behaviour in response to the risk of liability. If the threat of liability were to be removed, as a consequence of, say, the introduction of a scheme of no-fault compensation, would doctors become less careful, or even careless? This is at least one implication of the evidence that was presented to the Pearson Commission by the medical profession.[19]

3. No-fault compensation

1.10   Increased medical malpractice litigation in the 1980s led the medical profession to call for the introduction of a no-fault compensation scheme specifically for the victims of medical accidents, amid claims about defensive medicine and criticism of the law of tort as a method of compensating for personal injuries and death. The problems with the action in tort are well-documented.[20] They include the following: (i) delay, which appears to be endemic in the adversarial system[21]; (ii) the cost of bringing an action, which is notoriously high, at least in relation to the sums recovered in damages[22]; (iii) limited access to the courts for injured patients, because the cost of bringing an action excludes many people from pursuing otherwise legitimate claims for negligence, and the financial restrictions on eligibility for civil Legal Aid mean that in practice only the poorest citizens qualify for assistance; (iv) success depends on proof of both negligence and causation (which can be particularly difficult in cases of medical negligence); (v) problems of proof making the outcome of legal proceedings unpredictable, and the effects of this can be quite arbitrary, some cases succeeding and others failing on grounds which may appear to have little connection with the substantive merits of the respective claims; and, finally (vi) awards of damages in the form of a lump-sum mean that if the plaintiff's circumstances change it is not possible to adjust the award, a situation which can result in either over-compensation or under-compensation.[23]

---

[19] *Royal Commission on Civil Liability and Compensation for Personal Injury*, Cmnd. 7054 (1978), Vol. I, paras. 1342–1343; see § 1.11.

[20] See the *Royal Commission on Civil Liability and Compensation for Personal Injury*, Cmnd. 7054 (1978) and the *Civil Justice Review*, Cmnd. 394 (1988).

[21] The most recent estimate put the average time from accident to trial at over five years in the High Court and almost three years in the County Court (*Civil Justice Review*, Cmnd. 394 (1988), para. 421). Delay in medical negligence cases tends to be greater, on average, than in other types of personal injuries action (*Royal Commission on Civil Liability and Compensation for Personal Injury*, Cmnd. 7054 (1978), Vol. II, Table 129 and para. 242), and individual cases of over 10 years duration are not unknown.

[22] The *Royal Commission on Civil Liability and Compensation for Personal Injury*, Cmnd. 7054 (1978), Vol. I, para. 83 put the administrative costs of the tort system at 85 per cent. of the amounts paid in damages, whereas the cost of running the social security system came to 11 per cent. of the total paid out (para. 121). The *Civil Justice Review*, Cmnd. 394 (1988), paras. 427–432, estimated that legal costs alone amounted to up to 75 per cent. of the sums recovered in the High Court and up to 175 per cent. of the sums recovered in the County Court.

[23] See § 9.07.

The problems with tort as a compensation mechanism apply to all **1.11** types of personal injuries action, whether the plaintiff's injuries were sustained on the road, at work or in a hospital, although in practice medical negligence plaintiffs often have a more difficult task in proving negligence and/or causation.[24] The Pearson Commission considered, and rejected, the idea of no-fault compensation specifically for medical accidents, although it was accepted that a change of circumstances might shift the balance of the arguments in favour of such a proposal.[25] The evidence from the medical profession to the Commission was overwhelmingly in favour of retaining the tort action. It was argued that:

> "Liability was one of the means whereby doctors could show their sense of responsibility and, therefore, justly claim professional freedom. If tortious liability were abolished, there could be some attempt to control doctors' clinical practice to prevent mistakes for which compensation would have to be paid by some central agency. It was said that this could lead to a bureaucratic restriction of medicine and a brake on progress. It was further argued that the traditions of the profession were not sufficient in themselves to prevent all lapses which, though small in number, might have disastrous effects. Some penalty helped to preserve the patient's opportunity to express disapproval and obtain redress."[26]

The Medical Defence Union commented that, although they paid **1.12** the compensation, their investigation into the circumstances brought home to the doctor the part he had played and encouraged a sense of personal responsibility.[27] By 1987 the British Medical Association had come to the view that what was needed was a non-statutory scheme of compensation which "within defined limits would provide compensation without apportionment of blame." The opening paragraph of the B.M.A. Report put the case succinctly:

> "As a caring profession we wish to see adequate arrangements to provide compensation and support to those who suffer personal injury, given according to need and not to cause. It is clear that patients with similar disabilities may receive different benefits under current provisions. A child may remain brain damaged following (a) encephalitis, (b) vaccine inoculation, (c) traumatic birth delivery. The needs of all three children may be similar. There will be great sympathy for all three sets of parents.

---

[24] The *Royal Commission on Civil Liability and Compensation for Personal Injury*, Cmnd. 7054 (1978), Vol. I, para. 78, estimated that about 85–90 per cent. of all tort claims that are brought are successful (although this represented only 6.5 per cent. of all accident victims in any one year), whereas only 30–40 per cent. of plaintiffs suing for medical negligence succeeded in recovering some damages (para. 1326). More recent evidence suggests that the success rate in medical negligence actions has fallen during the 1980s to approximately 25 per cent. Ham, Dingwall, Fenn and Harris, *Medical Negligence: Compensation and Accountability*, 1988, King's Fund Institute, p. 12; citing Hawkins and Paterson (1987) 295 B.M.J. 1533.

[25] *Royal Commission on Civil Liability and Compensation for Personal Injury*, Cmnd. 7054 (1978), Vol. I, paras. 1348–1371.

[26] *Ibid.*, para. 1342.

[27] *Ibid.*, para. 1343.

However, the available compensation will range through no compensation at all, through £20,000, to some hundreds of thousands of pounds. This cannot be legal, fair or sensible."[28]

While the moral force of this argument is undeniable, the statement is misleading since a no-fault compensation scheme would probably not change the outcome of this particular example. The child with encephalitis would not be compensated under any current no-fault scheme since illness and/or disease and congenital disability are excluded, and even the child with vaccine damage would probably not receive compensation under some no-fault schemes.[29] This highlights a major concern with any no-fault scheme for the victims of medical accidents, namely who would be eligible to claim?

1.13 The New Zealand no-fault compensation scheme, which applies to all cases of "personal injury by accident," has experienced some problems in relation to eligibility arising from medical accidents because of the difficulty of identifying what constitutes medical misadventure. An unsatisfactory outcome which is within the normal range of medical or surgical failure does not amount to medical misadventure. This excludes many injuries which in the true sense of the word are "accidental." An adverse reaction to a drug may be a known side-effect, in which case it is an inherent risk of the treatment, and so not medical misadventure. The scheme also has considerable difficulty in dealing with omissions to treat, because the damage or death resulting from errors of diagnosis and the consequent non-treatment may be characterised as attributable to disease or infection, and thus outside the definition of "personal injury by accident."[30] It is still a matter of some uncertainty whether non-disclosure of the risks of treatment, where the patient claims that he would not have agreed to undergo the procedure had he known of the risks, amounts to medical misadventure.

1.14 The Swedish Patient Insurance Scheme is probably more comprehensive than the New Zealand scheme, although it specifically excludes injury or disease which: (a) is a consequence of necessary risk-taking, from a medical point of view, for diagnosis or treatment of an injury or disease which if untreated is life-threatening or entails a risk of severe disability; (b) to a preponderant extent has its origin in or is caused by a disease in the patient (unless due to misdiagnosis); (c) is an unavoidable side-effect of a drug (a separate insurance scheme, financed by levies on pharmaceutical companies, applies to drug injuries); (d) was caused by an infection, where the treatment creates an increased risk of infection or is in an area which is bacteriologically unclean; and (e) does not cause more than 30 days illness, 10 days hospitalisation, or permanent disability or death.

---

[28] *Report of the B.M.A. No Fault Compensation Working Party*, 1987. The same point is made in the Report of the Royal College of Physicians, *Compensation for Adverse Consequences of Medical Intervention*, 1990, para. 3.3.

[29] In New Zealand if the injury were categorised as a known and foreseeable risk of the procedure it would not constitute medical misadventure for the purpose of a claim under the accident compensation scheme. The Swedish pharmaceutical insurance scheme, on the other hand, does cover injuries caused by known side-effects.

[30] See McGregor Vennell "Medical Misfortune in a No Fault Society," in Mann and Havard, *No Fault Compensation in Medicine*, 1989, Royal Society of Medicine.

The scheme proposed by the B.M.A. would exclude significant **1.15** categories of accidental medical injury, namely: (a) injuries which are a consequence of the progress of the disease under treatment; (b) diagnostic error which could only have been avoided by hindsight; (c) unavoidable complications, however carefully and competently the procedure was carried out; (d) infections arising under circumstances which made them difficult to avoid; and (e) complications of drug therapy carried out in accordance with the drug manufacturer's instructions.[31]

These restrictions on eligibility exclude injuries which can truly be **1.16** said to be accidental, and raise the question of whether such a scheme would compensate for accidental injury or would look for something equivalent to negligence. If "unavoidable complications," for example, are excluded then the test for eligibility is that the complication must have been avoidable, which might well be interpreted to mean avoidable with the exercise of reasonable care. The result would be that:

> " . . . the scheme would do little more than convert the negligence test into a statutory formula, thereby making it easier for the victims of negligence to obtain compensation, but doing nothing for those suffering medical injury from other causes."[32]

This illustrates the point that the problem of proving causation, which is frequently said to be a major hurdle facing a plaintiff bringing an action for medical negligence, will not be solved under a limited no-fault compensation scheme. A scheme limited to medical accidents must inevitably distinguish between injuries which are *caused* by a medical accident (however widely or narrowly this may be defined) and those which are not.

Accountability and no-fault

Lack of accountability, and a doctor's sense of individual respon- **1.17** sibility, were the principal reasons given by the medical profession for opposing the introduction of a no-fault scheme in its evidence to the Pearson Commission. There is little evidence that accountability to patients outside the tort system, through various complaint mechanisms, has radically improved since the 1970s. The Health Service Commissioner is specifically precluded from investigating complaints about the exercise of clinical judgment.[33] The procedure for hospital complaints that involve the exercise of clinical judgment is generally limited to complaints which are "substantial" but which are not likely to be the subject of legal action, and is conducted by two independent consultants.[34] General practitioners may be disciplined by the Family

---

[31] *No Fault Compensation Working Party Report*, 1991. The Report of the Royal College of Physicians, *Compensation for Adverse Consequences of Medical Intervention*, 1990, does not identify any eligibility criteria.

[32] *Royal Commission on Civil Liability and Compensation for Personal Injury*, Cmnd. 7054 (1978), Vol. I, para. 1366.

[33] National Health Service Act 1977, s.116, Sched. 13, para. 19(1).

[34] H.C. (88) 37, H.N. (F.P.) (88) 18 Annex B (first issued as part of H.C. (81) 5).

Health Service Authority only where the subject of the complaint amounts to a breach of the doctor's terms and conditions of service, which may or may not cover a particular question of clinical judgment.[35] The General Medical Council, which is the only body to exercise a disciplinary jurisdiction over all doctors whether in the N.H.S. or private practice, may discipline a registered medical practitioner who has been convicted of a criminal offence or is guilty of "serious professional misconduct."[36] A persistent criticism of the way in which the G.M.C. exercises its disciplinary powers is that it fails to deal with what by any standard is culpable conduct in the treatment of patients because it cannot be categorised as *serious* professional misconduct.[37]

1.18   Despite the evidence given to the Pearson Commission, the B.M.A. now questions whether a system of no-fault compensation "importantly diminishes the accountability of doctors."[38] This is not the view of the Royal College of Physicians, which accepts that a no-fault scheme could remove a source of medical accountability.[39] The Royal College recommended that a no-fault scheme should be accompanied by "a separate mechanism for the scrutiny of each claim in which doctors were involved to ensure that appropriate care had not been transgressed. If transgression is demonstrated, questions of professional discipline should be pursued." Although this recognises that the principle of medical accountability is important, it fails to address the point that the present mechanisms for accountability are inadequate. If transgression of "appropriate care" would result in the doctor being referred to the G.M.C. as it presently functions, it would only be the most flagrant instances of negligence that would be subject to accountability. Moreover, it has been claimed that the introduction of a no-fault compensation scheme would remove the deterrent effect of possible litigation, thereby tending to lower rather than raise health care standards.[40]

---

[35] For the detailed procedures see National Health Service (Service Committees and Tribunal) Regulations 1974 (S.I. 1974/455). The general practitioner's terms and conditions are set out in the National Health Service (General Medical and Pharmaceutical Services) Regulations 1974 (S.I. 1974/160), Sched. 1, as amended.

[36] Medical Act 1983, s.36. See also the G.M.C. guide to *Professional Conduct and Discipline: Fitness to Practise*, 1991.

[37] See, *e.g.*, Brazier, *Medicine, Patients and the Law*, 1987, pp. 10–14.

[38] Report of the *B.M.A. Working Party on No Fault Compensation*, 1991. It is argued that the tort action does not produce accountability because the worst cases of negligence never get to court, but are settled in private, with only the marginal claims being fought. The result is that there may be an unfair burden of publicity on doctors who may well have acted perfectly properly. This misses the point about accountability, however, which enables an individual patient to hold a doctor to account for his actions in law, whether this results in a settlement or a trial. The payment of compensation may be completely irrelevant.

[39] Report of the Royal College of Physicians, *Compensation for Adverse Consequences of Medical Intervention*, 1990, p. 21.

[40] Andrew Morrison, a Royal Society of Medicine Council member of the Medical Defence Union, in Mann and Havard *No Fault Compensation in Medicine*, 1989, p. 156. In New Zealand, where since 1974 the action in tort has been unavailable if the patient receives compensation under the no-fault scheme, complaints to the equivalent of the G.M.C. between 1974 and 1987 increased by 1800 per cent.: Dr. J.A. Wall in Mann and Havard, *op. cit.,* 1989, p. 72. There has been concern in New Zealand about the lack of accountability of doctors in the absence of tort litigation: Ham, Dingwall, Fenn and Harris, *Medical Negligence: Compensation and Accountability*, 1988, p. 23; McGregor Vennell "Medical Misfortune in a No Fault Society" in Mann and Havard, *op. cit.*, 1989, p. 40. See further Brown (1985) 73 Cal. L. Rev. 976.

Defensive medicine and no-fault

A no-fault compensation scheme would probably not change a **1.19**
doctor's defensive reaction to medical errors. The present tort system
has no direct financial effect on a doctor, since damages are paid by
the health authority or a defence organisation, and a negligent doctor
is not penalised financially. Thus, the deterrent effect of tort must be
linked to the perceived consequences of litigation on the doctor's
reputation. No-fault compensation removes the link between proving
fault and obtaining compensation, it does not remove "fault" from the
practice of medicine. Separating compensation from proof of fault
does not reduce the risk to a doctor's reputation if there is to be
genuine accountability. If a suitable system of accountability was
introduced along with no-fault, in which doctors who have been guilty
of blameworthy conduct are held accountable for their actions, doctors
would presumably still be inclined to practise "defensively" in order to
protect their reputation and avoid disciplinary proceedings.

Levels of compensation

The levels of compensation for patients under the no-fault schemes **1.20**
in operation in Sweden and New Zealand are very different. The
Swedish system opts for the same levels of compensation as tort
damages, but payments are comparatively modest because social
security benefits are high and the scheme is frequently merely topping
up the patient's pecuniary losses. The New Zealand scheme does not
attempt to replicate tort damages, but concentrates on compensating
economic losses subject to capping the loss of earnings element. Non-
economic losses are compensated at a very low level in comparison to
tort. The B.M.A. *No Fault Compensation Working Party Report*, 1991,
envisages compensation for loss of income up to a limit of twice the
national average wage, although it would seem that overall the
B.M.A. would aim at "awards about half the size of those which a
court would make in a successful action." From a patient's point of
view, the value of a no-fault compensation scheme must relate both to
the ease with which a claim can be made and the amount of
compensation available. If the levels of compensation were comparable with social security benefits, for example, many people might
prefer the tort action, with all its vagaries, for the chance of substantial
compensation.

Cost

Estimates of the overall cost of a no-fault scheme limited to medical **1.21**
accidents are little more than guesswork. There are three variables: (i)
how many claimants there will be; (ii) how much the average payment
of compensation will be; and (iii) how much the system will cost to
administer. There is virtually no information about either of the first

two variables, and thus costings are extremely speculative.[41] Administration costs are certainly likely to be lower, at least in terms of the percentage of compensation paid out, than under the tort system.[42]

Questions of principle

1.22   The deficiencies of the tort system have been apparent for a number of years. Moreover, most of the criticism which can be directed at the action in negligence as a means of compensating the victims of medical accidents applies with equal force to claims arising out of other types of accidents. It is not clear why no-fault compensation should be adopted for one, small category of accident victims to the exclusion of others with equally serious injuries sustained in other ways. In theory, the tort of negligence provides a conceptual basis for distinguishing between patients who are entitled to compensation and those who are not, in that negligence "identifies" an individual (or his employer) who is responsible in law for the inflicting of the patient's injury, and so in fairness ought to recompense the patient for that loss. This is not how the system works in practice, because it may not be possible to establish fault, and insurance (through the medical defence organisations and through N.H.S. indemnity) removes a large element of individual responsibility. On the other hand, the conceptual underpinning of a scheme of no-fault compensation rests on a theory of social responsibility for the victims of misfortune, namely those who suffer injury by "accident." It is not apparent why the victims of a particular type of accident (medical accidents) should receive compensation on a no-fault basis when other accident victims have to prove fault. This is particularly the case when only certain types of medical accident, those which qualify under the eligibility criteria, would be compensated under such a scheme. These issues become especially important when it is proposed to fund a no-fault scheme from general taxation to which everyone must contribute, whether they fall into the favoured category of accident victim of not.

1.23   The argument that the principle of no-fault compensation selects its beneficiaries on a fairer basis (namely "need" not "fault") than the tort of negligence is questionable. It selects them on a different basis, but it still draws arbitrary and unprincipled distinctions between those who will be compensated and those who will not. Clearly, the needs of a child with brain damage are no different, whether caused by congenital disability or medical intervention at birth. A no-fault compensation scheme would almost certainly provide compensation

---

[41] Ham, Dingwall, Fenn and Harris, *Medical Negligence: Compensation and Accountability*, 1988, p. 31, estimated between £177 million and £235 million, at 1988 prices. The B.M.A. *No Fault Compensation Working Party Report*, 1991, paras. 7.1 and 7.2, estimated a cost of £100.4 million, at 1990 prices, for the whole U.K. This was on the basis of awards at half the level of present tort damages, following a survey of claims rates in 10 per cent. of district health authorities in 1988. The Report did not attempt to quantify the possible increase in claims rates, but conceded that it was probable that there would be an exponential rise in the number of claims during the first decade of operating a no-fault scheme.

[42] See n. 22, *ante*. The administrative costs of the Swedish system are put at 16 per cent. of the premiums.

for more patients (depending upon how strict the eligibility criteria were), more quickly and more efficiently than the present tort system. It could provide readier access to compensation for patients who may not be in a financial position to sue; and it could provide for periodic payments so that the compensation reflects the patient's actual loss. On the other hand, if the problem is that too few patients succeed in recovering compensation because of the difficulties of proving fault, it would be possible to improve plaintiff success rates under the tort system by introducing strict liability and reversing the burden of proof.[43] This would also separate the question of compensation from the proof of fault.

No-fault compensation cannot stop doctors from acting negligently, **1.24** nor will it stop patients seeking to hold doctors to account for blameworthy conduct. Indeed, it would be strange if doctors were the only profession to be unaccountable in the courts. The Pearson Commission commented that " . . . there would have to be a good case for exempting any profession from legal liabilities which apply to others, and we do not regard the special circumstances of medical injury as constituting such a case."[44] The fact that during the 1980s patients have sued their doctors in larger numbers than ever before can hardly be considered a "good case," since this is true of every other professional group. Nor should no-fault compensation have any effect on the "malpractice crisis" or defensive medicine, except to the extent that these are problems of perception and a no-fault scheme might change the profession's perception of litigation. The claim that it is the law that is positively detrimental to the practice of medicine in this country cannot be accepted. When the rhetoric is stripped away, it is the tort of negligence that provides the bottom line: the *minimum* standard of acceptable professional conduct. In practice, medical negligence is a failure to live up to proper medical standards, and those standards are set, not by lawyers, but by doctors.

---

[43] The European Commission is considering a proposal which would have the effect of reversing the burden of proof in respect of the liability of suppliers of services for personal injuries: O.J. 1991, No. C 12/8, January 18, 1991.

[44] *Royal Commission on Civil Liability and Compensation for Personal Injury*, Cmnd. 7054 (1978), Vol. I, para. 1344.

CHAPTER 2

THE BASIS OF LIABILITY

2.01 The nature of the relationship between doctors and patients is determined largely by the practice of the medical profession, and shaped by a strong commitment to long-standing principles of medical ethics. The law plays a significant role, however, in providing a structure within which the doctor/patient relationship is conducted. Whether it is the civil law or the criminal law which is invoked, legal rules can only set the outer limits of acceptable conduct, *i.e.* a minimum standard of professional behaviour, leaving the question of "ideal" standards of practice to the profession itself. Some doctors seem to believe that the law sets too high a standard, which does not take account of the realities of medical practice, but the courts apply the same principles, whether they be from the law of tort, contract or equity, that are used for any other section of the community when disputes between individuals arise. Accordingly, the professional liability of medical practitioners is determined by the rules of tort, contract or equity.

2.02 In practice most claims for medical malpractice are brought in tort, and of these the vast majority are for the tort of negligence. This is reflected in the structure of this chapter, the bulk of which deals with the circumstances in which a doctor will be held to owe a duty of care in the tort of negligence. The chapter begins with a section on contractual liability which, in theory, governs the respective rights and responsibilities of patients and doctors in the private sector. It will be seen, however, that in practical terms there is very little difference between the obligations undertaken by a medical practitioner in private practice and those imposed on his colleagues working in the National Health Service. All doctors owe a duty to their patients to exercise reasonable care in carrying out their professional skills of diagnosis, advice and treatment,[1] and the situations in which a stricter duty will be applied are quite rare. In addition to the contractual or tortious duty to exercise reasonable care, a medical practitioner is subject to a duty of confidence in respect of information about his patients acquired in his capacity as a doctor, and this is dealt with in the final section of this chapter. With private patients the duty arises under the contract between doctor and patient, whereas in the absence of a contractual relationship the duty of confidence is imposed by

---

[1] The meaning of "reasonable care" is considered in Chaps. 3 and 4.

equity. This distinction has little relevance to the nature of the *duty* owed by the doctor, but it does have significant consequences for the remedies available, since there is considerable doubt, as to whether there can be an action for damages in respect of a past breach of confidence where the duty is non-contractual.[2]

I. Contract

Most patients treated under the N.H.S. do not enter into a contractual **2.03** relationship with their doctor or the hospital where they receive treatment, although it has been suggested that there is a contract between a patient and his general practitioner, since the addition of the patient's name to the general practitioner's list increases the doctor's remuneration under his contract with the Family Practitioner Committee,[3] and this might constitute consideration by the patient.[4] Patients receiving private medical treatment clearly do have contractual rights and may sue for breach of a relevant term. Since a doctor providing private treatment also owes a concurrent duty in tort to the patient, the patient's claim may be pleaded in both contract and tort, but in practice it is rare for much to turn on this, because the doctor's contractual obligations are usually no greater than the duties owed in tort.[5] The courts are understandably reluctant to draw a sharp distinction between the rights of patients treated privately and under the N.H.S. For example, in *Hotson* v. *East Berkshire Area Health Authority* Sir John Donaldson M.R. said that:

" . . . I am quite unable to detect any rational basis for a state of the law, if such it be, whereby in identical circumstances Dr. A

---

[2] See § 9.71. Where the patient has sustained personal injury as a result of the breach of confidence a claim for damages could be based on the tort of negligence: see *Furniss* v. *Fitchett* [1958] N.Z.L.R. 396.

[3] Family Practitioner Committees have been replaced by Family Health Service Authorities: National Health Service and Community Care Act 1990, s.2; S.I. 1990/1329.

[4] Jackson and Powell, *Professional Negligence*, 1987, 2nd ed., para. 6.03, n. 7; *cf.* the Royal Commission on Civil Liability and Compensation for Personal Injury, Cmnd. 7054 (1978) Vol. I, para. 1313, stating that there is no contract where treatment is provided under the N.H.S. Patients who pay a prescription charge for medicinal products supplied on prescription under the N.H.S do not obtain the products under a contract of sale, but by virtue of the pharmacist's statutory duty to supply them: *Pfizer Corpn.* v. *Ministry of Health* [1965] A.C. 512. Presumably, the position of patients who make a partial payment for services under the N.H.S. (*e.g.* for dental treatment) is similar.

[5] See, *e.g.*, *Thake* v. *Maurice* [1986] 1 All E.R. 479 and *Eyre* v. *Measday* [1986] 1 All E.R. 488 (where on appeal the claim in tort had been abandoned). *Edwards* v. *Mallan* [1908] 1 K.B. 1002 provides an early example of concurrent liability in the medical context. The recent trend away from imposing concurrent liability in both the tort of negligence and in contract heralded by the decision of the Privy Council in *Tai Hing Cotton Mill Ltd.* v. *Liu Chong Hing Bank Ltd.* [1986] A.C. 80, 107, and exemplified in such cases as *Greater Nottingham Co-operative Society Ltd.* v. *Cementation Pilings and Foundations Ltd.* [1988] 2 All E.R. 971, *Pacific Associates Inc.* v. *Baxter* [1989] 2 All E.R. 159 and *Norwich City Council* v. *Harvey* [1989] 1 All E.R. 1180, is irrelevant in the context of the doctor/patient relationship. These cases have sought to prevent the imposition, through the tort of negligence, of more extensive obligations than the parties to complex commercial transactions originally agreed to undertake in the contract. This issue simply does not arise in the case of private medical treatment, because the duty to exercise reasonable care in the tort of negligence is effectively the same as the implied term to exercise reasonable care in a contract to provide medical services. If anything, the stricter duties are to be found in the contract.

who treats a patient under the National Health Service, and whose liability thereby falls to be determined in accordance with the law of tort, should be in a different position from Dr. B who treats a patient outside the Service, and whose liability therefore falls to be determined in accordance with the law of contract, assuming, of course, that the contract is in terms which impose on him neither more nor less than the tortious duty."[6]

Where there are differences between contract and tort they tend to be minimised, which may partially explain the courts' attitude to strict contractual warranties in the medical context.[7]

1. Reasonable care

2.04   In the absence of an express term, a term will be implied into a contract to provide a service that the service will be performed with reasonable care and skill.[8] The standard of care required to satisfy this obligation is the same as in the tort of negligence.[9] The surgeon who contracts to perform an operation undertakes to carry out the operation with reasonable care; he does not guarantee that it will prove to be a success. If, however, he agrees to give the case his personal attention this means that he will perform the operation personally and pay such subsequent visits as are necessary for the supervision of the patient until the discharge of the patient.[10] Delegation of the operation

---

[6] [1987] 1 All E.R. 210, 216; see also, *per* Croom-Johnson L.J. at p. 222; and Sir John Donaldson M.R. in *Naylor* v. *Preston Area Health Authority* [1987] 2 All E.R. 353, 360d; *Gold* v. *Essex County Council* [1942] 2 K.B. 293, 297, *per* Lord Greene M.R.

[7] See §2.07. Nonetheless some technical differences between actions in contract and tort do remain, *e.g.* different rules on limitation periods (though special rules apply to actions for personal injuries in both contract and tort: see Chap. 10); different measures of damages; possibly different tests for remoteness of damage; possibly different approaches to claims involving "loss of a chance" following the House of Lords' ruling in *Hotson* v. *East Berkshire Area Health Authority* [1987] 2 All E.R. 909, see §§ 5.30 *et seq.* Moreover, there may be practical differences between the N.H.S. and private medicine which have legal consequences. See, *e.g,* the comments of Finlay J. in *Dryden* v. *Surrey County Council* [1936] 2 All E.R. 535, 539 on the different levels of staffing that could legitimately be expected in public and private hospitals.

[8] Supply of Goods and Services Act 1982, s.13; *Eyre* v. *Measday* [1986] 1 All E.R. 488; *Thake* v. *Maurice* [1986] 1 All E.R. 497; *Greaves & Co.* (*Contractors*) *Ltd.* v. *Baynham Meikle & Partners* [1975] 3 All E.R. 99, 103–104, *per* Lord Denning M.R.: "The law does not usually imply a warranty that [a professional man] will achieve the desired result, but only a term that he will use reasonable care and skill. The surgeon does not warrant that he will cure the patient. Nor does the solicitor warrant that he will win the case."

[9] *Roe* v. *Minister of Health* [1954] 1 W.L.R. 128, 131, *per* McNair J. In *Sidaway* v. *Bethlem Royal Hospital Governors* [1985] 1 All E.R. 643, 665, Lord Templeman said that: "The relationship between doctor and patient is contractual in origin, the doctor performing services in consideration for fees payable by the patient. The doctor . . . impliedly contracts to act at all times in the best interests of the patient." It is difficult to see how a duty to act in the patient's "best interests" can differ in any substantive way from a doctor's duty to exercise reasonable care in practising the skills of medicine.

[10] *Morris* v. *Winsbury-White* [1937] 4 All E.R. 494, 500, although Tucker J. doubted whether this obligation depended upon a specific undertaking by the surgeon; rather, it was part of the retainer in the ordinary case. In any event, the consent to treatment given by the patient is consent to surgery by a *specific* doctor (see *Michael* v. *Molesworth* (1950) 2 B.M.J. 171), unless he specifies otherwise. To deal with this problem the standard N.H.S. consent form now usually contains a clause stating that: "No assurance has been given to me that the operation/treatment will be performed or administered by any particular practitioner" (M.P.S. General Consent Form, 1988). See further § 6.11.

to another doctor would constitute a breach of contract. Contractual duties of care are "non-delegable," so the doctor is liable for a failure to exercise reasonable care by the person who performs the service, notwithstanding that reasonable care has been taken in selecting a competent person.[11] Even if the procedure was a success the patient would still be entitled to nominal damages for the breach.

Within the N.H.S. a doctor is under an obligation to provide **2.05** personal treatment to his patients, by virtue of the contract of employment in the case of hospital doctors, and under the contract with the Family Health Services Authority (formerly the Family Practitioner Committee) in the case of general practitioners. A patient would not be entitled to sue on that contract, but it does allow the F.H.S.A. to place reasonable limits on the use of a deputising service.[12] It would seem unlikely, however, that a general practitioner would be held to owe a non-delegable duty to ensure that reasonable care has been taken by a deputising doctor if sued in tort, although it is possible that health authorities owe non-delegable duties to their "patients."[13]

In most cases of private medical treatment the existence of a **2.06** contract does not affect the duties owed by the doctor in practical terms, since the same duties are owed in tort. There are, however, some circumstances in which the liabilities under the contract to differ from those in tort.

2. Express and implied warranties

It is theoretically possible for a doctor to give a contractual warranty **2.07** that he will achieve a particular result, but the court will be slow to infer such a warranty in the absence of an express term, because medicine is an inexact science and it is unlikely that a responsible doctor would intend to give such a warranty. This point was demonstrated by decisions of the Court of Appeal in two cases involving failed sterilisations. In *Eyre* v. *Measday*[14] the plaintiff underwent a sterilisation operation performed by the defendant. The defendant had explained the nature of the operation (a laparoscopic sterilisation), emphasising that it was irreversible, but he did not inform the plaintiff that there was a less than one per cent. risk of pregnancy occurring following such a procedure. Both the plaintiff and her husband believed that the operation would render the plaintiff completely sterile. The plaintiff subsequently became pregnant. She issued proceedings claiming that the defendant was in breach of a contractual term that she would be rendered irreversibly sterile and/or a collateral warranty to that effect which induced her to enter the contract. It was common ground that the contract was embodied partly in oral conversations and partly in the written consent form signed by the plaintiff. It

---

[11] Dugdale and Stanton, *Professional Negligence*, 1989, 2nd ed., para. 16.23.
[12] *R.* v. *Secretary of State for Health, ex parte Spencer* [1990] 1 Med.L.R. 225, D.Ct. On the contractual nature of the relationship between a general practitioner and the F.H.S.C. see *Roy* v. *Kensington and Chelsea and Westminster Family Practitioner Committee* [1990] 1 Med.L.R. 328, C.A.
[13] See §§ 3.83–3.85, 7.11, and 7.24 *et seq.*,
[14] [1986] 1 All E.R. 488.

was also common ground that the appropriate test as to the nature and terms of the contract was objective, not subjective. This does not depend upon what the plaintiff or the defendant thought were the terms of the contract, but on what the court objectively considers the words used by the parties must be reasonably taken to have meant. The Court of Appeal held that it was a contract to perform a particular operation, not a contract to render the plaintiff sterile. Additionally, there was neither an express nor an implied warranty that the procedure would be an unqualified success. Although the plaintiff could reasonably have concluded from the defendant's emphasis on the irreversible nature of the operation that she would be sterilised, it was not reasonable for her to have concluded that he had given her a guarantee that she would be absolutely sterile.[15]

2.08 In *Thake* v. *Maurice*[16] the Court of Appeal (Kerr L.J. dissenting) reversed the decision of Peter Pain J.[17] that the defendant had contracted to make the male plaintiff irreversibly sterile following a vasectomy operation. The defendant had given the plaintiffs a graphic demonstration of the nature of the procedure and its effects, but had failed to give his usual warning that there was a slight risk that the male plaintiff might become fertile again. Both Neill and Nourse L.JJ. concluded that, on a objective interpretation, the defendant had not guaranteed the outcome, relying on the observation that medicine is not an exact science and results are to some extent unpredictable.[18] Nourse L.J. said that a doctor cannot be objectively regarded as guaranteeing the success of any operation or treatment unless he says as much in clear and unequivocal terms.[19]

2.09 By contrast, in the Canadian case of *La Fleur* v. *Cornelis*[20] a plastic surgeon contracted to reduce the size of the plaintiff's nose, and drew a sketch to show the changes that would be made. After the operation the plaintiff had some scarring and deformity. Barry J. held the defendant strictly liable for breach of contract, stating that whilst there is usually no implied warranty of success, there is no law preventing a doctor from contracting to do that which he is paid to do. The defendant had said to the plaintiff that there would be "no problem, you will be very happy." This was held to constitute an express warranty of success.

---

[15] See also *Dendaas* v. *Yackel* (1980) 109 D.L.R. (3d) 455 (B.C.S.C.), where there was similar confusion between doctor and patient, the patient believing that the doctor's emphasis on the "irreversible" and permanent nature of the sterilisation procedure meant that there was no chance of a future pregnancy. Bouck J. held that since there was no clear meeting of minds on this essential term the claim in contract must fail; *Grey* v. *Webster* (1984) 14 D.L.R. (4th) 706, 713; see §§ 6.131 *et seq.* on the question of the failure to disclose the risk of future pregnancy.

[16] [1986] 1 All E.R. 479.

[17] [1984] 2 All E.R. 513.

[18] "Medicine, though a highly skilled profession, is not, and is not generally regarded as being, an exact science. The reasonable man would have expected the defendant to exercise all the proper skill and care of a surgeon in that speciality; he would not in my view have expected the defendant to give a guarantee of 100 per cent. success": [1986] 1 All E.R. 479 at p. 510, *per* Neill L.J.

[19] *Ibid.,* at p. 512. However, the plaintiffs' claim that the defendant was liable in negligence for failing to warn about the small risk that the male plaintiff would become fertile again succeeded. See § 6.133.

[20] (1979) 28 N.B.R. (2d) 569 (N.B.S.C.).

Accordingly, while it may be possible to establish that a doctor has **2.10** guaranteed a particular result,[21] this is likely to be a rare occurrence.[22] Indeed, the converse, a statement by the doctor that he could *not* guarantee the outcome, would seem to be a more likely event in practice.[23] It must be borne in mind, however, that some contractual terms have nothing to do with the exercise of reasonable care. If a defendant contracts to perform a specific act, such as to attend upon the patient,[24] or to use a particular procedure,[25] then he is liable for failing to carry it out irrespective of whether he exercised reasonable care.

Where the contract involves a transfer of goods there will be implied **2.11** terms as to the merchantable quality and fitness for purpose of the goods supplied.[26] For example, in *Samuels* v. *Davis*[27] the defendant dentist agreed to make a set of dentures for the plaintiff, but the dentures did not fit. It was held that there was an implied term that the dentures would be reasonably fit for their purpose. Similarly, in *Dodd* v. *Wilson*[28] an injection of a vaccine into a herd of cattle by a veterinary surgeon resulted in some of the cattle becoming ill. There was held to be an implied term in the contract between the vet and the farmer that the vaccine would be reasonably fit for its purpose. There is no reason why the same proposition should not apply to injections given to patients.

This principle could apply to many forms of treatment, such as the **2.12** supply of drugs, prosthetics, heart pacemakers or artificial heart valves.[29] It is also possible that the duty applies to the design of an article, so that there may be a warranty that the design is fit for its

---

[21] Both Pain J. and Kerr L.J. came to this conclusion in *Thake* v. *Maurice*.

[22] It may be that with elective procedures such as sterilisation operations and cosmetic surgery the courts will be more willing to find express warranties of a successful outcome. In *La Fleur* v. *Cornelis* (1979) 28 N.B.R. (2d) 569, *e.g.,* Barry J. said that a cosmetic surgeon was in a different position from an ordinary physician; he was selling a special service and was more akin to a businessman.

[23] A person cannot, however, by a contractual term or by notice exclude or restrict liability for death or personal injury resulting from negligence: Unfair Contract Terms Act 1977, s.2(1). Any attempt to exclude or restrict liability for other forms of loss or damage resulting from negligence is subject to a test of resonableness: *ibid.,* s.2(2). These provisions apply to persons who act "in the course of a business" (*ibid.,* s.1(3)(*a*)), but that the term is broad enough to include health care provided under the N.H.S.

[24] *Morris* v. *Winsbury-White* [1937] 4 All E.R. 494. See also the comments of Oliver J. in *Midland Bank Trust Co. Ltd.* v. *Hett, Stubbs & Kemp* [1979] Ch. 384, 434: "A contract gives rise to a complex of rights and duties of which the duty to exercise reasonable care and skill is but one."

[25] A dentist who contracts to employ his painless process of tooth extraction will be strictly liable for breach of contract if he fails to employ his painless process, but an allegation that the tooth was unskillfully extracted is a claim that the defendant failed to exercise reasonable care, which in substance may be treated as an action in tort: *Edwards* v. *Mallan* [1908] 1 K.B. 1002, 1005, C.A.

[26] Supply of Goods and Services Act 1982, s.9. For detailed discussion see Bell (1984) 4 L.S. 175.

[27] [1943] 1 K.B. 526.

[28] [1946] 2 All E.R. 691.

[29] It has been suggested, *e.g.,* that the circumstances of *Roe* v. *Minister of Health* [1954] 2 Q.B. 66 (see § 3.55) might be covered by the proposition: see Nathan, *Medical Negligence*, 1957, pp. 18–19. Pharmacists who supply non-prescription products or who supply products under a private prescription will be liable in contract to the purchaser if the product is not of merchantable quality or fit for its intended purpose: see §§ 8.05–8.08.

intended purpose.[30] The obligation is strict, in that the exercise of reasonable care is not a defence. If the goods are not of merchantable quality nor fit for their purpose there is a breach of contract. This does not mean, however, that the product must be effective in preventing the illness or producing a cure, which would be the equivalent of giving a guarantee. Rather the implied term is that the goods will be fit for their intended purpose, which they may not be if they cause harm.[31]

II. TORT

2.13 The vast majority of claims for medical malpractice are brought in the tort of negligence, where the issue will usually be whether the defendant was in breach of a duty of care and/or whether the breach caused damage to the patient.[32] Normally, there will be no difficulty in finding a duty of care owed by the doctor to his patient, at least where the claim is in respect of personal injuries, and this is true even where there is a contractual relationship.[33] The practitioner may also owe a duty of care to the patient in respect of pure financial loss. In addition, there are a number of circumstances where the doctor may owe a duty of care to a third party arising out of the treatment given to the patient, but the incidence and extent of such duties is more problematic.

2.14 In some instances an action for trespass to the person may be available, particularly in the form of the tort of battery. Battery is an intentional tort which requires "the actual infliction of unlawful force on another person."[34] The action is potentially relevant to any medical treatment or examination which involves a touching of the patient, since, with the exception of certain forms of unavoidable or socially accepted contacts (such as jostling in a busy street or engaging someone's attention), any unwanted touching without lawful excuse will constitute a battery. So the surgeon who performs an operation without the patient's consent commits a battery, even though his

---

[30] *Independent Broadcasting Authority* v. *EMI Electronics Ltd. and BICC Construction Ltd.* (1980) 14 Build.L.R. 1, 47–48, *per* Lord Scarman. This strict design duty only applies where the defendant has supplied or manufactured the article as well as designing it: *George Hawkins* v. *Chrysler (UK) Ltd. and Burne Associates* (1986) 38 Build.L.R. 36; see Dugdale and Stanton, *Professional Negligence*, 1989, 2nd ed., paras. 4.08–4.09. The circumstances in which this type of strict design liability might apply in a medical context are somewhat limited, but it could be relevant in appropriate circumstances to claims arising out of cosmetic surgery, for example. An allegation of *negligent* design in the conduct of breast reduction surgery was made in *White* v. *Turner* (1981) 120 D.L.R. (3d) 269, 279, but failed on the facts; see also *La Fleur* v. *Cornelis* (1979) 28 N.B.R. (2d) 569, § 2.09, *ante*.

[31] Note, however, that a product, such as a drug, may be of merchantable quality and fit for its purpose even though it carries an inherent risk of an adverse reaction from known "side-effects": see § 8.06, n.12.

[32] On this see Chaps. 3–5.

[33] See n. 5, *ante*. In some circumstances the patient may be owed a duty of care by the institution providing the health care, such as a hospital or health authority, in addition to the duties owed by individual health care professionals. This form of "direct" liability is discussed in Chap. 7.

[34] *Collins* v. *Wilcock* [1984] 3 All E.R. 374, 377. It is the act that constitutes the trespass (the touching) that must be intentional; an intention to cause the harm is not necessary: *Wilson* v. *Pringle* [1986] 2 All E.R. 440, 445.

intention is to benefit the patient.[35] Consent by the patient exculpates the doctor, and thus, invariably, the question turns upon whether the requirements for a valid consent have been satisfied, or whether the case falls within the circumstances in which consent may be dispensed with. These issues are considered in Chapter 6.

1. Duty of care

The tort of negligence consists of a legal duty to take reasonable **2.15** care, and breach of that duty by the defendant causing damage to the plaintiff.[36] The duty of care determines as a matter of policy whether the type of loss suffered by the plaintiff in the particular manner in which it occurred can ever be actionable, whereas breach of duty deals with the standard of care required of a defendant in the circumstances in order to satisfy the duty of care, and whether the defendant's conduct fell below that standard; in other words, whether the defendant was careless/negligent.

The usual starting point for any discussion of the duty of care in the **2.16** tort of negligence is the landmark decision of *Donoghue* v. *Stevenson*,[37] and the famous dictum of Lord Atkin.[38] Its significance in the context of medical negligence, however, is somewhat limited since the duty of care owed by a doctor to his patient long ante-dates *Donoghue* v. *Stevenson*, and the relationship between doctor and patient clearly satisfies any test based upon foreseeability of harm, proximity of the relationship between plaintiff and defendant, or, indeed, a requirement that it be just and reasonable to impose a duty of care.[39]

It is rare for the courts to invoke policy as a ground for denying a **2.17** patient a right of action against a negligent medical practitioner, although certain "policy" considerations may have some subtle influence at other points.[40] Certain types of claim have been barred on

---

[35] *F.* v. *West Berkshire Health Authority* [1989] 2 All E.R. 545, 564, *per* Lord Goff; *T.* v. *T.* [1988] 1 All E.R. 613, 625, *per* Wood J. It is assumed throughout this book that the doctor is acting in good faith.

[36] *Lochgelly Iron Co.* v. *M'Mullan* [1934] A.C. 1, 25, *per* Lord Wright.

[37] [1932] A.C. 562.

[38] "You must take reasonable care to avoid acts or omissions which you can reasonably foresee would be likely to injure your neighbour. Who, then, in law is my neighbour? The answer seems to be persons who are so closely and directly affected by my act that I ought reasonably to have them in contemplation as being so affected when I am directing my mind to the acts or omissions which are called in question": *ibid.*, p. 580.

[39] This tripartite test for the existence of a duty of care derives from a series of appellate court decisions in the 1980s: see *Peabody Donation Fund* v. *Sir Lindsay Parkinson & Co. Ltd.* [1984] 3 All E.R. 529; *Yuen Kun-yeu* v. *A.-G. of Hong Kong* [1987] 2 All E.R. 705; *Smith* v. *Bush* [1989] 2 W.L.R. 790, 816, *per* Lord Griffiths; *Caparo Industries plc* v. *Dickman* [1990] 1 All E.R. 568; *Pacific Associates Inc.* v. *Baxter* [1989] 2 All E.R. 159, 189, *per* Purchas L.J. These cases (and others) represent a retreat from what has been perceived to be the unacceptable implications of a wide formulation of the test for the duty of care by Lord Wilberforce in *Anns* v. *Merton London Borough Council* [1978] A.C. 728, 751–2, a process that has culminated in the overruling of that decision by the House of Lords in *Murphy* v. *Brentwood District Council* [1990] 2 All E.R. 908. Although these decisions deal with the duty of care in general terms, they are virtually exclusively concerned with liability for pure economic loss and have little relevance in the context of medical malpractice litigation.

[40] In particular, in the form of an unquantifiable reluctance on the part of the courts to make findings of negligence against doctors, possibly due to fears about defensive medicine or the effects of such a finding on the defendant's professional reputation: see §§ 1.06–1.09, 3.91–3.93 and 3.119–3.120.

policy grounds, most of them arising from congenital injury to unborn children. Thus, "wrongful life" claims on the part of a child whose congenital disabilities the defendant negligently failed to diagnose are not actionable.[41] On the other hand, the mother may have an action in these circumstances for being deprived of the opportunity to have the pregnancy terminated. But where the foetus has reached a stage of development such that an abortion would not be lawful under the Abortion Act 1967, the action for loss of opportunity to have an abortion will be denied on policy grounds, since the plaintiff could not put the lost opportunity to benefit without breaking the law.[42] The basis for barring such actions seems to rest on the maxim *ex turpi causa non oritur actio* or some analogous principle, but a denial of a duty of care simply on the ground of "policy" is equally effective in practice. Thus, where potential claims arise out of the negligent performance of procedures which are unlawful the likelihood is that they will be barred on the grounds of policy.[43] It has also been suggested that actions in respect of suicides and attempted suicides should be denied on similar policy grounds, but it seems that such a defence is only likely to succeed where the suicide was "wholly sane" and his judgment was not impaired.[44]

2. Duty to the patient

2.18   From ancient times the medical practitioner has been held account-able for a failure to exercise reasonable care in treating his patient, independently of any contractual relationship with the patient. The surgeon, like the inn keeper or common carrier exercised a "common calling" which gave rise to a duty to exercise proper care and skill.[45] Today the duty arises from the tort of negligence, but it does not depend upon the doctor's status, qualifications or expertise. Rather it is imposed by law when the doctor undertakes the task of providing advice, diagnosis or treatment. It is irrelevant who called the doctor to the patient or who pays his bill.[46] In *R.* v. *Bateman* Lord Hewart C.J. said:

---

[41] *McKay* v. *Essex Area Health Authority* [1982] Q.B. 1166; see § 2.32.

[42] *Rance* v. *Mid-Downs Health Authority* [1991] 1 All E.R. 801. Following the amendment of the Abortion Act 1967 by the Human Fertilisation and Embryology Act 1990, s.37 there is no time limit where the termination is necessary to prevent grave permanent injury to the health of the woman, where the pregnancy involves risk to her life, or where there is a substantial risk that the foetus would be seriously handicapped. Where any of these grounds applied, the causation issue in *Rance* would be irrelevant. The time limit under s.1(1)(*a*) of the Abortion Act 1967 is 24 weeks. In *Udale* v. *Bloomsbury Area Health Authority* [1983] 2 All E.R. 522 Jupp J. held that damages should not be awarded for the birth of a healthy child following a failed sterilisation operation for reasons of policy, but the Court of Appeal has rejected this approach in *Emeh* v. *Kensington and Chelsea and Westminster Area Health Authority* [1984] 3 All E.R. 1044, reasoning that since a sterilisation operation is lawful there were no good policy reasons for denying a plaintiff's claim for the financial loss resulting from a negligent failure to perform the operation properly, whether or not the child is healthy; see further Symmons (1987) 50 M.L.R. 269; §§ 4.68, 9.55–9.57.

[43] Possible examples would be an unlawful organ transplant operation contrary to the Human Organ Transplants Act 1989, or a procedure connected with surrogate mother-hood in breach of the Surrogacy Arrangements Act 1985. The principle of public policy that would preclude the cause of action applies equally to claims in contract or tort.

[44] See §§ 4.100–4.101.

[45] Holdsworth, *History of English Law*, Vol. III, pp. 385–386; Winfield (1926) 42 L.Q.R. 184, 186–7; *cf.* Fifoot, *History and Sources of the Common Law*, pp. 157–158.

[46] *Gladwell* v. *Steggal* (1839) 5 Bing. (N.C.) 733: " . . . this is an action *ex delicto,*" per Tindal C.J.; *Pippin* v. *Sheppard* (1822) 11 Price 400; *Edgar* v. *Lamont* 1914 S.C. 277, 279.

"if a person holds himself out as possessing special skill and knowledge and he is consulted, as possessing such skill and knowledge, by or on behalf of a patient, he owes a duty to the patient to use due caution in undertaking the treatment. If he accepts the responsibility and undertakes the treatment and the patient submits to his direction and treatment accordingly, he owes a duty to the patient to use diligence, care, knowledge, skill and caution in administering the treatment. No contractual relation is necessary, nor is it necessary that the service be rendered for reward."[47]

It follows that, although there is no legal obligation upon a doctor to play the "Good Samaritan" and render assistance to a stranger who has been involved in an accident, a doctor who chooses to do so will owe a duty of care to the "patient."[48] The duty arises from the performance of the act. In *Everett* v. *Griffiths*[49] Atkin L.J. said that the duty of the medical practitioner to the person whom he undertakes to treat is not based on contract or implied contract: **2.19**

"It would apply to a doctor treating a member of the household of the other party to the contract, as it would, in my judgment, apply to a doctor acting gratuitously in a public institution, or in the case of emergency in a street accident; and its existence is independent of the volition of the patient, for it would apply though the patient were unconscious or incapable of exercising a conscious volition."[50]

Morevoer, the person who does not possess the relevant qualifications, expertise or skill comes under the same duty of care, since by undertaking the treatment he effectively represents that he does have these attributes.[51] In an emergency, such as a road accident, the position may well be different since a layman does not profess any specialist skill. It is doubtful, however, whether a court would con- **2.20**

---

[47] (1925) 94 L.J.K.B. 791 at p. 794; *Lindsey County Council* v. *Marshall* [1937] A.C. 97, 121. In *Cassidy* v. *Ministry of Health* [1951] 2 K.B. 348, 359 Denning L.J. said that: "If a man goes to a doctor because he is ill, no one doubts that the doctor must exercise reasonable care and skill in his treatment of him: and that is so whether the doctor is paid for his services or not."

[48] Though in an emergency less may be expected of the doctor to achieve the standard of reasonable care: see §§ 3.87–3.90.

[49] [1920] 3 K.B. 163, 213; *Banbury* v. *Bank of Montreal* [1918] A.C. 626, 657, *per* Lord Atkinson.

[50] See also *Goode* v. *Nash* (1979) 21 S.A.S.R. 419, where the doctor was liable for negligence in the course of conducting a public screening for the detection of glaucoma, notwithstanding that he "was engaged in a valuable community service, entirely on a voluntary basis."

[51] *R.* v. *Bateman* (1925) 94 L.J.K.B. 791, 794, *per* Lord Hewart C.J.: "the unqualified practitioner cannot claim to be measured by any lower standard than that which is applied to a qualified man"; *Pippin* v. *Sheppard* (1822) 11 Price 400, 409. See *Ruddock* v. *Lowe* (1865) 4 F. & F. 519 and *Jones* v. *Fay* (1865) 4 F. & F. 525 (which were both cases against alleged quacks) where it was said that it was not necessary that the defendant held himself out as a qualified doctor; the question is whether the defendant undertook the treatment of the plantiff and did so negligently. With one or two notable exceptions, such as the Abortion Act 1967, s.1(1) and the Nurses, Midwives and Health Visitors Act 1979, s.17 (attendance on a woman in childbirth), there is no prohibition on the unregistered practice of medicine, although it is a criminal offence for an unregistered person to represent himself as a registered medical practitioner: Medical Act 1983, s.49; Nurses, Midwives and Health Visitors Act 1979, s.14.

clude that no duty of care was owed in this situation; rather it may be that the standard required to satisfy the duty would be quite low. For example, a trained volunteer who offers first-aid medical help, such as a St. John's Ambulance volunteer, owes a duty of care to those to whom he renders first-aid.[52] The duty derives from the fact that he holds himself out as someone competent to render first-aid, and he undertakes a legal responsibility to that extent. Thus, the standard of care required of a first-aider is not that of a doctor but the standard of an ordinary skilled first-aider exercising and professing to have the special skill of a first-aider.[53] There must be a distinction, however, between a lay person who embarks upon "treatment," and one who merely gives "advice" (such as "take an aspirin and go to bed") in circumstances where it is clear that no responsibility is undertaken. Only if the circumstances are such as to indicate a genuine undertaking of responsibility for the patient's medical care will a duty arise.[54]

2.21   Although it may be trite to state that a doctor owes a duty of care to his patient, it is not so simple to state precisely when the relationship of doctor and patient begins. This is important because it is equally true to say that a doctor is under no legal obligation (whatever the moral or ethical position) to render assistance by way of examination or treatment to a stranger. This stems from the "mere omissions" rule: one who chooses to act must do so carefully so as to avoid inflicting harm on others; but, as a general rule, the tort of negligence does not compel a person to take positive steps to confer a benefit on others. There is no legal obligation to rescue someone in danger, even if rescue would involve little or no effort and no danger to the rescuer.[55] A "stranger" for these purposes is a person with whom the doctor is not and has never been in a professional doctor/patient relationship. Clearly, if such a relationship does exist a doctor may be liable for failing to attend or treat the patient, just as much as for careless treatment.[56]

2.22   Once a patient is accepted for treatment a duty of care will arise.[57] This, to some extent, begs the question of what is meant by the term "accepted for treatment." A person accepted onto a general practitioner's list is clearly the doctor's patient, even if the practitioner has never seen that person in a professional capacity.[58] Moreover, in an emergency the general practitioner may have an obligation to treat persons who are not on his list.[59] Similarly, where a person presents himself at a hospital casualty department complaining of illness or

---

[52] *Cattley* v. *St. John's Ambulance Brigade* (1988) (unreported), Q.B.D.

[53] See § 3.81.

[54] See Nathan, *Medical Negligence*, 1957, pp. 14–15. There is an analogy here with liability under *Hedley Byrne & Co. Ltd.* v. *Heller & Partners Ltd.* [1964] A.C. 465.

[55] For discussion of the rule see: Linden (1971) 34 M.L.R. 241; Weinrib (1980) Yale L.J. 247; Smith and Burns (1983) 46 M.L.R. 147; Logie [1989] C.L.J. 115.

[56] See §§ 4.04–4.08.

[57] *Jones* v. *Manchester Corporation* [1952] 2 All E.R. 125, 131, *per* Denning L.J. The duty would, of course, apply to any member of the medical team which is providing the treatment.

[58] See the National Health Service (General Medical and Pharmaceutical) Regulations 1974 (S.I. 1974/160) (as amended; see in particular S.I. 1989/1897).

[59] *Ibid.*, Sched. 1, para. 4(1)(*h*). In *Barnes* v. *Crabtree, The Times*, November 1 and 2, 1955 counsel for the defendant general practitioner conceded that the doctor's duty under the N.H.S. was to treat any patient in an emergency, whether his own patient or not.

injury, the staff in the department will owe a duty of care to that person even before he is treated or received into the hospital wards.[60] On the other hand, a "patient" is not entitled to demand that he be given a particular treatment where a doctor has decided that it would be inappropriate,[61] or where a health authority does not have the resources to provide the treatment.[62]

The position of consultants and doctors engaged in private practice **2.23** is less clear cut. Within the N.H.S. patients are normally referred to a consultant through their general practitioner. It is uncertain whether the doctor/patient relationship can be said to begin when the consultant "accepts" the patient for treatment, *e.g.* by letter, or whether some contact between doctor and patient, in the form of a consultation, is necessary. It may also be unclear precisely when the doctor/patient relationship ends. If the treatment has been completed, but problems recur at a later date, is the relationship a continuing one, or is a new relationship entered into when the patient re-presents with his complaint? Moreover, in the case of specialists there must be an implied limitation to the extent of the duty created by the doctor/patient relationship. An orthopaedic surgeon, for example, would not normally be responsible for failing to diagnose a patient's heart condition. The position of doctors engaged in private practice is even more problematic, because there is no equivalent to the general practitioner's "list" of N.H.S. patients. The extent of the doctor's responsibility would depend upon the terms, whether express or implied, of the contract of retainer.[63]

Financial loss

Whilst it is clear that a doctor owes a duty of care to his patient in **2.24** respect of any physical or psychological harm that may result from negligent diagnosis, advice or treatment, the position with respect to purely financial loss sustained by the patient as a result of negligent diagnosis or advice is less clear. In *Stevens* v. *Bermondsey and Southwark Group Hospital Management Committee*[64] the plaintiff was involved in an accident for which he had a claim against the local authority. He visited hospital and was seen by a casualty officer, who considered that there was nothing much wrong with him. On the strength of this the plaintiff settled his claim against the local authority for a small sum. It was subsequently discovered that he was suffering

---

[60] *Barnett* v. *Chelsea and Kensington Hospital Management Committee* [1968] 1 All E.R. 1068, 1072. See also the comments of O'Halloran J.A. in *Fraser* v. *Vancouver General Hospital* (1951) 3 W.W.R. 337, 340 (B.C.C.A); aff'd [1952] 3 D.L.R. 785 (S.C.C.), cited in § 4.05.

[61] *R.* v. *Ethical Committee of St. Mary's Hospital, ex parte Harriott* (1988) 18 Fam. Law 165.

[62] *R.* v. *Secretary of State for Social Services, ex parte Hincks* (1979) 123 S.J. 436; aff'd (1980) (unreported) C.A.; *R.* v. *Central Birmingham Health Authority, ex parte Walker, The Times*, November 26, 1987, C.A.; *R.* v. *Central Birmingham Health Authority, ex parte Collier* (1988) (unreported) C.A.

[63] See Nathan, *Medical Negligence*, 1957, pp. 39–40, suggesting that with general practitioners in private practice, at least, the question might turn upon whether according to ordinary usage the person could be regarded as a patient.

[64] (1963) 107 S.J. 478.

from spondylolisthesis, a congenital condition activated by the accident. He sued the defendants, alleging that if the doctor's diagnosis had not been negligent he would have claimed and received a larger sum from the local authority. Paull J. held that a doctor's duty was limited to the sphere of medicine and had nothing to do with the sphere of legal liability unless he conducted the examination with an eye to liability. In the absence of special circumstances, a doctor was not required to contemplate any question connected with a third party's liability to his patient.[65]

2.25 This situation would now seem to fall directly under the principle of *Hedley Byrne & Co. Ltd.* v. *Heller & Partners Ltd.*[66] Where the defendant is so placed that others could reasonably rely upon his judgment, skill, or upon his ability to make careful enquiry, and the defendant takes it upon himself to give information or advice to, or allows the information or advice to be passed on to, a person that he knows or should know will place reliance upon it, then a duty of care will arise.[67] In *Hedley Byrne* Lord Devlin considered that if the law were not developed to allow recovery for pure economic loss consequent upon a negligent statement relied upon by the plaintiff the consequences would be very odd. To illustrate this he gave the example of a doctor who advised the patient wrongly that his medical condition was such that he should give up work, it subsequently being discovered that there was no need for this.[68] It would be absurd, said his Lordship, that the fee-paying patient should have an action in these circumstances if the N.H.S. patient had none. There is no reason in principle why the medical profession alone should be immune from claims under *Hedley Byrne*. It may be that the distinction, if any, between Lord Devlin's example, which surely would be the subject of a *Hedley Byrne* duty, and *Stevens* v. *Bermondsey and Southwark Group Hospital Management Committee* is that a hospital casualty officer does not undertake to give advice to a patient with regard to his financial position, and so it would not be reasonable for the patient to rely on the advice for that purpose.[69] The difficulty with this argument is that it is clearly reasonable for a patient to "rely" on a casualty officer's diagnosis where a negligent diagnosis causes personal injury. Both forms of loss are foreseeable. To take a different view of the proximity of the relationship when the loss is purely financial is to resort to a distinction which the House of Lords considered to be

---

[65] The decision apparently rested on the view that the plantiff's claim against the council was either a *novus actus interveniens* or severed the chain of causation. See also *Pimm* v. *Roper* (1862) 2 F. & F. 783, where the plaintiff was examined by a surgeon employed by a railway company, following a train collision. The surgeon said that his injuries were slight, and relying on this the plaintiff accepted £5 in compensation from the railway company. The plantiff subsequently claimed that his injuries were much more serious, but his action against the doctor failed on the basis that the examination did not cause any injury to the plaintiff.

[66] [1964] A.C. 465.

[67] *Ibid.*, at p. 503, *per* Lord Morris. Note that in *Caparo Industries plc* v. *Dickman* [1990] 1 All E.R. 568, the House of Lords restated the duty of care that may arise under *Hedley Byrne* in more restricted terms. See in particular the speeches of Lord Bridge and Lord Oliver at pp. 576 and 589 respectively.

[68] *Ibid.*, at p. 517.

[69] *cf.* where a medical report is prepared for the purpose of litigation: *McGrath* v. *Kiely and Powell* [1965] I.R. 497.

untenable in *Hedley Byrne* itself. Nor does it help to speak in terms of what a casualty officer voluntarily "undertakes" to do, since it is now clear that an undertaking of responsibility is in reality the imposition of a duty of care by law where the defendant behaves in a particular manner.[70]

3. Duty to third parties

There are a number of circumstances in which the medical practi- **2.26** tioner may owe duties to persons other than his patient. In some instances it may be unclear whether a doctor/patient relationship has been created, but nonetheless it is possible to say that the doctor owes a duty of care to the person whom he is examining or advising or reporting upon. For example, where a doctor conducts a medical examination at the request of an employer, prospective employer, or insurance company there can be no doubt that, in addition to the duty owed to the person making the request, the doctor owes a duty of care to the subject of the examination. In *Thomsen* v. *Davison*,[71] for example, it was held that a doctor who, in a situation in which the relationship of doctor and patient does not exist, undertakes the examination of a person in order to assess his state of health, has a duty of care not merely to his employer but also to that person to conduct the examination competently, and not do or omit anything in the course of performing the examination which is likely to cause the latter damage.[72] This includes a duty to inform himself of the results of pathological tests and advise the person to undergo investigation and treatment if they are adverse. Similarly, in *Stokes* v. *Guest, Keen and Nettlefold (Bolts & Nuts) Ltd.*[73] Swanwick J. held that a factory medical officer was under a duty to institute six-monthly medical examinations of certain employees, given his knowledge of the risk to those employees of contracting cancer from the work in which they were engaged.

In addition, the doctor may owe a duty of care to third parties which **2.27** arises out of treatment or advice given to someone who is undoubtedly

---

[70] In *Smith* v. *Bush* [1989] 2 W.L.R. 790, 813, Lord Griffiths said that in the context of liability under *Hedley Byrne & Co. Ltd.* v. *Heller & Partners Ltd.* [1964] A.C. 465 a voluntary assumption of responsibility "can only have any real meaning if it is understood as referring to the circumstances in which the law will *deem* the maker of the statement to have assumed responsibility to the person who acts upon the advice" (emphasis added). See also *Banbury* v. *Bank of Montreal* [1918] A.C. 626, 657, where Lord Finlay L.C. said that: "There is in point of law no difference between the case of advice given by a physician and advice given by a solicitor or banker in the course of his business. By undertaking to advise he makes himself liable for failing to exercise due care in the discharge of his duty to the person who has entrusted him, and the fact that he undertook it gratuitously is irrelevant."

[71] [1975] Qd R. 93. In *Leonard* v. *Knott* [1978] 5 W.W.R. 511, 513 (B.C.S.C.) Kirke Smith J. held that where employees underwent annual health checks conducted by a doctor who was engaged by their employer for the purpose, the doctor/patient relationship existed between the doctor and the examinees.

[72] A similar duty is owed to persons whom a doctor certifies to be of unsound mind for the purpose of involuntary admission to hospital under the Mental Health Act 1983: see §§ 2.56–2.58.

[73] [1968] 1 W.L.R. 1776; see also *Lawton* v. *BOC Transhield Ltd.* [1987] 2 All E.R. 608 in which it was said that where A gives advice to B about C (in this case a reference on a former employee), A owes a duty to C to exercise reasonable care in giving that advice.

a patient. The circumstances in which such duties will be imposed are considered in the following paragraphs.

(i) Congenital disability

2.28   Although accepted in other common law jurisdictions, for many years there was no case in the United Kingdom in which it was decided that a duty of care was owed to an unborn child.[74] Finally it has been held that such a duty does exist at common law,[74a]although the point had been put beyond doubt by the Congenital Disabilities (Civil Liability) Act 1976 for births occuring after it came into force. The Act confers a right of action on a child who is born alive and disabled in respect of the disability,[75] if it is caused by an occurrence which affected either parent's ability to have a normal healthy child, or affected the mother during pregnancy, or affected the mother or child in the course of its birth, causing disabilities which would not otherwise have been present.[76] A defendant is liable to the child if he is or would, if sued in time, have been liable in tort to the parent, and it is no answer that the parent has suffered no actionable injury.[77] Thus, the child's action is derivative, in that it depends on a tortious duty owed to the parent, except that it is not necessary to show that the parent suffered any actionable injury. A child damaged by a drug taken by its mother during pregnancy, for example, can sue the manufacturer even though the mother did not suffer any harm, if there was a breach of a duty of care owed to the mother. Section 1A, which was added by the Human Fertilisation and Embryology Act 1990, s.44, effectively extends the provisions of section 1 of the Act to children born disabled as a result of damage to an embryo or to gametes in the course of infertility treatment, by the placing in a woman of an embryo, or of sperm and eggs or of artificial insemination. Where the disability results from an act or omission in the course of the selection, or the keeping or use outside the body, of the embryo carried by the woman or of the gametes used to bring about the creation of the embryo, and a person is answerable under the section to the child in respect of the act or omission, the child's disabilities are to be regarded as damage resulting from the wrongful act of that person. A person is answerable under section 1A if he was, or would if sued in due time have been,

---

[74] The point was conceded by counsel for the defendant in *Williams* v. *Luff, The Times*, February 14, 1978, and in *McKay* v. *Essex Area Health Authority* [1982] Q.B. 1166. A duty was assumed to exist in the thalidomide cases: *Distillers Co.* (*Biochemicals*) *Ltd.* v. *Thompson* [1971] A.C. 458, and in *Whitehouse* v. *Jordan* [1981] 1 All E.R. 267. See *Montreal Tramways* v. *Leveille* (1933) 4 D.L.R. 339 and *Duval* v. *Seguin* (1972) 26 D.L.R. (3d) 418 (Canada); *Watt* v. *Rama* [1972] V.R. 353 and *Pratt* v. *Pratt* [1975] V.R. 378 (Australia); *Presley* v. *Newport Hospital* (1976) 365 A. 2d 748 (U.S.A.).

[74a] *B.* v. *Islington Health Authority* [1991] 1 All E.R. 825; *De Martell* v. *Merton & Sutton Health Authority* [1991] 2 Med. L.R. 209. The births in both of these cases pre-dated the commencement of the Congential Disabilities (Civil Liability) Act 1976.

[75] Disability means "being born with any deformity, disease or abnormality, including predisposition (whether or not susceptible of immediate prognosis) to physical or mental defect in the future": Congenital Disabilities (Civil Liability) Act 1976, s.4(1).

[76] Congenital Disabilities (Civil Liability) Act 1976, s.1(1), (2). The child's mother is specifically excluded by s.1(1) as a potential defendant, except where the injury is attributable to her negligent driving of a motor vehicle: s.2. For detailed discussion of the legislation see Pace (1977) 40 M.L.R. 141.

[77] *Ibid.*, s.1(3).

liable in tort to one or both of the parents, and it is no answer that the parent suffered no actionable injury.[78]

The fact that a duty to the child depends upon a duty owed to the **2.29** parent may create difficulties, however, in some circumstances. Where, for example, there is a conflict between the interests of the mother and those of the child during labour a doctor will owe a duty to the mother to exercise reasonable care for her health and safety. It is irrelevant that what has to be done in the mother's interests involves a risk of harm to the child, since if the doctor has exercised reasonable care there is no tort against the mother (whether damage is caused or not), and so the child can have no claim under the Act.[79] This would also be the position where the mother refused to accept recommended treatment, a Caesarian section for example, since she is entitled to refuse to give her consent to any treatment and the doctor commits no tort by accepting her decision. Indeed, there is no legal mechanism by which the mother's rights could be overridden,[80] and the doctor who attempted to do so would commit the tort of battery. Even where there is no conflict of interest between mother and child there may be circumstances where there is no breach of a duty owed to the mother, but there has been negligence with respect to the child.[81]

The derivative nature of the duty is also apparent from the defences **2.30** available. The child is bound by a contractual exclusion or limitation clause that would have applied to the parents' action.[82] Damages may be reduced to take account of the parent's share of the responsibility for the child being born disabled.[83] Finally, where the disability is the result of an occurrence preceding the time of conception which affects the parents' ability to have a normal, healthy child, the defendant is not responsible to the child if either or both of the parents knew of the risk of disability, except that if the child's father is the defendant and he knew of the risk but the mother did not he will be answerable to the

---

[78] For discussion of some of the difficulties that may arise under this section see Morgan and Lee, *Blackstone's Guide to the Human Fertilisation and Embryology Act 1990,* 1991, pp. 171–174.

[79] See Eekelaar and Dingwall [1984] J.S.W.L. 258.

[80] There is no power to make a foetus a ward of court, *e.g.: Re F.* (*in utero*) [1988] 2 All E.R. 193. Some jurisdictions in the U.S.A. have made orders requiring women to undergo Caesarian sections against their wishes: see *Jefferson* v. *Griffin Spalding County Hospital* (1981) 274 S.E. 2d 457 (Georgia); *Re AC* (1988) 533 A. 2d 611 (District of Columbia).

[81] Cane (1977) 51 A.L.J. 704, 708 gives an example of a drug manufacturer who warns the mother of adverse side-effects which might cause her injury but negligently fails to warn about potential harm to the foetus. If the mother takes the drug and suffers no injury, but the child is injured, the child has no claim under the Act because, although the manufacturer owes a duty to the mother, there is no breach of duty against her (because a warning may discharge the manufacturer's duty: see §§ 8.32 *et seq.* As Cane comments, this is "unfortunate."

[82] *Ibid.,* s.1(6). However, a contractual exclusion clause which sought to exclude liability for death or personal injury caused by negligence would be ineffective: Unfair Contract Terms Act 1977, s.2(1).

[83] Congenital Disabilities (Civil Liability) Act 1976, s.1(7); except where the mother causes the damage in the course of driving a motor vehicle: s.2. If a woman discovers during the course of pregancy that the child is likely to be born disabled it is not unreasonable for her to refuse to undergo an abortion: *Emeh* v. *Kensington and Chelsea and Westminster Area Health Authority* [1984] 3 All E.R. 1044. Moreover, the mother's decision to decline an abortion does not contribute to the child's disabilities; rather it results in the birth of the child. This is not a ground for saying that the mother "shares responsibility" for the child's disabilities.

child.[84] Under this provision the parents' knowledge apparently defeats the child's claim, even where objectively it would be reasonable for them to attempt to have a normal, healthy child (e.g. if the defendants' negligence has created a one per cent. chance of them producing a disabled child).

2.31   The Act applies only to children born alive, the claim effectively crystallising at birth. If the defendant's negligence causes the death of the foetus *in utero* there can be no claim by the child, though either or both parents may have an action in appropriate circumstances.[85] Moreover, the action is limited to "disabilities which would not otherwise have been present." This wording was intended to exclude so-called "wrongful life" actions in which a child who is born with non-tortiously inflicted disabilities claims that, due to the defendant's negligence in failing to diagnose that the child was likely to be born disabled, the child has been deprived of an opportunity to be aborted (hence "wrongful entry into life").

2.32   This issue arose for resolution under the common law in *McKay* v. *Essex Area Health Authority*.[86] Tests conducted on a pregnant woman failed to disclose that she had contracted rubella, and her child was born severely disabled. The Court of Appeal held that a doctor did not owe a duty of care *to the child* to advise the mother of the serious consequences for the child of exposure to rubella and of the desirability of an abortion, although such a duty was owed to the mother. The child's action claimed a right to be aborted (effectively a right not to enter the world with disabilities), and this was contrary to public policy as a violation of the sanctity of human life. This view overstates the nature of the child's claim somewhat, since the doctor could not compel a pregnant woman to have an abortion. At its highest, the child's claim is that through the defendant's negligence the mother has been deprived of the opportunity to make a choice on the child's behalf as to whether it would be in the child's interests either to be born with disabilities or not to be born at all (a point apparently accepted by Griffiths L.J.). This is an interest which is implicitly recognised by the Abortion Act 1967 itself, which permits abortion where there is a substantial risk that the child would have disabilities which would cause it to be seriously handicapped.[87] Moreover, Stephenson L.J. did concede that there might be some "extreme cases"

---

[84] *Ibid.*, s.1(4). A specific version of this defence applies to actions arising out of errors in the course of assisted conception. By s.1A(3) a defendant is not answerable to the child if at the time the embryo, or the sperm and eggs, are placed in the woman, or at the time of her insemination, either or both parents knew the risk of their child being born disabled, *i.e.* the particular risk created by the act or omission. See further Morgan and Lee, *op. cit., ante*, n. 78, at pp. 172–173. The other defences in the Act apply to actions under s.1A: s.1A(4).

[85] See, *e.g., Kralj* v. *McGrath* [1986] 1 All E.R. 54; *Bagley* v. *North Hertfordshire Health Authority* [1986] New L.J. 1014, where damages were awarded to a mother for a stillborn child, although Simon Brown J. held that there can be no claim for damages for bereavement under the Fatal Accidents Act 1976, s.1A(2), which provides a fixed statutory sum for the parents of an unmarried minor child. A foetus cannot be said to be a "minor child" since it only attains the status of a legal person at birth, not before: *C.* v. *S.* [1987] 1 All E.R. 1230, 1234h, *per* Heilbron J. On claims by parents arising out of *in vitro* fertilisation see Hill (1985) 25 Med. Sci. and Law 270.

[86] [1982] Q.B. 1166. The child was born before the Act came into force.

[87] Abortion Act 1967, s.1(1)(*d*), as amended. This point was acknowledged by Stephenson L.J. in *McKay* at pp. 1179–1180.

where it could be said that it would be better for the child not to be born.[88] Thus, this policy argument against wrongful life actions is by no means clear-cut.

The Court of Appeal also took the view if the child's action were to **2.33** be allowed the court would have to engage in the impossible task of assessing damages by comparing the value of non-existence (of which the court has no knowledge) with the value of existence in a disabled state, although it could be said in reply that the courts do not find any particular difficulty in assessing many other imponderable forms of loss. Finally, it was suggested that allowing the wrongful life action might lead to claims by children born handicapped against their mothers for not having an abortion, an argument which would seem to have more force,[89] although, again, this objection is not insuperable since such claims could be barred on policy grounds. Paradoxically, it was accepted in *McKay* that a doctor would owe a duty of care to the mother in these circumstances to advise her of her right to an abortion under the Abortion Act.[90] Thus, an action on behalf of the parents may provide some redress for families in this situation.[91]

The Congenital Disabilities (Civil Liability) Act 1976 replaces the **2.34** common law for births after its commencement, but curiously only in respect of a defendant's potential liability for causing the child's disabilities.[92] Accordingly, although it is not possible to bring a wrongful life action under the Act, it is arguable that the legislation did not remove the possibility of bringing an action at common law. Such a claim is not an action in "respect of disabilities with which it might be born," but rather a claim not to have been born at all, which theoretically could be brought by a healthy child. The Court of Appeal in *McKay*, however, took the view that the Act did prevent *all* wrongful life claims for births after its commencement. With respect, this seems to misread the legislation, particularly section 4(5). Of course, even if such an action is not precluded by the Act, a common law claim would have to overturn the decision in *McKay*.[93]

---

[88] His Lordship cited the example of *Croke* v. *Wiseman* [1981] 3 All E.R. 852; see also *Re B. (a minor) (wardship: medical treatment)* [1981] 1 W.L.R. 1421, 1424, where Templeman L.J. said that the court, in exercising its wardship jurisdiction, might refuse to authorise life saving medical treatment where the child's life would be demonstrably awful, an exercise that involves weighing the quality of the child's potential life; *Re J (a minor) (wardship: medical treatment)* [1990] 3 All E.R. 930. For a similar Canadian case see *Re Superintendent of Family & Child Service and Dawson* (1983) 145 D.L.R. (3d) 610.

[89] See the *Royal Commission on Civil Liability and Compensation for Personal Injury*, Cmnd. 7054 (1978), Vol. I, para. 1465. See also Teff (1985) 34 I.C.L.Q. 423, and Symmons (1987) 50 M.L.R. 269 for discussion of the policy factors raised by "wrongful life" and "wrongful birth" actions.

[90] This assumes that she would be entitled to an abortion under the legislation. If not, the claim against the doctor will fail on the grounds of causation and public policy: see *Rance* v. *Mid-Downs Health Authority* [1991] 1 All E.R. 801. Note, however, that there is now no time limit under the Abortion Act 1967, where there is a substantial risk that the child would be seriously handicapped.

[91] See Robertson (1982) 45 M.L.R. 697; Symmons (1987) 50 M.L.R. 269. This type of claim may be categorised as a "wrongful birth" action, analogous to claims for failed sterilisation.

[92] " . . . in respect of any such birth it replaces any law in force before its passing, whereby a person could be liable to a child in respect of disabilities with which it might be born . . ." : Congenital Disabilities (Civil Liability) Act 1976, s.4(5). The Act came into force on July 22, 1976.

[93] See Fortin [1987] J.S.W.L. 306 and Slade (1982) 132 New L.J. 874 for the arguments; *cf.* Law Com. No. 60, Cmnd. 5709, 1974.

2.35   Section 1(2)(a) of the Act provides that an "occurrence" includes
one which "affected either parent of the child in his or her ability to
have a normal healthy child," which does allow for the possibility of an
action by the child in respect of pre-conception negligence. This
appears to recognise a form of legal interest in not being conceived.[94]
However, this would probably be limited to claims arising from
physical harm to one or both of the parents.[95] Negligent genetic
counselling, for example, in which parents are wrongly advised that it
is safe for them to conceive, because the risk of bearing a child with a
genetic disability is minimal, would normally give rise to a wrongful
life claim by the child since if the correct advice had been given (and
acted upon) the result would have been that the parents would not
have conceived, *i.e.* the child would not have been born at all. The
correct advice would not have resulted in the child being born without
disabilities. Where the negligence concerns not simply the question
whether to conceive or not but the precautions required to conceive a
healthy child, the position is more complicated. If precautions would
have prevented damage *to that child* then there could be a claim under
the Act, but if the precautions (such as recommending an amniocentesis test) would simply have revealed that the foetus had an abnormality and the mother would have had an abortion, the child has no
claim because this is wrongful life.[96] There is, of course, no reason why
a parent should not have an action in respect of negligent genetic
counselling, with the damages reflecting the additional cost of raising a
handicapped child over and above the cost of raising a healthy child, or
if an abortion is carried out damages for the disappointment of being
unable to complete the pregnancy, and pain and suffering.[97]

2.36   Probably the most difficult aspect of bringing an action under the
Congenital Disabilities (Civil Liability) Act 1976 is the problem of
proving causation. The Pearson Commission, for example, considered
that only a "minute proportion" of children born with congenital
defects would succeed in proving both negligence and causation.[98]

(ii) Infectious disease

2.37   Where a doctor has negligently permitted a person to come into
contact with a contagious disease there would be no difficulty in
establishing a duty of care, whether that person was the doctor's

---

[94] See Pace (1977) 40 M.L.R. 141, 153.

[95] Examples of this type on injury would include exposure of the mother or father to
radiation causing gene mutations; a congenital disease, such as syphilis, caused by a
blood transfusion negligently given to the mother before conception; or the supply of
contaminated sperm for artificial insemination: see Law Com. No. 64, Cmnd. 5709,
1974, para. 77. Brazier, *Medicine, Patients and the Law*, 1987, p. 165 cites the example
of mismanagement of a previous pregnancy with the result that Rhesus incompatibility
goes undiscovered and untreated, causing damage to a subsequent foetus.

[96] See Brazier, *Medicine, Patients and the Law*, 1987, pp. 170–171, who points out that
realistic examples of the former circumstances are difficult to indentify.

[97] Damages can be awarded for failed sterilisation operations to compensate the
plaintiff for the cost of rearing the child, whether the child is healthy or handicapped: see
§§ 9.55–9.57.

[98] *Royal Commission on Civil Liability and Compensation for Personal Injury*, Cmnd.
7054 (1978), Vol. I, para. 1452, and Annexes 12 and 13; Law Com. No. 60, Cmnd. 5709
(1974), para. 28.

patient or not. In *Lindsey County Council* v. *Marshall*[99] the House of Lords held the defendants liable for negligently failing to warn the plaintiff of the risk of infection by puerperal fever when she was admitted to their maternity home, following a recent outbreak of the disease. Similarly, if a doctor negligently discharged an infectious patient from hospital and, as a result, a third party contracted the disease, the doctor would undoubtedly owe a duty of care to the third party.[1]

By analogy it is arguable that a doctor, such as a general practi- **2.38** tioner, might be under a duty of care to warn the sexual partner(s) of a patient who has Acquired Immune Deficiency Syndrome or who is diagnosed as HIV positive about the patient's condition and the potential risk to their health, if the patient refused to consent to the disclosure. If the sexual partner was also the doctor's patient there would probably be little difficulty in finding a duty of care, since a "duty to inform" could be seen as part and parcel of the doctor's more general duty to exercise reasonable care to safeguard the health of his patient. It would be somewhat arbitrary, however, if the doctor's liability in this situation turned upon whether the sexual partner happened also to be one of his patients. Arguably the duty would arise irrespective of the sexual partner's status, on the basis that serious physical harm was foreseeable as a real risk.[2]

In any event, a plaintiff in this position would face considerable **2.39** difficulty in proving causation, since it would have to be shown that the infection occurred after the time at which the doctor ought reasonably to have disclosed the risk, and, given the substantial interval between an individual becoming HIV positive and developing AIDS, it would be unlikely that the plaintiff could pinpoint the exact time of infection.

There may well be other circumstances in which it is foreseeable that **2.40** a patient could be a potential hazard to third parties where a doctor would be held to owe a duty of care. If, for example, a patient's medical condition (such as epilepsy) or the side-effects of a drug that

---

[99] [1937] A.C. 97; *Heafield* v. *Crane, The Times*, July 31, 1937. See also *McDaniel* v. *Vancover General Hospital* (1934) 152 L.T. 56, where the plaintiff was a patient being treated for diphtheria in the defendant hospital, and contracted smallpox by cross-infection from other patients. The hospital was held not liable because, having conformed to accepted practice, there was no negligence.

[1] See *Evans* v. *Liverpool Corporation* [1906] 1 K.B. 160, where on essentially similar facts a claim against the hospital authority failed on the ground that, as the law then stood, the defendants were not vicariously liable for the acts of the physician. In the U.S. this form of liability is commonplace: *Hofmann* v. *Blackmon* 241 So. 2d 752 (1970), where there was a failure to diagnose tuberculosis in the father; the doctor was liable to the daughter infected by the patient; *Fosgate* v. *Corona* 330 A. 2d 355 (1974), where there was liability for the discharge of infectious tuberculosis patients without warnings to persons indentifiable as at risk (*i.e.* relatives).

[2] This view is not unproblematic, however, since disclosure would be a breach of the doctor's duty of confidence to the patient which would have to be justified by the public interest defence; see Jones (1990) 6 P.N. 16, 22, and § 2.103; Casswell (1989) 68 Can. Bar Rev. 225. The National Health Service (Venereal Diseases) Regulations 1974 (S.I. 1974/29) create a specific statutory duty of confidence with respect to venereal disease, which may apply to AIDS patients: *X.* v. *Y.* [1988] 2 All E.R. 648, 656. AIDS is not a notifiable disease under the Public Health (Control of Disease) Act 1984, s.10, but see the Public Health (Infectious Diseases) Regulations (S.I. 1988/1546) which extend ss. 35, 37 and 38 (allowing for compulsory medical examination, removal to or detention in a hospital) to persons suffering from AIDS, though not persons diagnosed as HIV positive. As to whether AIDS should be a notifiable disease see Keown (1989) 5 P.N. 121.

---

the doctor has prescribed render certain conduct (such as driving a motor vehicle) hazardous, the doctor will be under a duty to warn the patient. If he fails to do so and as a result the patient causes an accident injuring others, there could be little doubt that the doctor would owe a duty of care, both to the patient and the third parties.[3]

(iii) Rescuers

2.41   As a general rule a person is not obliged to undertake a rescue, but the courts are likely to be favourably disposed to a plaintiff who does attempt to rescue someone endangered by the defendant's negligence and who is injured in the process.[4] Thus, a duty of care is owed to a person who is foreseeably likely to intervene to assist a person put in danger by the defendant, provided the rescuer did not act with wanton disregard for his own safety. Foreseeability of the particular emergency that arose is unnecessary, provided some emergency is foreseeable[5] or, alternatively, provided the emergency is of the same "kind or class" as that which is foreseeable.[6]

2.42   The circumstances in which this principle can be applied in the context of medical negligence will probably be rare. The issue did arise, however, in the Canadian case of *Urbanski* v. *Patel*.[7] The defendant removed an ectopic kidney from his patient during the course of a sterilisation operation, mistakenly believing it to be an ovarian cyst. It was then discovered that the patient had only one kidney, and the effect of removing it was much more serious than would have been the case had she had the normal complement of two. Her father, Mr. Urbanski, donated one of his kidneys for transplant ("as what father would not?" remarked the trial judge, Wilson J.) in what turned out to be an unsuccessful attempt to alleviate his daughter's condition. In an action by the father for the expenses of and the pain and suffering involved in the operation the doctor was held liable by analogy to the rescue principle. An argument that the donation was unforeseeable was rejected, as was the suggestion that the plaintiff's conduct was voluntary and intentional, and so broke the chain of causation.[8]

2.43   It is probable that an English court would follow the approach adopted in *Urbanski* v. *Patel*, although it may be that claims would be

---

[3] See Giesen, *International Medical Malpractice Law*, 1988, para. 255; *Freese* v. *Lemmon* (1973) 210 N.W. 2d 576 (S.C. of Iowa).

[4] "Danger invites rescue. The cry of distress is the summons to relief. The law does not ignore these reactions of the mind in tracing conduct to its consequences. It recongnises them as normal. It places their effects within the range of the natural and probable. The wrong that imperils life is a wrong to the imperilled victim; it is a wrong also to his rescuer . . . The risk of rescue, if only it be not wanton, is born of the occasion. The emergency begets the man. The wrongdoer may not have foreseen the coming of a deliverer. He is accountable as if he had," *per* Cardozo J. in *Wagner* v. *International Railway Co.* (1921) 232 N.Y. 176, 180, cited with approval by Willmer L.J. in *Baker* v. *T.E. Hopkins & Sons Ltd.* [1959] 3 All E.R. 225, 241, and by Lord Wright in *Bourhill* v. *Young* [1943] A.C. 92, 108–109.

[5] *Videan* v. *British Transport Commission* [1963] 2 Q.B. 650, 669.

[6] *Knightley* v. *Johns* [1982] 1 All E.R. 851, 860.

[7] (1978) 84 D.L.R. (3d) 650 (Manitoba Q.B.).

[8] This type of argument has been consistently rejected in rescue cases: see, *e.g.*, *Haynes* v. *Harwood* [1935] 1 K.B. 146; *Baker* v. *T.E. Hopkins & Son Ltd.* [1959] 3 All E.R. 225.

limited to donations by close family members who are clearly more foreseeable as potential donors, and who would feel a greater sense of moral obligation to the patient.[9] This view is reinforced by section 2 of the Human Organ Transplants Act 1989, which prohibits the transplantation of an organ from a living donor who is not genetically related to the donee, except where authorised by regulations made by the Secretary of State.[9a] Moreover, it is probably the element of moral compulsion that undermines the argument that the plaintiff was a volunteer or that the decision to donate broke the chain of causation. One issue that might have to be addressed is the possibility that if the first transplantation proved to be unsuccessful further donations could take place. Is the defendant liable to all the donors? Possibly there would come a point at which the damage would be regarded as too remote or the donation would be treated as a *novus actus interveniens* but there is nothing in either principle or logic which would dictate this, since if the first donation is both a foreseeable and reasonable consequence of the defendant's negligence then subsequent donations merit the same categorisation.

(iv) Nervous shock[10]

It is now well-established that a tortfeasor who has negligently killed **2.44** or injured A may be liable to B for a psychiatric illness resulting from A's death or injury. There can be no claim for emotional distress, anguish or grief unless this leads to a positive psychiatric illness (such as an anxiety neurosis or reactive depression) or physical illness (such as a heart attack)."[11] There is no need for any direct impact to the plaintiff or fear of immediate personal injury to the plaintiff.[12]

The difficulty that the courts have had to face in dealing with cases **2.45** of nervous shock is how wide the scope of liability should be drawn. Initial scepticism about the nature of "psychiatric damage" and the danger of fraudulent claims led to more or less strict limits as to who

---

[9] See Spencer [1979] C.L.J. 45; Robertson (1980) 96 L.Q.R. 19. See also Giesen, *International Medical Malpractice Law*, 1988, para. 1331, discussing a similar German case in which the donor succeeded in an action against the doctor. Curiously, in the U.S. the courts have denied claims by organ donors against the original tortfeasor: *Sirianni* v. *Anna* 285 N.Y.S. 2d 709 (1969); *Moore* v. *Shah* 458 N.Y.S. 2d 33 (1982); *Petersen* v. *Farberman* 736 S.W. 2d 441 (1987).

[9a] See the Human Organ Transplants (Unrelated Persons) Regulations 1989, (S.I. 1989/2480); § 6.126.

[10] The term is used by lawyers to describe a medically recognised psychiatric illness, although it has been described as a "misleading and inaccurate expression," *per* Bingham L.J. in *Attia* v. *British Gas* [1987] 3 All E.R. 455, 462. "Psychiatric damage" encompasses "all relevant forms of mental illness, neurosis and personality change": *ibid.*

[11] *McLoughlin* v. *O'Brian* [1982] 2 All E.R. 298, 311, *per* Lord Bridge; *Hinz* v. *Berry* [1970] 2 Q.B. 40, 42. If, however, the plaintiff's mental distress or grief exacerbates other injuries which the plaintiff sustained in the same incident, preventing the plaintiff from making a recovery as quickly as would otherwise have occurred, this can be reflected in the award of damages in respect of the other injuries. In *Kralj* v. *McGrath* [1986] 1 All E.R. 54, 62, Woolf J. said: " . . . if the situation is one where the plaintiff's injuries have on her a more drastic effect than they would otherwise because of the grief which she is sustaining at the same time in relation to the death of a child who died in the circumstances in which Daniel died, that is something which the court can take into account." See also *Bagley* v. *North Hertfordshire Health Authority* (1986) 136 New L.J. 1014.

[12] *Hambrook* v. *Stokes Bros.* [1925] 1 K.B. 141.

could recover and in what circumstances. Thus, the nature of the relationship between the accident victim and the person who suffered the shock was important. A parent or spouse of a victim would more readily be accepted as a person likely to be affected, and accordingly within the range of a duty of care owed by the defendant. A bystander who is a total stranger to the accident victim will be treated as an unforeseeable plaintiff,[13] although a plaintiff who comes to the rescue at an accident will be given more favourable consideration if he subsequently sustains shock at the scene he has witnessed.[14]

2.46 A further restriction was that the shock must be the product of what the plaintiff perceived with his own unaided senses. There would be no action in respect of shock sustained as a result of what the plaintiff was told by others.[15] The effect was to limit claims to plaintiffs who were in fairly close physical proximity to the accident, although it was not essential that they had seen the accident itself.[16]

2.47 Athough it was said that the test of liability for shock is foreseeability of injury by shock,[17] it is clear that "foreseeability" was being given a restricted meaning in order to limit the potential number of claimants, first by excluding those who did not witness the event and secondly by excluding bystanders not related in some way to the victim.

2.48 In *McLoughlin* v. *O'Brian*[18] the House of Lords reconsidered the principles to be applied to actions for nervous shock. The plaintiff's husband and her three children were involved in a road accident caused by the defendant's negligence. One child was killed, and her husband and other two children were badly injured. The plaintiff was informed about the accident two hours after the event, and she was taken to the hospital where she was told about the death of her child and saw the injuries to her family in distressing circumstances. The House of Lords was unanimous in holding that the plaintiff's claim for nervous shock should succeed, but there was a difference of opinion as to the appropriate test of liability. Lords Wilberforce and Edmund-Davies considered that foreseeability of injury by shock was not the sole requirement. There must be some additional limits based on: (a) the class of person who could sue—the closer the emotional tie the greater the claim for consideration; (b) physical proximity to the accident, which must be close both in time and space, though this could include persons who did not witness the accident but came upon the "aftermath" of events—persons who would normally come to the scene, such as a parent or spouse, would be within the scope of the duty; (c) the means by which the shock

---

[13] *Bourhill* v. *Young* [1943] A.C. 92.

[14] *Chadwick* v. *British Railways Board* [1967] 1 W.L.R. 912; *Wigg* v. *British Railways Board, The Times,* February 4, 1986; *Mount Isa Mines Ltd.* v. *Pusey* (1970) C.L.R. 383; though see also *Dooley* v. *Cammell Laird & Co. Ltd.* [1951] 1 Lloyd's Rep. 271, where a workman succeeded in recovering damages for nervous shock having witnessed an incident in which he anticipated injury to fellow employees, although none in fact occurred.

[15] *Hambrook* v. *Stokes Bros.* [1925] 1 K.B. 141; *cf. Schneider* v. *Eisovitch* [1960] 2 Q.B. 430.

[16] *Boardman* v. *Sanderson* [1964] 1 W.L.R. 1317, where the plaintiff heard the accident and saw the aftermath; *Chadwick* v. *British Railways Board* [1967] 1 W.L.R. 912, where the plantiff saw the aftermath of a major train crash; *Benson* v. *Lee* [1972] V.R. 879.

[17] *King* v. *Phillips* [1953] 1 Q.B. 429, 441, *per* Denning L.J.

[18] [1982] 2 All E.R. 298.

is caused—it must come through the plaintiff's own sight or hearing of the event or its immediate aftermath; communication by a third party would not be sufficient.

Lords Bridge and Scarman preferred a test based upon foreseeability **2.49** alone, "untrammelled by spatial, physical or temporal limits," which would be largely arbitrary in their application. The factors included in Lord Wilberforce's "aftermath test" would have a bearing on the degree to which shock was foreseeable but they would not necessarily preclude a claim. Lord Bridge could see no logic in denying an action to a mother who read a newspaper report of a fire at a hotel where her children were staying, and who subsequently learnt of their deaths, simply because "an important link in the chain of causation of her psychiatric illness was supplied by her imagination of the agonies of mind and body in which her family died, rather than direct perception of the event."[19] Lord Russell, without expressly agreeing with Lord Bridge, concluded that if the shock to Mrs McLoughlin was foreseeable there was no justification for not finding the defendant liable, while conceding that policy might be relevant in an appropriate case to limit the scope of foreseeability.

Some courts now regard liability for nervous shock as turning on **2.50** foreseeability of shock alone.[20] On the other hand, in *Attia* v. *British Gas*[21] Bingham L.J. interpreted *McLoughlin* v. *O'Brian* as still permitting the court to deny recovery for foreseeable shock on policy grounds. Nonetheless, the Court of Appeal could see no grounds of policy in that case to prevent the plaintiff succeeding in an action for nervous shock sustained as a result of witnessing a fire which caused extensive damage to her home, although there were no personal injuries to anyone else and the plaintiff had not been at risk of physical injury to herself. If witnessing damage to property can give rise to an action for nervous shock, it is difficult to see what policy grounds could possibly justify denying liability where the plaintiff sustains foreseeable shock as a result of being told about the death or injury of a loved one, even if the plaintiff does not witness Lord Wilberforce's "aftermath."[22]

In *Jones* v. *Wright*, [22a] however, the Court of Appeal applied Lord Wilberforce's "aftermath test" to a number of claims for nervous shock which arose out of the Hillsborough stadium tragedy, in which 95 people were killed and over 400 injured. The events were shown in a live television broadcast, and some scenes were repeated as recorded news items. It was held that the class of persons who could maintain a claim for nervous shock was limited to spouses and persons in a

---

[19] *Ibid.*, p. 320. This may be a more likely cause of shock than witnessing the events: Teff (1983) 99 L.Q.R. 100, 107. See, however, *Jones* v. *Wright* [1991] 3 All E.R. 88, § 2.50.

[20] *Jaensch* v. *Coffey* (1984) 54 A.L.R. 417 (H.C. of Aus.); *Wigg* v. *British Railways Board*, *The Times*, February 4, 1986. See, however, Kidner (1987) 7 L.S. 319, 325 suggesting that here foreseeability has a "coded meaning."

[21] [1987] 3 All E.R. 455.

[22] See, *e.g.*, *Jaensch* v. *Coffey* (1984) 54 A.L.R 417, 463; Trindade [1986] C.L.J. 476, 484–485. In *Attia* v. *British Gas* [1987] 3 All E.R. 455 the Court of Appeal took the view that it was a question of fact, to be determined by the medical evidence, whether the psychiatric damage was reasonably foreseeable. Teff (1983) 99 L.Q.R. 100 comments that, from a medical viewpoint, the crucial determinant of whether the plaintiff is likely to suffer nervous shock is almost invariably the nature of his relationship with the victim.

[22a] [1991] 3 All E.R. 88. This decision is under appeal.

parent-child relationship, though looking to the factual relationship rather than simply the legal relationship between the plaintiff and the victim. More remote relationships were excluded on the basis that such individuals would be expected to show reasonable fortitude and so would not be foreseeably affected. Secondly, it was said that the "aftermath" did not extend to a plaintiff who went to the mortuary to identify his son's body. Mrs. McLoughlin's visit to the hospital was in a different category because the scene at the hospital was "part of the catastrophe itself for none of the victims had been cleaned up or attended to."[22b] Finally, the court held that witnessing events through a live television broadcast was equivalent to being told about the events by a third party and thus was outside the scope of compensation. Nolan L.J. took the view that an action for nervous shock must be based on a reaction to an immediate impact, even though this does not necessarily correspond to medical understanding of the mechanisms by which psychiatric injury may occur.[22c]

2.51   The full implications of these issues have yet to be worked out in the context of medical negligence. It is clear that damages for nervous shock may be awarded against a doctor. In *Kralj* v. *McGrath*[23] the plaintiff suffered physical injuries as a result of "horrific treatment" by the defendant in the course of delivering a baby. She also suffered shock on being told about the baby's injuries and seeing the child for the eight weeks that it survived. Woolf J. held that she was entitled to be compensated for this "nervous shock," although no specific psychiatric illness was identified. It is difficult to extrapolate too far from this case, because the plaintiff was undoubtedly owed a duty of care, as the doctor's patient, and she also suffered physical injury. It is unclear how far the concept of foreseeability and/or the "aftermath" will be stretched for non-patients. Does it extend, for example, to a relative who sees the injured patient in hospital after the events which caused the patient's injuries? *Kralj* v. *McGrath* might appear to suggest that it does, although the plaintiff in that case was actually present "at the scene" of the event, even if she was not aware of the injury to the child at the time. In *McLoughlin* v. *O'Brian* some emphasis was placed on the fact that the plaintiff saw her family at the hospital in a distressed state, before they had been fully attended to by the medical staff (a point that was reiterated by the Court of Appeal in *Jones* v. *Wright*). This is unlikely to be the case where the injuries are the result of

---

[22b] *Ibid.*, at p. 97, *per* Parker L.J.; see also, *per* Nolan L.J. at p. 123. In *Hevican* v. *Ruane* [1991] 3 All E.R. 65 Mantell J. held that a plaintiff who had identified his son's body at the mortuary was entitled to succeed for psychological trauma, even though he was not present at the scene of the accident or the aftermath, and in *Ravenscroft* v. *Rederiaktiebolaget Transatlantic* [1991] 3 All E.R. 73 Ward J. concluded that a mother who was called to the hospital, and when she arrived was told that her son was dead, was entitled to recover for a reactive depression. Neither of these cases would appear to be reconcilable with the decision of the Court of Appeal in *Jones* v. *Wright*.

[22c] *Ibid.*, at p. 123. See also *Rhodes* v. *Canadian National Railway* (1990) 75 D.L.R. (4th) 248, 298, *per* Taylor J.A. (B.C.C.A.) and *Campbelltown City Council* v. *Mackay* (1989) 15 N.S.W.L.R. 501, 503, *per* Kirby P. (N.S.W.C.A.) on this point.

[23] [1986] 1 All E.R. 54. In the American case of *Molien* v. *Kaiser Foundation Hospitals* (1980) 616 P. 2d 813 a doctor was held liable for a negligent diagnosis which led to the break up of the plaintiff's marriage. See also Norrie (1985) 34 I.C.L.Q. 442, 463 discussing the possibility of claims for nervous shock following unauthorised post-mortems, and, by extension, following the unauthorised removal of organs for transplantation contrary to the Human Tissue Act 1961.

medical negligence, at least where the injuries occur in the hospital itself.

Would psychiatric damage, for example clinical depression, which is **2.52** attributable to the plaintiff having to live with the fact that a loved one is permanently disabled as a result of the defendant's negligence, be actionable? No case has gone that far in this country, although in *Beecham* v. *Hughes*[24] the British Columbia Court of Appeal has contemplated such a claim. The plaintiff suffered from reactive depression which commenced some time after a motoring accident which rendered his common law wife permanently brain damaged. The defendant, who was responsible for the accident, was found not liable because the length of time between the accident and the onset of the plaintiff's depression cast doubt on the causal connection. The majority stated, however, that if the plaintiff's reactive depression had resulted from the stress of seeing his wife, day after day, in a condition utterly unlike her condition before the accident, the damage would have been foreseeable.[25] This conclusion would represent an extension of the present law, but such an extension would not necessarily be unwarranted on the grounds either of foreseeability or policy.

A further question concerns the potential liability of the person who **2.53** communicates the information to the plaintiff, as a result of which the plaintiff sustains nervous shock. It has been said that if the statement is true there is no obligation to break bad news gently, even if it is foreseeable that the person will be shocked by it.[26] This proposition has been questioned, however, at least where the circumstances are such that the impact of the news is needlessly exacerbated.[27] This could be significant for doctors, who frequently have to give bad news, both to patients and relatives. Where the information is false a doctor will be responsible for nervous shock suffered by the recipient. In *Jinks* v. *Cardwell*[28] a doctor who falsely told a wife that her husband had committed suicide by drowning in a bath because it would look better for the hospital was held liable for her "physical and emotional distress."[29] At best he was negligent, said the judge, at worst callous and unfeeling.[30]

When applying the test of foreseeability of injury by shock, it has to **2.54** be demonstrated that the plaintiff is a person of reasonable fortitude and is not unduly susceptible to some form of psychiatric reaction.[31]

---

[24] (1988) 52 D.L.R. (4th) 625 (B.C.C.A.).

[25] *cf. Rhodes* v. *Canadian National Railway* (1990) 75 D.L.R. (4th) 248, 298 (B.C.C.A.) and *Jones* v. *Wright* [1991] 3 All E.R. 88, 123, *per* Nolan L.J. requiring that the plaintiff's nervous shock be caused by a reaction to a specific *event*. This would seem to exclude psychiatric damage caused in other ways, such as depression caused by caring for an injured relative: see *Jaensch* v. *Coffey* (1984) 54 A.L.R. 417, 428–9.

[26] *Mount Isa Mines Ltd.* v. *Pusey* (1970) C.L.R. 383, 407.

[27] *Winfield & Jolowicz on Tort*, 13th ed., 1989, p. 110. In *Furness* v. *Fitchett* [1958] N.Z.L.R. 396 it was accepted that a doctor may be under a duty of care to his *patient* not to inform her about her medical condition. The defendant was held liable for harm to the plaintiff's psychiatric health even though the information was true.

[28] (1987) 39 C.C.L.T. 168 (Ont. H.C.).

[29] *cf. Guay* v. *Sun Publishing Co.* [1953] 4 D.L.R. 577, where a newspaper was held not liable for the shock suffered by the plaintiff on reading a false report of the family's death published negligently by a newspaper.

[30] A deliberate lie which causes shock might be actionable under the principle in *Wilkinson* v. *Downton* [1897] 2 Q.B. 57.

[31] *Bourhill* v. *Young* [1943] A.C. 92, 110; *McLoughlin* v. *O'Brian* [1982] 2 All E.R. 298, 309.

This excludes persons who are abnormally sensitive to shock. If, however, a person of ordinary fortitude would have sustained shock in the circumstances, the plaintiff who was particularly sensitive can also recover[32]; and, moreover, he is entitled to damages for the full extent of his injuries, even if they are exacerbated by a predisposition to mental illness or disorder and thus are more severe than an ordinary individual would have experienced.[33]

(v) Psychiatric patients

2.55   There can be no doubt that a doctor, such as a psychiatrist or clinical psychologist, will owe a duty of care to his psychiatric patients, and that this duty may require the doctor to take reasonable steps to protect the patient from harming himself, including, in some instances, the prevention of suicide attempts.[34] Moreover, a hospital authority may be responsible for injuries inflicted on a patient by a fellow patient where the injuries are the result of a failure to provide adequate control and supervision.[35] There are, however, at least two other situations in which a duty of care may arise which is owed to someone other than the patient. First, where a doctor certifies that a person is insane, and secondly, possibly, where a psychiatric patient has injured a third party in circumstances in which the damage was foreseeable.

(a) *Certificates of "insanity"*

2.56   Applications to commit patients compulsorily to hospital under Part II of the Mental Health Act 1983 must be supported by the recommendations of (normally) two doctors, one of whom must be an approved specialist in mental disorder, although an approved specialist will not necessarily be a qualified psychiatrist.[36] Under section 2 of that Act a person may be detained for 28 days for assessment, during which time he may receive some treatment without his consent. The doctors must certify that the patient is suffering from a mental disorder of a nature or degree which warrants detention for assessment, and that he ought to be detained in the interests of his own health or safety or for the protection of other persons.[37] In an emergency the application for admission for assessment needs the support of only one doctor, who does not have to be an approved specialist.[38] Under section 3 a person may be compulsorily detained for treatment, initially for up to six months. The doctors must certify:
  (a) that the person is suffering from mental illness, severe mental impairment, psychopathic disorder or mental impairment and

---

[32] *Jaensch* v. *Coffey* (1984) 54 A.L.R. 417.
[33] *Brice* v. *Brown* [1984] 1 All E.R. 997; *Benson* v. *Lee* [1972] V.R. 879.
[34] See §§ 4.89 *et seq.*
[35] *Wellesley Hospital* v. *Lawson* (1977) 76 D.L.R. (3d) 688 in which the Supreme Court of Canada proceeded on the basis that such a common law duty existed, though the case was concerned with the interpretation of a provision in the Ontario Mental Health Act 1970. An analogous case is *Ellis* v. *Home Office* [1953] 2 All E.R. 149 in which the prison authorities were held to owe a duty of care to a prisoner assaulted by another prisoner. On the facts the defendants were not found negligent since the attack was unforeseeable.
[36] Hoggett, *Mental Health Law,* 3rd ed., 1990, p. 100.
[37] Mental Health Act 1983, s.2(2).
[38] *Ibid.,* s.4.

his condition is of a nature or degree which makes medical
treatment in hospital appropriate;
(b) that, in the case of psychopathic disorder or mental impairment,
the treatment is likely to alleviate or prevent a deterioration of
his condition; and
(c) it is necessary for the health or safety of the patient or for the
protection of other persons that he should receive such treatment which cannot be provided unless he is detained.[39]

These procedures clearly contemplate that the person detained will **2.57**
not necessarily be a patient of the doctor(s) supporting admission,
since the Act specifies that one of the doctors must, *if practicable*, have
"previous acquaintance" with the person.[40] There is little doubt,
however, that the doctors owe a duty of care to that person in giving
the certificate and may be liable in an action for negligence.[41] In *De
Freville* v. *Dill*[42] McCardie J. was apparently opposed to the existence
of such a duty but felt compelled to hold that a duty of care did exist
on the balance of authority, particularly the majority decision of the
Court of Appeal in *Everett* v. *Griffiths*.[43] The House of Lords held in
Everett v. *Griffiths*[44] that the defendant doctor was not liable on the
facts, without expressing a concluded view on the decision of
Crompton J. in *Hall* v. *Semple*[45] in which a duty had been held to exist.

If a doctor owes a duty not to issue a certificate negligently, it would **2.58**
also follow that there may be liability for negligently *failing* to issue a
certificate if the person is in fact of unsound mind and through the
absence of certification and restraint, he inflicts injury on himself. This
point was acknowledged by McCardie J., obiter, in *De Frevill* v. *Dill*.[46]

(b) Injury to third parties

Is a doctor who is aware or ought reasonably to be aware that a **2.59**
psychiatric patient constitutes a serious risk of harm to others under a
duty of care to the third parties to take steps to prevent the harm or
minimise the risk? If, for example, a patient has threatened to kill
someone, does the doctor have a duty to warn either that person or the
police, or to initiate the compulsory detention procedures under the
Mental Health Act 1983.[47] If so, the doctor could be liable in damages

---

[39] See also s.7 of the Mental Health Act 1983 on reception into guardianship; and the
National Assistance Act 1948, s.47 and the National Assistance (Amendment) Act 1951
which require medical evidence in support of compulsory removal procedures.
[40] ss.12(2), 4(3).
[41] *Hall* v. *Semple* (1862) 3 F. & F. 337; *De Freville* v. *Dill* (1927) 96 L.J.K.B. 1056;
Everett v. *Griffiths* [1920] 3 K.B. 163, C.A.; [1921] 1 A.C. 631, H.L.; *Harnett* v. *Fisher*
[1927] A.C. 573; *Buxton* v. *Jayne* [1960] 1 W.L.R. 783; [1962] C.L.Y. 1167. On the
procedural restrictions to bringing such an action see Mental Health Act 1983, s.139,
post §§ 4.104 *et seq.*
[42] (1927) 96 L.J.K.B. 1056.
[43] [1920] 3 K.B. 163.
[44] [1921] 1 A.C. 631.
[45] (1862) 3 F. & F. 337.
[46] (1927) 96 L.J.K.B. 1056, 1060–1061. In *Everett* v. *Griffiths* [1920] 3 K.B. 163, 196
Scrutton L.J., in a dissenting judgment, considered that the prospect of such a duty
being owed was a reason for *not* imposing a duty generally in the granting of certificates.
[47] Note that there is a difference between saying that the statutory grounds for
compulsory detention are satisfied, and that the doctor owes a common law duty of care
to a third party to detain the patient.

to a victim of the patient if he negligently failed to take the appropriate steps.

2.60   This question has not arisen directly for decision in this country, but in *Tarasoff* v. *Regents of the University of California*[48] the Supreme Court of California held that a psychologist owed a duty of care to a woman murdered by the psychologist's patient. The patient had expressed an intention to kill the woman, who was a former girlfriend. The court accepted that there was a balance to be drawn between the public interest in effective treatment of mental illness and the consequent requirement of protecting confidentiality, and the public interest in safety from violent assault. Nonetheless, the protection of confidentiality must end where the public peril begins.[49]

2.61   This duty of care is not as wide as might at first appear. First, in *Tarasoff* it was recognised that the nature of the "psychotherapeutic dialogue" may lead patients to express threats of violence, few of which are ever executed, and a therapist should not be encouraged routinely to reveal such threats. Secondly, the California Supreme Court has subsequently distinguished *Tarasoff* in a case where a patient made general threats of violence against children, on the basis that *Tarasoff* involved a known and specifically foreseeable and identifiable victim.[50]

2.62   It is debatable whether *Tarasoff* would be followed in this country. In the one case which comes closest to it, *Holgate* v. *Lancashire Mental Hospitals Board*,[51] a hospital was held liable for negligently releasing on licence a dangerous patient who had been compulsorily detained following convictions for violent offences. The patient entered the plaintiff's home and assaulted her. The trial judge seemed to assume that a duty of care existed and the report deals largely with the question whether there had been negligence. The case may be justified on the basis of the degree of control exercised by the defendants over the dangerous patient, a control analogous to the relationship between gaoler and prisoner which may give rise to a duty of care.[52] This is the basis upon which a hospital authority may be held liable for injuries to a patient inflicted by a fellow patient as a result of negligent supervision, and there is no obvious reason why this duty should be owed only to patients, and not, for example, to visitors to the hospital.[53] However, in *Home Office* v. *Dorset Yacht Co. Ltd.*[54] Lord Diplock specifically reserved his opinion on *Holgate* v. *Lancashire Mental*

---

[48] (1976) 551 P. 2d 334; see de Haan (1986) 2 P.N. 86.

[49] "In this risk-infected society we can hardly tolerate the further exposure to danger that would result from a concealed knowledge of the therapist that his patient was lethal. If the exercise of reasonable care to protect the threatened victim requires the therapist to warn the endangered party or those who can reasonably be expected to notify him, we see no sufficient societal interest that would protect and justify concealment. The containment of such risks lies in the public interest," *per* Tobriner J. (1976) 551 P. 2d 334, at 347.

[50] *Thompson* v. *County of Alameda* 614 P. 2d 728 (1980); see also *Brady* v. *Hopper* 751 F. 2d 329 (1984); *cf. Jablonski* v. *U.S.* 712 F. 2d 391 (1983).

[51] [1937] 4 All E.R. 19.

[52] See *Home Office* v. *Dorset Yacht Co. Ltd.* [1970] A.C. 1004; *Ellis* v. *Home Office* [1953] 2 All E.R. 149.

[53] See *Wellesley Hospital* v. *Lawson* (1977) 76 D.L.R. (3d) 688 (S.C.C.) where the duty was said to be owed to "third persons," not simply patients. See also *Partington* v. *Wandsworth London Borough Council, The Independent*, November 8, 1989.

[54] [1970] A.C. 1004, 1062–1063.

Hospitals Boards, and it has been suggested that the case is of doubtful authority today on the basis that the discretion to admit or release a patient under the Mental Health legislation constitutes the exercise of a statutory power for which there can be civil liability only where the exercise of the power is *ultra vires*.[55]

An independent psychiatrist does not exercise this degree of control **2.63** over the patient, and thus some alternative basis for a duty of care would have to be established. It has been argued that this is to be found in the doctor's unique capacity to influence the patient's behaviour, whether through treatment or advice.[56] This is questionable, however, given that the doctor's ability to influence the patient may be limited, and in some circumstances it may be virtually nonexistent.

The basis of any potential duty of care must be the foreseeability of **2.64** harm to the victim. Foreseeability alone is not, however, sufficient to impose a duty of care. There must also be a proximate relationship between plaintiff and defendant, and it must be just and reasonable in the circumstances to impose a duty.[57] The more foreseeable the harm the more likely it is that a court will find the relationship between the parties to be proximate.[58] Thus, if a patient made genuine threats of serious injury to an identified third person and there was a real risk that the threats would be carried out, it is arguable that a doctor would come under a duty of care to the potential victim. The duty, if any, arises from the defendant's knowledge of the foreseeable danger of serious physical harm to the third party.[59]

There are difficulties, however with imposing such a duty.[60] There is **2.65** no general obligation in the tort of negligence to take positive steps to confer a benefit on others by preventing harm befalling them, and there is no obligation to rescue someone in danger, even if rescue would involve little or no effort and involves no danger to the

---

[55] Hoggett, *Mental Health Law*, 3rd ed., 1990, p. 248, citing *Anns* v. *Merton London Borough Council* [1978] A.C. 728. Presumably where the release was *ultra vires* an action could lie, particularly if there were negligence at what Lord Wilberforce termed the "operational level": see *Anns* v. *Merton London Borough Council* [1978] A.C. 728, 754 and the speech of Lord Diplock in *Home Office* v. *Dorset Yacht Co. Ltd.* [1970] A.C. 1004. Query whether this aspect of Lord Wilberforce's speech in *Anns* is still applicable following the overruling of that decision in *Murphy* v. *Brentwood District Council* [1990] 2 All E.R. 908. See, however, *Re HIV Haemophiliac Litigation*, (1990) 140 New L.J. 1349, where Ralph Gibson L.J. said that: "Although it was difficult to prove a negligent breach of duty when the party charged with negligence was required to exercise discretion and form judgments on the allocation of public resources, that was not sufficient to make it clear that there could be no claim in negligence."

[56] See de Haan (1986) 2 P.N. 86, 88.

[57] *Caparo Industries plc.* v. *Dickman* [1990] 1 All E.R. 568, 573–574, *per* Lord Bridge; *Smith* v. *Bush* [1989] 2 W.L.R. 790, 816, *per* Lord Griffiths; *Pacific Associates Inc.* v. *Baxter* [1989] 2 All E.R. 159, 189, *per* Russell L.J.

[58] *Caparo Industries plc* v. *Dickman* [1989] 1 All E.R. 798, 803, *per* Bingham L.J.

[59] There is an analogy with the infection cases here, since it is the doctor's failure to warn the third party or the failure to isolate the patient which leads to the spread of the infection, and the duty must be based on foreseeability of the risk see §§ 2.37–2.40. In *De Freville* v. *Dill* (1927) 96 L.J.K.B. 1056, 1060–1061 McCardie J., discussing the liability of a doctor who negligently certifies that a person is of unsound mind, raised the prospect of liability for negligently failing to issue a certificate where the person is in fact of unsound mind, and as a result the person inflicts injury on himself that could have been avoided by treatment or restraint. Such a duty, owed to someone who is not the doctor's patient, is not so far removed from the situation in *Tarasoff*.

[60] For more detailed discussion see Jones (1990) 6 P.N. 16, 21.

rescuer.[61] In the absence of a special relationship giving the defendant some degree of control over the patient, there is nothing upon which to base a duty to intervene, other than the mere foreseeability of the harm, which in the case of damage caused by a third party (here the patient) is not normally sufficient to impose a duty of care.[62]

2.66   A second objection might be that imposing a duty of care could create a conflict of duties for the doctor, between the duty of confidence owed to the patient and the duty of care owed to a third party. It is true that where the imposition of a duty of care might lead to a defendant being subject to conflicting duties the courts may be reluctant to find a duty of care,[63] but where the public interest defence to an action for breach of confidence applies there is no duty to maintain confidentiality and so no conflict with a possible duty of care.[64] The public interest defence recognises that in some circumstances other, more valued, social considerations outweigh the confidentiality of the doctor/patient relationship, and it is arguable that the public interest in safety from individuals known to be lethal falls into this category. It was this point which the court considered to be persuasive in *Tarasoff*.

2.67   A third factor which a court might consider relevant in determining whether there should be a duty of care is the possibility of an alternative remedy for the victim under the Criminal Injuries Compensation Scheme.[65]

2.68   If a duty does arise the question would be: in what circumstances? If the doctor considered the patient to be "dangerous," but the patient had made no threats against specific individuals, the courts would probably not impose a duty of care, on the basis that the victim was merely a member of a large unascertained class.[66] This would be consistent with the approach of the American courts.[67] This is linked to a further problem, namely what would be required of the doctor in order to satisfy the duty of care. Although a duty to give a warning is not a particularly onerous duty for the "reluctant rescuer" to comply with,[68] the assumption, of course, is that it is possible to give an effective warning about a dangerous psychiatric patient, either to a hospital, the potential victim or the police. But where the patient is not

---

[61] See *ante* § 2.41.

[62] See Norrie (1984) 24 Med.Sci. & Law 26, 30, who argues that *Tarasoff* would not be followed in this country because of the objection to imposing an affirmative duty to act; Brazier, *Medicine, Patients and the Law*, p. 42; see also Giesen, *International Medical Malpractice Law*, 1988, pp. 160–161; *cf.* de Haan (1986) 2 P.N. 86, 88.

[63] *Clerk & Lindsell on Torts*, 16th ed., 1989, p. 622, n. 57.

[64] Though *cf.* Brazier, *Medicine Patients and the Law*, p. 42: "The doctor is faced with a stark conflict of duty." The doctor's problem is, arguably, not the conflict of duties but the difficulty of deciding where, on the facts of the case before him, his duty lies. For a graphic illustration of the problem see Langton and Torpy (1988) 28 Med.Sci. & Law 195. On the public interest defence see §§ 2.95–2.105.

[65] See *Hill* v. *Chief Constable of West Yorkshire* [1987] 1 All E.R. 1173, 1182, 1183; the lack of a conviction, *e.g.* for want of *mens rea*, does not prevent a claim under the scheme.

[66] In *Hill* v. *Chief Constable of West Yorkshire* [1988] 2 All E.R. 238, 243 the House of Lords held that the police owed no duty of care to the victim of a notorious serial murderer for allegedly negligently failing to apprehend him, partly on the ground that the victim "was one of a vast number of the female general public who might be at risk from his activities but was at no special distinctive risk . . . "

[67] See n. 50, *ante*.

[68] Logie [1989] C.L.J. 115.

compulsorily detained or has not made threats against specific individuals this may be difficult.[69]

(vi) Financial loss to third parties

There is, in theory, no reason why a doctor should not owe a duty of **2.69** care to a third party in respect of purely financial loss when giving advice to that third party as to a person's medical condition, under the principle in *Hedley Byrne & Co. Ltd.* v. *Heller & Partners Ltd.*[70] For example, a doctor who prepared a medical report on a patient for the purpose of an insurance company that was contemplating issuing a life policy on the patient would clearly owe a duty of care to the insurance company under this principle, whether or not the doctor was paid for the service.[71] The position would be similar where the report was for an employer or prospective employer of the patient as to his medical fitness to perform his job.[72]

III. THE DUTY OF CONFIDENCE

A doctor owes a duty of confidence in respect of information **2.70** concerning his patient which he acquires in his capacity as a doctor, whether from the patient himself or from others. This obligation is widely regarded as one of the cornerstones of the doctor/patient relationship, and this is reflected in a number of international ethical codes.[73] The most important statement of the medical profession's ethical duty is contained in the guidance provided in the General Medical Council's "Blue Book," which in paragraph 77 states that:

> "It is a doctor's duty, except in the case mentioned below, strictly to observe the rule of professional secrecy by refraining from disclosing voluntarily to any third party information about a patient which he has learnt directly or indirectly in his professional capacity as a registered medical practitioner. The death of the patient does not absolve the doctor from this obligation."[74]

---

[69] See, *e.g.*, Langton and Torpy, *op. cit.*, n. 64 at p. 198.

[70] [1964] A.C. 465; see § 2.25.

[71] Although, since a contract of insurance is a contract *uberrimae fidei*, the insurers would have a right to avoid the contract if the patient/insured had failed to disclose a material fact about his medical history, and in these circumstances would suffer no loss. The action against the doctor would only be relevant if the patient was unaware of his medical condition.

[72] See *Lawton* v. *BOC Transhield Ltd.* [1987] 2 All E.R. 608, where it was said that an employer owes a duty of care to an employee when providing a reference about the employee to a prospective employer, and it would seem to follow from this that he owes a duty to the prospective employer.

[73] See, *e.g.*, the *Hippocratic Oath*: "All that may come to my knowledge in the exercise of my profession or outside my profession or in daily commerce with men, which ought not to be spread abroad, I will keep secret and will never reveal"; *Declaration of Geneva*: "I will respect the secrets which are confided in me, even after the patient has died"; *International Code of Medical Ethics*: "A doctor shall preserve absolute secrecy on all he knows about his patients because of the confidence entrusted in him."

[74] General Medical Council, *Professional Conduct and Discipline: Fitness to Practise.* In *W.* v. *Egdell* [1989] 1 All E.R. 1089; [1990] 1 All E.R. 835, C.A. the G.M.C. guidelines were described by Scott J. as "valuable" in showing the approach of the G.M.C. to the breadth of the doctor's duty of confidence; and para. 77 was said by Bingham L.J. (at p. 849) to "accurately state the general rule as the law now stands."

2.71   The confidentiality of the doctor/patient relationship is protected in
law, although there is little in the way of caselaw where this issue has
had to be decided.[75] There are dicta which simply assume that this is
correct.[76] In *W.* v. *Egdell* Scott J. said of a psychiatrist who had
prepared a medical report on the plaintiff for use at a mental health
review tribunal: "The question in the present case is not whether Dr.
Egdell was under a duty of confidence; *he plainly was*. The question is
as to the breadth of that duty."[77]

2.72   A duty of confidence frequently arises from the relationship between
a professional person (such as a lawyer or accountant) and the client.
Usually, the duty will derive from the contract, as either an express or
implied term. Patients within the N.H.S. do not normally enter into a
contractual relationship with their doctor. But, apart from a duty in
contract, equity will intervene to protect confidences where three
requirements are satisfied, namely:

   (a) the information must have the necessary quality of confidence
       about it;
   (b) it must have been imparted in circumstances importing an
       obligation of confidence; and (c) there must be unauthorised
       use of that information to the detriment of the person who
       communicated it.[78]

If these requirements are satisfied, the burden lies upon the defendant to establish some justification for disclosure of the confidential
information.[79]

2.73   Medical information imparted in the context of the doctor/patient
relationship clearly satisfies the first two requirements. The question of
what amounts to "detriment" to a patient is more problematic and has
not been fully addressed. Does a patient who does not base his claim
for breach of confidence on a contractual relationship have to establish
that the breach has, or is likely to, cause financial or physical/
psychological harm, or is the disclosure of the information sufficient in
itself to constitute a detriment?

2.74   In *A.-G.* v. *Guardian Newspapers Ltd.* (No. 2)[80] there was a division
of opinion in the House of Lords on this issue, with Lord Griffiths in

---

[75] See, however, *Kitson* v. *Playfair*, *The Times*, March 28, 1986.

[76] "The law has long recognised that an obligation of confidence can arise out of
particular relationships. Examples are the relationships of doctor and patient, priest and
penitent, solicitor and client, banker and customer," *per* Lord Keith in *A.-G.* v.
Guardian Newspapers (No. 2) [1988] 3 All E.R. 545, 639f; see also *Goddard* v.
Nationwide Building Society [1986] 3 All E.R. 264, 271, *per* Nourse L.J.: "The equitable
jurisdiction is well able to extend, for example, to the grant of an injunction to restrain
an unauthorised disclosure of confidential communications between priest and penitent
or doctor and patient"; see also *Hunter* v. *Mann* [1974] Q.B. 767, 772, *per* Boreham J.:
". . . the doctor is under a duty not to disclose [voluntarily], without the consent of his
patient, information which he, the doctor, has gained in his professional capacity."

[77] [1989] 1 All E.R. 1089, 1102, emphasis added. In the Court of Appeal [1990] 1 All
E.R. 835, 848, Bingham L.J. said that: "It has never been doubted that the circumstances here were such as to impose on Dr. Egdell a duty of confidence owed to W . . .
It is not in issue here that a duty of confidence existed." See also *X.* v. *Y.* [1988] 2 All
E.R. 648, although the breach of confidence at issue in this case was the duty owed by a
hospital employee to his employers under a contract of employment, not the duty owed
by a doctor to his patient.

[78] *Coco* v. *A. N. Clark (Engineers) Ltd.* [1969] R.P.C. 41, 47, *per* Megarry J.; *Stephens*
v. *Avery* [1988] 2 All E.R. 477, 479; *A.-G.* v. *Guardian Newspapers* (No. 2) [1988] 3 All
E.R. 545, 649.

[79] *A.-G.* v. *Guardian Newspapers* (No. 2) [1988] 3 All E.R. 545, 649–650.

[80] [1988] 3 All E.R. 545.

favour of a requirement of some detriment, whereas Lord Keith considered that it was a sufficient detriment to the confider that the information given in confidence is to be disclosed to persons whom he would prefer not to know of it, even though the disclosure would not be harmful to him in any positive way. As a general rule, said his Lordship, it is in the public interest that confidences should be respected, and the encouragement of such respect may in itself constitute a sufficient ground for recognising and enforcing the obligation of confidence, even in the absence of specific detriment. Although Lord Griffiths insisted on some detriment, he did accept that the court would protect a marital confidence from disclosure on the ground that this might involve the loss of a friend, "and friends can be precious."[81] For Lord Keith the invasion of personal privacy in such a case was a sufficient reason for intervening. The disclosure of confidential medical information may, of course, result in the loss of a friend, or in extreme cases (as possibly with AIDS) substantial financial loss.[82]

The legal protection afforded to medical confidences should not, **2.75** however, depend upon this fortuitous and arbitrary circumstance or the artificial identification of hypothetical or notional losses, and for this reason Lord Keith's view is to be preferred.[83] There is clearly a public interest in the preservation of medical confidences, since full disclosure by a patient to his doctor of information about his medical condition is an essential requirement for diagnosis and treatment. Patients should not be afraid to speak frankly about embarrassing matters, or be deterred from obtaining necessary medical assistance by the fear of unauthorised disclosure.[84] This problem is likely to be most acute with illnesses such as venereal disease, AIDS (or HIV positive infection),[85] and psychiatric disorders.[86]

It is unlikely that a court would refuse to grant an injunction to **2.76** restrain a threatened breach of medical confidence on the ground that a patient has suffered no detriment. Given that the doctor/patient relationship is widely cited as the paradigm example of a confidential

---

[81] See *Argyll* v. *Argyll* [1965] 1 All E.R. 611.

[82] See, *e.g.,* Napier (1989) 18 I.L.J. 84; Wacks (1988) 138 New L.J. 254, 255.

[83] In *X.* v. *Y.* [1988] 2 All E.R. 648, 657, which is the one case in which the issue has arisen in relation to medical information, Rose J. said that detriment in the use of the information is not a necessary precondition to injunctive relief: "I respectfully agree with Megarry V.-C. [in *Coco* v. *A.N. Clark* (*Engineers*) *Ltd.* [1969] R.P.C. 41, 48] that an injunction may be appropriate for breach of confidence where the plaintiff may not suffer from the use of the information and that is borne out by more recent observations in the Court of Appeal and the House of Lords...which contain no reference to the necessity for detriment in use, and indeed point away from any such principle." His Lordship referred to *Lion Laboratories Ltd.* v. *Evans* [1984] 2 All E.R. 417; *Schering Chemicals Ltd.* v. *Falkman Ltd.* [1981] 2 All E.R. 321; and *British Steel Corporation* v. *Granada Television Ltd.* [1981] 1 All E.R. 417.

[84] *X.* v. *Y.* [1988] 2 All E.R. 648, 656, *per* Rose J.

[85] Venereal disease is the subject of a specific statutory duty of confidence: see the National Health Service (Venereal Diseases) Regulations 1974 (S.I. 1974/29). In *X.* v. *Y.* [1988] 2 All E.R. 648, 656, Rose J. seemed to assume that this statutory duty applied to AIDS patients.

[86] *cf.*, however, Scott J. in *W.* v. *Egdell* [1989] 1 All E.R. 1089, 1150, responding to the suggestion that if patients could not suppress unfavourable psychiatric reports they would not be wholly frank: "I do not think that this answer has much weight. The possibility of a lack of frankness must always be present when a psychiatric examination takes place. An experienced psychiatrist would, I think, expect to be able to detect it. And the lack of frankness itself would constitute material of interest to the psychiatrist."

relationship, the court would either strain to find something detrimental to the plaintiff on the facts or would simply accept that the disclosure itself is a detriment. If the patient's complaint concerns a past breach of confidence, however, the position may be different since there is considerable uncertainty about the availability of damages as a remedy for breach of a confidence which is not based on breach of contract, and even here, where the claim is for distress or invasion of privacy, damages may be nominal.[87] For this reason the disciplinary powers of the General Medical Council and the profession's ethical standards may be more effective in maintaining patient confidentiality.

2.77   The duty of confidence binds not only the first recipient of the information, but also anyone else to whom that information is communicated who knows or ought to know that the information which he has received is confidential in character.[88]

Scope of the duty of confidence

2.78   The duty of confidence is not absolute, and it is only by looking at the circumstances in which a breach of confidence can be justified in law that the scope of the duty can be appreciated. The British Medical Association *Handbook of Medical Ethics*[89] gives five exceptions, and the General Medical Council[90] lists eight exceptions where information about a patient may be disclosed. Some of these exceptions correspond to exceptions in law, and most of them do not give rise to difficulty. The public interest defence is more amorphous, however, and this is considered in greater detail below. The G.M.C. exceptions are as follows.

2.79   (1) Written consent by the patient or his legal adviser.

In law, consent need not be in writing to be valid and may be express or implied.[91] Thus, the right to confidentiality is the patient's not the doctor's.

2.80   (2) "Confidential information may be shared with other registered medical practitioners who participate in or assume responsibility for clinical management of the patient," and in appropriate circumstances this will extend to other health care professionals who are assisting and collaborating with the doctor in his professional relationship with the patient.

---

[87] See §§ 9.70–9.72. This discrepancy may mark a difference between private patients and patients treated under the N.H.S.

[88] Though the breadth and nature of the duty of confidence must be considered separately against each defendant, because "the third party recipient may be subject to some additional and conflicting duty which does not affect the primary confidant or may not be subject to some special duty which does affect the confidant. In such situations the equation is not the same in the case of the confidant and that of the third party and accordingly the result may be different," *per* Sir John Donaldson M.R. in *A.-G. v. Guardian Newspapers Ltd.* (No. 2) [1988] 3 All E.R. 545, 600, cited by Scott J. in *W. v. Egdell* [1989] 1 All E.R. 1089, 1101.

[89] (i) Consent by the patient; (ii) where it is undesirable on medical grounds to seek the patient's consent, but it is in the patient's own interests that confidentiality should be broken; (iii) where the doctor has an overriding duty to society; (iv) for the purpose of medical research, approved by a research ethics committee; (v) when information is required by due legal process.

[90] *Professional Conduct and Discipline: Fitness to Practise* 1991 § 78.

[91] *Hunter v. Mann* [1974] 1 Q.B. 767, 772. As to the patient's right of access to his medical records see §§ 10.67 *et seq.*

This would probably be regarded by a court as an instance of **2.81** implied consent by the patient, although in *W.* v. *Egdell*[92] Scott J. considered that the disclosure of an independent psychiatrist's report to the hospital where the plaintiff was detained was justified under this provision, even though the patient had expressly refused his consent. The Court of Appeal doubted whether this exception applied, however, because the psychiatrist did not have a continuing professional relationship with the plaintiff, although the circumstances of the disclosure fell within the letter of the exception. If Scott J.'s view were correct then implied consent could not be the basis for the exception.

Clearly, all the members of the health care team come under a **2.82** corresponding duty of confidentiality with regard to the information communicated to them about the patient.

(3) Where it is "undesirable *on medical grounds* to seek the patient's **2.83** consent, information regarding the patient's health may sometimes be given in confidence to a close relative or a person in a similar relationship to the patient . . .."

Apart from the case of children under the age of 16 years,[93] the legal **2.84** basis for this exception is doubtful. Whilst there may be rare circumstances in which there could be a duty of care not to reveal facts about the patient's condition to the patient,[94] it does not follow that in law the doctor is entitled to disclose the information to someone else, whether a relative or otherwise.

(4) "If in the doctor's opinion disclosure of information to a third **2.85** party other than a relative would be in the best interests of the patient, it is the doctor's duty to make every reasonable effort to persuade the patient to allow the information to be given. If the patient still refuses then only in exceptional cases should the doctor feel entitled to disregard his refusal."

This exception is even more dubious than the previous one, since it **2.86** contemplates disclosure to someone who is not in a close relationship with the patient and contrary to the patient's express instructions,

---

[92] [1989] 1 All E.R. 1089, 1104; [1990] 1 All E.R. 835, C.A.; see §§ 2.96–2.98 for the facts of this case.

[93] Paras. 80–82 of the G.M.C. "Blue Book" deal specifically with children under 16. If the doctor is not satisfied that the child has sufficient maturity and understanding to "appreciate what is involved" he may decide to disclose the information learned from the consultation to a parent, or another person *in loco parentis*; but if he does so he should inform the patient accordingly, and his judgment concerning disclosure should "always reflect both the patient's best medical interests and the trust the patient places in the doctor." This guidance is derived from the decision of the House of Lords in *Gillick* v. *West Norfolk and Wisbech Area Health Authority* [1985] 3 All E.R. 402, on which see §§ 6.30–6.34. On the other hand, where the child does have sufficient maturity and understanding the doctor must respect the confidentiality of the doctor/patient relationship.

[94] *Furniss* v. *Fitchett* [1958] N.Z.L.R. 396 provides an unusual example. The Data Protection Act 1984, s.21 and the Data Protection (Subject Access Modification) (Health) Order 1987 (S.I. 1987/1903) exempts from the general right of access to information conferred by that Act information as to the physical or mental health of a data subject, where, *inter alia*, access would be likely to cause serious harm to the physical or mental health of the data subject. The Access to Health Records Act 1990, s.5(1)(*a*) contains a similar provision. The circumstances in which these exceptions apply have yet to be considered by the courts. See also Supreme Court Act 1981, ss.33 and 34 under which disclosure of medical records can be limited to the applicant's legal advisers and/or any medical or other professional adviser of the applicant; see further §§ 10.69– 10.70, 10.76, 10.90.

purportedly in the patient's best interests. It would be difficult to provide a justification in law for this overtly paternalistic attitude. The "best interests of the patient" cannot be invoked to override a patient's express wishes every time a doctor disagrees with a patient's views.

2.87   (5) "Information may be disclosed to the appropriate authority in order to satisfy a specific statutory requirement, such as notification of an infectious disease."

2.88   There are a number of statutes under which the disclosure of information is compulsory, and doctors are not exempt from these requirements.[95]

2.89   (6) Where a doctor is directed to disclose information by virtue of an order of the court.[96]

2.90   Examples include the direction of a judge that a doctor must give evidence in court either orally or by producing documents under a subpoena *duces tecum*, and an order under section 33 or 34 of the Supreme Court Act 1981,[97] though in most cases the applicant seeking disclosure under these provisions will be the patient, who will effectively have consented to the disclosure. The G.M.C. cautions that where litigation is in prospect, unless the patient has consented to disclosure or a formal court order has been made for disclosure, information should not be disclosed merely in response to demands from other persons such as another party's solicitor or an official of the court. On the other hand, in *Walker* v. *Eli Lilly & Co.*[98] Hirst J. commented that health authorities and doctors who are not likely to be defendants should respond readily and promptly to requests for disclosure to avoid unnecessary expense and delay.

2.91   A judge has a discretion to allow a doctor to decline to answer a question when giving evidence in court. In *Hunter* v. *Mann*[99] Lord Widgery C.J. said that:

> " . . . if a doctor, giving evidence in court, is asked a question which he finds embarassing because it involves him talking about things which he would normally regard as confidential, he can seek the protection of the judge and ask the judge if it is necessary for him to answer."

The judge's exercise of this discretion clearly depends on the importance of the potential answer to the issues being tried.

2.92   (7) "Rarely, disclosure may be justified on the ground that it is in the public interest which, in certain circumstances such as, for example, investigation by the police of a grave or very serious crime, might override the doctor's duty to maintain his patient's confidence."

---

[95] See, *e.g.*, Public Health (Control of Disease) Act 1984, s.11; Abortion Act 1967, s.2 and the Abortion Regulations 1991 (S.I. 1991/499); Road Traffic Act 1988, s.172(2) (on which see *Hunter* v. *Mann* [1974] Q.B. 767); Police and Criminal Evidence Act 1984, ss.9–12; Misuse of Drugs Act 1971, s.23; Prevention of Terrorism (Temporary Provisions) Act 1989, s.18; National Health Service Act 1977, s.124 and the National Health Service (Notification of Births and Deaths) Regulations 1982 (S.I. 1982/286).
[96] Doctors do not enjoy a privilege equivalent to legal professional privilege: *A.-G.* v. *Mulholland and Foster* [1963] 1 All E.R. 767, 771. See also Matthews (1984) 1 L.S. 77.
[97] See §§ 10.84–10.90, 10.98.
[98] *The Times*, May 1, 1986.
[99] [1974] Q.B. 767, 775.

In law, the public interest defence is considerably wider than this example would suggest (see *post*).

(8) Disclosure may be made where it is necessary for the purpose of **2.93** a medical research project which has been approved by a recognised ethical committee.

The legal justification for this exception probably derives from the **2.94** public interest defence, in that it is in the public interest that properly regulated medical research should be conducted and that the results should be available to the scientific community.[1] Research should not normally be conducted without the patient's consent, however, and if the doctor can obtain consent to conducting the research there would seem to be no reason for not obtaining consent to disclosure of the results at the same time.

Disclosure in the public interest

The G.M.C.'s example of the public interest, disclosure to the police **2.95** investigating a grave or very serious crime, is but one instance of the principle that "there is no confidence as to the disclosure of iniquity,"[2] though the iniquity rule is itself only part of the wider principle of public interest which may justify disclosure. This inevitably involves the weighing of competing interests, as Lord Goff observed in *A.-G.* v. *Guardian Newspapers* (No. 2):

" . . . although the basis of the law's protection of confidence is that there is a public interest that confidences should be preserved and protected by the law, nevertheless that public interest may be outweighed by some other countervailing public interest which favours disclosure . . . It is this limiting principle which may require a court to carry out a balancing operation, weighing the public interest in maintaining confidence against a countervailing public interest favouring disclosure."[3]

The scope of the public interest defence in the specific context of the **2.96** doctor/patient relationship was considered in *W.* v. *Egdell*,[4] where the question was whether a psychiatrist who had prepared a medical report on a patient was entitled to disclose the contents of the report both to the hospital where the patient was detained and to the Home Secre-

---

[1] Researchers may not be able to maintain the confidentiality of their data, even where it is supplied to them on a confidential basis. In the litigation concerning claims that some children have sustained brain damage as a reaction to pertussis vaccine, the defendants sought access to the data contained in the National Childhood Encephalopathy Study, which had been provided to the researchers on a confidential basis by doctors and hospitals. Stuart-Smith J. held that the interests of justice outweighed both the interests of patients in maintaining confidentiality of their records and the public interest in conducting research, which could be damaged if doctors and patients who co-operated in research projects believed that the information they supplied would not be kept confidential. It was ordered that the data be produced, with patient anonymity preserved by referring to patients by number: *Kinnear* v. *Wellcome Foundation Ltd.*; *Loveday* v. *Renton*, both unreported on this point.
[2] *Frazer* v. *Evans* [1969] 1 All E.R. 8, 11, *per* Lord Denning M.R. citing Page Wood V.-C. in *Gartside* v. *Outram* (1856) 26 L.J. Ch. 113, 114.
[3] [1988] 3 All E.R. 545, 659.
[4] [1989] 1 All E.R. 1089; [1990] 1 All E.R. 835, C.A.

tary. W was detained as a patient in a secure hospital without limit of time following a conviction for manslaughter of five neighbours on the grounds of diminished responsibility. He was diagnosed as suffering from paranoid schizophrenia. 10 years after his detention he applied to a mental health review tribunal for a transfer to a regional secure unit with a view, ultimately, to obtaining a conditional discharge. W's solicitors instructed Dr. Egdell, a consultant psychiatrist, to produce an independent psychiatric report for the purpose of the tribunal hearing. Dr. Egdell referred to the possibility that W was suffering from a paranoid psychosis rather than paranoid schizophrenia, which meant that medication would be less effective in protecting against a relapse. Moreover, there was a possibility that W might have a psychopathic deviant personality.

2.97   In view of the report W's solicitors withdrew the application to the tribunal. Dr. Egdell then sent the report to the hospital, also urging the hospital to forward a copy to the Home Secretary. Subsequently the Home Secretary referred W's case to the mental health review tribunal under section 71(2) of the Mental Health Act 1983, and sent a copy of the report to the tribunal. W sought an injunction restraining the defendants from using or disclosing the contents of the report, and damages (including aggravated damages) against the hospital board and the Home Secretary. Scott J. held that Dr. Egdell's duty to W was not his only duty, since W was not an ordinary member of the public. He was a detained patient in a secure hospital subject to a regime whereby decisions concerning his future were to be taken by public authorities. In taking those decision W's interests would not be the only or even the main criterion. The safety of the public would be the main criterion. In those circumstances Dr. Egdell had a duty to the public to place the result of his examination before the proper authorities, if, in his opinion, the public interest so required. The public interest in disclosure outweighed W's private interest.[5]

2.98   The Court of Appeal agreed that Scott J. had struck the correct balance between the public interest in patients being able to make full and frank disclosure to their doctors in reliance on the doctors' obligation of confidence, and the public interest in the safety of members of the public who might be at risk if W were released:

> "Where a man has committed multiple killings under the disability of serious mental illness, decisions which may lead directly or indirectly to his release from hospital should not be made unless the responsible authority is properly able to make an informed judgment that the risk of repetition is so small as to be acceptable. A consultant psychiatrist who becomes aware, even in the course of a confidential relationship, of information which leads him, in the exercise of what the court considers a sound professional judgment, to fear that such decisions may be made

---

[5] The actions against the other defendants also failed, though Scott J. considered that even if the case against Dr. Egdell had succeeded the other defendants would have had a valid public interest defence in view of the nature of the statutory scheme created by the Mental Health Act 1983. The claims against the other defendants were not pursued on appeal. An argument that Dr. Egdell's report was the subject of legal professional privilege was rejected by Scott J., and dismissed almost peremptorily by the Court of Appeal.

on inadequate information and with a real risk of consequent danger to the public is entitled to take such steps as are reasonable in all the circumstances to communicate the grounds of his concern to the responsible authorities."[6]

Limits to the public interest

The public interest defence to a breach of confidence is potentially very **2.99** wide in its scope, but it is possible to indentify certain limitations on the application of the defence. First, it is well-settled that there is a distinction between what is interesting to the public and what is in the public interest. It does not follow that simply because information would be of interest to the public it is in the public interest to disclose it.[7]

Secondly, the public interest defence justifies disclosure to the **2.100** "proper authorities" not necessarily to the world at large.[8] If, for example, Dr. Egdell had sold his report to the newspapers he would undoubtedly have been in breach of his duty of confidence.[9]

Thirdly, the risk of danger to the public must be a "real risk."[10] It is **2.101** not clear what constitutes a real risk, though on the facts of *W.* v. *Egdell* a possibility of danger rather than a probability appears to be sufficient. It is for the court to determine whether the doctor's assessment of the risk is sound.[11]

A further issue concerns the meaning of the word "public." In *W.* v. **2.102** *Egdell* both Scott J. and the Court of Appeal spoke of the danger *to the public* as the criterion which justified disclosure. Although it might be argued that danger to a single individual does not constitute danger to the public, the public interest is broader in conception than simply "danger to the public." It is submitted that, on principle, even where the danger is merely to a single individual the public interest in protecting that individual from physical harm would justify disclosure.[12]

---

[6] [1990] 1 All E.R. 835, 852–3. See also *R.* v. *Crozier*, [1991] Crim.L.R. 138, C.A, where a psychiatrist instructed by the appellant acted reasonably and responsibly in showing his report on the appellant to prosecuting counsel, since he believed that the appellant suffered from a psychopathic disorder which made him a danger to the public. The public interest in disclosure outweighed the duty of confidence owed to the appellant.

[7] *X.* v. *Y.* [1988] 2 All E.R. 648.

[8] *W.* v. *Egdell* [1989] 1 All E.R. 1089, 1104; *A.-G.* v. *Guardian Newspapers* (No. 2) [1988] 3 All E.R. 545, 659; *Furniss* v. *Fitchett* [1958] N.Z.L.R. 396, 406.

[9] [1989] 1 All E.R. 1089, 1102 and, *per* Bingham L.J. at [1990] 1 All E.R. 835, 848.

[10] *W.* v. *Egdell* [1990] 1 All E.R. 835, 853, *per* Bingham L.J.

[11] "Where, as here, the relationship between doctor and patient is contractual, the question is whether the doctor's disclosure is or is not a breach of contract. The answer to that question must turn not on what the doctor thinks but on what the court rules. But it does not follow that the doctor's conclusion is irrelevant. In making its ruling the court will give such weight to the considered judgment of a professional man as seems in all the circumstances to be appropriate": *ibid.*, at p. 851, *per* Bingham L.J.

[12] *E.g.*, in *Schering Chemicals Ltd.* v. *Falkman Ltd.* [1981] 2 All E.R. 321, 327 Shaw L.J. said that: "If the subject matter is something which is inimical to the public interest or *threatens individual safety*, a person in possession of knowledge of that subject matter cannot be obliged to conceal it . . . " (emphasis added). See also Barrowclough C.J. in *Furniss* v. *Fichett* [1958] N.Z.L.R. 396, 405–406: "Take the case of a doctor who discovers that his patient entertains delusions in respect of another, and in his disordered state of mind is liable at any moment to cause death or grievous bodily harm to that other. Can it be doubted for one moment that the public interest requires him to report that finding to someone?"

2.103   This could be relevant not only in the case of psychiatric patients who constitute a danger to others, but also AIDS (and HIV positive) patients who, despite counselling, refuse either to tell their sexual partner(s) about their condition or to change their sexual behaviour so as to minimise the risk of infecting their partner(s). The B.M.A. favours a strict duty of confidence for AIDS patients, pointing out that the majority of infected individuals can be persuaded to inform their sexual partner(s) of their condition.[13] Nonetheless, it is arguable that there may be rare cases where even a strict ethic of confidentiality may be broken to protect the interests of others from a potentially fatal disease.[14] Few would doubt that the disclosure in the circumstances would be justified in law, in the public interest.

2.104   A final question concerning the limits of the public interest defence, which arises from *W. v. Egdell*, is whether different considerations apply to patients who are compulsorily detained under the provisions of the Mental Health Act 1983.[15] Scott J. expressly based his decision on the circumstances in which the psychiatric report had been commissioned, icluding the fact that W was subject to a restriction order under the Act. This, his Lordship concluded, placed W and persons like him "in a position in which the duty of confidence owed by their psychiatrists is less extensive than the duty that would be owed by psychiatrists to ordinary members of the public."[16] The limitation on W's rights was justified by the need that the hospital, the Home Secretary and the tribunal should be fully informed about W when considering his clinical management and possible discharge. However, Bingham L.J. said that restricted patients under the Mental Health Act 1983 should not enjoy different rights from any other patient with respect to the duty of confidence, except in so far as a breach of confidence could be justified in the public interest. In W's circumstances, decisions about his release from hospital should not be made unless the responsible authority was able to make an informed judgment that the risk was so small as to be acceptable. That consideration weighed the balance of public interest decisively in favour of disclosure.[17]

2.105   The problem for a doctor with a patient who is not subject to a restriction order lies in the difficulty of assessing the risk. With a patient in W's position then, arguably, the evidence of the potential danger is more readily apparent, and those to whom disclosure should be made are more readily identified, namely persons who have some degree of control over W's future conduct. It does not necessarily follow that the duty of confidence owed by psychiatrists varies with

[13] See (1987) 294 B.M.J. 1177.

[14] Gillon (1987) 294 B.M.J. 1675, 1676; Wacks (1988) 138 N.L.J. 283; *c.f.* Casswell (1989) 68 Can. Bar Rev. 225 Note that Gillon considers that this is "particularly clearly justified" if the sexual partner is also a patient of the doctor concerned. The General Medical Council does accept that disclosure may be made in exceptional circumstances, where the failure to disclose would put the health of any of the health care team at risk, or where it is necessary to safeguard sexual partners of the patient from a possibly fatal infection.

[15] ss.37 and 41; formerly Mental Health Act 1959, ss.60 and 65.

[16] [1989] 1 All E.R. 1089, 1105.

[17] The hospital, the Secretary of State and the tribunal were all engaged in public law functions in the exercise of statutory powers which placed a strong emphasis on public safety and, bearing in mind W's history, his status as a detained patient was, almost inevitably, a significant factor to be weighed in assessing the public interest.

different types of patient, except to the extent that each patient
different and accordingly the psychiatrist's professional judgment a
the risk presented to the public varies.

Discretion or duty

In *W.* v. *Egdell* Scott J.'s judgment was ambiguous about whether a **2.106**
doctor who forms the view that his patient constitutes a potential risk
to others merely has a discretion to breach the confidentiality of the
doctor/patient relationship (which would give him a defence to a claim
for breach of confidence by the patient) or whether he comes under a
duty to disclose the information. At one point Scott J. said that a
doctor in Dr. Egdell's position "owes a duty not only to his patient but
also a duty to the public. His duty to the public would require him, in
my opinion, to place before the proper authorities the result of his
examination if, in his opinion, the public interest so required."[18] The
Court of Appeal indicated that the defendant was justified in disclosing
the report, but the decision does not suggest that he was under a duty
to disclose it. This would seem to be the better view.[19]

---

[18] [1989] 1 All E.R. 1089, 1104e.

[19] It is unlikely that it would be a criminal offence to withhold such information, in the
absence of a specific statutory requirement for disclosure (as, *e.g.,* in *Hunter* v. *Mann*
[1974] 1 Q.B. 767). Similarly, it is difficult to see how such a duty could arise in equity or
by whom it would be enforced. Possibly Scott J. considered that Dr. Egdell was under
some "quasi public law duty" to disclose the report to the relevant authorities, in view of
the particular circumstances under which the report was prepared. In this sense it might
be argued that Dr. Egdell was engaged in a "public" function, even though the report
had been prepared at W's request and for the purpose of supporting his application to
the tribunal. Possibly Scott J. had a duty of care in negligence in mind when he referred
to Dr. Egdell's duty, but this is also doubtful given the context in which the words were
used, particularly the reference to a duty owed to the public. Duties of care are normally
expressed in much more restricted terms than this, being owed to persons who are
foreseeable as likely to be directly affected by the defendant's failure to exercise
reasonable care.

CHAPTER 3

STANDARD OF CARE—GENERAL PRINCIPLES

3.01 The standard of care, and whether the defendant has failed to meet that standard, are normally the central issues in an action for medical negligence. Essentially, the question is: was the defendant careless? In law, the test for breach of duty in the tort of negligence is whether the defendant's conduct was reasonable in all the circumstances of the case. If it was reasonable he was not negligent; if it was unreasonable he was. At this level of abstraction the test is almost meaningless, since it begs all the important questions, namely what *is* reasonable and which circumstances of the case have to be considered. It is only when the general is applied to the particular that the term "reasonable care in all the circumstances" acquires any significance.

3.02 Within the blanket term "reasonable care" it is possible to identify some general principles which the courts have employed in the decision-making process about what constitutes negligence. They are, however, in practical terms, no more than guidelines, and as often as not competing principles point to different outcomes. The question of where the balance between negligence and due care is to be drawn can only be appreciated by developing a common-sense "feel" for the way in which the courts use these guidelines. This chapter deals with the general principles applied to the issue of breach of duty, and Chapter 4 looks at specific types of medical negligence. There is, inevitably, some overlap between these two chapters, because they seek to provide different perspectives on the caselaw.

3.03 Medical evidence is invariably a vital element in an action for medical negligence, but the importance attached to expert opinion should not obscure the underlying basis for a finding that the defendant has been negligent, or not (as the case may be). This is that, in the light of the expert evidence, the defendant has taken an unjustified risk, for example, or has failed to keep up to date, or has undertaken a task beyond his competence, or conversely that the risk was justified by the potential benefit to the patient, or the harm was unforeseeable, and so on. In other words, expert opinion about the defendant's conduct (whether favourable or unfavourable) should itself be measured against the general principles applied to the question of breach of duty.

1. The basic principle

When jury trials were the norm in civil litigation the issue of whether **3.04** the defendant had been negligent was for the jury to decide, and so it was treated as a question of fact. There are two stages, however, in this process. First, there must be an assessment by the court of how, in the circumstances, the defendant *ought* to have behaved—what standard of care should he have exercised? This enquiry necessarily involves a value judgment which should be made by the court. That judgment may be conditioned, but should not necessarily be determined, by the evidence. It is here that the hypothetical "reasonable man" is employed, partly as a measure of careless conduct and partly as a device to obscure the policy element of a judicial decision.[1] In a famous dictum Alderson B. said: "Negligence is the omission to do something which a reasonable man, guided upon those considerations which ordinarily regulate the conduct of human affairs, would do, or doing something which a prudent and reasonable man would not do."[2] This judicial abstraction has also been described as the ordinary man, the average man, or the man on the Clapham omnibus.[3] The standard of care expected of the reasonable man is objective. It does not take account of the subjective attributes of the particular defendant.[4] Nor, despite references to the average man, is it necessarily determined by the average conduct of people in general if that conduct is routinely careless. Similarly, there is no concept of an "average" standard of care by which a defendant might argue that he has provided an adequate service on average and should not be held liable for the occasions when his performance fell below the norm. No matter how skilled the defendant's conduct was, he will be responsible for even a single occasion when he fell below the standard of reasonable care.[5]

The second stage requires a decision about whether on the facts of **3.05** the case (as determined from the evidence) the defendant's conduct fell below the appropriate standard. This is truly a question of fact. Although these two stages are logically discrete, in practice it may be difficult to separate findings of "fact" and value judgments about the defendant's conduct.

(i) The reasonable doctor

Since the ordinary or average man would be ill-equipped to judge **3.06** the competence of a professional, a person who professes a special skill is judged, not by the standard of the man on the Clapham omnibus,

---

[1] See, *e.g.*, P. Cane, *Atiyah's Accidents, Compensation and the Law*, 4th ed., 1987, pp. 37–39, 418–423.

[2] *Blyth* v. *Birmingham Waterworks Co.* (1856) 11 Exch. 781, 784.

[3] *Hall* v. *Brooklands Auto Racing Club* [1933] 1 K.B. 205, 217.

[4] *Glasgow Corporation* v. *Muir* [1943] A.C. 448, 457.

[5] *Wilsher* v. *Essex Area Health Authority* [1986] 3 All E.R. 801, 810, *per* Mustill L.J. The courts have not accepted a distinction between "ordinary" negligence and "gross" negligence (despite the efforts of Lord Denning: see § 3.119). In *Wilson* v. *Brett* (1843) 11 M. & W. 113 Rolfe B. said that there was no difference—"it was the same thing with the addition of a vituperative epithet." Thus, any failure to meet the standard of reasonable care constitutes a breach of duty: Dugdale and Stanton, *Professional Negligence*, 1989, 2nd ed., para. 15.04.

but by the standards of his peers. Thus, for the "reasonable man" is substituted the "reasonable professional," be it doctor, lawyer, accountant, architect, etc.[6]

3.07 The classic statement of the test of professional negligence is the direction to the jury of McNair J. in *Bolam* v. *Friern Hospital Management Committee.*[7] Now widely known as the "*Bolam* test," this statement of the law has been approved by the House of Lords on no fewer than three occasions in recent years as the touchstone of liability for medical negligence.[8] Moreover, the Court of Appeal has confirmed that the test is not restricted to doctors, but is of general application to any profession or calling which requires special skill, knowledge or experience.[9]

3.08 McNair J. explained the law in these terms:

"But where you get a situation which involves the use of some special skill or competence, then the test whether there has been negligence or not is not the test of the man on the Clapham omnibus, because he has not got this special skill. The test is the standard of the ordinary skilled man exercising and professing to have that special skill. A man need not possess the highest expert skill at the risk of being found negligent . . . it is sufficient if he exercises the ordinary skill of an ordinary competent man exercising that particular art."[10]

His Lordship agreed that counsel's statement that "negligence means failure to act in accordance with the standards of reasonably competent medical men at the time" was a perfectly accurate statement of the law, provided that it was remembered that there may be one or more perfectly proper standards:

"A doctor is not guilty of negligence if he has acted in accordance with a practice accepted as proper by a responsible body of medical men skilled in that particular art . . . Putting it the other way round, a doctor is not negligent, if he is acting in accordance with such a practice, merely because there is a body of opinion that takes a contrary view."[11]

3.09 In *Hunter* v. *Hanley* Lord President Clyde dealt with the question of different professional practices in these terms:

"In the realm of diagnosis and treatment there is ample scope for genuine difference of opinion and one man clearly is not negligent merely because his conclusion differs from that of other professional men, nor because he has displayed less skill or knowledge than

---

[6] "The public profession of an art is a representation and undertaking to all the world that the professor possesses the requisite ability and skill. An express promise or express representation in the particular case is not necessary": *per* Willes J. in *Harmer* v. *Cornelius* (1858) 5 C.B. (N.S.) 236, 246.

[7] [1957] 2 All E.R. 118.

[8] *Whitehouse* v. *Jordan* [1981] 1 All E.R. 267: treatment; *Maynard* v. *West Midlands Regional Health Authority* [1984] 1 W.L.R. 634: diagnosis; *Sidaway* v. *Bethlem Royal Hospital Governors* [1985] 1 All E.R. 643: information disclosure. See also *Chin Keow* v. *Government of Malaysia* [1967] 1 W.L.R. 813, P.C.

[9] *Gold* v. *Haringey Health Authority* [1987] 2 All E.R. 888, 894.

[10] [1957] 2 All E.R. 118, 121.

[11] *Ibid.*, p. 122.

others would have shown. The true test for establishing negligence in diagnosis or treatment on the part of a doctor is whether he has been proved to be guilty of such failure as no doctor of ordinary skill would be guilty of if acting with ordinary care."[12]

This statement of the law has also been approved by the House of Lords,[13] although it has been argued that there is a difference between this formulation and the *Bolam* test.[14] There is, moreover, a distinction between a test of negligence based on the standards of the ordinary skilled man and one based on the reasonably competent man. The former places considerable emphasis on the standards which are in fact adopted by the profession, whereas the latter makes it clear that negligence is concerned with departures from what *ought* to have been done in the circumstances, which is measured by reference to the hypothetical "reasonable doctor."[15] The point here is that it is for the court to determine what the reasonable doctor would have done, not the profession. Of course, what the profession does in a given situation will be an important indicator of what ought to have been done, but it should not necessarily be determinative. In other words, in the final analysis the court sets the standard of care in negligence, drawing, of course, upon the evidence presented. The *Bolam* test fails to make this important distinction between the ordinary skilled doctor and the reasonably competent doctor, and this has produced some confusion in the cases.[16] In the vast majority of cases the distinction is irrelevant, indeed it passes largely unnoticed in the courts. It does become significant, however, when the question arises whether compliance with common professional practice can be negligent.

Similar formulations of the standard of care required of the medical **3.10** profession can be found in other Commonwealth jurisdictions. In Canada one of the most widely cited statements is that of Schroeder J.A. in *Crits* v. *Sylvester*:

"Every medical practitioner must bring to his task a reasonable degree of skill and knowledge and must exercise a reasonable degree of care. He is bound to exercise that degree of care and skill which could reasonably be expected of a normal, prudent practitioner of the same experience and standing, and if he holds himself out as a specialist, a higher degree of skill is required of him than of one who does not profess to be so qualified by special training and ability."[17]

Again, in Australia King C.J. has said that:

"The standard of care is that to be expected of an ordinarily careful and competent practitioner of the class to which the practitioner belongs."[18]

---

[12] 1955 S.C. 200, 204–205.
[13] *Maynard* v. *West Midlands Regional Health Authority* [1984] 1 W.L.R. 634, 638; *Sidaway* v. *Bethlem Royal Hospital Governors* [1985] 1 All E.R. 643, 660, *per* Lord Bridge.
[14] See Howie [1983] J.R. 193; *cf.* Norrie [1985] J.R. 145.
[15] For critical discussion of *Bolam* see Montrose "Is Negligence an Ethical or a Sociological Concept?" (1958) 21 M.L.R. 259.
[16] Jackson and Powell, *Professional Negligence*, 1987, 2nd ed., para. 1.25.
[17] (1956) 1 D.L.R. (2d) 502, 508; aff'd (1956) 5 D.L.R. (2d) 601 (S.C.C.).
[18] *F.* v. *R.* (1982) 33 S.A.S.R. 189, 190.

3.11   Here, too, there is no clear demarcation between the ordinary doctor and the reasonable doctor. The assumption is that the terms express essentially the same standard. These epithets—the "reasonable" man, the "average" man, or the "ordinary" man—were introduced at a time when judges had to give juries guidance as to the appropriate standard to apply in deciding whether conduct was negligent. In many respects they do little more than give a "flavour" of a suitable test, which it was left to the good sense of the jury to apply. On the whole, they serve their purposes even where actions are tried by judge alone.

(ii) What is reasonable care?

3.12   Reasonable care can only be measured by reference to the defendant's conduct in the circumstances. In one sense it is meaningless to say that the standard required is reasonable care, without knowing the particular situation with which the defendant was confronted. Nonetheless, the term is frequently used to emphasise that doctors do not guarantee a favourable outcome to their efforts. The medical practitioner is not an insurer, and so cannot be blamed every time something goes wrong. Indeed, it is widely acknowledged that in medicine, in particular, things can go wrong in the treatment of a patient even with the very best available care. This has long been reflected in judicial statements of the law:

> "A surgeon does not become an actual insurer; he is only bound to display sufficient skill and knowledge of his profession. If from some accident, or some variation in the frame of a particular individual, an injury happens, it is not a fault in the medical man . . . . The plaintiff must show that the injury was attributable to want of skill; you are not to infer it."[19]

> " . . . the standard of care which the law requires is not insurance against accidental slips. It is such a degree of care as a normally skilful member of the profession may reasonably be expected to exercise in the actual circumstances of the case in question. It is not every slip or mistake which imports negligence and, in applying the duty of care to the case of a surgeon, it is peculiarly necessary to have regard to the different kinds of circumstances that may present themselves for urgent attention."[20]

3.13   The practitioner is not judged by the standards of the most experienced, most skilful, or most highly qualified member of the profession, but by reference to the standards of the ordinarily competent practitioner in that particular field.

> "Every person who enters into a learned profession undertakes to bring to the exercise of it a reasonable degree of care and skill. He does not undertake, if he is an attorney, that at all events you shall gain your case, nor does a surgeon undertake that he will

---

[19] *Hancke* v. *Hooper* (1835) 7 C. & P. 81, 84, *per* Tindal C.J.
[20] *Mahon* v. *Osborne* [1939] 2 K.B. 14, 31, *per* Scott L.J.; "To fall short of perfection is not the same thing as to be negligent": *Daniels* v. *Heskin* [1954] I.R. 73, 84.

perform a cure; nor does he undertake to use the highest possible degree of skill. There may be persons who have higher education and greater advantages than he has, but he undertakes to bring a fair, reasonable and competent degree of skill . . . ."[21]

The doctor "owes a duty to the patient to use diligence, care, knowledge, skill and caution in administering the treatment . . . . The jury should not exact the highest, or a very high, standard, nor should they be content with a very low standard. The law requires a fair and reasonable standard of care and competence."[22]

Nor is the doctor to be judged by the standards of the least qualified **3.14** or least experienced.[23] It is not a defence that he acted in good faith, to the best of his ability if he has failed to reach the objective standard of the ordinarily competent and careful doctor.

2. Common professional practice

As a general rule within the tort of negligence, where the defendant **3.15** has acted in accordance with the common practice of others in a similar situation this will be strong evidence that he has not been negligent.[24] People do not normally adopt systematic practices that pay careless disregard for the safety of others. Following a common practice is only *evidence*, however, it is not conclusive, since the court may find that the practice is itself negligent.[25] There may be many reasons, such as convenience, cost, or habit, why a particular practice is commonly followed, which have nothing to do with reasonable prudence against potential harm to others. In the graphic words of Lord Tomlin: "Neglect of duty does not cease by repetition to be neglect of duty."[26]

A central feature of medical negligence claims is the importance that **3.16** is attached to compliance with common or accepted practice. It will be recalled that in *Bolam* v. *Friern Hospital Management Committee* McNair J. directed the jury that:

"A doctor is not guilty of negligence if he has acted in accordance with a practice accepted as proper by a *responsible* body of medical men skilled in that particular art . . . . Putting it the other way round, a doctor is not negligent, if he is acting in accordance

---

[21] *Lanphier* v. *Phipos* (1838) 8 C. & P. 475, 479, *per* Tindal C.J. See also *Greaves & Co. (Contractors) Ltd.* v. *Baynham Meikle and Partners* [1975] 3 All E.R. 99 at 103–104, *per* Lord Denning M.R., cited at § 2.04, n. 8.

[22] *R.* v. *Bateman* (1925) 94 L.J.K.B. 791, 794, *per* Lord Hewart C.J., approved in *Gent* v. *Wilson* (1956) 2 D.L.R. (2d) 160 (Ont. C.A.) and *Parkin* v. *Kobrinsky* (1963) 46 W.W.R. 193 (Man. C.A.).

[23] See §§ 3.74 *et seq.*

[24] *Morton* v. *William Dixon Ltd.* 1909 S.C. 807, 809; *Morris* v. *West Hartlepool Steam Navigation Co. Ltd.* [1956] A.C. 552, 579.

[25] See, *e.g., Lloyds Bank Ltd.* v. *E. B. Savory & Co.* [1933] A.C. 201; *Cavanagh* v. *Ulster Weaving Co. Ltd.* [1960] A.C. 145; *General Cleaning Contractors* v. *Christmas* [1953] A.C. 180, 193, *per* Lord Reid.

[26] *Bank of Montreal* v. *Dominion Gresham Guarantee and Casualty Co.* [1930] A.C. 659, 666; *Carpenters' Co.* v. *British Mutual Banking Co. Ltd.* [1937] 3 All E.R. 811, 820, *per* Slesser L.J.

with such a practice, merely because there is a body of opinion that takes a contrary view."[27]

There is no reason in theory why the general approach taken by the courts to accepted practice should not also apply to actions for medical negligence. Within the *Bolam* test, attention would then focus on whether the practice which the defendant had followed was accepted by *responsible* medical opinion, with the court deciding whether on the evidence before it the body of opinion which approved of the defendant's conduct could be said to be responsible. There are, however, some judicial statements which appear to take the view that the practice of the medical profession is determinative of the issue, and that it is not open to the court to condemn as negligence a commonly adopted practice.

(i) Complying with

3.17   In *Vancouver General Hospital* v. *McDaniel*[28] Lord Alness said that a defendant charged with negligence can "clear his feet" if he shows that he has acted in accordance with general and approved practice. This view was repeated by Maugham L.J. in *Marshall* v. *Lindsey County Council*:

> "An act cannot, in my opinion, be held to be due to a want of reasonable care if it is in accordance with the general practice of mankind. What is reasonable in a world not wholly composed of wise men and women must depend on what people presumed to be reasonable constantly do."[29]

3.18   There are many cases in which actions for medical negligence have been dismissed on the basis that the doctor conformed to an accepted practice of the profession.[30] Where there is more than one common practice, as the *Bolam* test contemplates, compliance with one of the practices will normally excuse the defendant. In *Maynard* v. *West Midlands Regional Health Authority*[31] Lord Scarman, delivering the judgment of the House of Lords, expressed the position in the following terms:

> "A case which is based on an allegation that a fully considered decision of two consultants in the field of their special skill was negligent clearly presents certain difficulties of proof. It is not enough to show that there is a body of competent professional opinion which considers that theirs was a wrong decision, if there

---

[27] [1957] 2 All E.R. 118, 122, emphasis added; *Holmes* v. *Board of Hospital Trustees of the City of London* (1977) 81 D.L.R. (3d) 67, 91, *per* Robins J. (Ont. H.C.): "Where in the exercise of his judgment a physician selects one of two alternatives, either of which might have been chosen by a reasonable and competent physician, he will not be held negligent."

[28] (1934) 152 L.T. 56, 57–58.

[29] [1935] 1 K.B. 516, 540.

[30] *Vancouver General Hospital* v. *McDaniell* (1934) 152 L.T. 56; *Whiteford* v. *Hunter* [1950] W.N. 553; *Bolam* v. *Friern Hospital Management Committee* [1957] 2 All E.R. 118; *Chapman* v. *Rix* (1959) 103 S.J. 940, C.A.; aff'd *The Times*, December 22, 1960 H.L.; *Gold* v. *Haringey Health Authority* [1987] 2 All E.R. 888.

[31] [1984] 1 W.L.R. 634; *Belknap* v. *Meakes* (1989) 64 D.L.R. (4th) 452, 473–475 (B.C.C.A.).

also exists a body of professional opinion, equally competent, which supports the decision as reasonable in the circumstances . . . . Differences of opinion and practice exist, and will always exist, in the medical as in other professions. There is seldom any one answer exclusive of all others to problems of professional judgment. A court may prefer one body of opinion to the other: but that is no basis for a conclusion of negligence."[32]

This statement is unexceptional. In a later passage, however, Lord **3.19** Scarman appears to take the view that compliance with accepted practice will, without more, absolve a doctor from liability:

" . . . a judge's 'preference' for one body of distinguished professional opinion to another also professionally distinguished is not sufficient to establish negligence in a practitioner whose actions have received the seal of approval of those whose opinions, truthfully expressed, honestly held, were not preferred. If this was the real reason for the judge's finding he erred in law even though elsewhere in his judgment he stated the law correctly. For in the realm of diagnosis and treatment negligence is not established by preferring one respectable body of professional opinion to another. Failure to exercise the ordinary skill of a doctor (in the appropriate specialty, if he be a specialist) is necessary."[33]

Here, the "seal of approval" of a distinguished body of professional **3.20** opinion, held in good faith, acquits the defendant of negligence. Lord Scarman seems to equate a *competent* (or "responsible") body of professional opinion with "distinguished" or "respectable" in fact. He thus conflates accepted practice with the absence of negligence. This interpretation is supported by Lord Scarman's speech in *Sidaway* v. *Bethlem Royal Hospital Governors* where he said:

"The *Bolam* principle may be formulated as a rule that a doctor is not negligent if he acts in accordance with a practice accepted at the time as proper by a responsible body of medical opinion even though other doctors adopt a different practice. *In short, the law imposes the duty of care, but the standard of care is a matter of medical judgment.*"[34]

It is also apparent from earlier passages in his Lordship's speech in **3.21** *Sidaway* that he considered the *Bolam* test required the determination of whether there has been a breach of a doctor's duty of care to be conducted "exclusively by reference to the current state of responsible and competent professional opinion and practice at the time."[35] As Lord Scarman himself recognised "the implications of this view of the law are disturbing. It leaves the determination of a legal duty to the

---

[32] *Ibid.*, p. 638.
[33] *Ibid.*, p. 639.
[34] [1985] 1 All E.R. 643, 649, emphasis added; *cf.* Sir John Donaldson M.R. in the Court of Appeal, [1984] 1 All E.R. 1018, 1028: "The definition of the duty of care is a matter for the law and the courts. They cannot stand idly by if the profession, by an excess of paternalism, denies its patients a real choice. In a word, the law will not permit the medical profession to play God."
[35] *Ibid.*, p. 645.

judgment of doctors." It was this point which led Lord Scarman to dissent in *Sidaway* on the question of the standard to be applied to the disclosure of information to patients about the risks of treatment, but he was apparently content to apply the standard of "responsible medical judgment" (as his Lordship had identified it) to diagnosis and treatment.[36]

3.22   This was an interpretation of the *Bolam* test that was not accepted by Lord Bridge in *Sidaway* who said:

> " . . . the issue whether non-disclosure in a particular case should be condemned as a breach of the doctor's duty of care is an issue to be decided primarily on the basis of expert medical evidence, applying the *Bolam* test . . . . Of course, if there is a conflict of evidence whether a responsible body of medical opinion approves of non-disclosure in a particular case, the judge will have to resolve that conflict. But, even in a case where, as here, no expert witness in the relevant medical field condemns the non-disclosure as being in conflict with accepted and responsible medical practice, I am of opinion that the judge might in certain circumstances come to the conclusion that disclosure of a particular risk was so obviously necessary to an informed choice on the part of the patient that no reasonably prudent medical man would fail to make it."[37]

In other words, the court may condemn even a universally followed practice as to risk disclosure as negligent on the basis that the hypothetical reasonable doctor would not have adopted it. There, is, of course, no reason to confine this approach to risk disclosure since the majority of their Lordships in *Sidaway* v. *Bethlem Royal Hospital Governors* said that the *Bolam* test applied to all aspects of the doctor's duty of care: diagnosis, advice and treatment.

3.23   It is clear that outside the context of medical negligence the courts have had no difficulty with the notion that commonly adopted practices may themselves be negligent. This has been most apparent in cases of employers' liability,[38] but it is also evident in some cases involving professional liability. In *Lloyds Bank* v. *Savory & Co.*,[39] for example, Lord Wright rejected the proposition that a bank is not negligent if it takes all the precautions usually taken by bankers "in cases where the ordinary practice of bankers fails in making due provision for a risk fully known to those experienced in the business of banking." More recently, in *Edward Wong Finance Co. Ltd.* v. *Johnson, Stokes and Masters*[40] the Privy Council held that a particular conveyancing practice

---

[36] *Ibid.*, p. 649.

[37] *Ibid.*, pp. 662–663. See also Sir John Donaldson M.R. in *Sidaway* v. *Bethlem Royal Hospital Governors* [1984] 1 All E.R. 1018, 1028: " . . . in an appropriate case, a judge would be entitled to reject a unanimous medical view if he were satisfied that it was manifestly wrong and that the doctors must have been misdirecting themselves as to their duty in law." Thus, a practice must be "rightly" accepted as proper by the profession. His Lordship drew a specific analogy with the cases in which the courts had held the common practice of employers to be negligent: see n. 38.

[38] As, *e.g.*, in *Cavanagh* v. *Ulster Weaving Co. Ltd.* [1960] A.C. 145; *Morris* v. *West Hartlepool Steam Navigation Co. Ltd.* [1956] A.C. 552; *Stokes* v. *Guest, Keen & Nettlefold (Bolts & Nuts) Ltd.* [1968] 1 W.L.R. 1776, 1783.

[39] [1933] A.C. 201, 203.

[40] [1984] A.C. 296.

widely followed in Hong Kong was negligent because the practice had an inherent risk which would have been foreseen by a person of reasonable prudence, and there was no need to take this risk. The fact that virtually all other solicitors adopted the same practice was not conclusive evidence that it was prudent, nor did it make the risk less apparent or unreal.

It might be added that condemning accepted practice does not **3.24** depend upon the risks being "fully known to those experienced" in the profession, but may extend to those risks which ought reasonably to have been known, but were simply not addressed by the profession as a whole. This point may be illustrated by *Re The Herald of Free Enterprise*: *Appeal by Captain Lewry*,[41] which concerned an appeal by the captain of the *Herald of Free Enterprise* against the revocation of his master's certificate following the disaster at Zeebrugge harbour. The ferry had set sail with both the inner and outer doors to the main deck open, and capsized soon after leaving the harbour with a substantial loss of life. The Divisional Court found that the practice of failing to check that the doors had been closed was prevalent in respect of most, if not all, of the masters who commanded ferries of that class. The court concluded, however, that this was not evidence of the required standard of care, but rather of a general and culpable complacency, born perhaps of repetitive routine, and fostered by the shortcomings of the ships' owners and managers. There had been a failure to apply common sense in respect of elementary precautions required for the safety of the ship.

It would be strange if a different rule about the effect of complying **3.25** with common practice were to be applied to the medical profession from that which is applied to all other professions, particularly since the Court of Appeal has emphasised that the *Bolam* test applies to all professions equally.[42] In other Commonwealth jurisdictions the courts have been careful to ensure that, ultimately, decisions as to what constitutes negligence remain for the court to determine. In *Anderson* v. *Chasney*[43] Coyne J.A. commented that if general practice was a conclusive defence "a group of operators by adopting some practice could legislate themselves out of liability for negligence to the public by adopting or continuing what was an obviously negligent practice, even though a simple precaution, plainly capable of obviating danger which sometimes might result in death, was well known." Thus, expert evidence from doctors as to a general or approved practice could not be accepted as conclusive on the issue of negligence, especially where the conduct in question did not involve a matter of technical skill and experience. Similarly, in *Crits* v. *Sylvester*[44] Schroeder J.A. commented that:

> "Even if it had been established that what was done by the anaesthetist was in accordance with 'standard practice,' such

---

[41] *The Independent*, December 18, 1987, D.Ct.

[42] *Gold* v. *Haringey Health Authority* [1987] 2 All E.R. 888, 894: "I can see no possible ground for distinguishing between doctors and any other profession or calling which requires special skill, knowledge or experience," *per* Lloyd L.J. In *Whitehouse* v. *Jordan* [1981] 1 All E.R. 267, 276j Lord Edmund-Davies prefaced his restatement of the *Bolam* test with the comment that "doctors and surgeons fall into no special category."

[43] [1949] 4 D.L.R. 71, 85 (Man. C.A.); aff'd [1950] 4 D.L.R. 223 (S.C.C.).

[44] (1956) 1 D.L.R. (2d) 502; aff'd (1956) 5 D.L.R. (2d) 601.

evidence is not necessarily to be taken as conclusive on an issue of negligence, particularly where the so-called standard practice related to something which was not essentially conduct requiring medical skill and training either for its performance or a proper understanding of it . . . . If it was standard practice, it was not a safe practice and should not have been followed."[45]

3.26 King C.J. explained the justification for this in the Australian case of *F.* v. *R.*:

" . . . professions may adopt unreasonable practices. Practices may develop in professions, particularly as to disclosure, not because they serve the interests of the clients, but because they protect the interests or convenience of members of the profession. The court has an obligation to scrutinise professional practices to ensure that they accord with the standard of reasonableness imposed by the law. A practice as to disclosure approved and adopted by a profession or a section of it may be in many cases the determining consideration as to what is reasonable . . . . The ultimate question, however, is not whether the defendant's conduct accords with the practices of his profession or some part of it, but whether it conforms to the standard of reasonable care demanded by the law. That is a question for the court and the duty of deciding it cannot be delegated to any profession or group in the community."[46]

3.27 There are, moreover, some cases in this country in which, on the facts, compliance with common practice has been said to have been negligent. In *Clarke* v. *Adams*[47] the plaintiff was being treated for a fibrositic condition of the heel and he was warned by the physiotherapist to say if he felt anything more than a "comfortable warmth." He suffered a burning injury resulting in the leg being amputated below

---

[45] *Ibid.*, p. 514; *Reynard* v. *Carr* (1983) 30 C.C.L.T. 42, 68 (B.C.S.C.): "If that was the standard practice at the time, it was not good enough because it was 'inconsistent with provident precautions against a known risk.' Simply because it was 'usual and long established' is not a sufficient justification," *per* Bouck J.; *Winrob* v. *Street* (1959) 28 W.W.R. 118, 122 (B.C.S.C.); *Hajgato* v. *London Health Association* (1982) 36 O.R. (2d) 669, 693; *Goode* v. *Nash* (1979) 21 S.A.S.R. 419, 422 (S.C. of S. Aus.); see also *O'Donovan* v. *Cork County Council* [1967] I.R. 173, 193, *per* Walsh J.: "If there is a common practice which has inherent defects, which ought to be obvious to any person giving the matter due consideration, the fact that it is shown to have been widely and generally adopted over a period of time does not make the practice any the less negligent. Neglect of duty does not cease by repetition to be neglect of duty"; *Albrighton* v. *Royal Prince Alfred Hospital* [1980] 2 N.S.W.L.R. 542, 562–563, *per* Reynolds J.A. (N.S.W.C.A.): " . . . it is not the law that, if all or most of the medical practitioners in Sydney habitually fail to take an available precaution to avoid foreseeable risk of injury to their patients, then none can be found guilty of negligence."

[46] (1982) 33 S.A.S.R. 189, 194 (S.C. of S. Aus.), approved by Zelling J. in *Battersby* v. *Tottman* (1985) 37 S.A.S.R. 524, 537. In *F.* v. *R.* Bollen J. commented, at p. 201, that: "I respectfully think that some of the cases in England have concentrated rather too heavily on the practice of the medical profession."

[47] (1950) 94 S.J. 599; see also *Jones* v. *Manchester Corpn.* [1952] 2 All E.R. 125, 129, *per* Singleton L.J. citing Oliver J., the trial judge. Some commentators consider *Clarke* v. *Adams* to be of questionable authority on the basis that it predates *Bolam* v. *Friern Hospital Management Committee* [1957] 2 All E.R. 118: see Montgomery (1989) 16 J. of Law and Soc. 319, 323; Dugdale and Stanton, *Professional Negligence*, 1989, 2nd ed., para. 15.23, n. 5. The *Bolam* test, however, was not new, it simply encapsulated earlier statements of the law. This, at least, was Lord Diplock's interpretation: *Sidaway* v. *Bethlem Royal Hospital Governors* [1985] 1 All E.R. 643, 657.

the knee. Slade J. held the defendant liable for giving an inadequate warning to enable the plaintiff to be safe, although it was the very warning that the defendant had been taught to give. In *Hucks* v. *Cole* Sachs L.J. said that where the evidence indicates the existence of a lacuna in professional practice by which risks of great danger are knowingly taken then:

> "the courts must anxiously examine that lacuna—particularly if the risks can be easily and inexpensively avoided. If the court finds, on an analysis of the reasons given for not taking those precautions that, in the light of current professional knowledge, there is no proper basis for the lacuna, and that it is definitely not reasonable that those risks should have been taken, its function is to state that fact and where necessary to state that it constitutes negligence. In such a case the practice will no doubt thereafter be altered to the benefit of patients."[48]

Nonetheless, it will be rare for the courts to condemn as negligence **3.28** a commonly accepted practice. Only where the risk was, or should have been, obvious to the defendant so that it would be folly to disregard it will the courts take this step.[49] In *Gent* v. *Wilson* Schroeder J.A. said that:

> "If a physician has rendered treatment in a manner which is in conformity with the standard and recognised practice followed by the members of his profession, unless that practice is *demonstrably unsafe or dangerous*, that fact affords cogent evidence that he has exercised that reasonable degree of care and skill which may be required of him."[50]

Where the case does not involve difficult or uncertain questions of **3.29** medical or surgical treatment, or abstruse or highly technical scientific issues, but is concerned with whether obvious and simple precautions could have been taken, the question of the practice of experts should be largely irrelevant. The courts do not rely on expert rally drivers, for example, to say whether a motorist was negligent.[51]

---

[48] (1968) 112 S.J. 483, 484.

[49] *Paris* v. *Stepney Borough Council* [1951] A.C. 367, 382, *per* Lord Normand: "obvious folly"; *General Cleaning Contractors* v. *Christmas* [1953] A.C. 180, 193, *per* Lord Reid: "obvious danger"; *Morris* v. *West Hartlepool Steam Navigation Co. Ltd.* [1956] A.C. 552, 579, *per* Lord Cohen: "obvious risk"; *Stokes* v. *Guest, Keen & Nettlefold (Bolts & Nuts) Ltd.* [1968] 1 W.L.R. 1776, 1783; see also *O'Donovan* v. *Cork County Council* [1967] I.R. 173, 193, *per* Walsh J.; *Johnston* v. *Board of Governors of the Hospital for Sick Children* (1984) (unreported), Q.B.D., *per* Glidewell J.

[50] (1956) 2 D.L.R. (2d) 160, 165 (Ont. C.A.), emphasis added.

[51] "Ordinary common sense dictates that when simple methods to avoid danger have been devised, are known, and are available, non-use, with fatal results, cannot be justified by saying that others also have been following the same old, less-careful practice; and that when such methods are readily comprehensible by the ordinary person, by whom, also, the need to use them or not is easily apprehended, it is quite within the competence of court or jury, quite as much as of experts to deal with the issues; and that the existence of a practice which neglects them, even if the practice were general, cannot protect the defendant surgeon" *per* Coyne J.A. in *Anderson* v. *Chasney* [1949] 4 D.L.R. 71, 86–87 (Man. C.A.); aff'd [1950] 4 D.L.R. 223 (S.C.C.). Similarly, in *Chapman* v. *Rix* (1959) 103 S.J. 940 Morris L.J., in a dissenting judgment, said that: "The question whether the omission was negligent was one on which expert technical guidance was not needed. Medical witnesses had . . . stated that if similarly placed their

3.30   Moreover, before any question of complying with accepted practice can arise the court must be satisfied on the evidence presented to it that there is a responsible body of professional opinion which supports the practice. It is always open to the court to reject expert evidence applying the ordinary principles of credibility that would be applied in any courtroom, for example, that the evidence is internally contradictory, or that the witness was acting as an advocate rather than an impartial and objective expert.[52] In *Hills* v. *Potter* Hirst J. denied that the *Bolam* test allows the medical profession to set the standard of care: "In every case the court must be satisfied that the standard contended for . . . accords with that upheld by a substantial body of medical opinion, and that this body of medical opinion is both respectable and responsible, and experienced in this particular field of medicine."[53]

3.31   It is submitted that this is the proper approach to adopt in cases involving accepted professional practice. Following accepted practice, or one of several such practices, is strong evidence of the exercise of reasonable care, but ultimately it is for the court to determine what constitutes negligence.[54] It will be rare for the court to conclude that a common practice was negligent, but when this does happen it will be through a finding that the practice was not "responsible." Once the practice followed by the defendant is acknowledged to be a "responsible" practice it is not open to the court to hold that it was negligent, even where another body of "responsible" professional opinion is critical of the practice.

(ii) Departing from

3.32   Just as compliance with accepted practice is good evidence that the defendant has acted with reasonable care, a departure from accepted practice may be evidence of negligence,[55] but in neither case is the evidence conclusive.[56] If deviation from a common professional prac-

---

conduct would have been no different from that under review. But the duty still remained with the court to decide whether such conduct amounted in law to negligence."

[52] See § 3.126.

[53] [1983] 3 All E.R. 716, 728. See also, *per* Lord Diplock in *Sidaway* v. *Bethlem Royal Hospital Governors* [1985] 1 All E.R. 643, 659, stating that the court must be satisfied by the expert evidence that a body of opinion qualifies as a "responsible" body of medical opinion. See further *Nye Saunders & Partners* v. *Bristow* (1987) 37 Build.L.R. 92, C.A., where it was held that no responsible body of architects would have failed to warn clients about the risks of inflation when undertaking a building project.

[54] See Jackson and Powell, *Professional Negligence*, 1987, 2nd ed., para. 1.26; Dugdale and Stanton, *Professional Negligence*, 1989, 2nd ed., paras. 15.22–15.23; Norrie [1985] Jur. Rev. 145; *cf.* Montgomery (1989) 16 J. of Law and Soc. 319, 322, who argues that there has been a consistent refusal by the judges to set substantive standards for the medical profession, and that claims to the contrary "make too much of *obiter dicta* and too little of the sobering indications of judicial practice." (*Ibid.*, p. 323.)

[55] *Robinson* v. *Post Office* [1974] 2 All E.R. 737, 745. In *Thake* v. *Maurice* [1986] 1 All E.R. 497 the defendant surgeon carelessly forgot to give his own usual warning that there was a slight risk that the plaintiff might become fertile again after a sterilisation operation. In the absence of any other expert evidence the Court of Appeal held that the defendant's usual practice was evidence of what constituted "responsible" practice, and held him negligent for failing to comply with it.

[56] *Holland* v. *The Devitt & Moore Nautical College, The Times*, March 4, 1960, Q.B.D., where a slight departure from the standard textbook treatment was held not negligent, since the doctor had to treat a particular patient, whereas the textbooks deal with a subject generally.

tice was considered proof of negligence then no doctor could introduce a new technique or method of treatment without facing the risk of a negligence action if something went wrong. As Lord President Clyde commented in *Hunter* v. *Hanley* this "would be disastrous . . . for all inducement to progress in medical science would then be destroyed."[57] His Lordship suggested that there were three requirements to establish liability where deviation from normal practice is alleged. First, it must be proved that there is a usual and normal practice; secondly, it must be proved that the doctor has not adopted that practice; and thirdly, it must be established that the course which he adopted is one which no professional man of ordinary skill would have taken if he had been acting with ordinary care. In other words, the fundamental test remains whether the defendant acted with reasonable care in all the circumstances, and the significance of compliance with or deviation from common professional practice lies in its evidential value.

Sometimes, a departure from accepted practices may provide over- **3.33** whelming evidence of a breach of duty, particularly where the practice is specifically designed as a precaution against a known risk and the defendant has no good reason for not following the normal procedure. If the risk should materialise the defendant will have great difficulty in avoiding a finding of negligence. In *Clark* v. *MacLennan*,[58] for example, the plaintiff developed stress incontinence soon after the birth of her first child. Conservative treatment failed to improve the plaintiff's condition, and so a month after the birth the defendant gynaecologist performed an anterior colporrhaphy operation. The normal practice of gynaecologists was not to perform such an operation until at least three months after the birth, because the condition may in any event improve with the passage of time, and if it is clear that the operation is required there is a much greater chance of success after three months, since the risk of haemorrhage is smaller. This was not an absolute rule since there might be exceptional cases, but it was not a case where there were two schools of thought amongst gynaecologists. None of the witnesses could point to any instance where the operation had been performed at less than three months. The operation was not a success because a haemorrhage caused the repair to break down. Two further operations were necessary, neither of which were successful with the result that the plaintiff's condition became permanent. The defendant was held liable. Peter Pain J. said that a doctor owes a duty to his patient to observe the precautions which are normal in the course of the treatment that he gives. Where "there is but one orthodox course of treatment and he chooses to depart from that . . . one has to inquire whether he took all proper factors into account which he knew or should have known, and whether his departure from the orthodox course can be justified on the basis of these factors."[59]

---

[57] 1955 S.C. 200, 206. This proposition also receives statutory recognition in the Congenital Disabilities (Civil Liability) Act 1976, s.1(5), which provides that: "The defendant is not answerable to the child, for anything he did or omitted to do when responsible in a professional capacity for treating or advising the parent, if he took reasonable care having due regard to then received professional opinion applicable to the particular class of case; *but this does not mean that he is answerable only because he departed from received opinion*" (emphasis added).

[58] [1983] 1 All E.R. 416.

[59] *Ibid.*, p. 425.

3.34   His Lordship went further, however, suggesting that where there is a general practice to take a particular precaution against a specific risk but the defendant fails to take that precaution, and the very damage occurs against which the precaution is designed to be a protection, then the *burden of proof* lies with the defendant to show both that he was not negligent and that the negligence did not cause the damage.[60] This view, that negligence can be established merely by showing that some step which is designed to avert or minimise a risk has not been taken, was disapproved by Mustill L.J. in *Wilsher* v. *Essex Area Health Authority*,[61] though the decision in *Clark* v. *MacLennan* was described as, on its facts, "unimpeachable." Thus, although the burden of proving negligence remains with the plaintiff, in a case where the defendant has departed from the single orthodox procedure he will probably be found liable, unless there is evidence before the court which would justify the departure.[62]

3.35   Some instances of departure from accepted practices are quite clearly negligent even where they are performed consciously and routinely. For example, in *Chin Keow* v. *Government of Malaysia*[63] a doctor gave a patient an injection of penicillin without making any enquiry about the patient's medical history. Had he done so he would have discovered that she was allergic to penicillin. The patient died due to an allergic reaction to the drug. The doctor was aware of the remote possibility of this risk arising but he carried on with his routine practice of not making any enquiry because he had had no mishaps before. All the medical evidence was to the effect that enquiries, which would have taken no more than five minutes, were necessary. The Privy Council held the doctor liable.

3.36   In *Landau* v. *Werner*[64] a psychiatrist engaged in social contact with a female patient who had developed a strong and obsessive emotional attachment to him. This was a departure from recognised standards in the practice of psychiatry and led to a serious deterioration in the patient's mental health. Barry J. said that although the defendant had acted from the best of intentions he had made a tragic mistake; there was no body of professional opinion which would have adopted this course of conduct with a patient in these circumstances, indeed, the medical evidence was all one way in condemning social contacts. Accordingly the defendant was liable. This was upheld on appeal. Sellers L.J. said that:

> " . . . a doctor might not be negligent if he tried a new technique but if he did he must justify it before the court. If his novel or exceptional treatment had failed disastrously he could not complain if it was held that he went beyond the bounds of due care and skill as recognised generally. Success was the best justification for unusual and unestablished treatment."

3.37   In *Coughlin* v. *Kuntz*[65] the defendant adopted a method of performing an operation which was experimental, unsupported by clinical

---

[60] *Ibid.*, p. 427, relying on *McGhee* v. *National Coal Board* [1972] 3 All E.R. 1008.
[61] [1986] 3 All E.R. 801, 814, 815. The House of Lords also disapproved this approach to the proof of causation in *Wilsher* v. *Essex Area Health Authority* [1988] 1 All E.R. 871; see § 5.20.
[62] For discussion of the burden of proof and the evidential burden, see §§ 3.94 *et seq.*
[63] [1967] 1 W.L.R. 813.
[64] (1961) 105 S.J. 257 and 1008 (C.A.).
[65] (1987) 42 C.C.L.T. 142 (B.C.S.C.); aff'd [1990] 2 W.W.R. 737 (B.C.C.A.).

study, and favoured by no other orthopaedic surgeon. The procedure
was under investigation by the College of Physicians and Surgeons,
which had urged the defendant to undertake a moratorium on the
procedure. The defendant was held to have been negligent. Similarly,
in *Cryderman* v. *Ringrose*[66] the defendant took a biopsy at a time when
there was a "presumptive pregnancy." The normal practice would
have been to alert the plaintiff to the possibility of pregnancy and wait
until a more certain diagnosis could be made. In the circumstances the
biopsy was not medically justified since it could cause an abortion, and
the defendant was liable.

3. Experimental techniques

The practitioner who departs from the accepted methods of treat- **3.38**
ment will normally have to provide some justification for doing so if, as
a consequence, the patient suffers injury.[67] This could have an inhibit-
ing effect on doctors who seek to employ novel or experimental
methods in the interests of their patients where traditional techniques
have failed. Moreover, there is also an obligation to keep up to date
with new methods,[68] but, inevitably, someone has to be the first to try
the innovation. On the other hand, patients should not be recklessly
subjected to untried and potentially dangerous experimentation. The
law has to reach a delicate balance between these competing considerations. One response has been to say that in such circumstances the
courts should be careful not to make a finding of negligence simply
because the patient has sustained injury. In *Wilsher* v. *Essex Area
Health Authority*[69] Mustill L.J. said that where the doctor embarks on a
form of treatment which is still comparatively untried, with techniques
and safeguards which are still in the course of development, then "if
the decision to embark on the treatment at all was justifiable and was
taken with the informed consent of the patient, the court should . . .
be particularly careful not to impute negligence simply because something has gone wrong." It is debateable whether this adds much to the
usual *caveat* that the courts give against findings of negligence merely
because an error has occurred. It simply begs the question whether the
decision to proceed was indeed justifiable.

Lord Diplock has also touched upon this problem in *Sidaway* v. **3.39**
Bethlem Royal Hospital Governors:

> "Those members of the public who seek medical or surgical aid
> would be badly served by the adoption of any legal principle that
> would confine the doctor to some long-established, well-tried

---

[66] [1977] 3 W.W.R. 109; aff'd [1978] 3 W.W.R. 481 (Alta. S.C. Appellate Division).
See also *Zimmer* v. *Ringrose* (1981) 124 D.L.R. (3d) 215, 223, on a doctor's duty to
inform the patient that a new procedure or technique had not been approved by the
medical profession. A reasonable practitioner would have disclosed this since he would
realise that the information would be likely to influence the patient's decision whether to
undergo the procedure.
[67] *Clark* v. *MacLennan* [1983] 1 All E.R. 416; *Landau* v. *Werner* (1961) 105 S.J. 1008,
C.A.
[68] See § 3.46.
[69] [1986] 3 All E.R. 801, 812.

method of treatment only, although its past record of success might be small, if he wanted to be confident that he would not run the risk of being held liable in negligence simply because he tried some more modern treatment, and by some unavoidable mischance it failed to heal but did some harm to the patient. This would encourage 'defensive medicine' with a vengeance."[70]

3.40 This statement clearly reflects the public interest in allowing the medical profession to develop new, and more effective methods of health care, without the fear that they may be sued for negligence simply for trying something different from established practice. The passage also indicates one factor that would be relevant to the question of whether embarking on the new procedure would be justified, namely where the past record of success of the established treatment is small. However, his Lordship also appeared to suggest that the *Bolam* test protects the doctor in this situation by acknowledging that there may be a number of different accepted practices at any particular time. This view is open to question. There is likely to be a time-lag between the development of new methods and their acceptance by the profession.[71] Where the new treatment is not yet established as a practice accepted as proper by a responsible body of medical opinion a defendant will have to justify his decision simply by reference to the "reasonable doctor." This will depend to a large extent on the relative risk of the treatment in comparison to the alternative treatments and the nature of the illness for which is is prescribed. Where the patient's condition is very serious and the standard treatment is ineffective, a doctor will be justified in taking greater risks in an attempt to provide some effective treatment.

3.41 The question of experimental procedures has been considered by the Canadian courts. The use of an innovative technique will not be treated as negligence *per se*. In *Zimmer* v. *Ringrose* Prowse J.A. said that:

> "A physician is entitled to decide that the situation dictates the adoption of an innovative course of treatment. As long as he discharges his duty of disclosure, and is not otherwise in breach of his duties of skill and care, *e.g.* has not negligently adopted the procedure given the circumstances, the doctor will not be held liable for implementing such a course of treatment."[72]

3.42 The defendant's method of sterilisation was "experimental and quite unsupported by clinical study as a method acceptable for human beings."[73] He was held to have been negligent in failing to inform the plaintiff that the technique had not been approved by the medical profession, although this aspect of the claim failed on the grounds of causation (the plaintiff would have undergone the procedure in any event). In *Cryderman* v. *Ringrose*[74] the plaintiff agreed to be sterilised

---

[70] [1985] 1 All E.R. 643, 657.

[71] As, *e.g.*, in *Crawford* v. *Charing Cross Hospital, The Times*, December 8, 1953.

[72] (1981) 124 D.L.R. (3d) 215, 223–224 (Alta. C.A.); aff'g in part (1978) 89 D.L.R. (3d) 646.

[73] (1978) 89 D.L.R. (3d) 646, 652, *per* MacDonald J.; see also pp. 655–656; see also *Coughlin* v. *Kuntz* (1987) 42 C.C.L.T. 142 (B.C.S.C.); aff'd [1990] 2 W.W.R. 737 (B.C.C.A.), *ante*, § 3.37.

[74] [1977] 3 W.W.R. 109; aff'd [1978] 3 W.W.R. 481 (Alta. S.C. Appellate Division).

by the same defendant by the same experimental procedure, which involved introducing silver nitrate into the fallopian tubes through the uterus. The plaintiff was not informed that the procedure was unreliable or that it might damage the uterus. The plaintiff believed that she was sterile, although the defendant knew that the procedure had not been successful and he did not inform her. She became pregnant and later underwent an abortion. The trial judge rejected the plaintiff's argument that the defendant was negligent because there was a usual and normal practice which had been not followed, on the ground that it would impede medical progress. He also distinguished *Halushka* v. *University of Saskatchewan*[75] on the basis that that was a case of "pure medical experimentation," where different considerations would apply:

> "When an experimental procedure is employed the common law requires a high degree of care and also disclosure to the patient of the fact that the treatment is new and risky."[76]

The standard of care was, nonetheless, that of a reasonable doctor considering all the circumstances, including the seriousness of the condition, the risks, the patient's capacity to comprehend and decide the question involved and the likely effect on her of the knowledge of the risks involved. Moreover, the court should be alert to the risk of a conflict of interest between the patient's welfare and the interests of the doctor, particularly when the doctor is prescribing *his* new process (as distinct from the objectivity that was to be presumed in the use of someone else's new process).

A similar approach would probably be taken in this country. A **3.43** degree of care is expected which is commensurate with the risk involved, and innovative treatment would be regarded as inherently "risky" until it has become tried and tested. In *Independent Broadcasting Authority* v. *EMI Electronics Ltd. and BICC Construction Ltd.*[77] the House of Lords held that a defendant employed to design an experimental television mast had to demonstrate that he had exercised a high degree of care both in assessing the risks of the venture and the possible alternatives. He could not justify his actions simply by saying "we were taking a step into the unknown and so the risks were unforeseeable." There was an obligation to think things through and to assess the dimensions of the "venture into the unknown."[78]

---

[75] (1965) 53 D.L.R. (2d) 436; see further § 6.118.

[76] [1977] 3 W.W.R. 109, 118; *Crossman* v. *Stewart* (1977) 82 D.L.R. (3d) 677, 686; *Poole* v. *Morgan* [1987] 3 W.W.R. 217, 254, *per* Cawsey J. (Alta. Q.B.) stating that " . . . where the risks involved in the treatment are great, or the treatment is a new one, the standard of care is increased." It is submitted that the standard of care does not change, rather the precautions required to satisfy the standard of "reasonable care in all the circumstances" are greater.

[77] (1980) 14 Build. L.R. 1.

[78] *Ibid.*, p. 31, *per* Lord Edmund-Davies. Dugdale and Stanton, *Professional Negligence*, 2nd ed., 1989, para. 16.10, comment that: "In law the burden of proving lack of reasonable care in such circumstances remains on the plaintiff, but, in practice, once the plaintiff has shown that the work has proved to be faulty and that it diverged from the accepted professional approach to such issues, it will be for the defence to justify their actions."

3.44 This proposition would also apply to claims arising out of a systematic research project, whether therapeutic or non-therapeutic.[79] An allegation of negligence in conducting research would involve proving that the design, the performance or the follow-up of the experimental procedure was negligent, or that the disclosure of information concerning risks was inadequate.[80] A researcher has a duty to investigate fully the possible consequences of the research using existing published literature and animal experiments where appropriate, prior to conducting research on human subjects.[81] The research should be well-designed, and should seek to minimise the risks to the research subjects. This would include: the provision of a "stoppage rule" by which the project would be halted if a serious risk of harm became apparent; provision for emergencies; and careful periodic observation of the subjects.[82] It is also arguable that a research project which failed to comply with national or international ethical codes on medical experimentation could be found to have been conducted negligently, on the basis that the codes constitute evidence of what is reasonable care, by reference to the accepted practice of the profession.[83]

3.45 The Pearson Commission recommended that a volunteer for medical research or a clinical trial who suffers severe damage as a result should have a cause of action on the basis of strict liability.[84] This proposal has not been implemented, although *ex gratia* compensation may be available to a volunteer injured in a study sponsored by the Medical Research Council, or during drug trials.[85] In an appropriate case a research subject might have an action against a drug manufacturer

---

[79] Therapeutic research is an activity which has a therapeutic intention, as well as a research intention, towards the subjects of the research; the subjects are also patients. Non-therapeutic research is an activity which does not have a therapeutic intention. This is normally carried out on healthy volunteers, who are not patients. See further §§ 6.104–6.124. The Royal College of Physicians, *Guidelines on the Practice of Ethics Committees in Medical Research Involving Human Subjects*, 2nd ed., 1990 and *Research Involving Patients*, 1990 distinguish *research*, which is designed to develop or contribute to generalisable knowledge, from *innovative therapy*, where a clinician departs significantly from standard practice entirely for the benefit of a particular patient. The latter may not constitute research, although it may be described as experimental in the sense that it is novel and unvalidated.

[80] On the disclosure of information to research subjects see §§ 6.106–6.113, 6.118–6.119.

[81] *Vacwell Engineering Co. Ltd.* v. *BDH Chemicals* [1971] 1 Q.B. 88, where the defendant was negligent in failing to check all relevant publications dealing with a little known chemical prior to marketing it.

[82] *Zimmer* v. *Ringrose* (1978) 89 D.L.R. (3d) 646, 656.

[83] See Dugdale and Stanton, *Professional Negligence*, 2nd ed., 1989, para. 16.11. Both therapeutic and non-therapeutic medical research are governed by the guidelines of the *Declaration of Helsinki*, extracted in Kennedy and Grubb, *Medical Law Text and Materials*, 1989, pp. 864–866. See also the Royal College of Physicians, *Guidelines on the Practice of Ethics Committees in Medical Research Involving Human Subjects*, 2nd ed., 1990 and Royal College of Physicians, *Research Involving Patients*, 1990. On the potential liability of Research Ethics Committees see Brazier (1990) 6 P.N. 186. The decisions of ethics committees are subject to judicial review: *R.* v. *Ethical Committee of St. Mary's Hospital, ex p. Harriott* (1988) 18 Fam. Law 165.

[84] *Royal Commission on Civil Liability and Compensation for Personal Injury*, Cmnd. 7054 (1978) paras. 1339–1441.

[85] See the Association of the British Pharmaceutical Industry *Guidelines for Medical Experiments in Non-Patient Human Volunteers*, 1988 and the ABPI *Guidelines: Clinical Trials—Compensation for Medicine-Induced Injury*, 1983, extracted in Kennedy and Grubb *Medical Law: Text and Materials*, 1989, pp. 895–907, 912–913.

under Part I of the Consumer Protection Act 1987, but the chances of such a claim succeeding are small given the difficulty that the plaintiff would have in proving that the drug was defective, and the fact that the manufacturer could rely on the development risks defence.[86]

4. Keeping up to date

Professional practice may change over time so that what was once **3.46** accepted as the correct procedure is no longer considered to be respectable or responsible. In *Bolam* v. *Friern Hospital Management Committee* McNair J. pointed out that a medical practitioner cannot "obstinately and pigheadedly carry on with some old technique if it has been proved to be contrary to what is really substantially the whole of informed medical opinion."[87] Thus, there is an obligation on doctors to keep up to date with new developments in their particular field. This principle is easy enough to state, but it is more difficult to determine precisely when a new development will render adherence to the old method negligent. In the same passage McNair J. illustrated his point in this way: "Otherwise you might get men today saying: 'I don't believe in anaesthetics. I don't believe in antiseptics. I am going to continue to do my surgery in the way it was done in the eighteenth century.' That would clearly be wrong." No doubt patients will be relieved to know that they should not be subjected to the surgical methods of the eighteenth century, but this still leaves considerable scope for debate about when practices become outdated.

In *Crawford* v. *Charing Cross Hospital*[88] the plaintiff developed **3.47** brachial palsy in an arm following a blood transfusion. At first instance the defendants were held liable on the basis that the anaesthetist had failed to read an article published in *The Lancet* six months earlier, concerning the best position of the arm when using a drip. The Court of Appeal reversed this decision, taking the view that it would be too great a burden on a doctor to say that he has to read every article appearing in the current medical press.[89] Moreover, it was wrong to suggest that a practitioner was negligent simply because he did not immediately put into operation the suggestions made by a contributor to a medical journal, although the time might come when a recommendation was so well proved and so well accepted that it should be adopted.

Once the risks associated with the old procedure become generally **3.48** known, so that it can be said that an ordinary and reasonably competent practitioner would have changed his practice, it will be

---

[86] See §§ 8.64, 8.87.
[87] [1957] 2 All E.R. 118, 122.
[88] *The Times*, December 8, 1953.
[89] See also *Dwan* v. *Farquhar* [1988] Qd. R. 234, where an article in a journal concerning the risks of contracting AIDS from blood transfusions was published in March 1983, and a patient contracted AIDS from a blood transfusion performed in May 1983; it was held that there was no negligence. See further *H.* v. *Royal Alexandra Hospital for Children* [1990] 1 Med.L.R. 297 on this risk.

negligent to continue with that procedure.[90] The obligation is to make a reasonable effort to keep up to date. A doctor cannot realistically be expected to read every article in every learned medical journal,[91] but where a particular risk has been highlighted on a number of occasions the practitioner will ignore it at his peril.

3.49   Practices adopted in other countries are not necessarily evidence of the appropriate standard here. In *Whiteford* v. *Hunter*[92] the defendant mistakenly diagnosed prostate cancer without performing a biopsy or using a cystoscope, procedures which were both standard practice in the United States. The instrument was rare in England at the time and the defendant did not have one. Moreover, the evidence indicated that it was against approved practice in England to use a cystoscope where, as with the plaintiff, there was acute urinary retention. The House of Lords held that the defendant was not negligent.

3.50   There is an inevitable tension between the doctor's obligation to keep up to date, and the trite observation that doctors should not adopt any and every new idea until it has been proved to be both effective and safe. Doctors should not subject patients to untried methods of treatment unless the traditional approach has proved ineffective and the anticipated benefits are justified by the risks. On the other hand, despite the emphasis within many malpractice actions on complying with common practice, the courts are careful to avoid the suggestion that findings of negligence may stifle innovation.[93] A new technique may carry an unforeseen danger, notwithstanding the reasonable efforts of the profession to identify risks in advance, and this will not be held negligent.[94]

5. Errors of judgment

3.51   The view was sometimes expressed that there was a difference between negligence and an "error of professional judgment" or a "mere" error of judgment. In *Whitehouse* v. *Jordan*, for example, Lord Denning M.R., having commented on malpractice litigation in the United States and its consequences, said: "We must say, and say

---

[90] See, *e.g.*, *Roe* v. *Minister of Health* [1954] 2 Q.B. 66; *McLean* v. *Weir* [1977] 5 W.W.R. 609; aff'd [1980] 4 W.W.R. 330, *post*, § 3.55; *McCormick* v. *Marcotte* (1971) 20 D.L.R. (3d) 345 S.C.C., where a surgeon was liable for using an obsolete method of treating a broken bone (plate and screw) notwithstanding a specialist orthopaedic surgeon recommended a different procedure (the insertion of an intramedullary nail); *Reynard* v. *Carr* (1983) 30 C.C.L.T. 42, 67–68; rev'd in part on other grounds (1986) 38 C.C.L.T. 217 where the defendant was ignorant about the serious side-effects of a drug he was prescribing, although this was general knowledge within the profession.

[91] See, *e.g.*, the comments of Mustill J. in *Thompson* v. *Smiths Shiprepairers* (*North Shields*) *Ltd.* [1984] 1 All E.R. 881, 894 on the question of the time at which employers became negligent given the developing knowledge of risk to employees' hearing within the industry. A reasonable employer would demonstrate "proper but not extraordinary solicitude for the welfare of his workers"; *Stokes* v. *Guest, Keen & Nettlefold* (*Bolts & Nuts*) *Ltd.* [1968] 1 W.L.R. 1776, 1783—"where there is developing knowledge, he must keep reasonably abreast of it and not be too slow to apply it," *per* Swanwick J.

[92] [1950] W.N. 553.

[93] See §§ 3.38–3.40.

[94] "Doctors, like the rest of us, have to learn by experience; and experience often teaches in a hard way. Something goes wrong and shows up a weakness and then it is put right" *per* Lord Denning M.R. in *Roe* v. *Minister of Health* [1954] 2 Q.B. 66, 83.

firmly, that, in a professional man, an error of judgment is not negligent."[95] In the House of Lords this statement was strongly criticised. Lord Edmund-Davies said that:

> "To say that a surgeon committed an error of judgment is wholly ambiguous, for while some such errors may be completely consistent with the due exercise of professional skill, other acts or omissions in the course of exercising 'clinical judgment' may be so glaringly below proper standards as to make a finding of negligence inevitable."[96]

Referring to the *Bolam* test, his Lordship added that if a surgeon fails to measure up to the standard of the ordinary skilled man exercising and professing to have that skill in *any* respect ("clinical judgment" or otherwise), he has been negligent.

Lord Fraser adopted a similarly forthright approach, commenting **3.52** that merely to describe something as an error of judgment says nothing about whether it is negligent or not. Rather, whether an error of judgment is negligent or not depends on the nature of the error. If it is one that would not have been made by a reasonably competent professional man professing to have the standard and type of skill that the defendant held himself out as having, and acting with ordinary care, then it is negligent. If, on the other hand, it is an error that a man, acting with ordinary care, might have made, then it is not negligence.[97]

Subsequently, Lord Denning M.R. returned to this issue in *Hyde* v. **3.53** *Tameside Area Health Authority*,[98] repeating his comment that, in a professional man, an error of judgment is not negligent:

> "Not every error of judgment, of course, but only those errors which a reasonably competent professional man, acting with ordinary care, might commit. So explained I stand by every word I used in *Whitehouse* v. *Jordan*. It is of the first importance so that 'medical malpractice' cases should not get out of hand here as they have done in the United States of America."

So explained, the term "error of judgment" is redundant as a guide to what constitutes negligence. It merely represents the conclusion that, applying the *Bolam* test, the defendant has not been negligent.

---

[95] [1980] 1 All E.R. 650, 658. His Lordship took this approach for policy reasons: "Take heed of what has happened in the United States. 'Medical malpractice' cases there are very worrying, especially as they are tried by juries who have sympathy for the patient and none for the doctor who is insured. The damages are colossal. The doctors insure but the premiums become very high: and these have to be passed on in fees to the patients. Experienced practitioners are known to have refused to treat patients for fear of being accused of negligence. Young men are even deterred from entering the profession because of the risks involved. In the interests of all, we must avoid such consequences in England." See also, *per* Lawton L.J. at p. 659 referring to defensive medicine; *cf.* Donaldson L.J. at p. 662.

[96] [1981] 1 All E.R. 267, 276.

[97] *Ibid.*, p. 281. See also, *per* Lord Diplock in *Saif Ali* v. *Sydney Mitchell & Co.* [1980] A.C. 198 at 220 referring to the liability of barristers: "No matter what profession it may be, the common law does not impose on those who practise it any liability for damage resulting from what in the result turned out to be errors of judgment, unless the error was such as no reasonably well informed and competent member of that profession could have made."

[98] (1981), reported at (1986) 2 P.N. 26, 29.

3.54   The Canadian courts have apparently accepted that an "error of judgment" may excuse the defendant. In *Wilson* v. *Swanson*[99] Rand J. said that "An error of judgment has long been distinguished from an act of unskilfulness or carelessness or due to lack of knowledge . . . . The honest and intelligent exercise of judgment has long been recognised as satisfying the professional obligation." It has been treated as a specific defence,[1] although it may be that the term is used as a *post hoc* explanation of a finding that the doctor exercised reasonable care notwithstanding the occurrence of injury to the patient. On this basis it stands in the same category as statements that doctors cannot guarantee results, that they are not insurers, and so on.

6. Unforeseeable harm

3.55   It is axiomatic within the concept of negligence that if a particular danger could not reasonably have been anticipated, the defendant has not acted negligently, because a reasonable man does not take precautions against unforeseeable consequences. This is measured by reference to knowledge at the date of the alleged negligence, not with hindsight. The principle is illustrated by the decision of the Court of Appeal in *Roe* v. *Minister of Health*.[2] Anaesthetic was kept in glass ampoules which were stored in disinfectant. The anaesthetic had become contaminated by the disinfectant which had seeped through cracks in the glass that were invisible to the naked eye. The plaintiff suffered permanent paralysis due to the administration of the contaminated anaesthetic during the course of the operation. The risk of contaminating anaesthetic in this way was not known at the time of the accident in 1947. It was held that there was no negligence because the danger was not reasonably foreseeable. The court "must not look at the 1947 accident with 1954 spectacles," but it would have been negligence to have adopted the same practice in 1954 when the risk was more widely known.[3] In *McLean* v. *Weir*[4] a similar approach was taken in circumstances where the plaintiff sustained paralysis in the course of an angiogram, when too much contrast medium was introduced into the spinal cord. This specific risk was not appreciated within the profession at the time. Subsequently, it became known that a different procedure would have avoided the mishap. Accordingly the defendant had not been negligent, although it would have been negligent to adopt exactly the same procedure after the risk had been identified.

---

[99] (1956) 5 D.L.R. (2d) 113, 120 (S.C.C.); approved by Ritchie J. in *Vail* v. *MacDonald* (1976) 66 D.L.R. (3d) 530, 535 (S.C.C.).

[1] Picard, *Legal Liability of Doctors and Hospitals in Canada*, 2nd ed., 1984, pp. 239–243.

[2] [1954] 2 Q.B. 66.

[3] *Ibid.*, p. 86. Denning L.J. commented, at p. 83, that: "It is so easy to be wise after the event and to condemn as negligence that which was only misadventure. We ought always to be on our guard against it, especially in cases against hospitals and doctors."

[4] [1977] 5 W.W.R. 609; aff'd [1980] 4 W.W.R. 330 (B.C.C.A.). On complications resulting from an aortagram see *O'Malley-Williams* v. *Board of Governors of the National Hospital for Nervous Diseases* (1975) 1 B.M.J. 635; *Ferguson* v. *Hamilton Civic Hospitals* (1983) 144 D.L.R. (3d) 214.

This principle applies not merely to questions of factual knowledge **3.56** but also to the relevant standards of reasonable care, which will be judged by reference to professional practices at the time of the treatment, not those applicable at the time when the action is tried.[5] It should be noted, however, that if damage of the same "type" was foreseeable it does not matter that the particular damage which occurred was unforeseeable, and, similarly, it is not necessary that the precise manner in which the injury occurred be foreseeable if it is of a type which was foreseeable in a general way.[6]

7. Degrees of risk

A defendant is not negligent if the damage was not a foreseeable **3.57** consequence of his conduct. It does not follow, however, that a defendant is negligent if the damage was foreseeable. A reasonable man may "foresee the possibility of many risks, but life would be almost impossible if he were to attempt to take precautions against every risk which he can foresee. He takes precautions against risks which are reasonably likely to happen."[7] In determining the level of acceptable risk the courts engage in a balancing exercise in which the magnitude of the risk, the purpose of the defendant's conduct, and the cost or practicability of taking precautions is evaluated. In some circumstances it may be reasonable simply to ignore a small risk, because the chance of it materialising is remote and the cost of precautions high.[8] On the other hand, if the cost of avoiding the risk is minimal it may be negligent to ignore a remote risk.[9]

The law requires a degree of care commensurate with the risk **3.58** created by the defendant's conduct.[10] The greater the risk of harm the greater the precautions that must be taken. This principle applies just as much to professional liability as it does to any other category of negligence. In *Battersby* v. *Tottman* Jacobs J. expressed the point in this way:

" . . . there is a clear relationship between the magnitude of the risk and the duty of care, in particular the standard of care. The greater the risks involved in any proposed course of treatment, the more carefully and anxiously must the medical practitioner weigh and consider the possible alternatives before deciding to resort to the proposed treatment."[11]

---

[5] See, *e.g.*, *Gold* v. *Haringey Health Authority* [1987] 2 All E.R. 888, where the issue was the appropriate standard of disclosure prior to a sterilisation operation in 1979.

[6] See §§ 5.66–5.73.

[7] *Bolton* v. *Stone* [1951] A.C. 850, 863, *per* Lord Oaksey.

[8] As in *Bolton* v. *Stone* [1951] A.C. 850 itself.

[9] *Overseas Tankship (U.K.) Ltd.* v. *Miller Steamship Co. Pty. Ltd., The Wagon Mound* (No. 2) [1967] 1 A.C. 617, 642.

[10] *Read* v. *J. Lyons & Co. Ltd.* [1947] A.C. 156, 173, *per* Lord Macmillan.

[11] (1985) 37 S.A.S.R. 524, 542; *Glasgow Corporation* v. *Muir* [1943] A.C. 448, 456, *per* Lord Macmillan: "Those who engage in operations inherently dangerous must take precautions which are not required of persons engaged in the ordinary routine of daily life"; see also *O'Donovan* v. *Cork County Council* [1967] I.R. 173, 190, *per* Walsh J.; *Buchan* v. *Ortho Pharmaceuticals (Canada) Ltd.* (1986) 25 D.L.R. (4th) 658, 678–679, *per* Robins J.A. (Ont. C.A.).

3.59   For example, when an anaesthetist was handling a dangerous substance which was known to be highly inflammable and he knew of the hazard arising from electrostatic sparks in an operating room, the degree of care required from him was proportionately high and he was bound to take special precautions to prevent injury to his patient.[12]

3.60   The magnitude of the risk involves two elements. First, the likelihood that the harm will occur. The more remote the chance that any damage to the plaintiff will arise the more reasonable it will be to take fewer, or even no, precautions against the eventuality.[13] On the other hand, the degree of risk also takes into account the severity of the potential consequences. If the harm is likely to be serious, should it occur, then greater precautions must be taken. This principle applies to the individual plaintiff, so that if it is foreseeable that the damage *to this plaintiff* is likely to be severe, greater precautions will be required than for the average individual. In *Paris* v. *Stepney Borough Council*,[14] for example, the defendant employers knew that the plaintiff was blind in one eye. In the course of the plaintiff's work a chip of metal entered his good eye, rendering him totally blind. The House of Lords held the employers liable in negligence for failing to provide goggles, although it was not usual to do so for that type of work. The duty of care was owed to each particular employee and in determining the requisite degree of care the defendants ought to have taken into account the gravity of the consequences for each individual employee—an injury to the plaintiff's good eye was a much more serious consequence than a similar injury to a fully sighted man, and a reasonable man would take account of the risk of greater injury as well as the greater risk of injury. Thus, where a doctor has formed an opinion as to the appropriate diagnosis of a patient's condition, he should take into account the possibility that an alternative diagnosis would explain the symptoms, especially where the consequences of the alternative diagnosis, if correct, would be very serious.[15]

3.61   A similar principle applies where the plaintiff's peculiar susceptibility makes the risk of harm occurring greater than would be the case with a normal individual. For example, a person who digs a hole in the pavement must take reasonable precautions to avoid the risk that a blind person might fall into the hole. Precautions that would protect the fully sighted will not necessarily protect the blind.[16] Accordingly, "a measure of care appropriate to the inability or disability of those who are immature or feeble in mind or body is due from others, who know of or ought to anticipate the presence of such persons within the scope and hazard of their own operations."[17]

---

[12] *Crits* v. *Sylvester* (1956) 1 D.L.R. (2d) 502, 511 (Ont. C.A.); aff'd (1956) 5 D.L.R. (2d) 601 (S.C.C.).

[13] As, *e.g.*, in *Warren* v. *Greig* (1935) *The Lancet*, vol. 1, 330, where a patient died from excessive bleeding following an operation to remove his teeth. He was suffering from acute myeloid leukaemia which was a rare disease. It was held that a blood test was not necessary against such a remote possibility.

[14] [1951] A.C. 367.

[15] *Lankenau* v. *Dutton* (1986) 37 C.C.L.T. 213, 232 (B.C.S.C.), where a doctor failed to reassess his initial diagnosis of the cause of the patient's paralysis following major surgery, with the result that it became permanent.

[16] *Haley* v. *London Electricity Board* [1965] A.C. 778.

[17] *Glasgow Corporation* v. *Taylor* [1922] 1 A.C. 44, 67, *per* Lord Sumner, approved by Lord Reid in *Haley* v. *London Electricity Board* [1965] A.C. 778, 793.

The purpose of the defendant's conduct will also be taken into **3.62** account in assessing what is reasonable. If sufficiently important, it will justify the assumption of abnormal risk.[18] In *Watt* v. *Hertfordshire County Council*[19] it was held that it was not negligent to transport a heavy lifting jack on a vehicle that was not designed to carry it to an emergency where a woman was trapped under a lorry. A fireman was injured when the jack slipped. The risk had to be balanced against the end to be achieved and, said Denning L.J., the saving of life and limb justifies taking considerable risk. This proposition is of obvious importance to the medical profession, who, when entering upon a treatment will invariably be seeking to improve the patient's health, even if life or limb are not at stake. This does not mean, however, that the purpose of saving life and limb can justify taking any risk. It is a matter of balancing the risk against the consequences of not taking the risk. If, for example, the patient's condition is such that he will almost certainly die without some form of medical intervention, then treatment with a high degree of risk will be justified, unless, of course, there is an equally effective alternative treatment that carries less risk. Difficulty in assessing the reasonableness of the defendant's conduct may arise where the alternative treatment is less risky or has less debilitating consequences, but is possibly a less effective form of treatment.

A further factor to be considered in assessing whether the taking of **3.63** a foreseeable risk was justified is the practicability (or cost) of taking precautions. If the risk can be avoided at small cost or with a trivial expenditure of time and effort it will be unreasonable to run the risk. Conversely, some risks can only be eliminated or reduced at great expense. A reasonable man would only neglect a risk if he had a valid reason for doing so, for example, "that it would involve considerable expense to eliminate the risk. He would weigh the risk against the difficulty of eliminating it." But a reasonable man would not ignore even a small risk "if action to eliminate it presented no difficulty, involved no disadvantage and required no expense."[20]

This principle has been applied in cases of medical negligence. For **3.64** example, in *Hucks* v. *Cole*[21] Sachs L.J. said that when risks of great danger are knowingly taken as a matter of professional practice then, however small the risks, the court must carefully examine the practice, particularly where the risks can be easily and inexpensively avoided. In *Coles* v. *Reading and District Management Committee*[22] it was held to be negligent not to have given the patient an anti-tetanus injection, since it was a simple precaution, and the consequences of the infection

---

[18] *Daborn* v. *Bath Tramways Motor Co. Ltd.* [1946] 2 All E.R. 333, 336, *per* Asquith L.J. where the need for ambulances during wartime justified the use of a left-hand-drive vehicle, although it created greater risk of road accidents due to inadequate hand signals.
[19] [1954] 1 W.L.R. 835.
[20] *Overseas Tankship (U.K.) Ltd.* v. *Miller Steamship Co. Pty. Ltd., The Wagon Mound* (No. 2) [1967] 1 A.C. 617, 642; and in the medical context see *Chin Keow* v. *Government of Malaysia* [1967] 1 W.L.R. 813, P.C., § 3.35; *Leonard* v. *Knott* [1978] 5 W.W.R. 511, 516 (B.C.S.C.).
[21] (1968) 112 S.J. 483, 484.
[22] (1963) 107 S.J. 115.

are serious.[23] Again, in *Anderson* v. *Chasney* McPherson C.J.M. commented that:

3.65 "It is not sufficient for the surgeon to say: 'I never adopted the use of either of such precautions in operations of this nature.' By doing so he took an unnecessary risk, as both were available for his use on that occasion and he assumed full responsibility for the lack of use of the same, and I would hold that he was negligent in so doing."[24]

3.66 Some risks are unavoidable. In this situation the risks of proceeding have to be weighed against the disadvantages of not proceeding, also taking into account the expected benefits to the patient's health. Where the consequences of not treating the patient are potentially very serious then the doctor will normally be justified in taking greater risks.[25] Conversely, where the treatment is for a minor ailment even small risks should not be disregarded[26]; *a fortiori*, where a diagnostic test which carries a real risk of an adverse reaction is conducted when there are no clinical indications for performing such a test.[27]

3.67 This balancing exercise must take account of the individual patient. So, for example, the risks of a general anaesthetic are greater for an elderly patient than for a young, and otherwise fit, patient, and a surgeon or anaesthetist would have to take this into account in making a decision as to whether the risks involved in an operation outweighed the potential advantages. In *Battersby* v. *Tottman*[28] a doctor prescribed a very high dose of a particular drug to his patient who was suffering from a mental illness. He was aware that there was a risk of the drug causing serious and permanent eye damage, but he took the view that the benefits of the drug outweighed the risk from the side-effects, since without treatment the patient was "dangerously suicidal," and other methods of treatment had failed. It was held that in these circum-

---

[23] The patient died. See also *Robinson* v. *Post Office* [1974] 2 All E.R. 737, 745, *per* Orr L.J.: "It was, in our judgment, a very relevant consideration that, although the risks of tetanus having developed in the wound did not amount to any high probability, they could not be dismissed as unreal, and the consequence, if they had materialised, would be likely to be fatal unless ATS were administered."

[24] [1949] 4 D.L.R. 71, 75, aff'd [1950] 4 D.L.R. 223 S.C.C.; see further § 4.65; *Crits* v. *Sylvester* (1956) 1 D.L.R. (2d) 502, 511; aff'd (1956) 5 D.L.R. (2d) 601.

[25] *Davidson* v. *Connaught Laboratories* (1980) 14 C.C.L.T. 251, where the patient suffered an allergic reaction to a rabies vaccine, having come into contact with a rabid animal. Rabies is almost invariably fatal. Linden J. said, at p. 270, that: "Although the risk was only slight that the plaintiff might contract the disease as a result of that contact, the doctor was not negligent in advising caution when the consequences of not doing so were potentially severe." See also *H.* v. *Royal Alexandra Hospital for Children* [1990] 1 Med. L.R. 297, where it was held that even when the risk of transmitting AIDS through contaminated blood products became known it would not have been a practical or reasonable measure to recall or withdraw the products, given the level of risk and the need for the products.

[26] The obvious example would be cosmetic surgery, although there may well be room for disagreement as to the importance to the individual patient of removing certain cosmetic defects. On the performance of breast reduction surgery see *MacDonald* v. *Ross* (1983) 24 C.C.L.T. 242 (N.S.S.C.); *White* v. *Turner* (1981) 120 D.L.R. (3d) 269; (1982) 12 D.L.R. (4th) 319; and on cosmetic surgery that resulted in the death of a 7 year old boy, see Dyer (1986) 293 B.M.J. 686.

[27] *Leonard* v. *Knott* [1978] 5 W.W.R. 511 (B.C.S.C.), see § 4.10.

[28] (1985) 37 S.A.S.R. 524; see also Scott L.J. in *Mahon* v. *Osborne* [1939] 2 K.B. 14, 31 on the surgeon's problem of balancing competing risks and objectives when performing an operation.

stances the decision to prescribe a dosage that was far in excess of the recommended dosages was not negligent. Similarly, in *Whiteford* v. *Hunter*[29] the defendant doctor did not perform a biopsy to confirm his diagnosis of prostate cancer, since he considered there was a risk of perforating the bladder wall, and that if the condition were cancerous, an unhealing ulcer would supervene. It was held that he was not negligent.

8. Specialists

A specialist is expected to achieve the standard of care of a **3.68** reasonably competent specialist in that field. He must "exercise the ordinary skill of his specialty."[30] This is inherent in the *Bolam* test itself, as Lord Bridge recognised in *Sidaway* v. *Bethlem Royal Hospital Governors*:

> "The language of the *Bolam* test clearly requires a different degree of skill from a specialist in his own special field than from a general practitioner. In the field of neuro-surgery it would be necessary to substitute for the . . . phrase 'no doctor of ordinary skill,' the phrase 'no neuro-surgeon of ordinary skill.' All this is elementary, and . . . firmly established law."[31]

References to "a doctor" in the *Bolam* test are simply shorthand for **3.69** "a doctor undertaking this type of act or procedure." Thus, while a general practitioner must be judged by the standards of general practitioners and not specialists,[32] if a general practitioner were to undertake something that was considered a specialist task he would be judged by the standards of the specialty. If he is unable meet those standards then he will be held negligent for undertaking work beyond his competence.[33]

The standard of care within a specialist field is that of the ordinary **3.70** competent specialist, not the most experienced or most highly qualified within the specialty:

> "A medical practitioner who holds himself out as being a specialist in a particular field is required to attain the ordinary

---

[29] [1950] W.N. 553.

[30] *Maynard* v. *West Midlands Regional Health Authority* [1984] 1 W.L.R. 634, 638, *per* Lord Scarman.

[31] [1985] 1 All E.R. 643, 660. See also, *per* Lord Fraser in *Whitehouse* v. *Jordan* [1981] 1 All E.R. 267, 280: negligence meant "a failure . . . to exercise the standard of skill expected from the ordinary competent specialist having regard to the experience and expertise that the specialist holds himself out as possessing." See also *McCaffrey* v. *Hague* [1949] 4 D.L.R. 291; *Holmes* v. *Board of Hospital Trustees of City of London* (1977) 81 D.L.R. (3d) 67, 78, (Ont. H.C.); *Reitze* v. *Bruser* (No. 2) [1979] 1 W.W.R. 31; *Crits* v. *Sylvester* (1956) 1 D.L.R. (2d) 502, 508; aff'd (1956) 5 D.L.R. (2d) 601 (S.C.C.); *Wilson* v. *Swanson* (1956) 5 D.L.R. (2d) 113, 119, *per* Rand J. (S.C.C.): "What the surgeon by his ordinary engagement undertakes with the patient is that he possesses the skill, knowledge and judgment of the generality or average of the special group or class of technicians to which he belongs and will faithfully exercise them."

[32] *Langley* v. *Campbell*, *The Times*, November 6, 1975; *Sa'd* v. *Robinson* [1989] 1 Med. L.R. 41; see further § 4.20.

[33] See § 3.80. This has important implications for the question of expert testimony on the appropriate standard of care to be expected of a specialist practitioner: see § 3.124.

level of skill amongst those who specialise in the same field. He is not required to attain the highest degree of skill and competence in that particular field."[34]

3.71 If the defendant has knowledge of some fact that makes harm to the plaintiff more likely than would otherwise be the case, then as a reasonable man he must take account of that fact. A greater than average knowledge of the risks will entail more than the average or standard precautions.[35] This appears to require that the specialist must take greater precautions than the average doctor when undertaking the same task, if the specialist's actual knowledge and experience gives him a greater knowledge of risks that ought to be guarded against.[36] His conduct should not be judged by reference to lesser knowledge than in fact he had. On the other hand, he does not have to use a higher degree of skill than comparable specialists. There may come a point, of course, where a sub-discipline develops within a specialty such that it can be said that a practitioner undertaking that form of work must achieve the standards of the new "specialty."[37]

3.72 In *Duchess of Argyll* v. *Beuselinck*[38] Megarry J. questioned the proposition that a uniform standard of care would always apply to specialists:

> "But if the client employs a solicitor of high standing and great experience, will an action for negligence fail if it appears that the solicitor did not exercise the care and skill to be expected of him, though he did not fall below the standard of a reasonably competent solicitor? If the client engages an expert, and doubt-less expects to pay commensurate fees, is he not entitled to expect something more than the standard of the reasonably competent? I am speaking not merely of those expert in a particular branch of the law, as contrasted with a general practitioner, but also of those of long experience and great skill as contrasted with those practising in the same field of the law but being of a more ordinary calibre and having less experience."[39]

3.73 This higher standard would be based on an implied term in the contract of retainer to the effect that the solicitor will use the care and skill that he actually possesses rather than the care and skill of the average solicitor specialising in that field of law. There is no reason in principle why a client should not be able to purchase a higher standard of care, though this justification would confine the higher duties to actions in contract. Megarry J. distinguished contractual duties from the tort of negligence, where "the unusually careful and highly skilled

---

[34] *O'Donovan* v. *Cork County Council* [1967] I.R. 173, 190, *per* Walsh J. (Supreme Court of Ireland); *Giurelli* v. *Girgis* (1980) 24 S.A.S.R. 264, 277, *per* White J.; *F.* v. *R.* (1983) 33 S.A.S.R. 189, 205, *per* Bollen J.

[35] *Stokes* v. *Guest, Keen & Nettlefold (Nuts & Bolts) Ltd.* [1968] 1 W.L.R. 1776, 1783, *per* Swanwick J.; *Wilson* v. *Brett* (1843) 11 M. & W. 113, 115, *per* Rolfe B.: "If a person more skilled knows that to be dangerous which another not so skilled as he does not, surely that makes a difference in the liability."

[36] A point accepted as correct by Webster J. in *Wimpey Construction U.K. Ltd.* v. *Poole* [1984] 2 Lloyd's Rep. 499, 506–507.

[37] See, *e.g., Poole* v. *Morgan* [1987] 3 W.W.R. 217.

[38] [1972] 2 Lloyd's Rep. 172.

[39] *Ibid.*, p. 183.

are not held liable for falling below their own high standards if they nevertheless do all that a reasonable man would have done." Clearly, if this distinction was accepted, and applied to the medical profession, it could lead to differential duties being owed to patients in contract and tort, a position that the courts have been reluctant to countenance.[40] In *Wimpey Construction U.K. Ltd.* v. *Poole*,[41] however, Webster J. considered Megarry J.'s dictum and concluded that the *Bolam* test had been approved by the House of Lords and the Privy Council without qualification, and so should be applied without this gloss.

9. Inexperience

(i) The doctor

It is axiomatic that the standard of care expected of the reasonable **3.74** man is objective, not subjective. It eliminates the personal equation and takes no account of the particular idiosyncrasies or weaknesses of the defendant.[42] Thus, the defendant who is inexperienced or who is just learning a particular task or skill must come up to the standards of the reasonably competent and experienced person. His "incompetent best" is not good enough.[43] This principle applies with as much force to an inexperienced doctor as it does to an inexperienced motorist. In *Jones* v. *Manchester Corporation*[44] a patient died from an excessive dose of anaesthetic administered by a doctor who had been qualified for five months. In an action which was concerned with the respective responsibilities of the junior doctor and the hospital authority, the Court of Appeal made it clear that it was no defence to an action by a patient to say that she did not have sufficient experience to undertake the task, or to say that the surgeon in charge was also to blame:

> "The patient was entitled to receive all the care and skill which a fully qualified and well-experienced anaesthetist would possess and use. If Dr. Wilkes failed to exercise that care and skill, she would be liable to the patient or his widow for the consequences, no matter that the hospital authorities knew that she had not sufficient experience for the task and were much to blame for asking her to do it without proper supervision."[45]

This issue arose in the more recent case of *Wilsher* v. *Essex Area* **3.75** *Health Authority*.[46] A premature baby in a special-care baby unit received excess oxygen due to an error in monitoring its supply of

---

[40] See § 2.03.
[41] [1984] 2 Lloyd's Rep. 499, 506.
[42] *Glasgow Corporation* v. *Muir* [1943] A.C. 448, 457, *per* Lord Macmillan. There remains, however, a subjective element in that it is left to the individual judge to decide what is reasonable and what could have been foreseen: "What to one judge may seem far-fetched may seem to another both natural and probable." *Ibid.*
[43] *Nettleship* v. *Weston* [1971] 2 Q.B. 691, 698, 710.
[44] [1952] 2 All E.R. 125.
[45] *Ibid.*, p. 131, *per* Denning L.J. See also at p. 133: "Errors due to inexperience or lack of supervision are no defence as against the injured person . . .."
[46] [1986] 3 All E.R. 801.

oxygen. A junior and inexperienced doctor inserted a catheter (by which the blood oxygen pressure was to be measured) into a vein rather than an artery. This in itself was not negligent, since it was the sort of mistake that any reasonably competent doctor might have made in the circumstances. The position of the catheter in the body can be checked, however, by means of an X-ray. This was done and the doctor failed to spot that the catheter was mispositioned, though he did ask a senior registrar in the unit to check the X-ray. The registrar failed to notice the mistake. The baby was subsequently discovered to be suffering from retrolental fibroplasia which causes blindness, possibly as a result of the exposure to excess oxygen.[47] In the Court of Appeal there was a division of opinion as to the appropriate standard of care to be applied to the junior doctor.

3.76   Sir Nicolas Browne-Wilkinson V.-C., dissenting, said that the general standard of care required of a doctor is that he should exercise the skill of a skilled doctor in the treatment which he has taken on himself to offer. This being the general standard, it is normally no answer to say that the treatment was of a specialist or technical nature in which he was inexperienced: "In such a case, the fault of the doctor lies in embarking on giving treatment which he could not skilfully offer: he should not have undertaken the treatment but should have referred the patient to someone possessing the necessary skills."[48] The position was different, said his Lordship, in the case of a junior houseman in his first year after qualifying or of someone who has just started in a specialist field in order to gain the necessary skill in that field. Such doctors cannot in fairness be said to be at fault if, at the start of their time, they lack the very skills which they are seeking to acquire:

> "Of course, such a doctor would be negligent if he undertook treatment for which he knows he lacks the necessary experience and skill. But one of the chief hazards of inexperience is that one does not always know the risks which exist. In my judgment, so long as the English law rests liability on personal fault, a doctor who has properly accepted a post in a hospital in order to gain necessary experience should only be held liable for acts or omissions which a careful doctor with his qualifications and experience would not have done or omitted."[49]

3.77   With great respect, this view appears to confuse the concept of "fault" in the tort of negligence with moral blameworthiness. A finding of negligence in a court of law does not necessarily mean that the defendant was morally blameworthy, since negligence is treated as an objective measure of a standard of conduct without any inquiry into why the defendant failed to achieve that standard, as might occur in a

---

[47] The decision of the Court of Appeal on the causation issue was reversed by the House of Lords: [1988] 1 All E.R. 871; see §§ 5.19 *et seq.* There was no appeal on the question of the standard of care.

[48] [1986] 3 All E.R. 801, 833.

[49] *Ibid.* This statement seems to echo the comment of the Lord Chancellor in *Junor* v *McNicol, The Times*, March 26, 1959, that a house surgeon had a duty to "display the care and skill of a prudent qualified house surgeon, it being remembered that such a position was held by a comparative beginner." At what point, it might be asked, would the inexperienced doctor be deemed to have sufficient experience to be judged by the ordinary objective standard?

court of morals.[50] The majority of the Court of Appeal (Mustill and Glidewell L.JJ.) adhered to the objective standard. Mustill L.J. said that the notion of a duty tailored to the actor, rather than to the act which he elects to perform, has no place in the law of tort. The consequence of applying a subjective test would be that the standard of care that a patient would be entitled to expect would depend upon the level of experience of the particular doctor who, by chance, happened to treat him. However, having said that if a professional person assumes to perform a task, he must bring to it the appropriate care and skill,[51] his Lordship added that the standard of care should be related, not to the individual, but to the post which he occupies, though distinguishing "post" from "rank" or "status." It followed that:

> "In such a case as the present, the standard is not just that of the averagely competent and well-informed junior houseman (or whatever the position of the doctor) but of such a person who fills a post in a unit offering a highly specialised service. But, even so, it must be recognised that different posts make different demands. If it is borne in mind that the structure of hospital medicine envisages that the lower ranks will be occupied by those of whom it would be wrong to expect too much, the risk of abuse by litigious patients can be mitigated, if not entirely eliminated."[52]

This statement is puzzling, since, having rejected a subjective test of **3.78** negligence, his Lordship seems to reintroduce variable standards of care by reference to the "posts" occupied by different doctors. Glidewell L.J. simply applied the *Bolam* test, commenting that this was the standard by which to weigh the conduct of all the doctors in *Wilsher*: "In my view, the law requires the trainee or learner to be judged by the same standard as his more experienced colleagues. If it did not, inexperience would frequently be urged as a defence to an action for professional negligence."[53] With respect, it is submitted that

---

[50] "There are very few professional men who will assert that they have never fallen below the high standards rightly expected of them. That they have never been negligent. If they do, it is unlikely that they should be believed. And this is as true of lawyers as it is of medical men. If the judge's conclusion is right, what distinguishes Mr. Jordan from his professional colleagues is not that on one isolated occasion his skill deserted him, but that damage resulted. Whether or not damage results from a negligent act is almost always a matter of chance and it ill becomes anyone to adopt an attitude of superiority": *per* Donaldson L.J. in *Whitehouse* v. *Jordan* [1980] 1 All E.R. 650, 666. See also *Clark* v. *MacLennan* [1983] 1 All E.R. 416, 433, and 422, *per* Pain J.: "Counsel for the defendant has referred to Professor Turnbull's Olympian reputation. I hope Professor Turnbull will take comfort in the thought that even Apollo, the god of healing, and the father of Aesculapius, had his moments of weakness"; "My recollection of classical mythology is that the gods on Olympus were no strangers to error"; and *Thake* v. *Maurice* [1984] 2 All E.R. 513, 523.
[51] [1986] 3 All E.R. 801, 810.
[52] *Ibid.*, p. 813.
[53] *Ibid.*, p. 831; *Dale* v. *Munthali* (1977) 78 D.L.R. (3d) 588, 594; aff'd (1978) 90 D.L.R. (3d) 763. In *Wills* v. *Saunders* [1989] 2 W.W.R. 715 (Alta. Q.B.) a junior doctor took it upon himself to insert a central feeding line into the patient's subclavian vein, without supervision, resulting in loss of consciousness and permanent damage to the patient's vision. Power J., holding the defendant negligent, stated that the standard of care to be applied "should not be lower by reason of his inexperience."

this is the correct and long-established approach.[54] A single standard of care for patients can only be achieved by relating the reasonableness of the defendant's conduct to the task that is undertaken, and what is objectively reasonable does not change with the experience of the defendant, nor, for that matter, the post he holds.[55] This is at its most obvious if a doctor in a specialist "post" were to undertake some procedure which was completely outside the sphere of that specialty. He would be required to achieve the standard of the reasonably competent doctor in performing that procedure, and if it were a specialised procedure he would have to achieve the standards of the specialty. This has nothing to do with his post. The duty arises by virtue of the fact that he has undertaken to perform the act, and by doing so professes that he has the competence to perform it with skill and care, just as an unqualified person would be held to the standard of a reasonably competent surgeon if he undertook surgery.[56] Thus, undertaking work which is beyond one's competence will constitute negligence. As a matter of practice and common sense the inexperienced doctor will normally undertake less complex tasks than his experienced colleagues, but if he does perform tasks beyond the level of his competence the fault lies not so much in not having the skills, which by definition he does not possess, but in undertaking the task at all.

3.79   It has been suggested that it is "unrealistic" to demand identical standards of competence from persons who come from different ranks of the same profession, and, accordingly, that the appropriate standard of care for a professional person should be a combination of objective and subjective considerations, namely the "skill and care which is ordinarily exercised by reasonably competent members of the profession, who have the same rank and profess the same specialisation (if any) as the defendant."[57] What is not clear, however, is why a patient's claim to legal redress should differ where he receives the identical treatment from Dr. A (a consultant, say) and from Dr. B (a senior house officer), a situation which could arise if the standard of care varied with the "rank" of the defendant. It is submitted that it would be unrealistic to apply different standards to the performance of the same task: if the defendant cannot exercise reasonable care he should not undertake the task at all.

3.80   It must be emphasised that this principle is not limited to actions against newly qualified doctors. It can apply at any stage where a

---

[54] The headnote in the All E.R. of *Wilsher* states that the standard of care is to be determined in the context of the particular posts in a specialist unit, although tailored to the acts undertaken by the doctor rather than the doctor himself. Only Mustill L.J. was in favour of linking the standard to the post occupied by the defendant, and so it cannot be said that this forms part of the ratio of the majority (*i.e.* Mustill and Glidwell L.JJ.).

[55] See Dugdale and Stanton, *Professional Negligence*, 1989, 2nd ed., para. 15.16; and para. 15.20 making the same point in relation to the standard to be applied to specialists.

[56] " . . . the unqualified practitioner cannot claim to be measured by any lower standard than that which is applied to a qualified man . . . . It is, no doubt, conceivable that a qualified man may be held liable for recklessly undertaking a case which he knew, or should have known, to be beyond his powers, or for making his patient the subject of reckless experiment": *per* Lord Hewart C.J. in *R.* v. *Bateman* (1925) 94 L.J.K.B. 791, 794.

[57] Jackson and Powell, *Professional Negligence*, 1987, 2nd ed., para. 1.29. The authors concede that the term "rank" is not entirely satisfactory, but it is meant to describe different levels within hierarchical professions such as medicine. It is not, presumably, the same as "post."

doctor gets in above his head. The doctor who holds himself out as a specialist will be held to the standards of a reasonably competent specialist, "even if he is a novice specialist,"[58] and even where he is performing the procedure for the first time.[59] A doctor must recognise his limitations and where necessary seek the advice or supervision of more experienced colleagues, or refer the patient to a specialist.[60] The inexperienced doctor will discharge his duty of care by seeking the assistance of his superiors to check his work, even though he may himself have made a mistake. It was on this basis that the junior doctor was found not to have been negligent in *Wilsher* v. *Essex Area Health Authority*, although the registrar was held negligent.[61]

In an emergency it may well be reasonable for a practitioner **3.81** inexperienced in a particular treatment to intervene, or indeed for someone lacking medical qualifications to undertake some forms of treatment. For example, a bystander who renders assistance at a road accident does not necessarily hold himself out as qualified to do so. He would be expected to achieve only the standard that could reasonably be expected in the circumstances, which would probably be very low.[62] This approach is clearly borne of the emergency since if there was no urgency, the unqualified person who undertakes treatment which is beyond his competence would be held to the standard to be expected of the reasonably competent and experienced practitioner. A person who holds himself out as trained in first-aid must conform to the standards of "the ordinary skilled first-aider exercising and professing to have that special skill of a first-aider."[63] This will obviously be greater than the standard of a layman performing first-aid, and would

---

[58] *Poole* v. *Morgan* [1987] 3 W.W.R. 217, 254 (Alta. Q.B.). The defendant ophthalmologist was held to be inadequately qualified to use laser treatment, a procedure normally performed by a retina vitreous specialist, even though ophthalmologists were permitted to use laser treatment by their governing body.

[59] *McKeachie* v. *Alvarez* (1970) 17 D.L.R. (3d) 87 (B.C.S.C.), where a surgeon was held liable for severing a nerve which could have been seen and avoided, and of whose existence he should have been aware, even though this was the first occasion on which he had done this type of operation.

[60] See the comment of Browne-Wilkinson V.-C. in *Wilsher* v. *Essex Area Health Authority* [1986] 3 All E.R. 801, 833, quoted at § 3.76; *Fraser* v. *Vancouver General Hospital* (1951) 3 W.W.R. 337 (B.C.C.A.); aff'd [1952] 3 D.L.R. 785 (S.C.C.); *Payne* v. *St. Helier Group Hospital Management Committee, The Times*, July 12, 1952, where a casualty officer was held to be negligent in failing to detain a patient for examination by a doctor of consultant rank. See § 4.30.

[61] See also *Junor* v. *McNicol, The Times*, March 26, 1959, where the House of Lords held that a house surgeon who had acted on the instructions of a consultant orthopaedic surgeon was not liable; *Tanswell* v. *Nelson, The Times*, February 11, 1959, where McNair J. said that a dentist was entitled to rely on a doctor's opinion about a patient's response to antibiotics, unless that opinion was clearly inconsistent with the observed facts; *Leonard* v. *Knott* [1978] 5 W.W.R. 511 (B.C.S.C.), where it was held that a radiologist is entitled to rely on the judgment of the referring physician as to whether a radiological investigation is required, unless there is some obvious problem; *cf. Davy-Chiesman* v. *Davy-Chiesman* [1984] 1 All E.R. 321, 332, 335, stating that solicitors should not rely blindly on the advice of counsel, although in this case the solicitor had failed to detect an "obvious error."

[62] On the difficulties of laymen diagnosing mental illness see *Ali* v. *Furness Withy* [1988] 2 Lloyd's Rep. 379, where the question was the standard applicable to a ship's master diagnosing insanity in a crewman.

[63] *Cattley* v. *St. John's Ambulance Brigade* (1988) (unreported), Q.B.D., *per* Judge Prosser Q.C.: " . . . the true test for establishing negligence in a first-aider is whether he has been proved to be guilty of such failure as no first-aider of ordinary skill would be guilty of, if acting with ordinary care . . . ."

be relevant, for example, in a claim against paramedically trained ambulance crew.

3.82 The rule that inexperience is not a defence is a consequence of the objective nature of the standard of care in negligence, and applies to other factors as well as inexperience. If the defendant is unable to measure up to the objectively required standard for any reason, be it stress, overwork, tiredness, or ill-health he will nonetheless be found negligent.[64] In *Barnett* v. *Chelsea and Kensington Hospital Management Committee*[65] a casualty officer, who was himself unwell, refused to see three nightwatchmen who had presented themselves in the casualty department of a hospital, telling them to go home and call in their own doctors. One of the men subsequently died. Nield J. held that the doctor's failure to see and examine the deceased was negligent: "It is unfortunate that Dr. Banerjee was himself at the time a tired and unwell doctor, but there was no-one else to do that which it was his duty to do."[66]

(ii) The hospital authorities

3.83 Whatever the position of the inexperienced doctor, it is possible that a health authority could be in breach of a primary duty of care to the patient if they allow inexperienced staff to practise without adequate supervision. In *Jones* v. *Manchester Corporation*[67] a majority of the Court of Appeal held that the hospital board was liable to make contribution to the inexperienced doctor whose negligence caused the patient's death. Indeed, the board bore the brunt of the blame (80 per cent.), even though counsel for the doctor admitted that she had been negligent to a degree which was inexcusable even in an inexperienced person. The hospital board should not leave patients in inexperienced hands without proper supervision, said Denning L.J.:

> "It would be in the highest degree unjust that hospital authorities, by getting inexperienced doctors to perform their duties for them, without adequate supervision, should be able to throw all the responsibility on to those doctors as if they were fully experienced practitioners."[68]

3.84 This point was reiterated in *Wilsher* v. *Essex Area Health Authority*.[69] Sir Nicolas Browne-Wilkinson V.-C. recognised that applying a

---

[64] Old age or infirmity is not a defence for a negligent driver of a motor vehicle: *Roberts* v. *Ramsbottom* [1980] 1 All E.R. 7, 15. In *Nickolls* v. *Ministry of Health, The Times*, February 4, 1955 the surgeon who operated on the plaintiff was suffering from cancer. The question was whether he was in a fit condition to have undertaken the operation. It was held that on the facts he was, and therefore he was not negligent. Clearly, if the conclusion had been that he was unfit, it would have been negligent to operate.

[65] [1968] 1 All E.R. 1068.

[66] *Ibid.*, p. 1073. It is common for junior hospital doctors to have to work excessively long hours. If this was a factor in an error made by the doctor the health authority may also be responsible: see § 3.84. It is doubtful that overwork or the fact that resources are stretched would fall within the notion of "battle conditions" which Mustill L.J. has suggested could influence the court's assessment of negligence: see *Wilsher* v. *Essex Area Health Authority* [1986] 3 All E.R. 801, 812, § 3.87. The term seems to indicate something in the nature of an emergency, rather than the everyday circumstances in which doctors have to work, even if they themselves feel "embattled."

[67] [1952] 2 All E.R. 125.

[68] *Ibid.*, p. 133.

[69] [1986] 3 All E.R. 801.

subjective standard of care to inexperienced junior doctors might mean that the rights of a patient would depend on the experience of the doctor who treats him. This would not be the case, said his Lordship, because the health authority could be directly liable: "In my judgment, a health authority which so conducts its hospital that it fails to provide doctors of sufficient skill and experience to give the treatment offered at the hospital may be directly liable in negligence to the patient."[70] There was no reason why, in principle, the health authority should not be directly liable if its organisation was at fault. Arguably, this proposition would apply with equal, if not greater, force to other organisational failures which expose patients to serious risk of injury, such as requiring junior hospital doctors to work excessive hours, with the result that they become so fatigued that their judgment or competence becomes impaired. Whilst a claim that the doctor was overworked would not provide a defence for the doctor in an action by the patient, it is a good reason to place the burden of responsibility upon the health authority.[71]

There is, however, a problem with this line of argument. The **3.85** standard of care applicable to a health authority in determining whether it had been at fault in failing to provide either sufficient numbers of staff or staff with sufficient experience would be whether the authority had acted reasonably in the circumstances, and the circumstances may include the resources at the authority's disposal. This could make such an action difficult to sustain,[72] although N.H.S. indemnity makes the issue of less significance, at least to plaintiffs, since the health authority will be financially responsible for a doctor's culpable errors attributable to overwork.

In *Wilsher* v. *Essex Area Health Authority*[73] the Court of Appeal **3.86** rejected the concept of "team negligence" whereby each of the

---

[70] *Ibid.*, p. 833; see also, *per* Glidewell L.J. at p. 831. In *Dryden* v. *Surrey County Council* [1936] 2 All E.R. 535, 539 Finlay J. commented that it could not possibly be held that the mere presence of probationary nurses was evidence of negligence. Although, as it stands the statement is clearly correct, this must, presumably, be a matter of degree.

[71] Employers have a non-delegable duty to their employees to provide competent staff, a safe system of work, proper plant and equipment, and a safe place of work: *Wilsons & Clyde Coal Co. Ltd.* v. *English* [1938] A.C. 57; *McDermid* v. *Nash Dredging and Reclamation Co. Ltd.* [1987] 2 All E.R. 878. There is no obvious reason why a similar duty should not be owed to patients, otherwise health authority employees would be in a better position than patients with regard to questions of safety. In *Denton* v. *South West Thames Regional Health Authority* (1980) (unreported), Q.B.D., *e.g.,* a health authority was held liable to a nurse for a back injury sustained when a bed tipped over. There was no system for checking the safety of beds, and Parke J. held that, given the risk of injury to patients, there should have been. It may be that the advent of N.H.S. indemnity has removed much of the practical force of the distinction between primary and vicarious liability, since the health authority will be fully responsible for the financial consequences of a doctor's error, and will not seek to shift some of the loss to the doctor's defence organisation. This still leaves Browne-Wilkinson V.-C.'s point, that doctors should not be blamed for the organisational faults of the health authority, unanswered. See further §§ 7.15–7.32. Note that a health authority which requires a doctor to work an excessive number of hours, so damaging the doctor's health, may be liable to the doctor in its capacity as an employer: see *Johnstone* v. *Bloomsbury Health Authority* [1991] 2 All E.R. 293.

[72] See § 4.83.

[73] [1986] 3 All E.R. 801, 812–813. For criticism of the insistence on setting the legal standard by reference to individual professional responsibility, when the reality of modern health care is co-operative care by inter-disciplinary teams: see Montgomery (1989) 16 J. of Law and Soc. 319, 333.

persons who formed the staff of the unit held themselves out as capable of undertaking the specialised procedures which the unit set out to perform. It would not be right, said Mustill L.J., to attribute to each individual member of the team a duty to live up to the standards demanded of the unit as a whole, because that would expose a student nurse to an action in negligence for a failure to possess the skill and experience of a consultant. On the other hand, if "team negligence" sought to fix a standard for the performance of the unit as a whole, this was simply a reformulation of the direct liability theory.

10. Emergencies

3.87   In determining what was reasonable care the court will take account of the particular situation as it presented itself to the defendant, as part and parcel of "all the circumstances of the case." The defendant faced with a dilemma or an emergency, having to act on the spur of the moment will not be judged too critically simply because with hindsight a different course of action might have avoided the harm.[74] This clearly may apply to medical practitioners. In *Wilsher* v. *Essex Area Health Authority* Mustill L.J. said that:

> "full allowance must be made for the fact that certain aspects of treatment may have to be carried out in what one witness . . . called 'battle conditions.' An emergency may overburden the available resources, and, if an individual is forced by circumstances to do too many things at once, the fact that he does one of them incorrectly should not lightly be taken as negligence."[75]

3.88   This does not mean that a different standard of care is applied in an emergency situation, simply that reasonable care takes into account the circumstances in which a doctor has to operate. If the error is one which a reasonably competent doctor could have made in the circumstances the defendant is not negligent. Conversely, if a reasonably competent doctor would not have made that error the defendant will be liable, notwithstanding the fact that it occurred in the course of an emergency.[76]

3.89   In *Wilson* v. *Swanson*[77] there was uncertainty as to the correct diagnosis of the patient's condition, which could have been either cancer or a gastric ulcer. The defendant surgeon recommended an operation, which revealed a large gastric ulcer. He was unsure whether this was cancerous, and he requested an immediate pathological investigation, which took 10 or 20 minutes. The pathologist thought

---

[74] *Parkinson* v. *Liverpool Corporation* [1950] 1 All E.R. 367; *Ng Chun Pui* v. *Lee Chuen Tat* [1988] R.T.R. 298, 302 (both non-medical cases).

[75] [1986] 3 All E.R. 801, 812; *Rodych* v. *Krasey* [1971] 4 W.W.R. 358, where a doctor who examined a drunken accident victim at night, with no more than a flashlight and streetlamp to see by, and then referred the patient to hospital, was held not negligent in the manner of conducting the examination.

[76] *Cattley* v. *St. John's Ambulance Brigade* (1988) (unreported), Q.B.D.: "An objective standard must still be applied and a person's own judgment or impulse is still not the sole criterion. He may still be found negligent if, notwithstanding the emergency, his acts are found to be unreasonable" *per* Judge Prosser Q.C.

[77] (1956) 5 D.L.R. (2d) 113 (S.C.C.).

that cancer was probably present, but could not make a conclusive diagnosis at that stage. The defendant had to make an instant decision whether to bring the operation to a close and wait for a more accurate pathological diagnosis, or whether to proceed on the basis that there was cancer present. He decided to continue and removed a large section of the patient's stomach. Subsequently it was discovered that there was no cancer. The Supreme Court of Canada held that in the circumstances the defendant was not negligent.

On the other hand, where an emergency is foreseeable it may be **3.90** negligence to have an inadequate system for dealing with the known risks that the emergency is likely to create,[78] or in failing to have an essential piece of equipment readily available.[79]

11. Policy and defensive medicine

The increase in medical malpractice litigation in recent years has **3.91** been accompanied by claims that, in response to the threat of litigation, doctors now practise defensively. This involves undertaking procedures which are not medically justified for the patient's benefit but are designed to protect the doctor from a claim for negligence. The most commonly cited examples are unnecessary diagnostic tests, such as X-rays, and unnecessary Caesarian section deliveries. Given the nature of the *Bolam* test, however, these claims do not make a great deal of sense, because a reasonable doctor would not undertake an *unnecessary* procedure and so a doctor cannot avoid a finding of negligence by performing one; to the extent that the procedure carries some inherent risk the practitioner acting in this way may increase the chances of being sued. Moreover, there is little clear understanding within the medical profession of what "defensive medicine" means.[80] Nonetheless, the courts have apparently acknowledged the existence of the phenomenon of defensive medicine, despite the fact that there is virtually no empirical, as opposed to anecdotal, evidence of such practices in this country. In *Wilsher* v. *Essex Area Health Authority*,[81] for example, Mustill L.J. said that: "The risks which actions for professional negligence bring to the public as a whole, in the shape of an instinct on the part of a professional man to play for safety, are serious and are now well recognised," and in *Sidaway* v. *Bethlem Royal Hospital Governors*[82] Lord Scarman commented that "the danger of defensive medicine developing in this country clearly exists."

---

[78] *Bull* v. *Devon Area Health Authority* (1989) (unreported), C.A.
[79] *Meyer* v. *Gordon* (1981) 17 C.C.L.T. 1 (B.C.S.C.); or in failing to have a system to check the safety of equipment: *Denton* v. *South West Thames Regional Health Authority* (1980) (unreported), Q.B.D. (not a case involving an emergency).
[80] See Jones and Morris (1989) 5 J. of the M.D.U. 40; *cf.* Tribe and Korgaonkar (1991) 7 P.N. 2. "Defensive" may mean simply treating patients conservatively or even "more carefully," and this begs the question whether that treatment option is medically justified in the patient's interests.
[81] [1986] 3 All E.R. 801, 810. See also *Royal Commission on Civil Liability and Compensation for Personal Injury*, Cmnd. 7054 (1978), paras. 1318–1324.
[82] [1985] 1 All E.R. 643, 653.

Lord Denning, in particular, has been most vocal in his warnings about defensive medicine.[83]

3.92 What impact does this have on individual cases of medical negligence? In non-medical cases the courts have occasionally relied on the prospect of unduly defensive practices developing in response to a potential liability in order to deny the existence of a duty of care.[84] Clearly, this option is not available in the vast majority of medical negligence cases, since the doctor undoubtedly owes a duty of care to his patient. In *Barker* v. *Nugent*[85] counsel for the defendant doctor argued that as a matter of public policy, to avoid an escalation of defensive medicine, the courts should be slower to impute negligence to the medical profession than to others. Rougier J. rejected the argument, pointing out that comparisons with the position in the United States of America are not entirely sound. Moreover, his Lordship added:

"I can think of only one thing more disastrous than the escalation of defensive medicine and that is the engendering of a belief in the medical profession that certain acts or omissions which would otherwise be classed as negligence can, in a sense, be exonerated."

3.93 Similarly, in *Wilsher* v. *Essex Area Health Authority* Mustill L.J. responded to his own acknowledgement of the risks of defensive practice with the comment that "the proper response cannot be to temper the wind to the professional man. If he assumes to perform a task, he must bring to it the appropriate care and skill." This was immediately followed, however, by the statement that the courts must constantly bear in mind that the fact that in retrospect the choice actually made can be shown to have turned out badly is not in itself a proof of negligence, and that the duty of care is not a warranty of a perfect result. Whilst this is perfectly accurate as a statement of the law, the linking of comments about defensive medicine, however vague and imprecise that notion may be, to the frequent reminders that the courts feel constrained to give themselves about the inherent risks of medical treatment suggests that "defensive medicine" does sometimes play a role in medical litigation, as part of the judicial "mind set" which creates an additional, though unquantifiable, hurdle

---

[83] "We should be doing a disservice to the community at large if we were to impose liability on hospitals and doctors for everything that happens to go wrong. Doctors would be led to think more of their own safety than of the good of their patients. Initiative would be stifled and confidence shaken": *Roe* v. *Minister of Health* [1954] 2 Q.B. 66, 86–87; *Lim* v. *Camden and Islington Area Health Authority* [1979] 1 Q.B. 196, 217; *Whitehouse* v. *Jordan* [1980] 1 All E.R. 650, 658; *Hyde* v. *Tameside Area Health Authority* (1981) reported at (1986) 2 P.N. 26 (see the quotation in § 4.99); in *Hatcher* v. *Black, The Times,* July 2, 1954, Lord Denning compared an action for negligence against a doctor to having a dagger plunged into his back (see the extract in his *The Discipline of Law,* 1979, p. 243). See also, *per* Lawton L.J. in *Whitehouse* v. *Jordan* [1980] 1 All E.R. 650, 659; *Sidaway* v. *Bethlem Royal Hospital Governors* [1984] 1 All E.R. 1018, 1031, 1035, *per* Dunne and Browne-Wilkinson L.JJ.; *Robinson* v. *Post Office* [1974] 2 All E.R. 737, 745; *Fletcher* v. *Bench* (1973) 4 B.M.J. 117, 118, *per* Megaw L.J.; *De Freville* v. *Dill* (1927) 96 L.J.K.B. 1056, 1062.
[84] *Hill* v. *Chief Constable of West Yorkshire* [1988] 2 All E.R. 238; *Rowling* v. *Takaro Properties Ltd.* [1988] 1 All E.R. 163, 173; *Yuen Kun-yeu* v. *A.-G. of Hong Kong* [1987] 2 All E.R. 705, 715–716; *Saif Ali* v. *Sydney Mitchell & Co.* [1980] A.C. 198.
[85] (1987) (unreported), Q.B.D.

that plaintiffs have to overcome. This may be reflected in the standard of proof that plaintiffs have to achieve in practice, although the formal standard of proof remains the same. But as Kilner Brown J. observed in *Ashcroft* v. *Mersey Regional Health Authority*[86]: "the medical and social consequences of medical men being found guilty of negligence on insufficient evidence may be appropriate as a statement of probable consequences, but beg the question which has to be decided." In other words, the question remains as to what constitutes "sufficient" evidence.

12. Proof of breach

Burden of proof

The burden of proof, on the balance of probabilities that the **3.94** defendant has been negligent and that the negligence caused damage to the plaintiff, lies with the plaintiff.[87] It is not for the defendant to show that he was not negligent. If there are two equally possible explanations for an accident, one of which indicates that the accident occurred without negligence by the defendant, the plaintiff's action will fail.[88] On the other hand, the plaintiff does not have to adduce positive evidence to disprove every theoretical explanation, however unlikely, that the defendant might devise to explain what happened in a way which would absolve him of fault.[89] Cases should not normally be decided on the burden of proof, since a tribunal of fact should make findings of fact in relation to the matters before it, even where this might be difficult. Only in an exceptional case would a judge be obliged in conscience to say that he did not know where the truth lay, and decide the issue on the basis of the burden of proof.[90]

Where two people are simultaneously negligent, and only one of **3.95** them caused the damage but it is not possible to identify which of them, then in theory the plaintiff's action would fail because he would not be able to attribute responsibility to either of them on the balance of probabilities. This problem arose in *Cook* v. *Lewis*[91] when two people on a hunting trip simultaneously discharged their guns, and the

---

[86] [1983] 2 All E.R. 245, 247.
[87] On the proof of causation see §§ 5.10 *et seq.* The Civil Evidence Act 1968, s.11, provides that proof that a person has been convicted of an offence shall be taken as proof that he committed the offence unless the contrary is proved. Provided the conviction is relevant to the facts in issue this means that the defendant will have to disprove negligence. This provision will rarely be of any assistance in a medical negligence claim.
[88] *Jones* v. *Great Western Railway Co.* (1930) 47 T.L.R. 39, 45, *per* Lord Macmillan; *The Kite* [1933] P. 154; *Harrington* v. *Essex Area Health Authority, The Times*, November 14, 1984, Q.B.D., where Beldam J. felt unable to select either one of two possible explanations for the plaintiff's necrosis of the skin, and the plaintiff's action failed on the burden of proof; see also *Ashcroft* v. *Mersey Regional Health Authority* [1983] 2 All E.R. 245; aff'd [1985] 2 All E.R. 96, a case formally decided on the balance of probabilities, but seemingly resting on the burden of proof.
[89] *Bull* v. *Devon Area Health Authority* (1989) (unreported), C.A., *per* Dillon L.J.
[90] *Morris* v. *London Iron & Steel Co. Ltd.* [1987] I.R.L.R. 182, C.A. (a non-medical case).
[91] [1952] 1 D.L.R. 1.

plaintiff was hit by one of them, but he was unable to prove which one. The Supreme Court of Canada held that in these circumstances the burden of proof was reversed, and it was for the defendants to prove that they did not cause the damage. If neither could do so then both would be liable. This might be hard on the "innocent" defendant, but the alternative rule, putting the burden of proof on the plaintiff would be just as harsh on the innocent and injured plaintiff. It is not clear whether *Cook* v. *Lewis* would be followed in this country.[92] It has been suggested that if it were to be applied it would be confined to joint tortfeasors involving some element of concerted action.[93] In any event, where a defendant health authority is vicariously liable for the negligence of all the potential defendants (surgeon, anaesthetist, nurses, etc.) the plaintiff does not have to prove which particular defendant caused the harm.[94]

3.96 In *Clark* v. *MacLennan*[95] Peter Pain J. had suggested that where there is a general practice to take a particular precaution against a specific risk but the defendant fails to take that precaution, and the very damage against which it is designed to be a protection occurs, the burden of proof lies with the defendant to show both that he was not in breach of duty and that the breach did not cause the damage. The justification for this was that where a defendant has deliberately chosen to omit the usual precautions and has thereby significantly increased the risk of injury, it is unfair for the plaintiff to be defeated solely by the burden of proof.[96] This approach to the proof of negligence, as opposed to causation, was criticised by Mustill L.J. in *Wilsher* v. *Essex Area Health Authority*,[97] although his Lordship accepted that in some instances breach and causation may be so closely linked that in practice it may be difficult to maintain a different rule for proof of breach of duty when proof of causation is governed by *McGhee* v. *National Coal Board*.[98] However, when *Wilsher* v. *Essex Area Health Authority*[99] reached the House of Lords, their Lordships made it clear that the burden of proving *causation* remains with the plaintiff throughout, and any suggestion to the contrary amounted to a misreading of the effect of *McGhee*. It is highly unlikely that, if the matter were to be tested in the House of Lords, a different approach to the question of proving breach of duty would be adopted.

3.97 Of course, to say that the plaintiff has the burden of proof does not necessarily mean that he must provide direct evidence that the defendant has fallen below the requisite standard of care. He may rely upon any legitimate inferences that can be drawn from the proved facts, and in the absence of evidence to the contrary the inference may

---

[92] *cf. Baker* v. *Market Harborough Co-operative Society Ltd.* [1953] 1 W.L.R. 1472, 1475, *per* Somerville L.J. suggesting that it would not, and *Roe* v. *Minister of Health* [1954] 2 Q.B. 66, 82, *per* Denning L.J. implying that it would and citing *Baker* in support; *Bray* v. *Palmer* [1953] 1 W.L.R. 1455.
[93] *Salmond and Heuston on the Law of Torts*, 19th ed., 1987, p. 267.
[94] *Cassidy* v. *Ministry of Health* [1951] 2 K.B. 343.
[95] [1983] 1 All E.R. 416.
[96] His Lordship relied on *McGhee* v. *National Coal Board* [1972] 3 All E.R. 1008.
[97] [1986] 3 All E.R. 801, 814.
[98] [1972] 3 All E.R. 1008; for consideration of whether *McGhee* does affect the burden of proving causation see §§ 5.16 *et seq.*
[99] [1988] 1 All E.R. 871.

well be that the defendant has been negligent. Indeed, although the discussion of *McGhee* v. *National Coal Board* in *Wilsher* v. *Essex Area Health Authority* centred upon the issue of the location of the burden of proving causation, it may be that the crucial, and largely unanswered, question is in what circumstances the court will draw inferences of fact which support the plaintiff's version of events in the absence of direct evidence.[1] An inference is a deduction from the evidence, which, if it is a reasonable deduction, may have the validity of legal proof, as opposed to conjecture which, even though plausible, has no value, "for its essence is that it is a mere guess."[2]

Res ipsa loquitur

The principle of *res ipsa loquitur* is in essence an evidential principle, **3.98** which, in certain instances, allows the court to draw an inference of negligence. Although in some cases it has been suggested that the principle has the effect of reversing the burden of proof, the better view would seem to be that this is incorrect. The burden of proof remains with the plaintiff, but the defendant must adduce evidence to rebut the inference of negligence, in order to avoid a finding of liability.[3]

The maxim applies where an accident occurs in circumstances in **3.99** which accidents do not normally happen unless there has been negligence by someone. The fact of the accident itself may give rise to an inference of negligence by the defendant which, in the absence of evidence in rebuttal, would be sufficient to impose liability. There is no magic in the phrase *res ipsa loquitur*—"the thing speaks for itself." It is simply a submission that the facts establish a prima facie case against the defendant.[4] The value of this principle is that it enables a plaintiff who has no knowledge, or insufficient knowledge, about how the accident occurred to rely on the accident itself and the surrounding circumstances as evidence of negligence, and prevents a defendant who does know what happened from avoiding responsibility simply by choosing not to give any evidence.[5]

(a) *When does res ipsa loquitur apply?*

Res ipsa loquitur is intended to assist a plaintiff who, through no **3.100** fault of his own, is unable to adduce evidence as to how the accident

---

[1] See § 5.22.

[2] *Jones* v. *Great Western Railway Co.* (1930) 47 T.L.R. 39, 45, *per* Lord Macmillan.

[3] See § 3.112, *post.*

[4] *Roe* v. *Minister of Health* [1954] 2 Q.B. 66, 87–88, *per* Morris L.J.; *Ballard* v. *North British Railway Co.* 1923 S.C. 43, 56, *per* Lord Shaw: "If that phrase had not been in Latin, nobody would have called it a principle."

[5] *E.g.*, patients under a general anaesthetic are not aware of what is going on about them, and the facts are peculiarly within the knowledge of the anaesthetist and others attending them: *Crits* v. *Sylvester* (1956) 1 D.L.R. (2d) 502, 510, *per* Schroeder J.A. (Ont. C.A.); see also *Mahon* v. *Osborne* [1939] 2 K.B. 14, 50, *per* Goddard L.J.: "The surgeon is in command of the operation, it is for him to decide what instruments, swabs and the like are to be used, and it is he who uses them. The patient, or if he dies, his representatives, can know nothing about this matter . . . . If, therefore, a swab is left in the patient's body, it seems to me clear that the surgeon is called on for an explanation . . . ." Note that the use of interrogatories may assist a plaintiff to ascertain facts within the defendant's knowledge: see R.S.C., Ord. 26.

occurred. If all the facts about the cause of the accident are known the maxim does not apply. Rather, the question then is whether, on the known facts, negligence by the defendant can be inferred.[6]

3.101   The principle derives from the case of *Scott* v. *London & St. Katherine Docks Co.*,[7] in which several bags of sugar fell from a hoist onto the plaintiff below. Erle C.J. said that:

> " . . . where the thing is shown to be under the management of the defendant or his servants, and the accident is such as in the ordinary course of things does not happen if those who have the management use proper care, it affords reasonable evidence, in the absence of explanation by the defendants, that the accident arose from want of care."[8]

There are two main elements to this; first, the defendant, or someone for whom he is responsible, must have been in "control" of the thing or circumstances that caused the damage; and, secondly, the accident must be such as "in the ordinary course of things" does not happen without negligence.

3.102   **"Control"** In order to impute negligence to the defendant the circumstances must speak of negligence "*by the defendant*," which they will not do if the defendant is not in control. Thus, in *Morris* v. *Winsbury-White*,[9] where the patient's post-operative treatment was under the control of several people (nurses, and resident medical officers) as well as the defendant surgeon, it was held that *res ipsa loquitur* did not apply. On the other hand, where the defendant is responsible in law for all the staff who played some role in the plaintiff's treatment, this is sufficient control.[10] The test is whether outside interference was likely. If it is unlikely that some unauthorised person could have interfered with the thing that caused the damage, the defendant has sufficient control.[11] Where the events were under the control of two of more independent persons, but the plaintiff cannot say which, then possibly he is entitled to call on each of them for an explanation.[12] This could be important where a patient receives private treatment but is unable to identify which member of the medical team was negligent, because the hospital may not be vicariously liable for all the staff, for example where the patient engaged the surgeon himself. Unless the patient can call on each defendant for an explanation of events the action will fail, because he cannot prove which of two or more defendants was responsible.

3.103   **"Ordinary course of things"** The circumstances must be such that in the ordinary course of things accidents do not happen unless someone

---

[6] *Barkway* v. *South Wales Transport Co. Ltd.* [1950] 1 All E.R. 392; *Johnston* v. *Wellesley Hospital* (1970) 17 D.L.R. (3d) 139, 146 (Ont. H.C.).

[7] (1865) 3 H. & C. 596.

[8] *Ibid.*, p. 601; cited with approval by Singleton L.J. in *Cassidy* v. *Ministry of Health* [1951] 2 K.B. 343, 353–4.

[9] [1937] 4 All E.R. 494, 499; see also *McFadyen* v. *Harvie* [1942] 4 D.L.R. 647.

[10] *Cassidy* v. *Ministry of Health* [1951] 2 K.B. 343.

[11] *Lloyde* v. *West Midlands Gas Board* [1971] 1 W.L.R. 749; *Easson* v. *London & North Eastern Railway Co.* [1944] K.B. 421.

[12] *Roe* v. *Minister of Health* [1954] 2 Q.B. 66, 82, *per* Denning L.J.; *cf. Salmond and Heuston on the Law of Torts*, 19th ed., 1987, p. 270.

has been negligent. This is largely a "common-sense" judgment based on the common experience of life. Common experience indicates that barrels of flour do not normally fall from warehouse windows into the street in the absence of negligence.[13] On the other hand, financial losses on the commodity market are not, without more, evidence of negligence by brokers.[14]

It might be thought that, given that much of medical practice is **3.104** outside the common experience of life and given the courts' frequent reference to the inherent risks of medical treatment, *res ipsa loquitur* could not be invoked in the context of a medical negligence action.[15] This, however, is not the position. The principle may be relied upon in an appropriate case, but the courts are cautious about drawing inferences of negligence simply because something has gone wrong with the treatment. In *Hucks* v. *Cole*,[16] for example, Lord Denning M.R. said that it was not right to invoke *res ipsa loquitur* against a doctor "save in an extreme case."

When does *res ipsa loquitur* apply in a medical context? In *Cassidy* v. **3.105** *Ministry of Health*[17] the plaintiff was suffering from Dupuytren's contraction of the third and fourth fingers of his left hand. The hand was operated on and following the operation the hand and arm had to be kept in a rigid splint for eight to 14 days. When the hand was released from the splint it was found to be virtually useless. The two fingers which had been operated on were completely stiff and the trouble had spread to the other two good fingers as well. The Court of Appeal held that, on the basis that the hospital was responsible for all those who treated the plaintiff, the facts raised a case of *res ipsa loquitur*. It was impossible to come to any clear conclusion as to why the injury occurred, and the defendants, having chosen not to call any independant expert evidence, failed to rebut the prima facie inference of negligence. Singleton L.J. said that it was unnecessary for the plaintiff to indentify the particular employee who was at fault. As Denning L.J. commented:

> "If the plaintiff had to prove that some particular doctor or nurse was negligent, he would not be able to do it. But he was not put to that impossible task: he says, 'I went into the hospital to be cured of two stiff fingers. I have come out with four stiff fingers, and my hand is useless. That should not have happened if due care had been used. Explain it, if you can.' I am quite clearly of

---

[13] *Byrne* v. *Boadle* (1863) 2 H. & C. 722; *Scott* v. *London & St. Katherine Docks Co.* (1865) 3 H & C. 596; *Chaprôniere* v. *Mason* (1905) 21 T.L.R. 633, where stones were found in buns; *Skinner* v. *London, Brighton & South Coast Railway Co.* (1850) 5 Exch. 787, colliding trains.

[14] *Stafford* v. *Conti Commodity Services Ltd.* [1981] 1 All E.R. 691.

[15] See, *e.g.*, Scott L.J. in *Mahon* v. *Osborne* [1939] 2 K.B. 14, 23: "How can the ordinary judge have sufficient knowledge of surgical operations to draw such an inference, or . . . what does he know of the 'ordinary course of things' in a complicated abdominal operation?" Note, however, that on the question of applying *res ipsa loquitur* this was a dissenting judgment. In Canada the view that *res ipsa loquitur* had no application to malpractice cases was expressly rejected by the Supreme Court in *Nesbitt* v. *Holt* [1953] 1 D.L.R. 671.

[16] (1968) 112 S.J. 483.

[17] [1951] 2 K.B. 343.

opinion that that raises a prima facie case against the hospital authorities."[18]

3.106 This statement cannot be taken to suggest that the fact that a patient comes out of hospital in a worse condition than he went in constitutes proof of negligence by the hospital staff. It is widely accepted that medical treatment carries risks, and that the occurrence of injury is not necessarily evidence of a lack of reasonable care.[19] Thus, in *O'Malley-Williams* v. *Board of Governors of the National Hospital for Nervous Diseases*[20] the plaintiff went into hospital for an X-ray of his arteries and came out with a serious neurological injury. His argument that this indicated negligence was rejected by Bridge J. There is a distinction, however, between saying, on the one hand, that "things can go wrong in medicine," or "it is not an exact science and an untoward occurrence is not evidence of negligence," and, on the other hand, saying that this particular procedure carries a specific risk of a particular complication and that complication has occurred. The former statement makes a vague appeal to "risk" in general to deny the applicability of *res ipsa loquitur*. Such a claim would not necessarily be confined to medical treatment, and seeks in effect to deny the validity of the principle entirely. The latter approach indentifies a particular feature of the circumstances, an inherent and specific risk, which provides a reasonable explanation of how the injury could have occurred without negligence.

3.107 Even within medicine, then, there are some circumstances where harm to the patient does not normally occur in the absence of negligence and the maxim *res ipsa loquitur* will apply. Leaving swabs or surgical instruments inside the patient after an operation will normally speak of negligence.[21] In *Mahon* v. *Osborne* Goddard L.J. said that:

> "There can be no possible question but that neither swabs nor instruments are ordinarily left in the patient's body, and no one would venture to say that it is proper, although in particular circumstances it may be excusable, so to leave them. If, therefore, a swab is left in the patient's body, it seems to me clear that the surgeon is called on for an explanation, that is, he is called on to show not necessarily why he missed it but that he exercised due care to prevent it being left there. . . . If a patient on whom

---

[18] *Ibid.*, p. 365–366, citing Goddard L.J. in *Mahon* v. *Osborne* [1939] 2 K.B. 14, 50; see also *Fraser* v. *Vancouver General Hospital* (1951) 3 W.W.R. 337, 343, *per* O'Halloran J.A. (B.C.C.A.): " . . . the evidence is clear a man died who should not have died and it is a legitimate inference therefrom the man died because of negligence of some kind by the hospital. There was no duty upon respondent plaintiff to attempt to isolate the specific act or omission which started and continued the chain of events which led directly to the man's death."

[19] For similar comments in the context of *res ipsa loquitur* see: *Roe* v. *Minister of Health* [1954] 2 Q.B. 66, 80; *Holmes* v. *Board of Hospital Trustees of the City of London* (1977) 81 D.L.R. (3d) 67, 78; *Girard* v. *Royal Columbian Hospital* (1976) 66 D.L.R. (3d) 676, 691 (B.C.S.C.).

[20] (1975) 1 B.M.J. 635; see also *Fletcher* v. *Bench* (1973) 4 B.M.J. 17, C.A., a case of alleged negligence by a dentist where Megaw L.J. said that it would be facile to say "something plainly went wrong and what went wrong is unexplained. Therefore, the dentist must have been negligent."

[21] *Garner* v. *Morrell, The Times*, October 31, 1953, C.A.; *Nesbitt* v. *Holt* [1953] 1 D.L.R. 671 (S.C.C.).

had befallen such a misfortune as we are now considering were not entitled to call on the surgeon for an explanation, I cannot but feel that an unwarranted protection would be given to carelessness, such as I do not believe the profession itself would either expect or desire."[22]

In *Saunders* v. *Leeds Western Health Authority*[23] a child suffered **3.108** cardiac arrest lasting 30 to 40 minutes while undergoing an operation, suffering quadriplegia. The evidence was that the heart of a fit child does not arrest under anaesthesia if proper care is taken in the anaesthetic and surgical processes. The defendants accepted that prima facie this was correct but sought to explain the accident by suggesting that the child's normal pulse had suddenly stopped. This evidence was rejected as mistaken, and the inevitable inference was that proper monitoring of the pulse would have given a forewarning of the arrest, and that in those circumstances the anaesthetic procedure, or the system for monitoring it or the execution of it was performed negligently. Similarly, in *Holmes* v. *Board of Hospital Trustees of the City of London*[24] an anaesthetist who administered an anaesthetic requiring a method of artificial ventilation which involved injecting jets of high pressure oxygen through a needle into the trachea produced massive tissue emphysema in the patient. This was a known danger of the procedure if the needle was not in the trachea but it did not normally happen with the exercise of due care. The anaesthetist was held liable on the basis of *res ipsa loquitur*.

The maxim has been held to apply where a patient sustained a burn **3.109** from a high frequency electrical current used for "electric coagulation" of the blood[25]; where gangrene developed in the plaintiff's arm following an intra-muscular injection[26]; when a patient underwent a radical mastoidectomy and suffered partial facial paralysis[27]; where the defendant failed to diagnose a known complication of surgery on the patient's hand for Paget's disease[28]; where there was a delay of 50 minutes in obtaining expert obstetric assistance at the birth of twins when the medical evidence was that at the most no more than 20 minutes should elapse between the birth of the first and the second twin[29]; when a needle broke in the patient's buttock while he was being

---

[22] [1939] 2 K.B. 14, 50 (approved by Denning L.J. in *Cassidy* v. *Ministry of Health* [1951] 2 K.B. 343, 365–366). This was a dissenting judgment, but not on this point. MacKinnon L.J. apparently agreed (at p. 38, though the point is not entirely free from doubt: Brazier, *Street on Torts*, 8th ed., p. 217) that *res ipsa loquitur* was applicable, although he agreed with Scott L.J. that the verdict against the defendant must be set aside. Scott L.J. was opposed (at pp. 21–24) to applying *res ipsa loquitur*.
[23] (1984) 129 S.J. 225.
[24] (1977) 81 D.L.R. (3d) 67 (Ont. H.C.).
[25] *Clarke* v. *Warboys*, *The Times*, March 18, 1952, C.A.
[26] *Cavan* v. *Wilcox* (1973) 44 D.L.R. (3d) 42 (N.B.C.A.); rev'd on the facts (1974) 50 D.L.R. (3d.) 687 (S.C.C.); *Cox* v. *Saskatoon* [1942] 1 D.L.R. 74 (Sask. K.B.), in which the plaintiff's arm was badly damaged during the course of donating blood for an operation. The procedure took up to three-quarters of an hour when normally it took 10 minutes, and the hospital had 100 similar operations that week without such a disastrous result. Held that *res ipsa loquitur*.
[27] *Eady* v. *Tenderenda* (1974) 51 D.L.R. (3d) 79 (S.C.C.).
[28] *Reitze* v. *Bruser* (No. 2) [1979] 1 W.W.R. 31 (Man. Q.B.).
[29] *Bull* v. *Devon Area Health Authority* (1989) (unreported), C.A., *per* Slade L.J. However, Mustill L.J. doubted whether *res ipsa loquitur* would assist because "all the facts that are ever going to be known are before the court," but in the absence of a proved explanation for the "inordinate delay," the judge had no choice, said his Lordship, but to find the defendants liable.

given an injection[30]; where a spinal anaesthetic became contaminated with disinfectant as a result of the manner in which it was stored causing paralysis to the patient[31]; where an infection following surgery in a "well-staffed and modern hospital" remained undiagnosed until the patient sustained crippling injury[32]; and where an explosion occurred during the course of administering anaesthetic to the patient when the technique had frequently been used without any mishap.[33]

3.110 Conversely, *res ipsa loquitur* has been held not to apply in the following circumstances: when a dentist left part of the root of a tooth behind during an extraction and broke the plaintiff's jaw[34]; where a dental drill broke and was left embedded in the jaw resulting in a fracture[35]; where the plaintiff became incontinent following a prostate operation[36]; where a patient suffered permanent partial paralysis of the legs following anaesthesia[37]; where the patient suffered neurological complications leading to partial paralysis of his hand following the performance of an aortagram[38]; where a patient died from haemorrhage during the course of spinal disc surgery when the surgeon pierced an artery with a surgical instrument[39]; where paralysis occurred following a cervical laminectomy,[40] or following arteriography[41]; where a baby suffered cerebral palsy following a forceps delivery[42]; where a sterilisation operation failed to render the plaintiff sterile[43]; and where the treatment is under the control of several people.[44] As a general

---

[30] *Brazier* v. *Ministry of Defence* [1965] 1 Lloyd's Rep. 26, 30.

[31] *Roe* v. *Minister of Health* [1954] 2 Q.B. 66. See also *Brown* v. *Merton, Sutton and Wandsworth Area Health Authority* [1982] 1 All E.R. 650, C.A., where the plaintiff developed quadriplegia following the administration of an epidural anaesthetic, in the course of preparation for giving birth. The defendants, in their stock defence, initially denied that *res ipsa loquitur* was applicable, but on a request for further and better particulars of the facts that they would rely on to show that "this type of accident happens in the ordinary course of epidural anaesthesia when proper care is used" the defendants conceded that the maxim did apply.

[32] *Hajgato* v. *London Health Association* (1982) 36 O.R. (2d) 669, 682; aff'd (1983) 44 O.R. (2d) 264 (Ont. C.A.), although the mere occurrence of infection did not give rise to an inference of negligence.

[33] *Crits* v. *Sylvester* (1956) 1 D.L.R. (2d) 502 (Ont. C.A.); aff'd (1956) 5 D.L.R. (2d) 601 (S.C.C.); *cf. McFadyen* v. *Harvie* [1942] 4 D.L.R. 647 (S.C.C.); aff'g [1941] 2 D.L.R. 663 (Ont. C.A.).

[34] *Fish* v. *Kapur* [1948] 2 All E.R. 176; *cf. Lock* v. *Scantlebury, The Times,* July 25, 1963, where the dentist was found negligent for failing to discover that he had dislocated the patient's jaw during an extraction.

[35] *Fletcher* v. *Bench* (1973) 4 B.M.J. 17, C.A.; *Keuper* v. *McMullin* (1987) 30 D.L.R. (4th) 408.

[36] *Considine* v. *Camp Hill Hospital* (1982) 133 D.L.R. (3d) 11 (Nova Scotia S.C.).

[37] *Girard* v. *Royal Columbian Hospital* (1976) 66 D.L.R. (3d) 676 (B.C.S.C.): " . . . medical science has not yet reached the stage where the law ought to presume that a patient must come out of an operation as well or better than he went into it" *per* Andrews J. at p. 691.

[38] *O'Malley-Williams* v. *Board of Governors of the National Hospital for Nervous Diseases* (1975) 1 B.M.J. 635.

[39] *Kapur* v. *Marshall* (1978) 85 D.L.R. (3d) 566 (Ont. H.C.).

[40] *Rocha* v. *Harris* (1987) 36 D.L.R. 410 (B.C.C.A.).

[41] *Ferguson* v. *Hamilton Civic Hospitals* (1983) 144 D.L.R. (3d) 214.

[42] *Whitehouse* v. *Jordan* [1980] 1 All E.R. 650, 658, 661; *Goguen* v. *Crowe* (1987) 40 C.C.L.T. 212 (Nova Scotia S.C.).

[43] *Grey* v. *Webster* (1984) 14 D.L.R. (4th) 706; nor where the patient's ureter was damaged in the course of a tubal ligation operation: *Hobson* v. *Munkley* (1976) 74 D.L.R. (3d) 408; *Videto* v. *Kennedy* (1980) 107 D.L.R. (3d) 612; rev'd on other grounds (1981) 125 D.L.R. (3d) 127 (Ont. C.A.), that perforation of the bowel during the course of a laparoscopic sterilisation is not a case of *res ipsa loquitur.*

[44] *Morris* v. *Winsbury-White* [1937] 4 All E.R. 494, 499; *cf. Cassidy* v. *Ministry of Health* [1951] 2 K.B. 343.

rule, the maxim will not apply where the injury sustained by the plaintiff is of a kind recognised as an inherent risk of the treatment, since such accidents can occur without negligence.[45] In *Kapur* v. *Marshall*[46] Robins J. said that *res ipsa loquitur* only comes into play when common experience or the evidence in the case indicates that the happening of the injury itself may be considered as evidence that reasonable care had not been used, and this will not be the case where the complication is a recognised, even if rare, risk inherent in the operation.[47]

It does not follow that simply because the plaintiff is in a position to **3.111** invoke *res ipsa loquitur* his action will necessarily succeed. The inference of negligence may be rebutted by evidence adduced by the defendant which explains how the accident occurred without negligence on his part.[48]

(b) *What is the effect of invoking res ipsa loquitur?*

There are two possible views as to the consequences in law of a **3.112** successful plea of *res ipsa loquitur*. The first is that it raises a prima facie inference of negligence which requires the defendant to offer some reasonable explanation as to how the accident could have occurred without negligence by him. In the absence of such evidence the prima facie case is established, and he will be found liable. If the defendant does adduce evidence that is consistent with the absence of negligence on his part, then the inference of negligence is rebutted, and the plaintiff has to produce positive evidence that the defendant has acted without reasonable care.[49] In practice, it is unlikely that the plaintiff will be able to do this, since he would not have relied on *res*

---

[45] *O'Malley-Williams* v. *Board of Governors of the National Hospital for Nervous Diseases* (1975) 1 B.M.J. 635; *Guertin* v. *Kester* (1981) 20 C.C.L.T. 225, on complications following plastic surgery on the patient's eyelids; *Considine* v. *Camp Hill Hospital* (1982) 133 D.L.R. (3d) 11 (Nova Scotia S.C.), where the medical evidence indicated that the operation could produce incontinence in 1–4 per cent. of cases; *Videto* v. *Kennedy* (1980) 107 D.L.R. (3d) 612, 618; rev'd on other grounds (1981) 125 D.L.R. (3d) 127—statistics demonstrated that perforation injuries are an inherent risk of a laparoscopic sterilisation. Statistical evidence of this kind does not show, of course, how many of the cases in which complications ensue are the result of a lack of reasonable care (see, *e.g.*, *Dendaas* v. *Yackel* (1980) 109 D.L.R. (3d) 455, 463, *per* Bouck J.). On the other hand, where the risk is known but does not normally occur in the absence of negligence *res ipsa loquitur* will apply: *Holmes* v. *Board of Hospital Trustees of the City of London* (1977) 81 D.L.R. (3d) 67 (Ont. H.C.).

[46] (1978) 85 D.L.R. (3d) 566, 574 (Ont. H.C.).

[47] In *Chubey* v. *Ahsan* (1977) 71 D.L.R. (3d) 550, 552 Freedman C.J.M. (in a dissenting judgment) took a robust approach to the occurrence of remote risks: "If in 7,000 operations of this kind, 6,999 are performed without damage to the aorta one may safely conclude that the surgeons attained this happy result by the exercise of due care. What can successfully be done in 6,999 cases ought to have been also done in the 7,000th. That it was not done in the 7,000th case must be ascribed to lack of due care." A majority of the Manitoba Court of Appeal took the view that the injury was simply the result of an inherent risk of the operation for which the surgeon was not liable.

[48] See, *e.g.*, *Roe* v. *Minister of Health* [1954] 2 Q.B. 66, where an anaesthetic was contaminated by the passage of phenol through invisible cracks in the glass ampoules in which the anaesthetic was stored, and this risk was unknown at the time; *Brazier* v. *Ministry of Defence* [1965] 1 Lloyd's Rep. 26, where a needle broke in the patient due to a latent defect in the needle rather than negligence in administering the injection; *Wilcox* v. *Cavan* (1974) 50 D.L.R. (3d) 687 (S.C.C.); *Hajgato* v. *London Health Association* (1982) 36 O.R. (2d) 669; aff'd (1983) 44 O.R. (2d) 264 (Ont. C.A.).

[49] *Ballard* v. *North British Railway Co.* 1923 S.C. 43, 54, *per* Lord Dunedin.

ipsa loquitur if he had positive evidence of the defendant's careless-ness. On this basis, the burden of proof does not shift to the defendant. If the probabilities are equally balanced that the defendant was or was not negligent, the plaintiff's action fails. So, for example, in *Colevilles Ltd.* v. *Devine*[50] it was said that the defendants had to show that the accident was just as consistent with their having exercised reasonable care as with negligence. It was not suggested that their explanation had to be more likely than the inference of negligence raised by applying the maxim, which would be the position if the burden of proof was reversed. This interpretation treats *res ipsa loquitur* as "no more than an exotic, although convenient, phrase to describe what is in essence no more than a common sense approach, not limited by technical rules, to the assessment of the effect of the evidence."[51]

3.113 The alternative view is that when *res ipsa loquitur* applies it has the effect of reversing the burden of proof, so requiring the defendant to show that the harm was not the product of his carelessness. The case which provides the strongest support for this proposition is the decision of the House of Lords in *Henderson* v. *Henry E. Jenkins & Sons*,[52] in which both Lord Reid and Lord Donovan specifically stated that the burden of proof lay with the defendants, and the effect of the majority finding that the defendants were liable was clearly that they had failed to discharge the burden of proof which lay upon them. A similar result was achieved in *Ward* v. *Tesco Stores Ltd.*,[53] where the only evidence before the court was that the plaintiff had slipped on some yoghurt in the defendants' store. There was no evidence as to how long the spillage had been there or as to whether the defendants had been careless in failing to clean it up. As Ormrod L.J. pointed out, in a dissenting judgment, the accident might have occurred no matter how careful the defendants had been.

3.114 In the most recent ruling of an appellate court on this issue the Privy Council has explicitly stated that the burden of proof does not shift to the defendant, but rests throughout the case with the plaintiff. In *Ng Chun Pui* v. *Lee Chuen Tat*[54] Lord Griffiths, delivering the opinion of the Board, said that in an appropriate case the plaintiff can establish a prima facie case by relying upon the fact of the accident. However, the "so-called doctrine of *res ipsa loquitur* . . . is no more than the use of a Latin maxim to describe the state of the evidence from which it is proper to draw an inference of negligence."[55] If the defendant adduces no evidence there is nothing to rebut the inference of negligence and the plaintiff will have proved his case. But if the defendant does adduce evidence, that evidence must be evaluated by the court:

> "Loosely speaking this may be referred to as a burden on the defendant to show he was not negligent, but that only means that

---

[50] [1969] 1 W.L.R. 475, 479, *per* Lord Donovan.
[51] *Lloyde* v. *West Midlands Gas Board* [1971] 1 W.L.R. 749, 755, *per* Megaw L.J., approved by the Privy Council in *Ng Chun Pui* v. *Lee Chuen Tat* [1988] R.T.R. 298, 301; see also the same judge in *Ward* v. *Tesco Stores Ltd.* [1976] 1 W.L.R. 810, 816.
[52] [1970] A.C. 282.
[53] [1976] 1 W.L.R. 810; *Moore* v. *R. Fox & Sons* [1956] 1 Q.B. 596; Atiyah (1972) 35 M.L.R. 337; see also, *per* Goddard L.J. in *Mahon* v. *Osborne* [1939] 2 K.B. 14, 50 stating that the defendant is required to show that he exercised due care.
[54] [1988] R.T.R. 298.
[55] *Ibid.*, p. 300.

faced with a prima facie case of negligence the defendant will be found negligent unless he produces evidence that is capable of rebutting the prima facie case."[56]

The duty of the court is to examine all the evidence and decide whether on the proved facts and legitimate inferences negligence has been established. Thus, the defendant's position is no different from that which arises when he is faced with positive evidence from the plaintiff raising an inference of negligence.

Certainly, this is the view that has been taken by the Canadian **3.115** courts on the effect of *res ipsa loquitur* in medical malpractice cases. In *Holmes* v. *Board of Hospital Trustees of the City of London* Robins J. explained the position in these terms:

> "The fact of the happening is, as I view *res ipsa loquitur*, simply a piece of circumstantial evidence justifying an inference of the defendant's negligence. The weight to be given that inference, like that to be given any other circumstantial evidence, will depend on the particular factual circumstances of the case. The strength of the inference may vary: it may be very strong or it may be sufficiently potent only to present a prima facie case and prevent the plaintiff from being non-suited. . . . What evidence, if any, the defendant need adduce will depend on the strength of the inference raised against him. The burden of proof remains with the plaintiff throughout; *res ipsa loquitur* does not shift the onus to the defendant or create a legal presumption in favour of the plaintiff which the defendant must disprove before he can escape liability."[57]

But an explanation of how the events could have occurred without **3.116** negligence will not necessarily rebut the inference of negligence, particularly where the explanation is a remote or unusual eventuality.[58] The plaintiff does not have to disprove every theoretical explanation, however unlikely, that might be devised to explain what happened in a way which absolves the defendant.[59] Just as the plaintiff is not entitled to rely on conjecture or speculation to establish his case on the balance of probabilities, so the defendant cannot resort to this when he is called upon for an explanation of events.

---

[56] *Ibid.*, p. 301. This is sometimes referred to as the defendant's "evidential burden," meaning that faced with a prima facie case of negligence he has a burden to give an explanation of the accident which is consistent with the absence of negligence.

[57] (1977) 81 D.L.R. (3d) 67, 79 (Ont. H.C.); *Crits* v. *Sylvester* (1956) 1 D.L.R. (2d) 502, 510 (Ont. C.A.); *Kapur* v. *Marshall* (1978) 85 D.L.R. (3d) 566, 574 (Ont. H.C.); *Girard* v. *Royal Columbian Hospital* (1976) 66 D.L.R. (3d) 676, 691 (B.C.S.C.); *MacDonald* v. *York County Hospital* (1972) 28 D.L.R. (3d) 521, 542; rev'd in part 41 D.L.R. (3d) 321 (Ont. C.A.); aff'd *sub nom. Vail* v. *MacDonald* (1976) 66 D.L.R. (3d) 530 (S.C.C.). In *Wilcox* v. *Cavan* (1974) 50 D.L.R. (3d) 687, 695 the Supreme Court of Canada said that: " . . . in medical cases where differences of expert opinion are not unusual and the sequence of events often appears to have brought about a result which has never occurred in exactly the same way before to the knowledge of the most experienced doctors, great caution should be exercised to ensure that the rule embodied in the maxim *res ipsa loquitur* is not construed so as to place too heavy a burden on the defendant."

[58] *Holmes* v. *Board of Hospital Trustees of the City of London* (1977) 81 D.L.R. (3d) 67, 82.

[59] *Bull* v. *Devon Area Health Authority* (1989) (unreported), C.A., *per* Dillon L.J.; *Ballard* v. *North British Railway Co.* 1923 S.C. 43, 54, *per* Lord Dunedin, that the defendant's explanation must be a reasonable one.

3.117   The differences between the two views of the effect of *res ipsa loquitur* have probably been exaggerated. It is a fine line between the probabilities being equally balanced and tipping the scale one way or the other. The issue turns upon the cogency that the court attributes to particular pieces of evidence, and this is necessarily a subjective judgment which it is virtually impossible to quantify.[60]

Standard of proof

3.118   The standard of proof in cases of medical negligence is, in theory, the same as for any other case of negligence, *i.e.* the general standard applicable in civil cases, namely "on the balance of probabilities." This standard tends to conceal the fact that the cogency of the evidence that the courts require in order to satisfy the test can vary with the issues at stake.[61] It is more difficult, for example, to establish that the defendant has behaved fraudulently than to prove that he was negligent.[62] It has been suggested that cases of professional negligence create particular problems for the courts and, in practice, this may result in what is effectively a higher standard of proof than for "ordinary" cases of negligence. In *Dwyer* v. *Roderick* May L.J. said that:

> "Professional men . . . are entitled to no special preference before the law, to no rule requiring a higher standard of proof on the balance of probabilities than any other. But it is to shut one's eyes to the obvious if one denies that the burden of achieving something more than that mere balance of probabilities is greater when one is investigating the complicated and sophisticated actions of a qualified and experienced lawyer, doctor, accountant, builder or motor engineer than when one is enquiring into the momentary inattention of the driver of a motor car in a simple running-down action."[63]

3.119   The disclaimer that professionals are entitled to no special treatment clearly belies what follows in this passage. There is, however, a suspicion that this judicial attitude is largely confined to the medical profession.[64] Most prominent amongst the judges taking this approach to the medical profession was Lord Denning, who was concerned both for the effect that findings of negligence might have on the reputation

---

[60] In *Levinkind* v. *Churchill-Davidson* (1983) (unreported), Kenneth Jones J., denying the applicability of the maxim to a medical negligence action, remarked that he should not allow himself to be "trammelled by the logical intricacies associated with *res ipsa loquitur.*"

[61] See Pattenden (1988) 7 C.J.Q. 220.

[62] *Hornal* v. *Neuberger Products Ltd.* [1957] 1 Q.B. 247.

[63] *The Times*, November 12, 1983; (1983) 127 S.J. 806.

[64] Jackson and Powell, *Professional Negligence*, 1987, 2nd ed., para. 6.21: "In practice, however, the medical profession seems to fare better before the courts than most other professions. The defence of 'non-negligent mistake' succeeds more often." The authors attribute this to the *Bolam* test as it has been applied to the medical profession, and the greater degree of deference which the courts show to expert witnesses in medical negligence actions. See also Robertson (1981) 44 M.L.R. 457, 459 commenting on the "strong pro-defendant policy" evident in many medical negligence cases; and Montgomery (1989) 16 J. of Law and Soc. 319 for an insight into why this happens.

of individual defendants, and with the more general consequences of medical malpractice litigation for the conduct of medicine.[65] In *Hucks* v. *Cole* these concerns were reflected in his view of the standard of proof:

> "A charge of professional negligence against a medical man was a serious charge, on a different footing to a charge of negligence against a car driver. As the charge was so grave, so should the proof be clearer. The burden of proof was correspondingly greater. A doctor was not to be held negligent simply because something went wrong. He was not liable for mischance, or misadventure; nor for an error of judgment. He was only liable if he fell below the standards of a reasonably competent practitioner in his field, so much so that his conduct was deserving of censure or inexcusable."[66]

This approach to allegations of negligence against doctors is also **3.120** apparent in the frequent reiteration of the point that medical procedures often carry unavoidable risks, not all errors connote negligence, there is no liability for mere "errors of judgment," judgment with hindsight should be avoided, doctors are not insurers of a favourable result, and so on. The law reports are replete with such comments. It may be that the difference between motorists and doctors is that in a medical negligence action the doctor's professional reputation is perceived to be in issue, and the courts hesitate before impugning the conduct of a member of a highly respected profession. On the other hand, some judges have taken a more robust attitude to this issue. In *Ashcroft* v. *Mersey Regional Health Authority* Kilner Brown J. doubted the validity of such an approach:

> "Furthermore, the suggestion that a greater burden rests on a plaintiff alleging negligence against a doctor is plainly open to question. . . . If there is an added burden, such burden does not rest on the person alleging negligence; on the contrary, it could be said that the more skilled a person is the more care that is expected of him."[67]

The question for consideration, said his Lordship, was whether on a **3.121** balance of probabilities it has been established that a professional man has failed to exercise the care required of a man possessing and professing special skill in circumstances which require the exercise of that special skill. Similarly, in *Whitehouse* v. *Jordan*,[68] Donaldson L.J. pointed out that very few professionals can claim never to have been

---

[65] See *Roe* v. *Minister of Health* [1954] 2 Q.B. 66, 86–87; *Hatcher* v. *Black, The Times,* July 2, 1954; *Whitehouse* v. *Jordan* [1980] 1 All E.R. 650, 658; *Hyde* v. *Tameside Area Health Authority* (1981) reported at (1986) 2 P.N. 26.

[66] (1968) 112 S.J. 483, 484. This repeats his direction to the jury in *Hatcher* v. *Black, The Times,* July 2, 1954, where he said that a doctor should not be found negligent unless his conduct was deserving of censure. Similarly, in *Whitehouse* v. *Jordan* [1980] 1 All E.R. 650, 659 Lawton L.J. commented that: "The more serious the allegation the higher the degree of probability that is required. In my opinion allegations of negligence against medical practitioners should be considered as serious."

[67] [1983] 2 All E.R. 245, 247.

[68] [1980] 1 All E.R. 650, 666 (see § 3.77, n. 50); see also *Clark* v. *MacLennan* [1983] 1 All E.R. 416, 433; *Thake* v. *Maurice* [1984] 2 All E.R. 513, 523.

negligent, and that often the only difference between those who are sued and their colleagues is that the error happens to have caused harm to the plaintiff.

3.122   Some instances of negligence are so glaring that they do warrant censure, but many departures from the standard of reasonable care can be attributed to understandable human error. The fact that errors are understandable does not mean, however, that they should be condoned, nor that patients should face a higher standard of proof in order to preserve the chimera of professional reputation.

Expert evidence and the role of the court

3.123   Expert witnesses have a vital function in medical negligence actions, but the emphasis that is sometimes placed on accepted professional practice can obscure their true role, which is to provide the evidence upon which the court decides whether there has been negligence or not. This is not for the witnesses to determine. This was forcefully expressed by Bollen J. in the Australian case of *F*. v. *R*.:

> "Expert evidence will assist the court. But in the end it is the court which must say whether there was a duty owed and a breach of it. The court will have been guided and assisted by the expert evidence. It will not produce an answer merely at the dictation of the expert evidence. It will afford great weight to the expert evidence. Sometimes its decision will be the same as it would have been had it accepted dictation. But the court does not merely follow expert evidence slavishly to a decision. The court considers and weighs up all admissible evidence which it has received. If the court did merely follow the path apparently pointed by expert evidence with no critical consideration of it and the other evidence, it would abdicate its duty to decide, on the evidence, whether in law a duty existed and had not been discharged."[69]

3.124   In *Sidaway* v. *Bethlem Royal Hospital Governors*[70] Lord Diplock said that in matters of diagnosis and treatment the court has to rely on and evaluate expert evidence (remembering, however, that it is no part of its task of evaluation to give effect to any preference it may have for one responsible body of professional opinion over another), provided it is satisfied by the expert evidence that both qualify as responsible bodies of medical opinion. This is a consequence of the *Bolam* test, a point which was made abundantly clear in *Maynard* v. *West Midlands Regional Health Authority*.[71] Lord Diplock's proviso, however, is crucial. The court must be satisfied that the experts' view constitutes a "responsible" body of professional opinion, experienced in the particular field of medicine concerned.[72] Thus, on questions of liability it is

[69] (1982) 33 S.A.S.R. 189, 201; see also *Anderson* v. *Chasney* [1949] 4 D.L.R. 71, 81–82; aff'd [1950] 4 D.L.R. 223 (S.C.C.); *Goode* v. *Nash* (1979) 21 S.A.S.R. 419, 422 (S.C. of S. Aus.).
[70] [1985] 1 All E.R. 643, 659.
[71] [1984] 1 W.L.R. 634; see § 3.18.
[72] *Hills* v. *Potter* [1983] 3 All E.R. 716, 728.

important to obtain expert opinion in the appropriate specialty, and conversely the evidence of a specialist may be of little assistance in an action against a general practitioner.[73] Where conflicting bodies of opinion are not "equally competent" or responsible the court is entitled to prefer the evidence of one body of professional opinion over another.[74]

The court may accept or reject in whole or in part the evidence of **3.125** any witness on the grounds of credibility or plausibility. On the other hand, on complicated technical matters, where acquaintance with and experience of matters such as anatomy and physiology are essential, the court may not be justified in disregarding expert testimony or reaching conclusions contrary to those of the experts.[75] Conversely, where the case does not involve such considerations it will be easier for the court to form its own view of the circumstances. Where the medical evidence is equivocal, or where, for example, there is a conflict of evidence as to whether a responsible body of medical opinion supports a particular practice, the judge has to resolve that conflict.[76] In resolving the conflict the judge should not invent his own version of the facts which is not based on the evidence.[77]

The cogency of the expert evidence can be affected by a number of **3.126** factors such as the unimpressive demeanour of the witness or the defective logic of an argument advanced by the witness.[78] In *Caldeira* v. *Gray*[79] the Privy Council had no doubt that in assessing the value of the testimony of expert witnesses their demeanour, their personality, and the impression they make upon the trial judge, *e.g.* whether they confined themselves to giving evidence or acted as advocates, may powerfully and properly influence the mind of the judge who sees and hears them in deciding between them. Again, in *Joyce* v. *Yeomans*, speaking of the advantage that a trial judge has over an appellate court in seeing a witness, even an expert witness, give evidence, Brandon L.J. observed that:

"Sometimes expert witnesses display signs of partisanship in a witness box or a lack of objectivity. This may or may not be

---

[73] *E.g.*, in *Wilson* v. *Swanson* (1956) 5 D.L.R. (2d) 113, 119 the plaintiff's expert's evidence was described as "a collection of elementary views on the diagnosis of cancer by one who is a virtual stranger to the exercise of such a medical and surgical judgment." See the comments of Brooke J. in *Scott* v. *Bloomsbury Health Authority* [1990] Med. L.R. 214 on the use of expert witnesses who have retired from practice; and on this question see also (1990) 6 J. of the M.D.U. 25, 33–34; *A.V.M.A. Medical & Legal Journal* (1990) No. 3, p. 10. Solicitors who have difficulty in finding an expert in the relevant specialty should contact Action for the Victims of Medical Accidents.
[74] *Poole* v. *Morgan* [1987] 3 W.W.R. 217, 253.
[75] *Anderson* v. *Chasney* [1949] 4 D.L.R. 71, 81–82, *per* Coyne J.A.; *McLean* v. *Weir* [1977] 5 W.W.R. 609, 620, *per* Gould J. (B.C.S.C.); aff'd [1980] 4 W.W.R. 330.
[76] *Sidaway* v. *Bethlem Royal Hospital Governors* [1985] 1 All E.R. 643, 663, *per* Lord Bridge; *Fincham* v. *Anchor Insulation Co. Ltd.*, *The Times*, June 16, 1989, Q.B.D., stating that the judge has a duty to make a legal diagnosis where the medical experts were unable to agree on whether the plaintiff was suffering from asbestosis.
[77] *McLean* v. *Weir* [1977] 5 W.W.R. 609, 620, *per* Gould J. (B.C.S.C.); aff'd [1980] 4 W.W.R. 330; *Hajgato* v. *London Health Association* (1982) 36 O.R. (2d) 669, 683; *cf. Hotson* v. *Fitzgerald* [1985] 3 All E.R. 167, where Simon Brown J. appeared to adopt a compromise theory about causation.
[78] *Maynard* v. *West Midlands Regional Health Authority* (1981) (unreported), C.A., *per* Sir Stanley Rees. See, *e.g.*, *Hotson* v. *Fitzgerald* [1985] 3 All E.R. 167, 173.
[79] [1936] 1 All E.R. 540, 542.

obvious from the transcript, yet it may be quite plain to the trial judge. Sometimes an expert witness may refuse to make what a more wise witness would make, namely, proper concessions to the viewpoint of the other side. Here again this may or may not be apparent from the transcript."[80]

3.127 On the other hand, where the crucial issue of negligence turns upon an inference drawn from the primary facts which depends on the evidentiary value that the trial judge gave to the witnesses' evidence and not on their credibility or demeanour, an appellate court is in just as good a position as the judge to determine the proper inference to be drawn and is entitled to form its own view.[81]

3.128 There is a tendency (not unnatural) for defendants to rely not on their recollection of what they actually did or said in the case, because with the passage of time they are unable to remember, but on what was their usual practice in similar cases. In some instances the court will be willing to accept this as cogent evidence, drawing an inference (since there is no direct evidence) that the defendant did what he normally does.[82] The Supreme Court of Canada, however, has taken a more sceptical approach to this form of evidence. In *Martel* v. *Hotel-Dieu St.-Vallier*[83] Pigeon J. took the view that the defendant's testimony was not convincing "because he did not have an exact recollection of this particular case. It was not because he remembered exactly what he had done that he swore that the had not committed an error, but it was only because he was convinced that he did what he always does." Conversely, the plaintiff, for whom the incident is unique and therefore far more memorable, may have a better recollection of events. Against this has to be set the fact that the plaintiff may not recall the details because he was distressed at the time, lacked the necessary technical knowledge, or may simply have no knowledge of the crucial facts because, for example, he was under anaesthetic at the time.

3.129 In *Whitehouse* v. *Jordan*[84] both the House of Lords and the Court of Appeal were critical of the manner in which some of the expert

---

[80] [1981] 1 W.L.R. 549, 556, cited with approval in *Maynard* v. *West Midlands Regional Health Authority* [1984] 1 W.L.R. 634, 637.

[81] *Whitehouse* v. *Jordan* [1981] 1 All E.R. 267, H.L. For criticism of the manner in which this principle was applied to the facts of *Whitehouse* v. *Jordan* see Robertson (1981) 44 M.L.R. 457. See also, *per* Lord Bridge in *Wilsher* v. *Essex Area Health Authority* [1988] 1 All E.R. 871, 883, speaking of a conflict of expert evidence on the question of causation: "Where expert witnesses are radically at issue about complex technical questions within their own field and are examined and cross-examined at length about their conflicting theories, I believe that the judge's advantage in seeing them and hearing them is scarcely less important than when he has to resolve some conflict of primary fact between lay witnesses in purely mundane matters."

[82] See, *e.g.*, *Sidaway* v. *Bethlem Royal Hospital Governors* [1985] 1 All E.R. 643; *Chatterton* v. *Gerson* [1981] 1 All E.R. 257; *Hills* v. *Potter* [1983] 3 All E.R. 716; *Belknap* v. *Meakes* (1989) 64 D.L.R. (4th) 452, 465–466 (B.C.C.A.). For an alternative inference to be drawn from the defendant's failure to recall events see *Holmes* v. *Board of Hospital Trustees of the City of London* (1977) 81 D.L.R. (3d) 67, 92 (Ont. H.C.), in an unusual case where almost immediately the possibility of litigation was recognised and proceedings were commenced within 6 months, the details of the treatment given to the particular patient should be more memorable. The failure to testify, and to remember, left the impression that "the whole story has not been told and requires that more inferences be drawn than should be necessary in a case involving professional standards of care."

[83] (1969) 14 D.L.R. (3d) 445, 449 (S.C.C.); *cf. Wilcox* v. *Cavan* (1974) 50 D.L.R. (3d) 687, 694; rev'g (1973) 44 D.L.R. (3d) 42, 54 (N.B.C.A.).

[84] [1981] 1 All E.R. 267; [1980] 1 All E.R. 650, 655.

evidence was prepared. Medical reports should not be "settled" by counsel. While some degree of consultation between experts and legal advisers is entirely proper, expert evidence should be, and should be seen to be, the independent product of the expert; it should not be tailored to the exigencies of the litigation.[85] This leaves open precisely what degree of consultation is proper, but presumably solicitors or counsel are entitled to point out any errors in a report, seek clarification of issues, and suggest alternative lines of enquiry to the expert. The crucial factor is that the report should reflect the witness's own independent expert opinion. If it smacks of advocacy this may well reflect on its credibility.

---

[85] *Ibid.*, p. 276, *per* Lord Wilberforce.

CHAPTER 4

STANDARD OF CARE—SPECIFIC INSTANCES

4.01 The circumstances which can give rise to a claim for medical negligence are as diverse as the practice of medicine itself. It is possible for any diagnosis or treatment to be performed in a careless fashion, or for some essential step to be negligently omitted. Some situations seem to recur, however, on a regular basis and it may be helpful to discuss the law in terms of these "types" of error. This chapter attempts to translate into legal categories the wide variety of forms of negligence that may arise in practice. It must be remembered, however, that these specific instances of error must always be measured against the general test for negligence embodied in the *Bolam* test. It does not follow that simply because in one case a doctor has been held negligent for omitting to take a particular precaution, that it will always be negligent to omit that precaution. The test is whether the defendant has acted as a reasonably competent doctor in all the circumstances of the case, and this is essentially a question of fact.[1] There must be some precedential value in previous cases, however, and where a particular practice has been found to be negligent in the past a defendant who has adopted that practice should at least be required to indicate how the circumstances of this case differ from that of the earlier case. In addition, practices change over time and what was once accepted and proper practice may now be negligent in the light of new knowledge.[2]

4.02 The doctor's duty to his patient encompasses diagnosis, advice and treatment, but these components can be further divided.[3] Thus, diagnosis should be preceded by the taking of a full history from the patient, a physical examination, and where necessary diagnostic tests. It is obvious that this may be difficult if the doctor fails to attend the patient, as "remote" diagnosis is a potentially risky exercise. Diagnosis should also be kept under review if the patient is failing to respond to the treatment. Diagnosis will normally be followed by advice, which may range from an assurance that there is nothing wrong with the

---

[1] See *Qualcast (Wolverhampton) Ltd.* v. *Haynes* [1959] A.C. 743, where the House of Lords cautioned against relying too heavily on previous cases as precedents for what constitutes negligence.

[2] *Roe* v. *Minister of Health* [1954] 2 Q.B. 66.

[3] See *Sidaway* v. *Bethlem Royal Hospital Governors* [1985] 1 All E.R. 643, 660, *per* Lord Bridge. This division is for the purpose of exposition; it is not to imply that different criteria apply to the different components: see *ibid.*, p. 657, *per* Lord Diplock.

112

patient, through the prescription of medication together with a suggestion that the patient take the tablets, to a recommendation that the
patient undergo major surgery. Treatment is almost too varied to be
categorised, although some common types of error are apparent.
Treatment clearly extends to post-operative care.

This chapter is divided into six main sections, which, initially at **4.03**
least, reflect the major generic forms of negligence: failure to attend or
treat the patient; errors of diagnosis; failures of advice and communication; and errors in treatment. These four sections are followed by a
section on mental health, which deals with the particular malpractice
issues raised by that topic, and finally by a brief section on the defence
of contributory negligence by the patient.

I. Failure To Attend Or Treat

A doctor who fails to attend his patient or who is dilatory in attending **4.04**
may be guilty of negligence if a reasonable doctor would have
appreciated that his attendance was necessary in his patient's interests.
But this will depend upon the precise circumstances of the case: how
serious was the patient's condition; what was the doctor told; what
commitments to other patients did he have at the time? For example,
in *Smith* v. *Rae*[4] the defendant doctor had undertaken to attend the
plaintiff at her confinement. He was summoned at 7.30 p.m., but
because he had other patients to deal with he said that he could not be
there until 8.30 p.m. An experienced midwife who was with the patient
predicted that the birth would not be until 11.00 p.m. The child died
during birth which occurred before 8.30 p.m. Middleton J., finding
that there had been no negligence, said that in these circumstances a
doctor does not undertake "to drop all other matters in hand to attend
the patient instantly upon receiving notification. The doctor must, having
regard to all the circumstances, act reasonably. Here the first message
received did not indicate any emergency. . . . The doctor had other
patients who had some claim upon his time and attention."[5] In *Kavanagh*
v. *Abrahamson*[6] a general practitioner's patient had moved house without
notifying him of the new address. He was asked to visit the patient who
was said to be suffering from influenza. When he visited the old address

---

[4] (1919) 51 D.L.R. 323 (Ont. S.C. Appellate Div.).

[5] *Ibid.*, at pp. 325–326; see also *Cavan* v. *Wilcox* (1973) 44 D.L.R. (3d) 42, 53
(N.B.C.A.), where the information the doctor received over the telephone was not
sufficiently serious to alert him to the emergency; *Lobley* v. *Nunn* (1985) (unreported),
C.A., where it was alleged that a general practitioner's receptionist was negligent in not
having a small child, who had been brought into the surgery, seen immediately by the
doctor as an emergency. The action failed because the parents had not, initially at least,
brought home to the receptionist the urgency of the situation; *Elder* v. *Greenwich &
Deptford Hospital Management Committee, The Times* March 7, 1953, where a general
practitioner who did not visit a patient with abdominal pains (which turned out to be
appendicitis), because she had already been seen by a hospital casualty officer, was held not
negligent; *Barnes* v. *Crabtree, The Times*, November 1 and 2, 1955, discussed in Nathan,
Medical Negligence, 1957, p. 37; *cf. Ball* v. *Howard, The Lancet*, February 2, 1924, p. 253,
Q.B.D., where a doctor was held negligent for "not attending at once to the patient's call"
when the patient had appendicitis.

[6] (1964) 108 S.J. 320.

he got no response, but did not make further efforts to ascertain the patient's new address. The patient had bronchitis and subsequently died in hospital. Atkinson J. held that the general practitioner was not negligent in not doing more to track down the new address.

4.05 A hospital casualty department that opens its doors to the public undertakes the task of providing an emergency service and will be liable for negligently failing to do so. In *Fraser v. Vancouver General Hospital*[7] O'Halloran J.A. said that:

> "The operation of a public hospital is for the public good; the carrying on of an emergency ward therein is a general invitation to the public without unreasonable limitations or reservations, and thus it is bound to the utmost extent to serve the public with that skill and professional knowledge the hospital holds out to the public that it possesses, and without negligence."[8]

This is illustrated by *Barnett v. Chelsea and Kensington Hospital Management Committee*,[9] in which three nightwatchmen had become ill after drinking some tea. They attended hospital, clearly appearing ill, and a nurse was informed that they had been vomiting. The nurse telephoned the casualty officer, who did not see the men, but said that they should go home and see their own doctors. They left, and about five hours later one of the men died from arsenic poisoning. Nield J. held that in these circumstances the casualty officer should have seen and examined the deceased, and was negligent in failing to do so.[10] The deceased should have been admitted for observation and diagnosis. It could not be said, however, that a casualty officer must always see a caller at the department. If, for example, the receptionist discovered that the visitor was already attending his own doctor and merely wanted a second opinion, or if the caller had a small cut which could be dressed by a nurse, the casualty officer need not be called.

4.06 A hospital which offers obstetric services has a duty to provide an adequate system for securing the attendance, within a reasonable time, of doctors with sufficient expertise to deal with an emergency during the course of delivery.[11] There is no reason, of course, why this duty should be limited to obstetric services. It will apply to any service offered by a hospital in which a foreseeable emergency may arise.

4.07 The duty to treat extends to post-operative treatment. In *Corder v. Banks*[12] a plastic surgeon who allowed the plaintiff to go home after an

---

[7] (1951) 3 W.W.R. 337 (B.C.C.A.); aff'd [1952] 3 D.L.R. 785 (S.C.C.).

[8] *Ibid.*, p. 340. If, on the other hand, the hospital simply closes the doors of the casualty department there is no longer an undertaking of responsibility and there will be no liability for failing to treat.

[9] [1968] 1 All E.R. 1068.

[10] The action failed, however, on the ground that the negligence did not cause the death, since there was no effective treatment that could have been given in time to prevent it: see § 5.04.

[11] *Bull v. Devon Area Health Authority* (1989) (unreported), C.A.

[12] *The Times*, April 9, 1960; see also *Videto v. Kennedy* (1980) 107 D.L.R. (3d) 612, 616–617; rev'd on other grounds (1981) 125 D.L.R. (3d) 127 (Ont. C.A.), where the arrangements made by the defendant doctor for post-operative care in the event of complications were "just about non-existent." The defendant had a duty to "ensure that his patient would get attention in an emergency situation and, if he did not make those arrangements, to himself communicate with the plaintiff or her relatives as to her condition," *per* Grange J. (Ont. H.C.).

operation on the plaintiff's eye-lids, but failed to make any arrangements for the plaintiff to contact him if bleeding occurred during the first 48 hours after the operation, was found to have been negligent. The duty to provide post-operative attendance does not extend, however, to supervising routine procedures carried out by nursing staff.[13]

In some circumstances the duty to examine and/or treat the patient **4.08** may arise independently of any request by or on behalf of the patient. For example, in *Stokes* v. *Guest, Keen and Nettlefold* (*Bolts & Nuts*) *Ltd.*[14] it was held that a factory medical officer should have instituted six monthly medical examinations, given his knowledge of the risk to employees of contracting cancer from their working conditions and the fact that early diagnosis gave a significantly better chance of successful treatment. The employers were held vicariously liable for the medical officer's negligence in failing to implement a system of screening employees for the disease. In this case the duty arose out of the relationship between the employer and employee, and the fact that the doctor's function was partially to discharge the employer's duty to the employees. It might be more difficult, however, to establish a general duty to engage in preventive medicine, on the part of general practitioners, for example, giving rise to a claim in negligence. If it became standard practice for general practitioners to conduct screening exercises for a particular disease, such as cervical cancer, then it would be easier to argue that the failure to do so constituted negligence.[15]

II. Errors In Diagnosis

Diagnostic errors can arise for various reasons, such as the following: **4.09** an inadequate medical history; errors in examining the patient; errors of judgment in interpreting the patient's symptoms; a failure to spot something "serious"; the failure to conduct tests or refer the patient for specialist consultation; or a failure to monitor treatment and revise the diagnosis where the treatment is proving ineffective.

1. Failure to take a full medical history

The necessity for taking a full medical history before embarking **4.10** upon treatment ought to be obvious, and the failure to do so can have

---

[13] *Morris* v. *Winsbury-White* [1937] 4 All E.R. 494.

[14] [1968] 1 W.L.R. 1776.

[15] The new terms of service of general practitioners include a greater element of "preventive medicine": see the National Health Service (General Medical and Pharmaceutical Services) Amendment (No. 2) Regulations 1989 (S.I. 1989/1897) (amending S.I. 1974/160). See also *Sutton* v. *Population Services Family Planning Programme Ltd.*, *The Times*, November 7, 1981, where a nurse was negligent in failing to detect the plaintiff's cancer. (Note, however, the distinction between examining the patient and failing to detect the disease, and not examining the patient at all, for which there will be no liability unless the defendant ought reasonably to have examined the patient in the circumstances.)

tragic consequences. In *Chin Keow* v. *Government of Malaysia*[16] a doctor did not make any inquiry into the patient's medical history before giving an injection of penicillin, and the patient died from an allergic reaction to the drug. The defendant was aware of the remote possibility of danger, but nevertheless carried on with his normal practice of not making any inquiry because he had not had any mishaps before. The Privy Council considered that this was a clear case of negligence, given that the precautions required to avoid the risk could easily have been taken. In *Leonard* v. *Knott*[17] the defendant physician, who conducted annual "executive health examinations" for client corporations, referred a patient for a radiological examination of the kidneys and urinary tract by means of an intravenous pyelogram (IVP). This was simply part of the "package" included in the annual check-up, and at that stage the defendant had never even met the patient, let alone examined him, taken a medical history, done any routine tests, such as urine analysis, or sought any information from the family doctor. The patient died from an allergic reaction to the contrast medium used in the IVP, a risk which was known and foreseeable to the medical profession. The defendant was held liable for exposing the deceased to such a risk without taking a history, examining him, or consulting the family doctor. The medical evidence indicated that 99 per cent. of problems can be determined from a comprehensive history and a proper physical examination, and the deceased had never had any signs or symptoms relating to the kidneys or urinary tract.

4.11   The patient's medical history may include not only the signs and symptoms of the illness or injury for which the patient is seeking treatment, but also details of any previous treatment either for the same condition or, in appropriate circumstances, a previous injury or disease. For example, in *Coles* v. *Reading and District Hospital Management Committee*[18] a patient who had sustained a crushing injury to his finger subsequently died of toxaemia due to tetanus infection. He had attended a cottage hospital for treatment where he was given first aid treatment by a nurse but he was not given an anti-tetanus injection. He was instructed to go to Battle hospital for further treatment but he did not go to the hospital, either because it was not clearly explained to him or because he was suffering from shock. Later he saw his own doctor, who made no inquiries as to what had happened at the hospital but simply redressed the wound. If the patient had been given an anti-tetanus injection he would probably not have died. Sachs J. held both the cottage hospital and the general practitioner liable. The general practitioner probably assumed that the hospital had done everything that was necessary, but he should have made inquiries of the hospital or the deceased. If he had decided against giving the anti-tetanus injection on the basis that it was unnecessary he would have been negligent for neglecting

---

[16] [1967] 1 W.L.R. 813.
[17] [1978] 5 W.W.R. 511 (B.C.S.C.).
[18] (1963) 107 S.J. 115. See also *Chute Farms* v. *Curtis*, *The Times*, October 10, 1961, in which a veterinary surgeon was held negligent for failing to give a yearling colt an anti-tetanus injection after it went lame.

an elementary precaution. Similarly, in *Meyer* v. *Gordon*[19] it was held that the failure of hospital staff to take details of the patient's obstetric history, which would have revealed that her previous labour had been a rapid one and put the staff on notice that the labour must be closely monitored, contributed to hypoxia suffered by the baby, which led to brain damage.

The duty to take a full history obviously requires the doctor to **4.12** *listen* to what the patient is saying. Sometimes, particularly if the patient is considered to be "difficult," a doctor may disregard or discount what the patient is telling him and this can colour the diagnosis. A failure to listen to a patient who is describing symptoms which would affect diagnosis and treatment will amount to negligence, where harm results. The Australian case of *Giurelli* v. *Girgis*[20] provides a vivid illustration. The plaintiff sustained a broken leg which was operated on by the defendant orthopaedic surgeon, who fixed a steel plate to the front outer surface of the tibia. The plaintiff complained on a number of occasions about serious pain in the leg and an inability to put any weight on the leg. The surgeon took the view that the plaintiff was a difficult patient, with a propensity for histrionics, who exaggerated his complaints. When the steel plate was removed and the plaintiff attempted to put weight on the leg, it gave way. A further operation was required to repair the fracture. White J. held that the surgeon was liable, because he had failed to take into account the possibility that the fracture was not uniting satisfactorily and had dismissed the plaintiff's complaints without making any proper investigation. The plaintiff was not believed or given sufficient time or opportunity to describe his symptoms, or the defendant did not ask sufficient questions. He had allowed only 5 to 10 minutes for consultations, but "pressure of time did not justify the risk of not listening and inquiring."[21] Complaint of serious pain is a significant indicator of movement at the fracture site and the possibility of non-union, and the full facts were vital to a correct diagnosis. As White J. observed:

> "I do not think that it was disputed that listening to the patient's history is as much a part of the art of medicine as clinical examination. Modern aids to diagnosis no doubt assist the medical practitioner in varying degrees depending upon the circumstances, but they can hardly take the place of listening to the patient's history."[22]

---

[19] (1981) 17 C.C.L.T. 1; *Schanczi* v. *Singh* [1988] 2 W.W.R. 465 (Alta. Q.B.), in which a surgeon was held liable for performing spinal disc surgery without first trying conservative management, having failed to take a full history, either from the patient or the referring doctor.

[20] (1980) 24 S.A.S.R. 264.

[21] *Ibid.*, p. 270.

[22] *Ibid.*, pp. 276–277; see also *Cassidy* v. *Ministry of Health* [1951] 2 K.B. 343, 349 on the question of medical staff ignoring the plaintiff's complaints of intense and excessive pain; *Saumarez* v. *Medway and Gravesend Hospital Management Committee* (1953) 2 B.M.J. 1109; *Reitz* v. *Bruser* (No. 2) [1979] 1 W.W.R. 31, where it was held that a doctor should not attribute the plaintiff's complaints of pain to "anxiety" until all the possible causes of the symptoms have been explored.

4.13   Of course, the patient also bears some responsibility to give truthful and frank replies when questioned by a doctor. If the information given by the patient is misleading the doctor will not be held accountable for acting upon it, at least where it is reasonable to rely upon the information.[23] It may not be reasonable where what the patient says is clearly contradicted by the symptons.

2. Wrong diagnosis

4.14   As with any form of medical error, an error of diagnosis will not necessarily be negligent. Ultimately, this is determined by the requirements of the *Bolam* test and whether the defendant acted as a reasonable doctor in the circumstances. It will depend to a large extent upon the difficulty of making the diagnosis given the symptoms presented, the diagnostic techniques available such as tests or instruments, and the dangers associated with the alternative diagnoses. This last point is well illustrated by *Maynard* v. *West Midlands Regional Health Authority*,[24] in which the plaintiff alleged that two consultants were negligent in failing to diagnose tuberculosis, and subjected her to an unnecessary operation. They recognised that turberculosis was the most likely diagnosis, but there was a possibility that the plaintiff was suffering from Hodgkin's disease, which at the time was likely to be fatal unless the patient received early treatment. They decided that a diagnostic operation, a mediastinoscopy, should be performed. This operation carried certain inherent risks even when performed correctly, and one of these risks, damage to the plaintiff's left laryngeal recurrent nerve, did materialise. The plaintiff's case was that the evidence of tuberculosis was so strong that it was negligent to defer the diagnosis and subject her to the operation. The House of Lords held that a responsible body of professional opinion approved of what the defendants had done and accordingly they were not negligent, applying the *Bolam* test. Clearly, a factor that weighed heavily in this assessment was the seriousness of the consequence if the condition proved to be Hodgkin's disease.

4.15   The difficulty of making a diagnosis will often excuse a defendant, and *a fortiori* where other doctors have in fact made the same mistake with the patient.[25] The diagnosis must be judged in the light of the pertinent facts at the time the practitioner rendered his professional opinion; he cannot be expected to possess the sharper vision and

---

[23] See, *e.g.*, *Venner* v. *North East Essex Area Health Authority*, *The Times*, February 21, 1987, where the plaintiff assured the defendant gynaecologist immediately before a sterilisation operation that she could not be pregnant. The defendant did not perform a dilatation and curettage (D. and C.) which probably would have terminated any pregnancy. The plaintiff was in fact pregnant at the time of the sterilisation operation, and subsequently gave birth to a healthy child. Tucker J. held that the defendant was not negligent in not performing a D. and C. as a matter of course.

[24] [1984] 1 W.L.R. 634.

[25] In *Pudney* v. *Union-Castle Mail SS Ltd.* [1953] 1 Lloyd's Rep. 73 rheumatoid arthritis was found to be very difficult to diagnose in its early stages; *Crivon* v. *Barnet Group Hospital Management Committee*, *The Times*, November 19, 1958, C.A., where an expert in the field of breast cancer said that he would have made the same diagnosis as the defendant in the circumstances.

higher wisdom of hindsight.[26] In *Hulse* v. *Wilson*[27] it was held that the failure to diagnose cancer of the penis was not negligent, given that in a young man it was extremely rare. Finnemore J. commented that: "The dangers of making a diagnosis too quickly are just as great as making a diagnosis too slowly." On the other hand, it is not necessarily negligent mistakenly to diagnose cancer.[28] In *Whiteford* v. *Hunter*[29] the House of Lords held that the defendant, who had diagnosed the plaintiff to be suffering from terminal cancer, was not liable for omitting to use a diagnostic instrument that was rare in England at the time; nor was it negligent to fail to take a biopsy when that involved a serious risk of perforating the bladder wall, which would have caused an unhealing ulcer if the condition was cancerous.

When making a diagnosis much depends on the symptoms observed: **4.16** obviously, where symptoms do not indicate the illness from which the patient is in fact suffering the doctor cannot be blamed for failing to identify the specific illness.[30] On the other hand, even where the particular condition cannot be diagnosed the symptoms may be such as to indicate that the plaintiff is suffering from something serious which needs further investigation,[31] or indeed the difficulty of making a diagnosis may in itself suggest that the doctor take additional precautions such as admitting the patient for observation, or conducting further testing.[32]

A number of cases in which doctors have been held responsible for **4.17** negligent diagnosis concern missed fractures. In *McCormack* v. *Redpath Brown & Co. Ltd.*[33] a casualty officer who failed to discover a

---

[26] *Holmes* v. *Board of Hospital Trustees of the City of London* (1977) 81 D.L.R. (3d) 67, 91 (Ont. H.C.); *Wilkinson Estate (Rogin)* v. *Shannon* (1986) 37 C.C.L.T. 181 (Ont. H.C.); *Roe* v. *Minister of Health* [1954] 2 Q.B. 66, 83, *per* Denning L.J.: "It is so easy to be wise after the event and to condemn as negligence that which was only misadventure. We ought always to be on our guard against it, especially in cases against hospitals and doctors."

[27] (1953) 2 B.M.J. 890; *cf. Sutton* v. *Population Services Family Planning Programme Ltd.*, *The Times*, November 7, 1981 on the diagnosis of cancer.

[28] *Crivon* v. *Barnet Group Hospital Management Committee*, *The Times*, November 19, 1958, C.A.; *Graham* v. *Persyko* (1986) 27 D.L.R. (4th) 699, 703–704, where a doctor who mistakenly diagnosed Crohn's disease was held to be not negligent.

[29] [1950] W.N. 553.

[30] *Sadler* v. *Henry* (1954) 1 B.M.J. 1331, where in the absence of symptoms of meningitis a general practitioner was not negligent in diagnosing hysteria; *Barker* v. *Nugent* (1987) (unreported), Q.B.D., where a general practitioner was not negligent, on the facts, in failing to diagnose meningitis in a baby; but on the diagnosis of meningitis see *Dale* v. *Munthali* (1976) 78 D.L.R. (3d) 588; aff'd (1978) 90 D.L.R. (3d) 763, § 4.20, *post; Serre* v. *de Tilly* (1975) 8 O.R. (2d) 490, where a patient died from a brain haemorrhage; the defendant's diagnosis of hysteria was a reasonable mistake given the symptoms.

[31] See § 4.20.

[32] *Barnett* v. *Chelsea and Kensington Hospital Management Committee* [1968] 1 All E.R. 1068, 1073. In *Seyfert* v. *Burnaby Hospital Society* (1968) 27 D.L.R. (4th) 96 a casualty officer who discharged a patient who had presented with a stab wound in the abdomen after 1–2 hours was held to have been negligent; observation of patients with abdominal stab wounds was normally for a minimum of 24 hours due to the risk of penetration of the peritoneum, which could result in the very dangerous condition of peritonitis.

[33] *The Times*, March 24, 1961; see also *Newton* v. *Newton's Model Laundry*, *The Times* November 3, 1959, on a failure to diagnose a compound fracture of the patella of the left knee after the plaintiff had fallen 12 feet onto a concrete floor; the defendant was held to be negligent; *Saumarez* v. *Medway and Gravesend Hospital Management Committee* (1953) 2 B.M.J. 1109, on a fracture of the distal phalanx of the left middle

depressed fracture of the skull and penetration of the bone into the brain tissue was found negligent. Head injuries were common at the hospital and the casualty officer had assumed, without checking, that this was just another cut head. Similarly, in *Wood* v. *Thurston*[34] a casualty officer examined a patient who was in an intoxicated condition and had been involved in an accident. The patient was allowed to go home, but he died the next day. The postmortem showed a fractured collar bone, 18 fractured ribs and congested lungs, which the defendant had failed to diagnose. He claimed that the deceased's state of intoxication had dulled his sensation to pain and prevented him from giving an accurate account of events. Pritchard J. held the casualty officer liable, because although the patient's intoxication might have deceived a doctor as to the patient's true condition, the examination should have been more thorough in the circumstances. The use of a stethoscope, for example, would have revealed the deceased's condition. Whilst it may not be negligent to fracture a patient's jaw when extracting a tooth,[35] a dentist who failed to notice that he had dislocated the patient's jaw, either at the time of the extraction or at one of the patient's subsequent visits, was held to be negligent.[36]

4.18   The failure of a hospital casualty officer to diagnose appendicitis in a child who presented with pain on the right side of the abdomen and vomiting has been held to be negligent,[37] as has a failure to diagnose the early stages of pneumonia in a baby on the basis that the defendant general practitioner had not examined the baby closely enough.[38] In *Wipfli* v. *Britten*[39] it was said that the failure of a general practitioner to diagnose twins was not necessarily negligent, but on the facts there were sufficient indications of a possible multiple gestation to have aroused the defendant's suspicions, and he should have investigated the possibility more carefully.

4.19   Where a practitioner has diagnostic aids available it may be negligence not to use them. In *Holmes* v. *Board of Hospital Trustees of the City of London*[40] the doctors responsible for the plaintiff's treatment

finger. The defendant, who ignored the patient's complaints about pain in the finger, was held to be negligent; *Fraser* v. *Vancouver General Hospital* (1951) 3 W.W.R. 337 (B.C.C.A.); aff'd [1952] 3 D.L.R. 785 (S.C.C.) on the failure to identify a dislocated fracture of the neck apparent on the X-rays; *Hotson* v. *East Berkshire Area Health Authority* [1987] 2 All E.R. 909, on a failure to identify an acute traumatic fracture of the femoral epiphysis.

[34] *The Times,* May 5, 1951. See also Medical Defence Union *Annual Report 1988*, p. 43 on intoxicated patients presenting in a casualty department.

[35] *Fish* v. *Kapur* [1948] 2 All E.R. 176.

[36] *Lock* v. *Scantlebury, The Times*, July 25, 1963.

[37] *Edler* v. *Greenwich & Deptford Hospital Management Committee, The Times*, March 7, 1953; on a failure to diagnose appendicitis see also *Bergen* v. *Sturgeon General Hospital* (1984) 28 C.C.L.T. 155, § 4.23; *Reeves* v. *Carthy* [1984] I.R. 348 (Supreme Court of Ireland), where there was an alleged failure to diagnose an abdominal perforation as a result of an inadequate medical examination.

[38] *Riddett* v. *D'Arcy* (1960) 2 B.M.J. 1607; *Duggan* v. *Tameside and Glossop Health Authority* (1987) (unreported), Q.B.D., where a failure to diagnose infection in the plaintiff's foot due to an inadequate examination was held to be negligent; *Moffatt* v. *Witelson* (1980) 111 D.L.R. (3d) 712 (Ont. H.C.), where an ophthalmologist who failed to recognise the serious danger of a penetrating wound of the cornea causing an infection of the anterior chamber of the eye was held to be negligent. On a failure to diagnose diabetes see Medical Defence Union *Annual Report 1990*, p. 26, and *Yepremian* v. *Scarborough General Hospital* (1980) 110 D.L.R. (3d) 341 (Ont. C.A.).

[39] (1982) 28 C.C.L.T. 104; aff'd (1984) 13 D.L.R. (4th) 169 (B.C.C.A.).

[40] (1977) 81 D.L.R. (3d) 67 (Ont. H.C.).

ordered X-rays to be carried out but then delayed for five days before examining them. They were held negligent for failing to inform themselves of the factual data (which included X–rays and nursing notes) which they had themselves identified as pertinent and necessary to the plaintiff's diagnosis, and which they knew or ought to have known was available. Robins J. said that in a complex medical situation a physician would be expected to conduct more frequent and more extensive examinations, and would be expected in making his assessment to seek all ancillary assistance (*e.g.* by means of tests).

3. Failure to spot something "serious"

In some cases, although the practitioner cannot be faulted for failing **4.20** to identify the specific illness or disease from which the patient is suffering, the patient's condition is so serious that he ought to have realised that either further tests were required for a more accurate diagnosis, or the patient should have been referred on to a specialist who was capable of making the diagnosis. In *Dale* v. *Munthali*,[41] for example, the defendant diagnosed the patient as suffering from influenza, when in fact he had meningitis. It was held that there was no negligence in failing to diagnose meningitis, but the patient was so extremely ill that the defendant should have realised that it was more than gastro-intestinal 'flu. The defendant's examination should have been more thorough, and the severity of the symptoms demanded that the patient should have been admitted to hospital for further tests.[42] Similarly, In *Langley* v. *Campbell*[43] the patient presented with symptoms of fever, headache and alternate sweating and shivering. His general practitioner diagnosed influenza, but the patient subsequently died from malaria, having recently returned from Uganda. The medical evidence was that, in the absence of complications, a patient with ordinary influenza began to feel better after three or four days. A patient who had no complications yet deteriorated should be the cause of special concern. General practitioners did not normally come across malaria, but in these circumstances it should have entered the defendant's head that it might be a tropical disease of some kind (particularly since the patient's family had told him that the patient had suffered from malaria during the war, and had suggested blood tests). He might not be capable of diagnosing malaria, but he should have been alerted to the possibility that it might not be an indigenous disease.

4. Failure to revise initial diagnosis

A doctor should always keep the diagnosis under review as the **4.21** treatment progresses, and keep an open mind about the causes of the

---

[41] (1976) 78 D.L.R. (3d) 588; aff'd (1978) 90 D.L.R. (3d) 763 (Ont. C.A.).

[42] See also *Barnett* v. *Chelsea and Kensington Hospital Management Committee* [1968] 1 All E.R. 1068, 1073.

[43] *The Times*, November 6, 1975. See also *Sa'd* v. *Robinson* [1989] 1 Med. L.R. 41, where a general practitioner was negligent in failing to refer immediately to hospital a child who had sucked hot tea from the spout of a teapot.

patient's condition if it does not respond to treatment. The dangers of acquiring "tunnel vision" are well demonstrated in the Canadian case of *Layden* v. *Cope*.[44] The plaintiff, who had a history of gout, saw his general practitioner complaining of a sore foot. The doctor made a tentative diagnosis of gout, arranged for some tests and prescribed medication. After some improvement the condition deteriorated and the plaintiff was admitted to a local hospital and seen by another general practitioner, who confirmed the diagnosis of gout. The foot continued to deteriorate and the plaintiff experienced fever, but the doctors continued with the treatment for gout. Eventually the plaintiff was transferred to another hospital and seen by a specialist who diagnosed a staphylococcal and/or streptococcal infection. The infection was so serious that a few days later the plaintiff's leg had to be amputated below the knee. Rowbotham J. held that the general practitioners were negligent on the basis that they had failed to reconsider their diagnosis or treatment, or both, and had failed to consult with, or refer the patient to, a specialist. In the light of the patient's prolonged period of hospitalisation and the obviously rapid deterioration of his overall medical condition, they should have been willing to revise their diagnosis. The need to explore all the alternative diagnoses was especially important when it became increasingly evident that the original diagnosis may have been incomplete or erroneous.

4.22   The need to consider alternatives was stressed by Hewak J. in *Reitz* v. *Bruser* (No. 2):

> "It is not sufficient in my view for a medical practitioner to say 'of the two or three probable diagnoses I have chosen diagnosis (A) or diagnosis (B) or (C).' It must be expected that the practitioner would choose diagnosis (A) over (B) or (C) because *all* of the facts available to that practitioner and *all* of the methods available to check the accuracy of those facts and that diagnosis had been exercised with the result that diagnosis (A) remains as the most *probable* of all. For example, if there were symptoms of persistent pain and puffiness associated with a limb encased in a cast and if that cast was split in an attempt to eliminate the cast as the source and cause of the pain and puffiness then if the symptoms of pain and puffiness still persisted an alternative procedure or check would be indicated to determine an alternative cause."[45]

This point becomes even more important where the consequences of the alternative diagnosis, if it turns out to be the correct diagnosis, are likely to be serious. In *Lankenau* v. *Dutton*[46] the medical evidence was that a surgeon confronted with a patient with paralysis after major surgery should not only attempt to diagnose the cause but also "should make a differential diagnosis, that is to say that he should consider other likely causes of her condition and test them against her symptoms and be ready with an alternative theory to direct her treatment if

---

[44] (1984) 28 C.C.L.T. 140 (Alta. Q.B.).
[45] [1979] 1 W.W.R. 31, 47 (emphasis in original).
[46] (1986) 37 C.C.L.T. 213 (B.C.S.C.).

his first diagnosis and treatment should fail to produce an improvement in her condition."[47] The defendant had diagnosed aortic dissection occurring during surgery, which initially was a reasonable diagnosis. As the patient's symptoms progressed, however, he failed to reassess the diagnosis, which resulted in the paralysis becoming permanent. He clung to the original diagnosis although the symptoms should have made him question it; he failed to test his theory by X-ray, and he failed to seek the assistance of neurological experts quickly enough. The surgeon was held negligent.

Similarly, in *Bergen* v. *Sturgeon General Hospital*[48] a female patient **4.23** was admitted to hospital complaining of pains in her abdomen. The provisional diagnosis was acute gastroenteritis, with appendicitis to be checked out. A general surgeon made a tentative diagnosis of pelvic inflammatory disease and referred the patient to a gynaecologist, who confirmed that diagnosis. The patient did not respond to treatment, and indeed deteriorated. She died from a ruptured appendix, following an emergency operation which was too late to save her. The defendants were held to have been negligent, not for the wrong diagnosis itself "for everyone will make mistakes," but for failing to take account of the fact that there was no improvement in the patient's condition after 48 hours of massive doses of penicillin (for the pelvic inflammation), and for failing to take any steps to rule out appendicitis when it explained all the symptoms and they had the facilities to do so by means of an exploratory laparotomy, bearing in mind that appendicitis is life-threatening. Indeed the evidence was that where there is doubt as to whether or not a person has appendicitis, it is such a dangerous condition that an appendectomy will be performed, and hospitals themselves expect 15 per cent. to 20 per cent. of appendectomies to yield healthy appendixes. As Hope J. observed:

> "Ordinary common sense must dictate that when you are dealing with a life-threatening malady that has been brought to your attention for the purpose of ruling it out, you do not ignore these precautions in the face of such signs, symptoms and information."[49]

5. Failure to arrange for tests for diagnosis

Where diagnostic aids would assist a doctor in reaching an **4.24** accurate diagnosis it may well be negligent to fail to use them, if available,[50] although, again, this is not necessarily the case.[51] Where a

---

[47] *Ibid.*, p. 231, *per* Spencer J.

[48] (1984) 28 C.C.L.T. 155 (Alta. O.B.).

[49] *Ibid.*, p. 174.

[50] *Bergen* v. *Sturgeon General Hospital* (1984) 28 C.C.L.T. 155; *Lankenau* v. *Dutton* (1986) 37 C.C.L.T. 213.

[51] *Whiteford* v. *Hunter* [1950] W.N. 553, see § 4.15. Writing over 30 years ago Lord Nathan, *Medical Negligence*, 1957, p. 45, suggested that X-rays were now so commonplace that there would be a grave danger of a finding of negligence if they are not used in a case where there was a real possibility of fractures or dislocations. This may be questioned, however, since the test is whether a reasonable doctor would have ordered an X-ray in the circumstances. They are unnecessary where the doctor is able to make a diagnosis on the basis of his clinical examination of the patient, or where the result of the X-ray would not normally affect the treatment given (*e.g.* as is often the case with a broken nose).

gynaecologist was aware of the possibility that his patient could be pregnant he should have conducted tests before subjecting the uterus to X-rays.[52] In some instances the patient's condition may be such that he should be admitted to hospital for observation and tests.[53]

4.25 Where tests have been carried out there may be negligence in failing to interpret the results properly,[54] or in mislaying or mixing up the samples, or where the pathologist fails to inform the doctor properly or at all of the test results,[55] or where the doctor fails to read the report.[56]

4.26 In addition to diagnostic tests, the nature of the treatment or medication being given to the patient may require that the patient be tested in advance for an allergic reaction or that the patient be carefully monitored for an adverse drug reaction. In *Robinson* v. *Post Office*,[57] for example, a doctor who departed from standard practice at the time by giving the plaintiff an anti-tetanus injection without first administering a test dose for an allergic reaction was held to have been negligent, although the action failed on the issue of causation. Similarly, in *Male* v. *Hopmans*[58] the plaintiff became deaf due to a side-effect of a drug administered to treat an infection in his knee. The manufacturer's instructions warned the doctor that the drug was particularly dangerous in the presence of impaired renal function, and the plaintiff exhibited some evidence of kidney dysfunction which, it was held, should have been investigated further by testing. The manufacturer also suggested that audiometric tests of hearing should be made prior to and during the course of therapy, because evidence of impairment to hearing can be detected by the audiometer before clinical signs develop. This precaution was particularly important when excessive doses were being given. The doctor was found negligent in failing to prescribe such tests either before or during the course of

---

[52] *Zimmer* v. *Ringrose* (1981) 125 D.L.R. (3d) 215, (Alta. C.A.) aff'g (1978) 89 D.L.R. 646, 656–657, where the defendant had diagnosed the patient's pelvic pain as constipation; *Gardiner* v. *Mounfield* [1990] 1 Med. L.R. 205, where the defendant dismissed the possibility that the plaintiff, who was overweight and had a history of amenorrhoea, was pregnant; *Bagley* v. *North Hertfordshire Health Authority* (1986) 136 New L.J. 1014, on failure to perform blood tests during pregnancy when it was known that the plaintiff suffered from blood incompatibility.

[53] *Dale* v. *Munthali* (1976) 78 D.L.R. (3d) 588; aff'd (1978) 90 D.L.R. (3d) 763 (Ont. C.A.); *Barnett* v. *Chelsea and Kensington Hospital Management Committee* [1968] 1 All E.R. 1068, 1073.

[54] See, *e.g.*, *Fraser* v. *Vancouver General Hospital* (1951) 3 W.W.R. 337 (B.C.C.A.); [1952] 3 D.L.R. 785 (S.C.C.), on the negligent interpretation of X-rays; *Rance* v. *Mid-Downs Health Authority* [1991] 1 All E.R. 801, on an allegedly negligent failure to interpret an ultrasound scan of a foetus, which was subsequently discovered to be suffering from spina bifida.

[55] Allegations to this effect were made in *McKay* v. *Essex Area Health Authority* [1982] Q.B. 1166; see also *Thomsen* v. *Davison* [1975] Qd. R. 93, on the pathologist's duty to communicate the results of testing to the doctor; *Gregory* v. *Pembrokeshire Health Authority* [1989] 1 Med. L.R. 81, C.A., on the doctor's duty to communicate results to the patient (see § 4.38, n. 85).

[56] *Fredette* v. *Wiebe* [1986] 5 W.W.R. 222 (B.C.S.C.).

[57] [1974] 2 All E.R. 737. For a discussion of allergic reactions associated with anaesthesia see Fisher (1990) 6 J. of the M.D.U. 4, stating that test dosing in this context is inherently invalid, though the availability of resuscitation facilities and drugs may affect the patient's chance of survival to such a reaction.

[58] (1967) 64 D.L.R. (2d) 105, 113–115 (Ont. C.A.).

treatment, even though facilities for conducting them were readily available at the hospital.[59]

Where a risk associated with the treatment is remote it will probably **4.27** not be negligent to omit to test for the condition.[60]

6. Failure to consult or refer patient to a specialist

Where a doctor is unable to diagnose or treat the patient he will be **4.28** under a duty either to seek advice from an appropriate specialist or refer the patient on to a specialist. If he attempts to diagnose or treat the patient himself he is, in effect, undertaking work beyond his competence, for which he will be held liable if harm results.[61] For example, in *Poole* v. *Morgan*[62] the defendant ophthalmologist was inadequately trained in the use of a laser, although he had often used it in his practice. The treatment that he gave to the plaintiff was usually performed by a retina vitreous specialist. The defendant had to come up to the standard of that specialty, and since he was unable to do so he had a duty to refer the plaintiff to such a specialist. It has also been said that where a doctor suspects cancer he should immediately refer the patient to a specialist or arrange for an immediate biopsy. A failure to do so was held to be negligent.[63]

In *MacDonald* v. *York County Hospital*[64] the plaintiff sustained a **4.29** severe fracture of the ankle in a road traffic accident. The defendant, a general surgeon, performed a closed reduction of the fracture and put the leg in a cast as a temporary measure, intending to perform an open reduction at a later stage. At the time of the emergency treatment there was no pulse in the ankle, and this was put down to a spasm of the artery resulting from the trauma which was expected to clear up in a few hours. The next day the condition of the plaintiff's foot and toes caused concern to the nurses, which they expressed to the defendant when he visited the plaintiff on two occasions. The defendant did nothing about the condition of the foot, which ultimately had to be amputated because it became gangrenous as a result of circulatory impairment. The conclusion was that the defendant knew that he did

---

[59] See also *Marshall* v. *Rogers* [1943] 4 D.L.R. 68 (B.C.C.A.), § 4.43; *cf. Battersby* v. *Tottman* (1985) 37 S.A.S.R. 524, where following a failure to monitor the known side-effects of a drug (a risk of serious and permanent eye damage) the defendant was held not negligent in the circumstances.

[60] *Warren* v. *Greig* (1935) *The Lancet*, Vol. 1, 330, where a patient who was suffering from acute myeloid leukaemia, which was a rare disease, died from excessive bleeding following an operation to remove his teeth. The defendants were not liable for not testing the patient's blood prior to the operation.

[61] See § 3.78. It may well be a nice question whether a doctor does have sufficient experience in the relevant field: see, *e.g.*, *Mose* v. *North West Hertfordshire Health Authority* (1987) (unreported), C.A.

[62] [1987] 3 W.W.R. 217; *Layden* v. *Cope* (1984) 28 C.C.L.T. 140, 148 (§ 4.21, *ante*), *per* Rowbotham J.: "Their most critical error in judgment was their failure, when faced with a medical problem they were unable to resolve, to consult with or refer the patient to a medical specialist until it was too late to save the patient's foot"; *Lankenau* v. *Dutton* (1986) 37 C.C.L.T. 213.

[63] *Wilson* v. *Vancouver Hockey Club* (1983) 5 D.L.R. (4th) 282, 288; aff'd (1985) 22 D.L.R. (4th) 516 (B.C.C.A.). On the failure to diagnose cancer see *Sutton* v. *Population Services Family Planning Programme Ltd.*, *The Times*, November 7, 1981.

[64] (1973) 41 D.L.R. (3d) 321 (Ont. C.A.); aff'd *sub nom. Vail* v. *MacDonald* (1976) 66 D.L.R. (3d) 530 (S.C.C.).

not know the cause of the impairment and he should have taken the advice of a cardiovascular specialist or had the plaintiff attended by a specialist:

" . . . when he found himself unable to diagnose the cause of the symptoms displayed in the plaintiff's foot, I consider that he failed in his duty to the plaintiff in not seeking the advice or colloboration of such a specialist, or at least in failing to recommend the desirability of such a course of action . . . "[65]

4.30 The difficulty for inexperienced practitioners is that their very lack of experience may prevent them from knowing when they are out of their depth.[66] Nonetheless, they will be held responsible for negligently failing to refer patients to more senior or experienced colleagues. In *Payne* v. *St. Helier Group Hospital Management Committee*[67] a casualty officer allowed a patient who had been kicked in the stomach by a horse to leave the casualty department and go home. The patient subsequently died from peritonitis, and the casualty officer was found to have been negligent in not admitting the patient for examination by a consultant. Similarly, in *Fraser* v. *Vancouver General Hospital*[68] a patient who attended the casualty department of a hospital following a road accident presented with cuts on his forehead and pain and stiffness in the back of his neck. He was examined by the junior doctors in charge, X-rays were taken and examined by the doctors. The patient was then discharged from the hospital, but later he died as a result of a dislocated fracture of the neck which was apparent on the X-rays but went unnoticed by the doctors at the hospital. The defendants were held liable. The patient should not have been discharged. In view of their limited knowledge and experience, it was negligence to attempt to read the X-rays at all. If the doctors were not competent to read the X-rays then they ought to have called in one of the specialist radiologists who were available for such an eventuality.

7. Overtesting

4.31 Claims that are sometimes made about defensive medicine suggest that defensive practices tend to be manifested in the form of unnecessary diagnostic tests. If a diagnostic test or procedure is unnecessary by

---

[65] *Ibid.*, pp. 349–350, *per* Dubin J.A. See *Ares* v. *Venner* (1970) 14 D.L.R. (3d) 4 (S.C.C.), which also involved the amputation of the plaintiff's leg as a result of the defendant negligently ignoring the classic symptoms of circulatory impairment. The normal practice of the profession in such cases was to split the cast, and if no relief is obtained refer to a specialist or, if equipped to do so, explore further to ascertain the cause of the problem; *Badger* v. *Surkan* (1970) 16 D.L.R. (3d) 146 (Sask. Q.B.); *Bayliss* v. *Blagg* (1954) 1 B.M.J. 709.

[66] See the comments of Browne-Wilkinson V.-C. in *Wilsher* v. *Essex Area Health Authority* [1986] 3 All E.R. 801, 833.

[67] *The Times*, November 12, 1952; *cf. Parkinson* v. *West Cumberland Hospital Management Committee* (1955) 1 B.M.J. 977, where a newly qualified casualty officer discharged a patient who had complained of chest pains, and the patient died of a coronary thrombosis 15 minutes later. The casualty officer was held not to have been negligent, either to discharge the patient or by refraining from seeking a more experienced view.

[68] (1951) 3 W.W.R. 337 (B.C.C.A.); aff'd [1952] 3 D.L.R. 785 (S.C.C.).

reference to the standards of the medical profession, *i.e.* according to the standards of the reasonably competent doctor exercising and professing to have that skill, it will be negligence to perform it, and it will be actionable if the patient suffers injury as a consequence.[69] This was the essence of the plaintiff's claim in *Maynard* v. *West Midlands Regional Health Authority*,[70] namely that the defendants had undertaken an unnecessary diagnostic operation during which an inherent risk of the procedure materialised, causing her injuries. The action failed because on the evidence a responsible body of professional opinion agreed that the operation was justified in the circumstances. It was not suggested in *Maynard* that the doctors were acting "defensively," but ultimately the issue of "defensive medicine" is merely a question of the doctor's motive for performing the procedure, and motives may be mixed.[71] It matters not whether the doctor was misguidedly seeking to protect himself from litigation or whether he simply misjudged the nature of the patient's symptoms; if no doctor of ordinary skill and acting with ordinary care would have considered the procedure to be called for it is negligence to perform it. This would apply with as much force to unnecessary diagnostic tests, such as X-rays, as it would to unnecessary operations, such as Caesarian sections.[72]

III. Failure Of Advice And Communication

A lack of communication is often said to be at the heart of many **4.32** medical negligence actions. This comment is usually directed to the fact that a patient who has suffered a medical accident may initiate proceedings because following the incident health care professionals have refused to discuss the circumstances frankly with the patient or his family. This results in a breakdown of the doctor/patient relationship, and the patient is left with the feeling that the only way to find out what happened is to resort to the courts.[73] Failures of communication, however, whether between doctor and patient or between practitioners, may frequently be the source of the initial injury.

---

[69] *Leonard* v. *Knott* [1978] 5 W.W.R. 511 (B.C.S.C.); see § 4.10, *ante*.

[70] [1984] 1 W.L.R. 634.

[71] See, *e.g.* *Robinson* v. *Post Office* [1974] 2 All E.R. 737, 743–744. Orr L.J. said, at p. 745, that it would be "asking too much of human nature" that the doctor should have excluded the possibility of being sued from his mind when he decided to give the patient an anti-tetanus injection, but he also weighed up the competing medical considerations in reaching his decision. In *Schanczi* v. *Singh* [1988] 2 W.W.R. 465 (Alta. Q.B.) the defendant was held negligent for failing to attempt conservative treatment before resorting to spinal surgery. The operation was "unnecessary" in the circumstances, but this was not attributed to defensive practice.

[72] The Royal College of Radiologists and the National Radiological Protection Board have estimated that unnecessary X-rays cause between 100 and 250 deaths a year: see *Patient dose reduction in diagnostic radiology*, H.M.S.O., 1990; Gifford (1990) 301 B.M.J. 451. Poor management, excessive dosages and unnecessary repeat X-rays are blamed.

[73] *E.g.*, in *Stamos* v. *Davies* (1985) 21 D.L.R. (4th) 507, 519 Krever J. commented that: " . . . the underlying cause of both the misadventure and of the litigation is a less than satisfactory physician-patient relationship arising out of the failure on the part of the physician to take the patient into his confidence . . . ." See further, Simanowitz, "Medical Accidents: The Problem and the Challenge" in Byrne (ed.), *Medicine in Contemporary Society*: *King's College Studies* 1986–87, p. 117.

1. Failure to warn about risks

4.33   It is axiomatic that a patient will normally need some information about the nature of his medical condition and the form of treatment that the doctor proposes in order to decide whether to accept the treatment. This is required both for the purpose of the patient giving a valid consent to treatment and as part of the doctor's duty of care to advise of the inherent risks of the proposed treatment, so that the patient can make an informed decision. The legal consequences of this type of communication failure are considered in Chapter 6.

4.34   In addition, however, to the doctor's duty of care to warn patients in advance of the risk of treatment, it is possible that in some circumstances the practitioner will come under a duty to inform the patient that something has gone wrong with the treatment. In *Gerber* v. *Pines*[74] Du Parcq J. said that as a general rule a patient was entitled to be told at once if the doctor had left some foreign object in his body. This view was disapproved, however, in the Irish case of *Daniels* v. *Heskin*,[75] where it was said that there was no abstract duty to tell patients what is wrong with them, or in particular to say that a needle had been left in their body. Everything depended upon the circumstances—the character of the patient, her health, her social position, her intelligence, the nature of the tissue in which the needle is embedded, the possibility of subsequent infection, the arrangements made for future observation and care, and so on.[76] The disclosure of such information was, accordingly, a matter within the discretion of the doctor's professional judgment.

4.35   It may be that this approach reflects the attitudes of an earlier age, when medical paternalism was more widely accepted than it is today. The more recent trend is for the courts to insist that patients do have a right to know what has been done to them, particularly where something has gone wrong, just as they have the right to know what is going to be done to them prior to treatment. For example, in *Lee* v. *South West Thames Regional Health Authority*[77] Sir John Donaldson M.R. pointed out that following *Sidaway* v. *Bethlem Royal Hospital Governors*[78] a doctor has a duty to answer a patient's questions about proposed treatment, and he could see no reason why the position should be any different where the patient asks what treatment he has in fact had. Why, asked his Lordship, is the duty before the treatment different from that afterwards?[79] Subsequently, in *Naylor* v. *Preston Area Health Authority*[80] his Lordship said that:

> "I personally think that in professional negligence cases, and in particular in medical negligence cases, there is a duty of candour resting on the professional man . . . . In my judgment, still admittedly and regretfully *obiter*, it is but one aspect of the

---

[74] (1934) 79 S.J. 13.
[75] [1954] I.R. 73, Supreme Court.
[76] *Ibid.*, p. 87, *per* Kingsmill Moore J.
[77] [1985] 2 All E.R. 385.
[78] [1985] 1 All E.R. 643; see § 6.71.
[79] [1985] 2 All E.R. 385, 389; see the quotation in § 10.95.
[80] [1987] 2 All E.R. 353, 360.

general duty of care, arising out of the patient/medical practitioner or hospital authority relationship and gives rise to rights both in contract and in tort."

In Canada the courts have treated this issue as part and parcel of the **4.36** doctor's duty of care to the patient. In *Stamos* v. *Davies*[81] the defendant, while performing a lung biopsy, punctured the plaintiff's spleen. The plaintiff asked what the defendant had obtained from the biopsy, and the defendant said simply that he had not obtained what he wanted, but he did not inform the plaintiff of the ruptured spleen. The plaintiff was discharged from hospital but had to be admitted as an emergency three days later, due to the bleeding into his abdominal cavity. The spleen was removed surgically, and the plaintiff recovered uneventfully. Krever J. said that he found the reasoning of Sir John Donaldson M.R. in *Lee* compelling, and held that the defendant was under a duty to inform the plaintiff that the spleen had been punctured. The defendant's failure to be candid was a breach of that duty.

The difficulty with any case of this nature is proving that the breach **4.37** of duty caused the plaintiff damage. The plaintiff's ignorance that something untoward has occurred will rarely contribute to any further loss, and since the damage has already occurred the failure to be candid is not a cause of the harm.[82] This was the position in *Stamos* v. *Davies*, where it was held that there was no causal connection; informing the patient of the damage to his spleen in the course of biopsy would not have saved the spleen, which was doomed from the moment it was injured.[83]

In an appropriate case, however, the failure to inform may be **4.38** causative of further injury if, for example, the patient takes a risk that he would otherwise have avoided, or if the patient's ignorance leads to delay in diagnosis (resulting in additional harm) if an emergency should subsequently arise as a result of the injury of which he is unaware. This point was accepted in *Daniels* v. *Heskin* where Kingsmill Moore J. said that a doctor would not always be justified in keeping such knowledge to himself, since he has a duty to take precautions against further injury to the patient. The nature of the precautions will vary with the circumstances of the case, but might include informing the patient to enable him to avoid unnecessary

---

[81] (1986) 21 D.L.R. (4th) 507 (Ont. H.C.).

[82] *Daniels* v. *Heskin* [1954] I.R. 73, 81, 88. Even in *Gerber* v. *Pines* (1934) 79 S.J. 13 the plaintiff was awarded only £5 damages.

[83] The defendant was found liable on a different ground; see § 4.42, *post*. See also *Keuper* v. *McMullin* (1987) 30 D.L.R. (4th) 408, where a dentist left a small piece of a drill bit in the patient's tooth without informing her and without discussing with her the various alternatives open. The tooth remained asymptomatic for 18 months. The New Brunswick Court of Appeal held that the defendant was under a duty to disclose the incident to the patient since she was alert and able to be consulted about the alternatives, but the action failed on the grounds of causation. A reasonable person in the plaintiff's position would have accepted the defendant's advice; see further *Fletcher* v. *Bench* (1973) 4 B.M.J. 17, C.A., on broken drill bits.

risks.[84] A failure to inform the patient that diagnostic tests have failed to produce any results may constitute negligence.[85]

4.39 Cases in which, due to the defendant's negligence, the plaintiff is unaware that she is or might become pregnant, do not present the same causation difficulties. For example, in *Scuriaga* v. *Powell*[86] the defendant performed a lawful abortion on the plaintiff, but failed to terminate the pregnancy. She subsequently gave birth to a healthy child. After the abortion operation the defendant assured the plaintiff that all was well, although he had found no evidence of foetal parts and believed that she had a potentially dangerous disorder. When the plaintiff became aware that she was still pregnant the defendant told her that the operation had failed because she had a structural defect. "In fact," said Watkins J. "the doctor botched the operation, then seized on a speculative and dangerous explanation for his failure. He should have placed the matter before a consultant without delay." If he had told the plaintiff the true position within two or three weeks she would have agreed to a second operation, but the delay had increased the risk to her health. She refused a second termination and gave birth to a healthy child. The defendant was held liable for the plaintiff's loss of earnings, loss of marriage prospects and pain and suffering.[87]

4.40 Similarly, in *Cryderman* v. *Ringrose*[88] the defendant doctor failed to inform the plaintiff that a sterilisation operation had not succeeded, and she believed she was sterile. She subsequently became pregnant and underwent an abortion by hysterectomy. If the plaintiff had been aware of the unreliability of the procedure used by the defendant, and had been told that the treatment had not rendered her sterile (as the defendant knew) she could have tried other methods of contraception or sterilisation. The defendant was held liable for this omission.

2. Failure to give proper instructions to the patient

4.41 A doctor will frequently need the patient's co-operation, in performing an examination, for example, or administering the treatment. This

---

[84] [1954] I.R. 73, 88; see also *Stamos* v. *Davies* (1985) 21 D.L.R. (4th) 507, 523: "There is no suggestion in the evidence that anything the plaintiff did at home caused the spleen to rebleed and thus cause its removal." Clearly, if there was evidence to this effect the result would have been different.

[85] In *Gregory* v. *Pembrokeshire Health Authority* [1989] 1 Med. L.R. 81, C.A. a patient who was never informed that an amniocentesis test had failed to produce a result subsequently gave birth to a Down's Syndrome baby. She alleged that if she had been informed she would have insisted on a second test being performed, and, had it proved positive, would have had an abortion. The omission to inform, the result of an administrative mix-up, was held negligent, but the action failed on the ground of causation. On the evidence, she would have accepted the doctor's advice not to have the test repeated at a late stage in her pregnancy. See also *Fredette* v. *Wiebe* [1986] 5 W.W.R. 222 (B.C.S.C.) (n. 87, *post*), where the failure to inform the patient stemmed from the doctor's negligence in not reading the pathologist's report.

[86] (1979) 123 S.J. 406; aff'd (1980) (unreported), C.A. See also Medical Defence Union *Annual Report 1988*, p. 47.

[87] *Fredette* v. *Wiebe* [1986] 5 W.W.R. 222 (B.C.S.C.) is another example, where the plaintiff was unaware that an abortion operaton had failed to terminate her pregnancy, and subsequently decided to continue with the pregnancy. The defendant doctor was also unaware that the abortion had not succeeded because she negligently failed to examine a post-operative pathologist's report; *Cherry* v. *Borsman* (1991) 75 D.L.R. (4th) 668 (B.C.S.C.).

[88] [1977] 3 W.W.R. 109; aff'd [1978] 3 W.W.R. 481 (Alta. S.C. Appellate Div.).

may be as simple as requiring the patient to keep still or instructing the patient about taking medication in the right quantity and at the right times of day. It may also be necessary to give the patient a warning as to any danger signs that he should look out for (*e.g.* as to the side-effects of a drug or the symptoms that indicate that his condition is deteriorating) with instructions as to what should be done if they occur, such as stopping the medication or seeking medical assistance immediately.[89] Sometimes this will be absolutely vital. In these circumstances the doctor will be under a duty to take special care in giving the patient instructions in comprehensible terms, making sure that the patient understands both the instructions and the importance of strictly adhering to them.

4.42 A failure to inform the patient how to avoid the potential dangers involved in the treatment will be negligence. In *Stamos* v. *Davies*[90] the defendant was performing a lung biopsy, a procedure which required complete co-operation by the patient, in effect, to keep still while it was carried out. The defendant punctured the patient's spleen because, the judge held, the patient moved. The defendant was held negligent because he had failed to take the patient into his confidence by more, and effective, communication with him about what was required of him in this situation. Again, in *Clarke* v. *Adams*[91] the plaintiff was being treated for a fibrositic condition of the heel. He sustained a burning injury resulting in the leg being amputated below the knee. The defendant physiotherapist had given a warning to the plaintiff before administering the treatment in these terms: "When I turn on the machine I want you to experience a comfortable warmth and nothing more; if you do I want you to tell me." Slade J. held the defendant liable on the basis that the warning, although the very warning that he had been taught to give, was inadequate to enable the plaintiff to be safe, because the words used would not indicate to a reasonable person that his safety depended on his informing the defendant as soon as he felt more than a comfortable warmth: "The warning must be couched in terms which made it abundantly clear that it was a warning of danger." Similarly, where it is unwise for a patient to engage in certain types of activity following the treatment, he must be warned of the danger.[92]

4.43 A number of cases concern the failure of doctors to warn patients about the significance of the side-effects of drugs, and what they should do if the symptoms appear.[93] In *Crichton* v. *Hastings*[94] the

---

[89] See, *e.g.*, *Crossman* v. *Stewart* (1977) 82 D.L.R. (3d) 677, where the defendant doctor was held negligent for failing to identify the indications of side-effects. For the position where the risk of further injury is the result of something having gone wrong with the patient's treatment see § 4.34.

[90] (1986) 21 D.L.R. (4th) 507.

[91] (1950) 94 S.J. 599.

[92] *Brushett* v. *Cowan* (1987) 40 D.L.R. (4th) 488; aff'd (1990) 69 D.L.R. (4th) 743 (Newfd. C.A.), where the plaintiff was given crutches to use following a biopsy on her leg, but she was not warned that she should not bear weight on the leg. While engaging in ordinary activity without the crutches the leg broke at the site of the biopsy. The doctor was held negligent.

[93] "The physcian cannot always be in constant attendance upon his patient, who may have to be left to his own devices; and if the former knows of some specific danger and the possibility of its occurring, it may well be part of his duty to his patient to advise him of the proper action in such emergency," *per* Winter J. in *Murrin* v. *Janes* [1949] 4 D.L.R. 403, 405–406 (Newfd. S.C.).

[94] (1972) 29 D.L.R. (3d) 692 (Ont. C.A.).

plaintiff was prescribed an anti-coagulant drug, but she was given no warning about the dangerous side-effects (haemorrhage), nor any instructions as to the importance of immediately reporting the appearance of these side-effects to her doctor. This was held to be negligent. Similarly, in *Sheridan* v. *Boots Co. Ltd.*[95] a doctor who prescribed a potent anti-inflammatory drug, but failed to give the patient a warning that if he experienced any stomach trouble he should stop taking the drug and consult a doctor immediately was said to have been negligent.[96] In some instances the risk associated with the treatment may be so great that it will be negligence for the doctor to rely on the patient accurately reporting his symptoms. In *Marshall* v. *Rogers*[97] a diabetic patient wanted to reduce his dependence on insulin, so the defendant put him on a strict diet, and reduced the insulin dosage. The defendant told the patient to report any symptoms of the changed diet. The new treatment failed and the patient became ill. The defendant claimed that the damage was caused by the patient's negligence in failing to report his symptoms. The British Columbia Court of Appeal held that the defendant was negligent. He had admitted that the method he adopted was dangerous, and thus it was negligent not to perform daily tests on the patient and watch over the patient very carefully. Fisher J.A. said that:

" . . . in a case such as this, where admittedly a dangerous remedy was being tried . . . the appellant was negligent in delegating to the patient himself the duty of deciding what his real condition was from time to time from what might be called only his subjective symptoms without having daily tests made."[98]

4.44   If the patient's treatment has not been completed he should be told of this and advised to return for further treatment or to seek treatment elsewhere. The doctor has a responsibility to bring home to the patient the importance of obtaining further treatment and the dangers involved in failing to do so.[99] Where there is a risk that a patient who has been discharged from hospital following an operation may start bleeding again, or that some other emergency may arise, the surgeon should make suitable arrangements for the plaintiff to contact him.[1]

3. Failure to communicate with other health care professionals

4.45   A breakdown in essential communication between health care professionals with responsibility for the patient can have dangerous

---

[95] (1980) (unreported), Q.B.D.

[96] The claim failed because the omission did not cause the injury. The plaintiff contracted Stevens-Johnson syndrome, causing blindness. He did not suffer any symptoms of stomach disorder, and so even if he had been given the warning about stomach trouble he would not have gone back to the doctor earlier than he did.

[97] [1943] 4 D.L.R. 68 (B.C.C.A.).

[98] *Ibid.*, at p. 77; *cf. Battersby* v. *Tottman* (1985) 37 S.A.S.R. 524, where, in the circumstances, a failure to monitor the known and serious side-effects of a drug was held not negligent.

[99] *Coles* v. *Reading and District Hospital Management Committee* (1963) 107 S.J. 115, where the patient should have been warned of the importance of having an anti-tetanus injection.

[1] *Corder* v. *Banks*, *The Times*, April 9, 1960; *Videto* v. *Kennedy* (1980) 107 D.L.R. (3d) 612, 616–617; rev'd on other grounds (1981) 125 D.L.R. (3d) 127 (Ont. C.A.); *cf. Murrin* v. *Janes* [1949] 4 D.L.R. 403, where the plaintiff's delay in seeing a doctor to deal with excessive bleeding following the extraction of some teeth was held to be the sole cause of his misfortune.

consequences for the patient. These errors may be the result of isolated acts of carelessness or they may be the product of some organisational failure. The system of communication may be so poor that mistakes are almost inevitable, or the methods adopted may fail to take into account the risks of human error by providing some mechanism for checking.

A hospital authority must have an adequate system for summoning **4.46** specialist assistance when needed,[2] and there must be a system for dealing with a surgeon's patients when the surgeon goes away for a week-end.[3] It is also to be expected that there will be a system for communication between hospitals or between a hospital and general practitioners about the treatment that a patient has received. In *Coles* v. *Reading and District Hospital Management Committee*[4] a patient died of toxaemia due to tetanus infection because he had not received an anti-tetanus injection. The cottage hospital where he received his initial treatment told the patient to go to Battle hospital for further treatment, but he did not do so. He subsequently saw his own doctor, who made no inquiries as to what had happened at the hospital but simply redressed the wound. Sachs J. held the cottage hospital and the general practitioner negligent on the basis that they had omitted an elementary precaution of giving the anti-tetanus injection, and on the ground that the system of communication was inadequate. The patient should have been given a document to take to Battle hospital saying what treatment he had received. The responsibility for ensuring that there was a proper system of communication between hospitals rested on the hospital authorities not on individual nurses.[5]

This case can be contrasted with *Chapman* v. *Rix*[6] in which a patient **4.47** who had suffered a knife wound in the stomach visited a cottage hospital, where the defendant diagnosed wrongly that the wound had not penetrated the peritoneum. He sent the patient home, telling him to see his own doctor that evening and tell him what had happened. When the patient saw his own doctor he had symptoms of pain and nausea. He told the doctor that he had been told at the hospital that the wound was "superficial." The general practitioner, thinking that the patient had attended a general hospital accepted this statement and

---

[2] *Bull* v. *Devon Area Health Authority* (1989) (unreported), C.A., where Slade L.J. described the system of summoning expert obstetric assistance as "operating on a knife edge." The length of the delay pointed strongly either to inefficiency in the system or to negligence by some individual in working the system; *Denton* v. *South West Thames Regional Health Authority* (1980) (unreported), Q.B.D., where the lack of a system to check the safety of equipment was held to be negligent.

[3] *Cassidy* v. *Ministry of Health* [1951] 2 K.B. 343, 359, *per* Singleton L.J.; *Crichton* v. *Hastings* (1972) 29 D.L.R. (3d) 692, 700 (Ont. C.A.), held that a doctor who is going away and relinquishing to others the care of his patient should arrange for the patient to be given adequate warning of the dangers of developing side-effects from the prescribed medication; *Ball* v. *Howard, The Lancet*, February 2, 1924, p. 253, Q.B.D.

[4] (1963) 107 S.J. 115; see also *Schanczi* v. *Singh* [1988] 2 W.W.R. 465, (Alta. Q.B.) on a specialist's failure to obtain adequate information about a patient from the referring doctor before proceeding to surgery.

[5] "The N.H.S. had been developed on the basis that a patient might well be transferred for treatment from one person to another so that the responsibility for the patient shifted . . . Any system which failed to provide for adequate communication was wrong and negligently wrong," *per* Sachs J.

[6] (1959) 103 S.J. 940, C.A.; *The Times*, December 22, 1960, H.L.; see also *Seyfert* v. *Burnaby Hospital Society* (1986) 27 D.L.R. (4th) 96 on the diagnosis of penetrating stab wounds.

treated the patient for dyspepsia. Five days later the patient died of peritonitis, the wound having penetrated the small intestine. The trial judge had found the defendant liable on the basis that he had failed to communicate directly with the patient's own general practitioner. This was reversed on appeal. With hindsight it would have been better if the defendant had sent a letter to the patient's doctor, but that was not the kind of precaution which in practice was regularly adopted between general practitioners, and the expert witnesses approved of the defendant's conduct.

4.48 Breakdowns in communication between doctors, or doctors and nurses can also occur within hospitals if there is an inadequate system of consultation between them. A doctor who fails to read the nursing notes will probably be found negligent.[7] Relying too heavily on casual exchanges can also cause problems, and this was criticised in the Canadian case of *Bergen* v. *Sturgeon General Hospital*:

> "There appears to be an accepted practice of what is referred to as 'Curbstone Consultations.' This appears to happen when doctors casually meet in such places as hospital corridors and discuss a patient. In my opinion, this is bad practice and to be discouraged. It seems to me that when an attending physician calls in a specialist for a 'consultation' the least that might be expected is for those physicians to have a meaningful discussion between them, or among them, as the case may require, whereby each advises the other of what they did, when they did it, and what should be done. In this way each would be fully aware of the procedure of the other, the findings of the other and the reasons for the diagnosis arrived at by the other. In this case, such a consultation did not take place which, in my opinion, contributed to the bad result."[8]

4.49 Communication errors can occur from simply mishearing or misreading an instruction, sometimes with catastrophic consequences. This may be attributable to a single lapse of concentration by a doctor or nurse, but the further question may then arise as to whether there was any system for checking for such errors, given that it is known that mistakes do sometimes happen. In *Collins* v. *Hertfordshire County Council*[9] a patient died after being injected with cocaine instead of procaine as a local anaesthetic. The surgeon had told a junior, unqualified medical officer over the telephone his requirements for the operation the next day, and the word "procaine" was misheard for "cocaine." The pharmacist dispensing the drug at the hospital pharmacy did not question the order for an "unheard-of dosage" of a dangerous drug, and the surgeon did not check prior to injecting the solution that he was in fact injecting what he had ordered. It was held

---

[7] *Holmes* v. *Board of Hospital Trustees of the City of London* (1977) 81 D.L.R. (3d) 67, 94 (Ont. H.C.).

[8] (1984) 28 C.C.L.T. 155, 175, *per* Hope J.

[9] [1947] 1 K.B. 598; in *Strangeways-Lesmere* v. *Clayton* [1936] 2 K.B. 11 where a nurse who misread her instructions and gave an excess dose was held to be negligent.

that both the surgeon and the medical officer were liable, as was the hospital authority for having an unsafe system for dispensing.[10]

A doctor who prepares a report or medical notes which he is aware **4.50** may be relied upon by others for the treatment of the patient has a duty to exercise reasonable care in writing the report.[11] This also applies to the writing of a prescription which should be reasonably legible. For example, in *Prendergast* v. *Sam and Dee Ltd.*[12] the defendant general practitioner wrote a prescription for Amoxil for the plaintiff's chest infection. The pharmacist misread the doctor's writing, taking the word Amoxil for Daonil, a drug used to control diabetes. The plaintiff suffered symptoms of hypoglycaemia as a result of taking Daonil, since he was not a diabetic, and he was left with permanent brain damage. It was held that both the doctor and the pharmacist were negligent. A doctor has a duty to his patients to write a prescription clearly, and must allow for some mistakes or carelessness on the part of a busy chemist. Standing on its own the prescription could reasonably have been read incorrectly, and thus the doctor was liable, notwithstanding that there were other factors which should have alerted the pharmacist to the possibility of error. The pharmacist has a duty to give some thought to the prescriptions he is dispensing and should not dispense them mechanically; if there is doubt he should contact the doctor for clarification. If he had been paying attention he would have realised that there was something wrong with the prescription, since the dosage and the small number of tablets were unusual for Daonil; moreover, the plaintiff paid for the prescription whereas drugs for diabetes were free under the N.H.S.[13]

A pathologist who has been given specimens for testing or analysis **4.51** owes a duty to the patient not only to conduct the test in a proper manner but also to take reasonable steps to communicate the results to the referring doctor, and it is irrelevant that the doctor also has a corresponding duty to find out the results.[14]

IV. ERRORS IN TREATMENT

Errors in treatment can take a multitude of forms. They may arise **4.52** from the defendant's lack of knowledge (*e.g.* as to the generally known

---

[10] *cf. Fussell* v. *Beddard* (1942) 2 B.M.J. 411, in which a patient received a fatal overdose of anaesthetic because the nurse misheard the anaesthetist's instructions about the strength of the dose. The patient received a 1 per cent. solution of decicaine instead of 0.1 per cent. Lewis J. said that when the nurse is inexperienced the surgeon and the anaesthetist should take care to see that she is carrying out or is competent to carry out the duties assigned to her, but when the nurse is experienced they are entitled to rely on her to carry out their instructions. His Lordship held that neither the anaesthetist nor the nurse had been negligent, but that an unfortunate mistake had been made. It would be difficult to support such a remarkable conclusion on negligence today.

[11] *Everett* v. *Griffiths* [1920] 3 K.B. 163, 213.

[12] [1989] 1 Med. L.R. 36, C.A.

[13] For similar cases of negligence by a pharmacist failing to spot prescription errors see *Collins* v. *Hertfordshire County Council* [1947] 1 K.B. 598 and *Dwyer* v. *Roderick, The Times*, November 12, 1983; McKevitt (1988) 4 P.N. 185.

[14] *Thomsen* v. *Davison* [1975] Qd. R. 93; see also *McKay* v. *Essex Area Health Authority* [1982] Q.B. 1166 on an alleged omission to communicate test results; *Gregory* v. *Pembrokeshire Health Authority* [1989] 1 Med. L.R. 81, C.A.; *Fredette* v. *Wiebe* [1986] 5 W.W.R. 222.

adverse reactions of a drug[15]), a lack of skill in performing a particular procedure (*e.g.* where the doctor is inexperienced[16]), a momentary, inadvertent slip (*e.g.* with a surgical instrument during the course of an operation[17]) or a conscious decision by the doctor to depart from the standard procedure normally employed in the circumstances.[18] Categorising the defendant's conduct as an error or a mistake does not, however, determine the issue of negligence. The question remains whether the error was such as no reasonably competent doctor exercising ordinary care would have made, applying the *Bolam* test. Thus, even where it is proved that the defendant made a mistake and that the plaintiff's injury was caused by that mistake, the plaintiff must still show that it was an unreasonable mistake.

4.53 Where the doctor has made a conscious decision to depart from the standard treatment, this may be evidence of negligence, but it is not necessarily conclusive.[19] The decision may well be justified by the particular circumstances of the patient, it being remembered that doctors have to treat the individual patient and not the "standard" patient found in the textbooks.[20] On the other hand, a substantial departure from accepted practice, even undertaken consciously and in full knowledge of the potential risks, will place a heavy onus on the defendant to justify his decision. If he cannot do so he will be found liable.[21]

4.54 If the defendant has taken a conscious decision about the balance of risks and benefits attached to a proposed treatment, then he has exercised a "professional judgment." To describe a mistake as an "error of professional judgment" is unhelpful, however, in determining the question of negligence because some such errors "may be so glaringly below proper standards as to make a finding of negligence inevitable."[22] But, in the nature of things, if a doctor has taken a considered decision it may be more difficult to conclude that there has been negligence than where he has made an unintentional or inadvertent "error," since there has been no balancing of risks and benefits. For example, in *Goode* v. *Nash*[23] the Supreme Court of South Australia declined to characterise the defendant's conduct as a "mere error of professional judgment," because:

> "There was indeed no exercise of a decision-making process at all, nor the taking of a calculated risk. There was simply a failure, however unintentional and inadvertent, to observe the obvious but critical precaution of ensuring that the instrument was not too hot to place upon the patient's eye."

---

[15] See *Reynard* v. *Carr* (1983) 30 C.C.L.T. 42 (B.C.S.C.).

[16] *Jones* v. *Manchester Corporation* [1952] 2 All E.R. 125.

[17] *Gonda* v. *Kerbel* (1982) 24 C.C.L.T. 222.

[18] *Clark* v. *MacLennan* [1983] 1 All E.R. 416.

[19] See §§ 3.32–3.37. Remember also that there may be more than one accepted practice. Adopting one rather than another is not negligence.

[20] *Holland* v. *The Devitt & Moore Nautical College, The Times*, March 4, 1960, in which Streatfield J. held that a doctor whose treatment had departed from the recommendations of the textbooks was not negligent. A doctor was entitled to use his experience and common sense, and a slight departure from the textbook was not necessarily a mistake let alone negligence.

[21] *Clark* v. *MacLennan* [1983] 1 All E.R. 416; see § 3.33.

[22] *Whitehouse* v. *Jordan* [1981] 1 All E.R. 267, 276, *per* Lord Edmund-Davies; see § 3.51.

[23] (1979) 21 S.A.S.R. 419, 423.

On the other hand, it is not negligence if the decision, which is **4.55** probably the wisest one in the circumstances, is reached by accident rather than by design, even where the accident was created by faulty management procedures.[24]

Most instances of negligence probably arise from simple, inadvertent **4.56** errors that even the defendant would concede should not have been made (although he might not concede that the error amounted to negligence).[25]

1. Operations

Difficulties may arise in assessing negligence in performing oper- **4.57** ations because of the number of people involved (surgeon(s), anaesthetist, nurses) each with their own duties and responsibilities. In the case of operations under the N.H.S., from the patient's point of view it does not matter if he cannot identify the particular person at fault, provided he can prove fault on the part of someone for whom the hospital authorities will be vicariously liable.[26] With private treatment, where the patient has contracted with a specific surgeon for whom the hospital is not vicariously responsible, it may be more important for the patient to be able to identify the person at fault. Moreover, from the defendants' perspective it will always be relevant to determine who was to blame.

Normally, a doctor will not be responsible for the negligence of **4.58** others, such as nurses, in carrying out the instructions that have been given with regard to the patient's treatment.[27] Nursing staff remain the employees of the hospital:

" . . . the true ground on which the hospital escapes liability for the act of a nurse who, whether in the operating theatre or

---

[24] *Lachambre* v. *Nair* [1989] 2 W.W.R. 749 (Sask. Q.B.).

[25] This includes, *e.g.* damage caused by surgical instruments (*Leckie* v. *Brent & Harrow Area Health Authority* (1982) (unreported), Q.B.D., where a scalpel cut of a baby's face during the performance of a Caesarian section, was held to be negligent; *Gonda* v. *Kerbel* (1982) 24 C.C.L.T. 222, where the perforation of the plaintiff's bowel during a bowel examination by sigmoidoscope raised an inference of negligence) or during post-operative treatment (*Powell* v. *Streatham Manor Nursing Home* [1935] A.C. 243, where a patient's bladder was punctured by a catheter inserted by a nurse; see also *Cassidy* v. *Ministry of Health* [1951] 2 K.B. 343, 355, on post-operative care); unnecessary and gross cosmetic distortion following breast reduction surgery (*Mac-Donald* v. *Ross* (1983) 24 C.C.L.T. 242 (N.S.S.C.); see also *White* v. *Turner* (1981) 120 D.L.R. (3d) 269; (1982) 12 D.L.R. (4th) 319, on breast reduction surgery; and Medical Defence Union *Annual Report 1989* p. 43); administering the wrong anaesthetic (*Collins* v. *Hertfordshire County Council* [1947] 1 K.B. 598) or too much anaesthetic (*Jones* v. *Manchester Corporation* [1952] 2 All E.R. 125); prescribing the wrong dosage of a drug (*Dwyer* v. *Roderick, The Times,* November 12, 1983) or injecting the wrong dosage by mistake (*Strangeways-Lesmere* v. *Clayton* [1936] 2 K.B. 11); damaging a nerve while administering an injection (*Caldeira* v. *Gray* [1936] 1 All E.R. 540); allowing an elderly patient to fall off a trolley (*Smith* v. *Lewisham Group Hospital Management Committee* (1955) 2 B.M.J. 65; *cf. Robertson* v. *Smyth* (1979) 20 S.A.S.R. 184, where there was no duty to assist a patient descending from an examination table); failing to check the position of a catheter monitoring the blood oxygen level of a premature baby (*Wilsher* v. *Essex Area Health Authority* [1986] 3 All E.R. 801).

[26] *Cassidy* v. *Ministry of Health* [1951] 2 K.B. 343.

[27] *Perinowsky* v. *Freeman* (1866) 4 F. & F. 977; *Morris* v. *Winsbury-White* [1937] 4 All E.R. 494, 498. In *Wilsher* v. *Essex Area Health Authority* [1986] 3 All E.R. 801, 812–813, Mustill L.J. said that the law does not recognise the concept of "team negligence" (although this comment was directed at the standard of care to be expected from individual members of the team).

elsewhere, is acting under the instructions of the surgeon or doctor is, not that *pro hac vice* she ceases to be the servant of the hospital, but that she is not guilty of negligence if she carries out the orders of the surgeon, however negligent those orders may be."[28]

The fact that a nurse acts under the instructions of a doctor, however, does not mean that she is excused from making any professional judgment. There may be circumstances where a nurse could be negligent even though following a doctor's instructions. For example, if a doctor ordered an obviously incorrect and dangerous dosage of a drug, a nurse who administered it without obtaining confirmation from the doctor or higher authority might well be found negligent.[29] Similarly, a pharmacists has been held to be negligent for failing to check a request for an "unheard-of dosage" of cocaine.[30]

4.59 Conversely, the doctor may be negligent if he knows or ought reasonably to have known that another person in the team, whether it be the anaesthetist or a nurse, has done something which puts the patient at risk but fails to take any steps to remedy the error.[31] He will also have a responsibility to take into account the possibility of error by another, for example, by making some check of what he is about to inject into a patient.[32]

4.60 The courts have long recognised that the mere fact that something has gone wrong during the course of an operation is not *per se* indicative of negligence. Thus, where a surgeon accidentally cut the patient's retina in the course of an operation on his eye this was held not to be negligent, because the surgeon was working within an extremely small margin of error.[33] Similarly, the fact that a patient sustained damage to a facial nerve does not indicate that the surgeon

---

[28] *Gold* v. *Essex County Council* [1942] 2 K.B. 293, 299, *per* Lord Greene M.R.

[29] *Ibid.*, p. 313, *per* Goddard L.J., although his Lordship added that: "In the stress of an operation, however, I should suppose that the first thing required of a nurse would be an unhesitating obedience to the orders of the surgeon." See also the analogus case of *Davy-Chiesman* v. *Davy-Chiesman* [1984] 1 All E.R. 321, 332, 335, stating that solicitors should not rely blindly on the advice of counsel.

[30] *Collins* v. *Hertfordshire County Council* [1947] 1 K.B. 598.

[31] *Perinowsky* v. *Freeman* (1866) 4 F. & F. 977, 982; *Wilsher* v.*Essex Area Health Authority* [1986] 3 All E.R. 801, where the registrar was held to have been negligent in failing to spot the senior house officer's error. In *Jones* v. *Manchester Corporation* [1952] 2 All E.R. 125 the Court of Appeal took the view that the inexperienced doctor who administered the fatal injection was not as culpable as the experienced doctor who supervised her: "She administered the pentothal under his very eyes and to his entire approval. In these circumstances it seems to me that her share in the responsibility is much less than his," *per* Denning L.J. at p. 871.

[32] *Collins* v. *Hertfordshire County Council* [1947] 1 K.B. 598; see § 4.49.

[33] *White* v. *Westminister Hospital Board of Governors*, *The Times*, October 26, 1961; see also *Chubey* v. *Ahsan* (1977) 71 D.L.R. (3d) 550 (Man. C.A.), where an orthopaedic surgeon who inadvertently pierced the aorta and vena cava during spinal surgery was held not negligent because this was recognised as an inherent risk of the procedure, albeit a remote risk; *Kapur* v. *Marshall* (1978) 85 D.L.R. (3d) 567, 573, *per* Robins J. (Ont. H.C.): "That the accident happened in this case, when it so rarely does happen, does not compel, as in effect was argued, a finding of negligence. An unfavourable result is not synonymous with negligence. A surgeon is not an insurer"; *cf.* the comments of Freedman C.J.M. (dissenting) in *Chubey* v. *Ahsan* (1977) 71 D.L.R. (3d) 550, 552, cited at § 3.110, n. 47.

used excessive force in removing granulated tissue from the eardrum.[34] On the other hand, a surgeon who accidentally knocked out four of patient's teeth during a tonsilectomy had fallen below a proper standard of care.[35]

A doctor may be liable for proceeding to an operation too quickly **4.61** without considering the alternative treatments available. In *Schanczi* v. *Singh*[36] the defendant surgeon was held negligent for failing to attempt conservative treatment before resorting to spinal surgery:

> "For a specialist to plunge ahead and operate in the circumstances was exercising entirely undue haste . . ... A surgeon is retained to perform surgery, but also to avoid performing surgery in the appropriate circumstances."[37]

Conversely, a delay in recommending surgery may also be negligent. In *Powell* v. *Guttman*[38] the plaintiff developed a condition of avascular necrosis following an operation on her leg performed by the defendant orthopaedic surgeon. The defendant failed to advise the plaintiff to undergo an arthoplasty operation to correct this. A year after the first operation another surgeon performed the operation, and during the course of that operation the plaintiff sustained a rotary fracture of the femur. Due to the delay, the condition of the bone had deteriorated as a result of osteoporsis, and this was a "significant cause" of the fracture that occurred. The defendant was held liable on the basis that the delay in the second operation was attributable to his negligence, and this had caused an increase in the osteoporosis which rendered the femur more susceptible to fracture. This "materially increased the risk of the very fracture which did occur."[39]

Burns

Where a patient sustains burns in an operating theatre this is usually **4.62** indicative of negligence. Thus, anaesthetists have been held liable for an explosion caused by a spark igniting a mixture of ether and oxygen,[40] and for knocking a bottle of ether over onto an electric fire.[41]

---

[34] *Ashcroft* v. *Merseyside Regional Health Authority* [1983] 2 All E.R. 245; aff'd [1985] 2 All E.R. 96; *Whitehouse* v. *Jordan* [1981] 1 All E.R. 267, where the defendant was held not to have pulled too long and too hard in the course of a forceps delivery; *Goguen* v. *Crowe* (1987) 40 C.C.L.T. 212 (Nova Scotia S.C.). For discussion of the "obstetric nemesis" which it is claimed that *Whitehouse* v. *Jordan* has precipitated see Symonds (1989) 5 J. of the M.D.U. 52.

[35] *Munro* v. *United Oxford Hospitals* (1958) 1 B.M.J. 167.

[36] [1988] 2 W.W.R. 465 (Alta. Q.B.).

[37] *Ibid.*, p. 472, *per* Marshall J.; see also *Coughlin* v. *Kuntz* (1987) 42 C.C.L.T. 142 (B.C.S.C.); aff'd [1990] 2 W.W.R. 737, 744 (B.C.C.A.), on a failure to try conservative treatment before surgery; *Haughian* v. *Paine* (1987) 37 D.L.R. (4th) 625, 629–635 (Sask. C.A.). In *Goguen* v. *Crowe* (1987) 40 C.C.L.T. 212 (Nova Scotia S.C.) it was alleged that the defendant obstetrician had intervened prematurely with the use of forceps to deliver a baby who sustained cerebral palsy; this was found, with hindsight, to have been an "error of judgment" but not, on the facts, negligent.

[38] (1978) 89 D.L.R. (3d) 180 (Man. C.A.).

[39] *Ibid.*, p. 188; see further § 5.27 on the causation aspects of this decision.

[40] *Crits* v. *Sylvester* (1956) 1 D.L.R. (2d) 502; aff'd (1956) 5 D.L.R. (2d) 601 (S.C.C.).

[41] *Paton* v. *Parker* (1942) 65 C.L.R. 187. For discussion of appropriate anaesthetic practice in the course of a difficult intubation see *Chambers* v. *Southern Health and Social Services Board* [1990] 1 Med. L.R. 231.

It is negligence to allow a patient's arm to hang over the side of the operating table and come into contact with a hot water can,[42] and where alcohol used to sterilise the patient's body is ignited on the application of a diathermy electrode.[43] In *Clarke* v. *Warboys*[44] the plaintiff was undergoing an operation in which extensive bleeding was anticipated, and so electric coagulation was applied. This involved passing a high frequency electrical current through her body, and for this purpose a pad was placed on her buttock. She sustained a severe burn at the site of the pad. The Court of Appeal held the defendants liable, applying *res ipsa loquitur*. Such an accident did not normally happen if reasonable care was exercised. A patient who sustained burns on her face from the use of Grenz rays succeeded in an action against the radiotherapist who had omitted to cover the face with a protective cloth.[45]

"Swab" cases

4.63   The danger of swabs or surgical instruments being left inside the patient at the end of an operation is clearly something which must be guarded against. But, even in this type of case where the risk of harm to the patient is obvious, the doctor does not give a guarantee that this cannot happen. He is not absolutely liable for leaving a swab behind, but must exercise reasonable care to see that it does not happen. The consequences can be very serious and accordingly the degree of care required in order to satisfy the requirement of reasonableness may be very high indeed. The precautions which can be adopted with swabs include using swabs with tapes to flag their position, a count by nurses, and a search by the surgeon at the conclusion of the operation.

4.64   It is not negligence for a surgeon to delegate the task of counting swabs to a nurse, but the question remains as to the extent of his responsibility. A surgeon will not necessarily avoid liability by relying on the count by the nurse:

> "As it is the task of the surgeon to put swabs in, so it is his task to take them out, and in that task he must use that degree of care which is reasonable in the circumstances and that must depend on the evidence. If, on the whole of the evidence, it is shown that he

---

[42] *Hillyer* v. *Governors of St. Bartholomew's Hospital* [1909] 2 K.B. 820, although the case turned on the question of the hospital authority's liability for the negligence of its professional staff. A similar case is *Hall* v. *Lees* [1904] 2 K.B. 602, where a nurse negligently placed a hot water bottle against a patient still under the influence of anaesthetic. The report deals with the question of the liability of the nursing association who employed the nurse.

[43] *Crysler* v. *Pearse* [1943] 4 D.L.R. 738, where the excess alcohol should have been swabbed off or allowed to evaporate; *cf. McFadyen* v. *Harvie* [1941] 2 D.L.R. 663; aff'd [1942] 4 D.L.R. 647, where, in the process of cauterising an ulcer on the plaintiff's body, there was a flash. Alcohol had been applied to the site to sterilise it. A jury held that there was no evidence of how the accident occurred.

[44] *The Times*, March 18, 1952. Burns to the buttocks following surgery are, apparently, a common type of claim: Medical Defence Union *Annual Report 1990*, p. 45.

[45] *Gold* v. *Essex County Council* [1942] 2 K.B. 293; *McCaffrey* v. *Hague* [1949] 4 D.L.R. 291, where burns were caused by an excessive dose of X-rays; *Goode* v. *Nash* (1979) 21 S.A.S.R. 419, where a patient's eye was burned by an instrument placed on the eye before it had cooled sufficiently after being sterilised.

did not use that standard of care, he cannot absolve himself if a mistake be made, by saying 'I relied on the nurse.' "[46]

He must, at the very least, make some check by asking for confirmation that all the swabs are accounted for; he cannot assume this.[47] In some circumstances the surgeon may have to take additional precautions. In *Urry* v. *Bierer*[48] a surgeon conducting a Caesarian section relied almost exclusively on the count. He did not use swabs with tapes. Pearson J. held that in a routine operation it was negligent not to take any additional precautions, although different considerations might apply in an emergency. The nurses' count might be fallible, and was itself meant to be a secondary check on the procedure adopted by the surgeon for removing the swabs. This decision was affirmed by the Court of Appeal. There was no reason, it was said, why the surgeon should not make some mental effort to remember where he had placed the swabs, particularly since he had chosen not to use tapes.

In *Anderson* v. *Chasney*[49] the child patient died following an **4.65** operation to remove his tonsils because a sponge was left in the base of the child's nostrils causing suffocation. It was not the surgeon's practice to use sponges with tapes attached nor to have a nurse present to keep a count of the sponges used, although sponges with tapes were available and the hospital would supply a nurse, on request, to keep a count. The surgeon asked his assistant at the operation whether all the sponges were removed, and the assistant had replied, no. He felt for any remaining sponges and found none. When, after the operation, it was noticed that the child was not breathing a nurse managed to remove the sponge. The Manitoba Court of Appeal, holding the defendant liable, rejected the contention that since he had complied with the accepted practice at the hospital he was not negligent:

> "While the method in which the operation was performed may be purely a matter of technical evidence, the fact that a sponge was left in a position where it was or was not dangerous is one which the ordinary man is competent to consider in arriving at a decision as to whether or not there was negligence."[50]

On the other hand, although leaving a swab in the patient will be **4.66** strong evidence of negligence it is not necessarily conclusive. This point is emphasised in the judgment of Scott L.J. in *Mahon* v. *Osborne*,[51] where his Lordship identified some of the factors that might have to be taken into account:

> "It is not every slip or mistake which imports negligence and, in applying the duty of care to the case of a surgeon, it is peculiarly

---

[46] *Mahon* v. *Osborne* [1939] 2 K.B. 14, 47, *per* Goddard L.J. (dissenting). See also the extract from *James* v. *Dunlop* (1931) 1 B.M.J. 730, cited by Goddard L.J. at pp. 47–48; and MacKinnon L.J. at pp. 42–43.

[47] *Mahon* v., *Osborne* [1939] 2 K.B. 14; *James* v. *Dunlop* (1931) 1 B.M.J. 730, C.A., discussed in *Mahon* v. *Osborne*.

[48] *The Times*, July 15, 1955, C.A.

[49] [1949] 4 D.L.R. 71 (Man. C.A.); aff'd *sub nom. Chasney* v. *Anderson* [1950] 4 D.L.R. 223 (S.C.C.).

[50] *Ibid.*, p. 74, *per* McPherson C.J.M.

[51] [1939] 2 K.B. 14. Note, however, that Scott L.J. dissented on the question of whether *res ipsa loquitur* applied to a swab case.

necessary to have regard to the different kinds of circumstances that may present themselves for urgent attention. I will mention a few applicable to a major abdominal operation: (1) The multiform difficulties presented by the particular circumstances of the operation, (2) the condition of the patient and the whole set of problems arising out of the risks to which he is being exposed, (3) the difficulty of the surgeon's choice between risks, (4) the paramount need of his discretion being unfettered if he thinks it right to take one risk to avoid a greater, (5) at the penultimate stage (swab removal) he may, particularly where the patient has been taking the anaesthetic badly and is suffering from shock, be so anxious on surgical grounds to bring the operation to an end as rapidly as possible that, in the exercise of his discretion, perhaps unconsciously exercised, as soon as he has completed the removal of all swabs of which he is at that moment aware he asks the sister for the count and forthwith starts to close the wound."[52]

4.67   In *Anderson* v. *Chasney*[53] Coyne J.A. regarded *Mahon* v. *Osborne* as an unsatisfactory case which turned ultimately on a misdirection of the jury. There is, however, a significant difference between the two cases. In *Mahon* v. *Osborne* it was an emergency operation for a perforated duodenal ulcer which the surgeon performed alone. It was a complicated and urgent operation and there was a system for counting the swabs. But in *Anderson* v. *Chasney* it was a routine operation in which there was no system for counting. These circumstances may justify a different conclusion on negligence, although *Mahon* v. *Osborne* probably makes the position in swab cases seem more complicated than it is. In practice such cases are usually settled as indefensible, and most of the cases that are litigated end in a finding of negligence.[54] Even if, on the facts, the conclusion is that the surgeon was not negligent in leaving the swab inside the patient, the result will almost invariably be that the nurse conducting the count was negligent. The position will usually be the same in the case of a surgical instrument left inside the patient's body.[55]

---

[52] *Ibid.*, pp. 31–32. See also, *per* Adamson J.A. in *Anderson* v. *Chasney* [1949] 4 D.L.R. 71, 94: "If a surgeon places a foreign article or substance such as a sponge or instrument in the body of a patient and fails to remove it and the patient is thereby injured, it is evidence of lack of care. Whether it should be held to be negligence depends on the circumstances in each particular case."

[53] [1949] 4 D.L.R. 71 (Man. C.A.); aff'd *sub nom. Chasney* v. *Anderson* [1950] 4 D.L.R. 223 (S.C.C.).

[54] See, *e.g., James* v. *Dunlop* (1931) 1 B.M.J. 730, which is considered in *Mahon* v. *Obsorne* [1939] 2 K.B. 14; *Dryden* v. *Surrey County Council* [1936] 2 All E.R. 535; *Holt* v. *Nesbitt* [1951] 4 D.L.R. 478 where a dental patient died of asphyxia when a swab lodged in his windpipe; the dentist, who had made no count of swabs used and assumed that they had all been removed when he could see no swabs in the patient's mouth, was held liable; *Garner* v. *Morrell, The Times*, October 31, 1953, where on similar facts the Court of Appeal held the defendant liable on the basis of *res ipsa loquitur; Urry* v. *Bierer, The Times*, July 15, 1955; *Fox* v. *Glasgow South Western Hospitals* 1955 S.L.T. 337; *Cooper* v. *Nevill, The Times*, March 10, 1961 (P.C.).

[55] *Hocking* v. *Bell* [1948] W.N. 21 (P.C.), where part of a drainage tube was left *in situ*, following a thyroidectomy operation; the defendant was held negligent; *Gloning* v. *Miller* [1954] 1 D.L.R. 372, where a surgeon who left pair of forceps inside a patient was held negligent. No count was made, and no other precautions were taken at the time of the operation; *cf. McDonald* v. *Pottinger* [1953] N.Z.L.R. 196—another forceps case, where a jury found that the surgeon was not guilty of negligence.

Failed sterilisation

There have been a number of cases arising from an unwanted **4.68** pregnancy following a sterilisation operation. Despite some initial reluctance the courts have now accepted that there are no good policy grounds for refusing to award damages for the cost of raising an unplanned child, following a negligently performed sterilisation operation, irrespective of whether the child is healthy or has disabilities.[56] The cases tend to fall into two (not mutually exclusive) categories: (i) where the plaintiff alleges that the sterilisation operation itself was performed negligently[57]; and (ii) where, although the operation was performed with reasonable care, the defendant failed adequately to inform the plaintiff about the risks of the procedure failing to achieve the desired result of rendering the plaintiff sterile.[58] It is well-known, at least within the medical profession, that there is a risk that a sterilisation operation will prove to be unsuccesssful, and the risk varies with the type of operation and the time at which it is carried out.[59] The fact that these procedures carry a small, but quantifiable, failure rate can make it difficult to prove that there has been negligence in the performance of the operation itself.[60] Thus, in *Grey* v. *Webster*[61] the plaintiff's claim was unsuccessful because the evidence showed that a failed sterilisation can occur without negligence and the procedure adopted by the defendant was approved by expert evidence. But as Bouck J. commented in *Dendaas* v. *Yackel*,[62] referring to failure rates of 3 to 17 per 1,000 for tubal ligation "there was of course no indication as to how many of these resulted from improper or negligent

---

[56] *Emeh* v. *Kensington and Chelsea Area Health Authority* [1984] 3 All E.R. 1044, C.A., overruling *Udale* v. *Bloomsbury Area Health Authority* [1983] 2 All E.R. 522. For discussion of the policy considerations involved in the assessment of damages see § 9.56. The plaintiff's refusal to undergo an abortion when she discovers that she is pregnant does not amount to a *novus actus interveniens*: *Emeh* v. *Kensington and Chelsea Area Health Authority*, see § 5.60; see further Rogers (1985) 5 L.S. 296; Argent (1985) 25 Med. Sci. and Law 136.

[57] *Udale* v. *Bloomsbury Area Health Authority* [1983] 2 All E.R. 522; *Emeh* v. *Kensington and Chelsea Area Health Authority* [1984] 3 All E.R. 1044; *Dendaas* v. *Yackel* (1980) 109 D.L.R. (3d) 455. For unusual examples of failed sterilisation, where the procedure was experimental see: *Cryderman* v. *Ringrose* [1978] 3 W.W.R. 481 (Alta. C.A.), and *Zimmer* v. *Ringrose* (1981) 125 D.L.R. (3d) 215 (Alta. C.A.). On the negligent performance of an abortion see *Scuriaga* v. *Powell* (1979) 123 S.J. 406; aff'd (1980) (unreported), C.A., (§ 4.39, *ante*); *Fredette* v. *Wiebe* [1986] 5 W.W.R. 222 (B.C.S.C.); *Cherry* v. *Borsman* (1991) 75 D.L.R. (4th) 668 (B.C.S.C.).

[58] *Eyre* v. *Measday* [1986] 1 All E.R. 488; *Thake* v. *Maurice* [1986] 1 All E.R. 497; *Gold* v. *Haringey Health Authority* [1987] 2 All E.R. 888; *Dendaas* v. *Yackel* (1980) 109 D.L.R. (3d) 455; *Grey* v. *Webster* (1984) 14 D.L.R. (4th) 706; *Videto* v. *Kennedy* (1981) 125 D.L.R. (3d) 127 (Ont. C.A.—risk of bowel perforation). On the non-disclosure of the risk of the sterilisation failing see § 6.131.

[59] See, *e.g*, *Eyre* v. *Measday* [1986] 1 All E.R. 488, 490–491; *Gold* v. *Haringey Health Authority* [1987] 2 All E.R. 888, 890; *Videto* v. *Kennedy* (1980) 107 D.L.R. (3d) 612, 618 (Ont. H.C.).

[60] In *Udale* v. *Bloomsbury Area Health Authority* [1983] 2 All E.R. 522 liability was admitted, and the report was concerned only with the assessment of damages. Similarly, the report in *Emeh* v. *Kensington and Chelsea Area Health Authority* [1984] 3 All E.R. 1044 proceeds on the assumption that the defendants' negligence had been established.

[61] (1984) 14 D.L.R. (4th) 706 (N.B.Q.B.); *Videto* v. *Kennedy* (1980) 107 D.L.R. (3d) 612, 618 (Ont. H.C.). Similarly, an allegation that the sterilisation had been negligently performed was rejected by the trial judge in *Gold* v. *Haringey Health Authority* [1987] 2 All E.R. 888, and abandoned by the plaintiff in *Eyre* v. *Measday* [1986] 1 All E.R. 488.

[62] (1980) 109 D.L.R. (3d) 455 (B.C.S.C.).

technique and how many came about because of matters beyond the control of the surgeon." In that case the defendant was held liable for the negligent performance of the operation itself, because in a subsequent tubal ligation performed on the plaintiff the surgeon found inadequate cauterisation of the fallopian tubes, and the judge was able to conclude that, on the balance of probabilities, for reasons unknown, the defendant did not properly cauterise the tubes.

2. Causing or failing to prevent infection

4.69   The commonest type of case falling into this category is that of a patient who acquires an infection during a stay in hospital. More rarely a patient may be discharged from hospital in an infectious condition and infect someone else with whom he comes into contact. About 10 per cent. of patients pick up infections while they are in hospital, and this costs the N.H.S. more than £110 million a year. Some of these cases are unavoidable, but some are due to medical staff ignoring basic hygiene rules.[63] Cases may arise from cross-infection, with patients acquiring a disease from another patient, or they may result from surgical intervention.

4.70   In *Lindsey County Council* v. *Marshall*[64] the plaintiff was admitted to the defendant's maternity home notwithstanding an outbreak of puerperal fever in the home a week earlier. Neither the plaintiff nor her doctor was informed of the outbreak. The House of Lords held the defendants liable on the basis of a breach of the general duty owed by occupiers of premises to entrants to ensure that premises are reasonably safe. Lord Wright said that he did "not put the obligation as high as that of a warranty; but the gravity of the risk must emphasise the gravity of the precautions proper to be taken to guard against it."[65] Similarly, in *Heafield* v. *Crane*[66] the plaintiff was admitted to a cottage hospital for her confinement. After the birth she was moved from the maternity ward to a general ward where a patient was suffering from puerperal fever, and the plaintiff caught the infection from this patient. Singleton J. held that the hospital authorities were negligent in placing the plaintiff in a ward where there was a gravely suspicious case of infection, and in failing to warn the plaintiff. The plaintiff's doctor was negligent because he ought to have isolated the other patient (he was her doctor too) and when he found that the plaintiff had been placed in the same ward he should have had her moved to prevent her becoming infected.

4.71   In *Vancouver General Hospital* v. *McDaniel*[67] the plaintiff went into a hospital for infectious diseases for the treatment of diphtheria, and contracted smallpox. She claimed that the defendants were negligent in the system that they adopted, which involved the juxtaposition of smallpox patients to the plaintiff, and the attendance on the plaintiff by nurses who also nursed smallpox patients. On appeal to the Privy

---

[63] *The Times*, September 4, 1990. See also Cooke (1989) 5 J. of the M.D.U. 62.
[64] [1937] A.C. 97.
[65] *Ibid.*, p. 121.
[66] *The Times*, July 31, 1937.
[67] (1934) 152 L.T. 56.

Council it was held that the defendants had not been negligent to adopt a new system for managing infectious patients by sterilisation rather than isolation, because they had conformed to a practice accepted as proper by a responsible body of professional opinion.[68] At the time of this decision the plaintiff would have been unable to proceed against the hospital on the basis that it was vicariously liable for the negligence of the staff in implementing the system of sterilisation that had been adopted.[69] Today, however, such a claim could be made and it would be irrelevant that the plaintiff was unable to identify which employee was at fault.[70] Moreover, the stronger the evidence that the defendants' system was foolproof, the easier it is to infer that if cross-infection occurred it must have been caused by the negligence of one of the hospital staff in applying the system.[71] This point is illustrated by *Voller* v. *Portsmouth Corporation*[72] in which the plaintiff developed meningitis after the administration of a spinal anaesthetic. It was admitted that the illness must have been caused either by contamination of the anaesthetic or by an infection occurring during its administration. The court found that the anaesthetic was not contaminated, and the staff had taken the usual precautions to disinfected themselves prior to the operation, but nonetheless held the hospital liable. It could not be said precisely how the accident occurred but there must have been some failure to follow the appropriate sterilisation procedure resulting in contamination from the equipment used.

In the case of post-operative infection, the infection itself cannot be **4.72** treated as evidence of negligence, because no-one can guarantee that the post-operative infection will not occur.[73] On the other hand, it is not unreasonable to expect that specialists should be quick to recognise the development of complications following surgery, such as infection, at the earliest possible moment and to treat them accordingly.[74]

Discharging an infectious patient from hospital prematurely with the **4.73** result that others who come into contact with the patient contract the disease is negligent.[75]

Some cases of infection arise from the transplantation of human **4.74** organs or the transfusion of bodily fluids from a donor who carried the

---

[68] See §§ 3.15 *et seq.*

[69] Applying *Hillyer* v. *Governors of St. Bartholemews Hospital* [1909] 2 K.B. 820; see § 7.03.

[70] *Cassidy* v. *Ministry of Health* [1951] 2 K.B. 343.

[71] There is an analogy here with the inference that may be drawn as to negligence by an employee where a product has a construction defect and the manufacturer claims that the manufacturing or quality control system is designed to be foolproof: see § 8.47.

[72] (1947) 203 L.T.J. 264.

[73] *Hajgato* v. *London Health Association* (1982) 36 O.R. (2d) 669, 681 (Ont. H.C.).

[74] *Reitze* v. *Bruser* (No. 2) [1979] 1 W.W.R. 31, 49–50, *per* Hewak J. (Man. Q.B.): "The fault lies not with the risk or development of infection but with the failure to recognise that it is present as quickly as possible and to take steps to treat it"; *Hajgato* v. *London Health Association* (1982) 36 O.R. (2d) 669, 682, where failure to detect and treat a post-operative infection before a crippling injury resulted, in a well-staffed and modern hospital, was held to be evidence of negligence, but on the facts the defendants' evidence rebutted the inference of negligence; see also *Hucks* v. *Cole* (1968) 112 S.J. 483 where the plaintiff developed fulminating septicaemia following the normal delivery of a child; the defendant was held negligent.

[75] *Evans* v. *Liverpool Corporation* [1906] 1 K.B. 160. The hospital authority was held not liable for the doctor's negligence on the basis that, as the law then stood, it was not vicariously liable for his negligence.

infection. One case has been commenced in this country by a patient who developed cancer following the transplantation of a cancerous kidney.[76] This involves allegations of negligence in failing to ensure that the kidney was healthy, failing to communicate the cause of the donor's death to the hospital where the transplant was performed, and failing to remove the kidney when it was discovered that the donor had suffered from cancer. Another potential source of infection stems from the donor insemination of sperm,[77] and the transfusion of bodily fluids, such as blood.[78] Haemophiliacs treated with imported HIV infected blood products commenced proceedings against the Department of Health, the Blood Products Laboratory and the National Blood Transfusion Service, alleging *inter alia* negligence in screening donors, failing to treat the blood products to minimise the risk of infection, failing to warn donors, and failing to achieve a self-sufficiency in blood products within the N.H.S.[79] The issue of negligence in such cases will, in general terms, turn upon the degree to which the risk of infection was known or foreseeable, and whether reasonably practicable steps could have been taken to eliminate or reduce the risk.[80]

3. Miscalculating drug reactions

4.75   Doctors must take account of manufacturers' instructions and known side-effects when prescribing drugs, although they should not necessarily rely on the manufacturer's information unthinkingly, since it is known that manufacturers are not always entirely frank about the contra-indications or risks associated with their product.[81] Where a doctor ignores the manufacturer's instructions and warnings, it is the

---

[76] *Sumners* v. *Mid-Downs Health Authority and South East Thames Health Authority*, see (1989) 298 B.M.J. 1544.

[77] For the risks of sexually transmitted disease and HIV infection associated with donor insemination see Barratt and Cooke (1989) 299 B.M.J. 1178, and 1531.

[78] The Law Commission identified an example of a successful claim in the German Supreme Court in respect of pre-natal injury for congenital syphilis caused by a negligent blood transfusion given to the mother before conception: Law Com. No. 60 Cmnd. 5709, 1974, para. 77. In *Morgan* v. *Gwent Health Authority*, *The Independent*, December 14, 1987, C.A., where a young unmarried woman was negligently given a transfusion of rhesus positive blood instead of rhesus negative blood following an operation, which raised the level of antibodies in her blood and put at risk any future pregnancy. She was awarded £20,000 in damages. For a case involving a negligent failure to carry out blood tests during pregnancy when it was known that the patient suffered from blood incompatibility see *Bagley* v. *North Hertfordshire Health Authority* [1986] N.L.J. Law Rep. 1014.

[79] *Re HIV Haemophiliac Litigation* (1990) 140 New L.J. 1349. This report, in which the Court of Appeal accepted that the plaintiffs had made out an arguable case of negligence, is concerned with discovery of documents. The litigation has subsequently been settled. For a comparable Australian case see *H.* v. *Royal Alexandra Hospital for Children* [1990] 1 Med. L.R. 297; and on infection with hepatitis from blood products see *Kitchen* v. *McMullen* (1989) 62 D.L.R. (4th) 481 (N.B.C.A.). On some of the problems involved in identifying blood donors see Grubb and Pearl (1991) 141 New L.J. 897 and 938.

[80] See Norrie (1985) 34 I.C.L.Q. 442 for discussion of both the principles of liability in negligence and the question of consent. As to whether the doctor who performs a blood transfusion can rely on the blood having been screened by the blood bank see *ibid.*, p. 446.

[81] See, *e.g.*, *Buchan* v. *Ortho Pharmaceuticals (Canada) Ltd.* (1986) 25 D.L.R. (4th) 658 (Ont. C.A.), §§ 8.34 and 8.36.

doctor who is responsible for any adverse reactions[82]; the manufacturer will not be liable since a warning addressed to the doctor will normally discharge the manufacturer's duty of care to the patient in the case of prescription drugs.[83]

Three types of case will tend to arise. First, where the doctor is **4.76** simply unaware of the known side-effects. If he ought reasonably to have known then he is negligent.[84] Secondly, where the doctor is generally aware of the dangers but makes an isolated error and gives an overdose or prescribes the wrong drug.[85] Thirdly, there may be cases where the doctor is aware of the risk from side-effects, but calculates that it is a reasonable risk to run in the circumstances, given the condition for which the drug is prescribed. If the calculation is correct by reference to the standards of the profession he is not negligent, but if the risk was unreasonable in the circumstances he will be liable.

For example, in *Battersby* v. *Tottman*[86] a doctor prescribed a very **4.77** high dose of melleril to a patient who was suffering from a mental illness. He knew that there was a danger that the drug could cause serious and permanent eye damage, but he took the view that the benefits of the drug outweighed the risk from the side–effects, since without treatment the patient was suicidal, and other methods of treatment had failed. The risk materialised, the patient suffering permanent eye damage. It was held that the decision to prescribe a dosage that was far in excess of the recommended dosages was not negligent; the risk was justified by the potential consequences of not using the drug.[87] By way of contrast, in *Graham* v. *Persyko*[88] the defendant gastroenterologist wrongly, but not negligently, diagnosed

---

[82] For a case in which it was alleged that a general practitioner had ignored the manufacturer's statement of contra-indications for giving a combined vaccination against cholera and typhoid see *King* v. *King* (1987) (unreported), C.A. The action was successful at first instance, but reversed on appeal. See also *Newman* v. *Hounslow & Spelthorne Health Authority* (1985) (unreported), Q.B.D., where the plaintiff suffered chronic adhesive arachnoiditis, a known reaction to myodil, a contrast agent used in myelography. The defendants negligently failed to spot this complication, and so failed to take the remedial measures indicated in the manufacturer's warning of adverse reactions; Herxheimer and Young (1990) 140 N.L.J. 859 on the adverse effects of minoxidil, including excessive hair growth and skin pigmentation.
[83] See § 8.33.
[84] In *Reynard* v. *Carr* (1983) 30 C.C.L.T. 42 (B.C.S.C.) the defendant was ignorant of the risks of avascular necrosis associated with prolonged use of prednisone, and apparently indifferent even to its other well-known side-effects; for a case of osteoporosis resulting from long term use of prednisolone see *A.V.M.A. Medical and Legal Journal* (1990) No. 3, p. 10; "Side-effects" can include the risk of the patient becoming dependent upon the drug, as has occurred with some patients taking benzodiazepines: (1988) 4 J. of the M.D.U. 46.
[85] See, *e.g.*, *Dwyer* v. *Roderick*, (1983) 127 S.J. 806; *The Times*, November 12, 1983, where a general practitioner negligently directed the patient to take an overdose in the prescription, and a pharmacist failed to spot the error; *McCaffrey* v. *Hague* [1949] 4 D.L.R. 291, where a doctor miscalculated the dosage of X-rays. See further *A.V.M.A. Medical and Legal Journal* (1990) No. 1, p. 11, reporting on the overdoses of radiation given to over 200 patients over a 6 month period at the Royal Devon and Exeter Hospital, due to the miscalibration of a mobaltron cobalt radiotherapy machine.
[86] (1985) 37 S.A.S.R. 524 (S.C. of S.Aus.).
[87] "It was a considered professional judgment made after consideration of all aspects and was supported by a body of medical evidence called by the respondent": *per* King C.J. at p. 526.
[88] (1986) 27 D.L.R. (4th) 699 (Ont. C.A.); (1986) 34 D.L.R. (4th) 160 (S.C.C.) leave to appeal refused.

that the plaintiff had Crohn's disease, and prescribed prednisone which caused avascular necrosis of the femoral heads. This is a rare but known complication of the drug. Prednisone is a very potent drug with a multitude of serious adverse effects, and, it was said, a low safety margin. When the defendant prescribed the drug the patient was asymptomatic, although the drug is only used to treat symptoms, since there is no cure for Crohn's disease. The defendant was found negligent; the risk from side-effects was disproportionate to the anticipated benefit to the patient.

4.78   It is also possible that the correct dosage of a drug may be undercalculated. A number of cases have arisen in which patients undergoing surgery have been awake and conscious of pain during the operation but unable to communicate with medical staff due to being paralysed by muscle relaxant drugs. This may or may not be due to a fault in the administration of the anaesthetic.[89]

4. Injections

4.79   Injections may be a source of problems because they are given in the wrong place, or the hypodermic may contain the wrong substance, or an excessive dose, or the needle may break. Not all errors, however, will give rise to a claim for negligence. In *Caldeira* v. *Gray*[90] damage to the sciatic nerve following an injection in the buttocks was found to have been caused by negligence, but in *Wilcox* v. *Cavan*[91] the Supreme Court of Canada held that where gangrene had developed in the plaintiff's arm following an intra-muscular injection, the nurse who administered the injection was not liable under the principle of *res ipsa loquitur*. Although there was no explanation as to how the injection had found its way into the plaintiff's circumflex artery, the defendant's version of events was consistent with the absence of negligence. It has been held that an injection into the patient's surrounding tissues instead of a vein is not necessarily negligent if the vein is difficult to find.[92] On the other hand, administering an excessive dose of a drug having misread the instructions is clearly negligent, [93] as is an excessive dose of anaesthetic given through misjudgment attributable to inexperience.[94]

---

[89] See *Ludlow* v. *Swindon Health Authority* [1989] 1 Med. L.R. 104; *Taylor* v. *Worcester and District Health Authority* [1991] 2 Med. L.R. 215; *Ackers* v. *Wigan Health Authority* [1991] 2 Med. L.R. 232. See further *A.V.M.A. Medical and Legal Journal* (1990) No. 1, pp. 13 and 16; No. 2, p. 15; Medical Defence Union *Annual Report 1990*, p. 18. This problem appears to have arisen most frequently in the case of women undergoing Caesarian section deliveries, but not all cases have involved "two patients": see Medical Defence Union *Annual Report 1989*, p. 21.

[90] [1936] 1 All E.R. 540; see also *Feist* v. *Gordon* (1990) 74 D.L.R. (4th) 140 (Alta. C.A.), where an opthalmologist was held liable for piercing the plaintiff's eyeball when administering an injection, having omitted a standard precaution.

[91] (1974) 50 D.L.R. (3d) 687 (S.C.C.); rev'g (1973) 44 D.L.R. (3d) 42 (N.B.C.A.).

[92] *Williams* v. *North Liverpool Hospital Management Committee, The Times*, January 17, 1959; *Prout* v. *Crowley* (1956) 1 B.M.J. 580; *Gent* v. *Wilson* (1956) 2 D.L.R. (2d) 160, where an allegation of negligence in selecting a site for vaccination of a child failed on the evidence.

[93] *Strangeways-Lesmere* v. *Clayton* [1936] 2 K.B. 11; *Smith* v. *Brighton and Lewes Hospital Management Committee, The Times*, May 2, 1958; *Sellers* v. *Cooke* [1990] 2 Med. L.R. 16, 19, where a "virtually barbaric" dosage of an intravenous drip was used in the performance of an abortion.

[94] As, *e.g.*, in *Jones* v. *Manchester Corporation* [1952] 2 All E.R. 125.

In *Collins* v. *Hertfordshire County Council*[95] a patient died following **4.80**
an injection of cocaine instead of procaine as a local anaesthetic, due
to a misunderstanding between the surgeon and the inexperienced
doctor who had been requested to prepare the anaesthetic. Hilbery J.
said that every surgeon must take responsibility for what he injects into
a patient as an infiltration or injection for a local anaesthetic, and this
required reasonable steps to make sure that he is injecting that which
he ordered, even allowing for the fact that the person to whom the
request was given was skilled in such things and that the solution was
made up in a hospital pharmacy:

> " . . . still there remains in him a residuum of obligation and duty
> as the surgeon who will make the injection . . . to make an
> efficient check to see that he is getting what he ordered, whoever
> has mixed it or however it has been mixed."[96]

It is not uncommon for needles to break in the course of giving an **4.81**
injection, but this is not necessarily an indication of negligence. In
Brazier v. *Ministry of Defence*[97] the court accepted that a needle which
broke in a patient's buttock was caused by a latent defect in the needle
for which the defendant was not responsible.[98] By contrast, in *Cardin*
v. *City of Montreal*[99] a doctor administered a vaccine by hypodermic
needle to a child who was struggling against his mother's efforts to
keep him still. The doctor insisted on proceeding with the injection
despite the mother's protestations and her offer to return another day
when the child was calmer, and the needle broke in the child's arm
with serious consequences. The Supreme Court of Canada held that
the doctor was negligent in not postponing the injection until the child
was in a less agitated state, since complete immobilisation of the arm
was an essential precaution.

5. Failure to monitor treatment

A doctor has a duty to monitor the treatment given to the patient, **4.82**
particularly where the treatment carries a high risk of an adverse

---

[95] [1947] 1 K.B. 598.

[96] *Ibid.*, p. 607; see also Medical Defence Union *Annual Report 1990*, p. 19 on a mix
up with an unlabelled syringe; Hill (1990) 6 J. of the M.D.U. 10; *cf. Fussell* v. *Beddard*
(1942) 2 B.M.J. 411, *ante,* § 4.49, n. 10; and *Bugden* v. *Harbour View Hospital* [1947] 2
D.L.R. 338, where, in the course of an operation, a doctor asked for novocaine, was
handed a bottle by a nurse, and without examining the label he injected it into the
patient. The solution was adrenalin and the patient died. It was held the doctor was not
negligent in failing to look at the label since it was a routine matter and there was
nothing about the circumstances to put him on inquiry, and he was entitled to rely on
experienced nurses. The nurse was negligent. This decision is difficult to reconcile with
Collins.

[97] [1965] 1 Lloyd's Rep. 26.

[98] See also *Gerber* v. *Pines* (1935) 79 S.J. 13; *Galloway* v. *Hanley* (1956) 1 B.M.J. 580;
Daniels v. *Heskin* [1954] I.R. 73: "It is certainly not open to a jury . . . to hold that the
breaking was caused by imperfection of technique on the ground that say in 60 per cent.
of cases of broken needles it is so caused . . ." *per* Lavery J. at p. 79.

[99] (1961) 29 D.L.R. (2d) 492 (S.C.C.).

reaction.[1] This duty obviously extends to post-operative conditions which the patient may develop. In *Bayliss* v. *Blagg*[2] the defendants were held negligent for failing to do anything about a marked deterioration in the condition of the patient's leg following the application of a plaster cast, and in *Poole* v. *Morgan*[3] it was held that a patient who had received laser treatment on his eye should be examined as soon as possible after the treatment. A delay of one month was too long, and negligent. Where a defendant had performed an "innovative" sterilisation procedure he was found negligent for failing to follow the patient's progress by conducting regular medical examinations.[4]

6. Lack of resources

4.83   Although there is no case in this country in which a hospital authority has been held liable in negligence for failing to provide adequate resources for the treatment of a patient, the possibility of such a claim has been canvassed in two recent Court of Appeal decisions. As a general rule, the defendant's resources, or lack of them, is not relevant to the question of liability in the tort of negligence. The burden, or cost, of taking precautions against a foreseeable risk is a factor to be taken into account in determining whether the defendant acted reasonably, but if on an objective assessment he ought reasonably to have taken precautions his impecuniosity is not a defence. In *Knight* v. *Home Office*[5] Pill J. held that prison authorities were not negligent in failing to provide the same level of staffing for prisoners suffering from a psychiatric illness that would be found in a psychiatric hospital outside prison. Thus, the standard of reasonable care "in all the circumstances" allows for different standards of medical care in a prison compared to a hospital. The lack of resources to provide a better staff/patient ratio, however, was not necessarily a complete defence. If, his Lordship observed, it was said that there were no funds to provide any medical facilities for prisoners there would be a breach of the duty of care, just as lack of funds would not excuse a public body which operated its vehicles on public roads without any system of maintenance, if an accident occurred due to lack of maintenance.

4.84   This, of course, is an extreme example, but in *Wilsher* v. *Essex Area Health Authority*[6] Browne-Wilkinson V.-C. suggested that "a health

---

[1] *Marshall* v. *Rogers* [1943] 4 D.L.R. 68, where a doctor who changed a diabetic's diet and reduced his insulin dosage should have conducted daily urine tests on the patient and have watched the patient very carefully; *Male* v. *Hopmans* (1967) 64 D.L.R. (2d) 105, 113–115 (Ont. C.A.), where a doctor was held negligent in failing to prescribe audiometric tests during the course of treating a patient with a drug for which the manufacturers recommended such testing; *Wilsher* v. *Essex Area Health Authority* [1986] 3 All E.R. 801, on negligence in monitoring the blood oxygen levels of a premature baby in a special care baby unit.

[2] (1954) 1 B.M.J. 709; see also *Ares* v. *Venner* (1970) 14 D.L.R. (3d) 4 (S.C.C.) on plaster casts; and on post-operative infection see *Reitze* v. *Bruser* (No. 2) [1979] 1 W.W.R. 31, 49–50.

[3] [1987] 3 W.W.R. 217.

[4] *Zimmer* v. *Ringrose* (1981) 125 D.L.R. (3d) 215, 225–226 (Alta C.A.), aff'g (1978) 89 D.L.R. (3d) 646.

[5] [1990] 3 All E.R. 237.

[6] [1986] 3 All E.R. 801, 833.

authority which so conducts its hospital that it fails to provide doctors of sufficient skill and experience to give the treatment offered at the hospital may be directly liable in negligence to the patient." Given the structure of hospital medicine within the N.H.S., in which very junior and overworked doctors are often stretched to the limit of their endurance and professional capacity, this is not in the least a far-fetched example. Such a claim, however, as his Lordship recognised, would raise "awkward" questions:

> "To what extent should the authority be held liable if (e.g. in the use of junior housemen) it is only adopting a practice hallowed by tradition? Should the authority be liable if it demonstrates that, due to the financial stringency under which it operates, it cannot afford to fill the posts with those possessing the necessary experience?"[7]

Both of these questions were touched upon in *Bull* v. *Devon Area* **4.85** *Health Authority*,[8] in which the health authority was held liable for implementing an unsatisfactory and unreliable system for calling expert assistance to an obstetric emergency. Either there was negligence in the operation of the system, or it was inadequate to cope with even minor hitches which fell short of the kind of major breakdown against which no system could be invulnerable. Counsel for the plaintiff did not argue that the levels of staffing were inadequate in terms of obstetric cover because the response would have been that the levels of staffing should be judged according to professional standards at the time, and the medical evidence was that the standards did not compare unfavourably with those that existed at other split-site hospitals in the provinces at the time. Mustill L.J. was disturbed by the implications of this reply which at one and the same time put the foetus at risk and claimed to be good enough to be "par for the course." It was not a question of highly specialist techniques or advanced equipment which it might be unrealistic to expect in provincial hospitals, but simply a matter of getting the right people together in the right place at the right time. Mustill L.J. was also unhappy about the (hypothetical) argument that the hospital was doing the best that could be expected with its limited resources:

> "I have some reservations about this contention, which are not allayed by the submission that hospital medicine is a public service. So it is, but there are other public services in respect of which it is not necessarily an answer to allegations of unsafety that there were insufficient resources to enable the administrators to do everything which they would like to do. I do not for a moment suggest that public medicine is precisely analogous to other public services, but there is perhaps a danger in assuming that it is completely *sui generis*, and that it is necessarily a complete answer to say that even if the system in any hospital was unsatisfactory, it was no more unsatisfactory than those in force elsewhere."

---

[7] *Ibid.*, p. 834.
[8] (1989) (unreported), C.A.

His Lordship acknowledged that these matters "raise important issues of social policy, which the courts may one day have to address." Dillon L.J. was content to observe that the level of staffing should be "reasonably sufficient for the foreseeable requirements of the patient." This leaves open the possibility of arguing that the provision of inadequate resources for a particular service constitutes negligence in itself.

4.86 There would be formidable obstacles, however, in mounting such a claim. From the perspective of the common law, there is a distinction to be drawn between undertaking a task with inadequate resources and being found negligent for failing to perform the task properly (which would be the form of an action in a situation analogous to *Bull* v. *Devon Area Health Authority*), and, on the other hand, not having the resources to perform the task at all, where the plaintiff claims that the failure to provide the service constitutes negligence. In the former circumstances a finding of negligence on the basis of inadequate resources would create the risk that, in reponse, a service might be withdrawn altogether, and the courts would hesitate long and hard before taking such a step.[9] The latter situation would almost certainly fall foul of the "mere omissions" rule, since there could be no common law duty to provide medical services, as opposed to acting carefully if one chooses to provide such services.[10] Moreover, decisions about the allocation of resources to a public service are normally taken in pursuance of statutory powers which confer a discretion on the decision-making body. An allegation that such a decision has been taken negligently must first establish that the discretion was exercised *ultra vires* the statutory power, applying public law principles.[11] The courts have demonstrated an extreme reluctance to become directly involved in resource allocation issues in the health service, and they are likely to take a highly sympathetic view of the health authority's position.[12]

4.87 The one situation in which a claim apparently based on a lack of resources would succeed is where a vital piece of equipment, which is normally available and should have been available, is absent or has

---

[9] In *Dryden* v. *Surrey County Council* [1936] 2 All E.R. 535, 539, Finlay J. said that it would be "most dangerous to hold that, because an increase of staff was recommended, therefore negligence by understaffing was established." His Lordship commented that it was impossible to receive in a public hospital the attention which a person will receive who is fortunate enough to be able to pay for the undivided attention of 1 or even 2 nurses. This remark pre-dates the foundation of the N.H.S., but nonetheless it may still be accurate in practical terms.

[10] So, *e.g.*, a casualty department of a hospital that opens its doors to the public "undertakes" the task of providing an emergency service and will be liable for negligently failing to do so: *Barnett* v. *Chelsea and Kensington Hospital Management Committee* [1968] 1 All E.R. 1068, 1073. If, on the other hand, it simply shuts down, there is no liability.

[11] See *Anns* v. *Merton London Borough Council* [1978] A.C. 728, 754; *Dorset Yacht Co. Ltd.* v. *Home Office* [1970] A.C. 1004, 1067.

[12] See, *e.g, R.* v. *Secretary of State for Social Services, ex parte Hincks* (1979) 123 S.J. 436, aff'd (1980) (unreported), C.A.; *R.* v. *Central Birmingham Health Authority, ex parte Walker*, The Times, November 26, 1987, C.A.; *R.* v. *Central Birmingham Health Authority, ex parte Collier* (1988) (unreported), C.A. See, however, *Re HIV Haemophiliac Litigation* (1990) 140 New L.J. 1349, which involved allegations about the negligent allocation of resources, including a failure to achieve self-sufficiency in the supply of blood products within the N.H.S. This report of the case deals with discovery, not the substantive issue of negligence.

gone missing with the result that the patient sustains avoidable harm. An instrument which is essential for resuscitation in an emergency, for example, may have been negligently mislaid.[13] This is not a true example of a shortage of resources, rather it is mismanagement of the available resources.

V. Mental Health

A psychiatrist or clinical psychologist clearly owes a duty of care to his **4.88** psychiatric patients, which, as with any doctor/patient relationship covers diagnosis, advice and treatment in all its forms. Generally, there are no special rules applicable to psychiatric patients and the *Bolam* test will apply.[14] Thus, a psychiatrist was held negligent where he engaged in social contact with a female patient who had developed a strong and obsessive emotional attachment to him, leading to a serious deterioration in the patient's mental health.[15] This was a departure from recognised standards in the practice of psychiatry which no body of professional opinion would have supported. In some instances, however, the nature of the patient's illness makes him dangerous, either to himself or to others, and claims can arise out of an alleged failure to exercise control over the patient.

1. Failing to control the patient

A doctor undoubtedly has a duty to take reasonable steps to protect **4.89** a psychiatric patient from harming himself, and in an institutional setting a hospital authority may be responsible for injuries inflicted on a patient by himself,[16] or by a fellow patient where the injuries are the result of a failure to provide adequate control and supervision.[17] The duty can include an obligation to make reasonable efforts to prevent suicide attempts.[18] There will generally be two types of case: (i) where the patient is a known suicide risk; and (ii) where it is alleged that the

---

[13] As, *e.g.*, in *Meyer* v. *Gordon* (1981) 17 C.C.L.T. 1, 15.

[14] The plaintiff in *Bolam* v. *Friern Hospital Management Committee* [1957] 2 All E.R. 118 itself was a psychiatric patient who sustained serious physical injuries in the course of electro-convulsive therapy administered to treat depression. The defendant did not use relaxant drugs or strap the plaintiff down before administering the treatment. There were, however, two schools of thought about the use of relaxant drugs, which reduced the danger from fractures but carried a small risk of death. There were also two schools of thought about the degree of physical restraint that should be used, one taking the view that it reduced the risk of fractures the other taking the view that it increased the risk. A jury acquitted the defendant of negligence, following the direction of McNair J.; see § 3.08.

[15] *Landau* v. *Werner* (1961) 105 S.J. 257, and 1008, C.A.

[16] *Jinks* v. *Cardwell* (1987) 39 C.C.L.T. 168 (Ont. H.C.), where there was negligent supervision of a schizophrenic patient who was known to be prone to fainting spells as a reaction to his medication; the patient drowned accidentally in a bath.

[17] *Wellesley Hospital* v. *Lawson* (1977) 76 D.L.R. (3d) 688, where the Supreme Court of Canada assumed that such a common law duty existed. In *Ellis* v. *Home Office* [1953] 2 All E.R. 149 prison authorities were held to owe a duty of care to a prisoner assaulted by another prisoner, although on the facts the defendants were held not to have been negligent.

[18] Jones (1990) 6 P.N. 107.

medical staff ought to have realised that he was a suicide risk, but failed to do so.

(i) The known suicide risk

4.90   Here, the issue may turn upon how much supervision the patient should have been given, and this may in turn depend upon the degree of risk. How serious is the threat, and so, in legal terms, how foreseeable was the patient's behaviour?

4.91   In *Thorne* v. *Northern Group Hospital Management Committee*[19] the nursing staff on a medical ward of a general hospital were aware that a patient, who was a suspected depressive, had threatened suicide. The patient walked out of the hospital, went home and committed suicide while mentally ill but not legally insane. Her husband sued the hospital alleging that a failure to provide adequate supervision of his wife was negligent. Edmund-Davies J. held that there had been no negligence since in the circumstances constant supervision was not appropriate. His Lordship did comment, however, that the degree of care and supervision required of hospital staff in relation to a patient with known or, perhaps, even suspected suicidal tendencies was greater than that called for in relation to patients generally.

4.92   By contrast, in *Selfe* v. *Ilford and District Hospital Management Committee*[20] it was accepted that reasonable care demanded reasonable supervision of a suicide risk which included continuous observation by a nurse on duty in the ward. The plaintiff, when aged 17, was admitted to hospital following an attempted suicide by an overdose of sleeping tablets. The staff knew that he was a serious suicide risk, and he was put in a ground floor ward with 27 patients, four of whom were suicide risks. The expert evidence was that with four such patients a minimum of three nurses was required. There were three nurses on duty, but two of them were briefly absent from the ward, and the third was assisting a patient at the far end of the ward. The plaintiff climbed out of a window and jumped off a roof, causing serious injuries. Hinchcliffe J. held the defendants liable. The degree of care required was proportionate to the degree of risk, and in this case there had been a breakdown in proper nursing supervision, which had caused the accident.

4.93   In *Villemure* v. *L'Hôpital Notre Dame*[21] a patient was admitted on an emergency basis to the psychiatric section of a hospital (where the windows were barred) following an attempted suicide, but was subsequently moved to a semi-private room in the medical section (where the windows were not barred). The patient's pleas to be allowed to return to the psychiatric ward were ignored and no supervision or other precautions were taken to prevent a recurrence. The patient leapt to his death from the window of his room. The Supreme Court of Canada concluded that the defendants had been negligent. On the other hand, where the suicide attempt is unforeseeable there will be no liability.[22]

---

[19] (1964) 108 S.J. 484.

[20] (1970) 114 S.J. 935.

[21] (1972) 31 D.L.R. (3d) 454.

[22] *Lepine* v. *University Hospital Board* (1966) 57 D.L.R. (2d) 701 (S.C.C.), where a leap out of a hospital window by a patient suffering from post-epileptic automatism was found to be unforeseeable, and reasonable care did not demand that the plaintiff be either physically restrained or kept at ground level; *Stadel* v. *Albertson* [1954] 2 D.L.R. 328 (Sask. C.A.) where the defendant was not liable for the suicide of a patient whose symptoms did not suggest that he was a danger either to himself or anyone else.

Another factor which may have to be considered in the case of a **4.94** known suicide risk is the degree of restraint or supervision appropriate in the light of the patient's mental condition. A psychiatrist, for example, may take the view that imposing restraint on a patient may exacerbate the patient's condition, or at least inhibit effective treatment. If it is against the patient's wishes it might undermine the trust between doctor and patient. This judgment has to balance competing risks to the patient's health, including the risk of suicide. In *Haines* v. *Bellissimo*,[23] Griffiths J. said that the therapist must weigh the advantages and disadvantages of hospitalisation against the advantages of continuing out-patient treatment. If there is a real risk of suicide or if the therapist is in doubt about this, said the judge, he should opt for hospitalisation. On the other hand, close observation, restrictions, and restraint of the patient may be anti-therapeutic and aggravate the patient's sense of worthlessness, which in itself can increase the risk of suicide. On the facts, the defendants had not been negligent because hospitalisation, whether voluntary or involuntary, would have been a blow to the patient's self-esteem and pride, interfered with his long term rehabilitation, and, most significantly, would have destroyed the strong therapeutic bond which had developed.

(ii) The undiagnosed suicide risk

Where it is claimed that the medical staff negligently failed to **4.95** appreciate that the patient was a suicide risk the question will usually be cast in terms of whether non-specialist (*i.e.* non-psychiatric) staff (whether doctors or nurses) ought to have realised that the patient's mental condition was such that there was a genuine risk of a suicide attempt. This will not be judged by reference to whether a psychiatrist could have made this diagnosis, unless the patient is receiving psychiatric treatment, but whether in the defendant's position a reasonable doctor or nurse would have identified the risk.

In *Hyde* v. *Tameside Area Health Authority*,[24] the plaintiff was **4.96** admitted to hospital with a painful shoulder. 12 days later he jumped from a third floor window in an attempt to kill himself having convinced himself, erroneously, that he had cancer. The attempt failed, but he suffered catastrophic injuries. The alleged negligence consisted of a failure by the medical staff to identify the plaintiff's mental distress, and a failure to realise "that the hospital had a serious psychiatric case on its hands which called for psychiatric treatment." At first instance the defendants were held liable. The Court of Appeal reversed this decision, finding that on the particular facts of the case there was no negligence, merely, in the words of Watkins L.J., a "forgivable failure to achieve a standard approaching perfection."

The court will make allowance for the fact that a decision to **4.97** introduce psychiatric treatment for patients who are not being treated for a psychiatric illness or disorder is one that involves competing considerations. In *Hyde* v. *Tameside Area Health Authority* Watkins L.J. pointed out that many patients in hospital suffer from anxiety, and

---

[23] (1977) 82 D.L.R. (3d) 215 (Ont. H.C.).
[24] (1981), reported at (1986) 2 P.N. 26.

worry about their medical condition. They may need re-assurance, sometimes they need drugs to ease pain or stress, but to tell a patient who requires surgery that he also needs psychiatric help may be counter-productive. As Watkins L.J. put it: "A decision to use psychiatry may do more harm than good. An over-eager resort to, and an excessive use of, this branch of medicine in hospitals other than those where the mentally ill are treated could have unfortunate and unsettling consequences."[25]

4.98   It has been argued that, quite apart from the question of breach of duty, claims for negligence based on suicide or attempted suicide should not be permitted, on the grounds of causation, *volenti non fit injuria, ex turpi causa non oritur actio*, or simply for policy reasons. The causation argument states that the defendant's negligence merely provided the opportunity for the deceased's act of suicide, which amounted, in effect, to a *novus actus interveniens*, so breaking the chain of causation. In *Kirkham* v. *Chief Constable of Greater Manchester Police*[26] Tudor Evans J. rejected the causation argument on the basis that the suicide was the very thing that the defendants had a duty to take precautions against,[27] and concluded that on evidence the suicide would probably have been prevented.[28] His Lordship seemed to regard the deceased's state of mind as relevant to the question of causation: "Although the act of suicide was in a sense a conscious and deliberate act, the deceased's mental balance was, I am satisfied, affected at the time."[29] This leaves open the question whether, if the deceased's mind was not "affected," the suicide could be regarded as a *novus actus interveniens*.

4.99   In *Hyde* v. *Tameside Area Health Authority* Lord Denning M.R. was hostile to actions based on suicide or attempted suicide:

> "I feel it is most unfitting that the personal representatives of a suicide should be able to claim damages in respect of his death. At any rate, when he succeeds in killing himself. And I do not see why he should be in any better position when he does not succeed. By this act—in self-inflicting this grievous injury—he has made himself a burden on the whole community. Our hospital services and our social welfare services have done, and will do, all they can to help him and his family—in the grievous injury that he has inflicted on himself and them. But I see no justification whatever in his being awarded, in addition, the huge sum of

---

[25] *Ibid.*, p. 30.

[26] [1989] 3 All E.R. 882; aff'd [1990] 2 W.L.R. 987.

[27] Where the intervening conduct is the very thing that the defendant was under a duty to guard against, he cannot avoid liability by arguing that the conduct constituted an intervening act: *Haynes* v. *Harwood* [1935] 1 K.B. 146, 156; *Perl (Exporters) Ltd.* v. *Camden London Borough Council* [1984] Q.B. 342, 353. See also, *per* Farquharson L.J. in *Kirkham* v. *Chief Constable of Greater Manchester Police* [1990] 2 W.L.R. 987, 997 in relation to the defence of *volenti non fit injuria*.

[28] In *Hyde* v. *Tameside Area Health Authority* (1986) 2 P.N. 26 O'Connor L.J. said that he did not think that "the fact that a patient commits suicide or attempts suicide will necessarily break the chain of causation if breach of duty is established against the hospital. It all depends on the circumstances of an individual case." See also *Funk Estate* v. *Clapp* (1986), reported at 68 D.L.R. (4th) 229, and (1988) 54 D.L.R. (4th) 512 (B.C.C.A.), where it was held that *novus actus interveniens* was not a defence to claim following the suicide of a prisoner.

[29] [1989] 3 All E.R. 882, 889.

£200,000 because he failed in his attempt. Such a sum will have to be raised, in the long run, by society itself—a sum which it cannot well afford. The policy of the law should be to discourage these actions. I would disallow them altogether—at the outset—rather than burden the community with them."[30]

This view was clearly based on considerations of policy, and in particular Lord Denning's belief that " 'medical malpractice' cases should not get out of hand here as they have done in the United States of America." In *Kirkham* v. *Chief Constable of Greater Manchester Police*[31] Lloyd L.J. said that he did not share this view, noting that neither Watkins nor O'Connor L.JJ. expressed agreement with Lord Denning's comments.

The defendant in *Kirkham* also argued that damages should not be **4.100** awarded on the basis of the principle *ex turpi causa non oritur actio*. The Court of Appeal accepted that the *ex turpi causa* defence is not confined to criminal conduct, but would apply to illegal or immoral conduct by the plaintiff "if in all the circumstances it would be an affront to the public conscience to grant the plaintiff the relief which he seeks because the court would thereby appear to assist or encourage the plaintiff in his illegal conduct or to encourage others in similar acts."[32] The question, then, was whether awarding damages following a suicide would "affront the public conscience, or, as I would prefer to say, shock the ordinary citizen."[33] Their Lordships concluded that the answers should be "No." Thus, said Lloyd L.J., the defence of *ex turpi causa* is not available in suicide cases "at any rate where, as here, there is medical evidence that the suicide is not in full possession of his mind."[34] Farquharson L.J.. said that an action could hardly be said to be grounded in immorality where "grave mental instability" on the part of the victim has been proved, although "the position my well be different where the victim is wholly sane."

The meaning of the phrases "grave mental instability" and "wholly **4.101** sane" is a matter of some conjecture. It is not clear, for example, whether a person who is not insane, but whose judgment is impaired by an emotional, as opposed to a psychological, disturbance falls into the category of "not wholly sane." Similar difficulties are raised by the defence of *volenti non fit injuria*. Lloyd L.J. could see no reason why this should not provide a complete defence where a man "of sound mind" commits suicide or injures himself in an unsuccessful attempt. But this, again, leaves open the question of precisely what the term "of

---

[30] (1981), reported at (1986) 2 P.N. 26, 29–30.

[31] [1990] 2 W.L.R. 987, 995.

[32] *Euro-Diam Ltd.* v. *Bathurst* [1988] 2 All E.R. 23, 28–29, *per* Kerr L.J., cited by Lloyd L.J. in *Kirkham*; see also *Thackwell* v. *Barclays Bank* [1986] 1 All E.R. 676; and *Saunders* v. *Edwards* [1987] 2 All E.R. 651; *cf.* the test for *ex turpi causa* adopted by a majority of the Court of Appeal in *Pitts* v. *Hunt* [1990] 3 All E.R. 344: the defence applied to an illegal activity where the circumstances were such that it was impossible to determine a standard of care, and therefore there was no duty of care owed by the defendant to the plaintiff.

[33] [1990] 2 W.L.R. 987, 993, *per* Lloyd L.J.

[34] *Ibid.*, p. 994; see also *Funk Estate* v. *Clapp* (1986), reported at 68 D.L.R. (4th) 229, and (1988) 54 D.L.R. (4th) 512, where it was held that *ex turpi causa* was not a defence to an action by the widow of a prisoner who committed suicide, although there was no negligence on the facts.

sound mind" means. In *Kirkham*, although the deceased was legally sane and his suicide was a deliberate and conscious act, nonetheless he "was suffering from clinical depression. His judgment was impaired. . . . He was not truly *volens*."[35] Thus, insanity is not essential in order to defeat the *volenti* defence; some impairment of judgment will suffice,[36] but it may be that suicides who cannot be categorised as suffering from some form of mental illness will be met with the *volenti* defence. The decision in *Kirkham* highlights the importance in this type of case of medical evidence indicating that the suicide was not of sound mind or that his "judgment was impaired."

(iii) Harm to third parties

4.102   It is uncertain whether, in this country, a psychiatrist would be held responsible for foreseeable harm inflicted by a patient on a third party. Even if it were possible to identify reasonably practicable steps that a doctor could have taken (such as requesting compulsory admission for assessment or treatment under the Mental Health Act 1983) it is not clear that a duty of care would be held to exist. Where the patient is compulsorily detained, however, the greater degree of control exercised over the patient may be sufficient to tip the balance in favour of a duty of care.[37]

2. Negligent certification

4.103   A doctor who provides a written recommendation supporting the compulsory admission of a patient into hospital under Part II of the Mental Health Act 1983 must exercise reasonable care.[38] This necessarily requires that the doctor examine the patient,[39] and that he should make such further enquiries as are necessary.[40] On the one hand, the court must make due allowance for the difficulty in making an accurate diagnosis in some cases of mental illness, and on the other hand, they should require "very considerable care" where a person is being deprived of his liberty.[41]

3. Procedural bars

4.104   Section 139(1) of the Mental Health Act 1983 provides that no person shall be liable to any civil or criminal proceedings in respect of

---

[35] *Ibid.*, pp. 992–993, *per* Lloyd L.J. Farquharson L.J. said, at p. 997, that it was "quite unrealistic" to suggest that Mr. Kirkham was truly *volens*: "His state of mind was such that, through disease, he was incapable of coming to a balanced decision even if his act of suicide was deliberate."

[36] *cf. Robson* v. *Ashworth* (1987) 40 C.C.L.T. 164, (Ont. C.A.)., where the fact that the deceased took his life "knowingly and deliberately while he was sane" barred the action by his widow.

[37] See §§ 2.59–2.68; *Holgate* v. *Lancashire Mental Hospitals Board* [1937] 4 All E.R. 19.

[38] *Hall* v. *Semple* (1862) 3 F. & F. 337; *De Freville* v. *Dill* (1927) 96 L.J.K.B. 1056; *Everett* v. *Griffiths* [1921] 1 A.C. 631; *Harnett* v. *Fisher* [1927] A.C. 573; *Buxton* v. *Jayne* [1960] 1 W.L.R. 783; [1962] C.L.Y. 1167. See § 2.57.

[39] Mental Health Act, 1983, s.12(1).

[40] *Hall* v. *Semple* (1862) 3 F. & F. 337, 354, *per* Crompton J.

[41] *Ibid.*, at pp. 355–356.

any act purporting to be done under the mental health legislation unless the act was done in bad faith or without reasonable care. In addition, civil proceedings may not be instituted in respect of such an act without leave of the High Court.[42] Proceedings issued without leave are a nullity,[43] although the requirement for leave applies only to patients who are formally detained under the Act; voluntary patients need not seek leave to bring an action.[44]

The rationale for this provision has been said to be that "patients **4.105** under the Mental Health Act may generally be inherently likely to harass those concerned with them by groundless charges and litigation, and may therefore have to suffer modification of the general right of free access to the courts."[45] This justification has been strongly criticised.[46] Very few patients, even those compulsorily detained, are suffering from disorders which make it likely that they will harass others, and rather more of them are suffering from disorders which make it likely that they will not complain at all, even where complaint would be justified. Patients with a mental disorder are often in a "peculiarly powerless position which merits, if anything, extra safe-guards rather than the removal of those available to everyone else."[47]

Under section 141 of the Mental Health Act 1959 the court could **4.106** not grant leave unless it was "satisfied that there is a substantial ground for the contention that the person to be proceeded against has acted in bad faith or without reasonable care." The requirement that there be a "substantial ground" was omitted from section 139 of the Mental Health Act 1983.[48] In *Winch* v. *Jones*[49] the Court of Appeal accepted that this was intended to be a change of substance, reducing the protection given to persons purporting to act under the legislation. Otton J. had held that although the plaintiff's application was neither frivolous nor vexatious, nor an abuse of the process of the court, he should not grant leave under section 139 unless there was a prima facie case of negligence against the defendant. The Court of Appeal, allowing the plaintiff's appeal, rejected this approach because it would lead to a full dress-rehearsal of the action which is inappropriate to an application for leave to commence proceedings, and at that stage an applicant who has a reasonable suspicion that there has been negli-gence may be quite unable to put forward a prima facie case before discovery. Sir John Donaldson M.R. said that section 139 is *sui generis* and the question that has to be resolved is whether on the materials immediately available to the court "the applicant's complaint appears to be such that it deserves the fuller investigation which will be

---

[42] Mental Health Act, 1983, s.139(2). See R.S.C., Ord. 32, r. 9. This requirement does not apply to actions against the Secretary of State or a health authority: s.139(4).

[43] *Pountney* v. *Griffiths* [1976] A.C. 314.

[44] *R.* v. *Runighian* (1977) Crim.L.R. 361, holding that acts done to an informal patient are not done in pursuance of the Mental Health Act. This case is concerned with the earlier provision requiring leave, s.141 of the Mental Health Act 1959, but the differences in the wording of the section do not affect the point.

[45] *Pountney* v. *Griffiths* [1976] A.C. 314, 329, *per* Lord Simon.

[46] Hoggett, *Mental Health Law*, 3rd ed., 1990, p. 367.

[47] *Ibid.*

[48] s.141(2) of the Mental Health Act 1959 having been repealed and replaced by the Mental Health (Amendment) Act 1982, s.60, now consolidated in the Mental Health Act 1983, s.139.

[49] [1985] 3 All E.R. 97.

possible if the intended applicant is allowed to proceed."[50] Parker L.J. took the view that if an action is neither frivolous nor vexatious it is prima facie fit to be tried, and if it is fit to be tried leave ought to be given. The purpose of the section, said his Lordship, was to prevent harassment by clearly hopeless actions, it was not to see that only those actions which could be seen to be likely to succeed should go ahead. Defendants still have some protection under the section, however, in comparison to the procedure for striking out frivolous and vexatious claims, because the plaintiff has to take the initiative by obtaining leave.

VI. CONTRIBUTORY NEGLIGENCE

4.107 In many instances a doctor needs the patient's co-operation to enable him to make an accurate diagnosis or for the purpose of administering the treatment. Sometimes this will be absolutely vital. For example, the doctor will need reasonably accurate information regarding the patient's symptoms, and/or medical history (*e.g.* the patient may forget to mention that he is allergic to penicillin). Similarly, the co-operation of the patient may be essential in implementing a treatment regime, for example, with regard to taking medication in the right quantity and at the right times of day, or returning for further treatment or tests. If the patient fails to follow proper instructions and this is a cause of his injuries then it will be possible to argue that the patient has been contributorily negligent, or in an extreme case that his conduct is the sole cause of the damage.[51]

4.108 Where damage is attributable partly to the fault of the defendant and partly to the fault of the plaintiff then the award of damages may be reduced by reason of the plaintiff's contributory negligence.[52] The reduction will be to such extent as the court thinks just and equitable having regard to the plaintiff's share in responsibility for the damage.

4.109 Fault means "negligence, breach of statutory duty or other act or omission which gives rise to a liability in tort or would, apart from this Act, give rise to the defence of contributory negligence."[53] The legislation clearly applies to the tort of negligence, although there has been uncertainty as to whether it also applies to actions for battery. The balance of authority is now in favour of the view that it can apply to actions in trespass to the person.[54] Similarly, there has been some

[50] *Ibid.*, p. 102.

[51] *Venner* v. *North East Essex Area Health Authority, The Times*, February 21, 1987; *Murrin* v. *Janes* [1949] 4 D.L.R. 403, 406 (Newfd. S.C.), where a plaintiff's delay in seeing a doctor to deal with excessive bleeding following extraction of his teeth, was the sole cause of his misfortune.

[52] Law Reform (Contributory Negligence) Act 1945, s.1. The defence must be specifically pleaded: *Fookes* v. *Slaytor* [1979] 1 All E.R. 137; R.S.C., Ord. 18, r. 8. In *Brown* v. *Merton, Sutton and Wandsworth Area Health Authority* [1982] 1 All E.R. 650, 652 counsel for the defendants intimated that he would rely on the defence of inevitable accident. This defence is generally regarded as limited to actions in trespass, and in any event it is confined to accidents that could not have been avoided by the exercise of reasonable care. Thus, in an action for negligence a plea of inevitable accident is, in effect, a denial of negligence.

[53] *Ibid.*, s.4.

[54] *Barnes* v. *Nayer, The Times*, December 19, 1986, C.A.; *Wasson* v. *Chief Constable of the Royal Ulster Constabulary* [1987] 8 N.I.J.B. 34; *Murphy* v. *Culhane* [1977] Q.B. 94; *cf. Lane* v. *Holloway* [1968] 1 Q.B. 379; Hudson (1984) 4 L.S. 332.

controversy about the extent to which the legislation applies to actions in contract. The Act is open to different interpretations and this has produced conflicting authorities.[55] It has now been held that where the defendant's negligent breach of contract would have given rise to liability in the tort of negligence independently of the existence of the contract, damages may be apportioned for the plaintiff's contributory negligence.[56] This means that the defence will be available in virtually all actions arising out of private medical treatment, since the obligations imposed by the contract are normally the same as the duty to exercise reasonable care in the tort of negligence. On the other hand, where (a) liability does not depend on negligence but arises from breach of a strict contractual duty; or (b) liability arises from breach of a contractual obligation which is expressed in terms of exercising reasonable care, but does not correspond to a common law duty of care which would exist independently of the contract; apportionment under the Act is not available.[57] Thus, if a patient was able to establish that the doctor had given a contractual warranty to achieve a particular result, this would fall into category (a), and the damages could not be apportioned for contributory negligence.[58] In the context of the relationship between doctor and patient, it is difficult to imagine contractual duties expressed in terms of exercising reasonable care which would not correspond to duties in the tort of negligence (category (b)), particularly since the courts have stressed that patients who receive treatment under the N.H.S. should not be placed at a disadvantage, in terms of their legal rights, in comparison with patients who receive treatment privately.[59]

Although, in theory, there is no reason why contributory negligence **4.110** should not apply in a claim for medical negligence, as with any other type of action for negligence, in practice the defence is rarely invoked successfully, and this is reflected in a comparative dearth of cases.[60] It may be that the plea is considered to be inappropriate in an action for medical negligence, given the inequality between the respective positions of doctor and patient. Patients do not generally question the advice or conduct of their doctors, a least initially, even when they are aware that their condition is deteriorating or not improving. Contributory negligence is measured by the standard of the reasonable, prudent man, which is meant to be the same standard of care as that applied to defendants.[61] In practice the courts tend to require less from plaintiffs in the way of prudence for their own safety than from defendants, and

[55] See Burrows, *Remedies for Torts and Breach of Contract*, Butterworths, 1987, pp. 73–78.
[56] *Forsikringsaktieselskapet Vesta* v. *Butcher* [1988] 2 All E.R. 43, C.A., approving the analysis of Hobhouse J. at [1986] 2 All E.R. 488, 508.
[57] *Ibid.*
[58] For the difficulties of proving this see § 2.07. If, in the case of a strict contractual warranty, the plaintiff has been guilty of "contributory" fault there is a risk that the court will conclude that the defendant's breach was not a cause of the loss, in which case the claim fails entirely: see, *e.g., Lambert* v. *Lewis* [1981] 1 All E.R. 1185.
[59] See § 2.03.
[60] There would appear to be no reported case in this country in which the court has had to make a finding of contributory negligence against a patient. See Giesen, *International Medical Malpractice Law*, 1988, para. 236; Picard, *Legal Liability of Doctors and Hospitals in Canada*, 2nd ed. 1984, pp. 243–247.
[61] *Jones* v. *Livox Quarries Ltd.* [1952] 2 Q.B. 608, 615.

this is likely to be even more apparent with patients, who rely heavily on the skills and knowledge of medical practitioners. If the patient has ignored his doctor's advice (*e.g.* by discharging himself from hospital or failing to return for further treatment) it may be easier to establish contributory negligence. It would have to be shown that a reasonable person would have been aware of the significance of the advice, which could depend upon the nature of the advice given by the doctor and whether the advice was clear to the patient.

4.111   By raising the plea of contributory negligence the defendant may highlight the extent of the doctor's duty to take special care in giving the patient instructions, and making sure that the patient understands both the instructions and the importance of strictly adhering to them.[62] In *Marshall* v. *Rogers*, [63] for example, the defendant alleged that the plaintiff's injury was caused by his own negligence in failing to follow the instructions that he had been given and to report his symptoms. It was held, however, that where a dangerous remedy was being attempted the doctor was negligent in delegating his own professional duty of deciding the true meaning of the patient's progressive symptoms to the patient himself, especially given that the patient had to make a subjective assessment of his symptoms. The defendant should have conducted daily tests.

4.112   Some Canadian courts have made findings of contributory negligence against careless patients. In *Brushett* v. *Cowan*[64] the plaintiff was contributorily negligent in engaging in ordinary activities without crutches following a bone biopsy on her leg, because she had failed to ask for clear instructions regarding the use of the crutches. A failure to have a post-operative check-up, as suggested by the doctor, has been held to be negligent,[65] and in *Crossman* v. *Stewart*[66] a patient who obtained prescription drugs from an unorthodox source, and continued to use the drugs on a prolonged basis without obtaining prescription renewals and without consulting the "prescribing" physician, was described as "foolhardy in the extreme." She was held to be responsible for two thirds of the damage to her eyesight caused by the side-effects of the drug.

---

[62] See §§ 4.41–4.44.

[63] [1943] 4 D.L.R. 68, 77.

[64] (1987) 40 D.L.R. (4th) 488; aff'd (1990) 69 D.L.R. (4th) 743 (Newfd. C.A.). In *Vancouver General Hospital* v. *McDaniel* (1934) 152 L.T. 56 it was suggested that the failure to be vaccinated against smallpox might constitute contributory negligence in a claim for infecting the patient with the disease, but this allegation was not pursued.

[65] *Fredette* v. *Wiebe* [1986] 5 W.W.R. 222 (B.C.S.C.).

[66] (1977) 82 D.L.R. (3d) 677, 686 (B.C.S.C.).

CHAPTER 5

CAUSATION AND REMOTENESS OF DAMAGE

In the tort of negligence damage is the gist of the action. If the plaintiff **5.01**
cannot show that he sustained injury as a result of the defendant's
breach of duty, there is no tort and the action fails. In contract a
plaintiff who proves that the defendant was in breach of contract is
entitled to nominal damages, but, again, he will not be awarded
substantial damages unless he establishes a causal link between the
breach and his loss. A similar principle applies to a claim in battery,
which, as an action in trespass to the person, is actionable *per se.*[1]

Causation is concerned with the physical connection between the **5.02**
defendant's negligence and the plaintiff's damage. No matter how
gross the defendant's negligence he is not liable if, as a question of
fact, his conduct did not cause the damage. Thus, there must be a
causal link between the defendant's breach of duty and the damage
sustained by the plaintiff.[2] This is essentially an explanatory inquiry:
how, in fact, did the damage occur? In medical malpractice litigation
this issue is largely a matter of medical and scientific evidence, for
example, about the pathology of a particular disease and the prospects
for successful treatment with proper care. The question is normally
dealt with by the "but for" test. In some instances there may be
several causal factors involved and the precise aetiology may be
unknown. This can leave a plaintiff with virtually insuperable difficulties of proof. Even if the "but for" test is satisfied, so that it is clear
that the defendant's negligence is *a* cause, there may be other sufficient
causes, or the negligence may form part of a sequence of events which
led to the plaintiff's injury. Here the question is whether the defendant's conduct is to be regarded as the cause in law of the loss. The
court may allocate causal responsibility to another cause, which is
treated as a supervening event or an intervening act which "breaks the
chain of causation."

Remoteness of damage is concerned with those situations where the **5.03**
defendant has undoubtedly caused the plaintiff's loss, but the damage
is not of the same type as would normally be anticipated in similar
circumstances, or the damage occurred in an unusual manner. There

---

[1] *Allan* v. *New Mount Sinai Hospital* (1980) 109 D.L.R. (3d) 634, 643 (Ont. H.C.).
For discussion of causation in the context of battery see § 6.97.
[2] See, generally, Hart and Honoré, *Causation in the Law*, 2nd ed., 1985.

has to be some limit, it is said, to a defendant's responsibility and it is considered to be unfair to hold a person liable for all the consequences of his negligence, however bizarre or freakish they might be.[3] In practice, while proof of factual causation can be a very real problem, questions of remoteness of damage are comparatively rare in medical negligence actions.

I. Causation in Fact

1. The "but for" test

5.04   If damage to the plaintiff would not have occurred "but for" the defendant's negligence then the negligence is *a* cause of the damage. It is not necessarily *the* cause because there may well be other events which are causally relevant. Putting this another way, if the loss would have occurred in any event, the defendant's conduct is not a cause. Two cases, both involving medical negligence, illustrate this point. In *Barnett* v. *Chelsea and Kensington Hospital Management Committee*[4] three nightwatchmen attended hospital, clearly appearing ill, and they informed a nurse that they had been vomiting. The nurse telephoned the casualty officer, who did not see the men, but said that they should go home and see their own doctors. They left, and about five hours later one of the men died from arsenic poisoning. Nield J. held that in these circumstances the casualty officer was negligent in failing to have seen and examined the deceased. It could not be said, however, that but for the doctor's negligence the deceased would have lived, because the medical evidence indicated that even if the patient had received prompt treatment it would not have been possible to diagnose the condition and administer an antidote in time to save him. Thus, the negligence did not cause the death.

5.05   Similarly, in *Robinson* v. *Post Office*[5] a doctor was found to have been negligent in the manner in which he administered a test dose to test for an allergic reaction to an anti-tetanus vaccination. He waited

---

[3] The term "remoteness" is also sometimes used to describe a causation problem, rather than being confined to setting the limits of actionability for damage which was clearly caused by the defendant's negligence. Where there has been an intervening event, for example, and the question is whether the defendant's negligence can still be treated as a cause of the plaintiff's loss, the damage may be described as "too remote." This is simply a way of saying that the defendant's conduct was not a cause in law of the damage.

[4] [1968] 1 All E.R. 1068. In *Kerry* v. *England* [1898] A.C. 742, P.C. the defendants' negligence accelerated the death of the patient, "but not to any appreciable extent"; it was held, in effect, that there was no causal connection because it was within the principle *de minimis non curat lex*; *Stamos* v. *Davies* (1985) 21 D.L.R. (4th) 507 (Ont. H.C.), where the defendant failed to tell the plaintiff that during the course of performing a lung biopsy the plaintiff's spleen had been punctured. The failure to be candid was held to be a breach of duty, but there was no causal connection between the breach and the damage, namely the loss of the spleen, because the spleen "was doomed from the moment it was injured"; see also *Serre* v. *de Tilley* (1975) 58 D.L.R. (3d) 362, 365 (Ont. H.C.), where Stark J. commented that it was "only conjectural that the treatment could have been sufficiently speedy and effective to prevent" the brain haemorrhage which resulted in the patient's death; *Wilson* v. *Vancouver Hockey Club* (1983) 5 D.L.R. (4th) 282; aff'd (1985) 22 D.L.R. (4th) 516 (B.C.C.A.).

[5] [1974] 2 All E.R. 737.

only a minute after giving the test before giving the patient the injection, although the standard procedure at the time was to wait half an hour. Nine days after being injected with the vaccine the plaintiff suffered a serious allergic reaction to the vaccine, which caused encephalitis and brain damage. The Court of Appeal held that the failure to administer a proper test was not causally related to the plaintiff's damage, because the test was not, in any event, a complete guarantee against a subsequent reaction, and the circumstances of the plaintiff's reaction were such that a test involving a delay of half an hour would probably not have produced a reaction in time to alert the doctor to the danger.

Where the defendant has made an error in diagnosis, but the correct **5.06** diagnosis would not have produced any difference in the treatment or management of the patient, the error has not caused any damage for which the defendant is responsible, even if he was negligent.[6]

In many cases, though not all, it may be easier to determine what **5.07** would have happened in the absence of negligence by the defendant, where events depend upon physical reactions which are amenable to objective scientific proof. Where the question depends upon how a person would have behaved, the issue is to some extent more speculative, but this will not prevent the court from drawing an inference of fact. In *McWilliams* v. *Sir William Arroll & Co. Ltd.*,[7] for example, a steel erector who was not wearing a safety belt fell to his death. His employers were in breach of a duty to supply a safety belt for his use, but the deceased had rarely, if ever, used a belt in the past, and the natural inference, said the House of Lords, was that he would not have used one on this occasion if it had been available. Thus, the breach of duty did not cause the death which would have occurred in any event.

This type of causation problem arises in a medical context whenever **5.08** a plaintiff alleges that but for the doctor's negligence he would have opted for an alternative course of treatment. Where, for example, the plaintiff claims that he was not properly informed about the risks of the treatment he has received and/or of the alternatives, he still has to show that had he been given the information he would not have accepted the treatment which he received. This may be difficult for the plaintiff to establish because the courts are wary of disappointed patients forming judgments about what they would have done with the benefit of hindsight.[8] Similarly, where the plaintiff alleges that the defendants negligently failed to communicate to her the test results following an amniocentesis test during her pregnancy, she must prove to the satisfaction of the court that, had she been informed that the test indicated that the foetus would be handicapped, she would have

---

[6] *Fish* v. *Kapur* [1948] 2 All E.R. 176, 178, where a dentist who failed to diagnose a patient's broken jaw, was held not liable because there was no treatment that could have been given in the circumstances, and thus the plaintiff did not suffer any additional pain or discomfort as a result of the failure to diagnose the fracture.

[7] [1962] 1 W.L.R. 295.

[8] *Chatterton* v. *Gerson* [1981] Q.B. 432; [1981] 1 All E.R. 257, 267; *Hills* v. *Potter* [1983] 3 All E.R. 716; see further § 6.97.

undergone an abortion.[9] This issue is not limited to circumstances where the question is what the plaintiff would have done, but for the breach of duty. For example, in *MacDonald* v. *York County Hospital*[10] hospital nurses were found to have been negligent in failing to inspect a patient's condition at frequent intervals when the classic symptoms of circulatory impairment began to appear, and in failing to notify the defendant doctor about these symptoms. The doctor gave evidence, however, that even if he had been informed he would not have taken any action at that time, and accordingly the nurses' negligence was held not to be a contributory cause of the patient's injury.

5.09   The "but for" test operates as a preliminary filter to exclude events which did not affect the outcome. It cannot, however, resolve all the problems of factual causation. In the case of two simultaneous wrongs to the plaintiff, each of which would have been sufficient to cause the damage, the test produces the ludicrous conclusion that neither wrong caused the harm.[11] The only sensible solution here is to say that both caused the damage, but it should be recognised that this decision involves a policy judgment. Similarly, the "but for" test may be inapplicable in the case of successive sufficient causes, although this depends upon the nature of the respective causes.[12] Policy issues are also apparent in the courts' attitude to the proof of causation. In *Cook* v. *Lewis*,[13] for example, two people on a hunting trip simultaneously discharged their guns and the plaintiff was hit by one of them, but he was unable to prove which one. The Supreme Court of Canada held that in these circumstances the burden of proof was reversed, and it was for the defendants to prove that they did not cause the damage. If neither could do so then both would be liable. The defendants' combined negligence had removed the plaintiff's opportunity to prove which of them had shot him, and it would be unjust to deprive him of a remedy through the operation of the burden of proof.

2. Proof of causation

5.10   It is for the plaintiff to prove, on the balance of probabilities, that the defendant's breach of duty caused the damage. In some instances the precise cause of the damage may be unknown, and this tends to be a particular problem with some types of medical injury, where the pathology of the patient's condition may be surrounded in mystery or be the subject of intense scientific dispute. The Pearson Commission reported that:

---

[9] See *Gregory* v. *Pembrokeshire Health Authority* [1989] 1 Med. L.R. 81, C.A., where the plaintiff's action failed on this ground. The test had failed to produce a result, and so the plaintiff had to show both that if she had known about this she would have insisted on a further test, and that if that test were positive she would have had the abortion. The difficulties inherent in this exercise in speculation about hypothetical events were highlighted by Nicholls L.J., who commented that: "this unhappy case turns on Mrs. Gregory's hypothetical response to Mr. Davies's hypothetical advice given at a hypothetical consultation."

[10] (1973) 41 D.L.R. (3d) 321 (Ont. C.A.); aff'd *sub nom. Vail* v. *MacDonald* (1976) 66 D.L.R. (3d) 530, 536 (S.C.C.).

[11] See Strachan (1970) 33 M.L.R. 386, 391.

[12] See *Baker* v. *Willoughby* [1970] A.C. 467, and *cf. Jobling* v. *Associated Dairies Ltd.* [1982] A.C. 794, *post*, §§ 5.46–5.47.

[13] [1952] 1 D.L.R. 1.

"The Medical Research Council said that while future research was likely to establish more causal relationships it would also reveal increasingly complex interactions which would heighten the problems of proving causation in the individual case."[14]

Faced with this kind of factual uncertainty the plaintiff may have an **5.11** impossible burden of proving causation on the balance of probabilities, although it should be remembered that the plaintiff does not have to achieve scientific standards of proof.[15] In *Kay* v. *Ayrshire and Arran Health Board*,[16] for example, the plaintiff was unable to prove that an overdose of penicillin could ever cause deafness. The plaintiff was a child suffering from meningitis who was negligently injected with 30 times the correct dose of penicillin. He recovered from the short term toxic effects of the overdose but was subsequently found to be deaf. One consequence of meningitis can be deafness, and the overwhelming weight of medical opinion was to the effect that penicillin did not cause deafness.[17] Similarly, in *Loveday* v. *Renton*[18] the plaintiff failed to show, on a balance of probabilities, that pertussis vaccine could cause brain damage in young children, although it was "possible" that it did because the contrary could not be proved either. Medical and expert opinion was deeply divided on this issue. The evidence from the National Childhood Encephalopathy Study supported the conclusion that the vaccine sometimes caused febrile convulsions, but did not provide evidence that such convulsions following the vaccine caused permanent brain damage. Stuart-Smith L.J. identified several factors that might explain a close temporal association between administration of the vaccine and subsequent neurological damage, without establishing a causal link.

Even where it is possible in principle to establish a connection **5.12** between the type of harm suffered by the plaintiff and a specific hazard, it may be very difficult to show that the individual plaintiff's condition was *caused* by exposure to that hazard rather than some other factor for which the defendant was not responsible. An obvious example is the problem of proving that an individual contracted cancer as a result of exposure to radiation, rather than other causes, although it is well known that radiation can cause cancer.[19]

---

[14] *Royal Commission on Civil Liability and Compensation for Personal Injury*, Cmnd. 7054, (1978), Vol. I, para. 1364; see also para. 1449: "As the boundary of knowledge increases, so does the area of uncertainty."

[15] This is something that should be borne in mind when instructing scientific and medical experts, who may feel uncomfortable with the notion of a standard of "proof" which depends upon the event having been "more likely than not," rather than the more rigorous standards of proof required in scientific inquiry. See the comments of the Supreme Court of Canada on this point in *Snell* v. *Farrell* (1990) 72 D.L.R. (4th) 289, 301–302.

[16] [1987] 2 All E.R. 417.

[17] For criticism of the approach of the House of Lords to the medical evidence in *Kay* see Logie 1988 S.L.T. 25.

[18] [1990] 1 Med. L.R. 117. The Ontario High Court came to the same conclusion on pertussis vaccine in *Rothwell* v. *Raes* (1988) 54 D.L.R. (4th) 193. For discussion of the scientific evidence presented in *Loveday* v. *Renton* see Powers and Harris, *Medical Negligence*, 1990, paras. 14.57–14.63.

[19] See Brahams (1988) 138 New L.J. 570; and Gifford (1990) 301 B.M.J. 451 on reducing the exposure of patients to radiation during diagnostic radiology. On the problems of establishing causation in cases of man-made, usually industrial, disease see Stapleton, *Disease and the Compensation Debate*, 1986, O.U.P., Chap. 3.

5.13   In such circumstances, where the scientific evidence is equivocal, the crucial issue from the plaintiff's point of view is whether the court will be prepared to draw an appropriate inference that there must have been some causal connection, since proof of causation in the medical sphere rests inevitably on the drawing of an inference of fact. In *Jones* v. *Great Western Railway Co.* Lord Macmillan put the matter in this way:

> "The dividing line between conjecture and inference is often a very difficult one to draw. A conjecture may be plausible, but it is of no legal value, for its essence is that it is a mere guess. An inference in the legal sense, on the other hand, is a deduction from the evidence, and if it is a reasonable deduction it may have the validity of legal proof. The attribution of an occurrence to a cause is, I take it, always a matter of inference. The cogency of a legal inference of causation may vary in degree between practical certainty and reasonable probability. Where the coincidence of cause and effect is not a matter of actual observation there is necessarily a hiatus in the direct evidence, but this may be legitimately bridged by an inference from the facts actually observed and proved."[20]

The burden of proof, is, ultimately, a burden of persuading the court to attribute legal responsibility for the plaintiff's injuries to the defendant. This is patent in the case of causation in law, where the court must select from a number of causative factors the event or events that it considers to have been decisive. This is also the position, although maybe less obviously so, with the proof of causation in fact. The readiness of the court to draw an inference of fact, assisted where appropriate by principles of law, depends to some extent on the court's subjective assessment of the evidence, which in turn may be influenced by the underlying policy objectives of the law.

Material contribution to the damage

5.14   The courts have gone some way to relieving a plaintiff from the rigours of the "but for" test where the difficulty of establishing causation has been a product of scientific uncertainty. In *Bonnington Castings Ltd.* v. *Wardlaw*[21] the House of Lords held that the plaintiff does not have to establish that the defendant's breach of duty was the main cause of the damage provided that it materially contributed to the damage. The plaintiff contracted pneumoconiosis from inhaling air which contained silica dust at his workplace. The main source of the dust was from pneumatic hammers for which the employers were not in breach of duty (the "innocent dust"). Some of the dust (the "guilty dust") came from swing grinders for which they were responsible by failing to maintain the dust-extraction equipment. There was no evidence as to the proportions of innocent dust and guilty dust inhaled by the plaintiff. Indeed, such evidence as there was indicated that

---

[20] (1930) 47 T.L.R. 39, 45.
[21] [1956] A.C. 613.

much the greater proportion came from the innocent source. On the evidence the plaintiff could not prove "but for" causation, in the sense that it was more probable than not that had the dust-extraction equipment worked efficiently he would not have contracted the disease. Nonetheless, the House of Lords drew an inference of fact that the guilty dust was a contributory cause, holding the employers liable for the full extent of the loss. The plaintiff did not have to prove that the guilty dust was the sole or even the most substantial cause if he could show, on a balance of probabilities, the burden of proof remaining with the plaintiff, that the guilty dust had materially contributed to the disease. Anything which did not fall within the principle *de minimis non curat lex* would constitute a material contribution. Subsequently, in *Nicholson* v. *Atlas Steel Foundry & Engineering Co. Ltd.*,[22] on virtually identical facts, the House of Lords held the defendants liable for an employee's pneumoconiosis, even though, in the words of Viscount Simonds, it was "impossible even approximately to quantify" the respective contributions of guilty and innocent dust.

These cases were significant in easing the plaintiff's burden of proof **5.15** for two reasons. First, they were a departure from "but for" causation—the plaintiff does not have to prove that he would not have suffered the "damage" (*i.e.* the injury or illness) but for the breach of duty. What has to be proved is redefined as a "material contribution" to the injury or illness, and, notwithstanding this redefinition of the "damage" to which the plaintiff must establish a causal link in more limited terms than the outcome, the plaintiff still recovers *damages* for the whole loss, *i.e.* the outcome, having proved causation in respect of a part only of that loss.[23] Secondly, the courts were willing to draw an *inference* of fact that there had been a material contribution when it was in reality impossible to say whether there had been any such contribution, or even to make a statistical guess.

Material contribution to the risk

Subsequently, the House of Lords appeared to take *Bonnington* **5.16** *Castings Ltd.* v. *Wardlaw*[24] one step further. In *McGhee* v. *National Coal Board*[25] the plaintiff, who worked at the defendants' brick kilns, contracted dermatitis as a result of exposure to brick dust. The employers were not at fault for the exposure during working hours, but they were in breach of duty by failing to provide adequate washing facilities. This increased the period of time during which the plaintiff was exposed to contact with the brick dust while he bicycled home. It was agreed that the brick dust had caused the dermatitis, but the current state of medical knowledge could not say whether it was probable that the plaintiff would not have contracted the disease if he had been able to take a shower after work. Thus, he could not

---

[22] [1957] 1 W.L.R. 613; [1957] 1 All E.R. 776. See also *Clarkson* v. *Modern Foundries Ltd.* [1957] 1 W.L.R. 1210; [1958] 1 All E.R. 33, applying *Bonnington Castings Ltd.* v. *Wardlaw* [1956] A.C. 613.

[23] See Stapleton (1988) 104 L.Q.R. 389, 404–5.

[24] [1956] A.C. 613.

[25] [1973] 1 W.L.R. 1; [1972] 3 All E.R. 1008.

establish "but for" causation in respect of the "guilty" exposure. At best it could be said that the failure to provide washing facilities materially increased the risk of the plaintiff contracting dermatitis. The House of Lords held the defendants liable on the basis that it was sufficient for a plaintiff to show that the defendants' breach of duty made the risk of injury more probable even though it was uncertain whether it was the actual cause.

5.17   A majority of their Lordships treated a "material increase in the risk" as equivalent to a "material contribution to the damage." Lord Simon, for example, said that "a failure to take steps which would bring about a material reduction of the risk involves, in this type of case, a substantial contribution to the injury."[26] Lord Wilberforce explicitly recognised that this process involves overcoming an "evidential gap" by drawing an inference of fact which, strictly speaking, the evidence does not support (as was done in *Bonnington Castings*), and, moreover, that this "fictional" inference is drawn for policy reasons. Why, his Lordship asked, should a man who is able to show that his employer should have taken certain precautions, because without them there is a risk or an added risk of injury or disease, and who in fact sustains exactly that injury or disease, have to assume the burden of proving more? In many cases it is impossible to prove causation because medical opinion cannot segregate the causes of an illness between compound causes:

> "And if one asks which of the parties, the workman or the employers, should suffer from this inherent evidential difficulty, the answer as a matter of policy or justice should be that it is the creator of the risk who, *ex hypothesi*, must be taken to have foreseen the possibility of damage, who should bear its consequences."[27]

5.18   The potential in this line of reasoning for reversing the burden of proof of causation was enormous—the plaintiff does not have to show that the defendant's breach of duty caused his injury, merely that it increased the risk of injury.[28] Indeed, Lord Wilberforce appeared to suggest that the burden of disproving causation would shift to the defendant in such cases. The implications of *McGhee* became apparent in *Clark* v. *MacLennan*,[29] a case of medical negligence, where the principle was extended to proof of breach of duty. Pain J. held that where there is a general practice to take a particular precaution against a specific, known risk but the defendant fails to take that precaution, and the very damage against which it is designed to be a protection occurs, then the burden of proof lies with the defendant to show both that he was not in breach of duty and that the breach did not cause the damage. This approach to the question of proving negligence, as opposed to causation, was criticised by Mustill L.J. in *Wilsher* v. *Essex Area Health Authority*,[30] although his Lordship accepted that in some

---

[26] [1972] 3 All E.R. 1008 at p. 1014; see also, *per* Lords Reid and Salmon at pp. 1011, 1017.
[27] *Ibid.*, p. 1012.
[28] See Weinrib (1975) 38 M.L.R. 518.
[29] [1983] 1 All E.R. 416.
[30] [1986] 3 All E.R. 801, 814.

instances breach and causation are so closely linked that in practice it may be difficult to maintain a different rule for proof of breach of duty when the *McGhee* rule is applicable to proof of causation.

In *Wilsher* itself the question was whether *McGhee* could be applied **5.19** to a case where there were up to five discrete causes of the plaintiff's injury any one of which might have caused the damage. The plaintiff was a premature baby who, through the defendants' negligence, received an excessive concentration of oxygen. It is known that excessive oxygen can damage the retina of a premature baby leading to a condition called retrolental fibroplasia (RLF) which results in blindness. The plaintiff contracted RLF. However, RLF can occur in premature babies who have not been given additional oxygen and there is evidence of some correlation between RLF and several other conditions from which premature babies can suffer (apnoea, hypercarbia, intraventricular haemorrhage, parent ductus arteriosus), all of which afflicted the plaintiff. As Mustill L.J. put it: "What the defendants did was not to enhance the risk that the known factors would lead to injury, but to add to the list of factors which might do so."[31] The majority of the Court of Appeal held that *McGhee* could apply in these circumstances, recognising that this represented an extension of that case. Mustill L.J. expressed the principle in the following terms:

> "If it is an established fact that conduct of a particular kind creates a risk that injury will be caused to another or increases an existing risk that injury will ensue, and if the two parties stand in such a relationship that the one party owes a duty not to conduct himself in that way, and if one party does conduct himself in that way, and if the other party does suffer injury of the kind to which the [risk] related, then the first party is taken to have caused the injury by his breach of duty, even though the existence and extent of the contribution made by the breach cannot be ascertained."[32]

Browne-Wilkinson V.-C., dissenting, took the view that the position was wholly different from that in *McGhee*:

> "A failure to take preventive measures against one out of five possible causes is no evidence as to which of those five caused the injury."[33]

The House of Lords reversed the decision of the Court of Appeal on **5.20** this issue, approving the judgment of the Vice-Chancellor.[34] It was held that *McGhee* did not establish any new principle of law and did not have the effect of reversing the burden of proof. The burden of proof remains with the plaintiff throughout, and he must establish that the

---

[31] *Ibid.*, p. 828.
[32] *Ibid.*, p. 829, as corrected at [1987] 2 All E.R. corrigenda; see also, *per* Glidewell L.J. at p. 832.
[33] *Ibid.*, p. 835.
[34] *Wilsher* v. *Essex Area Health Authority* [1988] 1 All E.R. 871. See also *Murray* v. *Kensington and Chelsea and Westminster Area Health Authority* (1981) (unreported), C.A. where the plaintiff failed to establish a causal link between the excess oxygen he had received and RLF.

breach of duty was at least a material contributory cause of the harm, applying *Bonnington Castings* v. *Wardlaw*. What the House of Lords did in *McGhee*, said Lord Bridge, was to adopt a robust and pragmatic approach to the undisputed primary facts of the case and draw a legitimate, common-sense, inference of fact that the additional period of exposure to brick dust had probably materially contributed to the plaintiff's dermatitis.[35]

5.21 The decision of the House of Lords in *Wilsher* leaves a practical problem of how these cases should be applied. *McGhee*, it seems, is still good law, subject to the formal requirement that the burden of proof remains with the plaintiff. It must, presumably, still be open to a plaintiff to argue that proof of a material increase in the risk of harm due to the defendant's negligence is sufficient proof of a material contribution to the damage, at least when the court can be persuaded to take a robust or pragmatic approach to the drawing of inferences of fact. In theory, a material contribution to the damage is one step beyond a material increase of risk in a chain of logical reasoning about causation, since identifying the existence of the risk does not in itself prove that the risk has materialised and caused damage. In practice, however, where the evidence is so uncertain, it is simply unreal to attempt to draw a sensible distinction between them.[36] Indeed, bearing in mind the paucity of the evidence on which the House of Lords held that a material contribution to the damage had been proved in *Bonnington Castings* it might seem to be a matter of semantics whether the test should be material contribution to the damage or material increase of the risk. Certainly, the correlation between these concepts, which was made explicit in *McGhee* had been anticipated in *Nicholson* v. *Atlas Steel Foundry & Engineering Co. Ltd.*[37] by both Viscount Simonds and Lord Cohen.

5.22 This still leaves unanswered the question of what constitutes a "material contribution" to the damage, and when it is legitimate to draw *admittedly fictional* inferences about causation when confronted by factual uncertainty. The inference is no less fictional simply for being described as "common sense" or "pragmatic," as Lord Bridge, in *Wilsher*, explained the decision in *McGhee*. If the court is prepared to draw such an inference the burden of proof is *irrelevant*, because the defendant, faced with the same factual uncertainty as the plaintiff, will be unable to adduce evidence which would rebut the inference.

5.23 In what circumstances, then, will *Bonnington Castings* and/or *McGhee* be applied? First, there must be uncertainty about the causal connection between the defendant's negligence and the plaintiff's damage. Where the extent of the defendant's contribution is known

---

[35] *Ibid.*, pp. 880, 881–2. This interpretation of *McGhee* does not address the issue raised by both *McGhee* and *Bonnington Castings* of how the plaintiff can succeed in recovering his whole loss from the defendant while establishing causation in respect of an indeterminate part only of that loss: see Stapleton (1988) 104 L.Q.R. 389, 404.

[36] See, *per* Lord Salmon in *McGhee* at pp. 1017, and 1018f. This was the point of Pain J.'s decision in *Clark* v. *MacLennan* [1983] 1 All E.R. 416.

[37] [1957] 1 W.L.R. 613; [1957] 1 All E.R. 776, at pp. 781 and 782 respectively.

the defendant is liable to that extent and no more.[38] Secondly, in *Fitzgerald* v. *Lane*[39] the Court of Appeal held that *McGhee* was not limited to factual uncertainties due to gaps in medical knowledge about the cause of injuries or diseases, but could apply to other types of factual uncertainty. This proposition seems still to be correct after *Wilsher*.

Thirdly, there would appear to be a distinction of some kind **5.24** between cumulative causes and discrete causes. In *Bonnington Castings* the guilty dust and the innocent dust were concurrent and, it was presumed, cumulative causes. In *McGhee* the innocent and guilty periods of exposure to brick dust were consecutive. They might both have contributed to the cause of the disease (cumulative effect) or, one or other may have been the sole (discrete) cause, although in *Wilsher*[40] Lord Bridge seems to have presumed that the inference drawn in *McGhee* was that they contributed cumulatively to the dermatitis. In *Wilsher* there were five possible discrete causes, and the House of Lords regarded this as an important distinction from *McGhee*. It is possible that *McGhee* will apply where the specific risk which has materialised, for which there would have to be some prima facie evidence, has been enhanced by the defendant's breach of duty, but not where the negligence enhanced a general risk to the plaintiff. This requires a narrow interpretation of the word "risk." So, for example, in *Wilsher* the risk created by the defendants was "RLF caused *by excess oxygen*," not simply an enhancement of an existing risk of RLF from other causes. Until it can be shown that the RLF was caused by excess oxygen the injury cannot be said to fall squarely within the risk created by the defendants.[41] Thus:

> "*McGhee* saves the court from the impossibility of separating the 'guilty' and 'innocent' components of a single risk, not from the impossibility of determining the causal impact of distinct risks, even if these risks may have the same consequences on maturity."[42]

It has been suggested that the distinction between *McGhee* and **5.25** *Wilsher* does not rest on the presence of more than one competing

---

[38] See *Thompson* v. *Smiths Shiprepairers (North Shields) Ltd.* [1984] 2 W.L.R. 522; [1984] 1 All E.R. 881, where the plaintiff suffered progressive hearing impairment due to industrial noise; the defendants were held liable only for that part of the deafness occurring after the exposure to noise became a breach of duty; see also *Torrison* v. *Colwill* (1987) 42 C.C.L.T. 51, 62 (B.C.S.C.) stating that *McGhee* is irrelevant in circumstances where there is evidence on which the court finds that, on the balance of probabilities, there is no causal connection.

[39] [1987] 3 W.L.R. 249; [1987] 2 All E.R. 455.

[40] [1988] 1 All E.R. 871, 880.

[41] [1986] 3 All E.R. 801, 835, *per* Browne-Wilkinson V.-C. In *Kay* v. *Ayrshire and Arran Health Board* [1987] 2 All E.R. 417 the House of Lords made it clear that an overall contribution to "the risk of damage" was insufficient to invoke *McGhee* where the negligence created a risk of a different kind of damage from that which occurred. Lord Mackay (at p. 425) said that: "In my opinion, it is not right to ask whether [the overdose] materially increased the risk of neurological damage when the evidence available distinguishes between different kinds of neurological damage . . . I cannot accept that it is correct to say that because evidence shows that an overdose of penicillin increases the risk of particular types of neurological damage found in these cases that an overdose of penicillin materially increases the risk of a different type of neurological damage, namely that which causes deafness when no such deafness has been shown to have resulted from such overdose"; see also, *per* Lord Griffiths at p. 422.

[42] Boon (1988) 51 M.L.R. 508, 513. It may be that this is simply a variation on the distinction between cumulative and discrete causes.

cause of injury in *Wilsher* but on the absence of a finding that excess oxygen had materially contributed to the plaintiff's condition. Had there been evidence that excess oxygen materially increases the risk of RLF, "and a consequential finding on the primary facts that excess oxygen was more likely than not to have materially contributed to the plaintiff's condition, he might then have relied on the judgment in *McGhee* for a finding that that cause rather than other possible causes was in fact the cause of his sad injury."[43] With respect, this argument appears to understate the plaintiff's difficulty in *Wilsher*. If there had been a finding of fact that the excess oxygen materially contributed to the RLF, he would not have had to rely on *McGhee,* and it is irrelevant what other causes may or may not have contributed. He would have established causation under *Bonnington Castings Ltd.* v. *Wardlaw*.[44] The plaintiff needed *McGhee in order to reach the finding of fact* (by the drawing of an inference) that the excess oxygen had made a material contribution to the RLF, and the issue in *Wilsher* was in precisely what circumstances a plaintiff could resort to *McGhee* in order to overcome the evidential difficulty of establishing a material contribution to the damage. The House of Lords said that this could be done only where there is an enhancement of an existing risk, not the addition of a discrete risk factor, and thus, where there is "more than one competing cause of the injury" the plaintiff simply cannot rely on *McGhee.* Of course, if it is possible to say that the defendant's negligence enhanced the specific risk which, on the balance of probabilities, has materialised and materially contributed to the plaintiff's injury, it is irrelevant that there were other discrete risk factors. In practice, however, the presence of other risk factors will probably make it impossible for the plaintiff to prove exactly which risk has materialised, and he will be unable to overcome the causation hurdle.

5.26   It is not entirely clear why the courts should want to make such fine distinctions when dealing with different types of factual uncertainty. It may be pure chance whether a defendant's negligence enhances an existing risk or adds a new risk factor, even if it is possible to distinguish between such risks. In some cases it may simply be unknown whether an illness is the result of a cumulative effect or of a single event the risk of which has been enhanced by the defendant.[45] In the face of such uncertainty it would seem strange to attach much significance to the distinction between cumulative and discrete causes,[46] although it may be conceded that in practice, if not in logic, it may be easier to infer that "there must have been some contribution" in cases of cumulative causes and/or the enhancement of a single risk factor. The decisions in *McGhee, Wilsher* (in the Court of Appeal), and *Fitzgerald* v. *Lane* were quite explicitly based upon policy considerations of fairness to plaintiffs faced with otherwise insuperable problems of proof.[47] On the other hand, in *Wilsher* Lord Bridge considered that

---

[43] *Clerk & Lindsell on Torts*, 16th ed., 1989, para. 11–25.

[44] [1956] A.C. 613.

[45] See, *e.g., Bryce* v. *Swan Hunter Group plc.* [1988] 1 All E.R. 659, 665, where mesothelioma was caused by exposure to asbestos dust.

[46] See Stapleton (1988) 104 L.Q.R. 389, 402 and 406, n. 40.

[47] In *Fitzgerald* v. *Lane* [1987] 2 All E.R. 455, 464, Nourse L.J. commented that: "A benevolent principle smiles on these factual uncertainties and melts them all away." See also Fleming, *The Law of Torts,* 7th ed., 1987, p. 175 observing that: "Whatever the technical allocation and standard of proof, in practice causal uncertainty is apt to be resolved by the strong sympathetic bias for the victim of a proven wrongdoer."

the forensic process would be rendered "still more unpredictable and hazardous by distorting the law to accommodate the exigencies of what may seem hard cases."[48]

In Canada the principle in *McGhee* has had a mixed reception. In **5.27** *Powell* v. *Guttman*[49] the plaintiff developed a condition of avascular necrosis following an operation on her leg performed by the defendant orthopaedic surgeon. The defendant negligently failed to advise the plaintiff to undergo an arthoplasty operation to correct this. When another surgeon performed the operation, the plaintiff sustained a rotary fracture of the femur because the delay had caused the condition of the bone to deteriorate as result of osteoporosis. The question was whether the negligence was a cause of the fracture. The defendant was held liable because his negligence had caused an increase in the osteoporosis which rendered the femur more susceptible to the fracture. This materially increased the risk of the very fracture which did occur. O'Sullivan J.A. applied the principle of *McGhee*:

> "However, I think the law in Canada is that where a tortfeasor creates or materially contributes to a significant risk of injury occurring and injury does occur which is squarely within the risk thus created or materially increased, then unless the risk is spent, the tortfeasor is liable for injury which follows from the risk, even though there are other subsequent causes which also cause or materially contribute to that injury."[50]

The Saskatchewan Court of Appeal has also applied this principle.[51] **5.28** On the other hand, in *Wilkinson Estate (Rogin)* v. *Shannon*[52] Anderson J. was not convinced that *McGhee* represented the law of Ontario, and in *Wilson* v. *Vancouver Hockey Club*[53] Murray J. declined to apply *McGhee* in a case of alleged medical negligence. In *Snell* v. *Farrell*[54] the trial judge concluded that *McGhee* did shift the onus of proof to the defendant. The defendant had been "asking for trouble" by operating on the plaintiff's eye when he knew that his patient had a retrobulbar bleed. The increased risk was followed by injury in the same area of risk, and this was sufficient to establish causation. On appeal to the Supreme Court of Canada,[55] however, it was held that the burden of proof remained with

---

[48] *Wilsher* v. *Essex Area Health Authority* [1988] 1 All E.R. 871, 883.

[49] (1978) 89 D.L.R. (3d) 180 (Man. C.A.).

[50] *Ibid.*, p. 192.

[51] *Nowsco Well Service Ltd.* v. *Canadian Propane Gas & Oil Ltd.* (1981) 122 D.L.R. (3d) 228, a non-medical case. See also *Meyer* v. *Gordon* (1981) 17 C.C.L.T. 1, 41–2 (B.C.S.C.), where *McGhee* was relied upon as an "additional ground" since the judge had already found that the negligence probably caused the damage. The negligence had "materially increased the risk of injury to the child and materially increased the risk of fetal distress and the resulting hypoxia." In *Wipfli* v. *Britten* (1982) 145 D.L.R. (3d) 80 (B.C.S.C.); aff'd (1984) 13 D.L.R. (4th) 169 (B.C.C.A.) the trial judge had relied on *McGhee* to establish causation, but the British Columbia Court of Appeal considered that this was unnecessary, since causation had been established on a balance of probabilities from the evidence. It was a reasonable inference that had the physicians attending the labour known that there were twins the labour would not have been allowed to continue for so long, and this would have avoided or materially lessened the effects of the prolonged labour on the second twin.

[52] (1986) 37 C.C.L.T. 181 (Ont. H.C.).

[53] (1983) 5 D.L.R. (4th) 282, 288; aff'd (1985) 22 D.L.R. (4th) 516 (B.C.C.A.), citing *Murray* v. *Shaughnessy Hospital* (1982) 15 A.C.W.S. (2d) 389, where Esson J. said that he doubted whether *McGhee* applied in British Columbia.

[54] (1986) 40 C.C.L.T. 298, 312–313 (N.B.Q.B.).

[55] (1990) 72 D.L.R. (4th) 289 .

the plaintiff throughout, applying the interpretation of *McGhee* adopted by the House of Lords in *Wilsher*. Nonetheless, though the burden of proof does not change, the court was entitled to draw an inference to establish causation, notwithstanding that causation was not proved by positive evidence:

> "In many malpractice cases, the facts lie particularly within the knowledge of the defendant. In these circumstances, very little affirmative evidence on the part of the plaintiff will justify the drawing of an inference of causation in the absence of evidence to the contrary."[56]

Moreover, the court was entitled to draw such an inference even where there was no firm expert opinion supporting the plaintiff's theory of causation, since medical experts normally determine causation in terms of certainties whereas the courts deal with the matter on the balance of probabilities.

3. Loss of a chance

5.29   The plaintiff's complaint in a medical negligence action is frequently not that the doctor has inflicted "additional" injury, but that as a result of the defendant's negligence his medical condition has not been improved or has been allowed to deteriorate. Accordingly, the plaintiff has been deprived of the opportunity of making a full or proper recovery from the illness or injury for which he first sought treatment. Applying the "but for" test of causation, if on the balance of probabilities competent treatment would have prevented the deterioration which has occurred, or would have produced an improvement, the negligence is causally linked to the damage and the defendant is responsible. Where, however, the patient's prospects of a successful outcome to the treatment were estimated to be less than 50 per cent., the patient cannot satisfy the "but for" test, because even with proper treatment the damage would probably (*i.e.* more likely than not) have occurred in any event.

5.30   An alternative approach to cases involving this type of factual uncertainty is to deal with them in terms of the measure of damages by reference to the chance of loss, rather than determining liability on an all or nothing basis (using the "but for" test). In *Hotson* v. *East Berkshire Area Health Authority*[57] the plaintiff suffered an accidental injury to his hip in a fall which created a 75 per cent. risk that he would develop a permanent disability through avascular necrosis of the femoral epiphysis. Due to negligent medical diagnosis the hip was not treated for five days, and the delay made the disability inevitable. The plaintiff contended that the doctor's negligence had deprived him of a 25 per cent. chance of making a good recovery, whereas the defendant argued that the plaintiff had failed to prove, on the balance of probabilities, that the negligence caused the disability. The trial judge held that where a "substantial chance" of a better medical result had been lost it was not necessary to prove that the adverse medical result was directly attributable to the

---

[56] *Ibid.*, p. 300.
[57] [1987] 1 All E.R. 210, C.A.

breach of duty because the issue was the proper quantum of damage rather than causation. The plaintiff could prove causation of the lost chance and accordingly he was entitled to damages on the basis of 25 per cent. of the value of the claim for the full disability.[58] This approach was upheld by the Court of Appeal, where Sir John Donaldson M.R. characterised the plaintiff's claim as the loss of the *benefit* of timely treatment, rather than the *chance* of successful treatment. The use of the word "chance" complicated the issue, because it imported probabilities, and opened the way for the defendant's argument. It was also inaccurate, said his Lordship, because it elides the identification of the loss with the valuation of the loss, which are distinct processes. Just as the categories of negligence are never closed, there was no reason why the categories of loss should be closed either.[59]

It is clear that there was a strong element of policy in the Court of **5.31** Appeal's decision. Sir John Donaldson M.R. commented that:

> "As a matter of common sense, it is unjust that there should be no liability for failure to treat a patient, simply because the chances of a successful cure by that treatment were less than 50 per cent. Nor, by the same token, can it be just that, if the chances of a successful cure only marginally exceed 50 per cent., the doctor or his employer should be liable to the same extent as if the treatment could be guaranteed to cure. If this is the law, it is high time that it was changed . . . ."[60]

The House of Lords, however, reversed the Court of Appeal on the **5.32** basis that the judge's finding that there was a high probability, put at 75 per cent., that even with correct diagnosis and treatment the plaintiff's disability would have occurred, amounted to a finding of fact that the accidental injury was the sole cause of the disability.[61] In other words this was not a "lost chance" case, it was an "all or nothing case"—either the fall or the misdiagnosis caused the disability, and on the balance of probabilities it was the fall. The valuation of a "lost chance" would only arise once causation had been established. As has been pointed out, however, this decision fails to address the essence of the plaintiff's argument, which was whether a claim formulated as a loss of a chance was acceptable.[62] If the nature of the damage could be redefined as the loss of a *chance* of a successful outcome, rather than the outcome itself (the disability), then on a traditional causation test the defendants' negligence clearly did cause the damage (*i.e* the lost chance). Logically, the question of whether the defendant's negligence caused damage is an issue that can only be dealt with *after* the nature of the damage has been defined.

---

[58] *Hotson* v. *Fitzgerald* [1985] 3 All E.R. 167.

[59] [1987] 1 All E.R. 210, 216–217.

[60] *Ibid.*, pp. 215–216. Dillon L.J. observed, at p. 219, that: "If counsel is right, and the chance is lost through a negligent failure of the doctor to examine the patient properly or to diagnose correctly, with the result that the treatment which alone might have saved the patient is not undertaken, the patient will have no remedy unless he can show that the chance of the treatment, if undertaken, proving successful was more than 50 per cent. That to my mind is contrary to common sense."

[61] [1987] 2 All E.R. 909.

[62] Stapleton (1988) 104 L.Q.R. 389, 393. This point was not lost on Sir John Donaldson M.R. in the Court of Appeal.

5.33   The decision of the House of Lords in *Hotson* had been anticipated in the Scottish case of *Kenyon* v. *Bell*,[63] where an infant sustained an accidental injury to her eye. It was alleged that due to negligent treatment of the eye by a casualty officer the eye was lost, or alternatively that proper treatment would have given the child a "materially greater chance of the eye being saved." The pursuer argued that the loss of a chance of saving the eye was in itself damage, and that the only difficulty was in the assessment of appropriate damages. This argument was rejected by Lord Guthrie as "extravagant and contrary to principle" because the pursuer would be entitled to damages "although on the evidence the balance of probability was that the loss of the eye was not caused by the defender." The pursuer had to show that but for the negligence the eye would have been saved.[64]

5.34   In some jurisdictions of the United States claims for loss of a chance have been accepted. In *Herskovits* v. *Group Health Co-operative of Puget Sound*[65] H died from cancer. When he was first seen, the defendants failed to diagnose his tumour. At that stage, if the tumour had been detected, H had a 39 per cent. chance of survival for more than five years. By the time his tumour was discovered and treated his chance of surviving for more than five years was only 25 per cent. The court allowed the case to go to the jury on the question of proximate cause, although the "loss" constituted the 14 per cent. reduction in the chance of survival, and any damages would be limited to the loss attributable to the premature death, not the death itself. As Dore J. pointed out:

> "To decide otherwise would be a blanket release from liability for doctors and hospitals any time there was less than a 50 per cent chance of survival, regardless of how flagrant the negligence was."[66]

5.35   This comment was echoed in the observations of the Court of Appeal in *Hotson* that applying the all or nothing approach to a patient whose chances of a successful outcome to his treatment were less than 50 per cent. means that the patient has no action against the doctor no matter how negligent he has been. This creates what is, in effect, an unenforceable duty to exercise reasonable care, a factor which had influenced both Lord Simon and Lord Salmon to impose liability *McGhee*.

5.36   One of the problems confronting a plaintiff in this type of case is the courts' attitude to statistical evidence. In *Hotson* v. *East Berkshire Area Health Authority* Croom-Johnson L.J. explained the difficulty:

> "If it is proved statistically that 25 per cent. of the population has a chance of recovery from a certain injury and 75 per cent. does not, it does not mean that someone who suffers that injury and who does not recover from it has lost a 25 per cent. chance. He may have lost nothing at all. What he has to do is prove that he was one

---

[63] 1953 S.C. 125.

[64] This he subsequently failed to do: see *Hotson* v. *East Berkshire Area Health Authority* [1987] 2 All E.R. 909, 915, *per* Lord Mackay.

[65] (1983) 664 P. 2d 474 (Washington S.C.). This decision was discussed by Lord Mackay in *Hotson* v. *East Berkshire Area Health Authority* [1987] 2 All E.R. 909, 916–919. See also *Hicks* v. *United States* (1966) 368 F. 2d 626 (4th Cir.); *Jeanes* v. *Milner* (1970) 428 F. 2d 598 (U.S.C.A. 8th Cir.); *Hamil* v. *Bashline* (1978) 481 Pa. 256 (Pennsylvania S.C.); Price (1989) 38 I.C.L.Q. 735.

[66] *Ibid.*, p. 477.

of the 25 per cent. and that his loss was caused by the defendant's negligence. To be a figure in a statistic does not by itself give him a cause of action. If the plaintiff succeeds in proving that he was one of the 25 per cent. and that the defendant took away that chance, the logical result would be to award him 100 per cent. of his damages and not only a quarter . . . ."[67]

The plaintiff's problem, of course, is that by definition he cannot prove that he would have been one of the 25 per cent. because if he could, he would be able to show that on a balance of probabilities the defendant did indeed cause the damage. Moreover, he cannot prove this because *as a result of the defendant's negligence* it will never be known whether he would have made a full recovery. It is the defendant's negligence which prevents the plaintiff from establishing "but for" causation. This in itself might be thought a good policy reason for permitting an action for a lost chance.[68] Lord Bridge acknowledged that in some cases, "perhaps particularly medical negligence cases, causation may be so shrouded in mystery that the court can only measure statistical chances," although "that was not so here."[69]

The question of whether it would ever be possible to claim for loss of a **5.37** chance in tort was specifically left open by their Lordships in *Hotson*. Lord Mackay took the view that while *McGhee* v. *National Coal Board*[70] was still good law it would be unwise to lay down as a rule of law that a plaintiff could never succeed by proving a loss of a chance in a medical negligence case. A material increase of the risk of a particular result was "equivalent to a material decrease in the chance of escaping" the result.[71] It is uncertain whether *Wilsher* v. *Essex Area Health Authority*[72] has made any difference to Lord Mackay's observation. Arguably, nothing has changed since *Wilsher* did not overrule *McGhee*, it merely explained it as a particular application of *Bonnington Castings Ltd.* v. *Wardlaw*.[73] It has been suggested that following *Wilsher* "there is no longer room for argument that in a case where the material facts lie in the past, anything less than proof of causation on a balance of probability suffices to discharge the necessary burden."[74] This statement is perfectly true, but does not address the question of exactly *what* may be the subject of proof of causation, on a balance of probability. If a loss of chance is actionable, the plaintiff would still have to prove, on a balance of probabilities, that the breach of duty caused him to lose the chance, or, in Sir John Donaldson's phrase, the benefit of timely treatment.

This leaves the relationship between *McGhee* v. *National Coal Board*[75] **5.38** and potential lost chance claims unclear. Would *McGhee* apply where it

---

[67] [1987] 1 All ER 210, 223; see also Lord Mackay's discussion of statistics at [1987] 2 All E.R. 909, 918; see further Hill (1991) 54 M.L.R. 511, arguing that there is a distinction between the loss of a statistical chance and the loss of a chance that was personal to the plaintiff; *cf.* Stapleton (1988) 104 L.Q.R. 389, 399, n. 23.

[68] *cf. Cook* v. *Lewis* [1952] 1 D.L.R. 1, § 5.09 *ante*, where the Supreme Court of Canada considered that this was a good reason for reversing the burden of proof.

[69] *Hotson* v. *East Berkshire Area Health Authority* [1987] 2 All E.R. 909, 913.

[70] [1973] 1 W.L.R. 1; [1972] 3 All E.R. 1008.

[71] [1987] 2 All E.R. 909, 916.

[72] [1988] 1 All E.R. 871.

[73] [1956] A.C. 613; see § 5.14, *ante*.

[74] Powers and Harris, *Medical Negligence*, 1990, para. 14.36.

[75] [1973] 1 W.L.R. 1; [1972] 3 All E.R. 1008.

was impossible to determine the extent of the increased risk,[76] but the lost chance approach when the risk was quantifiable, with the result that the less that was known about the risk the greater the potential award of damages, since under *McGhee* the damages are not discounted?[77] Could the facts of *Hotson* be reformulated in terms of a "material contribution to the damage," treating the disability as having two causes, the fall and the negligent delay in treatment.[78]

5.39　It is long established that a lost chance may be actionable in contract.[79] Where, for example, through a solicitor's negligence a client has lost the opportunity to bring proceedings (*e.g.* because the limitation period has been allowed to expire), the client in an action against the solicitor does not have to prove that he would have won the other case, merely that he has lost "some right of value, some chose in action of reality and substance."[80] Damages are then discounted to reflect his chances of success in the original action. It scarcely seems arguable that the basis of a distinction between *Kitchen* and *Hotson* is that one was a claim in contract and the other in tort, when the duties in each instance are the same, namely a duty to exercise reasonable skill and care. It would lead to the untenable result that, in identical circumstances, a patient who had received treatment privately might have a claim but a patient who received treatment under the National Health Service would not.[81]

5.40　In the House of Lords the analogy of *Kitchen* was dismissed as irrelevant, though it is not entirely clear why it was irrelevant, particularly as their Lordships did not give any reasons. Lord Bridge thought that the analogy with *Kitchen* was "superficially attractive," but considered that there were "formidable difficulties in the way of accepting the analogy."[82] The trial judge, on the other hand, was unable to see any sensible distinction between the solicitor/client relationship and the doctor/patient relationship in these circumstances.[83]

---

[76] Provided, of course, that it was possible to infer that the increase in risk must have resulted in a material contribution to the damage: see § 5.21.

[77] In *Seyfert* v. *Burnaby Hospital Society* (1986) 27 D.L.R. (4th) 96 (B.C.S.C.) McEachern C.J.S.C. adopted a lost chance approach (referring specifically to *Hotson* v. *Fitzgerald*) for this very reason, namely that *McGhee* would place the whole loss upon the defendant. The defendant was negligent in failing to diagnose that the patient had a stab wound which had penetrated the peritoneum, causing a wound to the transverse colon. There were three possible ways of treating this type of injury if diagnosed quickly enough, one of which did not involve a colostomy and delayed recovery. McEachern C.J. held that the plaintiff was "entitled to recover damages representing the loss of the chance he had of avoiding the risk of a colostomy, a second operation and an extended period of convalescence . . . I would fix that chance at 25 per cent., making it necessary that the plaintiff's damages be reduced by 75 per cent" (at p. 102).

[78] See, *per* Lord Bridge at [1987] 2 All E.R. 909, 913. The case was not argued on this basis. See also *Clerk & Lindsell on Torts*, 16th ed., 1989, para. 1–104, apparently unable to distinguish between *Hotson* and *McGhee*.

[79] *Chaplin* v. *Hicks* [1911] 2 K.B. 786, on loss of a chance to compete for a prize amongst a limited number of contestants.

[80] *Kitchen* v. *Royal Air Force Association* [1958] 1 W.L.R. 563; *cf. Sykes* v. *Midland Bank Executor & Trustee Co. Ltd.* [1971] 1 Q.B. 113, although this decision appears to be an exception to the general approach exemplified by *Kitchen:* see Jackson and Powell, *Professional Negligence*, 1987, 2nd ed., paras. 4.130–4.131.

[81] See *Hotson* v. *East Berkshire Area Health Authority* [1987] 1 All E.R. 210, at pp. 216, 219 and 222, *per* Sir John Donaldson M.R., Dillon L.J. and Croom-Johnson L.J. respectively.

[82] [1987] 2 All E.R. 909, 914–915.

[83] [1985] 3 All E.R. 167, 176; *cf.* Hill (1991) 54 M.L.R. 511, 519, arguing that *Kitchen* was not a lost chance case.

One possible explanation is that *Hotson* was concerned with uncer- **5.41**
tainty as to past facts whereas *Kitchen* was concerned with uncertainty
about hypothetical facts.[84] Uncertainty about the past is decided on the
balance of probabilities. Anything that is more probable than not is
treated as certain.[85] On the other hand, where "the uncertainty is as to
the facts that would have occurred had there been no negligence, *i.e.*
hypothetical facts, English Law has been prepared to regard the plaintiff's
loss as that of the chance of a favourable outcome."[86] With great respect,
this distinction does not seem so clear-cut, because in each case the issue
can be reformulated as uncertainty about either "hypothetical facts" or
"past facts." In *Hotson*, for example, the uncertainty was as to what
would have happened in the absence of negligence ("hypothetical fact"),
namely whether the plaintiff would have fallen into the category of the 25
per cent. of patients who, in his circumstances, would have benefited
from prompt treatment. Conversely, in *Kitchen*, the uncertainty could be
said to have concerned a past fact, namely whether the solicitor's
negligence caused the plaintiff's loss of the action. That question can only
be answered by answering another, hypothetical, question about what
would have happened in the absence of negligence. But this is true of any
causal inquiry which employs the "but for" test, because the test,
although apparently concerned with "facts," depends upon the answer to
an hypothetical question. For example, in *McWilliams* v. *Sir William
Arrol & Co. Ltd.*[87] the answer to the question "did the failure to supply
safety belts cause the workman's death?" (apparently uncertainty as to a
past fact), depended upon the answer to the further, and clearly
hypothetical, question "would he have worn a safety belt if it had been
supplied?" It seems doubtful, then, that the distinction between past and
hypothetical facts can explain the different approaches in *Hotson* and
Kitchen.

If, in appropriate circumstances, an action for loss of a chance were **5.42**
allowed the courts would have to determine whether cases should be
categorised as either claims for a lost chance (where damages would be
measured by a discount of the full value of the claim), or causation cases
(where damages would be awarded on an all or nothing basis).[88] Not all
cases would be categorised as lost chance claims, so it would not be open
to defendants to argue that damages should be discounted to the extent
that the plaintiff has failed to prove causation with 100 per cent.
certainty.[89] There remains, however, the question of whether it is ever
possible to claim in respect of a loss of chance in tort.[90] In view of the

[84] Dugdale and Stanton, *Professional Negligence*, 1989, 2nd ed., paras. 18.05–18.06.
[85] *Mallett* v. *McMonagle* [1970] A.C. 166, 176, *per* Lord Diplock, cited by both Lord
Mackay and Lord Ackner in *Hotson* [1987] 2 All E.R. 909, at pp. 915 and 921 respectively.
See also, *per* Lord Reid in *Davies* v. *Taylor* [1974] A.C. 207, 212–213.
[86] Dugdale and Stanton, *Professional Negligence*, 1989, 2nd ed., para. 18.06.
[87] [1962] 1 W.L.R. 295; *ante*, § 5.07.
[88] See the classification of Simon Brown J. in *Hotson* v. *Fitzgerald* [1985] 3 All E.R.
167.
[89] *Hotson* v. *East Berkshire Area Health Authority* [1987] 2 All E.R. 909, at pp. 914
and 922, *per* Lord Bridge and Lord Ackner respectively; *cf.* Stapleton (1988) 104 L.Q.R.
389, 396. In *Bagley* v. *North Hertfordshire Health Authority* (1986) 136 New L.J. 1014
Simon Brown J. awarded damages for negligence which resulted in a stillbirth, and
deducted 5 per cent. because, even without negligence, there was a 5 per cent. chance that
the child would not have survived. This approach was disapproved by Lord Ackner in
Hotson at p. 922.
[90] See, in general, Coote (1988) 62 A.L.J. 761; Hill (1991) 54 M.L.R. 511.

decision in *Hotson* it is difficult to envisage the circumstances in which a claim for a less than 50 per cent. chance would not be defeated by causation arguments: on the balance of probabilities the plaintiff has failed to show that but for the negligence he would not have sustained the harm. The conceptual obstacles that would be created by allowing a claim for loss of a chance in tort could be overcome, however, by a sympathetic court, sensitive to the policy issues at stake. The arguments about actions for loss of a chance are in reality arguments about whether the court should take any steps to ease the plaintiff's burden of proof in circumstances where, through no fault of the plaintiff, causation is uncertain and the plaintiff can prove no more than that he was "a figure in a statistic."

5.43   Where, on the other hand, it is possible to identify something specific that the plaintiff has lost as a result of a diagnostic error, rather than a "mere" statistical chance, then the plaintiff is entitled to compensation for that loss. Thus, in *Sutton* v. *Population Services Family Planning Programme Ltd.*[91] McCowan J. awarded damages for the premature onset of menopause and four "lost years" to a patient whose cancer was not detected early enough because of the negligence of a nurse. Early detection would not have prevented a recurrence of the cancer because it was of high grade malignancy, but it would have delayed the recurrence by four years, and the plaintiff would have led a normal life for four more years. There was no award for pain and suffering nor for the medical treatment required since the plaintiff would have had to face the same operations and treatment in any event, but four years later.

II. CAUSATION IN LAW

5.44 The "but for" test excludes those factors which cannot be said to have been *a* cause of the damage, but there may be more than one causal element that satisfies the "but for" test, in which case the court may have to choose which of two or more operative causes are to be treated as the cause *in law* of the plaintiff's damage. The question is whether the defendant's breach of duty was *the* cause, for the purpose of attributing legal responsibility. The court is not required to find that a single event was the sole legal cause, although there is a tendency for the courts to seek to identify a single cause, at least where the plaintiff has not been at fault (in which case responsibility will be apportioned under the Law Reform (Contributory Negligence) Act 1945). In practice this can be something of a fiction, and it is important to appreciate that there is an element of judicial policy at work in attributing causal connections.

5.45   "Common sense" is usually said to be the starting point in this process,[92] and judicial common sense is often filtered through a string of metaphors: was the "chain of causation" broken; was the causal link too remote; was the tort a "proximate" or "direct" or "substantial" or "effective" cause, the *causa causans* not merely the *causa sine qua non*? The use of such phrases should not obscure the fact that the court must

[91] *The Times*, November 7, 1981.
[92] *Cork* v. *Kirby MacLean Ltd.* [1952] 2 All E.R. 402, 407; *Yorkshire Dale Steamship Co. Ltd.* v. *Minister of War Transport* [1942] A.C. 691, 706.

make a choice, which may be conditioned by common usages of speech and may have only a tenuous connection with scientific notions of logic. As Lord Wright commented in *Liesbosch Dredger* v. *S.S. Edison*: "In the varied web of affairs, the law must extract some consequences as relevant, not perhaps on grounds of pure logic but simply for practical reasons."[93]

1. Successive sufficient causes

Where there are two independent events, each of which were sufficient **5.46** to have caused the damage sustained by the plaintiff, the determination of causal responsibility depends on the nature of the events and the order in which they occurred. Thus, where both events are tortious, responsibility will be attributed to the tort which occurred first in time.[94] In *Baker* v. *Willoughby*,[95] for example, the plaintiff sustained an injury to his leg as a result of the defendant's negligence. The plaintiff was subsequently shot in the same leg during an armed robbery at his place of work, resulting in the amputation of the leg. The defendant argued that the supervening amputation had submerged or obliterated the original injury, and that he should only have to compensate the plaintiff for the losses up to the date of the shooting. The House of Lords held that the defendant remained responsible for the initial disability even after the amputation. The person who shot the plaintiff would only have been liable for the *additional* loss that had been inflicted by the shooting, not the whole disability, and so the defendant's argument would have resulted in the plaintiff being undercompensated because he would have received no compensation at all for the initial disability caused by the defendant after the date of the amputation. It was wrong, said their Lordships, that the plaintiff should fall between two tortfeasors, receiving less in damages than he would have received had there been no interval between the torts.[96]

On the other hand, where the supervening event is not tortious the **5.47** defendant's responsibility for the injury ends when the event occurs. In *Jobling* v. *Associated Dairies Ltd.*[97] the plaintiff suffered a back injury as a result of his employers' negligence, reducing his earning capacity by 50 per cent. Three years later he developed a disease, unconnected with the accident, which rendered him wholly unfit for work. The House of Lords held that the employers were liable for the plaintiff's reduced earning capacity only for the three-year period. The supervening disease was treated as the sole cause of the plaintiff's inability to work, although the

---

[93] [1933] A.C. 449, 460. See also *Abbott* v. *Kasza and Ace Construction Co.* [1976] 4 W.W.R. 20, 28 (Alta. C.A.).

[94] *Performance Cars Ltd.* v. *Abraham* [1962] 1 Q.B. 33, where the defendant negligently damaged a motor vehicle which had previously been damaged by the negligence of another motorist; the defendant was held not liable for the cost of a respray because, having damaged an already damaged car, his negligence was not the cause of the loss.

[95] [1970] A.C. 467.

[96] cf. *Griffiths* v. *Commonwealth* (1985) 72 F.L.R. 260, 273, applying the preferred solution of the Court of Appeal in *Baker* v. *Willoughby* [1969] 2 W.L.R. 489 that the second tortfeasor is liable for the whole loss, having caused the plaintiff to "lose" his right of action against the original wrongdoer; Hudson (1987) 38 N.I.L.Q. 190–193.

[97] [1982] A.C. 794.

result was justified, not on the basis of causation, but on the ground of "vicissitudes." When assessing damages for future loss of earnings the award will be discounted for the possibility that other events might have reduced the plaintiff's earning capacity or working life, even if the tort had not occurred. A subsequent illness is one of these "vicissitudes of life," and, applying the principle that the court will not speculate about future events when the facts are known, the illness must be taken into account. Their Lordships were critical of the decision in *Baker* v. *Willoughby*, while recognising that a different approach could apply where the supervening event consisted of a tort.[98] Lord Keith rationalised the distinction by suggesting that a supervening tort might not be regarded as one of the ordinary vicissitudes of life, and so would not be taken into account, although Lord Wilberforce conceded that there was no logical justification.

2. Intervening acts

5.48   Where the act of another person, without which the damage would not have occurred, intervenes between the defendant's negligence and the plaintiff's damage, the court must decide whether the defendant is responsible or whether the intervening act constituted a *novus actus interveniens*. If the latter, then the act is regarded as having broken the causal connection between the negligence and the damage. This too is treated as a matter of common sense in which metaphor abounds.[99]

5.49   There are two broad approaches to this problem. The first asks whether the act was reasonable in the circumstances, which refers to the voluntariness of the act, not whether it was careless. The more voluntary the act the less reasonable it is, and therefore the more likely to be regarded as a *novus actus*, but even deliberate conduct may be "involuntary" in this sense, where, for example, a person is forced to make some conscious response to a situation brought about by the defendant's negligence.[1] The second approach looks to the foreseeability of the intervention. From this point of view, even where the intervening act is unreasonable it will not necessarily be treated as breaking the chain of causation. Accordingly, a negligent intervention, for example negligent medical treatment, will not automatically exculpate the original tortfeasor if it is a foreseeable consequence of the defendant's initial negligence.

(i) By third parties

5.50   Where there are two successive acts of medical negligence it may be a nice question whether the second incidence of negligence breaks the

---

[98] See also *Carslogie Steamship Co. Ltd.* v. *Royal Norwegian Government* [1952] A.C. 292, attributing the loss caused by a ship being laid up for repairs following a collision to the need to repair damage caused by a subsequent storm.

[99] So the question may be whether the intervening event was such as to "isolate" or "insulate" or "eclipse" the defendant's negligence, or whether it was merely a "conduit pipe" or "part of a transmission gear set in motion by" the defendant: *Weld-Blundell* v. *Stephens* [1920] A.C. 956, 986, *per* Lord Sumner; see also *The Oropesa* [1943] P. 32, 39, *per* Lord Wright.

[1] *The Oropesa* [1943] P. 32; *Emeh* v. *Kensington and Chelsea Area Health Authority* [1985] Q.B. 1012; [1984] 3 All E.R. 1044, *post*, § 5.60.

chain of causation between the first error and the patient's injury. As a general rule, a subsequent act of negligence will normally constitute an intervening act.[2] In *Hogan* v. *Bentinck West Hartley Collieries Ltd.*[3] the House of Lords held that an operation which had been unreasonably recommended by a doctor broke the chain of causation between the plaintiff's initial injury sustained at work and the amputation of his thumb. Lord Normand said that:

> "I start from the proposition, which seems to me to be axiomatic, that if a surgeon, by lack of skill or failure in reasonable care, causes additional injury or aggravates an existing injury and so renders himself liable in damages, the reasonable conclusion must be that his intervention is a new cause and that the additional injury or the aggravation of the existing injury should be attributed to it and not to the original accident. On the other hand, an operation prudently advised and skilfully and carefully carried out should not be treated as a new cause, whatever its consequences may be."[4]

The latter part of Lord Normand's statement makes it clear that where **5.51** appropriate medical treatment has been properly carried out, the original tortfeasor will be responsible for any complications arising out of the treatment.[5] This result can be justified, if justification were considered necessary, on the basis that:

  (i) the intervention was reasonable, arising in the ordinary course of events, and so did not break the chain of causation; or

 (ii) the unforeseeable consequences of a foreseeable and reasonable intervention are within the risk created by the defendant's negligence; or

(iii) some complication from medical treatment is foreseeable and it is not necessary to foresee the precise complication which occurred.

The first part of Lord Normand's statement, on the other hand, **5.52** suggests that negligence in the performance of corrective treatment will always break the chain of causation. This may now be doubtful. In *Price* v. *Milawski*,[6] for example, a doctor who negligently failed to identify a fracture of the patient's ankle was held liable for the subsequent negligence of another doctor in the treatment of the patient's condition. It was reasonably foreseeable that once the information generated by the defendant's negligent error got into the hospital records, other doctors subsequently treating the plaintiff might well rely on the accuracy of that information, *i.e.* that the X–ray showed no fracture of the ankle. It was also foreseeable that some doctor might do so without checking, even

---

[2] Although this will not always be the case: see *Rouse* v. *Squires* [1973] 1 Q.B. 889; and the discussion of this problem in *Knightley* v. *Johns* [1982] 1 W.L.R. 349; [1982] 1 All E.R. 851, § 5.53, *post.* Neither of these cases involved medical negligence.

[3] [1949] 1 All E.R. 588.

[4] *Ibid.*, p. 596.

[5] See *Robinson* v. *Post Office* [1974] 1 W.L.R. 1176; [1974] 2 All E.R. 737, § 5.79, *post; cf.* the South African case of *Alston* v. *Marine & Trade Insurance Co. Ltd.* 1964 (4) S.A. 112, where the plaintiff suffered a stroke as a result of an interaction between the drug he was prescribed for injuries caused by the defendant's negligence and cheese which he ate. In the light of the medical knowledge at the time it was not unreasonable to eat cheese. Nonetheless, it was held that eating the cheese constituted a *novus actus interveniens*, even though the plaintiff acted reasonably.

[6] (1977) 82 D.L.R. (3d) 130 (Ont. C.A.). See also *Reeves* v. *Carthy* [1984] I.R. 348 (Supreme Court of Ireland).

though to do so in the circumstances might itself be a negligent act. The Ontario Court of Appeal held that on the particular facts this was a risk that a reasonable doctor would not have brushed aside as far-fetched.

5.53   These cases illustrate the different approaches that are available to the courts in assessing the causative effect of intervening conduct, namely the reasonableness of the intervention and its foreseeability. Although *Price* v. *Milawski* is a Canadian case, the English courts have also used foreseeability as a basis for dealing with such problems. In *Knightley* v. *Johns*.[7] the Court of Appeal said that the question was whether the whole sequence of events was a natural and probable consequence of the defendant's negligence, and whether it was reasonably foreseeable, not foreseeable as a mere possibility.[8] In answering this question it was helpful but not decisive to consider which events were deliberate choices to do positive acts and which were mere omissions, which acts and omissions were innocent mistakes or miscalculations and which were negligent. Thus:

> "Negligent conduct is more likely to break the chain of causation than conduct which is not; positive acts will more easily constitute new causes than inaction. Mistakes and mischances are to be expected when human beings, however well trained, have to cope with a crisis; what exactly they will be cannot be predicted, but if those which occur are natural the wrongdoer cannot, I think, escape responsibility for them and their consequences simply by calling them improbable or unforeseeable. He must accept the risk of some unexpected mischances."[9]

In deciding which mischances amount to intervening events the court should apply "common sense rather than logic on the facts and circumstances of each case."

5.54   Where the subsequent negligence results in damage that cannot be said to be causally linked to the initial negligence, the first tortfeasor is not responsible, not because the later conduct intervened, but because the damage fails to satisfy the "but for" test. In *Yepremian* v. *Scarborough General Hospital*,[10] for example, doctor G was negligent in failing to diagnose the patient's diabetes. The plaintiff's subsequent cardiac arrest was caused by the negligent treatment given to the patient by another doctor, R, after the diabetes had been diagnosed. Thus, G's negligence was not a cause in fact of the cardiac arrest. If, however, said the Ontario

---

[7] [1982] 1 W.L.R. 349; [1982] 1 All E.R. 851, 865.

[8] See also, *per* Lord Reid in *Home Office* v. *Dorset Yacht Co. Ltd.* [1970] A.C. 1004, 1030: "Where human action forms one of the links between the original wrongdoing of the defendant and the loss suffered by the plaintiff, that action must at least have been something very likely to happen if it is not to be regarded as *novus actus interveniens* breaking the chain of causation."

[9] *Knightley* v. *Johns* [1982] 1 All E.R. 851, 865, *per* Stephenson L.J. The difficulty in making categorical statements about the effect of intervening negligence is illustrated by the different results reached by the Court of Appeal in *Knightley* v. *Johns* and *Rouse* v. *Squires* [1973] Q.B. 889, on essentially similar facts. In *Prendergast* v. *Sam & Dee Ltd.* [1989] 1 Med. L.R. 36, § 4.50, the Court of Appeal concluded that a pharmacist's negligence in misreading a doctor's prescription, and consequently supplying a patient with the wrong drug, did not break the chain of causation from the doctor's initial negligence in writing an illegible prescription. It was reasonably foreseeable that the prescription could be misread.

[10] (1980) 110 D.L.R. (3d) 513 (Ont. C.A.); the action was settled prior to the appeal hearing before the Supreme Court of Canada: (1981) D.L.R. (3d) 341.

Court of Appeal, the cardiac arrest had been part of the natural consequences of untreated diabetes, or even of ineffectively treated diabetes, then the subsequent negligence of R would not have prevented G's negligence from being regarded as a cause of the damage. G could not rely on R's failure to rescue the plaintiff from the consequences of G's negligence.

This latter point was the basis of the decision in *Thompson* v. **5.55** *Toorenburgh*,[11] where it was held that the failure of a doctor to provide an *actus interveniens* which would have saved the accident victim's life is not the same as committing an *actus interveniens* that caused her death. The defendant motorist who caused the deceased's initial injuries was liable, notwithstanding medical "mistreatment."[12] Robertson J.A. said that:

> "Mrs Thompson would almost certainly have recovered if proper treatment had been applied speedily; the doctors failed to apply that treatment and so failed to save her life, but they did not cause her death. They failed to provide an *actus interveniens* that would have saved her life, but that is not the same as committing an *actus interveniens* that caused her death."[13]

This approach to negligent omissions might be followed in this country. **5.56** In *Muirhead* v. *Industrial Tank Specialities Ltd.*[14] Goff L.J. suggested that a negligent failure by a third party to prevent damage caused by the negligence of the defendant would not exonerate the defendant. The defendant could escape responsibility "only where the act or omission of another was of such a nature that it constituted a wholly independent cause of the damage, *i.e.* a *novus actus interveniens*."[15] On this view it might be argued that a patient's refusal to accept medical treatment on, say, religious grounds does not break the chain of causation either, since, at worst, it represents an "unreasonable" (negligent) failure to intervene to prevent the damage caused by the defendant.[16]

On the other hand, it seems strange to attach significance to the fact **5.57** that the doctor's negligence consists of an omission to give life-saving treatment, and so amounts to a failure to provide an *actus interveniens* rather than constituting a *novus actus interveniens*, when it is patently clear that if the doctor were sued for negligence he would be held responsible for the death, at least where, on the balance of probabilities the evidence indicates that the patient's life would have been saved by prompt treatment.[17] Where the doctor has a duty of care to treat the patient, the courts have no difficulty in regarding an omission to treat as having causative effect. It is submitted that the better approach in this type of case is to treat both the first tort and the subsequent negligently performed medical treatment as causative of the patient's death, and to

---

[11] (1973) 50 D.L.R. (3d) 717 (B.C.C.A.).

[12] The court carefully avoided calling the medical treatment "negligent," although on the facts it is difficult to see how the treatment could not have been negligent.

[13] (1973) 50 D.L.R. (3d) 717, 721.

[14] [1985] 3 All E.R. 705, 718–719.

[15] *Ibid.* This rather begs the question of which acts or omissions are of such a nature that they constitute a wholly independent cause.

[16] See § 5.62, *post.*

[17] *cf. Barnett* v. *Chelsea and Kensington Hospital Management Committee* [1968] 1 All E.R. 1068, § 5.04, *ante.*

apportion liability accordingly. Thus, in *Commonwealth of Australia* v. *Martin*[18] M received injuries in a road traffic accident which were such that death was inevitable without proper corrective surgery. The medical treatment was performed negligently and he died four days later. It was held that both the negligent motorist and the negligent doctor had caused the death, and it was not necessary to show that the doctor's negligence constituted a *novus actus interveniens* before he could be held responsible.

5.58 Where a doctor's negligence has increased the susceptibility of the patient to sustaining further injury, he cannot avoid responsibility for a subsequent injury within the risk created by his negligence, even though there are other later causes which also caused or materially contributed to that injury.[19]

(ii) By the plaintiff

5.59 Medical treatment often depends upon the co-operation of the patient. Where the patient fails to co-operate this may amount to contributory negligence.[20] In an extreme case the patient's conduct may be sufficient to break the chain of causation.[21] The test for an intervening act by the plaintiff is normally whether he acted reasonably,[22] although it would be open to the court to conclude that a plaintiff who has acted unreasonably is guilty of contributory negligence, and apportion responsibility between the plaintiff and the defendant.[23] "Unreasonableness" is also used to indicate an element of voluntary conduct by the plaintiff, and so, where the plaintiff's capacity for rational judgment has been affected, this may remove the necessary voluntary element for an *actus interveniens*. It is on this basis that even suicide, which objectively would normally be regarded as an unreasonable act, will not necessarily amount to a *novus actus interveniens*.[24]

5.60 In *Emeh* v. *Kensington and Chelsea Area Health Authority*[25] the plaintiff brought an action in respect of the birth of a handicapped child

---

[18] (1985) 59 A.L.R. 439 (Fed. Ct. of Aus.).

[19] *Powell* v. *Guttman* (1978) 89 D.L.R. (3d) 180 (Man. C.A), § 5.27, *ante*, where the defendant was held liable for a fracture of the patient's leg which occurred in the course of a later operation performed by another doctor. The second doctor was found not to have been negligent.

[20] See § 4.107.

[21] *Venner* v. *North East Essex Area Health Authority, The Times*, February 21, 1987; *Murrin* v. *Janes* [1949] 4 D.L.R. 403, 406 (Newfoundland S.C.), where the plaintiff who delayed seeing a doctor to deal with excessive bleeding following the extraction of his teeth was held to be the sole cause of his misfortune. In *Stevens* v. *Bermondsey and Southwark Group Hospital Management Committee* (1963) 107 S.J. 478 the plaintiff claimed that a doctor's failure to diagnose the seriousness of his condition following a road traffic accident led to him settling his claim against the third party for a small sum. Paul J. dismissed the action against the doctor, partly on the ground that the action against the third party was a *novus actus interveniens*. This seems doubtful, however, and the decision may be better regarded as a case where there was no duty of care with respect to that particular damage; see §§ 2.24–2.25.

[22] *McKew* v. *Holland & Hannen & Cubitts (Scotland) Ltd.* [1969] 3 All E.R. 1621; *cf. Wieland* v. *Cyril Lord Carpets Ltd.* [1969] 3 All E.R. 1006.

[23] As, *e.g.* in *Sayers* v. *Harlow Urban District Council* [1958] 1 W.L.R. 623, or *The Calliope* [1970] P. 172. See also Millner (1971) 22 N.I.L.Q. 168, 176–179, criticising *McKew* v. *Holland & Hannen & Cubitts (Scotland) Ltd.* [1969] 3 All E.R. 1621 for not taking this approach.

[24] *Pigney* v. *Pointer's Transport Services Ltd.* [1957] 1 W.L.R. 1121; *Cotic* v. *Gray* (1981) 124 D.L.R. (3d) 641 (Ont. C.A.); see § 4.98; Jones (1990) 6 P.N.107, 110–112.

[25] [1984] 3 All E.R. 1044.

following a negligently performed sterilisation operation. She was about 20 weeks pregnant when she discovered the pregnancy. The trial judge had taken the view that the plaintiff's decision not to undergo an abortion was so unreasonable as to eclipse the defendants' wrongdoing, and amounted to a *novus actus interveniens*, and accordingly she was not entitled to damages for the events after she discovered that she was pregnant, except for the expense and pain and suffering of a further sterilisation operation. The Court of Appeal reversed this finding. Purchas L.J. said that it was unacceptable that the court should be invited to consider critically the decision of a mother whether to terminate a pregnancy which has been caused by the defendants' negligence. As Slade L.J. put it: "By their own negligence, they faced her with the very dilemma which she had sought to avoid by having herself sterilised."[26] The fact that she had exercised this particular option in this way did not show that it was an option which she wished to have. His Lordship doubted whether such a decision could ever constitute a *novus actus interveniens*:

> "Save in the most exceptional circumstances, I cannot think it right that the court should ever declare it unreasonable for a woman to decline to have an abortion, in a case where there is no evidence that there were any medical or psychiatric grounds for terminating the particular pregnancy."[27]

It might be added that if there are no medical or psychiatric grounds **5.61** for an abortion within the terms of section 1 of the Abortion Act 1967, the abortion would be unlawful, and it could not possibly be unreasonable for a woman to refuse to undergo an unlawful operation. It is unclear, then, what "exceptional circumstances" Slade L.J. had in mind which might justify the conclusion that such a refusal was unreasonable. Purchas L.J. appeared to suggest that where the sole motivation for the refusal to terminate the pregnancy was "commercial," in that the plaintiff continued the pregnancy merely in order to increase the damages that would be awarded in the action for the failed sterilisation, that would be a factor to be considered in deciding whether the chain of causation had been broken. Given the multiplicity of medical, social, emotional, moral, and economic factors which women take into account when making such a decision, it is highly unlikely that the financial prospects of promoting a civil action for damages could be shown to have been the sole motivation of any woman who decides to continue her pregnancy. Moreover, even in such extreme circumstances a decision that the plaintiff has acted unreasonably effectively stipulates that she was under a duty to abort in order to reduce the loss otherwise payable by the negligent doctor. The Abortion Act 1967 gives a woman the right to have an abortion in certain circumstances, if she chooses, but there is no law which imposes a duty to abort, and such a duty would appear to violate a principle of public policy upholding the sanctity of human life.[28] Thus, on principle it is submitted that a mother's decision not to undergo an abortion should never be held to constitute to a *novus actus interveniens*, irrespective of her motives.

---

[26] *Ibid.*, p. 1053.
[27] *Ibid.*
[28] *McKay v. Essex Area Health Authority* [1982] Q.B. 1166, see § 2.32.

5.62   Another situation which could result in a finding that the plaintiff acted so unreasonably as to break the chain of causation is where the patient refuses further medical treatment which would alleviate his condition or prevent it from deteriorating. It is clear that a plaintiff has an obligation to mitigate the damages, which may include seeking suitable medical treatment, except where there is a substantial risk of further injury or the outcome is uncertain.[29] Mitigation is a principle applied to the assessment of damages, but this stage will not be reached if the refusal of recommended treatment is categorised as an intervening act. In *R.* v. *Blaue*[30] the Court of Appeal held that a patient's refusal to undergo a blood transfusion on religious grounds did not break the chain of causation between a criminal assault and the patient's death, resulting in a charge of manslaughter.[31] It is clear, however, that this decision was based on policy considerations appropriate to the criminal law. Lawton L.J. suggested that, where the victim brought a civil claim, the concept of foreseeability could operate in the wrongdoer's favour, presumably by breaking the chain of causation; and, moreover, the wrongdoer was entitled to expect his victim to mitigate the damage by accepting treatment of a normal kind. It may be argued, however, that a refusal of medical treatment on religious grounds constitutes a failure to provide an *actus interveniens* that would have avoided the plaintiff's loss, which is not the same as committing a *novus actus interveniens* that caused the loss, an argument that has been accepted where a third party fails to intervene.[32] Moreover, the decision to refuse treatment would not necessarily be categorised as "unreasonable," even under the civil law. In *R.* v. *Blaue* Lawton L.J. responded to the suggestion that a Jehovah's Witness's decision not to have a blood transfusion was unreasonable:

> "At once the question arises—reasonable by whose standards? Those of Jehovah's Witnesses? Humanists? Roman Catholics? Protestants of Anglo-Saxon descent? The man on the Clapham omnibus?"[33]

5.63   A decision based on religious beliefs may well be regarded as reasonable because it is considered to be reasonable to conduct one's life according to a religious faith, even though those specific beliefs are not widely accepted within society. This view could be applied both to the question of whether the plaintiff's conduct amounts to a *novus actus interveniens* and to whether he has complied with his obligation to

---

[29] See § 9.21.

[30] [1975] 1 W.L.R. 1411.

[31] "It does not lie in the mouth of the assailant to say that his victim's religious beliefs which inhibited him from accepting certain kinds of treatment were unreasonable. The question for decision is what caused her death. The answer is the stab wound. The fact that the victim refused to stop this end coming about did not break the causal connection between the act and the death" *ibid.* at p. 1415, *per* Lawton L.J.

[32] See §§ 5.55–5.56, *ante*. The distinction between the duty to mitigate and the plaintiff's intervening act may be the difference between the plaintiff's unreasonable inaction (his failure to minimise loss) and the plaintiff's unreasonable action (his augmenting of the loss), respectively, although the principles are based on the same policy grounds and are sometimes used interchangeably: see Burrows, *Remedies for Torts and Breach of Contract*, 1987, p. 35.

[33] [1975] 1 W.L.R. 1411, 1415. See also *Malette* v. *Shulman* (1987) 47 D.L.R. (4th) 18; aff'd (1990) 67 D.L.R. (4th) 321 (Ont. C.A.), § 6.65, where a doctor who administered a blood transfusion contrary to the patient's instructions was held liable in battery.

mitigate the damage, which requires the plaintiff only to take reasonable steps in mitigation. It might also be argued that a plaintiff's refusal of treatment on religious grounds is foreseeable and so did not break the chain of causation, particularly in an action for medical negligence, where it could be expected that the doctor would have discussed with the patient in advance what medical treatment would be acceptable. Ultimately, this issue turns upon the courts' assessment of who should bear the burden of the plaintiff's religious beliefs.

III. REMOTENESS OF DAMAGE

Rules on remoteness of damage, at least in the tort of negligence, deal **5.64** with harm which occurs in some freakish or unpredictable fashion. In a system of fault liability, which depends upon foreseeability of the damage as a test of the defendant's breach of duty, it may seem unfair to hold the defendant responsible for all the damage that his negligence has caused, even where the damage is of a different type or occurred in a different manner from that which would normally be expected. There are two broad approaches to the problem of remoteness. The first takes the view that a defendant is liable for all the direct consequences of his negligence, no matter how unusual or unexpected. This treats remoteness as essentially a question of causation. At one time this was thought to be the appropriate rule in the tort of negligence,[34] and it remains the test in actions for trespass to the person.[35] The second approach holds that a person is only responsible for consequences that could reasonably have been anticipated, even where he has undoubtedly caused the damage in question. In theory, the test of remoteness in the tort of negligence is now foreseeability of the harm; if the damage was unforeseeable it is too remote.[36] This statement is deceptive, however, because in practice the issue is not that simple. The court must determine precisely what it is that has to be foreseen, and decisions about what falls within the realms of the foreseeable and what may legitimately be ignored in the sequence of events have a vital bearing upon the application of the rules on remoteness. Moreover, the courts have not abandoned the general

---

[34] *Re Polemis and Furness, Withy & Co. Ltd.* [1921] 3 K.B. 560.

[35] The defendant is liable for all the consequences which are a direct result of the tortious act whether they are foreseeable or not: "In battery, however, any and all damage is recoverable, if it results from the wrongful act, whether it is foreseeable or not. The limitation devices of foresight and remoteness are not applicable to intentional torts, as they are in negligence law" *per* Linden J. in *Allan* v. *New Mount Sinai Hospital* (1980) 109 D.L.R. (3d) 634, 643; see also *Chatterton* v. *Gerson* [1981] 1 All E.R. 257, 265.

[36] *Overseas Tankship (UK) Ltd.* v. *Morts Dock & Engineering Co., The Wagon Mound* [1961] A.C. 388, P.C. It is a matter of some uncertainty whether, and if so how, the test for remoteness of damage differs in the tort of negligence from that applied to actions in contract. It may be that the tests are in effect the same, at least for physical damage, following the decision of the Court of Appeal in *Parsons (Livestock) Ltd* v. *Uttley Ingham & Co. Ltd.* [1978] Q.B. 791; [1978] 1 All E.R. 525; see the excellent discussion in Burrows, *Remedies for Torts and Breach of Contract*, 1987, pp. 42–51. If there is a difference, the test in negligence is more generous to plaintiffs than that in contract (see *The Heron II* [1969] 1 A.C. 350), but this is probably of little or no practical significance in actions for medical negligence since the plaintiff with a contractual claim will also have a right of action in tort: see § 2.03.

principle that a tortfeasor must "take his victim as he finds him," which in practice means ignoring certain unforeseeable idiosyncrasies in the plaintiff which may have contributed to the damage. The result is that the limits of actionability set by the rules on remoteness of damage lie somewhere between the two approaches embodied in directness and foreseeability.

5.65   Once it is established that the damage sustained by the plaintiff was foreseeable, the likelihood that it would occur is irrelevant. In *The Heron II*[37] Lord Upjohn said that:

> "the tortfeasor is liable for any damage which he can reasonably foresee may happen as a result of the breach however unlikely it may be, unless it can be brushed aside as far-fetched."

The likelihood of the occurrence or the degree of foreseeability relates to the question of whether the defendant acted carelessly in the face of the risk.[38] To some extent this makes the test of remoteness of damage as close to a test based on causation as to one based on foreseeability, because many things which could be regarded as unlikely are foreseeable and yet are not necessarily far-fetched.[39] It is not sufficient, therefore, to say that the test of remoteness of damage is foreseeability. The court has scope to determine the outcome of a case through the definition of what, precisely, must be foreseen. The narrower the range of events or damage that must be anticipated the more difficult it will be for the plaintiff to overcome the remoteness hurdle. Following *The Wagon Mound* the courts soon came to the view that provided that the type or kind of damage could have been foreseen, it did not matter that its extent or the precise manner of its occurrence could not have been foreseen, and the eggshell skull rule,[40] which was retained after *The Wagon Mound*, is quite explicitly not based on foreseeability.

1. Manner of the occurrence

5.66   The fact that the damage occurred in an unforeseeable way does not necessarily mean that it was not foreseeable. The precise concatenation of events need not be anticipated if the damage is within the general range of what is reasonably foreseeable.[41] In *Hughes* v. *Lord Advocate*[42] some workmen negligently left a manhole open in the street, surrounded by paraffin lamps. Two young boys approached the manhole, out of curiosity, and one of the lamps was knocked into the hole. There was a

---

[37] [1969] 1 A.C. 350, 422.

[38] Although degrees of foreseeability are used in considering whether the chain of causation has been broken by an intervening act: see § 5.53.

[39] In *Emeh* v. *Kensington and Chelsea Area Health Authority* [1984] 3 All E.R. 1044, 1049 Waller L.J. concluded that a risk of 1 in 200–1 in 400 of a pregnant woman giving birth to a child with congenital abnormalities was "clearly one that is foreseeable, as the law of negligence understands it. There are many cases where even more remote risks have been taken to be 'foreseeable'." On variable degrees of foresight applied to both the duty of care in negligence and remoteness, see Kidner (1989) 9 L.S. 1.

[40] See § 5.76.

[41] *Stewart* v. *West African Terminals Ltd.* [1964] 2 Lloyd's Rep. 371, 375; *Wieland* v. *Cyril Lord Carpets Ltd.* [1969] 3 All E.R. 1006, 1009; *Sullivan* v. *South Glamorgan County Council* (1985) 84 L.G.R. 415.

[42] [1963] A.C. 837.

violent explosion in which one of the boys suffered severe burns. Expert evidence indicated that in these circumstances an explosion was unforeseeable, although burns from a conflagration if the lamp was knocked over could have been anticipated. The House of Lords held that the damage was not too remote. Lord Pearce considered that the accident was simply a "variant of the foreseeable," while Lord Reid took the view that, having been caused by a known source of danger, it was no defence that it was caused in an unforeseeable way. Lord Guest concluded that the precise details leading up to the accident do not have to be foreseen; it was sufficient if the accident was "of a type which should have been foreseeable by a reasonably careful person."

To a large extent this issue turns upon how the court frames the **5.67** question of what has to be foreseen. In *Hughes* v. *Lord Advocate* the question was "was injury by burning foreseeable?" to which the answer was "yes." If the question had been: "was injury by explosion foreseeable?", the answer would have been "no" and the damage would have been considered to be too remote. This is illustrated by the decision of the Court of Appeal in *Doughty* v. *Turner Manufacturing Co. Ltd.*,[43] in which an asbestos cover was knocked into a bath of molten liquid. Shortly after, due to a chemical reaction between the asbestos and the liquid which was unforeseeable at the time, there was an eruption of the liquid which burned the plaintiff who was standing nearby. It was held that burning by an unforeseeable chemical eruption was not a variant of burning by splashing, which was within the foreseeable risk created by knocking the cover into the liquid, distinguishing *Hughes* v. *Lord Advocate*. If the question had been "was injury by burning foreseeable?" as a consequence of knocking the cover into the liquid then the answer must have been "yes," and the court could have taken the view that the precise manner in which the injury occurred was irrelevant.[44]

2. Type of harm

The damage will be too remote if it is not of the same type or kind as **5.68** the harm that could have been foreseen. The problem is in defining the "type" of damage that must be foreseen. It would be possible to take a broad view of the classification of harm, dividing it into personal injury, damage to property and financial loss. Thus, if any personal injury were foreseeable the defendant would be liable for any type of personal injuries that occurred. The courts have not done this, although the eggshell skull rule as applied to personal injuries comes close to this result.[45] In practice a compromise position seems to have been adopted in which the courts insist that the damage must be of a foreseeable type or kind, whilst giving this term a comparatively wide meaning. In *Draper* v. *Hodder*,[46] for example, Edmund-Davies L.J. said that:

---

[43] [1964] 1 Q.B. 518.
[44] See also *Tremain* v. *Pike* [1969] 1 W.L.R. 1556; [1969] 3 All E.R. 1303 and *Crossley* v. *Rawlinson* [1981] 1 W.L.R. 369; [1981] 3 All E.R. 674, for examples of how narrowing the scope of the question produces the result that the harm was unforeseeable.
[45] See §§ 5.79–5.80.
[46] [1972] 2 Q.B. 556, 573.

" . . . the proper test in negligence is not whether the particular type of physical harm actually suffered ought reasonably to have been anticipated, but whether broadly speaking it was within the range of likely consequence."

5.69 This is illustrated in *Bradford* v. *Robinson Rentals Ltd.*[47] in which the plaintiff sustained frostbite, having been sent on a journey by his employers in a vehicle without a heater at a time of severe winter weather. Rees J. held that frostbite was damage of the same kind as that which was a foreseeable consequence of exposure to extreme cold. On the other hand, in *Tremain* v. *Pike*[48] a farm employee contracted a rare disease transmitted by contact with rats' urine, following an infestation of rats on the farm. Payne J. considered that the disease was damage of a different type from the foreseeable damage which could have occurred from rat bites or contamination of food. This decision, it is submitted, takes an unduly myopic view of what may be foreseeable. If the question had been whether illness from some rat-transmitted disease was a foreseeable consequence of an infestation of rats, the answer must surely have been that it was. Very few people would be capable of identifying in advance the specific disease that would be caused.

5.70 In *Sheridan* v. *Boots Co. Ltd.*[49] the plaintiff contracted Stevens-Johnson syndrome, causing blindness, as a side-effect of an anti-inflammatory drug, Butazolidin, which was known to have a number of side-effects ranging from gastro-intestinal disturbance, gastric ulcers and, in rare cases, blood dyscrazia which could take the form of aplastic anaemia, a very dangerous condition. Stevens-Johnson syndrome was known to be a possible side-effect, but this was not widely known. The manufacturer's literature published in the United States mentioned this possibility, but literature published in this country made no mention of it. Kenneth Jones J. held that the plaintiff's injury was too remote, because Stevens-Johnson syndrome was not damage of the same type as gastric disturbance. Stevens-Johnson syndrome involved ulceration over a widespread area of the body, which could affect the eyes. Gastric disturbance, on the other hand, involved localised ulceration in the stomach and does not affect the eyes:

> "It would seem contrary to common sense to say that a condition involving blindness is of the same kind as one causing gastric ulcer. When examined fully, the two conditions in their symptoms are wholly dissimilar."

5.71 Nor could it be said, his Lordship continued, that they arose through the same mechanism. This case can be contrasted with the decision of the Ontario Court of Appeal in *Graham* v. *Persyko*[50] in which a gastroenterologist was held to have been negligent in prescribing the drug prednisone for the patient's condition. The drug caused avascular necrosis of the femoral heads, which was a rare but known complication. Holland J. said that:

---

[47] [1967] 1 All E.R. 267.
[48] [1969] 3 All E.R. 1303.
[49] (1980) (unreported), Q.B.D.
[50] (1986) 27 D.L.R. (4th) 699 (Ont. C.A.); (1986) 34 D.L.R. (4th) 160 (S.C.C.) leave to appeal refused; see § 4.77.

"The complication of necrosis of femoral heads with a short dose of prednisone is known but unusual. There are a number of serious, known and more common side-effects. It may be that the particular side-effect that Mr. Graham suffered was not reasonably foreseeable but damage to Mr. Graham's health was foreseeable and liability results."[51]

Clearly, treating the type of damage that must be foreseen as "damage to health" takes a very broad view of what must be foreseen, and would be difficult to reconcile with *Sheridan* v. *Boots Co. Ltd*. Given the wide range of adverse effects which were foreseeable in *Graham* v. *Persyko* it would probably not have been difficult to categorise avascular necrosis as simply a variant of one of the foreseeable types of injury. Moreover, necrosis was a known complication "but unusual." It is arguable that this finding made the necrosis foreseeable, since it is well-established that for the purpose of remoteness the type of damage need only be foreseeable as a possible risk, it does not have to be likely or reasonably foreseeable.[52] Thus, in *Smith* v. *Brighton and Lewes Hospital Management Committee*[53] a patient who was negligently given 34 instead of 30 injections of streptomycin lost her sense of balance as a result. It was held that the defendant should have appreciated that some injury could be caused by giving an overdose, and she did not have to foresee the quality or extent of the damage. **5.72**

In *Kralj* v. *McGrath*[54] an unusual type of loss was said to have been foreseeable. Due to the defendant's negligence one child of twins was born with severe disabilities, and died eight weeks later. The plaintiff, the child's mother, said that she had always intended to have a family of three children, and as a result of the death she would have to undergo a further pregnancy, which would involve the discomforts involved in the pregnancy (including the fact that it would now have to be delivered by Caesarian section) and additional financial loss. The defendant argued that this was too remote because it was not reasonably foreseeable by the defendant. Woolf J. held that it was foreseeable that the plaintiff might want to have further children following the death of her child, and it was irrelevant that she had not specifically informed the defendant about this. **5.73**

3. Extent of the harm

If the type of harm and the manner of its occurrence were foreseeable, it is irrelevant that the physical extent of the damage was unforeseeable.[55] **5.74**

---

[51] *Ibid.*, p. 708, citing *Hughes* v. *Lord Advocate* [1963] A.C. 837. The known complications of the drug included: altering the patient's mental state, making some patients suicidal; effects on the cardiovascular system, and retention of salt and water; hypertension; cataracts and glaucoma; peptic ulcer; skin complaints; osteoporosis; reduction of the body's response to infection; diabetes; and, uncommonly, aseptic necrosis of hip joints and other joints.

[52] See § 5.65.

[53] *The Times*, May 2, 1958. In *Reeves* v. *Carthy* [1984] I.R. 348 (Supreme Court of Ireland) it was held that since it was foreseeable that, left untreated, peritonitis leads to circulatory weakness and hypotension it was also foreseeable that as a consequence of prolonged hypotension the plaintiff could suffer a stroke. Alternatively, even if the stroke was unforeseeable, it was damage of the same type as the foreseeable harm (circulatory damage and shock) notwithstanding its unforeseeable extent (see § 5.74).

[54] [1986] 1 All E.R. 54, 62.

[55] *Smith* v. *Leech Brain & Co. Ltd.* [1962] 2 Q.B. 405, 414, *per* Lord Parker C.J., stating that this proposition had not been changed by *The Wagon Mound* [1961] A.C. 388.

In *Hughes* v. *Lord Advocate* Lord Reid said that:

"No doubt it was not to be expected that the injuries would be as serious as those which the appellant in fact sustained. But a defender is liable, although the damage may be a good deal greater in extent than was foreseeable. He can only escape liability if the damage can be regarded as differing in kind from what was foreseeable."[56]

This principle applies to all forms of personal injury, including nervous shock,[57] and also to property damage.[58]

5.75 Liability for the unforseeable physical extent of otherwise foreseeable physical harm should be distinguished from the measure of damages required to compensate the plaintiff's loss. If the defendant injures someone with a high income, or damages a particularly valuable item of property, he must compensate the plaintiff to the full extent of his loss, and he cannot complain that the damages would have been less if the plaintiff had a low income or the property was of little value.[59]

4. The "eggshell skull" rule

5.76 Where the plaintiff suffers from a latent physical or psychological predisposition to a particular injury or illness which has been activated by the damage inflicted by the defendant, then the defendant is responsible for the additional, unforeseeable damage that his negligence has produced. This is usually referred to as the "thin skull" or the "eggshell skull" rule. If the plaintiff has an unusually thin skull, the defendant cannot complain if the injury is much more serious than would have been the case with a normal person.[60] Provided that some harm was foreseeable, so that it can be said that the defendant was in breach of duty, the defendant is responsible.[61] The same principle has been applied where the plaintiff had an unusually weak heart,[62] where he was a haemophiliac,[63]

---

[56] [1963] A.C. 837, 845. *Craig* v. *Soeurs de Charité de la Providence* [1940] 3 W.W.R. 336 (Sask. C.A.), where the patient suffered more extensive injuries than otherwise foreseeable from a burn by a hot water bottle because he was diabetic; the defendants were held liable for the full loss.

[57] *Brice* v. *Brown* [1984] 1 All E.R. 997. It is irrelevant that the plaintiff has a predisposition to nervous shock which, unknown to the defendant, increases the likelihood of more extensive harm than the ordinary individual would have experienced, provided that it was foreseeable that a person of ordinary fortitude would have sustained nervous shock: see § 2.54.

[58] *Vacwell Engineering Co. Ltd.* v. *B.D.H. Chemicals Ltd.* [1971] 1 Q.B. 88.

[59] *Smith* v. *London & South Western Railway Co.* (1870) L.R. 6 C.P. 14, 22–23; *The Arpad* [1934] P. 189, 202. As Fleming, *The Law of Torts*, 7th ed., 1987, p. 185 puts it, this is responsibility, not for unexpected consequences, but for the unexpectable cost of expected consequences.

[60] *Owens* v. *Liverpool Corporation* [1939] 1 K.B. 394, 401; *Dulieu* v. *White & Sons* [1901] 2 K.B. 669, 679, *per* Kennedy J.: " . . . it is no answer to the [plaintiff's] claim for damages that he would have suffered less injury, or no injury at all, if he had not had an unusually thin skull or an unusually weak heart."

[61] *Bourhill* v. *Young* [1943] A.C. 92, 109, *per* Lord Wright.

[62] *Love* v. *Port of London* [1959] 2 Lloyd's Rep. 541.

[63] *Bishop* v. *Arts & Letters Club of Toronto* (1978) 83 D.L.R. (3d) 107.

and even where he had an "eggshell personality."[64] The defendant does not, however, have to take the plaintiff's family as he finds them.[65]

The eggshell skull rule overlaps with the general principle that the **5.77** extent of the damage need not be foreseeable. Where the plaintiff's predisposition exacerbates the otherwise foreseeable type of harm then it provides the mechanism by which that principle comes into effect. It is arguable, however, that the eggshell skull rule goes beyond this by allowing recovery for harm of a different type from that which is foreseeable. In *Smith* v. *Leech Brain & Co. Ltd*[66] an employee was burned on the lip by a piece of molten metal. The burn was treated and healed, but due to a premalignant condition the burn promoted a cancerous growth which ultimately led to his death. Lord Parker C.J. held the defendants liable for the death:

> "The test is not whether these [defendants] could reasonably have foreseen that a burn would cause cancer and that [Mr. Smith] would die. The question is whether these [defendants] could reasonably foresee the type of injury he suffered, namely, the burn. What, in the particular case, is the amount of the damage which he suffers as a result of that burn, depends upon the characteristics and constitution of the victim."[67]

Lord Parker's reference to the "amount of the damage" suggests that **5.78** he regarded cancer and death as simply more extensive harm of the same type as the foreseeable harm, the burn. It is difficult, however, to see how these types of damage can be put into the same category. It is respectfully submitted that only if the harm is classified very broadly as "personal injury" could the death be regarded as merely more extensive damage of the same type as the foreseeable injury.

The eggshell skull rule predates the move to a test of remoteness based **5.79** on foreseeability, and the reality is that it is extremely difficult to provide a theoretical reconciliation of the two principles. Nonetheless, it has been confirmed on more than one occasion that the eggshell skull rule was not affected by the *The Wagon Mound*.[68] In *Robinson* v. *Post Office*[69] the plaintiff suffered a minor injury as a result of the defendants' negligence, but he suffered a serious allergic reaction to an anti-tetanus injection given by a doctor, causing brain damage. The Court of Appeal held the defendants responsible for the brain damage:

> " . . . the principle that a defendant must take the plaintiff as he finds him involves that if a wrongdoer ought reasonably to foresee

---

[64] *Malcolm* v. *Broadhurst* [1970] 3 All E.R. 508, where the injury aggravated a pre-existing nervous condition; see also the apparently irreconcilable decisions of *Meah* v. *McCreamer* [1985] 1 All E.R. 367 and *Meah* v. *McCreamer* (No. 2) [1986] 1 All E.R. 943.

[65] *McLaren* v. *Bradstreet* (1969) 113 S.J. 471; 119 New L.J. 484, where the plaintiffs could not recover for "family hysteria" resulting from the mother's neurotic reaction to minor injuries to her children caused by the defendant's negligence; *cf. Nader* v. *Urban Transit Authority of New South Wales* [1985] 2 N.S.W.L.R. 501.

[66] [1962] 2 Q.B. 405.

[67] *Ibid.*, p. 415.

[68] [1961] A.C. 388. See *Oman* v. *McIntyre* 1962 S.L.T. 168; *Warren* v. *Scruttons Ltd.* [1962] 1 Lloyd's Rep. 497; *Winteringham* v. *Rae* (1965) 55 D.L.R. (2d) 108, 112 (Ont. H.C.).

[69] [1974] 1 W.L.R. 1176; [1974] 2 All E.R. 737.

that as a result of his wrongful act the victim may require medical treatment he is, subject to the principle of *novus actus interveniens*, liable for the consequences of the treatment applied although he could not reasonably foresee those consequences or that they could be serious."[70]

5.80   There was no suggestion that the *type* of consequences had to be foreseeable, provided that the need for treatment was foreseeable. It may be that the Court of Appeal regarded "the consequences of medical treatment" as a specific "type" of damage, but since this would cover almost any form of personal injury (provided it is a potential consequence of medical treatment) it is difficult to see how different types of personal injury can be identified as being either foreseeable or unforeseeable consequences of an otherwise foreseeable harm. In other words, *Robinson* v. *Post Office* appears to support a very wide categorisation of the type of damage that must be foreseen, an approach that clearly favours plaintiffs. This may be justified by the observation that the eggshell skull rule contains a strong element of policy, particularly in the realm of personal injuries, for as Professor Fleming has commented: "human bodies are too fragile and life too precarious to permit a defendant nicely to calculate how much injury he might inflict."[71]

5.81   It may be arguable that a medical practitioner should be better able to foresee unusual complications arising from negligent medical treatment than other defendants. How many people would appreciate, for example, that if a doctor negligently removed a patient's ectopic kidney believing it to be an ovarian cyst, that this might turn out to be the patient's only kidney, with the result that she would need an organ transplant?[72] The doctor's liability for the consequences of this error can be justified on several grounds: that, as a doctor, this remote risk was foreseeable to him; that the damage was of the same type as the foreseeable harm, although the extent of the damage was unforeseeable; or, that the plaintiff came within the eggshell skull rule.

5.82   Where the defendant's negligence increases the plaintiff's susceptibility to further injury, and thus effectively renders the plaintiff thin-skulled, he may be held responsible when further injury is sustained by the plaintiff.[73]

5. Plaintiff's impecuniosity

5.83   The defendant is not responsible for losses which are attributable solely to the plaintiff's impecuniosity.[74] This rule is widely regarded as anomalous, and has been distinguished on a number of occasions.[75] Moreover,

---

[70] See also *Winteringham* v. *Rae* (1965) 55 D.L.R. (2d) 108 (Ont. H.C.), where on similar facts a tortfeasor was held liable for the plaintiff's rare reaction to anti-tetanus serum. Negligent medical treatment would normally constitute a *novus actus interveniens*, though in *Robinson* the doctor had been negligent but his negligence was not a cause of the harm: see § 5.05; *cf. Price* v. *Milawski* (1977) 82 D.L.R. (3d) 130.

[71] Fleming, *The Law of Torts*, 7th ed., 1987, p. 184.

[72] *Urbanski* v. *Patel* (1978) 84 D.L.R. (3d) 650 (Man. Q.B.), see § 2.42.

[73] *Powell* v. *Guttman* (1978) 89 D.L.R. (3d) 180, 190 (Man. C.A), § 5.27.

[74] *Liesbosch Dredger* v. *S.S. Edison* [1933] A.C. 449.

[75] *Martindale* v. *Duncan* [1973] 1 W.L.R. 574; *Jarvis* v. *T. Richards & Co.* (1980) 124 S.J. 793, holding that the rule was inapplicable where the impecuniosity is caused by the defendant's tort; *Dodd Properties (Kent) Ltd.* v. *Canterbury City Council* [1980] 1 All E.R. 928, rule inapplicable where a decision not to effect early repairs to property, because it would lead to financial stringency, is based on commercial prudence rather than lack of resources.

the plaintiff's impecuniosity will be taken into account in deciding whether the plaintiff has fulfilled his duty to mitigate the loss.[76] In practice this rule will rarely be relevant in an action for medical negligence, since it is limited to claims in respect of damage to property or pure economic loss. It might on occasion be suggested that the plaintiff's personal injuries could have been reduced by early medical treatment, which would have been available if the plaintiff had sought private treatment but the plaintiff was unable to afford the cost of private treatment. In theory the additional damage attributable to the delay is the product of the plaintiff's impecuniosity, but in practice it is thought that the court would approach this as a question of mitigation of damage. The plaintiff has a duty to take reasonable steps to mitigate his loss, but the court will take account of his financial position in determining what constitutes "reasonable steps."[77]

---

[76] *Dodd Properties (Kent) Ltd.* v. *Canterbury City Council* [1980] 1 All E.R. 928, 935, 941.

[77] See further § 9.23.

CHAPTER 6

CONSENT TO TREATMENT

6.01 Consent to medical treatment is widely regarded as the cornerstone of the doctor/patient relationship. As a general rule, patients cannot be required to accept treatment that they do not want no matter how painless, beneficial and risk-free the treatment may be and no matter how dire the consequences of a refusal of treatment. This proposition is recognised as both an ethical principle and a legal rule, and is founded, ultimately, on the principle of respect for the patient's autonomy, or, expressed in more compelling terms, on the patient's "right" to self-determination. Thus, the legal requirement for consent expresses respect for the patient's autonomy. In the famous words of Cardozo J.:

> "Every human being of adult years and sound mind has a right to determine what shall be done with his own body; and a surgeon who performs an operation without his patient's consent commits an assault . . . ."[1]

Patient autonomy is not the only value, however, that the requirement of consent protects. With patients who are unable to exercise autonomous choices, such as children and adults who do not have the relevant capacity to give a valid consent, it serves as a reminder that there must be some lawful justification for a medical procedure which would otherwise constitute the tort of battery. This affirms the ethical principle of respect for persons by giving legal protection to a patient's bodily integrity, irrespective of their mental capacity. There is also some evidence that obtaining the patient's consent may assist in the therapeutic process, by involving the patient in the treatment as an active participant.[2]

6.02 This chapter deals with the requirements for consent as a defence to the action for battery, and the distinct issue of the doctor's duty of care in negligence to supply the patient with information about any proposed treatment or diagnostic procedure. The patient's consent must be a "valid" consent, which means that it must be voluntary, the patient must have the mental capacity to understand the nature of the procedure to which he is consenting, and he must also have a certain

---

[1] *Schloendorff* v. *Society of New York Hospital* (1914) 211 N.Y. 125, 126.
[2] Teff (1985) 101 L.Q.R. 432; Brazier (1987) 7 L.S. 169, 176.

minimal amount of information about the nature of the procedure. Where the patient lacks the relevant capacity to give a valid consent the doctor needs some form of proxy consent, or a court order, or some other lawful justification, which may be either statutory or under the common law. There are three major problem areas: children; patients with mental disorder; and emergencies, where patients are temporarily incapacitated. The section on the duty of disclosure in negligence includes discussion of material from several Commonwealth jurisdictions, which may contribute to an understanding of English law. Canadian law differs in some marked respects from English law, although the position in Australia and New Zealand is very similar to that in this country. A section on causation covers both battery and negligence, and serves as a reminder that even where plaintiffs succeed in establishing culpable non-disclosure they may face considerable difficulty in proving that this was a cause of their damage. The final section deals with three special cases, where either the legal requirements for consent and information disclosure may be more extensive (research and transplantation of organs) or the subject has given rise to particular problems in practice (failed sterilisation).

I. BATTERY

The tort of battery has generally been regarded as unsuitable as a **6.03** method of providing compensation for the victims of medical accidents, partly because of its technical limitations, but principally because it is an intentional tort (which can overlap with the criminal offence of assault), and this is considered to be inappropriate in the context of the doctor/patient relationship. Nonetheless the tort is relevant because of the nature of medical practice which often involves physical contact with the patient's body. The courts have been anxious to restrict its application, particularly in the area of information disclosure, and more recently in the interpretation given to the defence of necessity.

Battery is a form of trespass to the person, and as such it is **6.04** actionable *per se*. Damage is not an essential requirement of the tort, although if a plaintiff seeks more than nominal damages he will have to establish that he has suffered loss. A battery consists of the infliction of unlawful force on another person.[3] It is an intentional tort, in the sense that the defendant must intend the act which inflicts the force, but an intention to cause injury is not necessary,[4] and the exercise of reasonable care is not a defence. Any direct[5] contact with the plaintiff,

---

[3] *Collins* v. *Wilcox* [1984] 3 All E.R. 374, 377, C.A.

[4] *Wilson* v. *Pringle* [1986] 2 All E.R. 440, 445.

[5] Note that the requirement of a "touching" (a direct application of force) makes battery unsuitable as a remedy for certain types of treatment where the patient alleges a lack of consent, *e.g.* drug injuries, where the patient alleges that his consent was invalid because he was given insufficient information, and the drug was taken orally rather than by injection: see *Malloy* v. *Shanahan* (1980) 421 A. 2d 803. The deliberate infliction of harm by indirect means would result in liability under the principle in *Wilkinson* v. *Downton* [1897] 2 Q.B. 57. For the requirements as to information disclosure for the purposes of battery see §§ 6.23–6.28.

no matter how trivial, is sufficient force,[6] and thus the tort protects a person not only from physical injury but also his personal dignity from any form of physical molestation.[7] An exception to this principle applies to unavoidable contacts which are generally accepted as a consequence of social life, such as casual jostling in a busy street or touching someone on the shoulder to engage his attention.[8] In *Wilson* v. *Pringle*[9] the Court of Appeal said that a touching must be "hostile" in order to constitute a battery. Hostility was said to be a question of fact, but would not be limited to acts of ill-will or malevolence nor "the obvious intention shown in acts like punching, stabbing or shooting." The court did not indicate, however, what would be considered hostile, except to say that the police officer who, in *Collins* v. *Wilcock*,[10] touched the plaintiff without any more hostile an intention than to restrain her temporarily was acting in a hostile manner, and therefore unlawfully, because the officer had no power to restrain her.

6.05   This issue is important in the medical context because it would probably be rare that the contact of doctor and patient in the course of an examination or treatment could be regarded as hostile. If hostility is a requirement of the tort, then battery would be largely irrelevant to a medical practitioner's civil liability. It is respectfully submitted that "hostility" is not, and has never been, an element of the tort of battery. In *F.* v. *West Berkshire Health Authority* Lord Goff addressed the point, doubting the suggestion that a touching must be hostile for the purpose of battery:

> "A prank that gets out of hand, an over-friendly slap on the back, surgical treatment by a surgeon who mistakenly thinks that the patient has consented to it, all these things may transcend the bounds of lawfulness, without being characterised as hostile. Indeed, the suggested qualification is difficult to reconcile with the principle that any touching of another's body is, in the absence of lawful excuse, capable of amounting to a battery and a trespass."[11]

6.06   In the Court of Appeal Lord Donaldson M.R. had observed that prima facie all, or almost all, medical treatment and all surgical treatment of an adult is unlawful, in the absence of consent, however beneficial that treatment might be.[12] Similarly, in *T.* v. *T.*[13] Wood J.

---

[6] "The least touching of another in anger is a battery": *Cole* v. *Turner* (1704) 6 Mod. 149, *per* Holt C.J.

[7] *Collins* v. *Wilcock* [1984] 3 All E.R. 374, 378, *per* Goff L.J.: "It has long been established that any touching of another person, however slight, may amount to a battery." Thus, battery may take the form of snatching something from the plaintiff's grasp: *Green* v. *Goddard* (1702) 2 Salk. 641; throwing water at him: *Pursell* v. *Horn* (1838) 8 A. & E. 602; or applying a tone rinse to his hair: *Nash* v. *Sheen* [1953] C.L.Y. 3726.

[8] *Collins* v. *Wilcock* [1984] 3 All E.R. 374, 378.

[9] [1986] 2 All E.R. 440.

[10] [1984] 3 All E.R. 374.

[11] [1989] 2 All E.R. 545, 564. See also *Re F.* (*Mental Patient: Sterilisation*) [1989] 2 W.L.R. 1025, 1051 and 1057, *per* Neill and Butler-Sloss L.JJ. respectively.

[12] "This is incontestable": *Re F.* (*Mental Patient: Sterilisation*) [1989] 2 W.L.R. 1025, 1034.

[13] [1988] 1 All E.R. 613, 625.

commented that the incision of the surgeon's scalpel need not be and is most unlikely to be hostile, but unless a defence or justification is established it falls within the definition of a trespass to the person. This view is consistent with the law in other common law jurisdictions, and provides the whole basis of the proposition that a patient's consent to medical treatment is an essential requirement in law. In *Allan* v. *New Mount Sinai Hospital*, for example, Linden J. said that:

> "Battery is the intentional application of offensive or harmful physical contact to a person. Any surgical operation is a battery, unless the patient consents to it."[14]

The requirement for consent means that the patient has the right to make a choice about whether or not to accept medical treatment, and this right of choice necessarily means that the patient has the right to refuse treatment. The right to decline treatment exists "even where there are overwhelming medical reasons in favour of the treatment and probably even where if the treatment is not carried out the patient's life will be at risk."[15]

1. Consent as a defence to battery

The patient's consent to medical treatment, or indeed any procedure **6.07** which involves a touching of the patient's body, is essential because it renders lawful what would otherwise constitute the tort of battery, and, indeed, a serious invasion of the person's bodily integrity.[16] Although battery is said to be an intentional tort, it must be emphasised that there is no need for the defendant to have intended to commit a tort. If, through some oversight, a doctor fails to obtain the patient's consent to the procedure in question he will be liable in battery. So, if he performs the wrong operation,[17] or operates on the wrong limb, or the wrong patient, he commits a battery. This is the position even where the doctor acts in all good faith, and is as much the victim of some administrative error as the patient. In *Schweizer* v. *Central Hospital*[18] the plaintiff consented to an operation on his toe,

---

[14] (1980) 109 D.L.R. (3d) 634, 641 (Ont. H.C.); see also Cardozo J. in *Schloendorff* v. *Society of New York Hospital* (1914) 211 N.Y. 125, 126, cited *ante*, § 6.01; *Schweizer* v. *Central Hospital* (1974) 53 D.L.R. (3d) 494, 507 (Ont. H.C.); *Parmley* v. *Parmley and Yule* [1945] 4 D.L.R. 81, 88 (S.C.C.); *Marshall* v. *Curry* [1933] 3 D.L.R. 260, 274.

[15] *Re F. (mental patient: sterilisation)* [1989] 2 W.L.R. 1025, 1050, *per* Neill L.J. Lord Donaldson M.R., at pp. 1041–1042, said that: "The ability of the ordinary adult patient to exercise a free choice in deciding whether to accept or to refuse medical treatment and to choose between treatments is not to be dismissed as desirable but inessential. It is a crucial factor in relation to all medical treatment." See also *Malette* v. *Shulman* (1990) 67 D.L.R. (4th) 321, 328 (Ont. C.A.); *cf. Re R (a minor) (wardship: medical treatment)* [1991] 4 All E.R. 177 on the question of overriding a competent minor's refusal of medical treatment.

[16] Consent to battery is not the same as the defence of *volenti non fit injuria*, which is a voluntary agreement by the plaintiff to absolve the defendant from the legal consequences of an unreasonable risk of harm created by the defendant, where the plaintiff has full knowledge of both the nature and extent of the risk. The patient who consents to medical treatment does not consent to run the risk of negligence by the doctor: see *Freeman* v. *Home Office* [1984] 1 All E.R. 1036, 1044, *per* Sir John Donaldson M.R.

[17] *E.g.* a circumcision instead of a tonsilectomy: see *Chatterton* v. *Gerson* [1981] 1 All E.R. 257, 265f.

[18] (1974) 53 D.L.R. (3d) 494.

but due to some mix up a spinal fusion operation was performed. The surgeon was held liable in battery.

6.08   Clearly, the patient's consent must relate to the procedure that the doctor performs. Just as a complete lack of consent will give rise to an action for battery, a doctor who exceeds the consent given by the patient will also be liable. Thus, a patient who consents to the administration of a particular type of anaesthetic does not consent to the administration of a different type of anaesthetic,[19] and a patient who consents to a procedure being performed on one limb does not consent to the same procedure on another limb, especially where the patient has specifically objected. In *Allan* v. *New Mount Sinai Hospital*[20] the plaintiff gave an anaesthetist specific directions that he should not touch her left arm because he would "have nothing but trouble there." In the past she had had some difficulty with attempts to find a vein in her left arm. The defendant replied that he knew what he was doing, and did administer the anaesthetic by needle in the plaintiff's left arm. During the operation the needle slipped out of the arm causing the anaesthetic to leak into the tissues interstitially, instead of through the vein. The normal consequence of this is that the patient has a sore arm for a few days, but the plaintiff suffered a severe reaction which was entirely unexpected. In the High Court of Ontario Linden J. held that although the defendant was not negligent in the way he administered and monitored the anaesthetic, he was liable in battery. The plaintiff had expressly refused her consent to having the needle inserted into her left arm:

"Without a consent, either written or oral, no surgery may be performed. This is not a mere formality; it is an important individual right to have control over one's body, even where medical treatment is involved. It is the patient, not the doctor, who decides whether surgery will be performed, where it will be done, when it will be done and by whom it will be done."[21]

If the defendant had thought that the plaintiff's view was inadvisable, it was his duty to discuss the matter with her and try to convince her to change her mind. Similarly, in *Mulloy* v. *Hop Sang*[22] a patient asked a doctor to repair his injured hand, but not to amputate it, as he preferred to have it looked at in his home town. When the doctor looked at the hand following administration of an anaesthetic he decided that it ought to be amputated, and proceeded to do so. He was held liable in battery because the amputation was contrary to the express objection of the patient.

---

[19] *Beausoleil* v. *La Communauté des Soeurs de la Charité de la Providence* (1964) 53 D.L.R. (2d) 65 (Quebec Q.B. Appeal Side).
[20] (1980) 109 D.L.R. (3d) 634; rev'd on a pleading point (1982) 125 D.L.R. (3d) 276.
[21] *Ibid.*, p. 642. In *White* v. *Turner* (1981) 120 D.L.R. (3d) 269, 282–283 (Ont. H.C.), aff'd (1982) 12 D.L.R. (4th) 319 (Ont. C.A.), Linden J. said that the law of battery remains available where there is no consent to the operation, where the treatment given goes beyond the consent, or where the consent is obtained by fraud or misrepresentation (citing *Reibl* v. *Hughes* (1980) 114 D.L.R. (3d) 1 (S.C.C.)).
[22] [1935] 1 W.W.R. 714 (Alta. C.A.).

Where a patient consents to the administration of an injection, the **6.09**
consent relates both to the act of inserting the needle and the contents
of the syringe. If what is injected is not the substance to which the
patient has given consent it is a battery. Thus, in *Potts* v. *North West
Regional Health Authority*[23] the plaintiff agreed to be vaccinated
against rubella, but unknown to the plaintiff the syringe also contained
the contraceptive drug Depo-Provera. The defendants were held liable
in battery. Consent to the vaccination injection did not amount to
consent to anything that the doctors considered to be appropriate
being injected into the patient.

In a number of cases women have been sterilised without their **6.10**
consent in the course of other operative procedures, such as Caesarian
sections. This may be because the surgeon has taken the view that it
would be better for the woman not to have any more children, or it
could be that there has been an administrative mix-up. In *Cull* v. *Royal
Surrey County Hospital*,[24] for example, an epileptic patient who was
pregnant went into hospital for a termination by curettage, but the
surgeon performed the major operation of hysterectomy with a view to
sterilising her. The patient had specifically refused consent to the
sterilisation, and her general practitioner had written to the hospital to
make this clear. The letter was mislaid by the hospital staff, although
the hospital admission book indicated for "curettage." The jury
awarded damages of £120 against the hospital for negligence, and
nominal damages for trespass against the surgeon. In *Devi* v. *West
Midlands Regional Health Authority*[25] a surgeon performed a sterilisation operation on the plaintiff in the course of an operation to repair a
perforation of the uterus which had been caused during an earlier
dilation and curettage. There had been no prior discussion with the
plaintiff about the possibility of sterilisation, the surgeon had simply
taken the view that it was in the patient's interests. The defendants
admitted liability for battery.[26] Similarly, in *Murray* v. *McMurchy*,[27] a
doctor, during the course of a Caesarean section, discovered fibroid
tumours in the patient's uterus which he believed would be a danger if
the patient were to become pregnant again, and so he performed a
sterilisation operation. He was held liable in battery. The sterilisation
could not be justified under the principle of necessity because there
was no immediate threat to the patient's health and it would not have
been unreasonable to postpone the operation. It was merely conven-

---

[23] (1983) (unreported), see *The Guardian*, July 23, 1983.
[24] [1932] 1 B.M.J. 1195.
[25] (1981) (unreported), C.A.
[26] Ormrod L.J. questioned whether battery was the appropriate cause of action rather
than a claim "on the basis of failure to give proper advice," and said that the case should
not be treated as authority on the question of battery, because it had not been discussed
in argument. Whatever the status of the case as an authority, it is respectfully submitted
that the sterilisation of a competent adult without her consent is undoubtedly a battery,
and there is no basis for treating it as simply an instance of negligence.
[27] [1949] 2 D.L.R. 442; *Winn* v. *Alexander* [1940] 3 D.L.R. 778; see also *Hamilton* v.
Birmingham Regional Health Board [1969] 2 B.M.J. 456, in which the plaintiff was
sterilised without her consent during a Caesarian delivery, which was her third
Caesarian. She was never asked whether she wanted to be sterilised. Liability was
admitted.

ient to perform the operation without consent as the patient was already under general anaesthetic.[28]

6.11 Prima facie the patient's consent will be limited to procedures to be performed by a particular doctor. Thus, in *Michael* v. *Molesworth*[29] a patient recovered nominal damages for breach of contract when an operation was performed by a doctor other than the doctor whom the patient had anticipated. The standard National Health Service consent form contained a clause stating that "No assurance has been given to me that the operation/treatment will be performed or administered by any particular practitioner," a provision which was specifically intended to cover the circumstances of *Michael* v. *Molesworth*.[30] There must be some limits, however, to the effectiveness of such a clause. It cannot be taken as an invitation to the whole world, for example, to perform surgery upon the patient. It is arguable that if a patient were to consent to surgery being performed by a person whom the patient mistakenly believed to be a registered medical practitioner, but who was in fact unqualified, the consent would be invalid because the qualifications of the person wielding the scalpel go to the *nature* of the transaction. By extension of this argument, it might be said that a patient's consent is not given simply to "a doctor" (any old doctor?), but to a doctor whom the patient believes to be qualified and competent to perform the procedure in question. Newly qualified junior doctors, for example, do not, and are not expected to, perform open heart surgery. A patient's signature on a standard consent form cannot be taken as consent to such a step.

Burden of Proof

6.12 It is unclear whether consent is a true defence to an action for battery, or whether it is part and parcel of the tort itself. Must the plaintiff prove that he did not consent in order to establish the cause of action, or is it sufficient to prove the direct interference, leaving the defendant to justify the act by asserting and proving that the plaintiff consented? This issue turns, essentially, upon who has the burden of proof. The traditional view has been that consent operates as a defence, and accordingly it is for the defendant to prove that the plaintiff consented. In *Freeman* v. *Home Office*,[31] however, McCowan J. held that the plaintiff has the burden of proof, a view which effectively redefines battery to mean an "unconsented to interference

---

[28] See also *Wells* v. *Surrey Area Health Authority*, *The Times*, July 29, 1978 (news report) in which a Roman Catholic woman was sterilised in the course of a Caesarian operation. She signed the consent form just before she went into the operating theatre. Croom-Johnson J. held that she had understood the nature of the operation and therefore consented to the sterilisation, but she had been inadequately counselled as to the implications of the operation. In particular the patient should have been told that there was no medical need for sterilisation, and that there was no urgency about the matter because it could be done at a later stage. The defendants were liable in negligence.
[29] [1950] 2 B.M.J. 171.
[30] The new standard N.H.S. consent form states that: "I understand that the procedure may not be done by the doctor/dentist who has been treating me so far," which does not appear to take the matter any further; see (1990) 301 B.M.J. 510.
[31] [1983] 3 All E.R. 589.

with another's bodily integrity." On the other hand, in *Collins* v. *Wilcock* Goff L.J. appeared to regard consent as a defence,[32] as did Neill L.J. in *Re F. (Mental Patient: Sterilisation)*,[33] and in Canada this is undoubtedly the case.[34]

2. Forms of consent

Consent may be either express or implied from the plaintiff's **6.13** conduct. If a doctor tells a patient that he wants to give him an injection and the patient silently bares his arm and holds it out for the needle he will be taken to have consented.[35] If the doctor reasonably believes that the patient has consented the patient cannot complain afterwards that there was no consent. Silence by a patient, however, is not necessarily consent; it will depend on the circumstances of the case, and whether the doctor's inference of consent was reasonable.[36]

Prior to most major surgical procedures the patient will be asked to **6.14** sign a written consent form. Standard consent forms state that the nature and purpose of the operation or treatment have been explained to the patient.[37] But such forms are not conclusive against the patient, they are merely evidence that the patient consented to the procedure in question. In *Chatterton* v. *Gerson* Bristow J. said that:

" . . . getting the patient to sign a *pro forma* expressing consent
to undergo the operation 'the effect and nature of which have
been explained to me' . . . should be a valuable reminder to
everyone of the need for explanation and consent. But it would

---

[32] [1984] 3 All E.R. 374, 378: "Generally speaking, consent is defence to battery"; see also *T.* v. *T.* [1988] 1 All E.R. 613, 625; Croom-Johnson L.J. in *Wilson* v. *Pringle* [1986] 2 All E.R. 440, 447 considered that consent was an example of "so-called 'defences.' "

[33] [1989] 2 W.L.R. 1025, 1050: "It is apparent therefore that the defence of consent is not a complete answer . . . " *Clerk & Lindsell on Torts*, 16th ed., 1989, para. 17–05 states that the burden of proving absence of consent lies with the plaintiff, citing *Freeman* v. *Home Office* [1983] 3 All E.R. 589; *cf.* Dugdale and Stanton, *Professional Negligence*, 1989, 2nd ed., para. 11.66 placing the onus of proving that the patient has given a valid consent on the doctor; and Trindade (1982) 2 O.J.L.S. 211, 229 to the same effect.

[34] *Beausoleil* v. *La Communauté des Soeurs de la Charité de la Providence* (1964) 53 D.L.R. (2d) 65, 69; *Hambley* v. *Shepley* (1967) 63 D.L.R. (2d) 94, 95 (Ont. C.A.); *Kelly* v. *Hazlett* (1976) 75 D.L.R. (3d) 536, 563 (Ont. H.C.); *Schweizer* v. *Central Hospital* (1974) 53 D.L.R. (3d) 494, 510; *Reibl* v. *Hughes* (1980) 114 D.L.R. (3d) 1, 9 (S.C.C.); *Allan* v. *New Mount Sinai Hospital* (1980) 109 D.L.R. (3d) 634, 641. See the discussion by Blay (1987) 61 A.L.J. 25.

[35] *Allan* v. *New Mount Sinai Hospital* (1980) 109 D.L.R. (3d) 634, 641. Provided, of course, that the syringe contains what the patient believed it to contain: *Potts* v. *North West Regional Health Authority* (1983) (unreported), § 6.09.

[36] *Ibid.*; see also *Schweizer* v. *Central Hospital* (1974) 53 D.L.R. (3d) 494, 508, *per* Thompson J.: "Consent may be implied where circumstances dictate that it is clearly indicated and it is manifest that the will of the patient accompanies such consent." A lack of objection may not be sufficient for the doctor to infer consent by the patient, a point that becomes significant in the context of the treatment of patients with mental handicap: see Gunn (1987) 16 Anglo-American L.R. 242, 246.

[37] The new N.H.S. consent form states that the patient agrees "to what is proposed which has been explained to me by the doctor/dentist named on this form"; see (1990) 301 B.M.J. 510. Where the patient receives treatment privately the contract between doctor and patient may be embodied partly in the written consent form and partly in the oral conversations between doctor and patient prior to the procedure, at which time the nature and effect of the operation should have been explained to the patient: *Eyre* v. *Measday* [1986] 1 All E.R. 488, 492.

be no defence to an action based on trespass to the person if no explanation had in fact been given. The consent would have been expressed in form only, not in reality."[38]

Thus, in *Coughlin* v. *Kuntz*[39] the patient signed consent forms but it was held that he did not understand and appreciate the nature of the procedure and therefore there was no valid consent. The defendant had not informed the patient that the procedure was novel, unique to the defendant, and under investigation by the College of Physicians and Surgeons, who had urged him to undertake a moratorium on the procedure.

6.15 It is not good practice to get patients to sign consent forms just before they have the operation when they have already been sedated. The drug may impair the patient's ability to comprehend, and render an apparent consent invalid. For example, in *Beausoleil* v. *La Communauté des Soeurs de la Charité de la Providence*[40] the plaintiff went into hospital for a back operation, and told the surgeon that she wanted a general anaesthetic, not a spinal anaesthetic. On the day of the operation she was sedated and taken to the operating theatre where she told the anaesthetist that she did not want a spinal anaesthetic. The anaesthetist then talked the plaintiff into accepting the spinal anaesthetic, without examining her or consulting the surgeon. This was administered with reasonable care, but after the operation the plaintiff was paralysed from the waist down, probably as a result of the spinal anaesthetic. It was held that the plaintiff had not given a valid consent. Due to the sedation the exchange between plaintiff and defendant "no longer had any real significance for the plaintiff and . . . [was] of no legal consequence."[41] Similarly, in *Kelly* v. *Hazlett*[42] the plaintiff consented to an osteotomy to correct a deformity in her elbow after the administration of a sedative. Morden J. commented that the giving of a consent in such circumstances, at the very least, leaves the validity of the consent open to question, although he concluded that, on the facts, the plaintiff had a sufficient understanding of the basic nature and character of the operation for the consent to be effective.[43]

6.16 Consent forms have usually included a clause confirming that the patient consents to "such further or alternative operative measures or treatment as may be found necessary during the course of the operation or treatment."[44] The effect of such a clause is highly

---

[38] [1981] 1 All E.R. 257, 265; *Hajgato* v. *London Health Association* (1982) 36 O.R. (2d) 669, 679; aff'd 40 O.R. (2d) 264 (Ont. C.A.): "While the plaintiff signed a standard form of authorisation and consent prior to the operation in which she acknowledged the nature of the operation had been explained to her satisfaction, the existence of that consent does not protect a doctor from liability unless the patient has been informed to the satisfaction of the court." See also *Bickford* v. *Stiles* (1981) 128 D.L.R. (3d) 516, 520; *Brushett* v. *Cowan* (1987) 40 D.L.R. (4th) 488; rev'd on the facts (1990) 69 D.L.R. (4th) 743 (Newfd. C.A.).
[39] (1987) 42 C.C.L.T. 142 (B.C.S.C.); aff'd [1990] 2 W.W.R. 737, 745 (B.C.C.A.).
[40] (1964) 53 D.L.R. (2d) 65 (Quebec Q.B. Appeal Side).
[41] *Ibid.*, *per* Rinfret J. at p. 76. See also *Wells* v. *Surrey Area Health Authority*, *The Times*, July 29, 1978 (news report), n. 28, *ante*.
[42] (1976) 75 D.L.R. (3d) 536 (Ont. H.C.).
[43] *Ibid.*, p. 563. The defendant was held liable in negligence for failing to inform the plaintiff about the risk of stiffness associated with the operation; see also *Ferguson* v. *Hamilton Civic Hospitals* (1983) 144 D.L.R. (3d) 214, 237, *per* Krever J., aff'd (1985) 18 D.L.R. (4th) 638 (Ont. C.A.).
[44] M.P.S. General Consent Form, 1988.

questionable, since if the "further or alternative" treatment was not justified in law under the principle of necessity,[45] it is unlikely that such a blanket consent would protect the doctor because the patient would probably be unaware of the nature of the treatment.[46] The consent form constitutes evidence of consent, but if in fact the patient does not understand the nature of the treatment the consent is invalid. The new N.H.S. model general consent form does not include such a "consent" but states that the patient understands "that any procedure in addition to the investigation or treatment described on this form will only be carried out if it is necessary and in my best interests and can be justified for medical reasons."[47] At best, this probably amounts to little more than providing information to the patient, bearing in mind that any procedure which was *not* in the best interests of the patient or could *not* be justified for medical reasons would run the risk of being held to be negligent. The model consent form also states that: "I have told the doctor or dentist about any additional procedures I would *not* wish to be carried out straightaway without my having the opportunity to consider them first."[48] The purpose of this provision is obscure, to say the least. Even if it were remotely practical for patients to identify all the potential procedures to which they did not wish to be subjected (which, clearly, it is not), there is no obligation in law for a patient to specify what he does not want to have done to him. In the absence of some valid justification, such as the patient's consent to the specific procedure that is contemplated, or necessity, all other procedures which involve physical contact with the person are unlawful, as battery. To suggest otherwise, even by implication, as the new model consent form appears to do, misrepresents the true position in law.

3. Consent must be valid

In order to be effective as a defence to a claim in battery the **6.17** patient's consent must be a valid consent. For this purpose the consent must be "real."[49] There are three elements to this. First, it must be voluntary and uncoerced. Secondly, the patient must be capable of understanding the nature of the procedure, *i.e.* he must have the capacity (or competence) to consent. Thirdly, he must have a certain minimum level of information concerning the "nature" of the procedure so that he knows what he is consenting to.

---

[45] See §§ 6.56–6.61.

[46] *cf.* Dugdale and Stanton, *Professional Negligence*, 1989 2nd ed., para. 11.70, suggesting that such a consent might justify more extensive intervention than would be lawful under the principle of necessity. In *Brushett* v. *Cowan* (1990) 69 D.L.R. (4th) 743 (Newfd. C.A.) the plaintiff signed a consent form authorising a muscle biopsy, and also consented to "such further or alternative measures as may be found to be necessary during the course of the operation." The defendant performed a muscle biopsy and a bone biopsy, and at first instance he was held liable in battery in respect of the bone biopsy (see (1987) 40 D.L.R. (4th) 488, 492). On appeal the decision was reversed, on the basis that the extent of the consent must be judged by looking at all the circumstances, not merely the consent form. The plaintiff had consented to a diagnostic procedure to determine the cause of her medical problem, and in the circumstances this was a sufficient consent to the bone biopsy.

[47] See (1990) 301 B.M.J. 510.

[48] *Ibid.*, emphasis in original.

[49] *Chatterton* v. *Gerson* [1981] 1 All E.R. 257, 264.

Voluntary consent

6.18   A person's consent must be voluntary.[50] Consent obtained by coercion or duress is invalid. In *Latter* v. *Braddell*[51] it was held that a housemaid, who, at the insistence of her employer, submitted to a medical examination protesting and sobbing throughout, had consented, even though she mistakenly believed that she was obliged to comply. The majority of the court took the view that the consent would be involuntary only where the plaintiff submitted through fear of violence. This decision was questionable at the time,[52] and would probably not be followed if the facts were to recur today. Thus, a mistaken belief as to the authority of the defendant may destroy in substance the plaintiff's freedom to choose.[53]

6.19   In *Freeman* v. *Home Office*[54] it was accepted that in some circumstances a person's apparent consent could be vitiated by the defendant's exercise of authority over him, without any threat of physical violence. The plaintiff, who was serving a term of life imprisonment, claimed that in the prison context it was impossible for there to be a free and voluntary consent by a prisoner to treatment by a prison medical officer, who was not merely a doctor but a prison officer within the meaning of the Prison Rules who could influence the prisoner's life and his prospects of release on licence. This created an atmosphere of constraint upon an inmate. McCowan J. rejected this contention as a proposition of law, taking the view that it is a question of fact in any particular case whether the patient's consent is voluntary. His Lordship added that where, in a prison setting, a doctor has the power to influence a prisoner's situation and prospects, a court must be alive to the risk that what may appear, on the face of it, to be a real consent is not in fact so.[55]

Capacity to consent

6.20   As a general rule, a person's capacity in law to enter into a transaction depends upon the nature of the transaction, so a person

---

[50] *Bowater* v. *Rowley Regis Corporation* [1944] K.B. 476, 479, *per* Scott L.J.: "A man cannot be said to be truly 'willing' unless he is in a position to choose freely, and freedom of choice predicates, not only full knowledge of the circumstances on which the exercise of choice is conditioned, so that he may be able to choose wisely, but the absence from his mind of any feeling of constraint so that nothing shall interfere with the freedom of his will." This remark was made in the context of the defence of *volenti non fit injuria*, but it has much force in relation to the defence of consent to battery: see *Freeman* v. *Home Office* [1983] 3 All E.R. 589, 592; [1984] 1 All E.R. 1036, 1042.
[51] (1881) 50 L.J.Q.B. 448, C.A.
[52] See the dissent of Lopes J. at (1880) 50 L.J.C.P. 166.
[53] *Clerk & Lindsell on Torts*, 16th ed., 1989, para. 17–08, citing *T.* v. *T.* [1964] P. 85, 99, 102; *cf.* Dugdale and Stanton, *Professional Negligence*, 1989, 2nd ed., para. 11.69, citing *Latter* v. *Braddell* (1881) 50 L.J.Q.B. 448.
[54] [1983] 3 All E.R. 589.
[55] *Ibid.*, p. 597; aff'd by the Court of Appeal [1984] 1 All E.R. 1036. See also *Kaimowitz* v. *Michegan Department of Mental Health* (1973) 42 U.S.L.W. 2063, where it was said that the capacity of an involuntarily detained mental patient to consent to psychosurgery was diminished by the very nature of his incarceration, which through the phenomenon of institutionalisation may strip the individual of the support which enables him to maintain his sense of self-worth.

may, at one and the same time, be competent in law for some purposes but not for others.[56] In the context of the doctor/patient relationship, capacity to consent to treatment depends upon the patient's ability to understand the nature of the treatment. This will be regarded as a question of fact in each case. The prima facie assumption with the vast majority of adult patients must be that they are competent to give a valid consent. The important corollary of this is that the vast majority of adult patients are competent to *refuse* treatment if they so choose.

How much understanding must a patient have in order to be treated **6.21** as having sufficient capacity, in law, to consent? In *Chatterton* v. *Gerson*[57] Bristow J. was confronted with the question of how much information a patient must be given before the consent can be regarded as valid. His Lordship said that:

> "In my judgment once the patient is informed in broad terms of the nature of the procedure which is intended, and gives her consent, that consent is real, and the cause of action on which to base a claim for failure to go into risks and implications is negligence, not trespass."[58]

If the patient need only be given information in broad terms as to the nature of the intended procedure, it must follow that the patient need only understand "in broad terms" the nature of the procedure in order to have sufficient understanding to be considered fully competent to give or withhold consent. This would appear to be quite a low level of understanding.[59]

In this country, the courts have not had to explore the precise **6.22** meaning of capacity in the context of medical treatment,[60] and the question is generally left to the good sense of the medical profession. If the issue were to arise, there are several possible tests that could be employed: was the patient's decision about whether to accept or reject treatment rational; was the outcome of the choice reasonable; did the patient have "full" understanding; was the patient's decision-making process rational/reasonable irrespective of the outcome?[61] The difficulty with most, if not all, of these tests is that there is a danger of categorising patients as incompetent simply because they have not chosen the medical option that some other person (whether it be the doctor, a relative or the court) would have chosen in the circumstances, and allowing that person to substitute their own paternalistic view of what is in the patient's best interests.[62] Respect for autonomy

---

[56] *E.g.*, a person may have sufficient understanding to enter into a contract of marriage but not to make a will: *Re Park's Estate* [1954] P. 89; see also *Re Beaney* [1978] 2 All E.R. 595.

[57] [1981] 1 All E.R. 257.

[58] *Ibid.*, p. 265.

[59] *cf.* the rule applied to children, which apparently requires a greater level of understanding than with adult patients: see §§ 6.32–6.33.

[60] With the exception of children as patients: see *Gillick* v. *West Norfolk and Wisbech Area Health Authority*, § 6.30, *post*. See Brazier (1990) 5 P.N. 25, 26 commenting that the courts have paid too little attention to the question of whether girls with a mental handicap were competent to refuse consent, before authorising sterilisation under the wardship jurisdiction.

[61] For more detailed discussion of this issue see Kennedy and Grubb, *Medical Law: Text and Materials*, 1989, Butterworths, pp. 190–215.

[62] There is thus a bias in favour of decisions to accept treatment: Gunn (1987) 16 Anglo-Am. L.R. 242, 251, citing Roth, Meisel and Lidz (1977) Am. J. of Psych. 279, 281.

and self-determination, which are said to be the foundations of the requirement for consent, must allow for patients to make unreasonable, irrational, or even silly decisions about their health care without the patient immediately being categorised as incompetent. In *Sidaway* v. *Bethlem Royal Hospital Governors*,[63] for example, Lord Templeman said that if a doctor advises a patient to submit to an operation "the patient is entitled to reject that advice for reasons which are rational, or irrational, or for no reason."[64]

Information

6.23 In order to be capable of understanding the nature of the procedure to which he is consenting, the patient must have some information about the procedure itself.[65] In *Chatterton* v. *Gerson*[66] the plaintiff suffered from chronic and intractable pain in the area surrounding an operation scar, following a hernia operation. The defendant was a specialist in the treatment of pain, and he operated on the plaintiff by administering an intrathecal injection of a solution of phenol and glycerine near the spinal cord with the object of destroying the pain-conducting nerves near the hernia operation site. The operation only relieved the pain temporarily, and the plaintiff had a second spinal injection given by the same surgeon. This was also unsuccessful in relieving the pain, but the plaintiff's right leg was rendered completely numb, which impaired her mobility. The defendant's practice was to explain to patients that the treatment involved numbness at the site of the pain and a larger surrounding area, and might involve temporary loss of muscle power. The plaintiff argued that because she had not been informed about the inherent risk of side-effects materialising from her treatment, her consent was vitiated and the doctor was liable in battery for all the adverse consequences of her treatment. Bristow J. said that in order to vitiate the reality of consent there must be a greater failure of communication between doctor and patient than that involved in a breach of duty if the claim is based on negligence. Accordingly, once the patient was "informed in broad terms of the nature of the procedure which is intended, and gives her consent, that consent is real," and the cause of action on which to base a claim for failure to discuss the risks and implications of a procedure was negligence, not trespass.[67] Miss Chatterton was under no illusion as to

[63] [1985] 1 All E.R. 643, 666.

[64] See also T.A. Gresson J. in *Smith* v. *Auckland Hospital Board* [1965] N.Z.L.R. 191, 219: "An individual patient must, in my view, always retain the right to decline operative investigation or treatment however unreasonable or foolish this may appear in the eyes of his medical advisers." In *Lepp* v. *Hopp* (1979) 98 D.L.R. (3d) 464, 470; aff'd (1980) 112 D.L.R. (3d) 67 (S.C.C.), Prowse J.A. said that: "Each patient is entitled to make his own decision even though it may not accord with the decision knowledgeable members of the profession would make. The patient has a right to be wrong"; Brazier (1987) 7 L.S. 169, 175.

[65] See the quotation from *Bowater* v. *Rowley Regis Corporation* [1944] K.B. 476, 479 cited *ante*, n. 50. A patient may be estopped from denying that he had the relevant information if he so acts as to lead the defendant reasonably to assume that the information was known to him: *Sidaway* v. *Bethlem Royal Hospital Governors* [1985] 1 All E.R. 643, 658, *per* Lord Diplock.

[66] [1981] 1 All E.R. 257.

[67] *Ibid.*, p. 265.

the general nature of the proposed procedure, and therefore her consent was not unreal.

Chatterton v. *Gerson* was the first attempt to introduce into this **6.24** country the doctrine of informed consent through the action for battery. From the plaintiff's point of view battery was perceived as having distinct advantages over a claim in negligence (with corresponding disadvantages for defendants). Battery, as a form of trespass, is actionable *per se* and so does not require proof of damage, although if the plaintiff seeks more than nominal damages he will have to establish that the loss was a direct result of the unlawful force. In the absence of consent it is clear that the medical procedure and any complications arising from it are the direct result of the battery. Secondly, once it is established that the patient's consent was invalid, it does not have to be proved that the patient would not have accepted the treatment had he been informed about the inherent risks of the procedure, which is an essential element of a claim based in negligence.[68] Thirdly, medical evidence as to the profession's usual disclosure practice is considered to be irrelevant to a claim based in battery, again because once the consent is vitiated the tort is committed.[69] A final factor, which was clearly influential in the courts' hostility to actions in battery, is the perception of trespass as an intentional tort. It was considered inappropriate that doctors, acting in good faith, should be held liable for an intentional tort.

The view that failure to discuss or explain the risks of the proposed **6.25** treatment, or alternatives to that treatment, goes to the doctor's duty of care in negligence, not trespass to the person, was adopted in *Hills* v. *Potter*[70] where it was held that the plaintiff's undoubted consent to the operation which was in fact performed negatived liability in battery.[71] This approach has been affirmed by the Court of Appeal. In *Sidaway* v. *Bethlem Royal Hospital Governors* Sir John Donaldson M.R. said that: "I am wholly satisfied that as a matter of English law a consent is not vitiated by a failure on the part of the doctor to give the patient sufficient information before the consent is given."[72] Once the patient has been informed in broad terms of the nature of the treatment, consent in fact amounts to consent in law.[73] A similar attitude to battery is apparent in the Canadian courts.[74]

---

[68] See § 6.97.

[69] This point assumes that medical evidence of what doctors normally tell patients *ought* to be relevant to the question of what patients have a right to know.

[70] [1983] 3 All E.R. 716, 728; *Freeman* v. *Home Office* [1983] 3 All E.R. 589, 593, *per* McCowan J.

[71] Hirst J. said that he deplored reliance on trespass to the person in medical cases of this kind, a dictum that was approved by Lord Scarman in *Sidaway* v. *Bethlem Royal Hospital Governors* [1985] 1 All E.R. 643, 650.

[72] [1984] 1 All E.R. 1018, 1026; see also, *per* Dunn L.J. at p. 1029 and Browne-Wilkinson L.J. at p. 1032.

[73] *Freeman* v. *Home Office* [1984] 1 All E.R. 1036, 1044, *per* Sir John Donaldson M.R.

[74] *Reibl* v. *Hughes* (1980) 114 D.L.R. (3d) 1, 10–11 (S.C.C.), *per* Laskin C.J.C.: "I can appreciate the temptation to say that the genuineness of consent to medical treatment depends on proper disclosure of the risks which it entails, but in my view, unless there has been misrepresentation or fraud to secure consent to the treatment, a failure to disclose the attendant risks, however serious, should go to negligence rather than battery." *White* v. *Turner* (1981) 120 D.L.R. (3d) 269, 283 (Ont. H.C.), *per* Linden J.; aff'd (1982) 12 D.L.R. (4th) 319 (Ont. C.A.): "The future use of battery is, therefore, limited to cases involving a real lack of consent. Where there has been a basic consent to the treatment, there is no place left for discussions of battery."

6.26   Thus, the courts have drawn a distinction between a lack of information which concerns the *nature* of the procedure (which gives rise to an action in battery) and a lack of information about the risks associated with the procedure (where the action must be based in negligence). It has been forcefully argued that this distinction is untenable, as it assumes an inherent difference in terminology and substance between the nature of the treatment and the risks inherent in the treatment.[75] Some risks may be so significant that they relate to the *nature* of the operation itself, so that non-disclosure of the risk would vitiate the consent and lead to liability in battery. It is not self-evidently apparent what the "nature" of any particular medical treatment consists of, nor that, for example, a high risk of serious consequences is not part and parcel of the "nature" of the procedure.[76] It depends, ultimately, on how one chooses to characterise the nature of any particular activity and the level of abstraction that is adopted.

6.27   A similar degree of confusion is apparent in relation to the exception for fraud and misrepresentation. It is said that if the patient's consent has been obtained by fraud or misrepresentation then it is not a valid consent.[77] Thus, in *Sidaway* v. *Bethlem Royal Hospital Governors* Sir John Donaldson M.R. said that:

> "It is only if the consent is obtained by fraud or by misrepresentation of the nature of what is to be done that it can be said that an apparent consent is not a true consent. This is the position in the criminal law . . . and the cause of action based on trespass to the person is closely analogous."[78]

It is not clear what would constitute fraud or misrepresentation. Must it relate to the nature of the procedure to vitiate consent, or will fraud as to the consequences or risks suffice? Sir John Donaldson M.R. appears to require misrepresentation as to the nature of the procedure: "only if the consent is obtained by fraud or by misrepresentation of the nature of what is to be done." But if the plaintiff does not consent to the *nature* of what is done, the consent is not real, *irrespective of the reason why.*[79] The defendant's motive, whether "fraudulent" or in good faith, is irrelevant. This might suggest that if the exception is to have any meaning it should also include fraud or misrepresentation as to consequences or risks. This certainly appears to have been the view of Laskin C.J.C. delivering the judgment of the Supreme Court of

---

[75] Tan (1987) 7 L.S. 149; see also Somerville (1981) 26 McGill L.J. 740, 742–52.

[76] "In some cases it may be difficult to distinguish, and separate out, the matter of consequential or collateral risks from the basic nature and character of the operation or procedure to be performed. . . . The more probable the risk the more it could be said to be an integral feature of the nature and character of the operation" *per* Morden J. in *Kelly* v. *Hazlett* (1976) 75 D.L.R. (3d) 536, 559; *cf.* the comments of Laskin C.J.C. in *Reibl* v. *Hughes* (1980) 114 D.L.R. (3d) 1, 9.

[77] "Of course, if information is withheld in bad faith, the consent will be vitiated by fraud," *per* Bristow J. in *Chatterton* v. *Gerson* [1981] 1 All E.R. 257, 265.

[78] [1984] 1 All E.R. 1018, 1026, citing *R.* v. *Clarence* (1888) 22 Q.B.D. 23 at 43; see also *Freeman* v. *Home Office* [1983] 3 All E.R. 589, 593, *per* McCowan J., aff'd [1984] 1 All E.R. 1036, 1044, *per* Sir John Donaldson M.R.

[79] Tan (1987) 7 L.S. 149, 156 makes this point: "There is no magic in the character of the conduct concealing or distorting medical advice for [the] purpose of the defence of consent. The misconduct only gives occasion to the concealment. What is material is the content of the medical advice that is concealed, not the mode of concealment."

Canada in *Reibl* v. *Hughes*: "unless there has been misrepresentation or fraud to secure consent to the treatment, *a failure to disclose the attendant risks*, however serious, should go to negligence rather than battery."[80] On this approach misrepresentation as to risks would vitiate the reality of the patient's consent.[81]

In the criminal law fraud vitiates consent only where the plaintiff's **6.28** mistake concerns the real nature of the transaction.[82] There is no obvious justification, however, for applying the criminal law rule in tort, since it is unduly favourable to the defendant.[83] The consequences of an act are often the crucial factor in the granting of a genuine consent. Except in a dire emergency, no one would consent to major surgery by someone who was not trained to perform it. If the defendant obtained the plaintiff's consent to an operation by misrepresenting his ability to carry it out, it is difficult to see why the plaintiff's consent should not be regarded as vitiated by the misrepresentation, even though there is no mistake as to the nature of the act (surgery).[84] Similarly, it is arguable that a deliberate lie in response to a specific question from the patient as to risks could be taken as evidence of bad faith which might vitiate the patient's consent. It seems likely, however, that the courts would seek to deal with this as an aspect of the doctor's duty of care in negligence in order to take account of the "therapeutic privilege" argument that disclosure of the information would have been harmful to the patient and, accordingly, the lie was in the patient's "best interests."[85]

4. Children

For the purpose of the law of consent, children fall into two **6.29**

---

[80] (1980) 114 D.L.R. (3d) 1, 10–11, emphasis added.

[81] Query whether a deliberate lie in the face of a specific question from the patient renders the consent "unreal"? See further *Halushka* v. *University of Saskatchewan* (1965) 53 D.L.R. (2d) 436 (Sask. C.A.), § 6.118. Note that there is a distinction between fraud, which implies bad faith, and misrepresentation, which does not. A misrepresentation may simply be negligent. In *Ferguson* v. *Hamilton Civic Hospitals* (1983) 144 D.L.R. (3d) 214, 243–244; aff'd (1985) 18 D.L.R. (4th) 638 (Ont. C.A.) it was argued that the non-disclosure of the risks of surgical treatment prior to conducting a *diagnostic* procedure (which might indicate a need for the treatment) constituted a misrepresentation of the nature of the diagnostic procedure. This argument was rejected, but it was not suggested that the defendant must have acted in bad faith for the "misrepresentation" exception to apply.

[82] Persuading a girl to have sexual intercourse by representing to her that it is a surgical operation, *e.g. R.* v. *Flattery* (1877) 2 Q.B.D. 410; *R.* v. *Williams* [1923] 1 K.B. 340; *cf. R.* v. *Clarence* (1888) 22 Q.B.D. 23—no offence when the defendant infected his wife with venereal disease, her consent was still valid.

[83] *Winfield & Jolowicz on Tort*, 13th ed., 1989, p. 686; *Clerk & Lindsell on Torts*, 16th ed., 1989, para. 17–07, take the view that the distinction may be applied to the civil law, citing *Hegarty* v. *Shine* (1878) 14 Cox C.C. 124 and 145, in which the plaintiff's action against her former lover for infecting her with venereal disease failed because she had consented to the sexual intercourse. The court also applied the maxim *ex turpi causa non oritur actio*, and was heavily influenced by the view that the plaintiff's conduct was unlawful and immoral, a view that would not be persuasive today. See, however, *Norberg* v. *Wynrib* [1988] 6 W.W.R. 305; aff'd (1990) 66 D.L.R. (4th) 553 for a modern example of the defence of *ex turpi causa* in the context of the doctor/patient relationship.

[84] This example is not hypothetical. Persons masquerading as doctors have been convicted of various criminal offences: see Eekelaar and Dingwall [1984] J.S.W.L. 258, 259, n. 5.

[85] See § 6.87. For consideration of the lawfulness of testing patients for HIV antibodies without their knowledge or consent see Sherrard and Gatt (1987) 295 B.M.J. 911; Keown (1989) 52 M.L.R. 790.

categories: either they have the capacity to make their own decisions about medical treatment, and can give a valid consent on their own behalf in precisely the same way as an adult; or they do not have capacity, in which case parental consent will normally be required. It is easy to state the principle; the difficulty lies in applying it to a particular case.

Children with capacity

6.30   By section 8(1) of the Family Law Reform Act 1969 children of 16 years or more are presumed to have the same capacity as an adult to consent to medical treatment.[86] This does not mean that children under the age of 16 do not have the relevant capacity. Section 8(3) of the same Act states that "Nothing in this section shall be construed as making ineffective any consent which would have been effective if this section had not been enacted." It was always assumed that this subsection was intended to make it clear that the legislation was without prejudice to the position at common law: if a child below the age of 16 did have the capacity to consent to medical treatment, section 8 did not change that. This interpretation was challeged in *Gillick* v. *West Norfolk and Wisbech Area Health Authority*,[87] where the plaintiff argued that no child under 16 could consent to medical treatment, and that section 8(3) merely preserved the parental right to consent for children of 16 or 17 years. Although accepted in the Court of Appeal, this argument was rejected by a majority in the House of Lords. Lord Fraser said that it was "verging on the absurd" to suggest that a girl or boy aged 15 could not effectively consent, for example, to have a medical examination of some trivial injury or even to have a broken arm set. Provided the patient is capable of understanding what is proposed, and of expessing his or her own wishes, there was no good reason for holding that he or she lacks the capacity to express them validly and effectively and to authorise the doctor to perform an examination or give treatment.[88]

6.31   Lord Scarman said that as a matter of law a minor child below the age of 16 will have the capacity to consent to medical treatment "when the child achieves a sufficient understanding and intelligence to enable him or her to understand fully what is proposed." This is a question of fact.[89] Lord Templeman agreed that a doctor may lawfully carry out some forms of treatment with the consent of an infant patient, even against the opposition of a parent based on religious or any other grounds.[90]

---

[86] S.8(1) provides that: "The consent of a minor who has attained the age of sixteen years to any surgical, medical or dental treatment which, in the absence of consent, would constitute a trespass to his person, shall be as effective as it would be if he were of full age; and where a minor has by virtue of this section given an effective consent to any treatment it shall not be necessary to obtain any consent for it from his parent or guardian . . . ." See also Mental Health Act 1983, s.131(2); Skegg (1973) 36 M.L.R. 370.

[87] [1985] 3 All E.R. 402.

[88] [1985] 3 All E.R. 402, 409; see also *Johnston* v. *Wellesley Hospital* (1970) 17 D.L.R. (3d) 139 (Ont. H.C.); Skegg (1973) 36 M.L.R. 370.

[89] *Ibid.*, p. 423. The child must also be capable of understanding the consequences of a failure to treat: *per* Lord Donaldson M.R. in *Re R (a minor) (wardship: medical treatment)* [1991] 4 All E.R. 177, 187.

[90] "The effect of the consent of the infant depends on the nature of the treatment and the age and understanding of the infant. For example, a doctor with the consent of an intelligent boy or girl of 15 could in my opinion safely remove tonsils or a troublesome appendix": *ibid.*, p. 432.

As with adults, the question arises as to how much the patient must **6.32** understand in order to have the relevant capacity. It will be recalled that an understanding "in broad terms" of the nature of the procedure is normally sufficient understanding to be considered fully competent to give or withhold consent.[91] In *Gillick*, however, their Lordships appeared to require a much greater level of understanding from a child under 16, at least with regard to contraceptive advice or treatment. Lord Scarman commented:

> "When applying these conclusions to contraceptive advice and treatment it has to borne in mind that there is much that has to be understood by a girl under the age of 16 if she is to have legal capacity to consent to such treatment. It is not enough that she should understand the nature of the advice which is being given: she must also have a sufficient maturity to understand what is involved. There are moral and family questions, especially her relationship with her parents; long-term problems associated with the emotional impact of pregnancy and its termination; and there are the risks to health of sexual intercourse at her age, risks which contraception may diminish but cannot eliminate. It follows that a doctor will have to satisfy himself that she is able to appraise these factors before he can safely proceed on the basis that she has at law capacity to consent to contraceptive treatment."[92]

Since, on this approach, the patient has to be able to appraise these **6.33** complex issues before "she has at law capacity to consent to contraceptive treatment" this clearly requires a greater degree of understanding than simply the nature of the procedure "in broad terms." It would seem to follow from this that when treating children a doctor has a greater duty to disclose information about the nature of the treatment and, indeed, the risks of the procedure, at the risk of being held liable in battery for non-disclosure, than is required when treating adults. Speaking specifically about contraceptive advice and treatment, Lord Fraser specified five factors that a doctor would have to consider:

> " . . . the doctor will, in my opinion, be justified in proceeding without the parents' consent or even knowledge provided he is satisfied on the following matters:
>
> (1) that the girl (although under 16 years of age) will understand his advice;
> (2) that he cannot persuade her to inform her parents or to allow him to inform the parents that she is seeking contraceptive advice;
> (3) that she is very likely to begin or to continue having sexual intercourse with or without contraceptive treatment;
> (4) that unless she receives contraceptive advice or treatment her physical or mental health or both are likely to suffer;

---

[91] *Chatterton* v. *Gerson* [1981] 1 All E.R. 257, 265; see § 6.23, *ante*.
[92] *Gillick* v. *West Norfolk & Wisbech Area Health Authority* [1985] 3 All E.R. 402, 424.

(5) that her best interests require him to give her contraceptive advice, treatment or both without the parental consent."[93]

Only the first point relates to the girl's *capacity* to consent, the remaining matters being more relevant to the doctor's assessment of whether providing the treatment is in her best interests in the circumstances. Lord Scarman clearly requires a higher level of understanding for the purpose of capacity to consent than Lord Fraser,[94] whereas Lord Templeman took the view that a child under the age of sixteen, although capable of consenting to some forms of treatment, could never have sufficient understanding to have the capacity to consent to contraceptive advice or treatment.[95]

6.34   The effect of *Gillick* is that there is no fixed age at which a child can be said to have the capacity to consent. It is a variable approach which depends upon the maturity of the child and the complexity or seriousness of the procedure required.[96] Even a very young child may having sufficient understanding to have capacity to consent to the dressing of a wound, but, conversely, an older child may possibly not be regarded as have sufficient understanding to decline, for example, life-saving treatment. "*Gillick* competence" is a developmental concept which does not fluctuate on a day-to-day or week-to-week basis. It involves an assessment of mental and emotional age, as contrasted with chronological age, but the test may not be appropriate where, as a result of mental illness, the child's understanding and capacity varies from day-to-day.[96a] Moreover, it may be that, even where a child has the capacity to consent to treatment, the parents have a concurrent power to consent notwithstanding that the child has refused treatment,[96b] and, whatever the position of a natural parent, it would appear that under the wardship jurisdiction the court has the power to authorise medical treatment of a "*Gillick* competent" ward who is refusing treatment.[96c]

---

[93] *Ibid.*, p. 413. On the doctor's duty of confidentiality owed to patients under the age of 16 see the General Medical Council, *Professional Conduct and Discipline*: *Fitness to Practise*, 1991, paras. 80–82, which are based to a large extent on the speeches of Lord Fraser and Lord Scarman in *Gillick*.

[94] See further Jones (1986) 2 P.N. 41.

[95] *Ibid.*, pp. 434–5. "I doubt whether a girl under the age of 16 is capable of a balanced judgment to embark on frequent, regular or casual sexual intercourse fortified by the illusion that medical science can protect her in mind and body and ignoring the danger of leaping from childhood to adulthood without the difficult formative transitional experiences of adolescence. There are many things which a girl under 16 needs to practise but sex is not one of them," *per* Lord Templeman at p. 432. It is apparent that Lord Scarman's views were also strongly influenced by the fact that the case was concerned with the controversial issue of contraception for girls under 16.

[96] See also the Children Act 1989, s.44(7), which provides that if a child is of sufficient understanding to make an informed decision he may refuse to submit to a medical or psychiatric examination ordered by the court when making an emergency protection order. Similarly, a supervision order may require a supervised child to submit to a medical or psychiatric examination or treatment, but again the child can refuse consent where he has sufficient understanding to make an informed decision: Children Act 1989, Sched. 3, paras. 4 and 5. See further *C.* v. *Wren* (1986) 35 D.L.R. (4th) 419, where the Alberta Court of Appeal concluded that a 16 year old girl had the capacity to consent to an abortion, and the fact that she was in disagreement with her parents on the issue did not mean that she lacked sufficient intelligence and understanding to make up her own mind.

[96a] *Re R (a minor) (wardship: medical treatment)* [1991] 4 All E.R. 177, 187, 192 *per* Lord Donaldson M.R. and Farquharson L.J. respectively.

[96b] *Ibid.*, p. 185 *per* Lord Donaldson M.R.; but query this, which seems inconsistent with *Gillick* and some provisions of the Children Act 1989; see above n. 96.

[96c] *Re R (a minor) (wardship: medical treatment)* [1991] 4 All E.R. 177, C.A.

Children lacking capacity

Where a child lacks the relevant capacity to consent to treatment, **6.35** parental consent will be required unless there is an emergency.[97] There must be some limits, however, to the parent's power to give or withhold consent. *Gillick* makes it clear that parental rights to control a child do not exist for the benefit of the parent. They exist for the benefit of the child, and they are justified only in so far as they enable the parent to perform his duties towards the child, and towards other children in the family.[98] Accordingly, the parental power to consent to treatment must be exercised in the best interests of the child.[99] Arguably, this means that a parent may only authorise procedures which are demonstrably for the benefit of the child. In *S.* v. *S.*,[1] however, the House of Lords considered that a parent would be entitled to require a young child to submit to a blood test for the purpose of determining who was the child's father in a paternity suit, even though the blood test could not be said to be in the child's medical interests and carried some, albeit extremely remote, risk of harm. Lord Reid considered that a parent could take into account the general public interest in the administration of justice and so "would not refuse a blood test unless he thought that would clearly be against the interests of the child."[2] An approach which permits parental consent to procedures which are "not against the child's interests" is clearly wider in its ambit than a test based solely on the child's "best interests," in that it reverses the assessment of the balance of interests, and curiously shifts from *best* interests to simply "interests." The change in emphasis may be significant, however, when considering the question of medical research on children or the transplantation of organs or bodily fluids.[3]

The parental power to consent on the child's behalf is a diminishing **6.36** one, as the child's understanding and intelligence develops to the stage at which he is capable of making up his own mind and thus acquires the capacity to consent himself.[4]

---

[97] *Gillick* v. *West Norfolk & Wisbech Area Health Authority* [1985] 3 All E.R. 402, 412, *per* Lord Fraser, and pp. 420, 423, *per* Lord Scarman. A local authority may exercise the power of consent to treatment when the child is in care and the authority has acquired parental responsibility: Children Act 1989, s.33(3). Parents do not lose parental responsibility (and therefore the power to consent to treatment) by virtue of the making of a care order (*ibid.* s.2), but where there is a conflict between the views of the parents and the local authority, the authority may restrict the extent to which the parents may exercise parental responsibility: Children Act 1989 s.33(3)(*b*). A person who does not have parental responsibility but has the care of the child may do what is reasonable for the purpose of safeguarding or promoting the child's welfare, which in appropriate circumstances would include giving a valid consent to medical treatment: *ibid.* s.3(5). The Act came into force on October 14, 1991: Children Act 1989 (Commencement and Transitional Provisions) Order (S.I. 1991/828).

[98] *Ibid.*, p. 410, *per* Lord Fraser.

[99] *Ibid.*, p. 432, *per* Lord Templeman. Note also that some procedures may be unlawful even with parental consent: see the Prohibition of Female Circumcision Act 1985; and also Lord Templeman's comments on sterilisation in *Re B.* (*a minor*) (*wardship: sterilisation*) [1987] 2 All E.R. 206, 214, § 6.37.

[1] [1970] 3 All E.R. 107.

[2] *Ibid.*, p. 112.

[3] See §§ 6.122 and 6.128–6.129. Note, however, that in *S.* v. *S.* [1970] 3 All E.R. 107 it could be said to be in the child's interests to have the question of paternity determined.

[4] *Gillick* v. *West Norfolk & Wisbech Area Health Authority* [1985] 3 All E.R. 402, 412, 423, *per* Lord Fraser and Lord Scarman respectively.

6.37   In *Re B. (a minor) (wardship: sterilisation)*[5] Lord Templeman suggested that parental consent would not be sufficient to authorise a doctor to perform a sterilisation operation on a girl under 18 years of age, and that a doctor who relied on parental consent might still be liable in criminal, civil or professional proceedings: a court exercising the wardship jurisdiction was the only authority empowered to author-ise such a drastic step after a full and informed investigation.[6] Although this view was not concurred in by the other members of the House, it is now the practice to seek the leave of the High Court in such cases.[7] The approval of the court is not necessary, however, where an operation, such as hysterectomy, is to be performed for therapeutic reasons even though sterilisation would be an incidental result.[7a] In these circumstances the parents can give a valid consent.

6.38   Under the wardship jurisdiction the High Court has the power to authorise or withhold permission for medical treatment for a ward of court. The welfare of the child is said to be the paramount considera-tion. This welfare principle is also expressed as "the best interests of the child."[8] In *Re J. (a minor) (wardship: medical treatment)*[9] Bal-combe L.J. said that in determining the child's best interests, the court should adopt the standpoint of the reasonable and responsible parent who has his or her child's best interests at heart. Both Lord Donaldson M.R. and Taylor L.J. appeared to endorse a form of "substituted judgment" test which requires the decision about whether to authorise medical treatment to be taken "from the assumed point of view of the patient."[10] It is clear that the court may authorise medical treatment of a ward notwithstanding an express refusal of consent by the parents, and may refuse to authorise treatment to which parents have given

---

[5] [1987] 2 All E.R. 206, 214.

[6] See also, *per* Neill L.J. in *Re F. (Mental Patient: Sterilisation)* [1989] 2 W.L.R. 1025, 1053, § 6.129 extending this to organ donation by children; and the dissenting speech of Lord Griffiths in *F. v. West Berkshire Health Authority* [1989] 2 All E.R. 545, 561–562 taking the view that sterilisation of mentally handicapped adults would only be lawful with the approval of the court.

[7] See *Practice Note (Official Solicitor: Sterilisation)* [1989] 2 F.L.R. 447, amended (1990) 140 New L.J. 1273; see § 6.55, n. 51; see *J. v. C.* [1990] 3 All E.R. 735. The House of Lords has held that the court may authorise the sterilisation of a mentally handicapped minor, in her "best interests": *Re B. (a minor) (wardship: sterilisation)* [1987] 2 All E.R. 206; *Re M. (a minor) (wardship: sterilisation)* [1988] 2 F.L.R. 497; *cf.* the approach of the Supreme Court of Canada in *Re Eve* (1986) 31 D.L.R. (4th) 1 taking the view that non-therapeutic sterilisation of a minor could never be authorised. See further Lee and Morgan (1988) 15 J. of Law and Soc. 229; Brazier (1990) 6 P.N. 25.

[7a] *Re E. (a minor), The Times,* February 22, 1991, *per* Sir Stephen Brown P.

[8] On the interpretation of the child's "best interests" see: *Re B. (a minor)(wardship: medical treatment)* [1981] 1 W.L.R. 1421; *Re C. (a minor) (wardship: medical treatment)* [1989] 2 All E.R. 782—the appropriate treatment for terminally ill infant; Roberts (1990) 106 L.Q.R. 218. It is likely that eventually "specific issue orders" under s.8 of the Children Act 1989 will be used to determine such issues rather than the wardship jurisdiction, though this procedure will be available only where the child is not in the care of the local authority: Children Act 1989, s.9. If, however, Lord Templeman's view in *Re B. (a minor) (wardship: sterilisation)* [1987] 2 All E.R. 206, 214 that parents could not give a valid consent to sterilisation of their child is correct, it would not fall within the concept of "parental responsibility" and so could not be the subject of a specific issue order under s.8. In that case wardship would continue to be the appropriate procedure to authorise sterilisations of minors who are not in care.

[9] [1990] 3 All E.R. 930; Wells, Aldridge and Morgan (1990) 140 New L.J. 1544.

[10] *Ibid.*, p. 938, *per* Lord Donaldson M.R. Taylor L.J. said, at p. 945, that: "The test must be whether the child in question, if capable of exercising sound judgment, would consider the life tolerable."

consent.[11] Moreover, under the wardship jurisdiction the court may authorise medical treatment even where the child is competent to refuse treatment and has done so.[11a]

A local authority can no longer invoke the wardship jurisdiction of **6.39** the High Court where a child is the subject of a care order,[12] nor can an authority apply for a specific issue order under section 8 of the Children Act 1989 with respect to a child who is in care.[13] This will not normally cause any difficulties in relation to consent to treatment because the authority will have acquired parental responsibility and so will be able to give a valid consent. Where, however, a child is in care but the local authority needs a court order to sanction a controversial medical procedure, such as sterilisation, the authority cannot rely on the wardship jurisdiction. In this situation the local authority may apply to the High Court (with the leave of the court) to exercise its inherent jurisdiction over the welfare of children for the purpose of authorising medical treatment provided that the result could not be achieved through an alternative procedure that the authority is entitled to use, and there is reasonable cause to believe that if the inherent jurisdiction is not exercised the child is likely to suffer significant harm.[14]

Emergency

In an emergency a doctor will be justified in providing medical **6.40** treatment to a child who lacks the capacity to consent, without parental consent or the authorisation of the court. The justification is analogous to that which applies to patients who are temporarily incapacitated, for example patients who are unconscious following an accident,[15] and is based on the principle of necessity. It may be, however, that in the case of children the concept of emergency is wider than that which would be applied to temporarily incapacitated adults. Thus in *Gillick* v. *West Norfolk and Wisbech Area Health Authority* Lord Scarman commented that:

> "Emergency, parental neglect, abandonment of the child or inability to find the parent are examples of exceptional situations justifying the doctor proceeding to treat the child without par-

---

[11] *Re P. (a minor)* (1982) 80 L.G.R. 301, an abortion in the child's best interests, contrary to the wishes of the parents; *Re B (a minor)*, *The Independent*, May 22, 1991, to the same effect; *Re B. (a minor) (wardship: medical treatment)* [1981] 1 W.L.R. 1421, on life-saving medical treatment of newborn baby with Down's Syndrome in the child's best interests, notwithstanding parents' refusal of consent; *Re D. (a minor) (wardship: sterilisation)* [1976] 1 All E.R. 326 sterilisation of an 11 year old girl with Soto's syndrome was not in child's best interests, despite the parent's consent.
[11a] *Re R (a minor) (wardship: medical treatment)* [1991] 4 All E.R. 177, C.A.
[12] Children Act 1989, s.100(2)(c).
[13] *Ibid.*, s.9(1), (5).
[14] *Ibid.*, s.100(4). It is thought that the court's inherent jurisdiction with respect to children is wider than the wardship jurisdiction, and that although the use of wardship by local authorities has been curtailed by the Children Act 1989 this residual jurisdiction is still available: see *S.* v. *McC.* [1972] A.C. 24, 47–50, *per* Lord MacDermott; *Re L.* [1968] 1 All E.R. 20, 24–25, *per* Lord Denning M.R. Indeed, this is the assumption made by subsection 100(4).
[15] See § 6.59.

ental knowledge and consent; but there will arise, no doubt, other exceptional situations in which it will be reasonable for the doctor to proceed without the parent's consent."[16]

If, for example, the parents were available but were refusing consent to life-saving treatment, perhaps on religious grounds, a doctor would be justified in performing the treatment, even in the face of an express parental prohibition. In *Gillick* Lord Templeman seemed to have such a situation in mind when he said:

"I accept that if there is no time to obtain a decision from the court, a doctor may safely carry out treatment in an emergency if the doctor believes the treatment to be vital to the survival or health of an infant and notwithstanding the opposition of a parent or the impossibility of alerting the parent before the treatment is carried out. In such a case the doctor must have the courage of his convictions that the treatment is necessary and urgent in the interests of the patient and the court will, if necessary, approve after the event treatment which the court would have authorised in advance, even if the treatment proves to be unsuccessful."[17]

6.41 Under the Children Act 1989 an emergency protection order may provide for medical or psychiatric examination (though not treatment) of the child.[18] While it is in force, however, an emergency protection order gives the applicant (normally the local authority) parental responsibility for the child,[19] which effectively confers the power to consent to medical treatment.

5. Patients with mental disorder

6.42 Most patients who suffer from mental disorder are subject to the same rules with respect to consent to medical treatment as any other adult. Part IV of the Mental Health Act 1983, ss.56–64, which deals with consent to treatment, applies only to patients liable to be detained under the Act,[20] and accordingly it does not apply to patients voluntarily admitted to hospital,[21] to mentally disordered patients who live in the community,[22] to patients subject to guardianship,[23] nor to certain

---

[16] [1985] 3 All E.R. 402, 424.

[17] *Ibid.*, p. 432. Parents are not free to make martyrs of their children before they have reached the age of full and legal discretion when they can make that choice for themselves: *Prince* v. *Massachusetts* (1944) 321 U.S. 158, 166 (Supreme Court). For an argument that the decision in *F.* v. *West Berkshire Health Authority* [1989] 2 All E.R. 545, § 6.59, provides a justification for routine medical treatment of children (*i.e.* "non-necessary" but medically desirable in the child's best interests) without parental consent see Lavery [1990] J.S.W.L. 375. See also Busuttil and McCall Smith [1990] J.S.W.L. 385 for discussion of the problem of medical examination of children who are suspected victims of sexual abuse without parental consent.

[18] Children Act 1989, s.44.

[19] *Ibid.*, s.44(4)(c).

[20] Mental Health Act 1983, s.56(1).

[21] With the exception of s.57 (requiring the patient's consent *and* a second opinion to surgical procedures for destroying brain tissue or the functioning of brain tissue) which is an additional safeguard for patients: Mental Health Act 1983, s.56(2).

[22] *R.* v. *Hallstrom, ex parte W.* (No. 2) [1986] 2 All E.R. 306.

[23] Mental Health Act 1983, s.8(5) providing that a patient received into guardianship ceases to be "liable to be detained."

patients who are liable to be detained but who are specifically excluded from Part IV.[24] The Act is concerned only with treatment of the patient's mental disorder, and it cannot be used to authorise treatment for other medical conditions, even in circumstances where the patient lacks the capacity to consent to such treatment.[25] Where the provisions of the Act do not apply, the power to give treatment depends upon the rules of the common law, which requires either a valid consent given by the patient or justification under the principle of necessity.[26]

The Mental Health Act 1983 does not assume that a patient with a mental disorder automatically lacks the capacity to consent to treatment under the Act, since both section 57 and section 58 provide for consent by the patient to some forms of treatment. But, by virtue of section 63, the consent of a patient is not required for any medical treatment given to him for the mental disorder from which he is suffering, not being treatment falling within section 57 or 58, if the treatment is given by or under the direction of the responsible medical officer.[27] This permits treatment without consent, or indeed notwithstanding the specific refusal of consent by a patient. Some forms of treatment are considered to be so controversial, however, that special safeguards are built into the Act. Under section 58 the patient's refusal of consent to electro-convulsive therapy cannot be disregarded unless an independent doctor has certified in writing that the treatment should be given; and under section 57 even consent by the patient is not itself sufficient where the treatment consists of destroying brain tissue. **6.43**

Section 57 (treatment requiring consent *and* a second opinion) provides that a patient cannot be given any form of medical treatment for mental disorder consisting of a surgical operation for destroying brain tissue or for destroying the functioning of brain tissue (and such other forms of treatment as may be specified in regulations by the Secretary of State[28]) unless he has consented to it, and it has been certified in writing by a registered medical practitioner (not being the responsible medical officer) and two other persons (not being registered medical practitioners) that the patient is capable of understanding the nature, purpose and likely effects of the treatment in question **6.44**

---

[24] Mental Health Act 1983, s.56(1); in effect, patients liable to be detained for short periods only.

[25] *F.* v. *West Berkshire Health Authority* [1989] 2 All E.R. 545; *T.* v. *T.* [1988] 1 All E.R. 613.

[26] "It goes without saying that, unless clear statutory authority to the contrary exists, no one is to be detained in hospital or to undergo medical treatment or even to submit himself to a medical examination without his consent. This is as true of a mentally disordered person as of anyone else," *per* McCullough J. in *R.* v. *Hallstrom, ex parte W.* (*No. 2*) [1986] 2 All E.R. 306, 314.

[27] For the definition of "responsible medical officer" see s.34(1).

[28] See the Mental Health (Hospital, Guardianship and Consent to Treatment) Regulations 1983 (S.I. 1983/893), reg. 16(1) specifying the surgical implantation of hormones for the purpose of reducing the male sex drive. These provisions do not apply to a drug reducing sexual drive which is neither a hormone nor surgically implanted: *R.* v. *Mental Health Commission, ex parte W.*, *The Times*, May 27, 1988, D.C. Other forms of treatment to which s.57 should apply may be specified in a Code of Practice: see Mental Health Act 1983, s.118(2). No other forms of treatment have been specified in the Code: see Fennell (1990) 53 M.L.R. 499, 507.

and has consented to it. It must also be certified by the registered medical practitioner that, having regard to the likelihood of the treatment alleviating or preventing a deterioration of the patient's condition, the treatment should be given. This provision means that competent patients can never be given such treatment without their consent, and the requirement for a second opinion is an additional safeguard. On the face of it section 57 would appear to rule out these forms of surgery for patients who are incapable of consenting.[29]

6.45   Section 58 (treatment requiring consent *or* a second opinion) applies to such forms of treatment for mental disorder as may be specified in regulations made by the Secretary of State,[30] and to the administration of medicine to a patient by any means (not being treatment consisting of a surgical operation for destroying brain tissue or for destroying the functioning of brain tissue) at any time during a period for which he is liable to be detained, if three months or more have elapsed since the first occasion in that period when medicine was administered to him by any means for his mental disorder. Under section 58 a patient cannot be given treatment to which the section applies unless he has consented to it, and a registered medical practitioner has certified in writing that the patient is capable of understanding its nature, purpose and likely effects and has consented to it; or an independent registered medical practitioner has certified in writing that the patient is not capable of understanding the nature, purpose and likely effects of the treatment or has not consented to it, but that, having regard to the likelihood of the treatment alleviating or preventing a deterioration of the patient's condition, the treatment should be given.

6.46   A patient who has consented to any treatment for the purposes of sections 57 and 58 can withdraw his consent at any time before the completion of the treatment.[31] This power to withdraw consent is subject to section 62(2), which provides for the continuation of treatment where, in the view of the responsible medical officer, discontinuance of the treatment would cause serious suffering to the patient.

6.47   In the case of "urgent treatment" sections 57 and 58 do not apply to any treatment:

(a) which is immediately necessary to save the patient's life; or

(b) which (not being irreversible) is immediately necessary to prevent a serious deterioration of his condition; or

(c) which (not being irreversible or hazardous) is immediately necessary to alleviate serious suffering by the patient; or

(d) which (not being irreversible or hazardous) is immediately necessary and represents the minimum interference necessary to pre-

---

[29] Given the wording of the section it seems doubtful that treatment would be justified under the common law principle of necessity, although the major premise of the decision of the House of Lords in *F.* v. *West Berkshire Health Authority* [1989] 2 All E.R. 545 was that incompetent patients should not be "deprived" of treatment that would otherwise be available to a competent adult.

[30] See the Mental Health (Hospital, Guardianship and Consent to Treatment) Regulations 1983 (S.I. 1983/893), reg. 16(2)(*a*) specifying electro-convulsive therapy.

[31] Mental Health Act 1983, s.60.

vent the patient from behaving violently or being a danger to himself or to others.[32]

Where a patient has been received into guardianship, the guardian can **6.48** require the patient to attend some specified place for the purpose of medical treatment,[33] but the guardian cannot require the patient to receive treatment, nor can he consent to the giving of treatment to which the patient does not himself consent.[34]

There is no power under the Act to give treatment to a mentally **6.49** disordered person who withholds his consent unless he is detained in hospital or has first been detained and been given leave of absence under section 17. Thus, in *R. v. Hallstrom, ex parte W.* (No. 2)[35] McCullough J. said that there is no provision in the Act to the effect that "a patient whose mental disorder is of a nature or degree which makes it appropriate that he should receive treatment as a hospital out-patient, but whose condition does not warrant his detention for treatment in hospital, may be treated as an out-patient, without his consent, if two registered medical practitioners are of the view etc." On the other hand, where a patient to whom the provisions of the Act do not apply lacks the capacity to consent to treatment (and hence the capacity to refuse consent to treatment) it is possible that a doctor will be justified in providing treatment for the mental disorder which is in the patient's "best interests," following the decision of the House of Lords in *F. v. West Berkshire Health Authority*.[36] This case was not concerned with the treatment of mental disorder, but the broad interpretation placed upon the common law principle of necessity by their Lordships may extend to this situation. This creates a potential conflict between the common law and the Mental Health Act 1983, since the Act is clearly concerned with restricting the circumstances in which treatment may be given compulsorily in order to protect the patient's rights, whereas in *F. v. West Berkshire Health Authority* the House of Lords was more concerned with facilitating treatment for patients with mental handicap, leaving the decision about the nature and purpose of treatment largely to the discretion of the medical profession.

The Mental Health Act 1983 deals with treatment for the patient's **6.50** mental disorder. It does not authorise treatment for anything other than mental disorder, even where the patient's capacity to give a valid consent is affected by that disorder. It had been generally assumed (or,

---

[32] Mental Health Act 1983, s.62. Treatment is irreversible if it has unfavourable irreversible physical or psychological consequences and hazardous if it entails significant physical hazard: s.62(3). S.62 merely removes the formal requirements for compliance with ss.57 and 58; it does not itself authorise treatment, which must be justified either under s.63, or at common law by the patient's consent or under the principle of necessity. See also National Assistance Act 1948, s.47, although it may be that this provision does not authorise medical treatment: Hoggett, *Mental Health Law* 3rd ed., 1990, pp. 136–143.
[33] Mental Health Act 1983, s.8(1)(*b*).
[34] *R. v. Hallstrom, ex parte W.* (No. 2) [1986] 2 All E.R. 306, 313; *T. v. T.* [1988] 1 All E.R. 613, 617. Under the Mental Health Act 1959, s.34(1) a guardian exercised the powers of a father of a child under 14 years of age, which meant that he could consent to treatment on the patient's behalf. The powers of the guardian were amended by the Mental Health (Amendment) Act 1982, ss.8 and 65(1), Sched. 3, para. 66. See generally Fisher [1988] J.S.W.L. 316. .
[35] [1986] 2 All E.R. 306, 313.
[36] [1989] 2 All E.R. 545; § 6.51.

at least, no one had sought to question it) that doctors were acting lawfully in giving medical treatment to adults who lacked the capacity to consent. The basis for that assumption was not tested in the courts in this country until cases involving the highly controversial issues of abortion and sterilisation of mentally handicapped women arose. In the case of girls under the age of 18 it was clear that the court, in the exercise of the wardship jurisdiction, may authorise an abortion or sterilisation of a minor where it is in her best interests.[37] The wardship jurisdiction is not available, however, once the child reaches the age of majority. In *T. v. T.*[38] the question was whether it would be lawful to perform an abortion and sterilisation on a 19 year old woman with a serious mental handicap. Wood J. considered and rejected a number of possible justifications, concluding that the operation would be lawful if it could be justified under the principle of necessity. Where there was no-one in a position to give consent for the patient, and where the patient was suffering from such mental abnormality as never to be able to give such consent, a doctor would be justified in taking such steps as good medical practice "demands."[39] By this term Wood J. envisaged "a situation where based on good medical practice there are really no two views of what course is for the best."[40] This approach leaves the substantive decision as to what is justified to the medical profession, but it is more restricted in its scope than the *Bolam* test since it does not allow for treatment when there are competing but "responsible" medical opinions about what should be done in the patient's best interests.

6.51   In *F. v. West Berkshire Health Authority*[41] the patient was a woman of 36 years who suffered from a serious mental disability. She was a voluntary in-patient at a mental hospital, and had formed a sexual relationship with a male patient. The psychiatric evidence was that F would not understand the meaning of pregnancy, labour or delivery, and would be unable to care for a baby if she had one. From a psychiatric point of view it would have been "disastrous for her to conceive a child." Other contraceptive methods were considered to be unreliable and/or to involve a risk of harm to her physical health. In these circumstances it was thought appropriate that F be sterilised. The Court of Appeal considered that the *Bolam* test (a practice accepted as proper by a responsible body of professional opinion) was an insufficiently stringent standard by which to measure necessity, though the test suggested by Wood J. in *T. v. T.* was rejected as too strict because there "will always or usually be a minority view and this approach, if strictly applied, would often rule out all treatment. On the other hand,

---

[37] *Re B. (a minor) (wardship: sterilisation)* [1987] 2 All E.R. 206; *Re P.* (1982) 80 L.G.R. 301; *Re D. (a minor) (wardship: sterilisation)* [1976] 1 All E.R. 326, where the decision went the other way on the facts; *cf.* the approach of the Supreme Court of Canada in *Re Eve* (1986) 31 D.L.R. (4th) 1, taking the view that the non-therapeutic sterilisation of a mentally handicapped minor could never be justified. The House of Lords were highly critical of this decision in *Re B. (a minor)* [1987] 2 All E.R. 206.

[38] [1988] 1 All E.R. 613; Fortin (1988) 51 M.L.R. 634. See also *Re X., The Times,* June 4, 1987, Q.B.D.

[39] *Ibid.,* p. 625. His Lordship distinguished patients with temporary incapacity, such as a person under an anaesthetic.

[40] *Ibid.,* p. 621.

[41] [1989] 2 All E.R. 545, H.L.; *Re F. (Mental Patient: Sterilisation)* [1989] 2 W.L.R. 1025, C.A.; Shaw (1990) 53 M.L.R. 91; Jones (1989) 5 P.N. 178.

the existence of a significant minority view would constitute a serious contra-indication."[42] The court was clearly concerned that patients who lack the capacity to consent to medical treatment are not simply the equivalent of competent adults who are unable to give an assent. They are also incapable of refusing treatment, and therefore "other things being equal there must be greater caution in deciding whether to treat and, if so, how to treat."[43]

The House of Lords agreed that the principle of necessity provided **6.52** the solution to the problem of patients who lack the capacity to consent, but considered that legal protection for patients was secondary to facilitating treatment. It was axiomatic, said Lord Bridge, that treatment which is necessary to preserve the life, health or well-being of the patient may lawfully be given without consent,[44] Lord Goff had no doubt that the common law recognised a principle of necessity which might justify action which would otherwise be unlawful, and Lord Brandon, without referring specifically to a general principle of necessity, said that the common law would be seriously defective if it failed to provide a solution to the problem created by an inability to consent to treatment.

Lord Brandon concluded that an operation or other treatment **6.53** performed on adult patients who are incapable, for one reason or another, of consenting, would be lawful provided that it is in the best interests of the patient. It will be in their best interests "if, but only if, it is carried out in order either to save their lives or to ensure improvement or prevent deterioration in their physical or mental health."[45] This statement of the patient's best interests is extremely wide. Procedures designed to "ensure improvement or prevent deterioration in . . . physical or mental health" would encompass virtually anything that a doctor might ever do to a patient. It would, for example, provide a blanket common law justification for the treatment of mental illness or disorder for which statutory provision is considered necessary in the Mental Health Act 1983, which provides specific safeguards for the patient. His Lordship was clearly concerned not to place constraints on the defence which might otherwise deprive patients of medical care which they need and to which they are entitled.[46] Lord Brandon used the same argument to justify adopting the *Bolam*[47] test as the appropriate standard for measuring the patient's best interests:

---

[42] [1989] 2 W.L.R. 1025, 1041–1042, *per* Lord Donaldson M.R.

[43] *Ibid.*, *per* Lord Donaldson M.R. See also, *per* Neill L.J. at p. 1053: "I would define necessary in this context as that which the general body of medical opinion in the particular speciality would consider to be in the best interests of the patient in order to maintain the health and to secure the well-being of the patient. One cannot expect unanimity but it should be possible to say of an operation which is necessary in the relevant sense that it would be unreasonable in the opinion of most experts in the field not to make the operation available to the patient."

[44] *F.* v. *West Berkshire Health Authority* [1989] 2 All E.R. 545, 548.

[45] *Ibid.*, p. 551.

[46] *Ibid.* See also at p. 548, *per* Lord Bridge, who was worried that a "rigid criterion of necessity" would deprive many patients of treatment which it would be entirely beneficial for them to receive. Lord Goff, at p. 566, said that in the case of a mentally disordered person the permanent nature of the incapacity calls for a wider range of treatment than would be appropriate in the case of temporary incapacity to be covered by the defence, including routine medical or dental treatment, and even simple care such as dressing and undressing and putting to bed.

[47] *Bolam* v. *Friern Hospital Management Committee* [1957] 2 All E.R. 118.

"If doctors were to be required, in deciding whether an operation or other treatment was in the best interests of adults incompetent to give consent, to apply some test more stringent than the *Bolam* test, the result would be that such adults would, in some circumstances at least, be deprived of the benefit of medical treatment which adults competent to give consent would enjoy. In my opinion it would be wrong for the law, in its concern to protect such adults, to produce such a result."[48]

6.54   Applying the *Bolam* test to the defence of necessity means that there may well be more than one view, or indeed several views, as to what is in the best interests of the patient and, accordingly, as to what course of conduct in relation to incompetent patients is justified in law, and none of these competing "responsible bodies of medical opinion" can be challenged in the courts. This assumes that decisions about medical treatment, even controversial treatment such as sterilisation, are matters solely within the discretion of the medical profession.

6.55   *F.* v. *West Berkshire Health Authority* raised a procedural problem. The House of Lords concluded that there was no equivalent of the wardship jurisdiction by which the court could exercise a power to consent on behalf of an incompetent adult. The ancient *parens patriae* jurisdiction of the Crown to protect the persons and property of those unable to do so for themselves was no longer available.[49] The court did not have jurisdiction to consent to medical treatment under Part VII of the Mental Health Act 1983, nor was there any residual inherent jurisdiction (in the absence of the *parens patriae* jurisdiction) to approve or disapprove of a proposed operation. Although it was not essential as a matter of law to obtain the approval of the court to a sterilisation operation on an incompetent adult,[50] nonetheless it would be good medical practice to obtain the "approval" of the court by means of an application for a declaration that the operation would be in the patient's best interests, and this is now the appropriate procedure.[51]

6. Emergency (temporary incapacity)

6.56   It is generally agreed that in an emergency, where an otherwise competent patient is unable to consent for some reason, doctors may

---

[48] *F.* v. *West Berkshire Health Authority* [1989] 2 All E.R. 545, 560; see also, *per* Lord Bridge at p. 549.

[49] [1989] 2 All E.R. 545, 552–3. For the history of this jurisdiction see Hoggett, "The Royal Prerogative in Relation to the Mentally Disordered: Resurrection, Resuscitation or Rejection" in Freeman (ed.), *Medicine, Ethics and the Law,* 1988, p. 85.

[50] *cf.* the dissent of Lord Griffiths on this point: *ibid.* at pp. 561–2.

[51] See the speech of Lord Brandon at [1989] 2 All E.R. 545, 558 and *Practice Note* (*Official Solicitor: Sterilisation*) [1989] 2 F.L.R. 447, amended (1990) 140 New L.J. Law Rep. 1273; *J.* v. *C.* [1990] 3 All E.R. 735. Lord Goff suggested, at p. 571, that if it became the invariable practice of the medical profession to seek a declaration before sterilising an incompetent adult there would be little practical difference between obtaining the court's approval under the *parens patriae* jurisdiction and obtaining a declaration. It is not necessary to obtain the approval of the High Court prior to performing an abortion on a mentally handicapped adult provided that the requirements of the Abortion Act 1967 are satisfied and it is in the patient's best interests: *Re S.G.* (*mental patient: abortion*) [1991] Fam. Law 309.

lawfully proceed to treat the patient without consent. Doctors have been acting on this supposition for years, every time an unconscious patient is wheeled into the casualty department of a hospital, for example. Moreover, it would be absurd if the law did not provide for this situation. As Lord Bridge observed in *F.* v. *West Berkshire Health Authority*,[52] doctors and other health care professionals would otherwise face an intolerable dilemma: if they administer the treatment which they believe to be in the best interests of the patient they might face an action for trespass to the person, but if they withhold that treatment they could be in breach of a duty of care in negligence.

One possible justification that has been canvassed in relation to **6.57** emergency procedures is implied consent.[53] The argument is that the unconscious patient, although unable to consent, would very probably consent to emergency treatment if he were able to do so and so his consent can be implied. The patient's "consent" is clearly fictional in these circumstances and this has been regarded as an unsatisfactory approach, particularly as it invites confusion with situations in which the patient is capable of exercising a capacity to consent, refrains from giving an express consent, and yet can be taken to have impliedly consented, for example, by his conduct.

Another approach was suggested in *Wilson* v. *Pringle*[54] where it was **6.58** said that a touching must be proved to be a "hostile touching" in order to constitute a battery. The Court of Appeal took the view that a general exception to the tort of battery, which embraces all physical contact which is generally acceptable in the ordinary conduct of daily life, provided:

> "a solution to the old problem of what legal rule allows a casualty surgeon to perform an urgent operation on an unconscious patient who is brought into hospital . . . Hitherto it has been customary to say in such cases that consent is to be implied . . . It is better simply to say that the surgeon's action is acceptable in the ordinary conduct of everyday life."[55]

This dictum was doubted by Wood J. in *T.* v. *T.*,[56] who commented that operative treatments and some more serious medical treatments did not seem to fall within the phrase "the ordinary conduct of daily life." In *F.* v. *West Berkshire Health Authority*[57] Lord Goff, whose judgment in *Collins* v. *Wilcock*[58] had been relied upon by the Court of Appeal in *Wilson* v. *Pringle*, confirmed that medical treatment, even treatment for minor ailments, does not fall into the category of "physical contact which is generally acceptable in the ordinary conduct of everyday life." Treatment given without consent has to be justified on some other principle—lack of "hostility" is not sufficient.

---

[52] *Ibid.*, p. 548.
[53] See, *e.g.*, Skegg (1974) 90 L.Q.R. 512; Brazier, *Medicine Patients and the Law*, 1987, p. 67; Mason and McCall Smith, *Law and Medical Ethics*, 3rd ed., 1991, p. 229; *Schweizer* v. *Central Hospital* (1974) 53 D.L.R. (3d) 494, 507.
[54] [1986] 2 All E.R. 440.
[55] *Ibid.*, p. 447.
[56] [1988] 1 All E.R. 613.
[57] [1989] 2 All E.R. 545, 564; see also *re F. (mental patient: sterilisation)* [1989] 2 W.L.R. 1025, 1051, *per* Neill L.J., though *cf.* the same judge at p. 1052; and see further § 6.05 *ante*.
[58] [1984] 3 All E.R. 374.

6.59   The third possible basis for justifying emergency treatment without consent is the principle of necessity.[59] The discussion of the defence of necessity in *F.* v. *West Berkshire Health Authority*[60] proceeded on the assumption that it applied in any situation where an adult was incapable of giving a valid consent to medical treatment, whether the capacity was permanent or temporary. Thus, treatment of a temporarily incapacitated patient in an emergency will be lawful if it is in the best interests of the patient, that is if, but only if, it is carried out in order either to save his life or to ensure improvement or prevent deterioration in his physical or mental health. Again, this will be measured by reference to the *Bolam* test. There are limits, however, to what may be done to the temporarily incapacitated patient. Lord Goff said that officious intervention cannot be justified; nor can intervention be justified when it is contrary to the known wishes of the assisted person, to the extent that he is capable of rationally forming such a wish.[61] Moreover, Lord Goff explicitly recognised that there was a difference between cases of permanent incapacity and temporary incapacity:

> "Where, for example, a surgeon performs an operation without his consent on a patient temporarily rendered unconscious in an accident, he should do no more than is reasonably required, in the best interests of the patient, before he recovers consciousness. I can see no practical difficulty arising from this requirement, which derives from the fact that the patient is expected before long to regain consciousness and can then be consulted about longer term measures."[62]

In the Court of Appeal Neill L.J. also drew a clear distinction between permanent and temporary incapacity. In an emergency situation treatment should be confined to "such treatment as is necessary to meet the emergency and such as needs to be carried out at once and before the patient is likely to be in a position to make a decision for himself."[63]

6.60   The Canadian courts distinguish between procedures which it would have been unreasonable to postpone in the circumstances, as opposed to being merely convenient to perform immediately. In *Marshall* v. *Curry*,[64] in the course of a hernia operation being performed under general anaesthetic, the surgeon discovered that his patient had a diseased testicle. It was held that he was justified in removing the testicle without first bringing the patient round to obtain his consent, because the organ could have become gangrenous and constituted a threat to the patient's life. The circumstances could not have been foreseen before the operation, and the doctor had acted in the best interests of his patient. The removal of the testicle was necessary

---

[59] See Skegg (1974) 90 L.Q.R. 512, 514, commenting that the principle is too vague.
[60] [1989] 2 All E.R. 545; see § 6.51.
[61] Leaving open the possibility of arguing that a patient who "unreasonably" refuses consent to treatment can be categorised as "irrational," thereby lacking the capacity either to consent or withhold consent. Are all beliefs, values, fears, prejudices upon which we base decisions rational, and if not does that mean that we lack the capacity to make those decisions? See Brazier (1987) 7 L.S. 169, 175.
[62] [1989] 2 All E.R. 545, 566.
[63] *Re F. (mental patient: sterilisation)* [1989] 2 W.L.R. 1025, 1050.
[64] [1933] 3 D.L.R. 260.

because it would have been unreasonable to postpone the procedure. On the other hand, in *Murray* v. *McMurchy*,[65] during the course of a Caesarean section, the doctor discovered fibroid tumours in the patient's uterus. He took the view that the tumours would be a danger if the patient were to become pregnant again, and so without reviving the patient from the general anaesthetic he performed a sterilisation operation. The doctor was held liable in battery, because it would not have been unreasonable to postpone the operation. There was no immediate threat to the patient's health; it was merely convenient to perform the operation without consent as she was already under general anaesthetic.[66]

In *F.* v. *West Berkshire Health Authority* Lord Goff apparently took **6.61** the view that the Canadian cases were restricted to the situation where a surgeon, in the course of an operation, discovers some other condition which he believes requires immediate attention although he has not obtained the patient's consent for that. It is not clear why the cases should be limited in this way, since the distinction could apply just as well to the patient who is incapacitated prior to the operation as the patient who is incapacitated during the operation itself. Thus, it is arguable that the measure of what is "reasonably required" under Lord Goff's approach to the temporarily incapacitated patient could be whether it would have been unreasonable to postpone the operation or procedure, as opposed to merely convenient to perform it without consent.[67]

The medical profession appears to have assumed for many years that **6.62** consent by a spouse or relative will suffice where an adult patient is incapable of consenting. While it may be "good medical practice" to consult relatives about a proposed treatment,[68] this probably has no effect in law.[69] If the procedure cannot be justified under the principle of necessity, the consent of a relative offers no protection, other than the practical observation that a patient may be less likely to litigate if the treatment had the approval of a relative.

7. Refusals of consent

The refusal of a competent patient to consent to medical treatment **6.63** is normally considered to be conclusive. The doctor must respect the

---

[65] [1949] 2 D.L.R. 442.

[66] See also *Parmley* v. *Parmley and Yule* [1945] 4 D.L.R. 81, 89 (S.C.C.). For an English case with similar facts to *Murray* v. *McMurchy* see *Devi* v. *West Midlands Regional Health Authority* (1981) (unreported), C.A. § 6.10.

[67] Whether this would prove, in practice, to be a more stringent test than the *Bolam* test depends upon expert evidence as to what was convenient and what was unreasonable. There is, in theory, a difference between whether it was unreasonable to postpone an operation and whether it was reasonable to proceed. Sometimes it may be reasonable to proceed (and therefore not negligent to do so) but also not unreasonable to postpone the operation until the patient could consent. In other words, the test is stricter than in negligence: see Skegg (1974) 90 L.Q.R. 512, 518. Note that since necessity is a defence the burden of proving that the treatment was necessary must lie with the defendant: *Clerk & Lindsell on Torts*, 16th ed., 1989, para. 17–09, n. 60.

[68] See Lord Goff in *F.* v. *West Berkshire Health Authority* [1989] 2 All E.R. 545, 567.

[69] See, *e.g.*, Skegg, *Law, Ethics and Medicine*, O.U.P., 1988, p. 73; see also *Paton* v. *British Pregnancy Advisory Service Trustees* [1978] 2 All E.R. 987, where the putative father was not entitled to intervene to prevent the mother undergoing an abortion; *cf. Wilson* v. *Pringle* [1986] 2 All E.R. 440, 447 where Croom-Johnson L.J. seemed to assume that the "next of kin" could consent for an unconscious patient.

patient's wishes, no matter how misguided he believes the patient to be, and no matter that he has only the patient's best interests in mind. The doctor who ignores the patient's refusal of consent risks a claim for battery.[70] Most patients want their medical condition to improve, if at all possible, and where differences between patient and doctor arise this is likely to be the product of differing assessments of the risks and benefits of the proposed treatment. Some situations arise, however, where the objectives of doctor and patient are at odds.

6.64   In *Leigh* v. *Gladstone*[71] it was held to be lawful for prison authorities to force-feed a prisoner on hunger strike. The decision was influenced by the fact that suicide, and attempted suicide, was a criminal offence at the time, although it is questionable whether the offence could be committed by omission. The case is now of doubtful authority, and the practice of force-feeding hunger strikers in British prisons has been discontinued.[72]

6.65   Jehovah's Witnesses, who object on religious grounds to surgical interventions which may involve the use of blood products, are entitled to decline treatment. Thus, in *Malette* v. *Shulman*[73] a surgeon administered blood to an unconscious patient admitted into a casualty department after a road accident. He was aware that she carried a card declaring that she was a Jehovah's Witness and that she was not willing to accept blood in any circumstances. Notwithstanding that the operation may well have saved the plaintiff's life, the defendant was held liable in battery. There was no concept of informed refusal of medical treatment, said Donnelly J.; the right to refuse treatment was not premised on the patient understanding the risks of refusal.[74] Arguably, the position of a person who has attempted suicide is analogous.

---

[70] "At common law a doctor cannot lawfully operate on adult patients of sound mind, or give them any other treatment involving the application of physical force however small . . . without their consent. If a doctor were to operate on such patients, or give them other treatment, without their consent, he would commit the actionable tort of trespass to the person," *per* Lord Brandon in *F.* v. *West Berkshire Health Authority* [1989] 2 All E.R. 545, 550–551; "There is no doubt that a person of full age and capacity cannot be ordered to undergo a blood test against his will . . . [because] English law goes to great lengths to protect a person of full age and capacity from interference with his personal liberty," *per* Lord Reid in *S.* v. *S.* [1970] 3 All E.R. 107, 111.

[71] (1909) 26 T.L.R. 139.

[72] See Zellick [1976] P.L. 153; see also *A.-G. of British Columbia* v. *Astaforoff* [1984] 4 W.W.R. 385, where the court refused to order treatment of a prisoner on hunger strike; Somerville (1985) 63 Can. Bar Rev. 59. American courts have declined to regard a patient's refusal of life-sustaining medical treatment (including tubal feeding) as equivalent to an attempt to commit suicide: see *Bouvia* v. *Superior Court* (1986) 225 Cal. Rptr 297 (Cal. C.A.); *Re Conroy* (1985) 486 A. 2d 1209 (New Jersey S.C.).

[73] (1987) 47 D.L.R. (4th) 18 (Ont. H.C.)); aff'd (1990) 67 D.L.R. (4th) 321 (Ont. C.A.).

[74] Damages were assessed at $20,000 for mental distress. In *R.* v. *Blaue* [1975] 1 W.L.R. 1411 the Court of Appeal touched upon this issue indirectly. The defendant had stabbed a young woman who subsequently refused a blood transfusion on religious grounds which would have saved her life. His appeal against a conviction for manslaughter on the ground that her unreasonable refusal of medical treatment broke the chain of causation between the attack and her death was dismissed. Lawton L.J. clearly considered that the woman's refusal to consent to a blood transfusion might be considered to be reasonable, although he accepted that there might be a difference between the criminal law and the civil law.

Provided the patient is competent to refuse consent to treatment, a doctor is not entitled to intervene.[75]

Some American courts have taken the view that it may be justifiable **6.66** to compel a person to accept medical treatment where this is essential to protect the life or health of a third party, particularly in the case of pregnant women. Thus, a pregnant woman has been ordered to undergo a blood transfusion contrary to her religious beliefs where this was considered necessary to save the life of a foetus of 32 weeks,[76] and women have been compelled to undergo Caesarian deliveries in circumstances where there was a high risk of death both to the child and the mother from a natural birth,[77] and even more disturbingly where the mother was dying from cancer and the operation was clearly contrary to her medical interests.[78] It is unlikely that the courts would resort to such drastic steps in this country, particularly in the light of the decision of the Court of Appeal in *Re F. (in utero)*[79] in which it was held that the wardship jurisdiction did not extend to a foetus.

Certain statutory provisions allow for an element of compulsion **6.67** where "patients" refuse consent. Most prominent of these is the Mental Health Act 1983, which authorises the compulsory admission to hospital of certain patients suffering from mental disorder for assessment or treatment.[80] The Public Health (Control of Disease) Act 1984, ss.35–38, provide for the compulsory medical examination, removal to hospital or detention in hospital of a person suffering from or carrying a notifiable disease, although there would appear to be no specific authorisation in the Act for compulsory medical treatment.[81] Finally, section 47 of the National Assistance Act 1948 allows for the removal to suitable accommodation of persons who are suffering from grave chronic disease or, being aged, infirm or physically incapacitated, are living in insanitary conditions and are not receiving proper care and attention.[82] This procedure overlaps to some extent with the procedures for compulsory admission to hospital under the Mental Health Act 1983, but again there is no express power to give medical treatment against the persons wishes.

---

[75] *cf.* Skegg, *Law, Ethics and Medicine*, O.U.P., 1988, pp. 110–112. In *re F. (mental patient: sterilisation)* [1989] 2 W.L.R. 1025, 1050 Neill L.J. appeared to leave open the possibility that there may be circumstances in which a doctor is entitled to give treatment in order to save the life of a patient who, having the capacity to make a choice, has refused treatment. Note, also, that a doctor may have a duty to prevent suicide attempts where the patient suffers from a "grave mental instability" or is not "wholly sane": see §§ 4.89–4.101; but in these circumstances it may be that the patient would not be regarded as competent.

[76] *Raleigh Fitkin-Paul Morgan Memorial Hospital* v. *Anderson* (1964) 201 A. 2d 537 (New Jersey S.C.).

[77] *Jefferson* v. *Griffin Spalding County Hospital Authority* (1981) 274 S.E. 2d 457 (Georgia S.C.).

[78] *Re AC.* (1988) 533 A. 2d 611 (District of Columbia C.A.).

[79] [1988] 2 All E.R. 193; see Morgan [1988] J.S.W.L. 197; *cf. D.* v. *Berkshire County Council* [1987] 1 All E.R. 20 allowing a local authority to proceed with care proceedings on an infant on the basis of the mother's behaviour during pregnancy (drug-addiction).

[80] Mental Health Act 1983, ss.2–6; see § 2.56. For detailed discussion see Hoggett, *Mental Health Law* 3rd ed., 1990, Chaps. 2–4.

[81] See, however, s.13(1)(*a*). Notifiable diseases are cholera, plague, relapsing fever, smallpox and typhus: s.10. The Public Health (Infectious Diseases) Regulations 1988 (S.I. 1988/1546) extend these provisions to AIDS, but not persons who are HIV positive.

[82] For discussion of this provision see Hoggett, *op. cit.*, pp. 136–141; Counsell (1990) 140 New L.J. 750.

II. NEGLIGENCE

6.68 Consent to medical treatment involves the exercise of a choice. The power to consent involves also the power to refuse consent, and it is argued that a person cannot make a real choice unless he has information about the options, so as to be able to make a reasoned choice. Hence it is said that the consent must be an "informed consent." In law, the question of a patient's consent to medical treatment is inextricably linked to the tort of battery, but the courts have stipulated that a minimal level of information must be conveyed to the patient for this purpose. The failure to go into risks and implications of a proposed treatment is an issue to be considered under the doctor's duty of care in negligence not battery.[83] It is thus a misnomer to speak of "informed consent," since a patient's right to the information which will enable him to make a meaningful choice about treatment options (including the option of no treatment) depends upon the nature of the doctor's duty to exercise reasonable care in performing his professional functions as a doctor. Although the doctor's duty to give the patient information only makes sense in the light of the patient's right to exercise a choice through the power to give or withhold consent,[84] the courts in this country have to a large extent separated these two issues, principally to curtail the use of actions for battery against medical practitioners.

6.69 The duty of care in negligence applies to diagnosis, treatment and advice, and there is no doubt that part of this duty involves giving information to the patient about the diagnosis of his medical condition and the prognosis, in the light of the various treatment options that are available. This inevitably requires some assessment of the prospects that treatment will be successful, and, it should follow, the prospects that treatment may be unsuccessful. The crucial question is how much or how little information must be disclosed to satisfy the doctor's duty of care, and by what standard this is to be judged.

1. The duty to disclose information

6.70 One aspect of the plaintiff's case in *Bolam* v. *Friern Hospital Management Committee*[85] was that he had not been warned of the risks involved in electro-convulsive therapy before he received the treatment. In directing the jury, McNair J. applied the same test to the question of warning the patient as applied to treatment, namely whether the defendant fell below a proper standard of competent professional opinion in deciding whether to warn or not. In the early 1980s a series of cases sought to challenge this approach, which states, in effect, that a patient is entitled only to such information as a reasonable doctor deems appropriate. In *Chatterton* v. *Gerson*[86] Bris-

---

[83] *Chatterton* v. *Gerson* [1981] 1 All E.R. 257, 265; § 6.23.
[84] See the comments of Lord Scarman in *Sidaway* v. *Bethlem Royal Hospital Governors* [1985] 1 All E.R. 643, 654.
[85] [1957] 2 All E.R. 118; see §§ 3.07–3.08, 4.88, n. 14.
[86] [1981] 1 All E.R. 257, 265; § 6.23.

tow J. held that it was the doctor's duty "to explain what he intends to do, and its implications, in the way a careful and responsible doctor in similar circumstances would have done" applying the *Bolam* test. If there was a real risk of a misfortune inherent in the procedure a doctor ought to warn of it. Hirst J. adopted the same approach in *Hills* v. *Potter*[87] in which the plaintiff had an operation on her neck to alleviate a deformity of the neck (spasmodic torticollis), and was left paralysed from the neck down after the operation. There was an inherent risk of paralysis from the operation even if performed competently. Death occurred in one per cent. to two per cent. of cases, but the risks of death were no worse than in neurosurgery generally. Good results were obtained in some 70 per cent. to 80 per cent. of cases. Hirst J. held that the proper standard of disclosure was the medical standard, in accordance with the *Bolam* test and *Chatterton* v. *Gerson*.[88]

6.71 The issue of the appropriate standard of disclosure was finally considered by the House of Lords in *Sidaway* v. *Bethlem Royal Hospital Governors*.[89] The plaintiff suffered from persistent pain in her neck and shoulders, and she was advised to have an operation on her spinal column to relieve the pain. The defendant surgeon warned the plaintiff of the possibility of disturbing a nerve root and the consequences of this, but he did not mention the possibility of damage to the spinal cord, although the operation would be within millimetres of the spinal cord. The overall risk of either of these events materialising was between one per cent. and two per cent., although the risk of spinal cord damage was less than one per cent. The potential consequences of these risks ranged from mild to severe, with the most severe consequence of spinal cord damage being partial paralysis. During the course of the operation, which was not performed negligently, the plaintiff sustained damage to the spinal cord resulting in severe disability from partial paralysis. She alleged that the defendant had been negligent in failing to inform her about this risk, and that had she known the true position she would not have accepted the treatment. The trial judge, Skinner J., applied the *Bolam* test and concluded that the defendant had acted in accordance with a practice accepted as proper by a responsible body of medical opinion by not informing the plaintiff of the risk of damage to the spinal cord. The decision was upheld by the Court of Appeal,[90] and the House of Lords affirmed this finding, although there was some disparity in their Lordships' reasoning.

6.72 Lord Scarman, in a strong dissenting speech, pointed out that applying the *Bolam* test to the question of how much information a patient is entitled to be given leaves the matter almost entirely to the discretion of the medical profession, which places too much judicial reliance on medical judgment instead of seeing the problem from the patient's point of view:

---

[87] [1983] 3 All E.R. 716.

[88] See also *Sankey* v. *Kensington and Chelsea and Westminster Area Health Authority* (1982) (unreported), Q.B.D., where the plaintiff sustained a stroke following a bilateral carotid arteriogram, performed with a view to identifying a lesion in the pituitary fossa. Tudor Evans J held that "the question of warning has to be judged by competent responsible medical opinion"; *O'Malley-Williams* v. *Board of Governors of the National Hospital for Nervous Diseases* (1975) 1 B.M.J. 635.

[89] [1985] 1 All E.R. 643.

[90] [1984] 1 All E.R. 1018.

"If one considers the scope of the doctor's duty by beginning with the right of the patient to make his own decision whether he will or will not undergo the treatment proposed, the right to be informed of significant risk and the doctor's corresponding duty are easy to understand, for the proper implementation of the right requires that the doctor be under a duty to inform his patient of the material risks inherent in the treatment."[91]

Accordingly, his Lordship preferred a standard of disclosure based on the "reasonably prudent patient test," which was derived from the American case of *Canterbury* v. *Spence*[92] and the decision of the Supreme Court of Canada in *Reibl* v. *Hughes*.[93] Under this test a doctor must disclose all material risks, and a risk is material "when a reasonable person, in what the physician knows or should know to be the patient's position, would be likely to attach significance to the risk or cluster of risks in deciding whether or not to forego the proposed therapy."[94] This requires the doctor to communicate the inherent and potential hazards of the proposed treatment, the alternatives to that treatment, if any, and the likely results if the patient remains untreated. The factors contributing significance to the dangerousness of a medical technique were said to be the incidence of injury and the degree of harm threatened. This standard of disclosure is subject to two exceptions. First, where there is a genuine emergency, for example, the patient is unconscious; and, secondly, where the information would be harmful to the patient, for example, where it might cause psychological damage,[95] or where the patient would become so emotionally distraught as to prevent a rational decision. This "therapeutic privilege" defence does not allow the doctor to remain silent about material risks simply because disclosure might prompt the patient to forego treatment that the doctor believes the patient needs in his best interests, otherwise the exception might become so wide as to undermine the requirement of disclosure.

6.73 Lord Diplock favoured applying the *Bolam* test. He pointed out that the only effect that mention of risks can have on the patient's mind will be in the direction of deterring the patient from undergoing the treatment which in the expert opinion of the doctor it is in the patient's interests to undergo:

"To decide what risks the existence of which a patient should be voluntarily warned, and the terms in which such warning, if any, should be given, having regard to the effect that the warning may have, is as much an exercise of professional skill and judgment as any other part of the doctor's comprehensive duty of care to the individual patient, and expert medical evidence on this matter should be treated in just the same way. The *Bolam* test should be applied."[96]

---

[91] [1985] 1 All E.R. 643, 654.
[92] (1972) 464 F. 2d 772 (U.S.C.A., District of Columbia).
[93] (1980) 114 D.L.R. (3d) 1.
[94] (1972) 464 F. 2d 772, 787.
[95] "Even if the risk be material, the doctor will not be liable if on a reasonable assessment of his patient's condition he takes the view that a warning would be detrimental to his patient's health," *per* Lord Scarman at [1985] 1 All E.R. 643, 655. For an unusual example of this see *Furniss* v. *Fitchett* [1958] N.Z.L.R. 396.
[96] [1985] 1 All E.R. 643, 659.

Lord Bridge, with whom Lord Keith agreed, accepted that a **6.74** conscious adult patient of sound mind is entitled to decide for himself whether or not he will submit to a particular course of treatment proposed by a doctor, particularly in the case of surgical treatment under general anaesthesia. His Lordship recognised "the logical force of the *Canterbury* doctrine" but regarded it as "quite impractical" for three reasons. First, it gives insufficient weight to the nature of the doctor/patient relationship. The doctor cannot educate the patient to his own standard of medical knowledge, and volunteering information about remote risks may lead to the risk assuming an undue significance for the patient. Secondly, it was "unrealistic" to confine the medical evidence to an explanation of primary medical facts and to deny the court evidence of medical opinion and practice on the particular question of disclosure. Thirdly, the objective *Canterbury* test of what a reasonable person in the patient's position would consider to be a significant risk was "so imprecise as to be almost meaningless."[97]

Lord Bridge realised that applying the *Bolam* test without qualifica- **6.75** tion to the question of what risks inherent in a proposed treatment should be disclosed carried the danger of medical paternalism which might not be controlled by the courts.[98] Nonetheless, he continued:

"I fully appreciate the force of this reasoning, but can only accept it subject to the important qualification that a decision what degree of disclosure of risks is best calculated to assist a particular patient to make a rational choice whether or not to undergo a particular treatment must primarily be a matter of clinical judgment. It would follow from this that the issue whether non-disclosure in a particular case should be condemned as a breach of the doctor's duty of care is an issue to be decided primarily on the basis of expert medical evidence, applying the *Bolam* test. But I do not see that this approach involves the necessity 'to hand over to the medical profession the entire question of the scope of the duty of disclosure, including the question whether there has been a breach of that duty.' Of course, if there is a conflict of evidence whether a responsible body of medical opinion approves of non-disclosure in a particular case, the judge will have to resolve that conflict. But even in a case where, as here, no expert witness in the relevant medical field condemns the non-disclosure as being in conflict with accepted and responsible medical practice, I am of opinion that the judge might in certain circumstances come to the conclusion that disclosure of a particular risk was so obviously necessary to an informed choice on the part of the patient that no reasonably prudent medical man would fail to

---

[97] *Ibid.*, p. 662. His Lordship did not explain why a test based on what a reasonable doctor would consider should be disclosed is any more precise or meaningful. See, however, the comments of Sir John Donaldson M.R. on the "prudent patient test" in the Court of Appeal in *Sidaway* v. *Bethlem Royal Hospital Governors* [1984] 1 All E.R. 1018, 1027.

[98] "To allow expert medical evidence to determine what risks are material and, hence, should be disclosed and, correlatively, what risks are not material is to hand over to the medical profession the entire question of the scope of the duty of disclosure, including the question whether there has been a breach of that duty": *per* Laskin C.J.C. in *Reibl* v. *Hughes* (1980) 114 D.L.R. (3d) 1, 13 (S.C.C.), cited by Lord Bridge at [1985] 1 All E.R. 643, 662.

make it. The kind of case I have in mind would be an operation involving a substantial risk of grave adverse consequences, as for example the 10 per cent. risk of a stroke from the operation which was the subject of the Canadian case of *Reibl* v. *Hughes* (1980) 114 D.L.R. (3d) 1. In such a case, in the absence of some cogent reason why the patient should not be informed, a doctor, recognising and respecting his patient's right of decision, could hardly fail to appreciate the necessity for an appropriate warning."[99]

6.76 It is not entirely clear what test for information disclosure Lord Templeman adopted. In his Lordship's view a doctor has an obligation to provide information which is adequate to enable the patient reach a balanced judgment about whether to submit to recommended treatment, subject to the doctor's obligation to say nothing which will be harmful to the patient.[1] The doctor, too, must make a balanced judgment:

"If the doctor making a balanced judgment advises the patient to submit to the operation, the patient is entitled to reject that advice for reasons which are rational or irrational or for no reason at all. The duty of the doctor in these circumstances, subject to his overriding duty to have regard to the best interests of the patient, is to provide the patient with information which will enable the patient to make a balanced judgment if the patient chooses to make a balanced judgment. A patient may make an unbalanced judgment because he is deprived of adequate information. A patient may also make an unbalanced judgment if he is provided with too much information and is made aware of possibilities which he is not capable of assessing because of his lack of medical training, his prejudices or his personality."[2]

His Lordship also considered that a patient who knows that a major operation may entail serious consequences cannot complain of lack of information unless he asks in vain for more information, or unless there is some danger which by its nature or magnitude or for some other reason is required to be separately taken into account by the patient in order to reach a balanced judgment in deciding whether or not to submit to the operation.[3] Thus, a doctor ought to draw the attention of a patient to a danger which may be special in kind or magnitude or special to the patient.[4] Lord Templeman emphasised that it is for the court to decide whether a doctor is in breach of his duty with respect to the disclosure of information to a patient, but if he conscientiously endeavoured to explain the arguments for and against the treatment the court would be slow to conclude that the doctor was negligent merely because he omitted some specific item of information.

---

[99] [1985] 1 All E.R. 643, 662–663.
[1] [1985] 1 All E.R. 643, 666.
[2] *Ibid.*
[3] *Ibid.*, p. 664.
[4] *Ibid.*, p. 665, citing the example of a 4 per cent. risk of death and 10 per cent. risk of stroke in *Reibl* v. *Hughes* (1980) 114 D.L.R. (3d) 1.

Notwithstanding the diversity of the speeches in *Sidaway*, it is **6.77**
submitted that the majority of their Lordships adopted the *Bolam* test
as the measure of a doctor's duty to disclose information about the
potential consequences and risks of proposed medical treatment. This
would seem to be the view of most commentators,[5] and indeed the
Court of Appeal has specifically endorsed this interpretation on two
occasions.[6] It has, however, been argued that *Sidaway* represents an
extension of *Bolam*. Professor Kennedy has suggested that the exception that Lord Bridge makes in the case of a non-disclosure of a
substantial risk of grave adverse consequences where a doctor could
hardly fail to appreciate the necessity for an appropriate warning
"cannot be very far from the reasonable or prudent patient test,"[7]
whereas Lord Diplock was in a minority of one.[8] This interpretation
appears to rest upon the assumption, which was explicit in Lord
Scarman's dissenting speech,[9] that the *Bolam* test depends solely upon
professional practice and that it is never open to the court to condemn
a common professional practice as negligent.

It is respectfully submitted that this view misstates the nature of the **6.78**
Bolam test. The objective nature of the test for negligence means that
it is always for the court to determine, ultimately, what constitutes
negligence on the basis of the evidence presented. The practices of a
profession may be good evidence of "reasonable care" but cannot be
conclusive.[10] Lord Bridge's "exception" for the non-disclosure of a
substantial risk of grave adverse consequences where a doctor could
hardly fail to appreciate the necessity for an appropriate warning is
simply an instance of the "obvious folly" test where it would be
appropriate for a court to condemn a common practice as negligent.[11]
This point was clear in the judgment of Sir John Donaldson M.R. in
the Court of Appeal, when his Lordship said that the definition of the
duty of care is a matter for the law and the courts, and that the duty is
fulfilled if the doctor acts in accordance with a practice *rightly* accepted
as proper by a body of skilled and experienced medical men.[12] In an

---

[5] Brazier (1987) 7 L.S. 169, 182; Norrie (1985) 34 I.C.L.Q. 442, 450; Tan (1987) 7
L.S. 149, 161, n. 42; Dugdale and Stanton, *Professional Negligence*, 1989, 2nd ed., para.
17.28; Jackson and Powell, *Professional Negligence*, 1987, 2nd ed., para. 6.90.

[6] *Gold* v. *Haringey Health Authority* [1987] 2 All E.R. 888; *Blyth* v. *Bloomsbury
Health Authority* (1987) reported at (1989) 5 P.N. 167, 171; see also *Worster* v. *City and
Hackney Health Authority*, *The Times*, June 22, 1987, *per* Garland J.; *Moyes* v. *Lothian
Health Board* [1990] 1 Med. L.R. 463, 469.

[7] Kennedy, *Treat Me Right*, 1988, O.U.P., p. 201. See also Teff (1985) 101 L.Q.R.
432, 448 who considers that *Sidaway* represents a modest modification of *Bolam*, almost
indistinguishable from *Bolam* in practice.

[8] Kennedy and Grubb, *Medical Law Text and Materials*, 1989, p. 249 identifies the
majority speeches in *Sidaway* as Lords Bridge, Keith and Templeman.

[9] See §§ 3.20–3.21.

[10] See §§ 3.22–3.31.

[11] See § 3.28, n. 49. Teff (1985) 101 L.Q.R. 432, 448, points out that in *Reibl* v.
Hughes (1980) 114 D.L.R. (3d) 1 the defendant had been found liable at first instance on
a professional judgment standard, and that it is difficult to envisage the example which
Lord Bridge cites from *Reibl* v.*Hughes* satisfying the *Bolam* test, by which, presumably,
he means that it is unlikely that a body of reasonable medical practitioners would accept
non-disclosure of such a risk (see further Dugdale and Stanton, *Professional Negligence*,
1989, 2nd ed., para. 17.28, n. 7 making the same point). The court would conclude that
no *responsible* body of professional opinion could have failed to disclose that degree of
risk: see the comment of Hirst J. in *Hills* v. *Potter* [1983] 3 All E.R. 716, 728 cited at §
3.30.

[12] *Sidaway* v. *Bethlem Royal Hospital Governors* [1984] 1 All E.R. 1018, 1028
emphasis in original.

appropriate case, said his Lordship, a judge would be entitled to reject a unanimous medical view if he were satisfied that it was manifestly wrong. Moreover, this qualification was "analogous to that which has been asserted in the context of treating a trade practice as evidencing the proper standard of care . . . and would be equally infrequently relevant."[13] Similarly, when Lord Bridge said that the issue whether non-disclosure in a particular case should be held to be negligent "is an issue to be decided *primarily* on the basis of expert medical evidence, applying the *Bolam* test," (emphasis added) he was not suggesting that normally the *Bolam* test applied but in exceptional circumstances it could be dispensed with. Rather he was stating the effect of the *Bolam* test itself, which relies *primarily* on expert evidence as to responsible professional practice, but, exceptionally, the court may decline to accept that evidence as a measure of the proper standard in law. Thus, the majority in *Sidaway* consisted of Lords Bridge, Keith and Diplock, who all applied the *Bolam* test.

Canada

6.79   In Canada the Supreme Court has established a standard of disclosure based on the "reasonably prudent patient." In *Hopp* v. *Lepp*[14] it was said that a surgeon should answer any specific questions posed by the patient as to the risks involved and should, without being questioned, disclose to him the nature of the proposed operation, its gravity, any material risks and any special or unusual risks attendant upon the performance of the operation. A risk which is a mere possibility, which ordinarily need not be disclosed, could be regarded as a material risk, requiring disclosure, if its occurrence carries serious consequences such as paralysis or death. Subsequently, in *Reibl* v. *Hughes*[15] the court explicitly rejected a professional medical standard for determining what are material risks and whether there has been a breach of the duty of disclosure:

> "To allow expert medical evidence to determine what risks are material and, hence, should be disclosed and, correlatively, what risks are not material, is to hand over to the medical profession the entire question of the scope of the duty of disclosure, including the question whether there has been a breach of that duty . . . The materiality of non-disclosure of certain risks to an informed decision is a matter for the trier of fact, a matter on which there would, in all likelihood, be medical evidence but also other evidence, including evidence from the patient or from members of his family."

6.80   In *Videto* v. *Kennedy*[16] the Ontario Court of Appeal summarised the effect of *Hopp* v. *Lepp* and *Reibl* v. *Hughes* in the following terms:
   (a) The question of whether a risk is material and whether there has been a breach of the duty of disclosure should not be

---

[13] *Ibid.*, citing *Cavanagh* v. *Ulster Weaving Co. Ltd* [1960] A.C. 145; *Morris* v. *West Hartlepool Steam Navigation Co. Ltd* [1956] A.C. 552; see § 3.23.
[14] (1980) 112 D.L.R. (3d) 67, 81 (S.C.C.).
[15] (1980) 114 D.L.R. (3d) 1, 13 (S.C.C.).
[16] (1981) 125 D.L.R. (3d) 127, 133–134 (Ont. C.A.).

determined solely by the standards of the profession. Professional standards are a factor to be considered.

(b) The duty of disclosure embraces what the surgeon knows or ought to know that the patient deems relevant to his decision whether or not to undergo the treatment. If the patient asks specific questions he is entitled to be given reasonable answers.

(c) A risk which is a mere possibility does not ordinarily have to be disclosed, but if its occurrence would have serious consequences it should be treated as a material risk.[17]

(d) The patient is entitled to be given an explanation of the nature of the operation and its gravity.

(e) Subject to this, other inherent dangers such as the dangers of anaesthetic or the risks of infection do not have to be disclosed.[18]

(f) The scope of the duty and whether it has been breached must be decided in the circumstances of each case.[19]

(g) The emotional condition of the patient may in certain cases justify the surgeon in withholding or generalising information which otherwise should be more specific.[20]

(h) The question of whether a particular risk is a material risk and whether there has been a breach of the duty is a matter for the trier of fact.

In *White* v. *Turner*[21] Linden J. explained that "material risks" are **6.81** significant risks that pose a real threat to the patient's life, health or comfort. The court must balance the severity of the potential result and the likelihood of its occurring. Even if there is only a small chance of serious injury or death, the risk may be considered material.[22] On the other hand, if there is a significant chance of slight injury this may also be held to be material.[23] "Unusual or special risks" are risks that

---

[17] See, *e.g.*, *Lachambre* v. *Nair* [1989] 2 W.W.R. 749.

[18] See, *e.g.*, *Hajgato* v. *London Health Association* (1982) 36 O.R. (2d) 669, 680. Note, however, that certain risks of infection, such as the risk of contracting hepatitis from blood products, may be an "unusual or special risk" which should be disclosed: *Kitchen* v. *McMullen* (1989) 62 D.L.R. (4th) 481 (N.B.C.A.).

[19] The patient may already know about the risks from a similar previous experience: *Goguen* v. *Crowe* (1987) 40 C.C.L.T. 212, 226 (N.S.S.C.). In addition to the risks of treatment a doctor should explain the consequences of leaving the ailment untreated, and the alternative means of treatment and their risks: *Haughian* v. *Paine* (1987) 37 D.L.R. (4th) 624, 639 (Sask. C.A.); *Schanczi* v. *Singh* [1988] 2 W.W.R. 465 (Alta. Q.B.).

[20] See, *e.g.*, *Hajgato* v. *London Health Association* (1982) 36 O.R. (2d) 669, 680.

[21] (1981) 120 D.L.R. (3d) 269, 284–285 (Ont. H.C.); aff'd (1982) 12 D.L.R. (4th) 319 (Ont. C.A.).

[22] Thus the risk of stroke, however minimal, is a material risk: *Forgie* v. *Mason* (1986) 30 D.L.R. (4th) 548, 558 (N.B.C.A.). A doctor does not satisfy his duty to warn of the risk of stroke by warning of the risk of death and assuming that mentioning the more serious risk, death, comprehended the less serious risk, stroke, because a reasonable patient may be prepared to run the risk of death but not the risk of stroke: *Ferguson* v. *Hamilton Civic Hospitals* (1983) 144 D.L.R. (3d) 214, 248; aff'd (1985) 18 D.L.R. (4th) 638 (Ont. C.A.). The risk of permanent loss or serious impairment of voice is a material risk in the context of the performance a carotid endarterectomy: *Casey* v. *Provan* (1984) 11 D.L.R. (4th) 708 (Ont. H.C.). A small risk of perforation of the bowel during the course of laparoscopic sterilisation and during a bowel examination by sigmoidoscope has been held not to be a material risk: *Videto* v. *Kennedy* (1981) 125 D.L.R. (3d) 127 (Ont. C.A.); *Gonda* v. *Kerbel* (1982) 24 C.C.L.T. 222.

[23] *Rawlings* v. *Lindsey* (1982) 20 C.C.L.T. 301, where a 5–10 per cent. risk of nerve damage and resultant numbness to the face following a wisdom tooth extraction was held to be a material risk; *cf. Diack* v. *Bardsley* (1983) 25 C.C.L.T. 159 (B.C.S.C.) where the plaintiff failed on causation.

are extraordinary or uncommon, but they are known to occur occasionally. Though rare, they should be described to a reasonable patient because of their unusual or special character. Thus, in the case of cosmetic surgery, where the operation can be described as elective, a doctor must be careful to make full disclosure of even remote risks of minor consequences since the patient may well decide that he would prefer to live with a blemish than to take the risk.[24]

Australia

6.82   In Australia the High Court has not yet had an opportunity to rule on the standard of disclosure to be applied to the medical profession. The leading case is probably *F.* v. *R.*[25] in which the Supreme Court of South Australia held that the duty was to be measured by the standards of the reasonable doctor. The duty applies not only to disclosure of real risks of misfortune inherent in the treatment but also to any real risk that the treatment, especially if it involves major surgery, may prove ineffective. What a careful and responsible doctor would disclose depends upon the circumstances, which includes the nature of the matter to be disclosed, the nature of the treatment, the desire of the patient for information, the temperament and health of the patient, and the general surrounding circumstances.[26] The duty was said to apply only to matters which might influence the decisions of a reasonable person in the situation of the patient. A risk of harm or of failure might be so slight in relation to the consequences of not undergoing the proposed treatment that no reasonable person would be influenced by it. The duty to disclose would not extend to such a risk. On the other hand, a small risk of great harm might call for disclosure although a greater risk of slight harm would not. The more drastic the proposed intervention, the more necessary it will be to keep the patient fully informed of the risks and likely consequences. Major surgery calls for special care in this regard. The existence of reasonably available alternative methods of treatment is also an important factor.

6.83   The doctor must also have regard to the patient's desire for information. An express and apparently seriously intended request for information necessary to make an informed decision will ordinarily place the doctor under an obligation to give a truthful and careful answer. There may be circumstances, however, where reasonable care for the patient may justify or even require an evasive or less than fully candid answer even to a direct request, and the doctor may reasonably judge that a patient has made an inquiry, not out of a desire for a frank answer, but out of a desire for reassurance. Similarly, the doctor can withhold information where he judges on reasonable grounds that the patient's health, mental or physical, might be seriously harmed by the information, or when the doctor reasonably judges that a patient's

---

[24] *White* v. *Turner* (1981) 120 D.L.R. (3d) 269; aff'd (1982) 12 D.L.R. (4th) 319 (Ont. C.A.); *Petty* v. *McKay* (1979) 10 C.C.L.T. 85 (B.C.S.C.); *Hankins* v. *Papillon* (1980) 14 C.C.L.T. 198, 203 (Que.S.C.); *Guertin* v. *Kester* (1981) 20 C.C.L.T. 225 (B.C.S.C.); *MacDonald* v. *Ross* (1983) 24 C.C.L.T. 242.

[25] (1983) 33 S.A.S.R. 189; see Manderson (1988) 62 A.L.J. 430.

[26] *Ibid.*, p. 191, *per* King. C.J.

temperament or emotional state is such that he would be unable to make the information a basis for a rational decision.[27] Finally, the doctor may also have regard to the surrounding circumstances in deciding what to disclose, for example, emergency conditions, the absence of an opportunity for detached reflection or calm counselling, and the existence of alternative sources of advice.

King C.J. did not accept that evidence of the usual practice of the profession should be decisive, although it would be of much assistance.[28] It was for the court to decide what a careful and responsible doctor would explain to the patient in the circumstances, and the opinions of the medical witnesses or the existence of a practice of non-disclosure in a section of the profession was not conclusive.[29] **6.84**

New Zealand

In *Smith* v. *Auckland Hospital Board*[30] the New Zealand Court of Appeal effectively applied a *Bolam* standard to the disclosure of information to a patient, even in response to a specific request for information by the patient. Barrowclough C.J. said that the court would, in most cases, require the assistance of expert medical evidence as to what is generally accepted medical or surgical practice.[31] **6.85**

2. What must be disclosed voluntarily?

Although it is the *Bolam* test which sets the standard of disclosure for the medical profession, it is nonetheless possible to identify some specific matters that either do or do not fall within the doctor's duty. In practice it is easier to identify the information that need not be disclosed. There is no obligation to inform a patient about the risk of death from general anaesthetic,[32] nor about other everyday risks that **6.86**

---

[27] *Ibid.*, p. 193; *cf.* Lord Templeman in *Sidaway* v. *Bethlem Royal Hospital Governors* [1985] 1 All E.R. 643, 666, § 6.76. In *Battersby* v. *Tottman* (1985) 37 S.A.S.R. 524 (S.C. of S.Aus.) it was held that the defendant was not liable for failing to warn a patient about the risk of blindness associated with the use of a particular drug in high doses because the plaintiff "was quite incapable by reason of her abnormal mental condition of using the information as the basis for calm or rational decision. She was likely to react hysterically and irrationally and to refuse treatment not on rational grounds or as a result of calm deliberation but as a result of distorted mental processes produced by her mental illness": *per* King C.J. at p. 527; *cf.* the forthright dissent of Zelling J. at pp. 534–535: "In my opinion it is no answer to the plaintiff's claim to say that the plaintiff might have had her treatment seriously affected or might have become suicidal if she had been told the truth. In my view no doctor is entitled to give a patient treatment which may blind her or seriously damage her eyesight without first discussing it with the patient and obtaining her consent to the treatment."

[28] "In many cases an approved professional practice as to disclosure will be decisive. But professions may adopt unreasonable practices": *ibid.*, p. 194; see further § 3.26.

[29] *Ibid.*, p. 196; see also, *per* Bollen J. at pp. 203–205.

[30] [1965] N.Z.L.R. 191 (N.Z.C.A.).

[31] *Ibid.*, p. 198; see also, *per* Turner J. at p. 205. It is uncertain whether the non-disclosure of risks of treatment falls within the definition of "medical misadventure" under New Zealand's system of no-fault accident compensation: see McGregor Vennell "Medical Misfortune in a No Fault Society," in Mann and Havard (eds.), *No Fault Compensation in Medicine*, 1989, Royal Society of Medicine, pp. 45–46. If it is not covered by the scheme the common law action would still be available to a patient.

[32] *Sidaway* v. *Bethlem Royal Hospital Governors* [1984] 1 All E.R. 1018, 1034, *per* Browne-Wilkinson L.J.: "It is of course obvious that the doctor is not under any duty to give information as to the ordinary risks normally attendant on any operation"; *Sidaway* v. *Bethlem Royal Hospital Governors* [1985] 1 All E.R. 643, 661, *per* Lord Bridge; *cf.* Lord Diplock at p. 658; *Considine* v. *Camp Hill Hospital* (1982) 133 D.L.R. (3d) 11, 39 (N.S.S.C.).

exist in all surgery, such as bleeding, pain, scars from an incision, or the risk of infection in any surgical procedure, because everyone is expected to know about them.[33] The doctor is not under a duty to tell the patient that if he is negligent in performing an operation he will cause damage,[34] nor that he is inexperienced in performing the particular procedure.[35]

6.87 There is no obligation to disclose information which the doctor believes will be medically harmful to the patient, or where the patient indicates that he does not want to know.[36] Under English law the notion of "therapeutic privilege" is not part of a defence to a claim for non-disclosure, it is incorporated within the duty of disclosure itself, applying *Sidaway* v. *Bethlem Royal Hospital Governors*. This allows for different levels of disclosure to different patients, within the doctor's exercise of clinical judgment. It is a "defence" only in the sense that if the medical evidence indicates that the normal practice of the profession is to disclose a particular risk, it will be for the defendant to justify non-disclosure to the patient. The doctor may take the view that a patient would be confused, frightened or misled by detailed information which he would be unable to evaluate at a time when he is suffering from stress, pain and anxiety.[37] There is an obvious danger in giving too wide an interpretation to this "exception" in that it could be used to undermine the patient's right to exercise a choice about whether to accept treatment. The mere fact that the doctor believes that if the patient were informed about the risks he would decline the treatment, which the doctor believes to be in the patient's best interests, would not justify withholding the information; otherwise, whenever the proposed treatment was medically appropriate, doctors would have no obligation to give patients information about risks.

6.88 The doctor does not have a duty to make the patient understand; it is a duty to make a reasonable effort to communicate information to the patient.[38] It is not an answer, however, for the doctor to say that he does not have the time to give seminars in medicine or that the

---

[33] *White* v. *Turner* (1981) 120 D.L.R. (3d) 269, 285, *per* Linden J. (Ont. H.C.); aff'd (1982) 12 D.L.R. (4th) 319 (Ont. C.A.). A failure to mention statistics should not be a factor in deciding whether the duty to inform has been breached: *Reibl* v. *Hughes* (1980) 114 D.L.R. (3d) 1, 13. In some circumstances certain infection risks, such as the risk of contracting AIDS from contaminated blood products, should be disclosed: see *H.* v. *Royal Alexandra Hospital for Children* [1990] 1 Med. L.R. 297, 324 (S.C. of N.S.W.)

[34] "The fundamental assumption is that he knows his job and will do it properly," *per* Bristow J. in *Chatterton* v. *Gerson* [1981] 1 All E.R. 257, 266; *Holmes* v. *Board of Hospital Trustees of the City of London* (1977) 81 D.L.R. (3d) 67, 83 (Ont. H.C.); *MacDonald* v. *Ross* (1983) 24 C.C.L.T. 242, 248.

[35] *Holmes* v. *Board of Hospital Trustees of the City of London* (1977) 81 D.L.R. (3d) 67, 83 (Ont. H.C.).

[36] *Sidaway* v. *Bethlem Royal Hospital Governors* [1984] 1 All E.R. 1018, 1034, *per* Browne-Wilkinson L.J. The doctor must identify the patient's "true wishes" and distinguish between patients who want information and patients who are only seeking reassurance, *per* Sir John Donaldson M.R. at p. 1027. If the information would be harmful to the patient the doctor could be in breach of a duty of care by disclosing it: see *Furniss* v. *Fitchett* [1958] N.Z.L.R. 396.

[37] *Sidaway* v. *Bethlem Royal Hospital Governors* [1985] 1 All E.R. 643, 664, *per* Lord Templeman; *Male* v. *Hopmans* (1967) 64 D.L.R. (2d) 105, 113 (Ont. C.A.).

[38] See *Kelly* v. *Hazlett* (1976) 75 D.L.R. (3d) 536, 565 (Ont. H.C.), *per* Morden J. stating that it is a duty to be reasonably satisfied that the patient is aware of the risks associated with the treatment of which he should be aware.

information is too complicated or technical for the patient to understand. The duty must be to give an explanation in terms which are reasonably comprehensible to a layman, although there can be no guarantee that the patient will in fact understand the information.[39] Where it is quite apparent to the doctor that the patient has not understood, he may have to make further efforts. The Canadian courts, for example, have taken the view that where the patient has language difficulties the doctor is under a special duty to be sure that the patient has understood.[40]

It is more difficult to state precisely what must be disclosed since **6.89** under the *Bolam* test this depends upon the practice of a responsible body of professional opinion at the time. One consequence of this is that patients will be entitled to more information as professional attitudes to the question of information disclosure change (assuming, of course, that changes in practice will reflect the growing concern that consent should be "informed"). It must be remembered that non-disclosure is not necessarily negligent merely because some doctors would have disclosed a particular risk, if other responsible practitioners would not have told the patient about it.[41] It is implicit from Lord Bridge's speech in *Sidaway* v. *Bethlem Royal Hospital Governors*,[42] however, that there must be some limits to the medical profession's discretion to withhold information. His Lordship cited *Reibl* v. *Hughes*,[43] in which there was a four per cent. risk of death and a 10 per cent. risk of stroke in the context of an operation intended to remove the risk of stroke, as an example of a case where a court could reasonably conclude that the disclosure of the risk was so obviously necessary to an informed choice on the part of the patient that no reasonably prudent doctor would fail to make it, notwithstanding the practice of the profession. In such a case, where there was a substantial risk of grave adverse consequences, a doctor could hardly fail to appreciate the necessity for an appropriate warning. In making this judgment there must inevitably be some degree of interrelationship between the chances of a successful outcome and the inherent risks of the procedure.[44] Similarly, there ought to be an interrelationship

---

[39] See Brazier (1987) 7 L.S. 169, 177 commenting on the intrinsic difficulty of communicating medical information to patients. One study found that between 2 and 5 days after an operation 27 per cent. of patients did not know which organ had been operated on, and 44 per cent. were unaware of the basic facts relating to the operation, *e.g.*, that a gall bladder had been removed: Byrne, Napier and Cuschieri (1988) 296 B.M.J. 839. See also McMahon, Clark and Bailie (1987) 294 B.M.J. 355, on the provision of drug information to patients.

[40] *Reibl* v. *Hughes* (1980) 114 D.L.R. (3d) 1, 34; *Schanczi* v. *Singh* [1988] 2 W.W.R. 465, 474 (Alta. Q.B.).

[41] See, *e.g.*, *Gold* v. *Haringey Health Authority* [1987] 2 All E.R. 888, where all the expert witnesses said that they would have disclosed the risk of a sterilisation operation failing to produce sterility, but that in 1979 there was a responsible body of professional opinion which would not have disclosed the risk; see also *Moyes* v. *Lothian Health Board* [1990] 1 Med. L.R. 463. Where there is no independent expert evidence as to professional practice the court may treat the defendant's own usual practice as evidence of the appropriate standard: *Thake* v. *Maurice* [1986] 1 All E.R. 497.

[42] [1985] 1 All E.R. 643, 662–663.

[43] (1980) 114 D.L.R. (3d) 1.

[44] "An operation with a very high success rate and a very low risk of paralysis may, rationally, be accepted much more readily than one where the prospects of success were more circumscribed, though the risk of paralysis was still slight," *per* Kirby P. in *Ellis* v. *Wallsend District Hospital* (1989) 17 N.S.W.L.R. 553, 561 (N.S.W. C.A.).

between the nature and severity of the potential risks and the purpose of the procedure. In the case of minor surgical operations the court could reasonably require doctors to disclose lower degrees of risk, whether measured by incidence or severity. Conversely, the more serious the patient's medical condition requiring treatment, the greater the level of risk the doctor could reasonably omit to disclose:

> "Moreover, the materiality of any particular risk must in the ordinary case depend on the relationship between the object to be achieved by the operation and the nature of the risks involved. If there is a half per cent. risk of total paralysis, that might well be a material risk in the context of an operation designed to get rid of a minor discomfort but not in the context of an operation required to avoid death. The decision as to the materiality of a risk does not depend simply on the difference between an elective operation and an essential operation: it depends on the balancing of benefits and risks."[45]

6.90 The courts in this country have been reluctant to accept a distinction between elective and non-elective procedures. Sir John Donaldson M.R. has said that the distinction is meaningless to a patient, because all operations are elective, *i.e.* the patient always has a choice.[46] Whilst on one level this is patently true, the concept of an elective medical procedure does seek to distinguish those situations where the patient's condition is such that there is in reality very little choice (all the evidence points to the treatment being accepted, possibly in an emergency[47]) from those where the options are more evenly balanced and there is time for considered reflection. In Canada, for example, cosmetic surgery has been treated as elective, requiring a greater degree of information disclosure about inherent risks.[48]

6.91 The Court of Appeal has also rejected a distinction between advice given in a therapeutic context and advice given in a non-therapeutic context. In *Gold* v. *Haringey Health Authority*[49] Schiemann J. attempted to avoid applying the *Bolam* test to the non-disclosure of the chance that a sterilisation operation might not render the plaintiff completely sterile, taking the view that in the context of a sterilisation for contraceptive purposes, as opposed to therapeutic purposes, there was no body of responsible professional opinion which would have omitted to give a warning. Alternatively, his Lordship held that the *Bolam* test did not apply in a non-therapeutic context, and accordingly

---

[45] *Sidaway* v. *Bethlem Royal Hospital Governors* [1984] 1 All E.R. 1018, 1034, *per* Browne-Wilkinson L.J. See also *H.* v. *Royal Alexandra Hospital for Children* [1990] 1 Med. L.R. 297, 324, *per* Badgery-Parker J.: "The greater the chance that the risk will eventuate, the more obviously will disclosure be necessary, even though the consequences of the happening of the risk may not be enormous. Conversely, where the possible consequence is disastrous, disclosure may be 'obviously necessary' even though the risk be quantified as tiny."

[46] *Ibid.*, p. 1028; see also *Gold* v. *Haringey Health Authority* [1987] 2 All E.R. 888, 894.

[47] See *Hills* v. *Potter* [1983] 3 All E.R. 716, 718, where Hirst J. observed that it was common ground in that case that it was not an emergency procedure "but was 'elective' in character, so that it was for the plaintiff to choose whether or not to undergo it."

[48] *White* v. *Turner* (1981) 120 D.L.R. (3d) 269 (Ont. H.C.); aff'd (1982) 12 D.L.R. (4th) 319 (Ont. C.A.); *cf. Gold* v. *Haringey Health Authority* [1987] 2 All E.R. 888, 894.

[49] [1987] 2 All E.R. 888; Montgomery (1988) 51 M.L.R. 245.

the defendant was negligent despite the medical evidence to the effect that a responsible body of professional opinion would not have given a warning. The Court of Appeal reversed this finding. Lloyd L.J. said that:

" . . . a distinction between advice given in a therapeutic context and advice given in a non-therapeutic context would be a departure from the principle on which the *Bolam* test is itself grounded. The principle does not depend on the context in which any act is performed, or any advice given. It depends on a man professing skill or competence in a field beyond that possessed by the man on the Clapham omnibus."[50]

The consequence of this appears to be that the *Bolam* test will be applied to the disclosure of information by doctors in all contexts, although it must remain arguable that even under the *Bolam* test a reasonable doctor should give patients more information about the inherent risks of a procedure which is "elective" (a term which would encompass "non-therapeutic") in the sense that it is not essential for the patient's well-being.

3. Asking questions

If a patient is only entitled to have volunteered the information that **6.92** a reasonable doctor considers to be appropriate in the light of the practices adopted by other responsible medical practitioners, it might be thought that he would be able to elicit more information by asking direct questions. In *Hatcher* v. *Black*[51] the defendant doctor deliberately lied to a patient because he did not want her to worry, telling her that there was no risk to her voice in the procedure that was to be performed when he knew that there was some slight risk. Denning L.J., in an instruction to a jury, said that the law only condemns a doctor when he falls short of the accepted standards of the profession, and he pointed out that none of the medical witnesses had criticised the defendant, saying "They did not condemn him; nor should we." In *Sidaway* v. *Bethlem Royal Hospital Governors*, however, Lord Bridge commented that:

" . . . when questioned specifically by a patient of apparently sound mind about risks involved in a particular treatment proposed, the doctor's duty must, in my opinion, be to answer both truthfully and as fully as the questioner requires."[52]

---

[50] *Ibid.*, p. 894. For criticism of a distinction between therapeutic and non-therapeutic sterilisation in a different context see *Re B. (a minor)* [1987] 2 All E.R. 206, 213, 214, *per* Lord Hailsham and Lord Bridge respectively; *cf. Re E. (a minor)*, *The Times*, February 22, 1991, where Sir Stephen Brown P. said, that there was a "clear distinction between an operation to be performed for a genuine therapeutic reason and one to achieve sterilisation."
[51] *The Times*, July 2, 1954.
[52] [1985] 1 All E.R. 643, 661.

Both Lord Diplock and Lord Templeman appeared to support this proposition.[53] Lord Bridge's dictum seems to preclude the judicially sanctioned white lie of *Hatcher* v. *Black*, but it is not entirely clear what his Lordship meant by the phrase "as fully as the questioner requires." In *Lee* v. *South West Thames Regional Health Authority* Sir John Donaldson M.R. suggested that a doctor has a discretion about the manner in which an answer to a patient's question should be given:

> "This duty is subject to the exercise of clinical judgment as to the terms in which the information is given and the extent to which, in the patient's interests, information should be withheld."[54]

6.93 The nature of the doctor's duty in response to questioning was considered by the Court of Appeal in *Blyth* v. *Bloomsbury Health Authority*.[55] The plaintiff was given an injection of the contraceptive drug Depo-Provera. She claimed that she was not given an adequate warning of the potential side-effects of the drug. The trial judge rejected the plaintiff's evidence that she had asked a series of specific questions, though he did accept that she had asked for some information and advice. The Court of Appeal reversed the decision that the defendants had been negligent, on the basis that the medical experts who gave evidence would not have given the plaintiff any more information than in fact she received, although no one suggested that information was withheld because it might have been harmful to the plaintiff. Kerr L.J. referred to the dicta of Lord Bridge and Lord Diplock in *Sidaway* and commented:

> "The question of what a plaintiff should be told in answer to a general enquiry cannot be divorced from the *Bolam* test, any more than when no such enquiry is made. In both cases the answer must depend upon the circumstances, the nature of the enquiry, the nature of the information which is available, its reliability, relevance, the condition of the patient, and so forth. Any medical evidence directed to what would be the proper answer in the light of responsible medical opinion and practice— that is to say the *Bolam* test—must in my view equally be placed in the balance in cases where the patient makes some enquiry, in order to decide whether the response was negligent or not . . . Indeed I am not convinced that the *Bolam* test is irrelevant even in relation to the question of what answers are properly to be given to specific enquiries, or that Lord Diplock or Lord Bridge intended to hold otherwise. It seems to me that there may always be grey areas, with differences of opinion, as to what are the proper answers to be given to any enquiry, even a specific one, in the particular circumstances of any case."[56]

---

[53] "No doubt, if the patient in fact manifested this attitude [of wanting to be fully informed of inherent risks] by means of questioning, the doctor would tell him whatever it was the patient wanted to know . . . ": *ibid.*, p. 659, *per* Lord Diplock. It is not clear whether this was simply Lord Diplock's expectation of what in fact would happen, or whether he considered that the doctor would be under a legal duty to inform his patient. Lord Templeman said that a patient would be entitled to complain of a lack of information if he asked in vain for more information: *ibid.*, p. 664.

[54] [1985] 2 All E.R. 385, 389.

[55] (1987) reported at (1989) 5 P.N. 167.

[56] (1989) 5 P.N. 167, 173.

Neill L.J. agreed that the *Bolam* test should apply, adding that neither Lord Bridge nor Lord Diplock had laid down a rule of law to the effect that where a patient asks questions a doctor is under an obligation to put the patient in possession of all the information on the subject which may have been available to the doctor. This decision may seem surprising in the light of the dicta in *Sidaway*, and may leave patients wondering just what they have to do in order to obtain full and truthful information.[57]

It is arguable that a doctor who did not answer questions truthfully **6.94** could be held liable in negligence even where there is a practice within the profession not to make full disclosure, on the basis that disclosure was so obviously necessary to an informed choice on the part of the patient that no reasonably prudent doctor would fail to make it.[58] Alternatively, it is possible that a deliberate lie might constitute a misrepresentation, vitiating the plaintiff's consent for the purpose of trespass to the person.[59] The difficulty with this argument, however, is that a misrepresentation as to the inherent risks of the treatment may not be interpreted as going to the *nature* of the procedure such as to render the patient's consent invalid.

In both Australia and New Zealand the courts have accepted that **6.95** medical practitioners must have some discretion as to the terms in which they deal with patients' questions. In *F.* v. *R.*[60] King C.J. said that if the plaintiff had asked a direct question the doctor would have had a duty to give full and frank advice. An express and seriously intended request for information would normally place the doctor under an obligation to give a truthful and careful answer. There might be circumstances, however, where reasonable care for the patient would justify or even require an evasive or less than fully candid answer even to a direct request, and the doctor may reasonably judge that a patient is merely seeking reassurance.[61] The plaintiff in *Smith* v. *Auckland Hospital Board*[62] asked whether there was any risk involved in aortography, in which a catheter was introduced into the femoral artery and guided into the aorta for the purpose of obtaining an X-ray. He was given a reassuring answer but was not told about the known risk of complications, which did in fact materialise and led ultimately to the amputation of his leg below the knee. The New Zealand Court of Appeal held the defendant liable on the basis that all the medical evidence indicated the defendant's answer fell below the appropriate

---

[57] Sir John Donaldson M.R. commented in *Sidaway* v. *Bethlem Royal Hospital Governors* [1984] 1 All E.R. 1018, 1027 that the doctor's duty of disclosure had to take account of the patient's "true wishes" because "it by no means follows that the expression of a wish for full information either generally or specifically represents the reality of the patient's state of mind." The patient might simply be seeking reassurance. Does the patient who asks questions have to convince the doctor that he wants a truthful answer? Can the doctor assume, unless there is evidence to the contrary, that the patient wants to be told lies?

[58] *Sidaway* v. *Bethlem Royal Hospital Governors* [1985] 1 All E.R. 643, 662–663, *per* Lord Bridge; §§ 6.75 and 6.78.

[59] See Montgomery (1988) 51 M.L.R. 245, 248 criticising the decision in *Blyth* v. *Bloomsbury Health Authority* (1987) reported at (1989) 5 P.N. 167.

[60] (1983) 33 S.A.S.R. 189, 196 (S.C. of S.Aus.); see also, *per* Legoe J. at p. 199, *per* Bollen J. at p. 207.

[61] *Ibid.*, p. 192.

[62] [1965] N.Z.L.R. 191 (N.Z.C.A.).

standard. The normal practice in response to such a question was to disclose the risk, and the defendant had departed from that practice.[63]

6.96 In Canada it may be that a stricter test applies to a doctor's response to questions. In *Hopp* v. *Lepp*[64] Laskin C.J.C. said that where a patient asks specific questions, not by way merely of general inquiry, the questions must be answered, even if they invite answers to merely possible risks. It is a question of fact how specific the questions are.

III. CAUSATION

6.97 One of the objections to using the tort of battery as the mechanism for ensuring that doctors disclose information concerning the risks of proposed treatment has been said to be that in battery the plaintiff does not have to prove causation. Thus, in *Chatterton* v. *Gerson* Bristow J. said that:

> "When the claim is based on negligence the plaintiff must prove not only the breach of duty to inform but that had the duty not been broken she would not have chosen to have the operation. Where the claim is based on trespass to the person, once it is shown that the consent is unreal, then what the plaintiff would have decided if she had been given the information which would have prevented vitiation of the reality of her consent is irrelevant."[65]

This is considered to be unfair to defendants because the plaintiff could in theory succeed in an action where, even if the risks had been disclosed in advance of treatment, the plaintiff would nonetheless have agreed to proceed and would therefore have sustained the very same injuries as a result of the materialisation of an inherent risk of the treatment.[66] It was this problem that led Bristow J. to assert that "justice requires that in order to vitiate the reality of consent there must be a greater failure of communication between doctor and patient than that involved in a breach of duty if the claim is based on

---

[63] "What is a proper answer will vary according to the circumstances of each case and it cannot always be said—especially when a patient is asking questions of his doctor—that the doctor is bound to give a full, complete and true answer. Much may depend on the effect of the answer on the health of the patient": *ibid.*, p. 198, *per* Barrowclough C.J.; see also Turner J. at p. 205 stating that a proper response must be measured by what other competent and experienced doctors would consider appropriate in the circumstances.

[64] (1980) 112 D.L.R. (3d) 67, 77 (S.C.C.); *Zimmer* v. *Ringrose* (1981) 124 D.L.R. (3d) 214, 221 (Alta. C.A.).

[65] [1981] 1 All E.R. 257, 265; *cf. Koehler* v. *Cook* (1975) 65 D.L.R. (3d) 766 (B.C.S.C.), where the defendant was held liable in trespass for non-disclosure of the risk of loss of smell, and Dryer J. went on to consider the causation issue, concluding that the plaintiff would have declined the operation to cure migraine headaches if she had known about the risk. This case must now be read in the light of *Reibl* v. *Hughes* (1980) 114 D.L.R. (3d) 1.

[66] In *Brushett* v. *Cowan* (1987) 40 D.L.R. (4th) 488 the defendant was held liable in battery for performing a bone biopsy without the patient's consent, although a claim in negligence failed because a reasonable patient would have consented to the biopsy had she been informed about it. The decision on battery was reversed on the facts, without affecting this point: see (1990) 69 D.L.R. (4th) 743 (Newfd. C.A.).

negligence."[67] It could be argued, however, that since consent to medical treatment is essentially concerned with the patient's right to exercise a choice about whether to accept or forego a particular treatment, the *reality* of that consent is intrinsically linked to the question of what the patient would have chosen to do had he been informed of the risks. If the information would not have altered his decision to accept treatment his consent was "real," whereas if disclosure of the risks would have caused him to change his mind about proceeding with the treatment his consent was not "real" and accordingly should be considered invalid. This approach would build the causation issue into the whole question of the reality of the patient's consent, and thus remove one of the objections to employing the tort of battery in this area. This argument does not appear to have been presented in any case where the problem has arisen, although the courts' clear hostility in this country to the use of actions in battery against doctors would probably lead to its rejection. On the other hand, where the defendant mistakenly fails to obtain the patient's consent, or exceeds the consent given, the present interpretation of "real consent" does not allow the defendant to plead that the patient would, in any event, have consented if he had known the situation.[68]

In battery the test of remoteness of damage is the directness of the **6.98** damage. The defendant is liable for all the consequences which are a direct result of the tortious act whether they are foreseeable or not. If no damage has been sustained the plaintiff is still entitled to nominal damages, because battery is actionable *per se*. Accordingly, in *Allan* v. *New Mount Sinai Hospital*[69] the defendant anaesthetist was held liable for the plaintiff's rare and unforeseeable reaction to the mishap occasioned by the needle slipping out of the plaintiff's vein, even though he was not negligent and in negligence the damage would probably have been regarded as too remote.[70]

Where the plaintiff brings an action in negligence for breach of the **6.99** doctor's duty to provide information, it is clear that he does have to establish causation by proving that had he been given a proper warning he would not have accepted the treatment.[71] In both *Chatterton* v.

---

[67] *Chatterton* v. *Gerson* [1981] 1 All E.R. 257, 265.

[68] See also Dugdale and Stanton, *Professional Negligence*, 1989, 2nd ed., para. 11.68, arguing that in any case where the plaintiff seeks substantial, as opposed to nominal, damages it should be open to the doctor to show that the damage would have been suffered irrespective of the failure to obtain consent.

[69] (1980) 109 D.L.R. (3d) 634 (Ont. H.C.); see § 6.08.

[70] "In negligence, the damage that occurs must be within the risk created by the negligent conduct or else there is no responsibility for it because it is too remote. In battery, however, any and all damage is recoverable, if it results from the wrongful act, whether it is foreseeable or not. The limitation devices of foresight and remoteness are not applicable to intentional torts, as they are in negligence law," *ibid.*, p. 643, *per* Linden J.

[71] See *Bolam* v. *Friern Hospital Management Committee* [1957] 2 All E.R. 118, 124. Thus, if the plaintiff already has the knowledge upon which he could base an informed decision about whether to accept treatment, the action will fail for lack of causation, even though he did not receive the information from his own doctor: *Davidson* v. *Connaught Laboratories* (1980) 14 C.C.L.T. 251, 272 (Ont. H.C.). Where the plaintiff has been warned about some, but not other, risks, and the combined, total risk of adverse consequences would have led him to refuse the treatment, he does not have to prove that the specific risk which has materialised was one about which he was not informed: *Moyes* v. *Lothian Health Board* [1990] 1 Med. L.R. 463, 467, *per* Lord Caplan. In other words, it would be possible for a plaintiff to succeed on causation even though he was warned about the particular complication that has occurred.

Gerson[72] and *Hills* v. *Potter*[73] the plaintiffs failed to convince the court that even if they had been given a fuller explanation about the risks of the procedure they would have declined to undergo it. In each of these cases the court adopted a subjective test for causation: would *this* plaintiff have accepted the treatment if adequately informed?[74] In *Reibl* v. *Hughes*,[75] on the other hand, the Supreme Court of Canada considered that a subjective test was too favourable to plaintiffs, creating the risk of self-serving testimony from patients who, with the benefit of hindsight, would invariably claim that they would have declined treatment had they known about the risks.[76] In order to deal with this perceived problem the court applied an objective test of causation: would a reasonable person in the plaintiff's position have declined the treatment? This makes it more difficult for the plaintiff to overcome the causation hurdle, because, even where he can demonstrate that he would not have accepted treatment, the action will fail if a reasonable person in his position would have gone ahead. The court recognised that this could place a premium on the doctor's assessment of the desirability of the treatment being undertaken, but concluded that merely because the recommended treatment was, objectively, medically appropriate it did not necessarily follow that a reasonable person in the plaintiff's position would agree to it, because the test takes account of the patient's particular situation. Thus in *Reibl* v. *Hughes* the plaintiff's action succeeded because although without the operation he had a continuing risk of suffering a stroke, the operation itself carried a 10 per cent. risk of stroke (which in fact materialised) and a four per cent. risk of death, and the plaintiff said that if he had known about these risks he would have delayed the operation in order to earn his full pension benefits at work. There was, moreover, no emergency making the surgery imperative, and the plaintiff was also under the mistaken impression that the operation would cure his headaches.

6.100   More generally, however, the effect of the objective test applied to causation in Canada has been that even where plaintiffs are successful in establishing a breach of the duty of disclosure, the action is much

---

[72] [1981] 1 All E.R. 257, 267.

[73] [1983] 3 All E.R. 716, 728.

[74] Leonard J. also applied a subjective test in *Blyth* v. *Bloomsbury Health Authority* (1985) (unreported) Q.B.D.; rev'd on other grounds (1987) C.A., reported at (1989) 5 P.N. 167. See also *Moyes* v. *Lothian Health Board* [1990] 1 Med. L.R. 463, 468. Note that even if the plaintiff fails to prove that if warned about the risk of complications he would have declined the treatment, he may nonetheless be entitled to compensation for the shock and depression consequent upon discovering, without prior warning that a complication has occurred: see *Smith* v. *Barking Havering and Brentwood Health Authority* (1989) 5 P.M.I.L.L. No. 4, § 9.52, n.42.

[75] (1980) 114 D.L.R. (3d) 1, 15–17.

[76] *White* v. *Turner* (1981) 120 D.L.R. (3d) 269, 286 (Ont. H.C.); aff'd (1982) 12 D.L.R. (4th) 319 (Ont. C.A.). Note that all testimony given by a plaintiff or defendant is potentially open to the criticism that it is self-serving. This is not necessarily a reason for adopting an objective test: *Ellis* v. *Wallsend District Hospital* (1989) 17 N.S.W.L.R. 553, 581, *per* Samuels J.A. (N.S.W.C.A.). Moreover, all reasoning about causation which relies upon the "but for" test is necessarily hypothetical and depends upon the drawing of appropriate inferences from other facts: see § 5.13.

more likely to fail on causation than to succeed.[77] Most of the cases in which plaintiffs have succeeded have involved procedures that could more readily be described as "elective" such as sterilisation[78] or cosmetic surgery,[79] where the balance of risks between the recommended treatment and the alternative treatments (or the alternative of foregoing any treatment) are more finely balanced, and the medical justification for proceeding is less overwhelming.[80] Similarly, it may be easier for a plaintiff to succeed on causation when the operation was designed to relieve chronic pain, where the plaintiff's discomfort is highly subjective, particularly where there were other treatment options which carried a lower, or no, risk.[81]

The objective test is open to the criticism that it represents a **6.101** departure from the principle that the individual patient is entitled to make the decision about whether to accept or reject medical treatment, a principle which the doctor's duty of disclosure is intended to serve.[82] If the success of the plaintiff's action depends upon what a

---

[77] Actions have failed on the grounds of causation in: *Bickford* v. *Stiles* (1981) 128 D.L.R. (3d) 516 (N.B.S.C.), where the incidence of vocal cord paralysis from mediastinoscopy was 0.5 per cent. and the alternative possible diagnosis was cancer; *Considine* v. *Camp Hill Hospital* (1982) 133 D.L.R. (3d) 11 (N.S.S.C.), where there was a risk of permanent incontinence of between 1–4 per cent. in the performance of a prostate operation; *Grey* v. *Webster* (1984) 14 D.L.R. (4th) 706, where evidence of failure rates for tubal ligation ranged from 1 in 300–500, or 2–5 per 1,000; *Stamos* v. *Davies* (1985) 21 D.L.R. (4th) 507, 521 (Ont. H.C.), where there was a risk of damage to the spleen during the performance of a lung biopsy, but the provisional diagnosis was of a life-threatening disease with a high mortality rate; *Poole* v. *Morgan* [1987] 3 W.W.R. 217, 263 (Alta. Q.B.), where there were risks inherent in laser treatment of the plaintiff's eye; *Petty* v. *McKay* (1979) 10 C.C.L.T. 85 (B.C.S.C.); *Hajgato* v. *London Health Association* (1982) 36 O.R. (2d) 669, 680; *Diack* v. *Bardsley* (1983) 25 C.C.L.T. 159, 170 (B.C.S.C.); aff'd (1984) 31 C.C.L.T. 308 (B.C.C.A.); *Ferguson* v. *Hamilton Civic Hospitals* (1983) 144 D.L.R. (3d) 214; aff'd (1985) 18 D.L.R. (4th) 638 (Ont. C.A.); *Casey* v. *Provan* (1984) 11 D.L.R. (4th) 708 (Ont. H.C.); *Kueper* v. *McMullin* (1986) 30 D.L.R. (4th) 408 (N.B.C.A.); *Rocha* v. *Harris* (1987) 36 D.L.R. 410 (B.C.C.A.); *Lachambre* v. *Nair* [1989] 2 W.W.R. 749 (Sask. Q.B.); *Kitchen* v. *McMullen* (1989) 62 D.L.R. (4th) 481 (N.B.C.A.). See further Dugdale (1986) 2 P.N. 108–111.

[78] *Dendaas* v. *Yackel* (1980) 109 D.L.R. (3d) 455; § 6.137.

[79] *White* v. *Turner* (1981) 120 D.L.R. (3d) 269 (Ont. H.C.); aff'd (1982) 12 D.L.R. (4th) 319 (Ont. C.A.), on breast reduction surgery; *cf. Petty* v. *McKay* (1979) 10 C.C.L.T. 85 (B.C.S.C.), where it was held that the plaintiff, an "exotic dancer," would have gone ahead with the operation (a modified abdominoplasty) even if the risks had been disclosed because she had a desire to attain a state of cosmetic perfection.

[80] See, *e.g.*, *Rawlings* v. *Lindsey* (1982) 20 C.C.L.T. 301, on failure to disclose 5–10 per cent. risk of nerve damage and resultant numbness to the face following a wisdom tooth extraction; the action succeeded on causation because the teeth were not giving any trouble at the time, they were merely superfluous; *cf. Diack* v. *Bardsley* (1983) 25 C.C.L.T. 159 (B.C.S.C.), where the teeth were causing problems.

[81] *Schanczi* v. *Singh* [1988] 2 W.W.R. 465 (Alta. Q.B.), where the plaintiff contracted arachnoiditis (inflammation of one of the membranes sheathing the spinal cord) which was caused by the dye used in the diagnostic myelogram, followed by the surgery (a disectomy performed in the lumbar spine). The option of conservative treatment had not been explored; *Haughian* v. *Paine* (1987) 37 D.L.R. (4th) 624 (Sask. C.A.), where there was small risk (c. 1 in 500) of paralysis associated with a laminectomy and discotomy, but the alternative treatment, conservative management, carried no risk; *Forgie* v. *Mason* (1986) 30 D.L.R. (4th) 548, 559 (N.B.C.A.). Note that the operations in the three English cases of *Sidaway* v. *Bethlem Royal Hospital Governors* [1985] 1 All E.R. 643, *Chatterton* v. *Gerson* [1981] 1 All E.R. 257 and *Hills* v. *Potter* [1983] 3 All E.R. 716, all involved treatment for chronic pain. Only in *Sidaway* did the plaintiff succeed on the causation issue.

[82] *Ellis* v. *Wallsend District Hospital* (1989) 17 N.S.W.L.R. 553, 560, *per* Kirby P. (N.S.W. C.A.).

"reasonable" patient would have done, then it can hardly be said that the patient can reject treatment "for reasons which are rational, or irrational, or for no reason."[83] Moreover, it is doubtful whether the objective test is, strictly speaking, a test of *causation* which, applying the general principles of the tort of negligence, is a question of whether *this* damage would have been suffered by *this* plaintiff but for the defendant's breach of duty.[84]

6.102   There have been occasional attempts to move away from the objective test in Canada. Thus, in *Buchan* v. *Ortho Pharmaceutical (Canada) Ltd.*[85] the Ontario Court of Appeal held that the objective test was "inappropriate" to the disclosure of information by a manufacturer in a products liability case, at least where the product was an oral contraceptive, because the selection of a method of preventing unwanted pregnancy in the case of a healthy woman was a matter, not of medical treatment, but of personal choice, and it was not unreasonable that notice of a serious potential hazard to users of oral contraceptives could influence her selection of another method of birth control. The court considered that a subjective test should be applied. In *Reynard* v. *Carr*[86] it was held that, although ordinarily the plaintiff has the burden of proving that if properly informed he would not have elected for the treatment, where the want of information is due not just to non-disclosure of the risk, but to culpable ignorance of its very existence, the plaintiff did not have to prove that he would not have consented if the doctor had known of the risk and had explained the nature of the risk to him.

6.103   The courts in this country have not considered whether an objective test should be applied to cases of non-disclosure,[87] and have been content to apply the subjective test. It may be that there is little difference in practice between the two approaches, since even under the subjective test the court will not simply accept uncritically the plaintiff's evidence that he would have declined treatment. The court must weigh the plaintiff's evidence against objective criteria in order to assess its credibility, and if a hypothetical reasonable patient would have accepted the treatment, given the balance of risks involved, this

---

[83] *Sidaway* v. *Bethlem Royal Hospital Governors* [1985] 1 All E.R. 643, 666, *per* Lord Templeman. See also, *per* T.A. Gresson J. in *Smith* v. *Auckland Hospital Board* [1965] N.Z.L.R. 191, 219; *Lepp* v. *Hopp* (1979) 98 D.L.R. (3d) 464, 470, *per* Prowse J.A.; aff'd (1980) 112 D.L.R. (3d) 67 (S.C.C.).

[84] See, *e.g.*, *McWilliams* v. *Sir William Arroll & Co. Ltd.* [1962] 1 W.L.R. 295, § 5.07; Nicholson (1990) 6 P.N. 83, 84–85.

[85] (1986) 25 D.L.R. (4th) 658, 685–7 (Ont. C.A.).

[86] (1983) 30 C.C.L.T. 42 (B.C.S.C.). See also *Grey* v. *Webster* (1984) 14 D.L.R. (4th) 706 (N.B.Q.B), where it was said that a subjective test should be applied to the disclosure of the risk that an operation (sterilisation) might not succeed in its purpose, whereas the objective test applied to the non-disclosure of the risk of additional harm being inflicted by the operation. Nonetheless, the action failed on causation; see § 6.139, n. 69.

[87] Although see *Hills* v. *Potter* [1983] 3 All E.R. 716, where Hirst J. concluded that the plaintiff's action failed on causation whether the test was subjective or objective. See further *Smith* v. *Barking, Havering and Brentwood Health Authority* (1989) 5 P.M.I.L.L. No. 4, where Hutchinson J. accepted that a subjective rest applied, though mediated by certain objective considerations.

will tend to undermine the plaintiff's credibility.[88] This point was made by Samuels J.A. in *Ellis* v. *Wallsend District Hospital*,[89] in which the New South Wales Court of Appeal adopted a subjective test of causation. In assessing the evidence the court would have regard to evidence about the plaintiff's temperament, the course of any prior treatment for the same or a similar condition, and the nature of the relationship between patient and doctor, including pre-eminently the degree of trust that the patient placed in the doctor. Clearly, the greater the trust, the greater the likelihood that the patient would have accepted the doctor's advice to undergo the treatment. Finally, the extent to which the procedure was elective or imposed by circumstantial exigency, and the nature and degree of the risk involved will also be relevant.[90] All of these factors could be relevant to an objective test which takes into account the plaintiff's particular situation. It would probably be rare, then, for a plaintiff to succeed on the subjective test but fail on the objective test.[91]

IV. SPECIAL CASES

1. Research

The fact that a person is the subject of medical research, as a **6.104** participant in a drug trial for example, may change the nature of the legal requirements for consent. Medical research is normally divided into two broad categories: therapeutic research, and non-therapeutic research. Therapeutic research is an activity which has a therapeutic intention, as well as a research intention, towards the subjects of the research. Thus, the subjects are also patients. Non-therapeutic research is an activity which does not have a therapeutic intention. This research is normally carried out on healthy volunteers, who are not patients. The legal principles applicable to these different categories of research may well differ, although there is a dearth of caselaw on the subject, and the most comprehensive statements of proper

---

[88] "I wholeheartedly accept that in retrospect she sincerely believes that she would have so declined. But, having regard to the evidence as to the gravity of her condition, I think it is more likely than not that she would have agreed to go ahead with the operation notwithstanding," *per* Hirst J. in *Hills* v. *Potter* [1983] 3 All E.R. 716, 728. Similarly, in *Chatterton* v. *Gerson* [1981] 1 All E.R. 257, 267 Bristow J. commented that: " . . . I would not have been satisfied that if properly informed Miss Chatterton would have chosen not to have it. The whole picture on the evidence is of a lady desperate for pain relief." In *Sidaway* v. *Bethlem Royal Hospital Governors* [1985] 1 All E.R. 643 the trial judge, Skinner J., did conclude that the plaintiff would have declined treatment had she known about the risks.

[89] (1989) 17 N.S.W.L.R. 553 (N.S.W. C.A.); Nicholson (1990) 6 P.N. 83. See also *Gover* v. *State of South Australia* (1985) 39 S.A.S.R. 543, 566; *H.* v. *Royal Alexandra Hospital for Children* [1990] 1 Med. L.R. 297, 324; and *Smith* v. *Auckland Hospital Board* [1965] N.Z.L.R. 191, where the New Zealand Court of Appeal apparently supported a subjective test of causation.

[90] *Ibid.*, p. 581, citing Robertson (1981) 97 L.Q.R. 102, 122.

[91] This did occur in *Considine* v. *Camp Hill Hospital* (1982) 133 D.L.R. (3d) 11 (N.S.S.C.).

safeguards for research subjects are to be found in national and international ethical codes.[92]

Therapeutic research

6.105   Therapeutic research involves medical treatment of the patient's illness or disability, and on this basis it may be that there is little or no difference in the requirements for an effective consent by the patient, or, indeed as to the doctor's duty to disclose information about the risks of the procedure. The patient's competence to consent for the purpose of the tort of battery would, presumably, be measured by the same criteria as are applied to any form of medical treatment, which depends upon his ability to understand the nature of the procedure.[93] Similarly, the voluntariness of the consent would be treated as a question of fact. Just as in a prison setting a court should be alive to the risk that what may appear, on the face of it, to be a real consent is not in fact so,[94] the court should also bear in mind that the stress of illness and the psychological pressures that a patient may experience in a "dependent" relationship with his doctor might affect the voluntariness of the patient's consent.[95] The patient may think, for example, that if he were to decline to participate, he would not subsequently be given the best available treatment or the most careful attention of the medical staff.[96] Thus, it is important that the patient is aware that he is free to decline to participate, and that this will not affect the treatment that he will receive.

6.106   The final issue concerns the question of how much information the patient must be given. It will be recalled that "once the patient is informed in broad terms of the nature of the procedure which is intended, and gives her consent, that consent is real."[97] If the treat-

---

[92] World Health Organisation, *Declaration of Helsinki* (1964, as amended in 1975 and 1983), extracted in Kennedy and Grubb, *Medical Law Text and Materials*, 1989, pp. 864–866. See also the Royal College of Physicians, *Guidelines on the Practice of Ethics Committees in Medical Research Involving Human Subjects*, 2nd ed., 1990 and Royal College of Physicians *Research Involving Patients*, 1990. For consideration of the standard of care to be applied to the conduct of research see §§ 3.28–3.44. For discussion of the potential liability of research ethics committees see Brazier (1990) 6 P.N. 186; and more generally Kirk (1986) 2 P.N. 186; Teff (1987) 3 P.N. 182.

[93] See §§ 6.20–6.22. Children of 16 or 17 years of age will be in the same position as adults by virtue of the Family Law Reform Act 1969, s.8(1). Children under 16 should have capacity if they have sufficient understanding, applying *Gillick* v. *West Norfolk & Wisbech Area Health Authority* [1985] 3 All E.R. 402. Query, however, whether a higher degree of understanding would be required for therapeutic research procedures than for simple "therapy," just as a high level of understanding is apparently required for contraceptive advice or treatment; see §§ 6.32–6.33.

[94] *Freeman* v. *Home Office* [1984] 1 All E.R. 1036, 1045; see § 6.19.

[95] In *Kaimowitz* v. *Michegan Department of Mental Health* (1973) 42 U.S.L.W. 2063 it was held that an involuntarily detained mental patient could not give a valid consent to experimental psychosurgery because the process of institutionalisation undermined the voluntary nature of the consent.

[96] The *Declaration of Helsinki*, para. I(10) provides that when obtaining consent the physician should be particularly cautious if the subject is in a dependent relationship to him, or may consent under duress. In such a case consent should be obtained by a doctor who is completely independent from the research project. Para. II(4) specifies that the refusal of the patient to participate in a study must never interfere with the physician-patient relationship.

[97] *Chatterton* v. *Gerson* [1981] 1 All E.R. 257, 265, § 6.23.

ment also has a research purpose the question is whether this alters the nature of the procedure, so that failure to tell the patient that he is part of a research study would vitiate the consent. Alternatively, it might be argued that a failure to inform the patient constitutes fraud or misrepresentation, on the basis that it involves withholding information in bad faith.[98] Here, everything turns on the meaning that is to be given to the term "nature of the procedure," and, in the absence of authority in this country, the answer must be largely speculative. If the court placed the emphasis on the therapeutic nature of the procedure, the fact that it was also experimental or part of a research project might be regarded as collateral to the therapy, to which consent "in broad terms" had been obtained. On this view, the doctor's research intention would be irrelevant to the validity of the patient's consent. On the other hand, it is arguable that the existence of the research intention does indeed change the nature of what is done, irrespective of any additional risk to which the patient may be exposed by virtue of the research aspect.[99] It is submitted that, on principle, the latter approach is correct, on the basis that no one, least of all patients who may be in a particularly vulnerable position, should be the subject of medical research without being aware of the circumstances and consenting to participate.

It has also been suggested that if the consent is to be valid the **6.107** patient must be informed of three further matters:

(1) that he may withdraw at any time from the research project, and will suffer no adverse consequences in terms of the treatment he will then receive;

(2) that he may be a member of a control group in a trial which is intended to test the effectiveness of a new therapy; and

(3) that the trial is a randomised controlled trial.[1]

The first matter relates to the question of the voluntariness of the consent: if the patient does not know that there is no compulsion to participate it may be arguable that his consent was involuntary. The second and third issues relate to the patient's knowledge of the treatment that he will receive. Although the patient will normally be unaware to which group he will be allocated, he should be informed of the nature of the treatment which each group will receive, otherwise he cannot consent, even in broad terms, to the nature of the procedure.

Notwithstanding that participation in therapeutic medical research **6.108** may increase the inherent risks of injury to a patient, it is unlikely that the courts would regard non-disclosure of risks as vitiating the reality of consent, given the general approach that has been taken to the tort of battery and the non-disclosure of risks. Clearly, a doctor would owe at least the same duty of care to inform a patient about the risks of

---

[98] See §§ 6.27–6.28.

[99] Kennedy and Grubb, *Medical Law Text and Materials*, 1989, p. 875.

[1] *Ibid.*, p. 876. Under a randomised controlled trial two or more groups of research subjects are given different treatments and the results are compared for any statistically significant difference in outcomes; subjects are allocated to the trial groups randomly in order to eliminate any bias in the selection of subjects for particular treatments. It has been found, however, that the majority of patients do not understand the process of randomisation when it is explained to them: see Simes *et al.* (1986) 293 B.M.J. 1065, 1067.

treatment as for any other form of treatment, applying *Sidaway* v. *Bethlem Royal Hospital Governors*.[2] The question is whether he would be under a duty to volunteer any additional information by virtue of a research intention.

6.109 In *Wilsher* v. *Essex Area Health Authority* Mustill L.J. observed that where the doctor embarks on a form of treatment which is still comparatively untried, with techniques and safeguards which are still in the course of development, then "if the decision to embark on the treatment at all was justifiable and was taken with the informed consent of the patient, the court should . . . be particularly careful not to impute negligence simply because something has gone wrong."[3] This leaves open the question of just how "informed" the patient should be, although, it may possibly be inferred that his Lordship contemplated a greater degree of disclosure than would be applied to the ordinary patient under *Sidaway*. It has been argued that *Sidaway* should not apply to therapeutic research because the reliance on what a responsible body of professional opinion would disclose is not relevant to the question of research, since the need for research is based on public policy, not professional opinion. What should be disclosed ought, therefore, to be a matter for the courts.[4] It could be said in reply that the patient's need for treatment is the consequence of his medical condition and any question of the potential benefits of research to the public is incidental.[5] Thus, the court could take the view that the risks entailed in the "research aspect" of the therapy have to be weighed in the balance by the doctor in deciding what information to give to the patient, just as with any other treatment, and accordingly that this is part and parcel of the doctor's clinical judgment, to which *Sidaway* should apply.

6.110 Moreover, the Court of Appeal has said that a distinction between advice given in a therapeutic and a non-therapeutic context was "elusive" and "wholly unwarranted and artificial."[6] This suggests that the test of negligence in any situation requiring the exercise of specialist skill, whether that of a doctor or a researcher, is the *Bolam* test and that therefore the standard of information disclosure is to be

---

[2] [1985] 1 All E.R. 643.

[3] [1986] 3 All E.R. 801, 812, emphasis added. In *R.* v. *Mental Health Commission, ex parte W., The Times*, May 27, 1988, D.C. Stuart-Smith L.J. said that "No doubt the consent has to be an informed consent in that he knows the nature and likely effect of the treatment. There can be no doubt that the applicant knew this. So too in this case, where the treatment was not routinely used for control of sexual urges and was not sold for this purpose, it was important that the applicant should realise that the use on him was a novel one and the full implications with use on young men had not been studied, since trials had only been involved with animals and older men."

[4] Kennedy and Grubb, *Medical Law Text and Materials*, 1989, p. 876. See also at p. 877, where it is suggested that in addition to the information necessary for the purpose of avoiding liability in battery a doctor would be required, in law, to disclose: (i) material risks; and (ii) material information necessary to enable the patient to make an "informed decision," *e.g.* any inconvenience associated with the fact that the patient is a research subject, such as additional hospital visits, additional tests, etc.

[5] The argument that a patient should not be informed that he is part of a research study because this would necessarily involve telling him other things about his condition which it would be better for him that he did not know is clearly without substance. If it is in the patient's interests not to be informed about his medical condition then this is an argument for excluding him from the study, not failing to inform him about it: see Kennedy, *Treat Me Right*, 1988, O.U.P., p. 223.

[6] *Gold* v. *Haringey Health Authority* [1987] 2 All E.R. 888; see § 6.91.

assessed by reference to what a reasonable doctor/researcher would have disclosed in the circumstances. Although the case was specifically concerned with the question of contraceptive advice, its implications may stretch to the question of research and, indeed, possibly to non-therapeutic research.

On the other hand, even if *Sidaway* were to be applied to cases of **6.111** therapeutic research, it could be argued that a failure to inform the patient that he was part of a research project is a matter that so obviously should have been disclosed that no reasonable doctor would fail to disclose it, applying Lord Bridge's dictum.[7] Alternatively, it might be said that the measure of what is responsible professional opinion should be determined not by the expert evidence of what in fact happens, but by the requirements of an ethical code, such as the Declaration of Helsinki. The Declaration states that a research subject "must be adequately informed of the aims, methods, anticipated benefits and potential hazards of the study and the discomfort it may entail." He should be informed that he is free to refuse to participate or to withdraw from participation at any time, and he should then give a free, informed consent, preferably in writing.[8]

The Canadian approach to this problem may be instructive. In **6.112** *Zimmer* v. *Ringrose*[9] the plaintiff was subjected to a novel and "experimental" method of sterilisation. At first instance the defendant was held liable because he had failed to inform the plaintiff that the technique had not been generally accepted by the medical profession, and had not informed her of the failure rate of up to 30 per cent. MacDonald J. applied *Halushka* v. *University of Saskatchewan*,[10] a case which was concerned with non-therapeutic research, holding the defendant liable in battery. The Alberta Court of Appeal reversed this decision, taking the view that the standard of disclosure required in *Halushka* was limited to non-therapeutic research:

"In the case of a truly 'experimental' procedure, like the one conducted in *Halushka* v. *University of Saskatchewan*, no therapeutic benefit is intended to accrue to the participant. The subject is simply part of a scientific investigation designed to enhance human knowledge. By contrast, the sterilization procedure performed by the appellant in this case was directed towards achieving a therapeutic end . . . [T]he silver nitrate method was experimental only in the sense that it represented an innovation in sterilisation techniques which were relatively untried . . . To hold that every new development in medical technology was 'experimental' in the sense outlined in *Halushka*

---

[7] [1985] 1 All E.R. 643, 663; see §§ 6.75 and 6.78.
[8] Para. I(9). However, this is qualified under para. II(5) (applying to therapeutic research) which provides that if the doctor considers it essential not to obtain informed consent, the specific reasons should be stated in the research protocol for consideration by a research ethics committee.
[9] (1978) 89 D.L.R. (3d) 646 (Alta. S.C.).
[10] (1965) 53 D.L.R. (2d) 436.

v. *University of Saskatchewan* would be to discourage advances in the field of medicine."[11]

6.113 Nonetheless, the defendant was found to have been negligent in failing to discuss alternative methods of sterilisation because the plaintiff was given no opportunity to measure the risks involved in the silver nitrate method against those involved in other forms of sterilisation. A reasonable practitioner would also have informed the plaintiff that the technique had not been approved by the medical profession, since he would realise that this information would be likely to influence the patient's decision whether to undergo the procedure.[12] Similarly, in *Coughlin* v. *Kuntz*[13] the defendant was held liable for failing to disclose that the contemplated operation was novel, unique to the defendant, and under investigation by a professional body, and for failing to inform the plaintiff that other medical experts had specifically advised against neck surgery.

6.114 The lawfulness of medical treatment given to adults who lack the capacity to give a valid consent depends upon the principle of necessity. This is measured by the patient's "best interests," and a medical procedure will be in the patient's best interests "if, but only if, it is carried out in order either to save their lives or to ensure improvement or prevent deterioration in their physical or mental health."[14] Given that the major premise of the decision in *F.* v. *West Berkshire Health Authority* was that incompetent patients should not be deprived of treatment that would be available to a competent adult, the courts would probably take the view that therapeutic research on incompetent adults can be justified if the treatment is in the patient's best interests. The *Bolam*[15] test will be applied to determine the patient's best interests: if a responsible body of professional opinion considers that the procedure was in the patient's best interests, it is irrelevant that others believed that the patient should not have been included in the research project.

6.115 Therapeutic research on children who lack the relevant capacity will be lawful where parental consent has been obtained, provided the procedure can be said to be in the child's best interests. To the extent that doctors have a duty to disclose additional information to competent patients when the treatment forms part of a research project, the parents would be entitled to a comparable degree of disclosure.

---

[11] (1981) 124 D.L.R. 215, 222–223, *per* Prowse J.A. See also *Cryderman* v. *Ringrose* [1977] 3 W.W.R. 109; aff'd [1978] 3 W.W.R. 481 (Alta. C.A.), in which the plaintiff agreed to be sterilised by the same defendant by the same experimental procedure. The plaintiff was not informed that the procedure was unreliable or that it might damage the uterus. The trial judge distinguished *Halushka* v. *University of Saskatchewan* (1965) 53 D.L.R. (2d) 436 on the basis that that was a case of "pure medical experimentation," where different considerations would apply.

[12] "When an experimental procedure is employed the common law requires a high degree of care and also disclosure to the patient of the fact that the treatment is new and risky," *per* Stevenson D.C.J. in *Cryderman* v. *Ringrose* [1977] 3 W.W.R. 109, 118. The claim for non-disclosure in *Zimmer* v. *Ringrose* failed on the ground that the plaintiff would have accepted the treatment in any event, although the action succeeded in respect of negligent after-care.

[13] (1987) 42 C.C.L.T. 142 (B.C.S.C.); aff'd [1990] 2 W.W.R. 737, 745 (B.C.C.A.).

[14] *F.* v. *West Berkshire Health Authority* [1989] 2 All E.R. 545, 551, *per* Lord Brandon; see § 6.53.

[15] *Bolam* v. *Friern Hospital Management Committee* [1957] 2 All E.R. 118.

Certain forms of research give rise to problems in the case of **6.116**
incompetent patients. In a randomised controlled trial, some patients
may well receive a treatment which the doctor does not believe to be
in their best interests medically. The consent of a competent patient to
participate may be taken to waive the doctor's duty to act in the
patient's best interests, but it is a matter of some doubt whether such a
waiver can ever apply where the patient is incapable of consenting.[16]

Non-therapeutic research

As with therapeutic research, the three central issues are the **6.117**
competence of the research subject to give a valid consent, the
voluntariness of the consent, and the appropriate level of information
disclosure. In the case of adults competence will be treated as a
question of fact, namely whether the subject understands the nature of
the procedure to which he is consenting. Children of 16 or 17 years
would not be presumed to be competent by virtue of section 8(1) of
the Family Law Reform Act 1969, since that section applies only to
"surgical, medical or dental *treatment*,"[17] but presumably *Gillick* v.
West Norfolk and Wisbech Area Health Authority[18] would apply to
determine the competence of children to consent to non-therapeutic
research. Possibly a higher degree of understanding would be required
from a child than in the case of medical treatment,[19] and the greater
the potential risk the greater the understanding that will be required.
The voluntary nature of the consent will also be treated as a question
of fact.[20]

The argument that the research subject should be fully informed is **6.118**
clearly much stronger in the case of non-therapeutic research. Withholding information about potential risks cannot be justified by reference to the research subject's medical condition or "best interests,"[21]
and so it is arguable that non-therapeutic research subjects should be
given full and complete information about the nature of the research
and the inherent risks. In *Halushka* v. *University of Saskatchewan*[22] the
plaintiff was a student who volunteered, for a fee, to undergo an
experimental test on a new anaesthetic. He was told that it was a safe
test which had been conducted many times before and that there was
nothing to worry about. This was untrue, since the anaesthetic had not

---

[16] See Kennedy, *Treat Me Right*, 1988, O.U.P., Chap. 10 for extended discussion of
the law on randomised controlled trials.

[17] See § 6.30, n. 86.

[18] [1985] 3 All E.R. 402.

[19] *cf.* the high level of understanding stipulated by Lord Scarman in *Gillick* v. *West
Norfolk and Wisbech Area Health Authority* [1985] 3 All E.R. 402, 424 before a child
under 16 could be said to have sufficient capacity to consent to contraceptive advice or
treatment: § 6.33.

[20] Where large financial inducements are provided to students or the unemployed this
may raise a question mark about the voluntariness of the consent: see, *e.g.*, *The
Observer*, October 2, 1988, and *The Times*, October 6, 1986. In 1984 2 student
volunteers in drug trials died in separate incidents: *The Times*, May 30, 1984, June 11,
1984, and April 25, 1985.

[21] It has been suggested, however, that "informed consent" may bias the results of a
clinical trial: Dahan *et al.* (1986) 293 B.M.J. 363; for criticism of this study see Launer
(1986) 293 B.M.J. 627–628.

[22] (1965) 53 D.L.R. (2d) 436 (Sask. C.A.).

previously been used or tested by the defendants. The plaintiff was not told that all anaesthetic agents involve a certain degree of risk, nor was he told that a catheter, which he knew would be inserted into a vein in his arm, would be advanced into his heart. The plaintiff suffered cardiac arrest, caused by the anaesthetic, and was unconscious for four days. The defendants were held liable in trespass to the person on the basis of a lack of consent, a finding upheld by the Saskatchewan Court of Appeal. Hall J.A. said that:

> "There can be no exceptions to the ordinary requirements of disclosure in the case of research as there may well be in ordinary medical practice. The researcher does not have to balance the probable effect of lack of treatment against the risk involved in the treatment itself. The example of risks being properly hidden from a patient when it is important that he should not worry can have no application in the field of research. The subject of medical experimentation is entitled to a full and frank disclosure of all the facts, probabilities and opinions which a reasonable man might be expected to consider before giving his consent."[23]

This statement specifies an objective test for disclosure, based upon the information that a "reasonable volunteer" would want to have. Arguably, in the case of non-therapeutic research the test should be subjective (what *this* volunteer would want to know) for the very reasons that Hall J.A. gives.

6.119   It is not clear whether a lack of information about risks, as opposed to the "nature" of the research procedure, would be treated in this country as relating to the researcher's duty of care in negligence rather than battery. It will be recalled that in *Gold* v. *Haringey Health Authority*[24] the Court of Appeal refused to draw a distinction between advice given in a therapeutic and a non-therapeutic context. The *Bolam* test did not, it was said, depend on the context in which advice was given, but on a man professing skill or competence in a field beyond that possessed by the man on the Clapham omnibus. Lloyd L.J. said that the *Bolam* test was not confined to a defendant exercising or professing the particular skill of medicine, and there was no basis for distinguishing between doctors and any other profession or calling requiring special skill, knowledge or experience. On this view, a research subject would only be entitled to be informed about the risks that a reasonably competent researcher would disclose. It is submitted that such an approach should be rejected and that the reasoning in *Gold* should not be extended to non-therapeutic research. The healthy volunteer has an ethical claim to full information about the anticipated risks of the procedure, and this should be reflected in the law.

6.120   Even where a volunteer is fully informed about the risks involved in an experimental procedure there may well be some limits to the risks

---

[23] *Ibid.*, p. 443.
[24] [1987] 2 All E.R. 888, 894, *per* Lloyd L.J., § 6.91.

which he can agree to accept, such that if the risks are too great an apparently valid consent might be ineffective.[25]

Where a potential research subject lacks the capacity to give a valid **6.121** consent the question arises whether it can ever be lawful for non-therapeutic research to be performed. By definition the research is not in the interests (whether these are categorised as "best interests" or merely "interests") of the research subject, and will normally carry some, albeit remote, risk of harm. On what legal basis could a proxy, whether it be a parent, the court or a doctor "authorise" a procedure that carried risk to the subject but was not intended to have any direct benefit for that person? In *F. v. West Berkshire Health Authority*[26] the House of Lords adopted a wide interpretation of the principle of necessity so as to facilitate the provision of medical treatment to permanently incapacitated adults. The rationale was that adults lacking the capacity to consent should not be in a worse position than competent adults, and should not be deprived of treatment that would be available to them if they were in a position to consent, provided that the treatment could be shown to be in their best interests. The same logic, that they should not be in a worse position than competent adults, would suggest that it would never be lawful to subject an incompetent adult to non-therapeutic research which carried any risk of harm, because otherwise the individual lacking capacity clearly is placed in a worse position than the competent adult who has the right and ability to refuse to participate. Moreover, their Lordships made it clear in *F. v. West Berkshire Health Authority* that the justification for providing treatment did not rest upon a proxy "consent" (which might give the proxy a limited power of choice or discretion) but on the principle of necessity, with the question of "necessity" to be determined, not by the needs of some other person or society in general, but by the best interests of the patient.

A similar problem arises in the case of non-therapeutic research on **6.122** children. How can a parent or indeed the court give a valid consent for research which by definition is not in the interests of the child, and may expose him to some risk, however small. The power of parents to exercise consent to medical treatment exists to protect the interests of children and must be exercised in their "best interests."[27] The view that non-therapeutic research on children is unlawful has been widely held by, *inter alia*, the Medical Research Council, the Medical Defence Union and the Medical Protection Society.[28] In more recent years, however, attitudes seem to have shifted and it has been argued that non-therapeutic research on children would be lawful in certain limited circumstances.[29] It remains to be seen how a court would respond to this question.

---

[25] *cf. Attorney-General's Reference* (No. 6 of 1980) [1981] Q.B. 715, that public policy may dictate that a consent is not valid in law, *e.g.*, in the course of a prize fight. The report of an Institute of Medical Ethics working group recommended that non-therapeutic research procedures on children should not be carried out if they involve "greater than minimal risk": Nicholson, *Medical Research with Children*, 1986, O.U.P., p. 233. For discussion of the problems involved in quantifying acceptable levels of risk in the conduct of research see *ibid.*, Chap. 5.

[26] [1989] 2 All E.R. 545, §§ 6.52–6.53.

[27] *Gillick* v. *West Norfolk and Wisbech Area Health Authority* [1985] 3 All E.R. 402, § 6.35. The same test is applied to the courts' exercise of the wardship jurisdiction: § 6.38.

[28] See Dworkin (1978) 53 Arch. Disease in Childhood 443.

[29] Dworkin, *op cit.*; Dworkin (1987) 13 Monash Univ. L.R. 189. For an extended discussion of this problem see Nicholson, *Medical Research with Children*, 1986, O.U.P.

Embryo research

6.123   The Human Fertilisation and Embryology Act 1990, s. 11, provides for the regulation of research on human embryos by a statutory Licensing Authority which may grant licences for the purpose of approved research projects. There are restrictions on the type and purpose of research that may be conducted.[30] Under section 12 one of the conditions for the grant of a licence is that the provisions of Schedule 3 concerning consent must be complied with. The consent required is the consent of each person whose gametes are used for the creation of an *in vitro* embryo, and the consent must specify the purpose for which the embryo may be used, namely treatment services or for the purposes of a project of research.[31] Consent is also required for the storage of gametes or embryos, but in any event embryos may not be stored for more than five years and gametes may not be stored for more than 10 years.[32] The consent must be in writing and may be varied or withdrawn, but not after the embryo has been used in research.[33] Before a person gives consent he must be given an opportunity to receive proper counselling about the implications and he must be "provided with such information as is proper," including his right to vary or withdraw consent.[34]

6.124   The Act does not confer any civil remedy for breach of the provisions concerning consent, although failure to comply with the consent requirements would be a breach of the licence conditions stipulated by section 12 and thus would be in contravention of section 3(1), constituting a criminal offence.[35] It might possibly be argued that a breach of the consent requirements should give rise to a tort of breach of statutory duty, although it could be replied that if Parliament had intended to grant a civil remedy for breach of the Act it could easily have made express provision to this effect.[36] Alternatively, it might be possible to argue that an action for nervous shock should be available, if, for example, a person's gametes or embryos were used for research purposes without his or her consent.[37] However, this is highly speculative, and would depend, *inter alia*, upon proving that the plaintiff had suffered from a genuine psychiatric illness as a consequence, not simply emotional distress or grief.

2. Transplantation

6.125   The live donation of organs must be limited to regenerative tissue such as blood or bone marrow, or paired organs such as kidneys,

---

[30] Human Fertilisation and Embryology Act 1990, s.3 and Sched. 2, para. 3.

[31] *Ibid.*, Sched. 3, para. 6.

[32] *Ibid.*, Sched. 3, para. 8, and s.14.

[33] *Ibid.*, Sched. 3, paras. 1, 4.

[34] *Ibid.*, Sched. 3, para. 3.

[35] *Ibid.*, s.41(2). It is a defence for the person charged to prove that he took all reasonable steps and exercised all due diligence to avoid committing the offence.

[36] For discussion of the problems surrounding the inference of the tort when Parliament has not expressly dealt with the matter see Stanton, *Breach of Statutory Duty*, 1986, Chap. 3.

[37] On nervous shock generally, see §§ 2.44–2.54.

where it is known that the donor can survive with a single organ. A donor could not give valid consent to the removal of an organ that would result in his death or serious disability.[38] The recipient of an organ transplant will be in the same position as any other patient receiving treatment with regard to consent and information disclosure, bearing in mind the degree of risk associated with the particular form of transplantation. It is arguable, however, that a much stricter standard of information disclosure is required for the donor of the organ. His position is analogous to that of a volunteer for non-therapeutic research, since the operation is of no medical benefit to the donor, and carries the risk of harm to his health. On this basis, it is submitted that there should be a full and frank disclosure of risks.[39]

This view has some statutory support in regulations made under the **6.126** Human Organ Transplants Act 1989. Under section 1, commercial dealings in human organs for transplantation are prohibited.[40] Section 2(1) prohibits the removal from a living person of an organ intended to be transplanted into another person, or the transplantation of an organ removed from a living person into another person, unless the donor is genetically related to the donee,[41] or the procedure satisfies the requirements of regulations made by the Secretary of State.[42] The Human Organ Transplants (Unrelated Persons) Regulations 1989[43] create an "Unrelated Live Transplant Regulatory Authority." The Regulations provide that section 2(1) of the Act shall not apply where the doctor who has clinical responsibility for the donor has referred the matter to the Authority and the Authority is satisfied that no payment has been made or is to be made in contravention of section 1, and (except where the primary purpose of removal of an organ from a donor is the medical treatment of that donor) that the following conditions are satisfied.

(a) The doctor has given the donor an explanation of the nature of the medical procedure for, and the risk involved in, the removal of the organ.

(b) The donor understands the nature of the medical procedure and the risks, and consents to the removal of the organ.

(c) The donor's consent was not obtained by coercion or the offer of an inducement.

(d) The donor understands that he is entitled to withdraw his consent, but has not done so.

---

[38] *Attorney-General's Reference* (No. 6 of 1980) [1981] Q.B. 715; see generally Dworkin (1970) 33 M.L.R. 353.

[39] See Norrie (1985) 34 I.C.L.Q. 442, 452. If the doctor's negligence is the cause of the need for the transplantation he may be liable to the donor for the consequences of the donation: *Urbanski* v. *Patel* (1978) 84 D.L.R. (3d) 650 (Man. Q.B.), § 2.42.

[40] "Organ" means any part of a human body consisting of a structured arrangement of tissues which, if wholly removed, cannot be replicated by the body: s.7(2). Thus, blood products and bone marrow, which do replicate, are not within the Act.

[41] "Genetically related" is defined in s.2(2). For the tests to be used to establish genetic relationship see the Human Organ Transplants (Establishment of Relationship) Regulation 1989 (S.I. 1989/2107).

[42] Human Organ Transplants Act 1989, s.2(3).

[43] S.I. 1989/2480. On the obligation of those conducting transplants of the heart, lung, pancreas, liver, or kidneys, to supply certain information to the South Western Regional Health Authority and the District Health Authority see the Human Organ Transplants (Supply of Information) Regulations 1989 (S.I. 1989/2108).

(e) The donor and recipient have been interviewed by a suitably qualified person, who has reported to the Authority on the conditions (a) to (d), and has included an account of any difficulties of communication with the donor or the recipient and an explanation of how the difficulties were overcome.

6.127 These statutory requirements for disclosure of the risks involved in transplantation apply only to non-related live donations, but it is submitted that a similar level of disclosure would be required at common law for all live organ donors.

6.128 The position of donors who are incapable of giving a valid consent is unclear. It would appear to be analogous to non-therapeutic research on children and incompetent adults. From one point of view, this would mean that organs can never be taken from such donors, since donation clearly creates risk to the donor, especially where it involves surgical intervention, and a parent cannot consent to procedures which are contrary to the interests of the child.[44] Some American courts have adopted an extended interpretation of an incompetent donor's "best interests" to include the psychological benefits that would accrue to the donor in order to justify donation between siblings.[45] Nine Canadian provinces have enacted legislation based on the Uniform Tissue Gift Act, which prohibits minors and mentally incompetent adults from making live donations of non-regenerative tissue.[46] Donation of regenerative tissue such as blood, bone marrow, or skin by minors is left to the common law, but there are no cases on the subject.

6.129 Similarly, there are no English cases on this issue, although in *Re F. (mental patient: sterilisation)* Neill L.J. did touch upon the point:

> "There are, however, some operations where the intervention of a court is most desirable if not essential. In this category I would place operations for sterilisation and organ transplant operations where the incapacitated patient is to be the donor. The performance of these operations should be subject to outside scrutiny. The lawfulness of the operation will depend of course on the question of whether it is necessary or not, but in my view it should become standard practice for the approval of the court to be obtained before an operation of this exceptional kind is carried out."[47]

His Lordship clearly contemplates that organ donation from incompetent donors could be lawful, subject to the supervision of the court,[48] depending upon whether it was "necessary or not." This rather begs the question, however, since the operation may well be necessary from

---

[44] See §§ 6.35 and 6.40; Norrie (1985) 34 I.C.L.Q. 442, 453.

[45] *Strunk* v. *Strunk* (1969) 445 S.W. 2d 145 (Kentucky App.); *Hart* v. *Brown* (1972) 289 A. 2d 386 (Conn.); *Little* v. *Little* (1979) 576 S.W. 2d 493 (Texas C.A.); Dickens (1981) 97 L.Q.R. 462, 476–477; *cf. Re Richardson* (1973) 284 So. 2d 388 (Louisiana C.A.); *Re Pescinski* (1975) 226 N.E. 2d 180 (Wisconsin S.C.); see Robertson (1976) 76 Columbia Law Rev. 48 discussing the principle of "substituted judgment" under which the decision-maker attempts to make the judgment about donation on behalf of the incompetent donor which the donor would have made if competent.

[46] Picard, *Legal Liability of Doctors and Hospitals in Canada*, 2nd ed., 1984, pp. 125–132.

[47] [1989] 2 W.L.R. 1025, 1053.

[48] A view which had been taken in *Hart* v. *Brown* (1972) 289 A. 2d 386, 391.

the recipient's point of view, but it might be extremely difficult to claim that it was *necessary* for the incompetent donor's welfare that he should give up one of his organs.

Cadaver donations are governed by the Human Tissue Act 1961, **6.130** which provides that authorisation for removal of organs for transplantation purposes may be given by the person "lawfully in possession" of the body in certain circumstances. There is considerable doubt as to whether there is any sanction for non-compliance with the requirements of the Act. In particular it is a matter of conjecture whether the unauthorised removal of tissue from a corpse would give rise to an action in tort by the relatives of the deceased person.[49]

3. Omission to warn about risk of sterilisation failing

It is widely accepted within the medical profession that there is a risk **6.131** that a sterilisation operation will fail to render the patient sterile. The risk varies with the type of operation and the time at which it is carried out.[50] The fact that sterilisation procedures carry a small, but quantifiable, failure rate can make it difficult to prove that there has been negligence in the performance of the operation itself. This has led to a number of cases in which plaintiffs have alleged that the surgeon was negligent in failing to inform them about the risks, although, with rare exceptions, these actions have been spectacularly unsuccessful. The early cases appear to have been pleaded solely in negligence, relying on the *Bolam* test, with the result that, if a responsible body of medical opinion would not have advised the plaintiff of the risk that the operation might not succeed in its objective, the action failed.[51]

There have been several attempts by plaintiffs to circumvent this **6.132** problem. In *Eyre* v. *Measday*[52] the defendant had emphasised that a sterilisation operation was irreversible, but he did not inform the plaintiff that there was a less than one per cent. risk of pregnancy occurring following such a procedure. The plaintiff claimed that the defendant was in breach of a contractual term that she would be rendered irreversibly sterile, and/or a collateral warranty to that effect which induced her to enter the contract. It was held that the contract was to perform a sterilisation operation, it was not a contract to render the plaintiff sterile, and there was neither an express nor an implied warranty that the procedure would be an unqualified success. In *Thake* v. *Maurice*[53] the Court of Appeal reached a similar conclusion that, on

---

[49] See Kennedy, *Treat Me Right*, 1988, O.U.P., Chap. 11, arguing that an action for nervous shock might be held to lie; and Norrie (1985) 34 I.C.L.Q. 442, 463–464 identifying Scottish cases which raised the possibility of claims for nervous shock following unauthorised post-mortems, and thus, by analogy, following unauthorised removal of organs for transplantation.

[50] See, *e.g.*, *Eyre* v. *Measday* [1986] 1 All E.R. 488, 490–491; *Gold* v. *Haringey Health Authority* [1987] 2 All E.R. 888, 890; *Videto* v. *Kennedy* (1980) 125 D.L.R. (3d) 612, 618 (Ont. H.C.).

[51] *Waters* v. *Park*, *The Times*, July 15, 1961; *Williams* v. *St. Helens and District Hospital Management Committee* (1977) (unreported), Q.B.D., where the defendant's omission to warn of a risk of failure of 1 in 300 was held to be not negligent where the evidence was that some gynaecologists gave a warning while others did not.

[52] [1986] 1 All E.R. 488; see § 2.07.

[53] [1986] 1 All E.R. 497; see § 2.08.

an objective interpretation, the defendant had not given a contractual guarantee that a vasectomy operation would render the male plaintiff irreversibly sterile, relying on the observation that medicine is not an exact science and results are to some extent unpredictable. The contractual approach is not entirely ruled out by these decisions; it is simply that it will be extremely difficult to prove that the defendant did in fact guarantee to achieve complete sterility.[54]

6.133 The defendant was, nonetheless, held liable for negligence in *Thake* v. *Maurice*. He had failed to give his usual warning that there was a slight risk that the male plaintiff might become fertile again. There was no independent evidence called by either party as to the general practice of the profession with regard to warnings at the time of the operation in 1975. The Court of Appeal held that in these circumstances the plaintiffs were entitled to rely on the defendant's own evidence (which was that he considered a warning to be necessary) as indicative of the appropriate standard of care, and that accordingly the defendant was negligent by inadvertently failing to give his usual warning.[55]

6.134 Where the plaintiff has not had the operation performed privately, the contractual guarantee argument is clearly not available. In *Worster* v. *City and Hackney Health Authority*[56] the plaintiff argued that, having signed a consent form which included the words " . . . and we understand that this means we can have no more children," the surgeon was liable for a negligent misrepresentation under the principle of *Hedley Byrne & Co. Ltd.* v. *Heller & Partners Ltd.*[57] It was suggested that the fact that the defendant did not inform her of the risk of the operation failing, combined with the wording of the consent form, constituted a representation that sterilisation was certain. Garland J. rejected this contention. *Hedley Byrne* did not avail the plaintiff since that case was concerned with establishing that a duty of care existed when giving gratuitous advice. Once the duty is established, the nature of the duty is governed by the *Bolam* test, and applying that test the action failed.[58]

6.135 The third attempt to avoid the implications of the *Bolam* test occurred in *Gold* v. *Haringey Health Authority*.[59] The plaintiff underwent a sterilisation operation the day after the birth of her third child which failed to render her sterile, and she subsequently had a fourth child. She alleged that the defendants were negligent in failing to warn her of the risks of failure. The evidence was that the failure rate for female sterilisation was in the range of 20 to 60 per 10,000, with

---

[54] In *Thake* v. *Maurice* both Pain J. and Kerr L.J. took the view that the plaintiff had established this on the evidence (see [1984] 2 All E.R. 513, 519–520 and [1986] 1 All E.R. 497, 503–506). Neill and Nourse L.JJ. came to a different conclusion.

[55] Presumably, if there had been some evidence that responsible practitioners did not give a warning, the defendant would have escaped liability, notwithstanding that he had inadvertently failed to follow his own usual practice and that he regarded a warning as necessary.

[56] *The Times*, June 22, 1987.

[57] [1964] A.C. 465.

[58] A claim for negligent misrepresentation was also rejected by the Court of Appeal in *Gold* v. *Haringey Health Authority* [1987] 2 All E.R. 888, 896. The plaintiff was not entitled to rely on the word "irreversible" as a representation that the operation would succeed, applying *Eyre* v. *Measday* [1986] 1 All E.R. 488.

[59] [1987] 2 All E.R. 888.

operations carried out post-partum at the higher end of the range. The failure rate for vasectomy was five per 10,000. The trial judge, Schiemann J., found that the defendants did not explain the risk of the operation failing to render the plaintiff sterile, and did not counsel her and her husband about the possibility of vasectomy, or explain the relative failure rates of the two operations. The medical experts were unanimous that although they themselves would have warned of the risk of failure, nonetheless a substantial body of responsible doctors would not have given any such warning in 1979. Thus, applying the *Bolam* test the plaintiff's action would fail. Schiemann J. drew a distinction, however, between advice given in a therapeutic context and advice given in a contraceptive context. In a therapeutic context there was a body of responsible medical opinion which would not have given a warning, but in a contraceptive context there was no such body of medical opinion. Moreover, even if there had been such a body of opinion, the defendants were still negligent because the *Bolam* test did not apply to advice given in a non-therapeutic context.

This decision was reversed by the Court of Appeal. Lloyd L.J. was **6.136** unconvinced by the distinction between therapeutic and non-therapeutic advice, finding it "elusive." The distinction between advice given in a therapeutic context and advice given in a non-therapeutic context was rejected as a departure from the *Bolam* test.[60] Accordingly, the defendant was not liable because there was a responsible body of medical opinion which would not have given any warning in 1979. *Gold* v. *Haringey Health Authority* would seem to bring all cases involving failure to warn about the risks of an operative procedure not succeeding within the *Bolam* test.

The decision in *Gold* may be contrasted with *Dendaas* v. *Yackel*[61] **6.137** where the defendant was held negligent for failing to discuss the relative failure rates of two different methods of female sterilisation (tubal ligation and the "abdominal method"). Bouck J. said that: "An average, prudent or reasonable woman who wished to be assured of sterility would probably have elected to follow the abdominal technique rather than the tubal ligation procedure since fear of future pregnancy was the overriding and dominant factor in such a choice."[62] The Supreme Court of South Australia distinguished *Dendaas* v. *Yackel* in *F.* v. *R.*[63] on the basis that in that case there were two medically acceptable sterilisation procedures available, each having some risk of failure. In *F.* v. *R.* the only operations having a lower failure rate were medically unacceptable merely for sterilisation purposes. The plaintiff's husband had asked specifically about the desirability of his having a vasectomy, and the defendant had said that there was no sense in him being operated on when his wife was being

---

[60] *Ibid.*, p. 894, *per* Lloyd L.J. (see the quotation at § 6.91). His Lordship continued: "The fact (if it be the fact) that giving contraceptive advice involves a different sort of skill and competence from carrying out a surgical operation does not mean that the *Bolam* test ceases to be applicable. . . . To dissect a doctor's advice into that given in a therapeutic context and that given in a contraceptive context would be to go against the whole thrust of the decision of the majority of the House of Lords in [*Sidaway*]."

[61] (1980) 109 D.L.R. (3d) 455 (B.C.S.C.).

[62] *Ibid.*, p. 462. The medical evidence of the failure rate for tubal ligation varied between 3 in 1,000 and 17 per 1,000.

[63] (1983) 33 S.A.S.R. 189.

sterilised, since the tubal ligation would be performed at same time as a Caesarian section. It was held that the non-disclosure of an overall failure rate for tubal ligation between a half a per cent. and one per cent. did not amount to negligence, particularly since in the defendant's hands the odds against failure were very much longer. The statistical risk referred to all tubal ligations wherever done and whatever the circumstances. The defendant was experienced and competent. She was entitled to expect that the operation done by her in a modern hospital would be successful. On the other hand, had there been an alternative procedure with even less chance of failure, the defendant would have been under a duty to offer more information, including the statistical rate of failure of the alternative procedure.[64]

6.138   Even if the plaintiff succeeds in proving that the defendant was negligent in failing to disclose the risk that the operation would not produce sterility, the plaintiff must still establish causation. Most patients who consider sterilisation for contraceptive purposes would probably undergo the operation even if informed about the remote risk of the procedure failing to achieve sterility, and it would be highly unlikely that they would continue with other contraceptive methods "just in case" the sterilisation had failed.[65] In *Gold* v. *Haringey Health Authority*[66] the point was that if the comparative failure rates had been discussed the male plaintiff would have had a vasectomy, and thus there would have been no difficulty in showing that the plaintiff would not have proceeded with the operation. In *Thake* v. *Maurice*,[67] on the other hand, the argument was not that if the plaintiffs had known of the risk of recanalisation the male plaintiff would not have had the vasectomy operation, since the failure rate was lower than for female sterilisation. Rather, it was that if they had realised that this was a possibility, the female plaintiff would have appreciated that she was pregnant earlier in the pregnancy than in fact she did and would have had an abortion at an early stage. The defendant's claim that this risk was unforeseeable and therefore too remote was rejected by the Court of Appeal.

6.139   Nonetheless, causation will remain a problem in most cases of failure to warn about the risk of the sterilisation not being effective,[68] unless the plaintiff can point to a medically acceptable alternative procedure which carried a lower failure rate,[69] or is in a position to

---

[64] *Ibid.*, p. 207, *per* Bollen J.

[65] *Grey* v. *Webster* (1984) 14 D.L.R. (4th) 706, 715 (N.B.Q.B).

[66] [1987] 2 All E.R. 888.

[67] [1986] 1 All E.R. 497.

[68] See, *e.g.*, *Zimmer* v. *Ringrose* (1981) 124 D.L.R. (3d) 215 (Alta. C.A.), where despite the fact that the defendant was held negligent in failing to disclose that his method of sterilisation was experimental, and had not been approved by the profession, the action for non-disclosure failed because a reasonable patient in the plaintiff's position would have accepted the treatment. The decisive factor in her case was that she wanted to avoid having to go into hospital to be sterilised when she had a young baby at home to look after.

[69] In *Grey* v. *Webster* (1984) 14 D.L.R. (4th) 706 (N.B.Q.B.) the plaintiff said that if she had known about the failure rate for tubal ligation she would have undergone a hysterectomy to ensure sterility. The medical evidence, however, indicated that hysterectomy was not a medically acceptable procedure merely for sterilisation purposes, and the action failed on causation.

adopt the argument in *Thake* v. *Maurice* that because she was not informed about the remote risk that the sterilisation might be ineffective she did not realise that she might be pregnant until it was too late safely to have an abortion. Where, on the other hand, the defendant knows that the sterilisation procedure has failed to render the plaintiff sterile, but fails to inform the plaintiff of that fact to give her the opportunity to take alternative contraceptive measures, there will be no difficulty in establishing both negligence and causation.[70]

---

[70] *Cryderman* v. *Ringrose* [1977] 3 W.W.R. 109; aff'd [1978] 3 W.W.R. 481 (Alta. C.A.). Note that where the sterilisation operation itself has been performed negligently (see § 4.68), there will be no difficulty in proving causation. The plaintiff's refusal to undergo an abortion when she discovers that she is pregnant does not amount to a *novus actus interveniens*: see *Emeh* v. *Kensington and Chelsea Area Health Authority* [1984] 3 All E.R. 1044, § 5.60.

CHAPTER 7

LIABILITY OF HOSPITALS AND CONTRIBUTION

7.01 In theory there are two grounds upon which a hospital authority may be held responsible for injury to patients. The first, and by far the most common, is by virtue of an employer's vicarious liability for the torts of an employee committed during the course of employment. Although in the past hospital authorities had an effective immunity from liability for the negligence of professional staff, for over 40 years now hospitals have been in the same position as other employers with respect to vicarious liability. The only lingering uncertainty concerns precisely which staff are considered to be employees. The second, and in some respects more speculative, ground is the concept of direct liability, by which a hospital is held liable not for the tort of an employee but for breach of its own duty owed directly to the patient. This may be the result of some organisational error, where, for example, there is an inadequate system for co-ordinating the work of staff which has put patients at risk. Alternatively, it may be that a hospital owes a primary, non-delegable duty to patients. Breach of such a duty renders the hospital liable to the patient whether it is occasioned by the conduct of an employee or of someone who is not an employee, such as an independent contractor. Thus, there can be some overlap between vicarious liability and a non-delegable duty. These two forms of liability are conceptually quite distinct, though in reality the purpose of imposing a non-delegable duty is simply to establish the responsibility of an "employer" for the negligence of independent contractors.

This chapter considers both the vicarious liability of a hospital authority and its potential direct liability to patients. It concludes with a brief section on contribution between tortfeasors.

I. VICARIOUS LIABILITY

7.02 An employer is vicariously liable for torts committed by his employees acting in the course of their employment.[1] Vicarious liability arises from the employer/employee relationship, it does not depend upon any

---

[1] See generally *Clerk & Lindsell on Torts*, 16th ed., 1989, Chap. 3.

272

personal fault by the employer. Liability is imposed on the employer, not for a breach of the employer's duty to the plaintiff, but for the employee's breach of a duty owed by the employee to the plaintiff. This can be distinguished from the situation in which the employee's act results in the breach of a primary duty owed by the employer to the plaintiff.

At one time it was thought that hospital authorities were not **7.03** vicariously liable for the negligence of their "professional" staff, whether doctors or nurses, in the performance of their professional duties. This stemmed from the ruling of the Court of Appeal in *Hillyer* v. *Governors of St. Bartholemews Hospital*,[2] which was based to some extent on the view that when acting on a professional judgment doctors exercised a discretion which the hospital authority could not control, and in the absence of control they were not employees.[3] The authority's responsibility was limited to exercising reasonable care in the selection of competent staff (which was a primary duty) and to vicarious liability for the performance of "purely ministerial or administrative duties, such as . . . attendance of nurses in the wards, the summoning of medical aid in cases of emergency, the supply of proper food and the like."[4]

The "control test" is no longer considered adequate as a determi- **7.04** nant of the employer/employee relationship in modern economic conditions, where employers often do not have the technical expertise to supervise and control the manner in which skilled employees perform their work.[5] The current approach to identifying the employer/ employee relationship is that there is no single test: the question depends upon weighing a number of possibly conflicting factors in order to decide whether the work is performed under a contract of service or a contract for services.[6]

The move away from the consequences of *Hillyer* began in *Gold* v. **7.05** *Essex County Council*,[7] where the Court of Appeal refused to accept the distinction between purely administrative duties and professional duties, holding the hospital authority vicariously liable for the negligence of a qualified radiographer employed under a contract of

---

[2] [1909] 2 K.B. 820; see also *Evans* v. *Liverpool Corporation* [1906] 1 K.B. 160, which was followed by the Court of Appeal in *Hillyer*; *Hall* v. *Lees* [1904] 2 K.B. 602, where a nursing association undertook to supply competent nurses, not to nurse the patient, and so were not liable for a nurse's negligence. In *Gold* v. *Essex County Council* [1942] 2 K.B. 293, 301 Lord Greene M.R. said that in *Hall* v. *Lees* the contract was a special one "and the case has nothing to do with hospitals or nursing homes."

[3] In *Cassidy* v. *Ministry of Health* [1951] 2 K.B. 343, 361 Denning L.J. suggested that the decision in *Hillyer* was attributable "to a desire to relieve the charitable hospitals from liabilities which they could not afford"; see also the comments of Lord Cooper in *MacDonald* v. *Board of Management for Glasgow Western Hospitals* 1954 S.C. 453, 476. Lord Denning has returned to this theme, but this time as a champion of financially beleaguered N.H.S. hospitals, on a number of occasions: see § 3.91, n. 83, and § 4.99.

[4] [1909] 2 K.B. 820, 829. *Hillyer* was followed in *Strangeways-Lesmere* v. *Clayton* [1936] 2 K.B. 11; *Dryden* v. *Surrey County Council* [1936] 2 All E.R. 535; and *Marshall* v. *Lindsey County Council* [1935] 1 K.B. 516 (C.A.). The House of Lords in *Lindsey County Council* v. *Marshall* [1937] A.C. 97 did not consider whether *Hillyer* was correctly decided.

[5] A point made 40 years ago by Kahn-Freund (1951) 14 M.L.R. 504.

[6] *Ready Mixed Concrete (South East) Ltd.* v. *Minister of Pensions and National Insurance* [1968] 2 Q.B. 497; *Market Investigations Ltd.* v. *Minister of Social Security* [1969] 2 Q.B. 173; *O'Kelly* v. *Trusthouse Forte plc.* [1983] I.R.L.R. 369.

[7] [1942] 2 K.B. 293.

service. Lord Greene M.R. approached the question in terms of the obligation to the patient undertaken by a hospital. It was not a duty simply to provide suitable equipment and facilities, and to take reasonable care in selecting competent staff. It was a duty to treat the patient with the apparatus provided, and this could not be avoided by employing someone to discharge the duty, irrespective of whether the procedure involved the use of skill. MacKinnon and Goddard L.JJ. simply took the view that since the radiographer was employed under a contract of service, and was therefore an employee, the hospital authority were vicariously liable for his negligence. The position of the hospital in the case of negligence by a doctor was left unresolved. Goddard L.J. considered that the hospital would be responsible for the negligence of doctors on the permanent staff, provided they were employed under a contract of service, although visiting surgeons and physicians were not employed under a contract of service, but rather a contract for services.[8] This was applied by Hilbery J. in *Collins* v. *Hertfordshire County Council*,[9] holding a hospital authority vicariously liable for the negligence of a resident junior house surgeon (employed on a temporary, but full-time basis). On the other hand, the authority was not responsible for the conduct of a visiting surgeon, although he had been engaged on similar written terms (but part-time) to the resident junior houseman.[10]

7.06   In *Cassidy* v. *Ministry of Health*[11] the Court of Appeal confirmed that a hospital authority will be held vicariously liable for the negligence of all staff, nurses and doctors alike, employed under a contract of service as part of the permanent staff of the hospital. Denning L.J. was clear that a hospital is in the same position as any other employer with respect to the torts of employees:

> "In my opinion authorities who run a hospital, be they local authorities, government boards, or any other corporation, are in law under the selfsame duty as the humblest doctor; whenever they accept a patient for treatment, they must use reasonable care and skill to cure him of his ailment. The hospital authorities cannot, of course, do it by themselves: they have no ears to listen through the stethoscope, and no hands to hold the surgeon's knife. They must do it by the staff they employ; and if their staff are negligent in giving the treatment, they are just as liable for that negligence as is anyone else who employs others to do his duties for him."[12]

---

[8] *Ibid.*, pp. 313 and 310. See also Lord Greene M.R. *ibid.* at p. 302, commenting that with consultants the nature of the work and their relationship with the hospital is such that the hospital does not undertake responsibility for their negligence. His Lordship expressly left open the position of a resident house surgeon.

[9] [1947] 1 K.B. 598, 614–620.

[10] *Ibid.*, p. 619. In *Cassidy* v. *Ministry of Health* [1951] 2 K.B. 343, 352 Somervell L.J. described the relationship between the visiting surgeon and the hospital in *Collins* as "obscure."

[11] [1951] 2 K.B. 343. The same view has been taken in Scotland: *MacDonald* v. *Board of Management for Glasgow Western Hospitals* 1954 S.C. 453; *Fox* v. *Glasgow South Western Hospitals* 1955 S.L.T. 337; Ireland: *O'Donovan* v. *Cork County Council* [1967] I.R. 173; Australia: *Samios* v. *Repatriation Commission* [1960] W.A.R. 219; and in Canada: *Fleming* v. *Sisters of St. Joseph* [1938] S.C.R. 172; *Fraser* v. *Vancouver General Hospital* (1951) 3 W.W.R. 337, 340, 347 (B.C.C.A.); aff'd [1952] 3 D.L.R. 785 (S.C.C.); *Martel* v. *Hotel-Dieu St.-Vallier* (1969) 14 D.L.R. (3d) 445 (S.C.C.); *Toronto General Hospital* v. *Aynsley* (1971) 25 D.L.R. (3d) 241 (S.C.C.).

[12] *Ibid.*, p. 360.

The position of a consultant surgeon or physician who is not an employee of the hospital was, however, expressly distinguished by Somervell and Singleton L.JJ.[13] Somervell L.J. suggested that a patient who is treated by a consultant is in much the same position as a private patient who has arranged to be operated upon by a specific doctor. Denning L.J. went further than the majority, taking the view that a hospital is under a non-delegable duty to treat patients, a duty which cannot be discharged by delegating its performance to a consultant under a contract for services. If this is correct the basis on which a consultant is engaged, whether as an employee or an independent contractor is, in practice, irrelevant: the hospital will be liable for his negligence.[14]

Subsequently, in *Roe* v. *Minister of Health*[15] the Court of Appeal **7.07** considered the question of a hospital authority's responsibility in respect of a part-time anaesthetist, and concluded that there would be vicarious liability, although on the facts there had been no negligence. Denning L.J. repeated the view he had expressed in *Cassidy* v. *Ministry of Health*, apparently conflating the question of vicarious and primary liability:

" . . . the hospital authorities are responsible for the whole of their staff, not only for the nurses and doctors, but also for the anaesthetists and the surgeons. It does not matter whether they are permanent or temporary, resident or visiting, whole-time or part-time. The hospital authorities are responsible for all of them. The reason is because, even if they are not servants, they are the agents of the hospital to give the treatment. The only exception is the case of consultants or anaesthetists selected and employed by the patient himself."[16]

Morris L.J., relying on the judgment of Lord Greene M.R. in *Gold* v. *Essex County Council*, said that the question depended upon what the hospital had undertaken to provide, and that this was a question of fact in each case. On the facts, the anaesthetists in *Roe* "were members of the 'organisation' of the hospital: they were members of the staff engaged by the hospital to do what the hospital itself was undertaking to do."[17] On this basis the principle of *respondeat superior* applied. It would seem that both Lord Greene M.R. and Morris L.J. considered that the hospital's "undertaking" was the basis for imposing *vicarious* liability, not as giving rise to a non-delegable duty. Under a non-delegable duty the hospital would be responsible for the conduct of a consultant (unless the consultant was privately engaged by the patient), but the consultant was specifically excluded from the hospital's responsibility by Lord Greene.

The cumulative effect of these cases is that a hospital authority will **7.08** be vicariously liable for the negligence of all full-time or part-time

---

[13] *Ibid.*, pp. 351 and 358 respectively.
[14] See §§ 7.24–7.25. There is, however, a possible difference between vicarious liability for employees and liability under a non-delegable duty for the acts of independent contractors, in that the employer is not liable for the "collateral negligence" of an independent contractor; see § 7.30.
[15] [1954] 2 Q.B. 66.
[16] *Ibid.*, p. 82.
[17] *Ibid.*, p. 91.

employees.[18] It is possible that visiting consultants do not fall into the category of employees,[19] although in *Razzel* v. *Snowball*[20] Denning L.J. said that since the introduction of the National Health Service the term 'consultant' does not denote a particular relationship between a doctor and a hospital. Rather, it is simply a title denoting his place in the hierarchy of the hospital staff: "He is a senior member of the staff but nevertheless just as much a member of the staff as the house surgeon."[21] This view has not had to be tested in the courts since in practice, whatever the legal niceties may be, health authorities within the National Health Service do not argue the point that a consultant is not an employee when engaged on N.H.S. work. Consultants clearly fall within the terms of H.C.(89)34 which introduces "N.H.S. indemnity," on the assumption that they are members of staff for whom the health authority will be vicariously liable.[22] This is also true of staff supplied to the hospital by outside agencies. It is arguable that an agency nurse, for example, remains the employee of the agency and does not become an employee of the health authority for the purpose of vicarious liability.[23] The health authority will accept responsibility for the negligence of agency staff, however, under the terms of N.H.S. indemnity.[24] The fact that N.H.S. hospital authorities accept vicarious responsibility for consultants and agency staff removes much of the practical import of the arguments about whether a hospital is under a non-delegable duty to patients.

Correct defendants

7.09   As a general rule, when suing a N.H.S. hospital the appropriate defendant will be the District Health Authority,[25] although some

---

[18] *Gold* v. *Essex County Council* [1942] 2 K.B. 293 (radiographer); *Collins* v. *Hertfordshire County Council* [1947] 1 K.B. 598 (resident house surgeon and pharmacist); *Cassidy* v. *Ministry of Health* [1951] 2 K.B. 343 (assistant medical officer); *MacDonald* v. *Board of Management for Glasgow Western Hospitals* 1954 S.C. 453 (resident medical officer); *Roe* v. *Minister of Health* [1954] 2 Q.B. 66 (anaesthetist); *Fox* v. *Glasgow South Western Hospitals* 1955 S.L.T. 337 (nurses). An employer will be vicariously liable for injury to an employee caused by the negligence of an occupational medical officer: *Stokes* v. *Guest, Keen and Nettlefold (Bolts & Nuts) Ltd.* [1968] 1 W.L.R. 1776, § 4.08.
[19] This was the view of Hilbery J. in *Collins* v. *Hertfordshire County Council* [1947] 1 K.B. 598, 619–620; see also *MacDonald* v. *Board of Management for Glasgow Western Hospitals* 1954 S.C. 453, 478, 485; *Higgins* v. *North West Metropolitan Hospital Board* [1954] 1 W.L.R. 411, 417.
[20] [1954] 1 W.L.R. 1382.
[21] *Ibid.*, p. 1386. See also Brazier, *Street on Torts*, 8th ed., 1988, p. 447, stating that consultants under the N.H.S., even where only engaged part-time or occasionally, are employees of the hospital authority.
[22] See §§ 7.38–7.39.
[23] For the effect of transferring employees between employers see *Mersey Docks and Harbour Board* v. *Coggins & Griffith (Liverpool) Ltd.* [1947] A.C. 1; *Bhoomidas* v. *Port of Singapore Authority* [1978] 1 All E.R. 956; *Gibb* v. *United Steel Companies Ltd.* [1957] 1 W.L.R. 668. Note, however, that staff supplied by an employment agency may not be employees of the agency: see *Ironmonger* v. *Movefield Ltd.* [1988] I.R.L.R. 461.
[24] See H.C. (89) 34, para. 8 and Annex A, para. 18. See Appendix.
[25] See the National Health Service Act 1977, ss.3 and 8, and Sched. 5, para. 15. Although consultants' contracts are with the Regional Health Authority the point is not taken by District Health Authorities: Capstick, *Patient Complaints and Litigation* 1985, p. 44.

hospitals are not within the District Health Authority's remit, in which case the hospital itself will be the correct defendant.[26] Where a claim arises out of the conduct of a service, such as the ambulance service, which is operated by the Regional Health Authority, then that authority will be the appropriate defendant.

Surgeons do not normally employ the nurses in the operating theatre **7.10** or on the ward and will not be responsible for their negligence in carrying out the instructions that have been given with regard to the patient's treatment.[27] Nursing staff remain the employees of the hospital, and if the hospital is not liable for the conduct of a nurse who is acting under the instructions of the surgeon or doctor, the reason is "not that *pro hac vice* she ceases to be the servant of the hospital, but that she is not guilty of negligence if she carries out the orders of the surgeon, however negligent those orders may be."[28]

General practice

General practitioners are not employees of Family Health Service **7.11** Authorities,[29] and so a claim for negligence against a general practitioner would have to be pursued against the individual doctor. General practitioners will be vicariously liable for the negligence of their employees, such as nurses or receptionists.[30] The position of a locum tenens is unclear. It seems likely that a deputising doctor would not be considered to be an employee, but would be categorised as an independent contractor.[31] It is doubtful whether a general practitioner would be under a non-delegable duty with respect to the negligence of a locum.

Private treatment

Where a patient has received treatment privately, he could sue the **7.12** hospital or clinic, who will be vicariously liable for the negligence of

[26] N.H.S. Trust hospitals established under the National Health Service and Community Care Act 1990, ss.5–11 and Sched. 2 and 3, are self-governing bodies corporate outside the control of District Health Authorities.

[27] *Perionowsky* v. *Freeman* (1866) 4 F. & F. 977; *Morris* v. *Winsbury-White* [1937] 4 All E.R. 494, 498.

[28] *Gold* v. *Essex County Council* [1942] 2 K.B. 293, 299, *per* Lord Greene M.R.; *Johnston* v. *Wellesley Hospital* (1970) 17 D.L.R. (3d) 139, 152 (Ont. H.C.). Note, however, that a nurse does not necessarily act with reasonable care by mechanically following a doctor's orders. If the instruction was obviously incorrect the nurse would have a duty to seek confirmation from the doctor, *per* Goddard L.J. at [1942] 2 K.B. 293, 313; see § 4.58.

[29] Family Health Service Authorities have replaced Family Practitioner Committees: National Health Service and Community Care Act 1990, s.2; S.I. 1990/1329. In *Wadi* v. *Cornwall and Isles of Scilly Family Practitioner Committee* [1985] I.C.R. 492 the E.A.T. held that the relationship between general practitioners and a Family Health Service Authority was not contractual but statutory. This is inconsistent with the later decision of the Court of Appeal in *Roy* v. *Kensington and Chelsea and Westminster Family Practitioner Committee* [1990] 1 Med. L.R. 328, holding that the relationship is contractual.

[30] See, *e.g.*, *Lobley* v. *Nunn* (1985) (unreported), C.A., where an action against a receptionist failed on the facts; *Hancke* v. *Hooper* (1835) 7 C. & P. 81, where a surgeon was held liable for the negligence of an apprentice.

[31] This was the conclusion of Osler J. in *Rothwell* v. *Raes* (1988) 54 D.L.R. (4th) 193, 262 (Ont. H.C.), who emphasised the independence of the locum's professional judgment. The locum's freedom of action as a medical practitioner was not circumscribed in any way, other than financially.

their employees, but, in practice, the doctor may not be employed by the hospital or clinic. Unless the hospital has held the doctor out to the patient as an employee,[32] they will not be liable for his negligence and the patient will have to sue the doctor individually. This may depend upon the construction placed on the contract between the hospital and patient. On the other hand, it is arguable that where the patient's contract is with the hospital then the hospital undertakes a non-delegable duty, at least where the contract is to provide treatment as opposed to merely providing facilities for treatment to be given by an independent doctor. This view derives some support from an observation by Morris L.J. in *Roe* v. *Minister of Health*:

> "While the requisite standard of care does not vary according as to whether treatment is gratuitous or on payment, the existence of arrangements entitling the plaintiffs to expect certain treatment might be a relevant factor when considering the extent of the obligation assumed by the hospital."[33]

7.13 Where a doctor who is not employed by the hospital has been engaged directly by the patient, the hospital will not be liable for the doctor's negligence. This applies both to vicarious liability and non-delegable duties.[34]

Acts in the course of employment

7.14 The vicarious liability of an employer is limited to the torts of an employee who is acting in the course of his employment. This is treated as a question of fact in each case. Provided that the employee is still engaged on the tasks he was employed to do, albeit he is doing it in a wrongful and unauthorised manner, he will be acting in the course of employment. This aspect of vicarious liability does not appear to have created problems in the context of medical negligence actions. In theory a surgeon who performed an operation beyond the sphere of his experience could be considered to be acting outside the scope of employment, but this is a question of degree, and the circumstances would probably have to be quite extreme before this would become a live issue.[35] Liability will not necessarily be limited to acts in the course of providing treatment itself, so, for example, the hospital may be responsible for negligence which leads to the patient falling out of bed.[36]

---

[32] See, *e.g.*, *Rogers* v. *Night Riders* [1983] R.T.R. 324, C.A., where a minicab hire firm were held to be under a non-delegable duty with regard to the safety of vehicles, although the vehicle drivers were independent contractors.

[33] [1954] 2 Q.B. 66, 89.

[34] See Denning L.J. in *Cassidy* v. *Ministry of Health* [1951] 2 K.B. 343, 362 and *Roe* v. *Minister of Health* [1954] 2 Q.B. 66, 82; *Johnston* v. *Wellesley Hospital* (1970) 17 D.L.R. (3d) 139, 152–153 (Ont. H.C.); *Crits* v. *Sylvester* (1956) 1 D.L.R. (2d) 504, 508 (Ont. C.A.); aff'd (1956) 5 D.L.R. (2d) 601 (S.C.C.), holding that a hospital authority is not liable if a doctor employed by the patient, not the hospital, fails to use the equipment available; the hospital is not required to oversee the use of appliances by a privately engaged doctor.

[35] H.C. (89) 34, Annex A, para. 12, introducing "N.H.S. indemnity" (see §§ 7.38–7.39 and Appendix), states that "actions in the course of N.H.S. employment" should be interpreted liberally.

[36] *Smith* v. *Lewisham Group Hospital Management Committee*, *The Times*, June 21, 1955; *Beatty* v. *Sisters of Misericorde of Alberta* [1935] 1 W.W.R. 651.

II. DIRECT LIABILITY

The concept of the direct liability of a hospital authority is used in two **7.15** distinct ways. First, where the authority is itself at fault in the manner in which it has performed its functions, although it may not be possible to identify any particular employee who was negligent. This may be categorised as some form of organisational failure. Secondly, direct liability is also used to describe the imposition of a non-delegable duty, for the purpose of establishing the authority's responsibility for the negligence of an independent contractor. As a general rule a person is not liable for the torts of an independent contractor, unless he authorised or ratified the tort,[37] or unless he has himself been negligent in selecting an incompetent contractor, or employing an inadequate number of men for the job,[38] or he has interfered with the manner in which the work was performed so causing the damage.[39] If an employer discovers that the contractor's work is being done in a foreseeably dangerous fashion, he may be liable if he condones the negligence.[40] In each of these instances the employer is personally at fault. There are, however, a number of circumstances in which a person may be liable for the negligence of an independent contractor without fault on his part. Here the employer is said to be under a non-delegable duty, which means that he may delegate the performance of the duty to another, but not the responsiblity for the manner in which the duty is performed. If the contractor is negligent, it is the employer's primary duty to the plaintiff that is broken.[41] In this situation there is no "personal" fault by the employer, and the concept of non-delegable duty simply means that the employer is liable for non-performance of the duty: it is no defence to show that he delegated the performance to another person, whether his employee or not, whom he reasonably believed to be competent to perform it.[42] The circumstances in which a non-delegable duty will be imposed are relatively fixed, but there is no guiding principle which determines precisely how and when such a duty arises.[43]

1. Organisational errors

The notion that a hospital authority may be directly liable for **7.16** negligence in the organisation of its services is not new. Actions have, in the past, been formulated in this way in order to overcome the argument that the hospital were not vicariously liable for the negli-

---

[37] *Ellis* v. *Sheffield Gas Consumers Co.* (1853) 2 E. & B. 767.
[38] *Pinn* v. *Rew* (1916) 32 T.L.R. 451.
[39] *McLoughlin* v. *Pryor* (1842) 4 M. & G. 48.
[40] *D. & F. Estates Ltd.* v. *Church Commissioners for England* [1988] 2 All E.R. 992, 1008.
[41] Sometimes referred to as a duty to see that care is taken, as opposed to a duty to exercise reasonable care: *cf. The Pass of Ballater* [1942] P. 112, 117; and *Stennett* v. *Hancock* [1939] 2 All E.R. 578.
[42] *McDermid* v. *Nash Dredging and Reclamation Co. Ltd.* [1987] 2 All E.R. 878, 887, *per* Lord Brandon.
[43] For discussion see McKendrick (1990) 53 M.L.R. 770.

gence of their professional staff. Thus, in *Vancouver General Hospital* v. *McDaniel*[44] the plaintiff went into a hospital for infectious diseases for the treatment of diptheria, and contracted smallpox. She claimed that the defendants were negligent in the system of infection control that they adopted, namely the juxtaposition of smallpox patients to the plaintiff, and the attendance on the plaintiff by nurses who also nursed smallpox patients. Lord Alness observed that the plaintiff had not alleged negligence on the part of an employee of the hospital:

> "The complaint is that the technique was adopted by the appellants, not that it failed in its execution. In other words, the case made against the appellant is one, not of vicarious, but of direct responsibility."[45]

7.17 This type of direct liability may take a number of forms. A hospital will be under a primary liability if it fails to provide suitable medical facilities or equipment,[46] or, it has been negligent in selecting incompetent staff.[47] A hospital also owes a duty to establish adequate procedures to safeguard patients from cross-infection,[48] and from the risk of errors in the administration of drugs.[49] In *Bull* v. *Devon Area Health Authority*[50] the health authority were held liable for instituting an unreliable system for calling expert assistance to an obstetric emergency. It was unclear precisely why the communication system had broken down, but the inference was that either there had been negligence in the operation of the system, or it was inadequate to cope with even minor hitches which it should have been possible to anticipate. This illustrates the point that a safety system may be either poorly designed or poorly implemented. Moreover, the stronger the evidence that the system is adequate to cope with all eventualities, the more compelling will be the inference that there must have been some negligence on the part of the hospital staff in implementing the procedure, for which the hospital authority will be vicariously liable.[51]

---

[44] (1934) 152 L.T. 56.

[45] *Ibid.*, p. 57.

[46] *Vuchar* v. *Trustees of Toronto General Hospital* [1937] 1 D.L.R. 298, 321 (Ont. C.A.), a case which applied *Hillyer* v. *Governors of St. Bartholemews Hospital* [1909] 2 K.B. 820; *Denton* v. *South West Thames Regional Health Authority* (1980) (unreported), Q.B.D., on failing to have a system to check the safety of equipment.

[47] *Wilsher* v. *Essex Area Health Authority* [1986] 3 All E.R. 801, 831, *per* Glidewell L.J. This was the limit of the hospital's duty in *Hillyer* v. *Governors of St. Bartholemews Hospital* [1909] 2 K.B. 820.

[48] *Vancouver General Hospital* v. *McDaniel* (1934) 152 L.T. 56; *Lindsey County Council* v. *Marshall* [1937] A.C. 97.

[49] *Collins* v. *Hertfordshire County Council* [1947] 1 K.B. 598, where a hospital failed to bring to the attention of an unqualified junior medical officer the requirements of their routine procedures for having a written prescription signed by a qualified person. Hilbery J. commented, at p. 614, that: "If they had had a proper system in operation, this solution could not have arrived at the theatre, let alone arrived at the body of the unfortunate patient." There may also be an obligation to have a system for informing patients about the side-effects of drugs: see the discussion of *Blyth* v. *Bloomsbury Health Authority* (1985) (unreported), Q.B.D., (1987) C.A., reported at (1989) 5 P.N. 167, by Montgomery (1987) 137 New L.J. 703.

[50] (1989) (unreported), C.A.; § 4.85. For discussion of the duty with regard to hospital casualty departments see § 4.05.

[51] See Nathan, *Medical Negligence*, 1957, p. 102; *Voller* v. *Portsmouth Corporation* (1947) 203 L.T.J. 264. In practice it may be impossible to identify whether the system was inadequate or whether individuals have been careless in implementing it: see, *e.g.*, *Cassidy* v. *Ministry of Health* [1951] 2 K.B. 343, 359, *per* Singleton L.J. This has the effect of blurring the distinction between the hospital's primary liability for organisational errors and vicarious liability.

The failure to enforce its own rules and regulations can amount to negligence on the part of the hospital.[52]

A hospital authority may be negligent by providing an inadequate **7.18** number of staff to care safely for the patients,[53] or in permitting an inexperienced doctor to administer anaesthetics without proper supervision.[54] Similarly, employing too many inexperienced staff can amount to negligence by the hospital. In *Wilsher* v. *Essex Area Health Authority* Browne-Wilkinson V.-C. said that:

> "In my judgment, a health authority which so conducts its hospital that it fails to provide doctors of sufficient skill and experience to give the treatment offered at the hospital may be directly liable in negligence to the patient. Although we were told in argument that no case has ever been decided on this ground and that it is not the practice to formulate claims in this way, I can see no reason why, in principle, the health authority should not be so liable if its organisation is at fault."[55]

An individual patient could face considerable difficulty, however, in proving negligence on this basis, a point that Browne-Wilkinson V.-C. acknowledged:

> "To what extent should the authority be held liable if (*e.g.* in the use of junior housemen) it is only adopting a practice hallowed by tradition? Should the authority be liable if it demonstrates that, due to the financial stringency under which it operates, it cannot afford to fill the posts with those possessing the necessary experience? But, in my judgment, the law should not be distorted by making findings of personal fault against individual doctors who are, in truth, not at fault in order to avoid such questions."[56]

In *Bull* v. *Devon Area Health Authority*[57] Slade L.J. considered that **7.19** an allegation about inadequate levels of staffing would have to be judged according to professional standards at the time, applying the

---

[52] *Bergen* v. *Sturgeon General Hospital* (1984) 28 C.C.L.T. 155 (Alta. Q.B.), on inconsistency between the hospital's policy on the keeping of accurate notes and records and what happened in practice; *Bernier* v. *Sisters of Service* [1948] 2 D.L.R. 468 (Alta. S.C.).

[53] *Laidlaw* v. *Lions Gate Hospital* (1969) 8 D.L.R. (3d) 730 (B.C.S.C.), where the hospital had provided a sufficient number of nurses per patient, but had failed to correct a lackadaisical attitude which had arisen among the nurses as to how many should be present in the post-anaesthesia recovery room; *Krujelis* v. *Esdale* (1971) 25 D.L.R. (3d) 557 (B.C.S.C.), where the hospital was held vicariously liable for the negligence of nurses, when 3 out of 5 on duty in the post-anaesthesia recovery room went for their coffee-break together. Employing insufficient staff may mean that existing staff have to work excessive hours. If this results in harm to an employee's health the health authority may be liable in its capacity as an employer: see *Johnstone* v. *Bloomsbury Health Authority* [1991] 2 All E.R. 293.

[54] *Jones* v. *Manchester Corporation* [1952] 2 All E.R. 125.

[55] [1986] 3 All E.R. 801, 833 citing *McDermid* v. *Nash Dredging and Reclamation Co. Ltd.* [1986] 2 All E.R. 676; [1987] 2 All E.R. 878, a case in which the House of Lords subsequently applied the principle that an employer's duty with respect to the safety of employees is non-delegable, *ibid.* Glidewell L.J. agreed, *ibid.* at p. 831, "that there seems to be no reason in principle why, in a suitable case different on its facts from this, a hospital management committee should not be held directly liable in negligence for failing to provide sufficient qualified and competent medical staff."

[56] *Ibid.*, pp. 833–834.

[57] (1989) (unreported), C.A.

Bolam test, and Dillon L.J. simply commented that the level of staffing should be "reasonably sufficient for the foreseeable requirements of the patient." Mustill L.J. had some reservations, however, about the argument that the hospital authority could not be expected to do more than their best, allocating their limited resources as favourably as possible. Although public medicine might not be precisely analogous to other public services, there was a danger in assuming that it was *sui generis*, and that it was necessarily a complete answer to say that even if the system in any hospital was unsatisfactory, it was no more unsatisfactory than those in force elsewhere.[58] Similarly, in *Re HIV Haemophiliac Litigation*[59] Ralph Gibson L.J. said that although it was difficult to prove negligence when the defendant was required to exercise discretion and form judgments on the allocation of public resources, that was not sufficient to make it clear that there could be no claim in negligence.

7.20   An action in negligence against a hospital authority which alleges that the plaintiff sustained injury through an inadequate provision of resources, whether it be staff, equipment, or funds for drugs, would have to prove that the lack of resources was a consequence of negligence in the *organisation* of the hospital itself.[60] It is not sufficient simply to point to the lack of resources, since this may well be a consequence of resource allocation decisions over which the hospital has no control. Moreover, challenges on public law grounds to decisions about resource allocation made by the Secretary of State or individual health authorities have been notably unsuccessful.

7.21   By virtue of section 3 of the National Health Service Act 1977 the Secretary of State has a duty to provide throughout England and Wales, to such extent as he considers necessary to meet all reasonable requirements, *inter alia*, hospital accommodation; medical, dental, nursing and ambulance services; services for the diagnosis and treatment of illness; facilities for the prevention of illness, the care and after-care of persons suffering from illness and facilities for the care of expectant and nursing mothers and young children.[61] In *R. v. Secretary of State for Social Services, ex parte Hincks*[62] four patients, who had been waiting for orthopaedic operations for some years, sought to challenge a decision to postpone the expansion of a local hospital due to the cost, relying on section 3. The application for judicial review failed. Lord Denning M.R. said that additional words had to be implied into section 3(1) which should read: "to such extent as he

---

[58] See § 4.85. See also *Knight* v. *Home Office* [1990] 3 All E.R. 237, 243, § 4.83, where Pill J. said that the lack of resources to provide a better staff/patient ratio was not necessarily a complete defence. Lack of funds would not justify a failure to provide *any* medical facilities for prisoners in a large prison.

[59] (1990) 140 New. L.J. 1349.

[60] In *Wilsher* v. *Essex Area Health Authority* [1986] 3 All E.R. 801, 833 Browne-Wilkinson V.-C. said: " . . . I can see no reason why, in principle, the health authority should not be so liable *if its organisation is at fault*" (emphasis added). See Montgomery (1987) 137 New L.J. 703, 705 who comments that: "To hold health authorities liable for inadequate systems would provide a mechanism whereby managers can be made accountable for the effects which their activities have on patient care."

[61] See also National Health Service Act 1977, ss. 4 and 5: provision of special hospitals for mental health, and provision of other services, including school medical services, contraceptive services, a microbiological service, and the conduct of research.

[62] (1979) 123 S.J. 436; aff'd (1980) (unreported), C.A.

considers necessary to meet all reasonable requirements *such as can be provided within the resources available.*" Bridge L.J. commented that there must be some limitation on the resources available to finance the health service and that limitation must be determined in the light of the current government economic policy. That was an implication which must be read into section 3(1).

This approach has been followed in two cases where parents sought **7.22** to require a hospital to provide the facilities and staff necessary to perform heart surgery on two young children. Both applications for judicial review were unsuccessful. In *R. v. Central Birmingham Health Authority, ex parte Walker*[63] Sir John Donaldson M.R. said that:

> "It is not for this court, or indeed for any court, to substitute its own judgment for the judgment of those who are responsible for the allocation of resources. This court could only intervene where it was satisfied that there was a prima facie case, not only of failing to allocate resources in the way in which others would think that resources should be allocated, but a failure to allocate resources to an extent which was *Wednesbury* unreasonable . . . [T]he jurisdiction does exist. But it has to be used extremely sparingly."

Subsequently, in *R. v. Central Birmingham Health Authority, ex parte Collier*[64] Stephen Brown L.J. considered that this would be the position even if the medical evidence were to establish that there was immediate danger to the child's health. Ralph Gibson L.J. commented that the courts have no role as a general investigator of social policy and of the allocation of resources. Rather, the court's jurisdiction was limited to dealing with breaches of duty under law, including decisions made by public authorities which are shown to be unreasonable.

These cases make it clear that an action which alleges that the failure **7.23** to provide adequate resources constitutes negligence would be unlikely to succeed. Decisions about the allocation of resources are made under statutory powers which confer a broad discretion upon the Secretary of State and health authorities. A claim that such a decision has been taken negligently must first establish that the discretion was exercised *ultra vires* the statutory power, applying public law principles,[65] but the courts are apparently reluctant to make such a finding in the context of health resources.[66]

2. Non-delegable duty

There are two grounds for suggesting that a hospital authority owes **7.24** a non-delegable duty to patients in the hospital.[67] The first stems to

---

[63] *The Times*, November 26, 1987, C.A.

[64] (1988) (unreported), C.A.

[65] See *Anns* v. *Merton London Borough Council* [1978] A.C. 728, 754; *Dorset Yacht Co. Ltd.* v. *Home Office* [1970] A.C. 1004, 1067. See further § 8.15 for a discussion of the distinction between policy and operational decisions.

[66] *cf. Meade* v. *London Borough of Haringey* [1979] 2 All E.R. 1016 where the Court of Appeal held that the parents of children could maintain an action for breach of statutory duty to secure that there should be sufficient schools to provide full-time education in the locality under s.8 of the Education Act 1944. The schools had been closed as a result of industrial action.

[67] Dugdale and Stanton, *Professional Negligence*, 1989, 2nd ed., para. 22.21.

large extent from *Cassidy* v. *Ministry of Health*[68] where Denning L.J. asserted that hospital authorities were under a primary, non-delegable duty to patients, at least where the doctor or surgeon, whether a consultant or not, was employed and paid, not by the patient but by the hospital authorities. It was irrelevant whether the contract under which he was employed was a contract of service or a contract for services; the hospital authorities were liable for his negligence in treating the patient:

" . . . the hospital authorities accepted the plaintiff as a patient for treatment, and it was their duty to treat him with reasonable care. They selected, employed, and paid all the surgeons and nurses who looked after him. He had no say in their selection at all. If those surgeons and nurses did not treat him with proper care and skill, then the hospital authorities must answer for it, for it means that they themselves did not perform their duty to him. I decline to enter into the question whether any of the surgeons were employed only under a contract for services, as distinct from a contract of service. The evidence is meagre enough in all conscience on that point. But the liability of the hospital authorities should not, and does not, depend on nice considerations of that sort. The plaintiff knew nothing of the terms on which they employed their staff: all he knew was that he was treated in the hospital by people whom the hospital authorities appointed; and the hospital authorities must be answerable for the way in which he was treated."[69]

7.25   His Lordship repeated this view in both *Roe* v. *Minister of Health*[70] and in *Jones* v. *Manchester Corporation*.[71] The authority of this proposition remains uncertain, since it is tolerably clear that the majority of the Court of Appeal in both *Cassidy* and *Roe* proceeded on the basis that the doctors concerned were employees for whom the health authority would be vicariously liable, and the question has not arisen directly for decision in this country.[72]

7.26   The view that the liability of a hospital to a patient is based on a personal non-delegable duty has been approved, *obiter*, on two occasions by the High Court of Australia.[73] In *Ellis* v. *Wallsend District Hospital*,[74] the one Australian case which has had to decide the issue,

---

[68] [1951] 2 K.B. 343, 362–365.

[69] *Ibid.*, p. 365.

[70] [1954] 2 Q.B. 66, 82.

[71] [1952] 2 All E.R. 125, 132.

[72] Both Dugdale and Stanton, *Professional Negligence*, 1989, 2nd ed., para. 22.21 and Jackson and Powell, *Professional Negligence*, 1987, 2nd ed., para. 6.56 doubt whether Lord Denning's approach represents the law. *Clerk & Lindsell on Torts* 16th ed., 1989, para. 11–24 accepts that the question remains undecided in England, though supporting the view that hospital authorities should be under a non-delegable duty (see also *ibid.* at para. 3–12.). See further the comments of Lord Jauncey in *Esso Petroleum Co. Ltd.* v. *Hall Russell and Co. Ltd.* [1989] 1 All E.R. 37, 61.

[73] *Commonwealth* v. *Introvigne* (1982) 56 A.L.J.R. 749, 755; *Kondis* v. *State Transport Authority* (1984) 55 A.L.R. 225, 234. The possibility of establishing a personal non-delegable duty owed by a hospital to a patient was accepted by the New South Wales Court of Appeal in *Albrighton* v. *Royal Prince Alfred Hospital* [1980] 2 N.S.W.L.R. 542, 561–562, although this would depend upon the facts proved. See further Whippy (1989) 63 A.L.J. 182.

[74] (1989) 17 N.S.W.L.R. 553 (C.A.); Nicholson (1990) 6 P.N. 83.

the New South Wales Court of Appeal was divided as to whether a non-delegable duty arose on the facts. The majority (Samuels and Meagher JJ.A.) distinguished between a hospital which functions merely as a provider of facilities pursuant to an arrangement between the doctor and the hospital, and a hospital which functions as a place where a person in need of treatment goes to obtain treatment.[75] In the latter case a non-delegable duty could arise,[76] but such a duty "does not extend to treatment which is performed by a doctor pursuant to a direct engagement with the patient, and not on behalf of the hospital."[77] The basis for establishing a non-delegable duty lies in the nature of the relationship between the patient and the hospital. Where the patient goes directly to the hospital for advice and treatment, the hospital, by accepting the patient, undertakes to make available all the therapeutic skill and devices which it is reasonably able to deploy:

> "If the hospital's response is to open the door and admit the patient to the benefits of the medical and surgical cornucopia within, it remains responsible to ensure that whatever treatment or advice the horn disgorges is given with proper care; its duty cannot be divested by delegation."[78]

The patient had been treated by a doctor who was an "honorary **7.27** medical officer" with privileges at the hospital. She had approached the doctor herself and he had arranged for her admission to the hospital and performed the surgery. In these circumstances a non-delegable duty did not arise. The hospital was merely a provider of the facilities for the treatment. Kirby P., dissenting, took the view that the hospital was not a "mere venue" for the performance of private medical procedures, it was an integrated institution and an honorary medical officer was part of it.[79] In his Lordship's opinion the hospital was vicariously liable for all its staff, whether the position was "honorary" or not, and directly liable by virtue of a non-delegable duty.

The courts in Australia have accepted that a hospital may come **7.28** under a non-delegable duty to its patients, albeit that there is a difference of opinion as to precisely when the duty arises. On the other hand, in *Yepremian* v. *Scarborough General Hospital*[80] the majority of a five judge Ontario Court of Appeal held that in Canada a hospital

---

[75] Relying on the judgment of Houlden J.A. in *Yepremian* v. *Scarborough General Hospital* (1980) 110 D.L.R. (3d) 513, 581 (Ont. C.A.).

[76] Thus, accounting for the dicta in *Albrighton* v. *Royal Prince Alfred Hospital* [1980] 2 N.S.W.L.R. 542, 561–562, which was a case where the patient had gone directly to the hospital for treatment.

[77] (1989) 17 N.S.W.L.R. 553, 604. Denning L.J. would have agreed that where the patient himself selects and employs the doctor or surgeon, the hospital authorities are not liable for his negligence, because he is not employed by them: *Cassidy* v. *Ministry of Health* [1951] 2 K.B. 343, 362.

[78] *Ibid.*, p. 605, *per* Samuels J.A.

[79] "He was integrated into the discipline and direction of the hospital. What he did in his rooms was his affair. But when he came into the hospital, he was part of the hospital. When working on its premises he was part of its integrated medical team": *ibid.*, p. 566.

[80] (1980) 110 D.L.R. (3d) 513 (Ont. C.A.). The action was settled before an appeal to the Supreme Court of Canada was heard: (1981) 120 D.L.R. (3d) 341.

does not undertake a non-delegable duty to a patient, whether he presents himself directly at the door of the hospital or not.[81]

7.29 The second ground for suggesting that under the N.H.S. a hospital authority is under a non-delegable duty to provide medical services to the patient derives from the statutory obligation placed on a health authority under the National Health Service Act 1977, through the duty placed on the Secretary of State. In *Razzel* v. *Snowball*[82] the Court of Appeal held that the duty placed on the Minister of Health by section 3(1)(c) of the National Health Service Act 1946 was not limited to merely providing competent specialists, but extended to providing treatment by means of their services. The effect of this particular ruling was that the defendant doctor was to be regarded as carrying out the Minister's duty and therefore he was entitled to claim the benefit of a one-year period of limitation that applied to acts done in pursuance or execution of any Act of Parliament or any public duty under section 21 of the Limitation Act 1939. It is arguable that the consequence of this is that the equivalent provision in section 3(1) of the National Health Service Act 1977 creates a non-delegable statutory duty to provide treatment services which is not discharged by the appointment of competent staff, whether as an employee or an independent contractor, such as a consultant.[83] This argument has not been tested in the courts, and it remains to be seen how the proposition would be received if advanced by a plaintiff.[84]

7.30 Even where a non-delegable duty is established, the employer is not liable for acts of collateral negligence by an independent contractor. This is negligence which is not committed in the performance of the very work which has been delegated, although in practice it can be very difficult to distinguish between collateral acts and acts which are simply a manner of performing the delegated work.[85] The distinction was accepted by Denning L.J. in *Cassidy* v. *Ministry of Health*,[86] but was said to be unimportant in that case "because we are not concerned with any collateral or casual acts of negligence by the staff, but

---

[81] cf. *Aynsley* v. *Toronto General Hospital* (1969) 7 D.L.R. (3d) 193, 209 (Ont. C.A.); aff'd (1971) 25 D.L.R. (3d) 241 (S.C.C.), where Aylesworth J.A. said that a hospital was liable for the negligence of a doctor even if he had been employed under a contract for services. This suggests that the hospital was under a non-delegable duty, since the negligence would have been that of an independent contractor. This was a case of private medicine, however, and a contractual relationship between the hospital and the patient may well create a non-delegable duty.

[82] [1954] 1 W.L.R. 1382; see also *Higgins* v. *North West Metropolitan Hospital Board* [1954] 1 W.L.R. 411.

[83] Dugdale and Stanton, *Professional Negligence*, 1989, 2nd ed., para. 22–22.

[84] One unusual feature of the case was that it was the plaintiff who argued that the Minister's duty was merely to provide the specialists and not the treatment, whereas it was the defendant who was claiming that he was performing the Minister's non-delegable duty. In *Yepremian* v. *Scarborough General Hospital* (1980) 110 D.L.R. (3d) 513, 565 Blair J.A. considered that the liability of hospitals in the U.K. "now rests on a clear statutory foundation," relying on *Razzel* v. *Snowball* [1954] 1 W.L.R. 1382. There is authority for the view that where a statute imposes an "absolute" duty, responsibility for its performance cannot be delegated: *Smith* v. *Cammell Laird & Co. Ltd.* [1940] A.C. 242; *The Pass of Ballater* [1942] P. 112. Whether a duty is "absolute" depends upon the construction of the statute, but it can apply to a duty to use "due diligence": *Riverstone Meat Co. Pty. Ltd.* v. *Lancashire Shipping Co. Ltd.* [1961] A.C. 807.

[85] See *Padbury* v. *Holliday & Greenwood Ltd.* (1912) 28 T.L.R. 494; *Holliday* v. *National Telephone Co.* [1899] 2 Q.B. 392.

[86] [1951] 2 K.B. 343, 365.

negligence in the treatment itself which it was the employer's duty to provide." There is no comparable restriction on an employer's vicarious liability, provided the employee's negligence occurred in the course of employment.

The underlying justification for imposing a non-delegable duty on **7.31** hospital authorities rests on the patient's expectations. Patients know nothing about the terms upon which the hospital engages its staff. They go to hospital for treatment, and if they suffer injury in the course of that treatment their entitlement to damages should not turn upon whether the negligence was inflicted by an employed nurse or an agency nurse, a house surgeon or a visiting consultant.[87] In *Yepremian* v. *Scarborough General Hospital*[88] Arnup J.A. was critical of the notion of non-delegable duties because it seemed to be a case of saying: "In all the circumstances, the hospital *ought* to be liable." This, however, is the very point, and it is as true of the principle of vicarious liability, and indeed most tort duties.

The policy that has been adopted with regard to negligent treatment **7.32** given in N.H.S. hospitals of, in effect, ignoring the distinction between employees and independent contractors provided that the plaintiff's injury was caused in the course of receiving N.H.S. treatment, has rendered much of the argument about non-delegable duties redundant. The health authority will accept vicarious liability for the negligence of consultants and agency staff irrespective of whether they are engaged under a contract of service or a contract for services. Moreover, even with private medical treatment, in practice it will rarely matter to the plaintiff whether the hospital owes a non-delegable duty since, if the doctor is proved to have been negligent, the patient will have a claim against him, and if he is not an employee but an independent contractor he will normally have insured against liability through a medical defence organisation. If the doctor is not negligent there would not in any event have been an action against the hospital for breach of its non-delegable duty. The issue becomes of practical importance to the plaintiff if the doctor has no, or limited, insurance cover,[89] or where the plaintiff has chosen to sue only the hospital and not the doctor.[90] The effect of imposing a non-delegable duty on a hospital is merely to make the hospital a guarantor of the independent contractor's solvency, or rather to place the risk of the contractor's insolvency or lack of insurance cover on the hospital rather than the plaintiff. If the contractor is negligent, the hospital will have either a contractual claim for indemnity or a right to contribution under the Civil Liability (Contribution) Act 1978.

---

[87] See Whippy (1989) 63 A.L.J. 182, 201. This point has been made by McKendrick (1990) 53 M.L.R. 770 in the wider context of employers' vicarious liability. Given the elusiveness of the distinction between a contract of service and a contract for services, and the difficulty that the courts have in identifying it, there is no obvious reason why an employer's responsibility should hang on this particular issue.

[88] (1980) 110 D.L.R. (3d) 513, 532 (Ont. C.A.).

[89] As was the case in *Ellis* v. *Wallsend District Hospital* (1989) 17 N.S.W.L.R. 553, 569.

[90] As occurred in *Yepremian* v. *Scarborough General Hospital* (1980) 110 D.L.R. (3d) 513 (Ont. C.A.).

III. JOINT LIABILITY AND CONTRIBUTION

7.33 Where two or more tortfeasors are liable for the same damage they will be entitled to claim contribution from each other under the Civil Liability (Contribution) Act 1978.[91] The Act allows for the apportionment of damages between the respective defendants; it does not operate as a defence to the plaintiff's claim. Similarly, judgment against one defendant is not a bar to a subsequent action against other defendants.[92] If the first judgment remains unsatisfied, the plaintiff can sue the other tortfeasors, subject to a possible penalty in costs.[93] Where the plaintiff does not sue all the persons responsible for the damage, a defendant may join the others in third party proceedings.[94]

7.34 The Act applies to any type of action; the defendants' liability need not be based on breach of the same obligation, so a defendant who is in breach of contract may seek contribution from a defendant who is in breach of a duty of care in tort provided that both contributed to the plaintiff's damage.[95] Section 2(1) provides that the amount of contribution shall be "such as may be found by the court to be just and equitable having regard to the extent of that person's responsibility for the damage in question."[96]

7.35 A settlement of the plaintiff's claim before judgment by one defendant does not remove his right to seek contribution from another defendant, irrespective of whether he is or ever was liable in respect of the damage, provided, however, "that he would have been liable assuming that the factual basis of the claim against him could be established."[97] Thus, settlement of a doubtful claim does not prejudice the defendant's claim to contribution provided the doubts concern issues of fact. Where the settlement is based on uncertainty about the law the defendant may have to prove that he was liable to the plaintiff in order to maintain the claim for contribution.[98] In these circumstances he may have to submit to judgment in order to protect his right to contribution.

7.36 Where a defendant has ceased to be liable to the plaintiff he is nonetheless still subject to a claim for contribution by another defendant, unless he ceased to be liable to the plaintiff by virtue of the expiry of a limitation period which extinguished the plaintiff's right of action against him.[99] Most limitation periods, including those applying to actions for personal injuries, do not extinguish the plaintiff's right of action but merely bar his remedy. Thus, the fact that a defendant would not be liable to the plaintiff because the plaintiff's limitation period has expired against him does not prevent another defendant

---

[91] See Dugdale (1979) 42 M.L.R. 182.
[92] Civil Liability (Contribution) Act 1978, s.3.
[93] *Ibid.*, s.4.
[94] R.S.C., Ord. 16.
[95] Civil Liability (Contribution) Act 1978, s.6(1).
[96] Although a defendant cannot be required to pay more by way of contribution than he would have been liable to pay the plaintiff: *ibid.*, s.2(3).
[97] Civil Liability (Contribution) Act 1978, ss.1(2), (4).
[98] Dugdale (1979) 42 M.L.R. 182, 184.
[99] Civil Liability (Contribution) Act 1978, s.1(3).

bringing a contribution claim against him.[1] If the plaintiff has sued the defendant to judgment, section 1(5) of the Civil Liability (Contribution) Act 1978 provides that the judgment is conclusive in contribution proceedings "as to any issue determined by that judgment" in favour of the person from whom contribution is sought. There is a potential conflict here between subsection 1(3) and subsection 1(5), since if the plaintiff's action failed because it was statute barred by the Limitation Act 1980 then subsection 1(5) appears to preclude a contribution claim by another defendant. This provision was intended to apply to a determination of the issue on the merits, not on a procedural point.[2]

The Act does not affect an express or implied contractual or other **7.37** right to indemnity, or an express contractual provision regulating or excluding contribution.[3] Thus, a defendant who is liable to make a contribution under the Act may recover this sum from another defendant under an indemnity clause.[4]

Although the contribution legislation has been used in medical **7.38** litigation,[5] its significance has been greatly reduced in the case of actions against N.H.S. hospital doctors since 1954 when Circular H.M. (54) 32 was introduced. This established a private arrangement between doctors' defence organisations and the Department of Health, by which payment to the plaintiff was apportioned between the defendants by agreement amongst themselves in each case, or (in the absence of agreement) in equal shares. The purpose of this Circular was to provide a formal, though not legally binding, mechanism which would reduce defendants' costs and at the same time present a united front to the plaintiff in the conduct of the litigation. This arrangement was replaced from January 1, 1990 with the introduction of "N.H.S. indemnity" under which health authorities have assumed responsibility for new and existing claims of medical negligence and no longer

---

[1] Similarly, where a defendant has settled the plaintiff's claim against him he may still be liable to make contribution to another defendant: *Logan* v. *Uttlesford District Council* (1984) 136 New L.J. 541. The limitation period for contribution proceedings under the Civil Liability (Contribution) Act 1978 is 2 years from the date of judgment or compromise: Limitation Act 1980, s.10.

[2] *Clerk & Lindsell on Torts*, 16th ed., 1989, para. 2–60. See, however, *Nottingham Health Authority* v. *Nottingham City Council* [1988] 1 W.L.R. 903, 906, where, without reference to subsection 1(5), Balcombe L.J. assumed that a defendant who was held not liable due to a successful limitation plea would still be liable to make contribution; and *R.A. Lister & Co. Ltd.* v. *E.G. Thomson (Shipping) Ltd.* (No. 2) [1987] 3 All E.R. 1032, 1039–1040, holding that a stay in proceedings or dismissal of an action for want of prosecution, which are procedural not substantive issues, do not fall within subsection 1(5) and so do not preclude contribution proceedings.

[3] Civil Liability (Contribution) Act 1978, s.7(3).

[4] *Sims* v. *Foster Wheeler Ltd.* [1966] 1 W.L.R. 769. An employer has no right to indemnity from an employee under the contract of employment if the employer has himself contributed to the damage or if he bears some part of the responsibility, where, *e.g.*, a more senior employee's negligence has contributed to the damage: *Jones* v. *Manchester Corporation* [1952] 2 All E.R. 125, 130, *per* Singleton L.J. Clearly, this rule does not apply to a claim for contribution under the Civil Liability (Contribution) Act 1978.

[5] See, *e.g.*, *Jones* v. *Manchester Corporation* [1952] 2 All E.R. 125, where the issue concerned the respective responsibilities of a junior and inexperienced anaesthetist whose negligence resulted in the death of a patient, and the hospital authority which failed to provide appropriate supervision. The Court of Appeal, taking the view that the hospital should bear the brunt of the responsibility, allocated 80 per cent. to the hospital and 20 per cent. to the doctor; *Collins* v. *Hertfordshire County Council* [1947] 1 K.B. 598, 623–625.

require their medical and dental staff to subscribe to a defence organisation.[6] The health authority's indemnity will cover only health authority responsibilities, namely their vicarious liability for the negligence of staff acting in the course of their employment, and there will be no attempt to seek contribution from the employee. This includes consultants and staff provided by by external agencies.

7.39   The new scheme was introduced as a result of substantial increases in the subscription rates of the medical defence organisations in the 1980s, and the growing pressure to relate subscription rates to the doctor's specialty, with high risk specialties paying a higher rate. It was considered that this could lead to distortion in pay and recruitment to the medical profession. N.H.S. indemnity does not apply to general practitioners except where the general practitioner has a contract of employment (*e.g.* as a clinical assistant at a hospital) with a health authority and the treatment is being given under that contract. If the health authority is essentially providing only hotel services and the patient remains in the general practitioner's care, the hospital authority will not be responsible. Where a case involves a claim against both a health authority and a general practitioner the possibility of a contribution claim exists, but the Circular requests health authorities and general practitioners' representatives to seek to reach agreement out of court as to the proportion of their respective liabilities, and to co-operate fully in the formulation of the defence. Nor does the scheme apply to private hospitals or private work performed by a consultant in a N.H.S. hospital. The Circular concedes, however, that where junior medical staff are involved in the care of private patients in N.H.S. hospitals, they would normally be doing so as part of their contract with the health authority.[7] Any work which is outside the scope of a junior doctor's employment (*e.g.*, reports for insurance companies or locum work for a general practitioner) will not be covered. Similarly, a "Good Samaritan" act of assisting at an accident is not covered, but negligence by a locum doctor, whether "internal" or provided by an external agency is within the scheme.

7.40   N.H.S. Trust hospitals[8] do not fall within N.H.S. indemnity. From April 1, 1991, N.H.S. Trusts have to bear their own losses arising out of claims for clinical negligence although, unlike health authorities, they are free to enter into private insurance arrangements to cover the risk.[9] The assumption is that in practice N.H.S. Trust hospitals will handle and the bear the cost of claims against their clinical staff arising in the course of employment and will not seek contribution against the doctors concerned, since they might otherwise have some difficulty in recruiting or retaining staff.

7.41   In practice, then, contribution claims under the Civil Liability (Contribution) Act 1978 will tend to be limited to actions arising out of

---

[6] See H.C. (89) 34, H.C. (89) (FP) 22; see Appendix; Brazier (1990) 6 P.N. 88; Tingle (1991) 141 New L.J. 630. The new arrangements are to be reviewed in 1992.

[7] Though as Brazier (1990) 6 P.N. 88, 89, n. 5 points out the position of a junior doctor told by a consultant to see to a private patient is particularly unclear.

[8] Introduced under the National Health Service and Community Care Act 1990, ss.5–11, Scheds. 2 and 3.

[9] E.L. (90) 195. The Secretary of State has the power under s.21 of the National Health Service and Community Care Act 1990 to establish a scheme for meeting all classes of liability falling on health authorities and N.H.S. Trusts.

private medicine, disputes between general practitioners and hospitals, and disputes between general practitioners and pharmacists.[10] Of course, it is always open to any defendants to seek to agree their respective responsibilities without recourse to the legislation.

[10] See, *e.g.*, *Dwyer* v. *Roderick* (1983) 127 S.J. 806; *The Times*, November 12, 1983, C.A., where a general practitioner negligently prescribed too high a dosage of a drug, and the pharmacist had negligently failed to spot the error in the prescription. On appeal, liability was apportioned 45 per cent. to the general practitioner and 55 per cent. to the pharmacist; *Prendergast* v. *Sam and Dee Ltd.* [1989] 1 Med. L.R. 36, C.A., where liability was apportioned 25 per cent. to the doctor who negligently wrote a prescription which could be misread, 75 per cent. to the pharmacist who misread the prescription and supplied the patient with the wrong drug.

CHAPTER 8

DEFECTIVE PRODUCTS

8.01 It was the tragedy of thalidomide that first brought to public attention
the problems confronting the victims of defective drugs in obtaining
compensation for their injuries. This provided the stimulus for tighter
control of drug marketing by the Medicines Act 1968, and ultimately
led to the setting up of the Pearson Commission to look into the
system of compensation for personal injuries. Actions in respect of
defective drugs are probably the most common form of medical
product liability claims, but they are not the only product which could
give rise to litigation in a health care setting. Claims have already been
made in respect of defective heart valves,[1] intra-uterine devices,[2] and
contaminated blood products,[3] and it would not be difficult to think of
other products which could provoke litigation if defective.[4]

8.02   The same legal principles apply whatever the product in question,
although drug injuries do appear to create their own special problems.
All drugs have some inherent risk. They are designed to interfere with
the body's chemistry, and some patients will have idiosyncratic reactions. Many drugs cannot be made completely safe for their intended
or ordinary use even when they are properly manufactured and are not
impure. Notwithstanding the medically recognisable risk of harm that
they present, the marketing of such drugs may be justified by their

---

[1] *Sunday Times*, March 10, 1985 reporting on deaths linked to a faulty valve, the
Bjork-Shiley valve, manufactured in the U.S. by a subsidiary of Pfizer; [1990] 32 Law
Soc. Gaz. 7.
    [2] Claims against A. H. Robins, the American pharmaceutical company that marketed
the Dalkon Shield, led to that company going into voluntary liquidation with an
estimated liability of $US 2.5 billion. See Ferrell (1988) 62 A.L.J. 92.
    [3] *Re HIV Haemophiliac Litigation* (1990) 140 New L.J. 1349. See also *H.* v. *Royal
Alexandra Hospital for Children* [1990] 1 Med. L.R. 297 (S.C. of N.S.W.).
    [4] *E.g.,* heart pacemakers; limb joints; tampons, which can cause toxic shock syndrome
(see (1990) 301 B.M.J. 257); donated organs (see *Sumners* v. *Mid-Downs Health
Authority and South East Thames Health Authority* discussed at (1989) 298 B.M.J. 1544);
contaminated or defective donated sperm. It is unclear whether human organs or bodily
fluids can be regarded as "products," at least for the purposes of the Consumer
Protection Act 1987 (see § 8.62), but so far as the tort of negligence is concerned liability
turns on the foreseeability of the risk of harm from contamination, rather than
categorisation as a product or otherwise.

utility.[5] Thus, it can be difficult to come to a judgment about what is a "defective" drug, since the risk of side-effects for a minority of patients may be acceptable in view of the benefits for the majority of patients. Where, on the other hand, an alternative, safe option is available a product which carries inherent risk may be categorised as defective.[6]

A further problem stems from the difficulty of proving causation. **8.03** This arises at two levels. First, it must be shown that the drug in question is capable of causing the type of harm from which the plaintiff is suffering. This will depend upon scientific evidence, which may be difficult to obtain and may be equivocal in its conclusions. Where, for example, there is a substantial delay in the injuries becoming manifest, (as can be the case with teratogenic injuries)[7] and/or where the adverse reactions constitute an addition to the background risk, so that it is extremely difficult, if not impossible, to distinguish drug injuries from other and often unknown causes, the difficulties of proving causation may be insurmountable.[8] Secondly, even where it is accepted that the drug is capable of causing the type of injury concerned, the plaintiff must still prove that *his* injury was attributable to the drug in question and not some other factor, such as the illness for which he was being treated, or an unforeseen interaction between a number of drugs taken at the same time. Where generic drugs or drugs from different manufacturers have been used over a number of years, there may be difficulties simply in identifying a defendant.[9]

Donoghue v. *Stevenson*[10] established that, in addition to any liability **8.04** in contract, there could also be liability in the tort of negligence for

---

[5] *Buchan* v. *Ortho Pharmaceutical (Canada) Ltd.* (1986) 25 D.L.R. (4th) 658, 668, (Ont. C.A.). Surprisingly, perhaps, there is no reported case in this country in which a court has had to make a finding of liability against a drug manufacturer. Claims have been made in respect of, *inter alia*, Thalidomide, Opren, Debendox, Myodil, pertussis vaccine, neomycin, and benzodiazepine, but the actions have, to date, either settled or failed for want of proof of causation (see *Davies* v. *Eli Lilly & Co.* (1987) 137 New L.J. 1183 and Dyer (1988) 296 B.M.J. 109 on the Opren settlement; and Orme (1985) 291 B.M.J. 918 on Debendox). Note that in the case of vaccine damage, compensation may be available under the Vaccine Damage Payments Act 1979, though the sums available are small in relation to the harm suffered (see s.1(1A), as inserted by the Social Security Act 1985, s.23 and the Vaccine Damage Payments Act 1979 Statutory Sum Order 1985 (S.I. 1985/1249), specifying £20,000) and there may still be problems in proving causation (see *Loveday* v. *Renton* [1990] 1 Med. L.R. 117). For discussion of the Act see Dworkin [1978–79] J.S.W.L. 330.

[6] *Nicholson* v. *John Deere Ltd.* (1986) 34 D.L.R. (4th) 542, 549, *per* Smith J., (Ont. H.C.): "A manufacturer does not have the right to manufacture an inherently dangerous article when a method exists of manufacturing the same article without risk of harm. No amount of or degree of specificity of warning will exonerate him from liability if he does."

[7] See, *e.g.*, *Sindell* v. *Abbott Laboratories* (1980) 607 P. 2d 924, *post*, § 8.51.

[8] *Kay* v. *Ayrshire and Arran Health Board* [1987] 2 All E.R. 417, where the plaintiff failed to prove that an overdose of penicillin could cause deafness; *Loveday* v. *Renton* [1990] 1 Med. L.R. 117, where the plaintiff failed to prove, on a balance of probabilities, that pertussis vaccine could cause brain damage in young children, although it was "possible" that there was a causal link; see also *Rothwell* v. *Raes* (1988) 54 D.L.R. (4th) 193, on the pertussis vaccine and causation; *D. and R.* v. *Schering Chemicals Ltd.* (1982) (unreported), Q.B.D. See also the *Royal Commission on Civil Liability and Compensation for Personal Injury*, Cmnd. 7054 (1978) Vol. I, para. 1364.

[9] See, *e.g.*, *Mann* v. *Wellcome Foundation Ltd.* (1989) (unreported), Q.B.D.; *cf.* the approach adopted to this type of problem by the California Court of Appeal in *Sindell* v. *Abbott Laboratories* (1980) 607 P. 2d 924, § 8.51, *post*.

[10] [1932] A.C. 562.

defective products. However, in spite of some cases which suggested that in certain circumstances a high standard of care would be required, the action has remained fault-based. The English courts have not followed the American example where strict liability in tort was established.[11] In the 1970s a number of law reform bodies recommended that strict liability for defective products should be introduced, and now, following a European Community initiative, the United Kingdom has a form of strict liability by virtue of the Consumer Protection Act 1987. Thus, liability for damage caused by defective products is a combination of liability in contract, the tort of negligence and under Part I of the Consumer Protection Act 1987.

I. CONTRACT

8.05 The ultimate consumer of a product will rarely be in a contractual relationship with the manufacturer, and this is particularly true of medicinal products. However, a defective product sold by a retailer may give rise to an action for breach of contract which may be traced back through the contractual chain of supply to the manufacturer in the form of indemnity claims. The contractual action is limited, by the doctrine of privity of contract, to the purchaser of the product and it is of no value to, for example, a member of the purchaser's family injured by the product. This is the major drawback of the claim in contract.

8.06 Where a contractual remedy is available it will often be more advantageous to the plaintiff than a claim in tort. A purchaser of goods will have the benefit of implied terms as to merchantable quality and fitness for purpose of the goods,[12] which in the case of "consumer" transactions cannot be excluded.[13] Liability is strict, in the sense that it does not have to be shown that the defect was attributable to the vendor's fault, and the exercise of reasonable care is not a defence. Moreover, the contractual action is available for products which are defective in quality, though not dangerous, if the defect is such as to constitute a breach of warranty. This type of claim is not available in the tort of negligence.

8.07 Thus, non-prescription products sold by retail pharmacists over the counter may be the subject of a contractual action if the purchaser sustains injury, as would drugs supplied on private (*i.e.* non-National Health Service) prescription. Products supplied under N.H.S. prescriptions, on the other hand, are not supplied under a contract between the pharmacist and the customer, but by virtue of the patient's statutory right to demand the product on payment of the prescription

---

[11] See *Restatement, Torts* (2d), § 402A.
[12] Sale of Goods Act 1979, s.14; Supply of Goods and Services Act 1982, s.4. Note that what is merchantable quality or fit for its purpose will be a matter of degree in the case of drugs which may have known side-effects; it does include, however, the packaging and instructions for use, so that if the instructions are wrong or misleading the goods are not merchantable or fit for their purpose: *Wormell* v. *R.H.M. Agriculture (East) Ltd.* [1986] 1 All E.R. 769.
[13] Unfair Contract Terms Act 1977, s.6.

charge and the Minister's statutory obligation to supply it.[14] The result is that, in practice, contractual claims arising from defective drugs are likely to be extremely rare.

A retailer sued in contract by the purchaser of defective goods will **8.08** normally have a contractual claim for indemnity against his own vendor (wholesaler or distributor), and so on, up the contractual chain to the manufacturer who produced the defective goods, subject to any valid exemption clauses. In this way, in theory at least, liability will rest with the person responsible for the defect. This contractual chain may break down if, for example, one link is missing, having gone into liquidation or is simply untraceable through lack of records.[15] The doctrine of privity of contract then prevents any further claims along the contractual chain.[16] From the plaintiff purchaser's point of view this will be irrelevant, unless it is the retailer who is no longer available to be sued, in which case the purchaser's contractual claim will be useless. This will leave the purchaser in the same position as all other plaintiffs injured by a defective product, having to rely on a claim in tort for negligence or under the Consumer Protection Act 1987.

II. TORT

1. Manufacturers' duty

In *Donoghue* v. *Stevenson*[17] the House of Lords held that the **8.09** manufacturers of a defective product owed a duty of care in negligence to the ultimate consumer of the product, notwithstanding the absence of any contractual relationship between the consumer and the manufacturer.[18] In the course of his speech Lord Atkin expressed the duty in these terms:

"A manufacturer of products which he sells in such a form as to show that he intends them to reach the ultimate consumer in the form in which they left him, with no reasonable possibility of intermediate examination, and with the knowledge that the absence of reasonable care in the preparation or putting up of the

---

[14] *Pfizer Corpn.* v. *Ministry of Health* [1965] A.C. 512; *Appleby* v. *Sleep* [1968] 2 All E.R. 265, 269.

[15] As occurred in *Lambert* v. *Lewis* [1981] 1 All E.R. 1185.

[16] There may be a claim, however, under the Civil Liability (Contribution) Act 1978. In addition, it has been held that economic loss suffered by a distributor in a chain of supply which consists of a liability to pay damages to the ultimate consumer for physical injuries, or to indemnify a distributor lower in the chain for his liability to the consumer for physical injuries, may be recoverable from the manufacturer under the principle of *Donoghue* v. *Stevenson* [1932] A.C. 562: see *Lambert* v. *Lewis* [1981] 1 All E.R. 1185, 1192; *Virgo Steamship Co. S.A.* v. *Skaarup Shipping Corpn.* [1988] 1 Lloyd's Rep. 352.

[17] [1932] A.C. 562.

[18] So removing the so-called "privity of contract" fallacy, which argued that the plaintiff was seeking to take the benefit of a contract (between manufacturer and wholesaler or retailer) to which he was not a party, attributed to *Winterbottom* v. *Wright* (1842) 10 M. & W. 109. For discussion of the privity of contract fallacy see *Dutton* v. *Bognor Regis Urban District Council* [1972] 1 Q.B. 373, 392–393.

products will result in injury to the consumer's life or property, owes a duty to the consumer to take that reasonable care."[19]

Lord Thankerton said that the defendant brought himself into a direct relationship with the consumer by placing his product upon the market in a form which precluded interference with or examination of the product by any intermediate handler, with the result that the consumer was entitled to rely on the exercise of reasonable care by the manufacturer to secure that the product should not be harmful.

8.10   The manufacturer's duty has been given a broad interpretation. "Product" includes almost any item capable of causing damage, such as underpants,[20] motor cars,[21] hair dye,[22] lifts,[23] and chemicals.[24] Similarly, "ultimate consumer" means anyone foreseeably harmed by the defective product. This includes the user of the product, such as a donee, a member of the purchaser's family, including a foetus *in utero*,[25] or an employee of the purchaser,[26] someone who handles the product, such as a storeman or a shopkeeper,[27] and a by-stander.[28]

8.11   The range of potential defendants has also been extended to include not only manufacturers, but also repairers,[29] and assemblers.[30] A supplier of goods, such as a retailer or wholesaler, may be liable if the circumstances are such that he ought reasonably to have inspected the goods or tested them.[31] Distributors who obtain goods from suppliers of doubtful reputation ought to test them,[32] and *a fortiori* when the manufacturers' instructions state that the product should be tested.[33] The duty does not arise in all cases of supply, only where the circumstances indicate that an inspection or test is reasonably required. Clearly, if the dangerous defect was in fact known to the supplier he ought, at least, to give a warning to the recipient.

8.12   An issue that arises in the context of pharmaceutical products is the possible liability of statutory regulatory agencies. Under the Medicines Act 1968 the manufacture and distribution of medicines in this country is regulated by a Licensing Authority, which consists of Health

---

[19] [1932] A.C. 562, 599. This duty applies to personal injuries and physical damage to other property, including economic loss consequential on the physical damage, applying the usual principles of the tort of negligence. Pure economic loss, which includes physical damage to the product itself, is not recoverable: *Murphy* v. *Brentwood District Council* [1990] 2 All E.R. 908; *Muirhead* v. *Industrial Tank Specialities Ltd.* [1985] 3 All E.R. 705.

[20] *Grant* v. *Australian Knitting Mills Ltd.* [1936] A.C. 85.

[21] *Herschtal* v. *Stewart & Arden Ltd.* [1940] 1 K.B. 155.

[22] *Watson* v. *Buckley, Osborne Garrett & Co. Ltd.* [1940] 1 All E.R. 174.

[23] *Haseldine* v. *Daw & Son Ltd.* [1941] 2 K.B. 343.

[24] *Vacwell Engineering Co. Ltd.* v. *BDH Chemicals Ltd.* [1971] 1 Q.B. 111.

[25] Congenital Disabilities (Civil Liability) Act, 1976; see §§ 2.28–2.29.

[26] *Davie* v. *New Merton Board Mills Ltd.* [1959] A.C. 604.

[27] *Barnett* v. *Packer (H. & J.) & Co. Ltd.* [1940] 3 All E.R. 575.

[28] *Stennett* v. *Hancock* [1939] 2 All E.R. 578.

[29] *Stennett* v. *Hancock* [1939] 2 All E.R. 578; *Haseldine* v. *Daw & Son Ltd.* [1941] 2 K.B. 343, 379.

[30] *Howard* v. *Furness Houlder Argentine Lines Ltd.* [1936] 2 All E.R. 781.

[31] *Andrews* v. *Hopkinson* [1957] 1 Q.B. 229; *cf. Hurley* v. *Dyke* [1979] R.T.R. 265. See also *Good-Wear Treaders Ltd.* v. *D. & B. Holdings Ltd.* (1979) 98 D.L.R. (3d) 59, holding that the supplier owes a duty not to supply a product to a purchaser whom he knows intends to misuse the product, thereby endangering the safety of third parties.

[32] *Watson* v. *Buckley, Osborne Garrett & Co.* [1940] 1 All E.R. 174.

[33] *Kubach* v. *Hollands* [1937] 3 All E.R. 907.

Ministers and Agriculture Ministers.[34] The Licensing Authority is advised by the Medicines Commission, and specialist committees set up under section 4 of the Act, including the Committee on the Safety of Medicines (C.S.M.) and the Committee on the Review of Medicines (C.R.M.).[35] The C.S.M. assesses product licence applications and the C.R.M. reviews product licences, which are granted only when the Licensing Authority is satisfied as to the safety, efficacy and quality of the product.[36]

The effect is that pharmaceutical products distributed in the United **8.13** Kingdom will have been scrutinised for safety by an independent statutory body. If the product is found to have a design defect it is arguable that the licensing authority should be responsible along with the manufacturer, for allowing a defective product to be marketed. The Medicines Act 1968 does not confer any general civil right of action for breach of its terms, nor does it grant any immunities from any action that would otherwise be available.[37] It is not certain, however, that the Licensing Authority would be held to owe a duty of care to members of the public in granting a licence.

Whilst the regulatory agencies have been sued,[38] the issue has been **8.14** considered by the courts only in the course of interlocutory proceedings. In *Department of Health and Social Security* v. *Kinnear*[39] claims were brought against the D.H.S.S. in respect of injuries alleged to have been caused by reaction to whooping cough vaccine. The D.H.S.S. adopted a policy of promoting immunisation against whooping cough in the bona fide exercise of a statutory discretion under the National Health Service Act 1946, s.26. Stuart-Smith J. held that since the policy was within the limits of the discretion it could not give rise to a cause of action.[40] Even allegations of negligence on the part of the department's servants, *e.g.* in failing to submit relevant reports to the persons taking the decisions prior to and leading up to the formulation of the policy, could not found a cause of action against the department.

On the other hand, claims that the D.H.S.S. had given negligent or **8.15** misleading advice to health authorities regarding the circumstances in which inoculations should be performed, and the factors to be applied in determining whether particular individuals should be inoculated, were not struck out as disclosing no reasonable cause of action. It was at least arguable that the alleged negligent advice fell within the

---

[34] Medicines Act 1968, ss.1, 6. The Act applies to "medicinal products" which means a substance or article (but not an instrument, apparatus or appliance) used for a medicinal purpose: see s.130 for a detailed definition. For discussion of the effectiveness of the regulatory scheme established by the Medicines Act see Teff (1984) 47 M.L.R. 303.

[35] *Ibid.*, ss.2–5.

[36] *Ibid.*, ss.19–20.

[37] Medicines Act 1968, s.133(2).

[38] *E.g.*, in the Opren litigation: *Davies* v. *Eli Lilly & Co.* [1987] 3 All E.R. 94 (the report deals only with the issue of costs); and in connection with the contamination of blood products with HIV virus: *Re HIV Haemophiliac Litigation* (1990) 140 New L.J. 1349.

[39] *The Times*, July 7, 1984.

[40] Applying *Anns* v. *Merton London Borough Council* [1978] A.C. 728, 754; *Dorset Yacht Co. Ltd.* v. *Home Office* [1970] A.C. 1004, 1067. See also *Bonthrone* v. *Secretary of State for Scotland* 1987 S.L.T. 34; *Ross* v. *Secretary of State for Scotland* [1990] 1 Med. L.R. 235.

operational category, in which negligence in the performance of a statutory power could give rise to a duty of care, adopting the operational/policy dichotomy used by Lord Wilberforce in *Anns* v. *Merton London Borough Council*.[41] It is not clear, however, whether this distinction between operational and policy decisions as a basis for determining negligence in the performance of statutory powers will continue to be used by the courts following the overruling of *Anns* in *Murphy* v. *Brentwood District Council*.[42] In *Re HIV Haemophiliac Litigation*[43] the Court of Appeal had to consider whether haemophiliacs who had been infected with the HIV virus as a result of receiving contaminated blood products, had a prima facie case in negligence against, *inter alia*, the Department of Health, the Licensing Authority under the Medicines Act 1968 and the C.S.M., in the course of proceedings for discovery of documents. Ralph Gibson L.J. commented that although it was difficult to prove negligence when the defendant was required to exercise discretion and form judgments on the allocation of public resources, that was not sufficient to make it clear that there could be no claim in negligence. This interlocutory decision appears simply to assume, without deciding the issue, that a duty of care could exist.

8.16 In a number of recent cases it has been held that certain regulatory authorities do not owe a duty of care to members of the public when performing their statutory functions.[44] Most, though not all,[45] of these cases were concerned with pure economic loss, rather than personal injuries and thus may not be directly applicable to actions against the Licensing Authority, the Medicines Commission or the C.S.M. Various other factors have been taken into account, however, in denying the existence of a duty of care, some of which would be relevant in this context. All of the cases deal with liability for the conduct of third parties, where the question will frequently be: what degree of control did the defendant have over the third party's conduct? The mere fact that the regulatory body could register or de-register the third party, and thus had some control over whether he could continue the operations which caused the plaintiff's loss, is not a ground for imposing a duty of care.[46] It has been said that the imposition of a duty of care might lead to a conflict of duties, in which the regulatory agency adopts an unusually conservative or defensive approach to its functions because of the fear of liability, a practice

---

[41] [1978] A.C. 728. Similarly, in *Rothwell* v. *Raes* (1988) 54 D.L.R. (4th) 193, 346 (Ont. H.C.) it was held that the Ontario Ministry of Health did owe a duty of care with regard to the implementation of a policy decision to establish a system for pertussis vaccination, although the Ministry had not been negligent on the facts. The trial judge relied on *City of Kamloops* v. *Neilsen* (1984) 10 D.L.R. (4th) 641, in which the Supreme Court of Canada had adopted Lord Wilberforce's operational/policy dichotomy.

[42] [1990] 2 All E.R. 908.

[43] [1990] N.L.J. Law Rep. 1349.

[44] See *Yuen Kun-yeu* v. *A.-G. of Hong Kong* [1987] 2 All E.R. 705; *Davis* v. *Radcliffe* [1990] 2 All E.R. 536; *Rowling* v. *Takaro Properties Ltd.* [1988] 1 All E.R. 163; *Minories Finance Ltd.* v. *Arthur Young* [1989] 2 All E.R. 105; *Mills* v. *Winchester Diocesan Board of Finance* [1989] 2 All E.R. 317; *Murphy* v. *Brentwood District Council* [1990] 2 All E.R. 908.

[45] *cf. Hill* v. *Chief Constable of West Yorkshire* [1988] 2 All E.R. 238.

[46] *Yuen Kun-yeu* v. *A.-G. of Hong Kong* [1987] 2 All E.R. 705; *Davis* v. *Radcliffe* [1990] 2 All E.R. 536.

which may not be in the public interest.[47] Where the plaintiff would
have an alternative remedy, even against another defendant,[48] or
where the plaintiff is merely a member of a large unascertained class of
potential plaintiffs, the courts may deny the existence of a duty of
care.[49]

In *Yuen Kun-yeu* v. *A.-G. of Hong Kong*[50] the Privy Council took **8.17**
the view that since the statutory framework which established the
particular regulatory system did not provide for compensation, it
would be "strange" for the courts to superimpose a common law duty
of care. Similarly, in *Murphy* v. *Brentwood District Council*[51] Lord
Oliver pointed to the absence of any specific provision in the legislation creating a private law right of action for breach of statutory duty,
as one reason for not imposing a duty of care on the local authority in
exercising its statutory powers to ensure that new buildings comply
with building regulations. Section 133(2) of the Medicines Act 1968
expressly provides that the Act does not confer a civil right of action,
and a court could adopt the reasoning of the Privy Council in *Yuen
Kun-yeu* in order to deny the existence of a duty of care.

In response it might be argued that most of these cases have been **8.18**
concerned with actions for pure economic loss, and that different
considerations apply where a statutory body can be said to owe a
statutory duty to the public with regard to public health and safety, as
is clearly the position under the Medicines Act 1968. This was, in
theory at least, the rationale for the decision in *Anns*, since the local
authority's duty was said to arise where there was a present or
imminent danger to the health or safety of the occupants of the
premises. This interpretation of the nature of the plaintiffs' loss in
Anns was finally shown to be mistaken in *Murphy* v. *Brentwood
District Council*,[52] where the damage to the plaintiff's house was
categorised as economic loss. Counsel for the local authority in
Murphy had conceded, however, that the local authority would owe a
duty of care with respect to any personal injuries sustained as a result
of the defendants' negligent failure adequately to perform their
statutory powers, although this concession was not necessarily
approved.[53]

These cases make it difficult to predict whether, if the matter had to **8.19**
be decided, the regulatory bodies established by the Medicines Act
1968 would be held to owe a duty of care to individual patients in

---

[47] *Yuen Kun-yeu* v. *A.-G. of Hong Kong* [1987] 2 All E.R. 705, 715–716; *Rowling* v.
Takaro Properties Ltd. [1988] 1 All E.R. 163, 173; *Hill* v. *Chief Constable of West
Yorkshire* [1988] 2 All E.R. 238, 243–244. On the risk of "defensive licensing" of
pharmaceutical products see Teff (1984) 47 M.L.R. 303, 310–311.

[48] *La Banque Financière de la Cité S.A.* v. *Westgate Insurance Co. Ltd.* [1988] 2
Lloyd's Rep. 513, 563; *Simaan General Contracting Co.* v. *Pilkington Glass Ltd.* (No. 2)
[1988] 1 All E.R. 791, 804–806.

[49] *Hill* v. *Chief Constable of West Yorkshire* [1988] 2 All E.R. 238, 243.

[50] [1987] 2 All E.R. 705, 713.

[51] [1990] 2 All E.R. 908, 937.

[52] [1990] 2 All E.R. 908; having been radically undermined in *D. & F. Estates Ltd.* v.
Church Commissioners for England [1988] 2 All E.R. 992.

[53] Lord Mackay (*ibid.*, p. 912) and Lord Keith (at p. 917) reserved their opinions on
whether any duty would be owed at all, and Lord Bridge (at p. 929) was prepared to
assume, but was by no means satisfied that the assumption was correct, that the local
authority's potential liability in tort was co-extensive with that of the builder.

performing their statutory function of authorising and reviewing the marketing of pharmaceutical products, although it may be argued that *Re HIV Haemophiliac Litigation*[54] does provide some support for the proposition. It is submitted that the regulatory framework established by the Medicines Act is clearly directed to the protection of members of the public from risks to their health, and that on principle the regulatory agencies should be held to owe a duty of care to individual patients who suffer injury as a consequence of negligence in the discharge of their statutory powers.

2. Intermediate inspection

8.20   The manufacturer's duty applies to products which are intended to "reach the ultimate consumer in the form in which they left him, with no reasonable possibility of intermediate examination."[55] The article need not reach the ultimate consumer in a sealed package for the duty to apply. It is sufficient if it was subject to the same defect as it had when it left the manufacturer, and the consumer used it as it was intended to be used.[56] The mere opportunity for inspection of the product after it has left the hands of the manufacturer will not excuse the defendant.[57] Lord Atkin's term "reasonable possibility" of inter-mediate inspection has been interpreted to mean "reasonable proba-bility" of intermediate inspection.[58] Thus, the manufacturer is liable if he has no reason to contemplate that an intermediate examination will occur, whether by a third party or the consumer. The question is whether a reasonable person would anticipate an examination before use which would avoid injury to the user.[59]

8.21   Where the manufacturer has given a warning, for example, to test a product before use, this may be sufficient to discharge his duty.[60] The effect of the warning will depend upon its terms. For example, the suggestion that the product be tested before use creates a reasonable probability of intermediate inspection, whereas a warning against using the product in certain circumstances (*e.g.* contra-indications for use of a drug) limits what can be regarded as ordinary use. Ignoring the

---

[54] (1990) 140 New L.J. 1349.

[55] *Donoghue* v. *Stevenson* [1932] A.C. 562, 599, *per* Lord Atkin.

[56] *Grant* v. *Australian Knitting Mills Ltd.* [1936] A.C. 85.

[57] *Herschtal* v. *Stewart & Arden Ltd.* [1940] 1 K.B. 155; *Griffiths* v. *Arch Engineering Co. Ltd.* [1968] 3 All E.R. 217.

[58] *Paine* v. *Colne Valley Electricity Supply Co. Ltd.* [1938] 4 All E.R. 803, 808–9; *Buckner* v. *Ashby and Horner Ltd.* [1941] 1 K.B. 321, 333; *Haseldine* v. *Daw & Son Ltd.* [1941] 2 K.B. 343, 376.

[59] *Gallagher* v. *N. McDowell Ltd.* [1961] N.I. 26, 42. In *Aswan Engineering Establish-ment Co.* v. *Lupdine Ltd.* [1987] 1 All E.R. 135, 153–4 Lloyd L.J. said that there is no independent requirement for the plaintiff to show that there was no reasonable possibility of intermediate examination. Rather, this is merely a factor, usually an important factor, which the court must consider when determining whether the damage was reasonably foreseeable.

[60] See further §§ 8.32–8.37. In *Holmes* v. *Ashford* [1950] 2 All E.R. 76 the manufacturers of a hair dye were held not liable when a hairdresser disregarded an instruction to test the product before using it on a customer; *Kubach* v. *Hollands* [1937] 3 All E.R. 907 the manufacturer of a chemical was held not liable to a schoolgirl injured in an explosion, having warned the retailer to examine and test the chemical before use. The retailer did not test the chemical or warn the teacher who purchased it that it should be tested.

warning might constitute a misuse of the product. It is clear that the warning need not necessarily be addressed to the ultimate consumer. A warning to an intermediary, such as a prescribing doctor or pharmacist, may be sufficient.[61]

The question of intermediate examination is closely related to the **8.22** concepts of causation and contributory negligence. It has been held that there is no liability if the plaintiff knew of the danger and ignored it,[62] nor if a third party knew of the danger, and, being under a duty to remove the product from circulation, failed to do so.[63] These cases can be explained in terms of causation rather than intermediate examination. The defendant's negligence was not the cause of the damage because the intervening conduct of the plaintiff or the third party broke the chain of causation.[64]

It is arguable, however, that a defendant who has created a **8.23** dangerous situation should not be excused merely because someone else, whether an intermediary or the plaintiff, has failed to remove the danger. If both have been at fault then both should be held responsible. In the case of a negligent intermediary this could be achieved by apportioning liability between the manufacturer and the intermediary under the Civil Liability (Contribution) Act 1978. If it is the plaintiff who has failed to use a reasonable opportunity to examine the goods, then it is a case of contributory negligence, for which damages can be apportioned. Knowledge of the danger will be irrelevant, however, if there were no practical steps that the plaintiff could take to avoid it.[65] In *Rimmer* v. *Liverpool City Council* the Court of Appeal said that an opportunity for inspection by the plaintiff will not exonerate the defendant unless the plaintiff "was free to remove or avoid the danger in the sense that it was reasonable to expect him to do so, and unreasonable for him to run the risk of being injured by the danger."[66] The circumstances in which a patient could be said to have a realistic opportunity for intermediate inspection of a medicinal product must be rare indeed.

If the consumer misuses the product in an unforeseeable fashion the **8.24** defendant will not be liable. This is not because of contributory negligence or causation, but because the manufacturer is responsible only for dangers arising from a product's contemplated use. If misused, the product cannot be said to be "defective," so there is no breach of duty.[67] On the other hand, where the misuse is foreseeable there will at least be an obligation to give a warning not to use the product in this manner, and in some instances there may be a duty not to supply a product which it is known will be misused.[68]

3. What is "defective"?

Defects may arise in the manufacture or design of the product, or in **8.25** its presentation with inadequate warnings or instructions for use. The

[61] See §§ 8.33–8.35, *post.*
[62] *Farr* v. *Butters Bros & Co.* [1932] 2 K.B. 606.
[63] *Taylor* v. *Rover Co. Ltd.* [1966] 1 W.L.R. 1491.
[64] *Grant* v. *Australian Knitting Mills Ltd.* [1936] A.C. 85, 105.
[65] *Denny* v. *Supplies and Transport Co. Ltd.* [1950] 2 K.B. 374.
[66] [1984] 1 All E.R. 930, 938.
[67] *Aswan Engineering Establishment Co.* v. *Lupdine Ltd.* [1987] 1 All E.R. 135, 154.
[68] See, *e.g., Good-Wear Treaders Ltd.* v. *D. & B. Holdings Ltd.* (1979) 98 D.L.R. (3d) 59.

standard of care required is the usual standard in all actions for negligence: reasonable care in all the circumstances of the case.

Manufacturing defects

8.26 Examples of manufacturing defects include construction faults, contamination of the product, errors in mixing compounds, and faulty packaging which cause the product to deteriorate. Manufacturers are almost invariably held liable for this type of error,[69] although they may escape responsibility where the defect could have been identified by intermediate inspection. Since the product fails to conform to the manufacturer's own design specification it is easier for the plaintiff to prove negligence. The defect must have arisen while under the defendant's control; intermeddling by a third party at a later stage will exculpate the manufacturer, unless the intermeddling ought reasonably to have been foreseen and guarded against.[70] For example, the manufacturer is not liable if the product has been stored improperly by a retailer causing it to deteriorate, or (in the context of an allegation of a failure to warn) if consumer information leaflets have been removed from the package after it left the manufacturer's control.

Design defects

8.27 Where the product has a design defect, it conforms to the manufacturer's specification but causes injury from ordinary use in a manner that was not anticipated at the time of design or manufacture. The product is intrinsically unsafe. Manufacturers undoubtedly have a duty to exercise reasonable care in the design of a new product,[71] which includes an obligation to be careful in conducting the research which goes into the design.[72] The courts are generally reluctant, however, to impose liability for negligent design. One of the difficulties is that the defect may not have been apparent before the product was marketed. For liability in negligence the defect must have been foreseeable at the time of design and manufacture: if the risk was unforeseeable in the light of the scientific and technical knowledge at the time there is no negligence.[73] Whilst a manufacturer is under a duty to keep abreast of

---

[69] See § 8.47.

[70] See also the Consumer Protection Act 1987, s.4(1)(d), which provides a defence where the defect arose after the supply by the defendant.

[71] *Hindustan Steam Shipping Co. Ltd.* v. *Siemens Bros. & Co.* [1955] 1 Lloyd's Rep. 167.

[72] *Vacwell Engineering Co. Ltd.* v. *BDH Chemicals Ltd.* [1971] 1 Q.B. 88, 99, *per* Rees J.: " . . . it was the duty of BDH to have established and maintained a system under which adequate investigation and research into the scientific literature took place in order to discover, *inter alia*, what hazards were known before a new, or little known, chemical was marketed"; see also at p. 109.

[73] For an example of this in the context of a medical product liability action see *Mann* v. *Wellcome Foundation Ltd.* (1989) (unreported), Q.B.D., where it was held that the risk of deafness from the application of neomycin spray to burns was unforeseeable in the light of the medical and scientific knowledge. Unforeseeable reactions may also be held to be too remote a consequence of the breach of duty: see *Sheridan* v. *Boots Co. Ltd.* (1980) (unreported), Q.B.D., in which the plaintiff contracted Stevens-Johnson syndrome as a side-effect of an anti-inflammatory drug, which was known to cause gastric ulcers. The injury was held to be too remote, because Stevens-Johnson syndrome was not damage of the same type as gastric disturbance. See further § 5.70.

medical and scientific discoveries,[74] the courts are wary of making judgments with the benefit of hindsight.[75]

On the other hand, manufacturers cannot automatically rely on the **8.28** innovative nature of their product, claiming that they were engaged on a "venture into the unknown" where the risks were unforeseeable because they were operating at the frontiers of human knowledge. In *Independent Broadcasting Authority* v. *EMI Electronics Ltd. and BICC Construction Ltd.*[76] the House of Lords held that the designers of a new type of television mast were negligent, even though it was the first such mast to be constructed anywhere in the world. Lord Edmund-Davies said that, although judgment on hindsight has to be avoided, the designers had a duty to identify and think through the problems presented by their lack of empirical knowledge so that the dimensions of the venture into the unknown could be adequately assessed:

> "And it is no answer to say . . . 'it wasn't obvious because it hadn't been considered.' The learned trial judge held that it should have been, and in my judgment he was right in saying so."[77]

The graver the danger, the greater the need for special care, and in some instances the risks may be so great or their elimination may be so difficult to ensure with reasonable certainty that the only reasonable course is to abandon the project altogether. "The law requires even pioneers to be prudent."[78]

The difficulty with medicinal products, and particularly drugs, is that **8.29** most if not all are recognised as carrying some degree of risk, from side-effects, allergic reactions, or other unforeseen consequences. The question of what is safe is inevitably a relative concept, particularly in this field. It is a question of whether a reasonable person would consider the relative risk acceptable given the objective desired in using the product, and the risks associated with alternative treatments or non-treatment. The risks that would be acceptable in producing a new analgesic would be far less than the risks attached to a new drug for the treatment of, say, cancer or AIDS. Provided that the risk-benefit ratio is acceptable, and provided the manufacturer has taken all reasonable care to eliminate risks (*e.g.* by proper scientific research, including volunteer and clinical

---

[74] *Stokes* v. *Guest, Keen & Nettlefold (Bolts & Nuts) Ltd.* [1968] 1 W.L.R. 1776, 1783; *Cartwright* v. *GKN Sankey Ltd.* [1972] 2 Lloyd's Rep. 242, 259; *Bolam* v. *Friern Hospital Management Committee* [1957] 2 All E.R. 118, 122.

[75] See, *e.g.,* the comments of Mustill J. in *Thompson* v. *Smiths Shiprepairers (North Shields) Ltd.* [1984] 1 All E.R. 881, 894, on the question of the time at which employers became negligent in failing to take precautions against hearing loss, given the knowledge within the industry: "One must be careful, when considering documents culled for the purpose of a trial, and studied by reference to a single isolated issue, not to forget that they once formed part of a flood of print on numerous aspects of industrial life, in which many items were bound to be overlooked. However conscientious the employer, he cannot read every textbook and periodical, attend every exhibition and conference, on every technical issue which might arise in the course of his business; nor can he necessarily be expected to grasp the importance of every single item which he comes across." *Mann* v. *Wellcome Foundation Ltd.* (1989) (unreported), Q.B.D., provides a similar example in the context of product liability; *cf.* also the "development risks" defence under the Consumer Protection Act 1987, s.4(1)(*e*), § 8.87, *post.*

[76] (1980) 14 Build. L.R. 1.

[77] *Ibid.*, p. 31.

[78] *Ibid.*, p. 28, *per* Lord Edmund-Davies.

trials, and full reference to published literature), it is not negligent to market the drug. Where the reaction is rare, but severe, it will be unlikely that studies will reveal this before marketing.[79] On the other hand, where a manufacturer had sold 20 million bottles of corn solvent to the public, it was said that one aspect of the danger to the public arose from the wide variation in tolerance by different individuals of the kerotolytic substance when applied to the skin as distinct from corns. Accordingly:

> "one must have in contemplation pretty well the whole scope of human variation in that vast market. There was a duty on the defendants to give some warning and to secure the bottle in some better way. . . ."[80]

8.30   The difficulty of proving negligence will be even greater where the plaintiff has sustained injury while taking part in a programme of research, whether in the form of pre-clinical or clinical trials. Adverse reactions are more likely to be regarded as unforeseeable and therefore unavoidable with the exercise of reasonable care. A plaintiff would probably have to establish negligence in the conduct of the research.[81]

Marketing defects

8.31   It is not necessarily enough for a manufacturer simply to produce an article that has a "safe" design and conforms to its design specification. There is an obligation to supply adequate information to the consumer to allow him to use the product safely. At its simplest this involves informing the consumer how the product should be used and, where necessary, warning against improper and potentially dangerous misuse. A warning may allow the user to avoid the danger altogether. Moreover, some products have an inherent and irreducible element of risk in their use, and a warning may give the user the opportunity to make an informed decision whether to expose himself to that risk. This is more likely to be the position in the case of drugs.

4. Warnings

8.32   An adequate warning may be sufficient to discharge the manufacturer's duty of care, as may a warning that in its existing condition a product is unsafe.[82] The explicitness of the warning will vary with the danger likely

---

[79] See, *e.g.*, Newdick (1985) 101 L.Q.R. 405, 418–9.

[80] *Devilez* v. *Boots Pure Drug Co. Ltd.* (1962) 106 S.J. 552, *per* Elwes J.

[81] See § 3.44. An *ex gratia* payment of compensation may be available to a healthy volunteer or a patient who sustains injury during the course of a drug trial: see § 3.45, n. 85.

[82] *Kubach* v. *Hollands* [1937] 2 All E.R. 907; *Holmes* v. *Ashford* [1950] 2 All E.R. 76. See the example of Goddard L.J. in *Haseldine* v. *Daw & Son Ltd.* [1941] 2 K.B. 343, 380. In *Hurley* v. *Dyke* [1979] R.T.R. 265 the House of Lords apparently accepted that a warning that a second hand car was sold "as seen and with all its faults" might have been sufficient to fulfil the defendant's duty even if he had known of a specific defect but had failed to advise the purchaser of the danger; *cf. Andrews* v. *Hopkinson* [1957] 1 Q.B. 229.

to be encountered in the ordinary use of the product,[83] although where a
method exists of manufacturing the same product without risk of harm
then no amount or degree of specificity of warning will exonerate the
manufacturer of an inherently dangerous article.[84]

It is not necessary that the warning be addressed directly to the **8.33**
consumer where a product is intended to be used under the supervision
of experts. A warning given to the expert will normally be sufficient to
discharge the manufacturer's duty of care.[85] In the case of prescription
products the prescribing doctor is clearly in the position of an
intermediary. In *Buchan* v. *Ortho Pharmaceuticals (Canada) Ltd.*
Robins J.A. commented that:

" . . . the manufacturer of drugs, like the manufacturer of other
products, has a duty to provide consumers with adequate warning
of the potentially harmful side-effects that the manufacturer
knows or has reason to know may be produced by the drug. . . .
In the case of prescription drugs, the duty of manufacturers to
warn consumers is discharged if the manufacturer provides prescribing physicians, rather than consumers, with adequate warning of the potential danger."[86]

Prescription drugs are available only on prescription and the pre- **8.34**
scribing doctor is in a position to take into account the propensities of
the drug and the susceptibilities of the patient. He has a duty to inform
himself of the benefits and potential dangers of the drug he is
prescribing, and he has to exercise an independent judgment as a
medical expert based on his knowledge of the patient and the drug.[87]
The duty to supply full information to the medical profession about
prescription drugs is greater than the doctor's duty to give information
to a patient, since the manufacturer's disclosure does not intrude upon

[83] *Lambert* v. *Lastoplex Chemical Co.* (1971) 25 D.L.R. (3d) 121 (S.C.C.).
[84] *Nicholson* v. *John Deere Ltd.* (1986) 34 D.L.R. (4th) 542, 549 (Ont. H.C.); see also
Good-Wear Treaders Ltd. v. *D. & B. Holdings Ltd.* (1979) 98 D.L.R. (3d) 59, held that
a warning may be inadequate where the manufacturer knows that the product will be
used in a dangerous manner.
[85] *Holmes* v. *Ashford* [1950] 2 All E.R. 76; *Kubach* v. *Hollands* [1937] 3 All E.R. 907.
[86] (1986) 25 D.L.R. (4th) 658, 669 (Ont. C.A.). See also *H.* v. *Royal Alexandra
Hospital for Children* [1990] 1 Med. L.R. 297 (S.C. of N.S.W.) on warnings about the
risks of infection with HIV virus from blood products.
[87] Under the Medicines Act 1968, s.96 products cannot be promoted to doctors unless
the doctor has been supplied with a data sheet about the product in prescribed form: see
Medicines (Data Sheet) Regulations 1972 (S.I. 1972/2076) (as amended by S.I.
1979/1760, S.I. 1981/1633 and by S.I. 1989/671) reg. 2(1)(*b*) and Sched. 2, para. 5. The
data sheet must inform the doctor of the contra-indications, any warnings that should be
given and the necessary precautions for safe administration. The information that has to
be given to patients in product leaflets is governed by regulations made under the
Medicines Act 1968: Medicines (Leaflets) Regulations 1977 (S.I. 1977/1055). Patient
leaflets will become compulsory for all products unless the necessary information is
available on the container or in the packaging: see E.C. Dir. 89/341/EEC. Despite all the
regulation it would seem that many doctors are inadequately informed about the drugs
they prescribe: see Teff (1984) 47 M.L.R. 303, 314–315.

the practice of medicine or the doctor patient relationship, and doctors need the information so that they can properly assess the situation.[88]

8.35 This principle, known as the "learned intermediary rule," has been held to be inapplicable to the manufacturers of oral contraceptives in some jurisdictions in the United States of America, where it has been held that, to be effective, a warning must reach the consumer/patient.[89] The rationale for this approach is that in the case of the contraceptive pill there is heightened participation of patients in the decision to use the drug; there may be substantial risks associated with its use; it is feasible for the manufacturer to give warnings direct to the user; there is frequently limited participation by the physician in the decision to take the pill; and there is a real possibility that patients may not be fully informed by their doctors. This view was followed *obiter* by the Ontario Court of Appeal in *Buchan* v. *Ortho Pharmaceuticals (Canada) Ltd.*,[90] where it was said that manufacturers of oral contraceptives should be obliged to warn the ultimate consumer as well as prescribing physicians about the risks associated with the pill.

What is an "adequate" warning?

8.36 An adequate warning should be communicated clearly and understandably in a manner calculated to inform the user of the nature of the risk and the extent of the danger; it should be in terms commensurate with the gravity of the potential hazard, and it should not be neutralised or negated by collateral efforts on the part of the manufacturer.[91] For example, promotional literature which seeks to minimise any suggestion of risk or promote the drug as "completely safe" would tend to negate the effectiveness of a warning.[92] The location and prominence of a warning may be a significant factor.[93] In *Buchan* v. *Ortho Pharmaceuticals (Canada) Ltd.* Robins J.A. said that:

> "Whether a particular warning is adequate will depend on what is reasonable in the circumstances. But the fact that a drug is

---

[88] *Davidson* v. *Connaught Laboratories* (1980) 14 C.C.L.T. 251, 276 (Ont. H.C.), where the manufacturer of a rabies vaccine was held to be negligent in failing to supply information to doctors about the risks associated with the vaccine. The action failed for lack of causation: see § 8.38. There is, of course, no guarantee that the doctor will pass on the information to the patient, since he may take the view that the patient would be unduly alarmed, or the risk may be so small that a reasonable doctor would not consider it appropriate to mention it: see *Sidaway* v. *Bethlem Royal Hospital Governors* [1985] 1 All E.R. 634, § 6.71 *et seq*.

[89] *MacDonald* v. *Ortho Pharmaceutical Corp.* (1985) 475 N.E. 2d 65 (Mass.); *Odgers* v. *Ortho Pharmaceutical Corp.* (1985) 609 F. Supp. 867 (D.C. Mich.); *Stephens* v. *G. D. Searle & Co.* (1985) 602 F. Supp. 379 (Mich.); *Lukaszewicz* v. *Ortho Pharmaceutical Corp.* (1981) 510 F. Supp. 961 (Wis.), holding that the manufacturer of oral contraceptives has a duty to provide the consumer with written warnings conveying reasonable notice of the nature, gravity, and likelihood of known or knowable side-effects, and advising the consumer to seek fuller explanation from the prescribing physician.

[90] (1986) 25 D.L.R. (4th) 658, 688–689 (Ont. C.A.).

[91] *Buchan* v. *Ortho Pharmaceuticals (Canada) Ltd.* (1986) 25 D.L.R. (4th) 658, 667.

[92] On misleading advertising campaigns by pharmaceutical companies see *The Times*, March 25, 1985, p. 8, which also suggested that regulation of advertising by the D.H.S.S. was ineffective; see also Teff (1984) 47 M.L.R. 303, 314. For the provisions regulating the contents of drug advertisements to doctors see S.I. 1978/1020.

[93] *Lambert* v. *Lastoplex Chemical Co.* (1971) 25 D.L.R. (3d) 121 (S.C.C.).

ordinarily safe and effective and the danger may be rare or involve only a small percentage of users does not necessarily relieve the manufacturer of the duty to warn. While a low probability of injury or a small class of endangered users are factors to be taken into account in determining what is reasonable, these factors must be balanced against such considerations as the nature of the drug, the necessity for taking it, and the magnitude of the increased danger to the individual consumer. Similarly where medical evidence exists which tends to show a serious danger inherent in the use of a drug, the manufacturer is not entitled to ignore or discount that information in its warning solely because it finds it to be unconvincing; the manufacturer is obliged to be forthright and to tell the whole story. The extent of the warning and the steps to be taken to bring the warning home to physicians should be commensurate with the potential danger—the graver the danger, the higher the duty."[94]

8.37 The defendant manufacturers in that case were held liable in negligence on the basis of a failure to give sufficient information to the medical profession about the risks of oral contraceptives. The fact that the manufacturers were aware that warnings had been circulated to the profession by the Canadian Food and Drugs Directorate on the instructions of the relevant Minister did not relieve them of their legal duty to warn the profession.[95] Thus, the duty to warn doctors cannot be delegated. The manufacturer cannot justify a failure to warn on the ground that doctors were in a position to learn about the risks inherent in the product from other sources. In *Davidson* v. *Connaught Laboratories* Linden J. observed that:

"A drug company cannot rely upon doctors to read all the scientific literature outlining the specific dangers involved in the many drugs they have to administer each day. . . . They have little time for deep research into the medical literature. They rely on the drug companies to supply them with the necessary data."[96]

In *Buchan* a significant factor in the conclusion that the defendants had negligently failed to give adequate warning to consumers was the fact that the defendants' associated companies in other countries (including the United Kingdom) had given a much more comprehensive warning.

5. Failure to warn and causation

8.38 Where the alleged negligence consists of a failure to warn either the consumer or an intermediary, such as a prescribing doctor, about the

---

[94] (1986) 25 D.L.R. (4th) 658, 678–9 (Ont. C.A.). See also *Rothwell* v. *Raes* (1988) 54 D.L.R. (4th) 193, 341–342 (Ont. H.C.), on inadequate warnings by the manufacturers of pertussis vaccine to the medical profession. The action failed on the ground that the vaccine did not cause the plaintiff's injuries.

[95] "The report of the advisory committee cannot be considered determinative of the nature and extent of the legal duty imposed on drug manufacturers to warn the medical profession. The duty to warn of a risk so grave as stroke . . . arose long before the report . . . .. The report did not release Ortho from its common law duty, limit its ability to discharge the duty, or fix a standard of disclosure to the medical profession": (1986) 25 D.L.R. (4th) 658, 680–1, *per* Robins J.A.

[96] (1980) 14 C.C.L.T. 251, 276 (Ont. H.C.). In the U.K. doctors' other sources of drug information, in addition to the manufacturers, include the *British National Formulary*, produced jointly by the B.M.A. and the British Pharmaceutical Society, *MIMS* (the *Monthly Index of Medical Specialities*), and *Prescribers' Journal*.

side-effects or contra-indications of a drug, for example, the plaintiff still has to prove that had the warning been given he would not have taken the drug. In other words he must demonstrate that the negligent omission caused or contributed to the damage. In the case of prescription drugs, where the evidence is that adequate warnings would have had no effect on whether or not the doctor would have prescribed the drug, the patient's claim against the manufacturer will fail on the ground of a lack of causation.[97] In *Davidson* v. *Connaught Laboratories*[98] the manufacturer of a rabies vaccine was found to have given an inadequate warning to doctors in its literature accompanying the vaccine. The manufacturer did not mention myelitis or neuritis; nor the possibility of paralysis or death; nor were there any figures relating to the risks, nor any source material. The defendants had known of these dangers for a long time. The manufacturer was held not liable, however, because:

   (a) the information would not have changed the doctors' decision to recommend use of the vaccine, because of the grave danger associated with rabies (it is normally fatal); and

   (b) the plaintiff had been given full information about the risks, in any event, by another doctor.

8.39   In *Buchan* v. *Ortho Pharmaceuticals* (*Canada*) *Ltd.*[99] the Ontario Court of Appeal held that the test of causation should be subjective not objective, contrary to the normal rule in Canada on the non-disclosure of risks associated with medical treatment.[1] It ought not to be incumbent on a plaintiff, said the court, to prove as part of her case what her doctor might or might not have done had he been adequately warned. One could assume that a doctor would not ignore a proper warning or fail to disclose a material risk or otherwise act negligently. Moreover, even if the evidence indicated that the doctor was negligent, the manufacturer would not be shielded from liability if the negligence was a forseeable consequence of the manufacturer's breach of duty to warn. This was said to be a rebuttable presumption. In this country the test of causation is, in any event, subjective, *i.e.* would *this* patient have taken the drug, and where causation depends upon what the prescribing doctor would have done had he been given an adequate warning, it is suggested that the test should also be subjective to *that* doctor and should not be determined by what a reasonable doctor would have done in the circumstances.

6. Continuing duty

8.40   Negligence depends upon foreseeability of injury. If at the time that a product was put onto the market the defect was unknown the

---

[97] *Buchan* v. *Ortho Pharmaceuticals* (*Canada*) *Ltd.* (1986) 25 D.L.R. (4th) 658, 682 (Ont. C.A.). See also *H.* v. *Royal Alexandra Hospital for Children* [1990] 1 Med. L.R. 297 (S.C. of N.S.W.), where it was held that the failure of the manufacturers of blood products in 1983 to warn doctors of the risk that the products could transmit the AIDS infection was negligent, but that such a warning would have had no effect on the decision of the doctors to use the products for treatment of a haemophiliac with a joint bleed, given the perception of the relative risks of treatment and non-treatment.

[98] (1980) 14 C.C.L.T. 251 (Ont. H.C.).

[99] (1986) 25 D.L.R. (4th) 658, 682 and 686–688.

[1] See § 6.99.

manufacturer was not negligent. If a danger becomes apparent (or ought to have been discovered) it will be negligent to continue to produce the same unmodified product, or at least to do so without attaching a warning.[2]

In addition, the manufacturer is under a continuing duty in respect **8.41** of products already in circulation which are now known to be defective. The manufacturer must take reasonable steps either to warn users of the danger or recall the defective products.[3] In *Buchan* v. *Ortho Pharmaceuticals (Canada) Ltd.*[4] the Ontario Court of Appeal applied this principle to the manufacturer of oral contraceptives with respect to warnings of side-effects to be given to doctors who pre-scribed the drug. Robins J.A. expressed the proposition in these terms:

> "A manufacturer of prescription drugs occupies the position of an expert in the field; this requires that it be under a continuing duty to keep abreast of scientific developments pertaining to its product through research, adverse reaction reports, scientific literature and other available methods. When additional dangerous or potentially dangerous side-effects from the drug's use are discovered, the manufacturer must make all reasonable efforts to communicate the information to prescribing physicians. Unless doctors have current, accurate and complete information about a drug's risks, their ability to exercise the fully informed medical judgment necessary for the proper performance of their vital role in prescribing drugs for patients may be reduced or impaired."[5]

A new drug which produces a high incidence of adverse reactions **8.42** (c. 1 in 300) should be spotted in pre-clinical or clinical trials. Less common reactions may only become apparent when the drug is in widespread use. It is almost inevitable, then, that some drug injuries will only be identified after the product has been marketed. The exercise of reasonable care clearly requires that manufacturers have an effective system for monitoring adverse reaction and for the recall of defective products, both for manufacturing defects (to identify faulty batches, for example) and for design defects, which may involve removing the product from the market altogether.[6] In a suitable case

---

[2] *Wright* v. *Dunlop Rubber Co. Ltd.* (1972) 13 K.I.R. 255, 272.

[3] *Walton* v. *British Leyland UK Ltd.* (1978) (unreported), Q.B.D., cited in Miller, *Product Liability and Safety Encyclopaedia*, Div. III, § 43.1; *Rivtow Marine Ltd.* v. *Washington Iron Works* (1973) 40 D.L.R. (3d) 530, 536 (S.C.C.); *Buchan* v. *Ortho Pharmaceuticals (Canada) Ltd.* (1986) 25 D.L.R. (4th) 658, 667 (Ont. C.A.).

[4] (1986) 25 D.L.R. (4th) 658.

[5] *Ibid.*, p. 678.

[6] The "yellow card scheme," in which doctors submit reports on adverse reactions to the C.S.M., is not particularly effective in identifying adverse reactions: see Teff (1984) 47 M.L.R. 303, 315. The anti-arthritis drug, Opren, was not suspended by the Licensing Authority under the Medicines Act 1968 until after more than 3,500 reports of adverse reactions, including 61 fatalities: Teff, *op. cit.*, at p. 304, n. 5. See further *The Lancet*, November 5, 1988, pp. 1059, 1060, on the withdrawal of "Merital" (nomifensine), suggesting that undue reliance on the yellow card scheme may result in insufficient emphasis on other preventive measures. The C.S.M. put pressure on the manufacturers to withdraw the drug following a sharp increase in reports under the scheme in 1985, but there had been suspicions about adverse reactions since 1979. See also *The Lancet*, January 31, 1987, p. 287, reporting the withdrawal of "Dorbanex" (danthron).

an appropriate warning may be sufficient to satisfy the manufacturer's duty. In this country it is a condition of the grant of a product licence for pharmaceutical products that such a procedure exists,[7] but nonetheless there might be negligence in implementing the recall procedure.[8]

7. Common practice

8.43   Where a manufacturer has complied with the standards normally adopted within the industry, this will usually be taken as good evidence that he has acted with reasonable care, just as a departure from common practice may be evidence of negligence.[9] Neither, however, is necessarily conclusive of the issue. In the case of pharmaceutical products manufacturers must comply with the statutory requirements of the Medicines Act 1968. Compliance will not be conclusive, but it will undoubtedly constitute strong evidence of the exercise of reasonable care. If an independent body, such as the C.S.M., has reached the same view as the manufacturer on the safety of a product or the adequacy of warnings this will inevitably influence the court's assessment of whether there has been negligence, assuming that the same information was available to both the C.S.M. and the manufacturer, and assuming, of course, that the C.S.M. has not been negligent.[10]

8.44   In *Budden* v. *B.P. Oil Ltd. and Shell Oil Ltd.*[11] it was alleged that children had sustained injuries attributable to inhaling petrol fumes containing lead, and they brought an action against the oil companies. The levels of lead in petrol complied with statutory regulations, and these levels had been set by the Secretary of State having received expert advice. The Court of Appeal took the view that in these circumstances the decision about lead levels must be presumed to be in the public interest, and accordingly the manufacturers or suppliers of petrol could not be said to be negligent if the limit to which they adhered was one which they were entitled reasonably to believe to be consistent with the public interest. It could not be said that:

> "a reasonable person, with the knowledge which the oil companies had or should have had, objectively weighing all relevant considerations, had failed in his duty owed to the children in complying with the requirements prescribed by the Secretary of State and approved, impliedly, by Parliament, after the investigation which had been made of the very matters which were relevant for the companies' decisions.[12]

---

[7] Medicines (Standard Provisions for Licences and Certificates) Regulations 1971 Sched. 1, para. 6 (S.I. 1971/972) as amended.

[8] See, *e.g., Nicholson* v. *John Deere Ltd.* (1986) 34 D.L.R. (4th) 542. The defendants "had a duty to devise a programme that left nothing to chance," *per* Smith J. at p. 549. The defendants' efforts to warn were deficient in that they were doomed to failure with respect to the vast majority of users.

[9] See §§ 3.17–3.37.

[10] See *Buchan* v. *Ortho Pharmaceuticals (Canada) Ltd.* (1986) 25 D.L.R. (4th) 658, 672–3, where the issue was raised, but not decided, whether compliance by the manufacturer with the requirements of the Canadian Food and Drug Directorate as to the warnings to be given directly to the users of oral contraceptives absolved them from liability. The trial judge had held that the statement required by the F.D.D. "amounted to no warning at all."

[11] [1980] J.P.L. 586.

[12] *Ibid.*, p. 587. The court was worried that if it were to make a finding of negligence there would be a constitutional anomaly, because the court would effectively be declaring a decision of Parliament to be unlawful. "The authority of Parliament must prevail."

The grant of product licences under the Medicines Act 1968 does not **8.45** depend upon express approval by Parliament, but nonetheless the logic of *Budden* v. *B.P. Oil Ltd. and Shell Oil Ltd.* could well be applied to pharmaceutical products licensed by the Licensing Authority.[13] Conversely, a failure by the manufacturer to comply with provisions of the Medicines Act 1968 must put the onus on the defendant to justify its conduct, although breach of the Act or regulations made under the Act is not negligence *per se*.[14]

8. Proof

The burden of proving negligence rests with the plaintiff. In **8.46** *Donoghue* v. *Stevenson*[15] Lord Macmillan said that there was no presumption of negligence nor any justification for applying the maxim *res ipsa loquitur* in such a case. Where, however, a defect has arisen in the course of construction it will be virtually impossible for a plaintiff to show by affirmative evidence what went wrong. In *Grant* v. *Australian Knitting Mills Ltd.*[16] this difficulty was recognised. Lord Wright said that:

> "[The manufacturing] process was intended to be foolproof. If excess sulphites were left in the garment, that could only be because someone was at fault. The appellant is not required to lay his finger on the exact person in all the chain who was responsible or to specify what he did wrong. Negligence is found as a matter of inference from the existence of the defects taken in connection with all the known circumstances."[17]

The effect of this is that in cases of manufacturing defects the **8.47** plaintiff will normally establish negligence by proving the existence of the defect, and that this was probably not a result of events that occurred after the product left the manufacturer's possession.[18] The possibility of intermediate deterioration or tampering with the product will be taken into account in terms of the degree of likelihood that the defect was present when it left the manufacturer.[19] It is irrelevant whether the inference of negligence is called *res ipsa loquitur* or not, because in some instances it amounts in practice to a form of strict liability. The greater the danger, the greater the precautions that will be required to discharge a duty of care.[20] The defendant may rebut the inference by proving how the defect occurred and showing that this was not due to lack of care on his part, but this may be difficult. Ironically, the stronger the evidence that his manufacturing system was "foolproof," the stronger is the inference that the defect arose as a

---

[13] *cf.* also Consumer Protection Act 1987, s.4(1)(*a*), § 8.80, *post,* providing a defence to strict liability under that Act where the defect was attributable to compliance with any statutory requirement or a European Community obligation.
[14] Medicines Act 1968, s.133(2).
[15] [1932] A.C. 562.
[16] [1936] A.C. 85.
[17] *Ibid.*, p. 101.
[18] *Mason* v. *Williams & Williams Ltd.* [1955] 1 W.L.R. 549.
[19] See, *e.g., Evans* v. *Triplex Safety Glass Co. Ltd.* [1936] 1 All E.R. 283.
[20] *Wright* v. *Dunlop Rubber Co. Ltd.* (1972) 13 K.I.R. 255, 273–4.

result of carelessness by one of his employees, for whose negligence he will be held vicariously liable.[21]

8.48   The plaintiff will have greater difficulty in proving negligence where the product is defective in design rather than manufacture. It is easier to demonstrate that a product is defective if it does not meet the manufacturer's own standards because something has gone wrong during manufacture. Where however, a product performs as it was designed and intended, there is no obvious standard against which to compare it.[22] The design may have been the result of a conscious compromise between cost and safety, or between efficacy and safety.[23] If the risk was a known risk it may be treated as an unavoidable side-effect which was acceptable because of the otherwise beneficial effects of the drug, either for the plaintiff or other users. Side-effects are simply part of the cost-benefit analysis undertaken when considering whether a drug has a safe design.

8.49   On the other hand, if a particular risk is unforeseeable it is not possible to take reasonable precautions against it by amending the design. This is especially true of products such as drugs, where, despite extensive pre-marketing research, it may not be possible to predict all the potential reactions that may occur in a large population. In addition to the problem of proving causation, this will make it difficult to prove that the manufacturer was negligent because at the time when the product was marketed the risk was unknown.[24] Thus, although design defects can be negligent, the courts are more reluctant to hold defendants liable in such cases.[25]

9. Causation in fact

8.50   In addition to any questions of causation which may arise from intermediate examination, the plaintiff has to prove that the defective product in fact caused the injury of which he complains, applying the usual principles of causation. This will tend to be more difficult with defective drugs.[26] There may be difficulty in isolating drug-induced harm from the background incidence of such injuries. Merely proving an increased risk of injury does not in itself establish causation. The question is whether one can infer a causal link, taking a "common sense" approach to attributing cause.[27] *McGhee* v. *National Coal*

---

[21] *Grant* v. *Australian Knitting Mills Ltd.* [1936] A.C. 85; *Hill* v. *Crowe (James) (Cases) Ltd.* [1978] 1 All E.R. 812, 816, criticising *Daniels* v. *White & Sons Ltd.* [1938] 4 All E.R. 258, where carbolic acid used in washing bottles contaminated lemonade, and the defendants were held not liable on proving the effectiveness of the system.

[22] Unless specifically governed by statute; see, *e.g.*, Consumer Protection Act 1987, s.11.

[23] "Most, if not all, drugs cannot be effective unless they are also powerful enough to be potentially harmful": Teff (1984) 47 M.L.R. 303, 309.

[24] *Mann* v. *Wellcome Foundation Ltd.* (1989) (unreported), Q.B.D. See also Newdick (1985) 101 L.Q.R. 405; and on the thalidomide tragedy see Teff and Munro, *Thalidomide: The Legal Aftermath*, 1976.

[25] Newdick (1987) 103 L.Q.R. 288, 300–4.

[26] See Newdick (1985) 101 L.Q.R. 405, 420; Stapleton (1985) 5 O.J.L.S. 248, 250 discussing the difficulties of proving causation with certain types of disease; and *Kay* v. *Ayrshire and Arran Health Board* [1987] 2 All E.R. 417; *Loveday* v. *Renton* [1990] 1 Med. L.R. 117; *Rothwell* v. *Raes* (1988) 54 D.L.R. (4th) 193, *ante*, §8.03, n. 8. See generally §§ 5.10 *et seq.*

[27] This is the effect of the interpretation placed upon *McGhee* v. *National Coal Board* [1972] 3 All E.R. 1008 by the House of Lords in *Wilsher* v. *Essex Area Health Authority* [1988] 1 All E.R. 871.

Board[28] was never a complete solution to this type of problem. There, it was known that excess exposure to brick dust could cause dermatitis; the only question was whether on the particular facts it was the negligent period of exposure that had caused the plaintiff's dermatitis. Where it is not known whether a drug can cause a particular reaction this approach cannot assist the plaintiff.[29] Nor does it solve the problem of multiple potential defendants in cases of generic prescribing, where it may be impossible for a plaintiff to say which manufacturer was responsible for the drug he took, especially if it was taken over a long period of time.[30]

This problem was addressed by the California Court of Appeal in **8.51**
Sindell v. *Abbott Laboratories*,[31] where, due to the very long delay in the teratogenic effects of the drug DES (diethylstilboestrol) becoming apparent, it was impossible for the plaintiff to identify the particular manufacturers of the drug taken by her mother during pregnancy. The court reversed the burden of proof, requiring the manufacturers to show that their product was not used, and in the absence of proof, damages were apportioned between the various defendants on the basis of their market share of sales of the drug.[32] It would seem highly unlikely, to say the least, that the courts could be persuaded to adopt such an approach in this country, in the light of the attitude taken to the proof of causation by the House of Lords in recent years.[33]

III. CONSUMER PROTECTION ACT 1987

Although in cases of manufacturing defects the liability of manufac- **8.52**
turers in negligence amounts, in effect, to a form of strict liability, the action for negligence remains essentially fault-based and subject to all the vagaries associated with such actions. Some plaintiffs simply fall through the compensation net due to an inability to prove negligence, particularly if the risk of injury was unforeseeable. Iatrogenic and teratogenic drug injuries are often in this category, and it was one of the most prominent and poignant examples of drug injuries, the thalidomide tragedy, which prompted calls for reform. Both the Law Commission and the Pearson Commission recommended the introduction of strict liability for defective products.[34] The Strasbourg Convention on Products Liability in regard to Personal Injury and Death 1977,

---

[28] [1972] 3 All E.R. 1008.
[29] As, *e.g.*, in *Loveday* v. *Renton* [1990] 1 Med. L.R. 117, and *Rothwell* v. *Raes* (1988) 54 D.L.R. (4th) 193.
[30] For an example of this type of problem see *Mann* v. *Wellcome Foundation Ltd.* (1989) (unreported), Q.B.D.
[31] (1980) 607 P. 2d 924.
[32] For discussion of this case see Newdick (1985) 101 L.Q.R. 405, 427–429; Teff (1982) 31 I.C.L.Q. 840; and see further *Hymowitz* v. *Eli Lilly & Co.* (1989) 73 N.Y. 2d 487, applying *Sindell* even where the defendants could prove that the plaintiff had not used their product.
[33] See in particular *Wilsher* v. *Essex Area Health Authority* [1988] 1 All E.R. 871; and *Hotson* v. *East Berkshire Area Health Authority* [1987] 2 All E.R. 909; §§ 5.19 *et seq.* and 5.29 *et seq.*
[34] Law Com. No. 82, Cmnd. 6831, 1977; *Royal Commission on Civil Liability and Compensation for Personal Injury*, Cmnd. 7054 (1978), Vol. I, Ch. 22.

and two draft European Community Directives, led finally to the European Community Directive on Liability for Defective Products 1985,[35] which required member states to implement its terms within three years. This was done by Part I of the Consumer Protection Act 1987 which came into force on March 1, 1988, and applies to damage caused by products which were put into circulation by the producer after that date.[36] Section 1(1) states that Part I of the Act "shall have effect for the purpose of making such provision as is necessary in order to comply with the product liability Directive and shall be construed accordingly." In the light of section 1(1), it is arguable that, where there is a conflict between the Act and the Directive, then the Directive should prevail.

8.53   In theory the Act introduces a regime of strict liability for injuries inflicted by defective products, but the very concept of a product which is "defective" involves resorting to much the same approach as when deciding whether there has been negligence, particularly where it is alleged that a product is defective in design.[37] This is even more apparent with the development risks defence, which effectively excludes liability for unforeseeable design defects. Moreover, the problem of proving causation remains intractable. Given that liability in negligence for most construction defects comes close to strict liability, since negligence tends to be inferred from the defect itself, it is unlikely that the Consumer Protection Act will produce a marked change from the action in negligence apart from the reversal of the burden of proof in one area.[38] Indeed, it is doubtful whether the victims of thalidomide, who provoked the initial cry for reform, would be in any better position under the Act than in the tort of negligence.

8.54   The Act has not replaced the common law; it is an additional remedy.[39] If for any reason the Act does not apply (if, for example, the special limitation periods under the Act have expired, or the product which caused the damage was put into circulation before the Act came into force on March 1, 1988) a claim for negligence may still be available.[40]

1. Plaintiffs

8.55   Section 2(1) provides that "where any damage is caused wholly or partly by a defect in a product, every person to whom subsection 2 below applies shall be liable for the damage." This section confers a

---

[35] Dir. 85/374/EEC.

[36] Consumer Protection Act 1987, s.50(7); S.I. 1987/1680.

[37] Clark (1985) 48 M.L.R. 325; Stapleton (1986) 6 O. J.L.S. 392.

[38] See Stapleton (1986) 6 O.J.L.S. 392; Newdick (1987) 103 L.Q.R. 288; Newdick [1988] C.L.J. 455.

[39] Consumer Protection Act 1987, s.2(6).

[40] Part II of the Consumer Protection Act 1987 lays down general requirements for the safety of certain consumer goods and gives the Secretary of State power to make specific safety regulations. Breach of these regulations is a criminal offence, and by s.41 an individual injured by an infringement of a safety regulation (but not the general safety requirement) can bring an action for breach of statutory duty. Part II replaces earlier legislation containing similar provisions (Consumer Safety Act 1978, which itself replaced the Consumer Protection Act 1961). This right of action appears not to have been widely used.

right of action on *any* person who suffers damage as a result of a defective product.[41] There is no need to establish that the plaintiff was foreseeable as likely to be affected by the defect, nor that the defendant was negligent. Proof that the product was "defective" and that the defect caused the damage puts the onus on the defendant to establish one of the specific defences.

2. Defendants

Section 2 imposes liability on four categories of defendant: (i) the producer of the product; (ii) anyone who holds himself out as the producer; (iii) an importer; and (iv) in certain circumstances, the supplier.[42] This creates the possibility of suing multiple defendants under the Act for a single injury. **8.56**

(i) A "producer" is the manufacturer of the product, or the person who won or abstracted a substance which has not been manufactured, or the processor where the "essential characteristics" of a product are attributable to an industrial or other process.[43] "Producer" also includes the manufacturer of a component part.[44] The component manufacturer will be liable together with the manufacturer of the finished product if the damage caused by the finished product is attributable to a defect in the component. On the other hand, it would seem that the component manufacturer is not liable for damage caused by the finished product if the component was not defective. This is the position where the defect in the finished product was wholly attributable to the design of that product, because section 4(1)(*f*) provides a specific defence for the component manufacturer. The Act does not deal with the position of the component manufacturer where the defect in the finished product is a construction defect or the result of a defective component supplied by another manufacturer, but under the Directive a person is liable only for products which he has supplied, and the component manufacturer does not supply the finished product. **8.57**

The definition of producer is wide enough to encompass, not only a large pharmaceutical company, but also the individual pharmacist or doctor who mixes small amounts of product to produce a compound or mixture, or the doctor who modifies an appliance, or uses an additive in an intravenous solution. **8.58**

(ii) A person holds himself out as the producer of the product "by putting his name on the product or using a trade mark or other distinguishing mark in relation to the product."[45] Whereas a retail supplier will not normally be liable, retailers who adopt the practice of putting their own brand name on goods produced by others will be liable for defects in those goods. This is now a common practice with large retail chain stores in the United Kingdom. Supermarkets and retail chemists who supply non-prescription medicines under their own brand name will be treated as the producer. However, it is not thought **8.59**

---

[41] Including ante-natal injuries: Consumer Protection Act 1987, s.6(3).
[42] *Ibid.*, ss.2(2), (3).
[43] *Ibid.*, s.1(2). "Essential characteristics" are not defined by the legislation.
[44] This is by virtue of the definition of "product" in s.1(2).
[45] Consumer Protection Act 1987, s.2(2)(*b*); the "own-brander."

that simply attaching a name and address to a product, which pharmacists and dispensing doctors are required to do by law, constitutes holding oneself out as the producer.

8.60 (iii) The importer of a product is liable if he imported it from a place outside the European Community into a member State in the course of any business of his, to supply it to another.[46] The importer from another member State into the United Kingdom is not liable under this subsection. So the importer of a defective product from Japan is liable for damage caused by the defect, but not the importer of a product from France. If the Japanese product had first been imported to France and then imported to the United Kingdom, the French importer would be liable, but not the U.K. importer.

8.61 (iv) The supplier of goods, whether a retailer or intermediate distributor, is not normally liable under the Act. A supplier will be liable, however, if he fails, within a reasonable period of receiving a request from the person who suffered the damage, to identify either the producer, "own-brander," importer, or the person who supplied the product to him.[47] The supplier is not liable under section 2(3) merely because he cannot identify who provided the component parts or raw materials in a finished product supplied to him,[48] rather it is the producer or supplier of the finished product that he must identify. The plaintiff's request must be made within a reasonable period after the damage occurs, and at a time when it is not reasonably practical for the plaintiff to identify them. This section is intended to give plaintiffs an identifiable defendant, and it puts the onus on suppliers, such as retail pharmacists and dispensing general practitioners, to keep accurate records of their own sources of supply. This may be a particular problem for pharmacists dispensing generic drugs. If the supplier complies with the request he is not liable under the Act, even if the plaintiff cannot pursue a remedy against the identified defendants, for example because they are in liquidation. The liability of suppliers in the tort of negligence is potentially wider than this.

3. Products

8.62 "Product" means any "goods or electricity" and includes a product which is comprised in another product whether as a component part or raw material.[49] It is not clear whether human organs or bodily fluids, such as blood, will be treated as "products" under the Act, although the Pearson Commission recommended that they should.[50]

8.63 Agricultural produce and game are excluded unless they have undergone an industrial process,[51] but there is no definition of an

---

[46] *Ibid.*, s.2(2)(*c*).

[47] *Ibid.*, s.2(3); on the meaning of "supply" see s.46.

[48] *Ibid.*, s.1(3).

[49] *Ibid.*, s.1(2). "Goods" includes substances, growing crops and things comprised in land by virtue of being attached to it, and any ship, aircraft or vehicle: s.45.

[50] Cmnd. 7054, Vol. I, para. 1276. *Clark & Lindsell on Torts*, 16th ed., 1989, para. 12–22, n. 5, suggests that human blood and tissue do not fall within the Act; *cf.* Morgan and Lee, *Blackstone's Guide to the Human Fertilisation and Embryology Act 1990*, 1991, pp. 174–176, discussing whether embryos or gametes could be regarded as "products."

[51] Consumer Protection Act 1987, s.2(4). Agricultural produce means "any produce of the soil, of stock-farming or of fisheries": s.1(2).

"industrial process." The processor is only liable as a producer if the "essential characteristics" of the product are attributable to an industrial or other process.[52] This requirement does not apply to other potential defendants in respect of processed products, the "own-brander," the importer or the supplier. Nor is it necessary that the defect in the product is the result of the industrial process itself. For example, food that is contaminated prior to processing can give rise to liability under the Act, once processed, whereas the same contaminated food sold to consumers unprocessed is not within the Act. This could be a relevant distinction with some forms of herbal remedy.

4. Defects

Liability under the Consumer Protection Act 1987 is strict, not **8.64** absolute. The plaintiff does not succeed simply by showing that the product caused damage; he must prove that the damage was caused by a defect in the product. By section 3(1) a product has a defect "if the safety of the product is not such as persons generally are entitled to expect." Safety includes safety with respect to component parts, and with respect to property damage as well as personal injury. The crucial question is: what are persons generally entitled to expect by way of safety? The answer, almost inevitably, must be: it all depends on the circumstances of the case.

They are entitled to expect that food and drink will not be **8.65** contaminated with decomposed snails or acid, that clothes and hair dye will not contain skin irritants, that motor cars will not have defective steering, that dangerous chemicals will be adequately labelled, and so on. But they are not necessarily entitled to expect that drugs will have no adverse side-effects, or that all motor cars will be as safe as modern technology can make them. Safety, like risk, is a relative concept, and this is just as true in determining what is "defective" as it is in deciding whether a manufacturer has been negligent. It is always a question of degree, in which levels of safety are traded off against both cost and the usefulness of the product, although this is more likely to be an intuitive judgment than a strict cost-benefit analysis.[53]

Section 3(2) provides that in determining what persons generally are **8.66** entitled to expect "all the circumstances shall be taken into account," including:

"(a) the manner in which, and purposes for which, the product has been marketed, its get-up, the use of any mark in relation to the product and any instructions for, or warnings with respect to, doing or refraining from doing anything with or in relation to the product;
(b) what might reasonably be expected to be done with or in relation to the product; and
(c) the time when the product was supplied by its producer to another;

---

[52] *Ibid.*, s.1(2).
[53] See Clark (1985) 48 M.L.R. 325.

and nothing in this section shall require a defect to be inferred from the fact alone that the safety of a product which is supplied after that time is greater than the safety of the product in question."

8.67 The types of defect which can arise fall into the same categories as are found with the tort of negligence, namely defects in the manufacture, design, or the presentation of the product with inadequate warnings or instructions for use. "Consumer expectations" are treated as a measure of defectiveness, but medicinal products almost invariably carry some risk of adverse reactions, even if in only a small minority of consumers. Thus, consumers are not necessarily entitled to expect that medical products will be risk-free. The risks have to be weighed against the anticipated benefits, and indeed against the "costs" of not using the product, such as the harm associated with the disease, and the risks and anticipated benefits of alternative treatments. This process is familiar from the assessment of what constitutes negligence. Similarly, consumer expectations may be limited by any warnings or contra-indications given by the manufacturer, either directly to the consumer or to an intermediary such as the prescribing physician. It does not make sense, however, to speak of warnings against dangers which were unknown or unforeseeable by the producer, and once the question of foreseeability arises the concept of reasonable care is reintroduced.[54] It seems likely that the adequacy of any warnings will be judged by the same criteria as used for negligence.

8.68 Misuse of the product by the consumer will be taken into account. If the product is used in a way which could not reasonably be expected then, as with negligence, it cannot be considered defective. Presumably, foreseeable misuse will make the product defective, subject to a possible defence of contributory negligence.

8.69 Section 3(2)(c) takes account of the time at which the product was supplied by the producer (not when supplied to the consumer) in assessing whether it was defective. The product may have deteriorated since it left the producer's hands, as a result of the passage of time, repeated use, misuse or mishandling. A product which has deteriorated in this way is not necessarily defective, though it is not necessarily safe either. It will depend upon the nature of the product, how much time has elapsed, how much use it has had, and so on. Keeping and using drugs after their expiry date may be an example of contributory negligence, but it may also indicate that the drugs were not even defective if the consumer was not entitled to expect that they would not deteriorate.

8.70 The proviso to section 3(2) states that the defectiveness of a product is not to be inferred simply from the fact that products which are supplied at a later date are safer than the product in question. In negligence, of course, carelessness is measured by reference to the knowledge and standards applicable at the time of the accident,

---

[54] Clark (1987) 50 M.L.R. 614, 617. Notwithstanding the introduction of strict product liability in the U.S., defective design cases and cases of failure to warn are treated as equivalent to actions in negligence: see *Feldman* v. *Lederle Laboratories* (1984) 479 A. 2d 374; *Brown* v. *Superior Court* (1988) 751 P. 2d 470.

ignoring subsequent improvements,[55] and the proviso appears to apply a similar standard. This must go to the question of proof, however, rather than creating a rule of law, otherwise all unforeseeable defects would be excluded from the ambit of the Act, as in negligence. Presumably a case such as *Roe* v. *Minister of Health*[56] is just the type of situation which ought to be covered by strict liability, since persons generally are entitled to expect that anaesthetics will not be contaminated with paralysing agents.[57] Once an improved product becomes available this may be relevant to whether the old product is defective-if the supply of the old product is *continued*, as in negligence, but this begs the question of what is meant by "improved." A new drug may have fewer side-effects, but be less effective, or it may be more effective, but have more side-effects. At what point can it be said that the drug is "improved"? This is all a matter of degree, and also depends upon knowledge about the new product, which it may take some time to acquire through clinical use.[58]

Moreover, it would appear that there is no equivalent under the Act **8.71** of a "continuing duty" parallel to that in the tort of negligence, requiring the manufacturer to recall products which were not known to be defective at the time of supply, where it has subsequently been discovered that the product does create an unacceptable risk of harm. Although the supply of similar products after the date of knowledge could result in the conclusion that they are defective, there is nothing in section 3 to indicate how a product that was "safe" at the time of supply can subsequently become defective, unless it can be said that some obligation to recall products forms part of consumer expectations. Indeed, there is a specific defence where the defendant can show that the defect did not exist in the product when he supplied it to another.[59]

The Act does not mention the cost of the product as a factor in **8.72** determining defectiveness. Where the defect is a construction defect or a failure to warn or provide adequate instructions for use, then cost is probably irrelevant, but it may well be a significant feature where it is claimed that the product is defective in design.[60]

Once it is established that the product was defective liability is strict, **8.73** in the sense that it is not a defence for the producer to show that he excercised reasonable care. It is arguable, however, that many of the factors taken into account in deciding whether a manufacturer has discharged a duty of care in negligence are incorporated into the decision-making process about whether a product is defective under the Act.

[55] *Roe* v. *Minister of Health* [1954] 2 Q.B. 66, § 3.55, but the duty does at least extend beyond the date of putting the product into circulation, requiring a manufacturer to warn about any subsequently discovered dangers or in an appropriate case to recall the product; see § 8.41.
[56] [1954] 2 Q.B. 66.
[57] See, however, the development risk defence, §§ 8.87–8.92, *post*.
[58] Drugs which are supplied as part of a clinical trial probably to fall within the ambit of the Act, but the fact that the product is still under research would have a bearing on whether it could be said to be defective. Moreover, the development risks defence would apply, effectively excluding the manufacturer's responsibility for unforeseeable reactions: § 8.87. See further §§ 3.44–3.45.
[59] See § 8.83.
[60] See Stapleton (1986) 6 O.J.L.S. 392, 404; Newdick (1987) 103 L.Q.R. 288, 300–4.

5. Types of loss

8.74 The Act is designed to protect consumer expectations in the safety of products, and therefore there is no liability in respect of pure economic loss, damage to commercial property or damage to the product itself, even if the product is potentially dangerous. For the purpose of liability under section 2, damage means "death or personal injury or any loss of or damage to any property (including land)."[61] Loss of or damage to the product itself is specifically excluded, as is loss of or damage to a product caused by a defective component product which had been supplied with the product.[62]

8.75 By section 5(3) property damage claims are limited to property which is (a) ordinarily intended for private use, occupation and consumption; and (b) intended by the person suffering the loss or damage mainly for his own private use, occupation or consumption. This excludes damage to business property. Actions in respect of property damage (but not personal injury) below £275 are also excluded.[63]

6. Causation

8.76 The plaintiff has the burden of proving that the product was defective and that the damage was caused "wholly or partly" by the defect.[64] The difficulty of proving factual causation in some instances will be just as great as in the tort of negligence, although there is no requirement to prove that the damage was of a foreseeable type, as in negligence.

8.77 The Act makes it clear that the producer remains liable where the damage is caused partly by the defect and partly by some other event. The other event may be entirely innocent or it may be the "faulty" conduct of a third party, for example, the failure of a third party to examine or test the product or heed warnings in the manufacturer's instructions for use. It will be recalled that, so far as the tort of negligence is concerned, the failure to take advantage of a reasonable opportunity for intermediate inspection may be treated as breaking the chain of causation. It is arguable that this will no longer be the position under the Act, because the damage is "partly" caused by the defective product and "partly" by the failure of the intermediate examination.[65] The manufacturer and the third party will be jointly and severally liable, and their respective responsibilities can be apportioned under the Civil Liability (Contribution) Act 1978. On the other hand, it is possible that where the manufacturer has good grounds for contemplating that an intermediate inspection will occur or that an intermediary will follow instructions, then the product will not be categorised as defective. Section 3(2) provides that instructions, warnings, and "what might reasonably be expected to be done with or in

---

[61] Consumer Protection Act 1987, s.5(1).
[62] *Ibid.*, s.5(2).
[63] *Ibid.*, s.5(4).
[64] *Ibid.*, s.2(1).
[65] Brazier, *Street on Torts*, 8th ed., pp. 310–11.

relation to the product" can be taken into account in determining what is defective. Thus, the effects of intermediate examination may simply have been shifted from the causation stage of the injury to the earlier point of deciding whether the product was unsafe in all the circumstances. If the product is categorised as defective, then the omission of an intermediate examination should not defeat the action on grounds of causation.

Logically, the same approach should apply to "faulty" conduct by **8.78** the plaintiff. If he misuses the product in an unforeseeable fashion or disregards a warning, the conclusion may simply be that the product was not defective. If it *is* found to be defective, the plaintiff's conduct should be treated as contributory negligence.

7. Defences

Once the plaintiff proves that the product was defective and caused **8.79** the damage the onus shifts to the defendant to establish one of the specific defences provided in section 4. One potential defence is expressly prohibited. By section 7 liability cannot be "limited or excluded by any contract term, by any notice or by any other provision." This prevents the manufacturer excluding liability under the Act to the injured consumer.[66] It does not, however, affect possible exclusion or limitation clauses in the contracts which constitute the chain of supply from manufacturer to distributor to retailer. Such clauses would not necessarily be caught by the Unfair Contract Terms Act 1977.[67]

Miscellaneous defences[68]

It is a defence for the defendant to show that: **8.80**

(i) The defect was attributable to compliance with any statutory requirement or European Community obligation.[69] Compliance with regulations made under the Medicines Act 1968 should not be an automatic defence, but this may be good evidence that the product conformed to what persons generally are entitled to expect by way of safety, as in the case of negligence.

(ii) He never supplied the product to another.[70] **8.81**

(iii) The only supply by him was otherwise than in the course of a **8.82** business, and if he is a producer, "own-brander" or importer that this is by virtue only of things done by him otherwise than with a view to profit.[71] Thus, free samples would not be within the defence, since they are distributed with a view, ultimately, to profit.

---

[66] An exclusion of liability for personal injuries caused by negligence will be invalid by virtue of the Unfair Contract Terms Act 1977, s.2(1).

[67] See *Thompson* v. *T. Lohan (Plant Hire) Ltd.* [1987] 2 All E.R. 631; *cf. Phillips Products Ltd.* v. *Hyland* [1987] 2 All E.R. 620. Of course, exclusion clauses in the chain of supply are irrelevant to the consumer's action.

[68] Note that special rules in respect of limitation periods apply to claims brought under the Consumer Protection Act 1987: see § 10.51.

[69] Consumer Protection Act 1987, s.4(1)(*a*).

[70] *Ibid.*, s.4(1)(*b*), *e.g.*, if it was stolen from him.

[71] *Ibid.*, s.4(1)(*c*).

8.83   (iv) The defect did not exist in the product when he supplied it to another.[72] If the defendant is a supplier, as opposed to a producer, an "own-brander" or an importer, it is a defence to show that the defect did not exist, not when *he* supplied it, but when it was last supplied by the producer, "own-brander" or importer.[73]

8.84   (v) A component manufacturer is not liable for a defect in the finished product which was wholly attributable to the design of the finished product (*e.g.* where the component product is normally safe in its contemplated use but is misused in the design of the finished product); nor where the defect is due to the compliance by the component manufacturer with instructions given by the manufacturer of the finished product.[74]

8.85   (vi) Contributory negligence is a partial defence.[75] Of course, misuse of the product by the plaintiff may be relevant to the question of whether the product was defective at all, or whether an otherwise defective product caused the plaintiff's damage. Conceptually these are distinct issues. If the product was defective, and if it was a cause, even a partial cause, of the damage, then the defendant is liable, and the plaintiff's fault is relevant only to apportionment of the damages. In practice, however, it may be difficult to separate these questions.

8.86   In theory, problems could arise as to the basis of apportionment of damages since the plaintiff is at fault and the defendant in breach of a strict duty which may not involve any negligence on his part. In such circumstances what is the "claimant's share in the responsibility for the damage"?[76] This is not likely to be a major obstacle, however, because the courts have considerable experience of apportionment in other areas where the defendant may have been in breach of a strict duty (*e.g.* employers' liability).

The "development risks" defence

8.87   Under section 4(1)(*e*) of the Consumer Protection Act 1987 it is a defence to prove that:

> "the state of scientific and technical knowledge at the relevant time was not such that a producer of products of the same description as the product in question might be expected to have discovered the defect if it had existed in his products while they were under his control."

The "relevant time" is the time when the defendant supplied the product to another, in effect, when it was put into circulation.[77]

8.88   This so-called development risks defence was one of the most controversial aspects of both the European Community Directive and the Consumer Protection Act 1987. Its effect is to excuse a defendant who can show that the defect was unknown and unforeseeable when he

---

[72] *Ibid.*, s.4(1)(*d*) and 4(2)(*a*).
[73] *Ibid.*, s.4(2)(*b*).
[74] *Ibid.*, s.4(1)(*f*).
[75] *Ibid.*, s.6(4).
[76] Law Reform (Contributory Negligence) Act 1945, s.1(1); see §§ 4.107–4.112.
[77] Consumer Protection Act 1987, s.4(2)(*a*).

put the product into circulation, the justification being that if defendants were held responsible for unknown and unknowable risks this might deter the development of new products which might be beneficial to the public at large. The objection to the defence is that it represents a policy of allowing individual consumers to bear these development risks should they materialise, when the possibility of loss spreading through insurance and the price mechanism is readily available. It amounts to a retreat into negligence theory at precisely the point that strict liability is most useful.[78]

Both the Law Commission and the Pearson Commission recom- **8.89** mended that this defence should not be available. Pearson, for example, commented that it would "leave a gap in the compensation cover, through which, for example, the victims of another thalidomide disaster might easily slip."[79] Indeed, the pharmaceutical industry will probably be one of the principal beneficiaries of this defence. There is a public policy argument in favour of the development and marketing of new drugs which are intended to save life and reduce pain and suffering, even where the drugs carry risks to the public. The central issue, however, is who should carry the burden of these development risks. If it is in the public interest then maybe the public should bear the risks, either through strict liability and the market mechanism or through a no-fault compensation scheme.[80]

The wording of the defence invites comparison with the scientific **8.90** and technical knowledge of a hypothetical producer of "products of the same description as the product in question." This is a subjective test of knowledge, by reference to the knowledge of the industry concerned, not general scientific and technical knowledge. The Act differs significantly from the Directive on this point. Article 7(e) of the Directive confers the defence where "the state of scientific and technical knowledge at the time when he put the product into circulation was not such as to enable the existence of the defect to be discovered." This version of the defence is narrower than section 4(1)(e) of the Act, since it is easier to prove that no producer of similar products could have discovered the defect, than to prove that no-one, considering the state of scientific and technical knowledge, could have discovered the defect.[81] This discrepancy has been referred to the European Commission on the basis that the Act does not fully implement the Directive, and it may be that the issue will have to be resolved by the European Court of Justice. On the other hand, section 1(1) states that Part I of the Act "shall have effect for the purpose of making such provision as is necessary in order to comply with the product liability Directive and shall be construed accordingly," and it is arguable that a domestic court should interpret provisions in the Act

---

[78] Although see Stapleton (1986) 6 O.J.L.S. 392, 408–13, arguing that even without a development risks defence the same considerations have to be taken into account in a scheme which bases liability on defectiveness.

[79] *Royal Commission on Civil Liability and Compensation for Personal Injury*, Cmnd. 7054 (1978), Vol. I, para. 1259.

[80] On no-fault compensation for drug injuries see Fleming (1982) 30 Am. J. Comp. Law 297.

[81] Crossick (1988) 138 New L.J. 223; *cf.* Newdick [1988] C.L.J. 455, 459–460 who argues that the Directive is ambiguous and that s.4(1)(e) is the correct interpretation of the ambiguity.

in accordance with the Directive, if there is any discrepancy between the Act and the Directive. As it stands, section 4(1)(e) effectively excuses the defendant when he has not been negligent in failing to discover the defect, and amounts to little more than a reversal of the burden of proving negligence.[82]

8.91 A major problem in applying section 4(1)(e) will be the interpretation of the words "scientific and technical knowledge." It is not clear when "information" becomes "knowledge." This could be when it is accepted as scientific fact; or when it is published in a scientific journal as a hypothesis; or when a researcher in a laboratory considers it to be a remote possibility. Where there are conflicting views within the scientific community, then which view must the manufacturer follow? How discoverable must the defect be? With the expenditure of moderate or reasonable or extensive resources? Indeed, is cost a relevant consideration at all? If the defect could have been discovered from existing information but the appropriate intellectual "connections" have not been made by researchers, is this "knowledge" from which the defect might be expected to have been discovered?[83] These issues await resolution by the courts.

8.92 It is not clear whether the defence applies to manufacturing defects. On the face of it the defence is concerned with the producer's knowledge of the possibility that the defect might exist, and excuses him from liability if he could not have known about the risk. Thus, it appears to be concerned with design defects rather than construction defects. It is arguable, however, that the defence might also apply to construction defects which it is known can occur, but the state of technical knowledge is such that it is impossible to devise a quality control system that will detect all defective items in the production line.[84] Although this argument runs contrary to the whole principle of strict liability for defective products, and so may not be accepted, the different treatment given to construction defects and design defects is itself illogical and arbitrary.[85] It is the development risks defence itself which, combined with the definition of defectiveness, undermines the principle of strict liability. The effect is that the Consumer Protection Act 1987 constitutes little more than a statutory version of negligence, with a reversed burden of proof.

---

[82] Newdick [1988] C.L.J. 455, 460, 475; indeed, in certain respects the standard required may be lower than in negligence: *ibid.,* p. 457, n. 11. See also Newdick (1985) 101 L.Q.R. 405, 406 commenting that: " . . . a state of the art defence would be sufficient to undermine the entire policy of a scheme of strict liability so far as it applied to drug damage."

[83] In *Independent Broadcasting Authority* v. *EMI Electronics Ltd. and BICC Construction Ltd.* (1980) 14 Build. L.R. 1, 36 Lord Fraser commented that: "The error arose not from difficulty of calculation but from the omission of what seems to me to have been a simple piece of reasoning about known facts"; *cf.* where the primary information has not been discovered.

[84] See Newdick [1988] C.L.J. 455, 469–73.

[85] Stapleton (1986) 6 O.J.L.S. 392.

CHAPTER 9

DAMAGES

Most actions against medical practitioners are claims in respect of **9.01**
personal injuries or death and the consequential financial loss, and
there is no difference in the principles applied to the assessment of
damages in medical negligence cases from other actions for personal
injuries. Injunctive relief is rarely relevant, with the possible exception
of actions for breach of confidence. Accordingly, this chapter concentrates almost exclusively on the principles adopted by the courts in the
assessment of damages for personal injuries and death, though the
final section deals with damages for breach of confidence.[1]

I. GENERAL PRINCIPLES

1. Types of damages

The fundamental principle applied to the assessment of an award of **9.02**
damages in tort is that the plaintiff should be fully compensated. He is
entitled to be restored to the position that he would have been in had
the tort not been committed, in so far as this can be done by the
payment of money.[2] In contract the plaintiff is entitled to be placed in
the position he would have been in had the contract been performed,
but in practice this is unlikely to produce a different measure of
damages in contract and tort in an action for personal injuries. In the
case of non-pecuniary loss the principle of restoring the plaintiff to his
pre-accident position is inappropriate. No amount of money can

---

[1] Strictly speaking, claims in respect of certain financial losses arising out of failed
sterilisations may not be categorised as actions for personal injuries (see *Pattison* v.
Hobbs, *The Times*, November 11, 1985, § 10.06) but they are nonetheless included in
this chapter. It is not possible to give more than an outline of the law on damages for
personal injuries here. For detailed discussion see Kemp & Kemp, *The Quantum of
Damages*; *McGregor on Damages*, 15th ed., 1988, Chaps. 33 and 34.
[2] *Livingstone* v. *Rawyards Coal Co.* (1880) 5 App.Cas. 25, 39. In torts actionable *per
se*, such as trespass to the person, a plaintiff could be awarded nominal damages where it
is clear that a tort has been committed but the plaintiff has suffered no loss. Similarly, in
contract nominal damages may be awarded where there has been a breach of contract
but no loss. In the tort of negligence damage is the gist of the action, and some
substantive damage must be proved for the action to lie. These distinctions will rarely, if
ever, be relevant to claims in respect of personal injuries.

restore a lost limb or take away the plaintiff's experience of pain. Here the principle applied by the courts is that damages for non-pecuniary loss should be "fair" or "reasonable." This is patently unhelpful, because it simply begs the question of what is a fair or reasonable sum. The award is inevitably an arbitrary one. In practice, the courts adopt a tariff or "going rate" for specific types of injury in an attempt to achieve some degree of consistency between plaintiffs with similar injuries and to provide a basis for the settlement of claims.

9.03 Inexact or unliquidated losses are compensated by an award of "general damages." In an action for personal injuries this includes the non-pecuniary losses which are compensated under the heads of pain and suffering, and loss of amenity. It also includes prospective pecuniary losses such as future loss of earnings and medical expenses. "Special damages" are the losses that are capable of being calculated with reasonable accuracy, and will normally consist of accrued pecuniary losses, such as loss of earnings and other expenses incurred from the date of the injury to the date of assessment. These distinctions are important for pleading and procedural purposes and for the purpose of determining the appropriate rate of interest, since different rates apply to special damages and general damages for non-pecuniary loss, and no interest will be awarded in respect of future pecuniary loss.[3] Although the court will assess damages under these broad heads, the court should also have regard to the appropriateness of the total award in order to avoid any overlapping of the different heads of damage, though it is doubtful whether there can be any overlap between pecuniary and non-pecuniary losses.[4]

9.04 Where damages are at large, that is where the award is not limited to the pecuniary loss that can be specifically proved,[5] the court may take into account the manner in which the tort was committed in assessing damages. If it was such as to injure the plaintiff's proper feelings of dignity and pride, then aggravated damages may be awarded.[6] Aggravated damages are compensatory, but they are higher than would normally be the case to reflect the greater injury to the plaintiff. In *Kralj* v. *McGrath* [7] Woolf J. held that aggravated damages should not be awarded in an action for negligence against a doctor, notwithstanding that the medical evidence indicated that the plaintiff's

---

[3] R.S.C., Ord. 18, r. 12, as amended by S.I. 1989/2427, provides that a plaintiff in an action for personal injuries must serve with his statement of claim a medical report substantiating all the personal injuries alleged in the statement of claim, which the plaintiff proposes to adduce in evidence at trial, and a statement of the special damages for expenses and losses (including loss of earnings and of pension rights) claimed. For an argument that this rule should not apply to medical negligence actions see Body and Levy, (1990) *A.V.M.A. Medical and Legal Journal*, No. 3, p. 8. On the payment of interest see § 9.18. Where possible, special damages should be agreed in advance of the hearing: *Practice Direction (Personal Injuries Action: Particulars of Special Damage)* [1984] 3 All E.R. 165.

[4] *Lim Poh Choo* v. *Camden and Islington Area Health Authority* [1980] A.C. 174, 191, 192; see also *Royal Commission on Civil Liability and Compensation for Personal Injury*, Cmnd. 7054, 1978, Vol. I, para. 759.

[5] *Rookes* v. *Barnard* [1964] A.C. 1129, 1221. This includes loss of reputation, injured feelings, pain and suffering or loss of amenity; *Broome* v. *Cassell & Co. Ltd.* [1972] A.C. 1027, 1073.

[6] *Jolliffe* v. *Willmett & Co.* [1971] 1 All E.R. 478—an "insolent and high-handed trespass" by a private investigator.

[7] [1986] 1 All E.R. 54.

treatment had been "horrific." If, on the other hand, the particular treatment increased the plaintiff's pain and suffering this should be reflected in a higher award under this head. As a matter of principle, it is difficult to see why doctors should be specifically excluded from the ambit of aggravated damages, which are compensatory not punitive, although as a question of fact it will be unlikely that mere negligence would be sufficient for such an award. In *Broome* v. *Cassell & Co. Ltd.*[8] Lord Reid said that the commission of a tort in a malicious, insulting or oppressive manner may aggravate the plaintiff's injury. It is arguable that some forms of treatment could be regarded as oppressive or insulting: sterilisation of a competent adult without consent, for example.[9] In *Barbara* v. *Home Office*[10] a remand prisoner was forcibly injected with a tranquillising drug by prison officers, and the defendants admitted liability for trespass to the person. The plaintiff was awarded £100 general damages and £500 aggravated damages, but a claim for exemplary damages was rejected. Mere negligence, it was said, did not justify an award of exemplary damages simply because it resulted in a trespass to the person which from the plaintiff's point of view could be regarded as oppressive.

Exemplary damages should be distinguished from aggravated **9.05** damages. Exemplary damages are punitive in nature and are awarded in addition to compensatory damages in order to teach the defendant that "tort does not pay." At common law exemplary damages may only be awarded in two categories of case, namely: (i) oppressive, arbitrary or unconstitutional action by servants of the government; and (ii) where the defendant's conduct has been calculated by him to make a profit for himself which may well exceed the compensation available.[11] The restricted availability of exemplary damages makes it highly unlikely that they would ever be awarded in an action for medical negligence, although they do feature in malpractice claims against doctors in some American and Canadian jurisdictions.

2. Lump sum awards

The plaintiff can only bring one action in respect of a single tort. He **9.06** cannot bring a second action based on the same facts simply because the damage turns out to be more extensive than was first anticipated.[12]

---

[8] [1972] A.C. 1027, 1085.

[9] See § 6.10. In *Devi* v. *West Midlands Regional Health Authority* (1981) (unreported), C.A., compensatory damages of £4,000 were awarded in a case of non-consensual sterilisation, without any reference to aggravated damages.

[10] (1984) 134 New L.J. 888. A similar allegation failed on the facts in *Freeman* v. *Home Office* [1983] 3 All E.R. 589; aff'd [1984] 1 All E.R. 1036.

[11] *Rookes* v. *Barnard* [1964] A.C. 1129; *Broome* v. *Cassell & Co. Ltd.* [1972] A.C. 1027.

[12] *Fetter* v. *Beale* (1701) 1 Ld Raym. 339, 692; *Bristow* v. *Grout, The Times*, November 9, 1987, C.A.; *cf. Brunsden* v. *Humphrey* (1884) 14 Q.B.D. 141, where the plaintiff was held to be entitled to bring two separate actions in respect of damage to property and personal injuries arising out of the same events, because they are two distinct rights. There cannot be two actions, however, for two separate forms of personal injury arising from a single negligent act, even where one of the injuries only comes to light after damages for the first injury have been recovered: see *Bristow* v. *Grout, The Times*, November 9, 1987.

Damages are normally assessed once-and-for-all and will be awarded in the form of a lump sum, both for accrued and prospective losses. The court has no power to require a defendant to make periodical payments nor to review the award at a later date if the estimate of the plaintiff's loss turns out to be either too low or too high.[13] A limited exception may apply where there is evidence of a change of circumstances after the trial of an action, but before an appeal. In these circumstances the Court of Appeal may admit the new evidence to mitigate the consequences of the lump sum system.[14] As a general rule, however, once the time limit for an appeal has expired, an appeal out of time on the basis of changed circumstances will not be permitted.

9.07 The rule that damages may only be awarded as a lump sum causes particular problems in cases of personal injuries, especially where the medical prognosis is uncertain, because the court has to assess damages based on assumptions about what will happen to the plaintiff in the future which may well turn out to be incorrect. The plaintiff's condition may become worse than could have been anticipated at the trial or it may improve. He may live longer than the predicted life expectancy and the damages may be inadequate or he may die sooner, with the result that the damages will not be used for their intended purpose and will result in a windfall for the beneficiaries of his estate. As Lord Scarman commented in *Lim Poh Choo* v. *Camden and Islington Area Health Authority*:

> "Knowledge of the future being denied to mankind, so much of the award as is attributed to future loss and suffering will almost surely be wrong. There is really only one certainty: the future will prove the award to be either too high or too low."[15]

9.08 When assessing damages the court will make an estimate of the chances that a particular event will or would have happened, and reflect those chances in the amount of damages awarded, irrespective of whether the chance was more or less than even.[16] The question is whether the chance is substantial. If it is a mere possibility or speculative it must be ignored, although the question of whether the chance is substantial or speculative should be decided without regard to legal niceties, but on a consideration of all the facts in proper perspective.[17]

9.09 There are now three mechanisms by which some of the problems caused by awarding damages only in the form of a lump sum can be ameliorated, though not removed entirely. These are: the possibility of

---

[13] *Fournier* v. *Canadian National Railway* [1927] A.C. 167, 169; *British Transport Commission* v. *Gourley* [1956] A.C. 185, 212; *Burke* v. *Tower Hamlets Health Authority*, *The Times*, August 10, 1989. For criticism of this rule and an argument that the courts should exercise a power to award damages by way of periodical payments see Croxon, (1990) *A.V.M.A. Medical and Legal Journal*, No. 3, p. 4.

[14] *Mulholland* v. *Mitchell* [1971] A.C. 666; *Lim Poh Choo* v. *Camden and Islington Area Health Authority* [1980] A.C. 174. In *Lim* Lord Scarman described this exception as "an unsatisfactory makeshift, and of dubious value in any case where the new facts are themselves in issue." See further R.S.C., Ord. 59, r. 10. The court may permit a party to argue a point that was not raised at trial where there has been a change in the law in the interim: see, *e.g.*, *McCamley* v. *Cammell Laird Shipbuilders Ltd.* [1990] 1 All E.R. 854, 864.

[15] [1980] A.C. 174, 183.

[16] *Mallett* v. *McMonagle* [1970] A.C. 166, 176, *per* Lord Diplock.

[17] *Davies* v. *Taylor* [1974] A.C. 207, 212, *per* Lord Reid.

claiming provisional damages; separate trials on liability and quantum; and the possibility of the parties agreeing to the compensation being paid in the form of a structured settlement.

Provisional damages

Section 32A of the Supreme Court Act 1981 introduced a procedure **9.10** for the award of provisional damages in cases where there is a "chance" that as a result of the tort the plaintiff will develop some serious disease or suffer some serious deterioration in his condition. In such cases the plaintiff may be awarded provisional damages assessed on the basis that the disease or deterioration will not occur. If the event subsequently materialises the plaintiff can then make an application for further damages in order to compensate for the loss that has now occurred. This procedure should, in theory, produce assessments of damages which more accurately reflect the loss that the plaintiff has sustained, since he will not be compensated for a risk that may never materialise, and moreover, if the risk does materialise the plaintiff will receive fuller compensation, instead of damages heavily discounted under the lump sum system on the basis that there is only a small risk that the loss may occur.

Under R.S.C., Ord. 37 a claim for provisional damages must be **9.11** pleaded by the plaintiff, and when making an order the court must specify the disease or type of deterioration which will entitle the plaintiff to make a further application for damages, and the period of time within which the second application should be made.[18] The plaintiff must apply for further damages within the specified period, giving the defendant three months notice of intention to apply, and only one application for further damages can be made.[19] Where an application for an award of provisional damages has been made, a defendant may at any time make a written offer agreeing to the making of an award and to tender a sum of money in satisfaction of the plaintiff's claim for damages assessed on the assumption that the plaintiff will not develop some serious disease or suffer a serious deterioration in his physical or mental condition. The tender must identify the disease or deterioration in question.[20]

Provisional damages are not appropriate in all, or even most, cases.[21] **9.12** Since the disease or type of injury for which the plaintiff is entitled to seek further damages must be specified when the plaintiff applies for provisional damages, the procedure does not cover a general deterioration in the plaintiff's condition, nor an unforeseen complication. The term "chance" can cover a wide range between something that is *de*

---

[18] R.S.C., Ord. 37, r. 8. See further *Practice Direction* (*Provisional Damages: Procedure*) [1985] 2 All E.R. 895; and *Practice Direction* (*Personal Injuries Actions: Provisional Damages: Default of Defence*) [1988] 2 All E.R. 102.

[19] R.S.C., Ord. 37, r. 10. The plaintiff may apply for an extension of the period before it expires: r. 8(3).

[20] R.S.C., Ord. 37, r. 9(1)(*a*), as amended by S.I. 1989/2427.

[21] An award of provisional damages is discretionary. The court will weigh up the possibility of doing justice by a "once-and-for-all" assessment against the possibility of doing better justice by reserving the plaintiff's right to return at a future date: *Willson* v. *Ministry of Defence* [1991] 1 All E.R. 638, 645.

minimis and something that is a probability, but it must be measurable rather than fanciful. Provided the chance is measurable it can fall within the procedure for provisional damages, however slim the chance may be.[22] "Serious deterioration" in the plaintiff's condition means "something beyond ordinary deterioration" and this is a question of fact depending on the circumstances of the case, including the effect of the deterioration on the plaintiff.[23]

9.13 "Chance" cases must be distinguished from cases where the medical evidence can forecast with a reasonable degree of certainty that the plaintiff's condition will deteriorate causing a reasonably probable degree of disability. A typical example of this situation occurs where it is possible to predict that over the years arthritis is likely to develop in a damaged joint. Here damages should be assessed on the single lump sum basis, discounting the award for the chance that arthritis will not occur. In *Willson* v. *Ministry of Defence*[24] it was held that the development of arthritis to the point at which surgery is required, or which requires the plaintiff to change his employment, did not fall within the definition of serious deterioration, rather it was "simply an aspect of a progression of this particular disease." Similarly, the chance that due to a disabling injury the plaintiff may sustain a further injury, even if that injury could be severe, did not call for provisional damages. The risk of a serious injury was not to be equated with a serious deterioration in the plaintiff's physical condition.

9.14 Provisional damages are limited to cases where there is a clear-cut event which will trigger an entitlement to further compensation, cases where there would be little room for later dispute whether or not the contemplated deterioration had actually occurred.[25] A claim for provisional damages cannot include a declaration that the plaintiff's surviving dependants should be entitled to bring a claim under the Fatal Accidents Act 1976 if the plaintiff should subsequently die as a result of a deterioration in his physical condition.[26]

Split-trial and interim payments

9.15 R.S.C., Ord. 33, r. 4 provides a procedure for separate trials on liability and damages, so that the assessment of damages can be made at a later date when the medical prognosis is more certain.[27] This procedure is only of value where the plaintiff's medical condition is unstable and needs time to settle. In an action for personal injuries the

---

[22] *Willson* v. *Ministry of Defence* [1991] 1 All E.R. 638, 642, *per* Scott Baker J.
[23] *Ibid.*
[24] *Ibid.*, pp. 642 and 643.
[25] *Ibid.*, p. 644; *Patterson* v. *Ministry of Defence* [1987] C.L.Y. 1194. Thus, they are appropriate for cases with "a clear and severable risk rather than a continuing deterioration, as is the typical osteoarthritic picture": *ibid.*, p. 644; *Allott* v. *Central Electricity Generating Board* (1988) (unreported), Q.B.D. The fact that there is disagreement in the medical evidence, however, about the risk of the plaintiff contracting cancer in the future does not preclude the court from making an award of provisional damages: *Hurditch* v. *Sheffield Health Authority* [1989] 2 All E.R. 869. The plaintiff will still have to establish causation, of course, when making the application for further damages.
[26] *Middleton* v. *Elliott Turbomachinery Ltd.*, *The Independent*, November 16, 1990 C.A.
[27] The test is whether it is just and convenient to order a split trial: *Coenen* v. *Payne* [1974] 1 W.L.R. 984.

court may at any stage of the proceedings, and of its own motion, make an order for the issue of liability to be tried before any issue concerning the question of damages.[28] This procedure can be combined with the power to seek an interim payment to meet the plaintiff's immediate needs, which is then deducted from the final award. Under R.S.C., Ord. 29, r. 11 an interim payment can be obtained where the defendant has admitted liability, or the plaintiff has obtained judgment for damages to be assessed, or "if the action proceeded to trial, the plaintiff would obtain judgment for substantial damages," provided that the defendant is insured against liability to the plaintiff, or is a public authority, or is a person whose means and resources are such as to enable him to make the interim payment.[29]

Structured settlements

A structured settlement allows the plaintiff to take the award of **9.16** damages in the form of periodic payments. This is a private arrangement between the plaintiff and the defendant's liability insurer under which the normal lump sum damages award can be varied or "structured" over a period of time.[30] The settlement may include a lump sum element plus periodic payments intended to meet the plaintiff's future losses. The payments can be for a fixed period or until the plaintiff's death, and they can be index-linked. The payments are financed by the purchase of an annuity by the liability insurer with the money, or part of it, that would have been paid to the plaintiff as a lump sum. The annuity is held by the insurer on behalf of the plaintiff and, as a result of a concession by the Inland Revenue, the payment is not taxable as income in the plaintiff's hands. Moreover, the insurer is not liable to tax on the annuity either. The result is that for large awards, where the tax liability on the income generated by investment of the lump sum damages would be high, the value of the arrangement to both plaintiff and insurer is substantially greater than the traditional lump sum award.[30a] The possibility of index-linking also removes the problem of inflation eroding the value of the award.

Structured settlements will undoubtedly prove to be of benefit to **9.17** some plaintiffs who have sustained serious personal injury and who will have a substantial claim for future pecuniary loss. They do not, however, constitute the form of periodic payments recommended by the Pearson Commission in order to remove some of the uncertainties in assessing future pecuniary losses.[31] They depend upon agreement between the parties; the court has no power to order a defendant to

---

[28] R.S.C., Ord. 33, r. 4, as amended by S.I. 1989/2427.

[29] It has been suggested, however, that the new rules on recoupment of social security benefits will curtail the usefulness of an application for an interim payment, because the benefits are liable to be recouped in full from any compensation payment: see (1990) 140 New L.J. 1661. On the recoupment of benefits see §§ 9.43 *et seq.*

[30] See Allen (1988) 104 L.Q.R. 448; Lewis (1988) 15 J. of Law and Soc. 392.

[30a] The sum awarded under a structured settlement should be smaller than with a straightforward payment of a lump sum, since there are tax savings which result in the same benefits accruing to the plaintiff: *Kelly* v. *Dawes, The Times,* September 27, 1990.

[31] *Royal Commission on Civil Liability and Compensation for Personal Injury,* Cmnd. 7054, 1978, Vol. I, para. 573; *cf.* Law Com. No. 56, H.C. 373, 1973, para. 28, rejecting the introduction of periodical payments.

accept this form of settlement.[32] It is still necessary to estimate what the lump sum award would be, applying the normal principles, before setting up a structured settlement, if only to advise the client whether the arrangement is appropriate in the circumstances. The periodic payments are only varied over time in accordance with the terms agreed at the outset; they cannot take account of unanticipated events which affect the plaintiff's future pecuniary expenditure.

3. Interest

9.18 Where damages for personal injuries or death exceeding £200 are awarded the court must award interest unless there are special reasons for not doing so.[33] In the case of special damages for accrued pecuniary loss interest will normally be awarded at half the special investment rate on money paid into court, running from the date of the accident to the date of trial, the reasoning being that part of the loss will have occurred immediately after the tort and part immediately before the assessment.[34] Interest at half the rate is a compromise. If, however, there are special circumstances which would make it unfair to apply this rule it may be possible to obtain interest at the full rate on certain items of special damage which have been incurred shortly after the accident.[35] No interest is awarded on future pecuniary loss, such as prospective loss of earnings or medical expenses, because the loss has not yet accrued.[36]

9.19 Interest on damages for non-pecuniary loss (pain and suffering and loss of amenity) is awarded at a modest rate, currently two per cent., for the period from the date of service of the writ to the date of trial.[37] This low rate is attributable to the fact that a large proportion of nominal interest rates is represented by inflation, and inflation is taken into account when the court assesses the damages for non-pecuniary loss by a general uprating of the tariffs or bands applied to different types of injury.[38] Interest at two per cent. represents an approximate

---

[32] *Burke* v. *Tower Hamlets Health Authority, The Times*, August 10, 1989.

[33] Supreme Court Act 1981, s.35A; County Courts Act 1984, s.69. A claim for interest must be specifically pleaded: R.S.C., Ord. 18, r. 8(4). The interest is not taxed as income: Income and Corporation Taxes Act 1988, s.329.

[34] *Jefford* v. *Gee* [1970] 2 Q.B. 130, 146; *Cookson* v. *Knowles* [1979] A.C. 556. In the case of a split-trial in a personal injuries action, where liability is agreed or determined first with damages to be assessed later, interest on the damages awarded under s.17 of the Judgments Act 1838 will run from the date of judgment on damages and not from the date of judgment on liability: *Thomas* v. *Bunn* [1991] 1 All E.R. 193, H.L.

[35] *Ichard* v. *Frangoulis* [1977] 1 W.L.R. 556. Private medical fees are one possible example: see *Dexter* v. *Courtalds Ltd.* [1984] 1 All E.R. 70, 73. In the "generality of personal injury cases," however, the principles laid down in *Jefford* v. *Gee* [1970] 2 Q.B. 130 should be applied: *ibid.*, p. 74, *per* Lawton L.J.; *cf. Prokop* v. *Department of Health and Social Security* (1983) (unreported), C.A., referred to in Kemp & Kemp, *The Quantum of Damages*, Vol. I, para. 16.07, where it is suggested that the decision in *Dexter* was reached *per incuriam*. A claim for the full rate of interest must be pleaded.

[36] *Cookson* v. *Knowles* [1979] A.C. 556; *Joyce* v. *Yeomans* [1981] 1 W.L.R. 549.

[37] *Birkett* v. *Hayes* [1982] 2 All E.R. 710; *Wright* v. *British Railways Board* [1983] 2 A.C. 773. Personal injury cases seem to be in a special category, since interest on damages for non-pecuniary loss will not be awarded in actions for deceit or false imprisonment: *Saunders* v. *Edwards* [1987] 2 All E.R. 651; *Holtham* v. *Commissioner of Police of the Metropolis, The Times*, November 28, 1987.

[38] It is arguable that this low rate should not apply to damages for bereavement under the Fatal Accidents Act 1976, s.1A (§ 9.64), because the amount of the award is fixed by statute and does not increase when tariffs are uprated: see *Prior* v. *Bernard Hastie & Co.* [1987] C.L.Y. 1219; *Sharman* v. *Sheppard* [1989] C.L.Y. 1190.

real rate of return for the plaintiff not having the use of his money. The fact that interest runs from the date of service of the writ provides a very good reason for both issuing and serving a writ early, even where negotiations are proceeding, since interest can amount to a substantial sum (notwithstanding the low interest rate) where the award of damages for non-pecuniary loss is likely to be high and the delay between initiating a claim and trial is likely to be lengthy, which may well be the case in a medical negligence action. Moreover, where the plaintiff has delayed in bringing a claim to trial the judge has a discretion to disallow interest on pre-trial damages.[39] Prompt issue and service of the writ also avoids problems with limitation periods and the time limits for service.

Where the plaintiff has received social security benefits which are **9.20** subject to the recoupment provisions of the Social Security Act 1989,[40] then the amount of the award of damages for the purpose of assessing interest on the award is treated as reduced by a sum equal to the relevant benefits.[41] The reduction takes effect first against the special damages, and then, if there is a remaining balance, against the general damages.

4. Mitigation of damage

The plaintiff is under a duty to mitigate the damage caused by the **9.21** defendant's tort, although he commits no wrong against the defendant if he fails to do so.[42] If he has lost his job as a result of the injury he should seek alternative employment, if he is capable of working. If he takes a lower paid job he can only recover from the defendant the difference between his previous earnings and his present earnings. The plaintiff should also seek medical attention which will improve his medical condition, although he will not be required to undergo a medical procedure where there is a substantial risk of further injury or the outcome is uncertain. The test is whether in all the circumstances, including particularly the medical advice received, the plaintiff acted reasonably in refusing the treatment.[43] Where the medical advice is conflicting, or the treatment involves some risk and the doctors prefer to leave the final decision to the plaintiff, a refusal of treatment will be considered to be

---

[39] *Birkett* v. *Hayes* [1982] 2 All E.R. 710, 717; *Spittle* v. *Bunney* [1988] 3 All E.R. 1031; *Corbett* v. *Barking Havering and Brentwood Health Authority* [1991] 1 All E.R. 498.

[40] See § 9.43.

[41] Social Security Act 1989, Sched. 4, para. 23 (added by the Social Security Act 1990, Sched. 1, para. 6).

[42] *Darbishire* v. *Warran* [1963] 1 W.L.R. 1067, 1075.

[43] *Selvanayagam* v. *University of West Indies* [1983] 1 All E.R. 824, 827, P.C.; *Marcroft* v. *Scruttons Ltd.* [1954] 1 Lloyd's Rep. 395; *McAuley* v. *London Transport Executive* [1957] 2 Lloyd's Rep. 500; *cf.* the more subjective approach of the Australian courts in *Glavonjic* v. *Foster* [1979] V.R. 536 and *Karabotos* v. *Plastex Industries Pty. Ltd.* [1981] V.R. 675, where the test was said to be whether a reasonable man in the plaintiff's particular circumstances and subject to the various factors that affected the plaintiff, would have refused the treatment; see further Hudson (1983) 3 L.S. 50. In *Marcroft* v. *Scruttons Ltd.* [1954] 1 Lloyd's Rep. 395, the Court of Appeal clearly had some sympathy for the plaintiff's subjective response to the recommended treatment, which was electro-convulsive therapy, but nonetheless applied an objective test.

reasonable.[44] The burden of proving that the plaintiff acted unreasonably in failing to mitigate the loss is the defendant's.[45]

9.22 If the plaintiff has acted unreasonably in refusing medical treatment a question arises as to how damages should be assessed where the treatment cannot guarantee an improvement in the plaintiff's condition. In *Ippolito* v. *Janiak*[46] the mitigating operation which the plaintiff had unreasonably refused to undergo had a 70 per cent. chance of success. A majority of the Ontario Court of Appeal held that, rather than assuming (on the basis of the balance of probabilities) that the operation would succeed, the 30 per cent. chance of the operation failing to alleviate the plaintiff's condition should be taken into account in assessing damages for prospective loss of earnings. It is unclear how the English courts would approach this problem because, although an action for the loss of a less than 50 per cent. chance of a successful medical outcome is unlikely to be accepted,[47] the courts have no difficulty in taking into account even small chances of future events when assessing damages. It is suggested that the chance of the treatment failing to achieve its purpose should be taken into account, particularly since it may well be this factor which persuades the plaintiff to refuse the treatment and notwithstanding that objectively the refusal is considered to be unreasonable.[48]

9.23 Where the plaintiff is unable, through impecuniosity, to mitigate the damage, the defendant is liable for the full loss.[49] This should be distinguished from the situation where the damage itself is the product of the plaintiff's impecuniosity, when it may be treated as too remote. In practice this distinction is not easy to draw, although it will rarely be relevant in a claim for medical negligence since the court would probably treat impecuniosity in the context of personal injuries as a question of mitigation rather than remoteness.[50]

---

[44] *Savage* v. *T. Wallis Ltd.* [1966] 1 Lloyd's Rep. 357; *McAuley* v. *London Transport Executive* [1957] 2 Lloyd's Rep. 500, 505; *Selvanayagam* v. *University of West Indies* [1983] 1 All E.R. 824. There is no obligation upon a plaintiff who has become pregnant following a negligently performed sterilisation operation to undergo an abortion to mitigate the loss: *Emeh* v. *Kensington and Chelsea Area Health Authority* [1984] 3 All E.R. 1044; § 5.60.

[45] *Steele* v. *Robert George & Co.* (1937) *Ltd.* [1942] A.C. 497; *Richardson* v. *Redpath, Brown & Co. Ltd.* [1944] A.C. 62, H.L. A dictum to the contrary effect in *Selvanayagam* v. *University of West Indies* [1983] 1 All E.R. 824 would seem to be incorrect: see McGregor (1983) 46 M.L.R. 758; Kemp (1983) 99 L.Q.R. 497.

[46] (1981) 126 D.L.R. (3d) 623.

[47] See §§ 5.29 *et seq.*

[48] In *McAuley* v. *London Transport Executive* [1957] 2 Lloyd's Rep. 500, 505 Jenkins L.J. said that: "damages ought to be assessed as they would properly have been assessable if [the plaintiff] had, in fact, undergone the operation and secured the degree of recovery to be expected from it." This permits the defendant to benefit from an assumption that a particular event would have occurred as a certainty, whereas plaintiffs normally have their future losses discounted for the chance that particular events might not have occurred, *e.g.* that they might not have continued working until retirement age. It is not clear why defendants should be in better position than plaintiffs in this respect.

[49] *Clippens Oil Co.* v. *Edinburgh & District Water Trustees* [1907] A.C. 291, 303; *Dodd Properties (Kent) Ltd.* v. *Canterbury City Council* [1980] 1 All E.R. 928, 935, 941.

[50] See § 5.83.

II. Personal Injuries: Pecuniary Losses

A plaintiff who sustains personal injuries will normally suffer two **9.24** distinct types of loss, pecuniary and non-pecuniary loss. Pecuniary loss is the damage that is capable of being directly calculated in monetary terms, whether accrued or prospective. It includes, for example, loss of earnings and pension rights, medical expenses, travelling expenses, the cost of special equipment and the cost of employing someone to carry out domestic duties which the plaintiff is no longer able to perform. Following *Jefford* v. *Gee*[51] damages in a personal injuries action must be particularised under at least three broad heads for the purpose of calculating interest, namely special damages, prospective pecuniary loss, and non-pecuniary damages, though in practice distinct items of loss are particularised in much greater detail. Care should be taken when identifying these items of loss to avoid overlap or duplication in the total assessment.

1. Medical and other expenses

The plaintiff is entitled to recover his medical and other expenses **9.25** (such as additional housing and travel costs) which are reasonably incurred.[52] Accrued expenses will be awarded as part of the special damages, whereas future medical expenses will be estimated by the multiplier method and awarded as general damages.[53] The possibility of avoiding medical expenses, or part of them, by taking advantage of National Health Service facilities is disregarded.[54] Thus, the plaintiff can insist on damages to cover the cost of private medical treatment at the defendant's expense, although the court does not exercise any control over how the plaintiff uses the award (except where he is a minor or of unsound mind). If it seems likely that the plaintiff will be unable to receive privately all the treatment that he needs, and will eventually have to enter a N.H.S. hospital, a deduction from the award for future medical expenses will be made to allow for this.[55] Where the plaintiff has in fact used N.H.S. facilities for medical treatment he cannot recover what he would have paid had he received private treatment.[56] Any saving to the plaintiff which is attributable to his maintenance wholly or partly at public expense in a hospital,

---

[51] [1970] 2 Q.B. 130.

[52] He is not entitled to the cost of an operation which he would have had to undergo in any event: *Cutler* v. *Vauxhall Motors Ltd.* [1971] 1 Q.B. 418.

[53] For discussion of the "multiplier method" in the context of future loss of earnings see § 9.32. When dealing with future nursing care or domestic assistance the multiplier may be higher than for the loss of earnings claim because the period during which nursing care is needed may well exceed the plaintiff's pre-accident working life expectancy.

[54] Law Reform (Personal Injuries) Act 1948, s.2(4). The Pearson Commission recommended repeal of this provision: *Royal Commission on Civil Liability and Compensation for Personal Injury*, Cmnd. 7054, 1978, Vol. I, para. 342.

[55] *Lim Poh Choo* v. *Camden and Islington Area Health Authority* [1980] A.C. 174; *Housecroft* v. *Burnett* [1986] 1 All E.R. 332, 342.

[56] *Harris* v. *Brights Asphalt Contractors Ltd.* [1953] 1 Q.B. 617, 635; *Lim Poh Choo* v. *Camden and Islington Area Health Authority* [1980] A.C. 174, 188.

nursing home or other institution will be set off against any income he has lost as a result of his injuries.[57] A similar rule applies to plaintiffs who make savings in domestic expenditure while being looked after in a private institution.[58]

9.26 If the plaintiff has to live in a special institution, such as a nursing home, or receive attendance at home, he is entitled to the cost of that, provided that it is reasonably necessary.[59] Where there is a choice as to where the plaintiff is cared for it is not necessarily a question of which option is the cheapest. Thus, a plaintiff who needs constant nursing care may be entitled to be cared for at home rather than in an institution, even if this is more expensive, provided it is reasonable in the circumstances.[60] Where the cost of care at home is substantially greater than that of care in an institution, the burden of proving that it is reasonable to incur this expense is the plaintiff's. The plaintiff can recover the cost of adapting accommodation to his special needs resulting from his disability, subject to a deduction for the added capital value of the property which would be recoverable on a sale.[61] If it is not possible to adapt existing accommodation, damages will be awarded in respect of the purchase of special accommodation, but they will be assessed, not on the basis of the capital cost of the property, but by reference to the additional annual cost over the plaintiff's lifetime of providing that accommodation, as compared with ordinary accommodation. This is because the award is intended to compensate for the plaintiff's loss, it should not enhance the capital value of the plaintiff's estate after death.[62]

9.27 Where a plaintiff suffers from a major disability as a result of his injuries, the items of additional expense can be numerous. They may include the cost of adapting a car; the extra costs of running a household such as higher costs attributable to having to run larger accommodation or accommodation adapted to the plaintiff's disability; additional laundry bills; the cost of clothes which may wear out more frequently; the expense of maintaining a car[63] or house which the plaintiff will no longer be able to do for himself; the cost of special equipment such as wheelchairs, and nursing or medical appliances; physiotherapy and other forms of rehabilitative therapy; the additional costs of going on holiday; and, where the plaintiff is incapable of managing his own affairs, the cost of administration of the damages fund by the Court of Protection.[64] The plaintiff is entitled to travelling expenses incurred in obtaining medical treatment, and also the travelling expenses attributable to relatives' visits to plaintiff, provided the

[57] Administration of Justice Act 1982, s.5.
[58] *Lim Poh Choo* v. *Camden and Islington Area Health Authority* [1980] A.C. 174.
[59] *Shearman* v. *Folland* [1950] 2 K.B. 43.
[60] *Rialas* v. *Mitchell, The Times*, July 17, 1984.
[61] *Roberts* v. *Johnstone* [1988] 3 W.L.R. 1247.
[62] *Ibid.*, pp. 1257–1258. Damages "are notionally intended to be such as will exhaust the fund, contemporaneously with the termination of the plaintiff's life expectancy." The Court of Appeal applied a rate of 2 per cent. of the capital value as the annual cost. This is then multiplied by the appropriate multiplier for the plaintiff's life expectancy.
[63] There is potentially a degree of overlap in the award of damages if the plaintiff receives a large sum for loss of earnings from which he may have purchased and run a car in any event. If he is claiming the cost of specially adapted transport there will clearly be an element of overlap which should be taken into account.
[64] *Jones* v. *Jones* [1984] 3 All E.R. 1003; *Rialas* v. *Mitchell, The Times*, July 17, 1984.

visits are of benefit to the plaintiff in mitigating the damage (but not where the sole justification is the plaintiff's comfort or pleasure).[65]

Where a non-earner, such as a housewife, is injured then, clearly, **9.28** she cannot claim for the earnings that she would have lost had she been in paid employment. But a housewife who is deprived of her ability to look after her family suffers a real loss, even though other members of the family now perform the tasks that she used to do, and she is entitled to compensation for this loss.[66] For the future, this loss is estimated on the basis of the cost of employing domestic help, irrespective of whether a housekeeper will be employed. Past loss, on the other hand, is compensated as an addition to the award of general damages if a housekeeper has not been employed.[67]

In many instances a third person, such as a relative or friend, bears **9.29** part of the cost of the plaintiff's injury, either in the form of direct financial payments or by providing gratuitous services, such as nursing assistance. A spouse or relative may give up paid employment to look after the plaintiff. The third party has no direct claim in tort against the defendant. The plaintiff can recover this cost, however, from the defendant, irrespective of whether he is under any legal or moral obligation to reimburse the third party. In *Donnelly* v. *Joyce*[68] the Court of Appeal held that this expense was the plaintiff's loss, and consisted of the need for nursing services or special equipment, not the expenditure of the money itself. The question of who has provided the service or purchased equipment, or whether the plaintiff has an obligation to repay,[69] are irrelevant to the defendant's liability. The measure of the loss is the "proper and reasonable cost" of supplying the plaintiff's needs. In the case of a relative who has given up paid employment this will be at least the relative's loss of earnings, subject to a ceiling of the commercial rate for supplying those services to the plaintiff.[70] It would seem that, normally, the full commercial rate should not be applied unless the relative has given up paid employment, the assumption being that where relatives look after the plaintiff out of love or a sense of duty the commercial rate is inappropriate.[71]

Where the plaintiff's injuries lead to the break up of his marriage the **9.30** financial consequences of the divorce are not recoverable, either on the basis that the loss is too remote or on the ground of public policy.[72]

---

[65] This curious head of damage stems from a dictum of Diplock J. in *Kirkham* v. *Boughey* [1958] 2 Q.B. 338, 343, and now appears to be well-established, although strictly speaking it is not the plaintiff's loss. The expenses are normally agreed, as *e.g.* in *Donnelly* v. *Joyce* [1974] Q.B. 454, and *Thomas* v. *Wignall* [1987] 1 All E.R. 1185, 1187.

[66] *Daly* v. *General Steam Navigation Co. Ltd.* [1981] 1 W.L.R. 120.

[67] This approach is criticised as illogical by Burrows, *Remedies for Torts and Breach of Contract*, 1987, p. 171.

[68] [1974] Q.B. 454, approved by the Pearson Commission: *Royal Commission on Civil Liability and Compensation for Personal Injury*, Cmnd. 7054, 1978, Vol. I, paras 343–351; *cf.* Burrows, *Remedies for Torts and Breach of Contract*, 1987, pp. 69–70.

[69] *cf. Cunningham* v. *Harrison* [1973] Q.B. 942, 952.

[70] *Housecroft* v. *Burnett* [1986] 1 All E.R. 332. In *Croke* v. *Wiseman* [1981] 3 All E.R. 852 the plaintiff's mother had given up her employment to look after him. Her loss of earnings included loss of pension rights in the job she had given up.

[71] *McCamley* v. *Cammell Laird Shipbuilders Ltd.* [1990] 1 All E.R. 854, 857, C.A.; see *Almond* v. *Leeds Western Health Authority* [1990] 1 Med. L.R. 370, where half the commercial rate was awarded for past care.

[72] *Pritchard* v. *J.H. Cobden Ltd.* [1987] 1 All E.R. 300, C.A., disapproving *Jones* v. *Jones* [1984] 3 All E.R. 1003. Subsequently in *Pritchard* v. *J.H. Cobden Ltd.* [1987] 2 F.L.R. 56, the same court held that the legal costs of the divorce *were* recoverable from the tortfeasor on the particular facts of the case.

On the other hand, loss of marriage prospects may be the subject of an award of general damages for pain and suffering.[73]

2. Loss of earnings

9.31 Loss of earnings will be calculated over two periods: the loss up to the date of assessment and the prospective loss, for which the multiplier method is used. Where the plaintiff's working life expectancy has been reduced, the prospective loss of earnings will have to be further divided into the period during which the plaintiff is expected to survive, and the period during which he would have been employed but is not now expected to survive (the "lost years"), because the basis of the calculation is different in these periods. Calculating the loss of earnings up to the date of assessment is usually a reasonably precise exercise, intended to measure the plaintiff's actual loss over the period that he has been unable to work. This is the net loss, after deducting the plaintiff's income tax[74] and national insurance contributions,[75] and the plaintiff's contributions to a compulsory pension scheme.[76] Any loss of pension rights resulting from the contributions not having been paid is calculated separately.[77] All forms of earnings are included, such as perquisites.[78] If the plaintiff's rate of pay would have changed during this period, then this is taken into account.[79] The accrued loss of earnings to the date of trial form part of the special damages. The plaintiff must give credit for the expenses he would have incurred had he been at work, for example, the cost of travel to and from work should be deducted.

Prospective loss of earnings

9.32 Calculating the plaintiff's future loss of earnings can cause real problems because the court will have to prophesy both what will happen to the plaintiff in the future and what would have happened if he had not been injured, in order to estimate the difference. This involves considering the plaintiff's life expectancy, his earnings, the chance that he may have increased his earnings through promotion or reduced them through redundancy or illness, and what financial benefits he will now receive. The starting point is to work out the plaintiff's net annual loss of earnings, as at the date of assessment, not the date of injury.[80] The net annual loss is known as the "multiplicand." This will be adjusted to take account of the plaintiff's individual prospects of a future increase in income (e.g. through a promotion[81]),

---

[73] See § 9.51.
[74] *British Transport Commission* v. *Gourley* [1956] A.C. 185. For criticism of this principle see Bishop and Kay (1987) 104 L.Q.R. 211.
[75] *Cooper* v. *Firth Brown Ltd.* [1963] 1 W.L.R. 418.
[76] *Dews* v. *National Coal Board* [1987] 2 All E.R. 545.
[77] *Auty* v. *National Coal Board* [1985] 1 All E.R. 930.
[78] *Kennedy* v. *Bryan*, *The Times*, May 3, 1984—company car.
[79] *Cookson* v. *Knowles* [1979] A.C. 556, 569, a Fatal Accidents Act case.
[80] *Cookson* v. *Knowles* [1979[A.C. 556.
[81] *Roach* v. *Yates* [1938] 1 K.B. 256; *Robertson* v. *Lestrange* [1985] 1 All E.R. 950.

but no allowance will be made for a general rise in real average earnings. This sum is then multiplied by a "multiplier" which is based on the number of years that the loss is likely to continue. The multiplier is discounted, however, to take account of the uncertainty of the prediction (e.g. the plaintiff might have lost his job in any event through redundancy or illness in the future), and the fact that the plaintiff receives the money immediately as a capital sum, instead of in instalments over the rest of his working life.[82] The plaintiff is then expected to invest the award of damages and use both the income and part of the capital over the expected period of the loss, so that at the end of that period the whole award will be exhausted (although part of his living expenses may have included provision for retirement). Thus, the plaintiff is compensated on an annuity basis. Where there is no, or an uncertain, pre-accident record of the plaintiff's earnings the claim for prospective loss of earnings will be more speculative, and the court may decide not to use the multiplier method and may simply award a lump sum for loss of earning capacity.[83] This will often be the position where young children suffer serious injury. Such an award is not "calculated" arithmetically but is largely impressionistic, and the sum will often be discounted quite heavily to allow for its inherent uncertainty.

The maximum multiplier used in the courts is 18 years, even where **9.33** the anticipated number of years loss of earnings is considerably greater, and it is rarely this high. The multipliers used are based on the assumption that a person who invests a capital sum will receive a return of approximately four-and-a-half per cent. after the effects of taxation and inflation have been taken into account.[84] It has been argued that this assumption is unrealistic, with the result that the multipliers are too low and plaintiffs are undercompensated.[85] The problem is greater in periods of high inflation, but the courts refuse to make any allowance for future inflation eroding the value of an award.[86] Protection against inflation is to be sought by careful investment, the assumption being that some capital appreciation of the money invested will offset increases in the cost of living.[87] In *Lim Poh Choo* v. *Camden and Islington Area Health Authority*[88] it was accepted, however, that in an exceptional case some allowance might be made if on the particular facts an award which ignored inflation would not result in fair compensation, although Lord Scarman commented that plaintiffs who receive a lump sum award "are entitled to no better

---

[82] No reduction is made for the fact that the plaintiff does not have to "earn" the money. For discussion of the multiplier to be applied to future loss of earnings where a young woman has been rendered paraplegic see *Hughes* v. *McKeown* [1985] 3 All E.R. 284 and *Housecroft* v. *Burnett* [1986] 1 All E.R. 332, 345 stating that the chance that she would have married and had children, thus giving up her employment, should be ignored; *cf.* the alternative approach in *Moriarty* v. *McCarthy* [1978] 2 All E.R. 213.

[83] See § 9.38.

[84] *Cookson* v. *Knowles* [1979] A.C. 556, 577, *per* Lord Fraser; *Auty* v. *National Coal Board* [1985] 1 All E.R. 930; *Robertson* v. *Lestrange* [1985] 1 All E.R. 950.

[85] See Kemp (1985) 101 L.Q.R. 556.

[86] See *Taylor* v. *O'Connor* [1971] A.C. 115; *Mitchell* v. *Mulholland* (*No. 2*) [1972] 1 Q.B. 65; *Cookson* v. *Knowles* [1979] A.C. 556; *Lim Poh Choo* v. *Camden and Islington Area Health Authority* [1980] A.C. 174.

[87] *Taylor* v. *O'Connor* [1971] A.C. 115, 143, *per* Lord Pearson.

[88] [1980] A.C. 174.

protection against inflation than others who have to rely on capital for their support."[89] His Lordship added that attempts to take inflation into account seek a perfection in the assessment of damages which is beyond the inherent limitations of the system.

9.34 A similar problem arises in connection with the effect of taxation. The award of damages in a personal injuries action is not itself liable to tax,[90] but the income produced by investing the award is taxable. Where the plaintiff receives a very large award it is possible that the income generated will be subject to higher rate tax, with the effect that the combined fund of capital and income from which the plaintiff must meet his annual loss may be inadequate. In *Hodgson* v. *Trapp*[91] the House of Lords held that it was not permissible, having selected a multiplier on the conventional basis, then to increase the multiplier to take account of the effects of higher rates of tax. Lord Oliver reiterated that the process of assessing future pecuniary loss cannot, by its nature, be a precise science. Future taxation was just as uncertain as future inflation, and so predicting what might happen to future political, economic or fiscal policies required not the services of an actuary or an accountant, but those of a prophet. There was no justification for singling out taxation for special treatment when it was merely one of the many imponderables that have to be taken into account in the conventional method of assessing damages.[92]

9.35 As in *Lim Poh Choo*, their Lordships accepted that there might be very exceptional cases where special allowance might have to be made for inflation and taxation, although Lord Oliver observed that it was difficult to envisage circumstances in which something so inherently uncertain could be proved to the satisfaction of the court. Possibly it could tip the balance in favour of the selection of a higher multiplier as part of the assessment of all the uncertain factors that have to be taken into account, but it would not be proper to make a specific addition to the multiplier on account of this one factor. Moreover, when considering the effect of higher rate tax on the damages award the court must be careful to look only at the damages awarded for future loss (whether for prospective loss of earnings or the cost of future medical or nursing care) to which the multiplier method is appropriate. Only the income from that fund would be relevant to the question of higher rate taxation. If, for example, the plaintiff chose to invest the damages awarded for non-pecuniary loss in order to supplement his income, and this put him into a higher tax bracket, that would not be a reason for increasing the award for loss of future earnings and future care.

The lost years

9.36 Where the plaintiff's life expectancy has been reduced by his injuries, this may well have reduced the period during which he would

---

[89] This view is inconsistent with the basic principle in assessing tort damages of restoring the plaintiff to his pre-accident position, because if he would have had better protection from inflation if he were in employment, then he is worse off as a result of the tort by now being forced to rely on investment income.

[90] Income and Corporation Taxes Act 1988, s.329.

[91] [1988] 3 All E.R. 870, overruling *Thomas* v. *Wignall* [1987] 1 All E.R. 1185.

[92] *Ibid.*, p. 884.

have been earning in the future. In *Oliver* v. *Ashman*[93] the Court of Appeal held that the losses incurred in these "lost years" (the period between his expected date of death and the date that he would have stopped working but for the tort) were not recoverable, on the basis that a plaintiff cannot suffer a loss during a period when he will be dead. This rule created a problem for plaintiffs with dependants because of the interrelationship with the Fatal Accidents Act. Normally, where the victim of a tort dies as a result of his injuries his dependants have a claim against the tortfeasor for their financial loss under the Fatal Accidents Act 1976. Such a claim is only available, however, where at the date of the death the victim would have had a right of action against the tortfeasor. If, while still alive the deceased had obtained a judgment against the tortfeasor or settled his claim, then on his death there is no subsisting right of action and the dependants have no claim under the Act. Thus, *Oliver* v. *Ashman* penalised the plaintiff's dependants, since their dependency in the lost years would generally have been met from the plaintiff's earnings during that period. It was this consideration which led the House of Lords to overrule *Oliver* v. *Ashman* in *Pickett* v. *British Rail Engineering Ltd.*[94] Damages for prospective loss of earnings will be awarded for the whole of the plaintiff's pre-accident life expectancy, subject to a deduction for the money that the plaintiff would have spent on his own (not his dependants') living expenses during the lost years. His own living expenses will not be incurred and therefore they are not a real loss.[95]

Although the objective of *Pickett* v. *British Rail Engineering Ltd.* **9.37** was, in effect, to protect the interests of dependants, there is no way of ensuring that the plaintiff does in fact use the damages to make provision for his dependants. Moreover, the plaintiff is entitled to an award covering the lost years even where he has no dependants. Where the plaintiff has an established pattern of earnings it will be easier to make an appropriate calculation. In the case of a young single person the award is likely to be modest to reflect the high degree of speculation involved.[96] Exceptionally a young child may have a claim for loss of earnings in the lost years,[97] but though in principle the loss is recoverable, the speculative nature of the loss will often result in an assessment of nil damages.[98]

Loss of earning capacity

Where a person suffers a permanent disability which affects his **9.38** ability to earn in the future at the same rate as he earned before the

---

[93] [1962] 2 Q.B. 210.

[94] [1980] A.C. 136.

[95] See *Harris* v. *Empress Motors Ltd.* [1983] 3 All E.R. 561, on the calculation of the living expenses; *White* v. *London Transport Executive* [1982] 1 All E.R. 410; *Adsett* v. *West* [1983] 2 All E.R. 985; *Wilson* v. *Stag* (1986) 136 New L.J. 47; Evans and Stanton (1984) 134 New L.J. 515, 553.

[96] *Harris* v. *Empress Motors Ltd.* [1983] 3 All E.R. 561; *Adsett* v. *West* [1983] 2 All E.R. 985. It may be that where the lost years claim is highly speculative, it is better simply to make a small adjustment to the multiplier (adding 1 or a half) as applied to the full multiplicand, rather than attempting to speculate on notional earnings and notional living expenses: *Housecroft* v. *Burnett* [1986] 1 All E.R. 332, 345, *per* O'Connor L.J.

[97] *Gammell* v. *Wilson* [1982] A.C. 27, 78.

[98] *Croke* v. *Wiseman* [1981] 3 All E.R. 852; *Connolly* v. *Camden and Islington Area Health Authority* [1981] 3 All E.R. 250.

injury, then he may or may not suffer a loss of earnings. The loss may be total if he is unable to work at all, or partial if he is able to take a less remunerative job. In some instances, although the injuries have affected the plaintiff's ability to earn, he suffers no loss of earnings because his employer continues to employ him at the same rate of pay. In these circumstances the plaintiff is entitled to damages for his loss of earning capacity if there is a real risk (as opposed to a fanciful or speculative risk) that he could lose his existing employment in the future, because his capacity to find a job with equivalent remuneration has been reduced, and he is now at a disadvantage in the labour market.[99] If the court makes a separate assessment for loss of earning capacity and loss of future earnings, care must be taken to avoid any duplication in the award.[1]

9.39   It has been said that there is no real difference between damages for loss of earning capacity and damages for future loss of earnings.[2] A reduction in the plaintiff's present earning capacity is ultimately likely to have some impact on the level of his future earnings. In practice, however, awards for loss of earning capacity are more impressionistic and less susceptible to the multiplier method of calculation. The assessment is particularly speculative in the case of children where there may be little or no evidence about what the child may eventually do for a living.[3] The solution is to award only moderate sums in this situation, although there is no tariff or conventional award for loss of earning capacity and each case must be considered on its own facts.[4] In *Foster* v. *Tyne and Wear County Council*,[5] for example, an award of £35,000 to an adult plaintiff under this head was upheld by the Court of Appeal.

3. Deductions

9.40   A person who suffers personal injury may receive financial support from a number of sources other than tort damages.[6] The most common

---

[99] *Smith* v. *Manchester Corporation* (1974) 17 K.I.R. 1; *Moeliker* v. *Reyrolle & Co. Ltd.* [1977] 1 All E.R. 9.

[1] *Clarke* v. *Rotax Aircraft Equipment Ltd.* [1975] 1 W.L.R. 1570.

[2] *Foster* v. *Tyne and Wear County Council* [1986] 1 All E.R. 567, 571–572; *Royal Commission on Civil Liability and Compensation for Personal Injury*, Cmnd. 7054, 1978, Vol. I, para. 338.

[3] See *S.* v. *Distillers Co. (Biochemicals) Ltd.* [1970] 1 W.L.R. 114; *Joyce* v. *Yeomans* [1981] 1 W.L.R. 549; *Croke* v. *Wiseman* [1981] 3 All E.R. 852; *Mitchell* v. *Liverpool Area Health Authority, The Times*, June 17, 1985. In *Cronin* v. *Redbridge London Borough Council, The Times*, May 20, 1987, the Court of Appeal complained that this was an exercise in unsatisfactory guesswork.

[4] *Page* v. *Enfield and Haringey Area Health Authority, The Times*, November 7, 1986. The court may be willing to use the multiplier method for assessment of loss of earnings of even a young child, based on a multiplicand of the national average wage: see *Croke* v. *Wiseman* [1981] 3 All E.R. 852; *Moser* v. *Enfield and Haringey Area Health Authority* (1983) 133 New L.J. 105. In *Aboul-Hosn* v. *Trustees of the Italian Hospital* (1987) 137 New L.J. 1164 an 18 year old with 4 "A" Levels and a place at university was held to have a good prospect of earning £18,000 per annum, plus a company car.

[5] [1986] 1 All E.R. 567.

[6] The Pearson Commission found that the tort system provided about 25 per cent. of the total compensation paid out to the victims of personal injury: *Royal Commission on Civil Liability and Compensation for Personal Injury*, Cmnd. 7054, 1978, Vol. I, para. 44.

source is social security benefits, but others include sick pay, pensions, private insurance and charitable donations. The compensatory principle applied to the assessment of tort damages should mean that in theory any receipt of financial assistance from another source is deducted in full from the award of damages, since they reduce the plaintiff's loss. There are, however, a number of competing policy factors which may justify non-deduction.

Social security benefits

In principle, benefits paid by the state in the form of social security **9.41** should be deducted from damages awards on the basis that damages are meant to be compensatory and the plaintiff should not be in a better financial position than he would have been but for the tort. By 1988 the common law had essentially reached the position that benefits should be fully deducted. The Social Security Act 1989, however, introduced a scheme for recoupment by the state from tortfeasors of certain social security benefits paid to plaintiffs. This means that there are now two sets of rules governing the deduction of social security benefits.

Under the old rules, which still apply to injuries that occurred before **9.42** January 1, 1989, the extent of deduction of benefits depended to a large extent upon whether the case was governed by statute or the common law. By section 2(1) of the Law Reform (Personal Injuries) Act 1948 (as amended) *half* the value of any rights which have accrued or probably will accrue to the plaintiff in respect of: (i) sickness benefit; (ii) invalidity benefit; (iii) severe disablement allowance; and (iv) disablement benefit, for a period of five years from the time when the cause of action accrued, is deducted from the damages for loss of earnings (including any award for loss of earning capacity[7]). After five years these benefits are not deducted at all.[8] Where the plaintiff is contributorily negligent the benefits are deducted from the damages before apportionment.[9] On the other hand, where the matter was free from statutory regulation the courts had increasingly taken the view that benefits should be deducted in order to avoid double recovery.[10] Most benefits have been held to be fully deductible, including attendance allowance and mobility allowance,[11] statutory sick pay,[12] unemployment benefit,[13] past receipts of supplementary benefit/income

---

[7] *Foster* v. *Tyne and Wear County Council* [1986] 1 All E.R. 567.

[8] *Jackman* v. *Corbett* [1987] 2 All E.R. 699. This view may have to be reconsidered, however, in the light of the decision of the House of Lords in *Hodgson* v. *Trapp* [1988] 3 All E.R. 870; see Burrows (1989) 105 L.Q.R. 366, 368. See, however, *Almond* v. *Leeds Western Health Authority* [1990] 1 Med. L.R. 370, where *Jackman* v. *Corbett* was applied.

[9] Law Reform (Personal Injuries) Act 1948, s.2(3).

[10] *Hodgson* v. *Trapp* [1988] 3 All E.R. 870, 876, *per* Lord Bridge. The Pearson Commission also recommended that there should be no overlap between tort damages and social security payments: *Royal Commission on Civil Liability and Compensation for Personal Injury*, Cmnd. 7054, 1978, Vol. I, para. 482.

[11] *Hodgson* v. *Trapp* [1988] 3 All E.R. 870, overruling *Bowker* v. *Rose* (1978) 122 S.J. 147.

[12] *Palfrey* v. *Greater London Council* [1985] I.C.R. 437.

[13] *Nabi* v. *British Leyland (UK) Ltd.* [1980] 1 All E.R. 667; *Westwood* v. *Secretary of State for Employment* [1985] A.C. 20.

support and family income supplement/family credit,[14] and, in a claim for the cost of maintaining a child following a failed sterilisation operation, child benefit.[15] State retirement pension may be an exception to the principle of full deductibility.[16]

9.43   The new rules on the recoupment of benefits apply to any compensation payment made after September 3, 1990[17] in respect of an accident or injury which occurred on or after January 1, 1989, or in the case of a disease where the first claim for benefit was made on or after that date. By section 22(6) of the Social Security Act 1989, except as provided in any other legislation, the amount of any "relevant benefit" paid or likely to be paid to or for the plaintiff is to be disregarded in assessing damages in respect of an accident, injury or disease. In other words, the benefit is *not* deducted in assessing damages. Relevant benefits are benefits specifically listed by the Secretary of State, namely: attendance allowance; disablement benefit (including disablement pensions); family credit; income support; invalidity pension and allowance; mobility allowance; benefits payable under schemes made under the Industrial Injuries and Diseases (Old Cases) Act 1975; reduced earnings allowance; retirement allowance; severe disablement allowance; sickness benefit; statutory sick pay; and unemployment benefit.[18] Any benefits which are not specifically prescribed will, presumably, continue to be subject to the common law rules on deduction from damages.

9.44   A person paying compensation[19] (the "compensator") in respect of an accident, injury or disease suffered by the "victim" shall not make the payment until the Secretary of State has furnished him with a certificate of the "total benefit."[20] The compensator must then deduct from the payment (not merely from the loss of earnings element) a sum equal to the gross amount of any relevant benefits paid or likely to be paid to or for the victim during the "relevant period" in respect of that accident, injury or disease.[21] This sum must be paid to the Secretary of State, and the victim provided with a certificate specifying

---

[14] *Lincoln* v. *Heyman* [1982] 2 All E.R. 819; *Gaskill* v. *Preston* [1981] 3 All E.R. 427. Supplementary benefit and family income supplement were replaced by income support and family credit respectively by the Social Security Act 1986, ss.20–22. The possibility of future receipts of these benefits should be ignored because an award of damages for prospective loss of earnings will probably remove the plaintiff's entitlement to the benefit: *Gaskill* v. *Preston, ante.*

[15] *Emeh* v. *Kensington and Chelsea Area Health Authority* [1984] 3 All E.R. 1044, 1051.

[16] *Hewson* v. *Downs* [1970] 1 Q.B. 73. It is doubtful, however, whether this decision can survive the reasoning in *Hodgson* v. *Trapp* [1988] 3 All E.R. 870.

[17] S.I. 1990/102.

[18] Social Security (Recoupment) Regulations 1990 (S.I. 1990/322), para. 2.

[19] A "'compensation payment" does not include the payment of costs: Social Security Act 1989, s.22(3), as amended by Social Security Act 1990, Sched. 1, para. 1.

[20] The Secretary of State must issue the certificate within four weeks of receipt of an application provided that the compensator has supplied the prescribed information (the prescribed information is listed in the Social Security (Recoupment) Regulations 1990 (S.I. 1990/322), reg. 9). If the certificate is not issued within the four week period the compensator's liability to make the relevant deduction of benefits becomes unenforceable: Social Security Act 1989, Sched. 4, para. 15. If, however, a subsequent compensation payment is made by the same or any other compensator, the relevant benefits which were not recovered from the earlier payment may be recouped against the later compensation payment: *ibid.*, para. 15(3).

[21] Social Security Act 1989, s.22(1).

the amount that has been deducted and paid to the Secretary of State. The relevant period is five years from the date of the accident or injury, or in the case of a disease five years from the first claim for a relevant benefit consequent upon the disease.[22] A payment of compensation in final discharge of the plaintiff's claim before the end of the five years brings the "relevant period" to an end. After the relevant period the recoupment provisions do not apply, but by virtue of section 22(6) the "relevant benefits" must nonetheless be disregarded in assessing damages and so will *not* be deducted. The effect of this is that a plaintiff will be better off financially in any case where his entitlement to benefit continues after the settlement of the damages claim (thereby encouraging early settlement where possible) and in any case where the entitlement to benefit exceeds five years, which will tend to be the cases involving more serious injury. To the extent that the common law had virtually reached the position that the Pearson Commission had recommended on the deduction of social security benefits, namely full deduction, this statutory departure from the principle of compensatory damages can be seen as a retrograde step.

The justification for recoupment of social security benefits is that the **9.45** deduction of benefits from damages in order to satisfy the compensatory principle produces a windfall for defendants, or rather their insurers, who are effectively subsidised by the taxpayer. Whatever the logic of this proposition (it is by no means clear that those who effectively have to pay the insurance premiums which fund the tort system are a significantly different group from taxpayers) it clearly makes no sense in relation to medical negligence claims which are met from N.H.S. funds, also provided by the taxpayer. Recoupment in this context simply means shifting taxpayers' money from one government department to another government department, while adding to administrative costs.

Under section 22(4) of the Social Security Act 1989 certain compen- **9.46** sation payments are exempted from the recoupment provisions. These include "small payments," which is where the compensation payment, or the aggregate of two or more connected compensation payments, does not exceed £2,500[23]; awards or settlements under the Fatal Accidents Act 1976 (s.4 of which provides that social security benefits are to be disregarded when assessing the loss of dependency); any payment under the Vaccine Damage Payments Act 1979 (though without prejudice to s.6(4) of that Act which provides for the deduction of such payments in the assessment of an award of damages); payments under accident insurance policies entered into by the victim before the accident; and any redundancy payments taken into account in assessing damages.[24] Section 2(1) of the Law Reform (Personal Injuries) Act 1948 now applies only to "small payments,"

---

[22] *Ibid.*, s.22(3). The legislation makes detailed provision for, *inter alia*, multiple compensation payments, multiple defendants, structured settlements, payments into court, administration, and appeals: see Social Security Act 1989, Sched. 4; Social Security Act 1990, Sched. 1; Social Security (Recoupment) Regulations 1990, (S.I. 1990/322).

[23] Social Security (Recoupment) Regulations 1990 (S.I. 1990/322), para. 3(1).

[24] The Act also exempts payments made under the Powers of Criminal Courts Act 1973, s.35; any award of criminal injuries compensation; and payments from certain trusts.

which are exempt from the recoupment provisions. One-half of the relevant benefits may be deducted from the award of damages, by virtue of section 2(1) (as amended) the deduction operating against the whole of the damages award, not merely loss of earnings.

Other collateral benefits

9.47   Where the plaintiff has received compensation or pecuniary benefits from a source other than social security, the question of deduction depends upon the nature of the benefit and the source. Prima facie, the recoverable loss is the net loss, and so financial gains accruing to the plaintiff which he would not have received but for the accident should be taken into account in mitigation of his loss.[25] There are, however, two well-established exceptions to this. First, the proceeds of a personal accident insurance policy taken out by the plaintiff are ignored, on the basis that otherwise the plaintiff's foresight and thrift would benefit the defendant rather than himself.[26] Secondly, gratuitous payments to the plaintiff from charitable motives are not deducted, again on the basis that the donor intended to benefit the plaintiff, not the defendant.[27]

9.48   In *Parry* v. *Cleaver*[28] the House of Lords held, by a bare majority, that an occupational disability pension should not be deducted from lost earnings, whether the pension was contributory or non-contributory. The majority of their Lordships took the view that the nature of a pension makes it analogous to private insurance effected by the plaintiff.[29] On the other hand, occupational sick pay will be deducted if it is paid as a term of the plaintiff's contract of employment, and this is the case whether or not the employer has taken out a policy of

---

[25] *Hussain* v. *New Taplow Paper Mills Ltd.* [1988] 1 All E.R. 541, 544–545, *per* Lord Bridge. A tax rebate under the PAYE system due to the fact that the plaintiff is not earning is deductible from the loss of earnings: *Hartley* v. *Sandholme Iron Co. Ltd.* [1975] Q.B. 600. Savings attributable to the fact that the plaintiff is being maintained in a public or private institution should be deducted from the loss of earnings claim: Administration of Justice Act 1982, s.5; *Lim Poh Choo* v. *Camden and Islington Area Health Authority* [1980] A.C. 174. Any savings from expenses which are no longer being incurred, such as travelling expenses to and from work, should be deducted.

[26] *Bradburn* v. *Great Western Railway Co.* (1874) L.R. 10 Ex. 1; *Parry* v. *Cleaver* [1970] A.C. 1, 14, *per* Lord Reid.

[27] *Redpath* v. *Belfast and County Down Railway* [1947] N.I. 167; *Parry* v. *Cleaver* [1970] A.C. 1, 14; *Hussain* v. *New Taplow Paper Mills Ltd.* [1988] 1 All E.R. 541, 545.

[28] [1970] A.C. 1.

[29] Lord Morris, dissenting, pointed out that in reality there is no difference between receipt of sick pay and receipt of a pension. The true loss of earnings in each case is the difference between what the plaintiff received prior to his injury and what he now receives by virtue of his contract of employment. Nor is it an answer to say that he "earned" his pension entitlement by his own efforts, since if he obtains alternative employment the plaintiff must account for his new earnings in mitigation of his lost earnings, notwithstanding that these receipts are "earned." In *Smoker* v. *London Fire and Civil Defence Authority* [1991] 2 All E.R. 449 the House of Lords has affirmed that *Parry* v. *Cleaver* was correctly decided, on the basis that pension benefits constitute deferred remuneration in respect of the plaintiff's past work, and the tortfeasor cannot appropriate the fruit of the plaintiff's past service. Where, however, the injury leads to a reduction of the plaintiff's retirement pension under his occupational pension scheme, because he is prevented from making full contributions, then disabilty pension payments which will be received after the plaintiff would have retired should be taken into account as mitigating the loss of pension: *Parry* v. *Cleaver* [1970] A.C. 1, 20–21, *per* Lord Reid.

insurance to cover the contractual commitment to pay sick pay, and irrespective of the fact that the entitlement to sick pay applies to long-term incapacity for work.[30] It has been argued, however, that where there is some direct or indirect link between the benefits received by the plaintiff and wages foregone, as part of the overall wage structure, for example, then the position is closer to *Parry* v. *Cleaver* in the sense that the plaintiff has "purchased" the benefits himself.[31] There would seem to be little in logic to justify the different approaches to occupational sick pay and occupational pensions, though in practice everything turns upon how the payment is characterised: if it is a "pension" it is not deducted, if it is "sick pay" it is deducted.

Where the plaintiff is under a contractual obligation to repay to his **9.49** employer any payments of sick pay if he is successful in an action for damages, then sick pay should not be deducted from the award.[32] Similarly, gratuitous payments of sick pay should not be deducted since they are analogous to charitable payments, although where the employer is also the tortfeasor it would seem that the payments should be deducted.[33] If the plaintiff is made redundant as a result of his injuries, in the sense that his disability makes him a more likely candidate for redundancy, any redundancy payment should be deducted.[34] But if he would have been redundant regardless of the accident the payment will not be deducted,[35] although this will clearly be a factor in calculating the loss of earnings attributable to the tort since it is known that the plaintiff would not have continued in that employment.

III. PERSONAL INJURIES: NON-PECUNIARY LOSSES

Non-pecuniary losses consist of the pain and suffering caused by the **9.50** injury itself, and the loss of amenity which is consequent upon any

---

[30] *Hussain* v. *New Taplow Paper Mills Ltd.* [1988] 1 All E.R. 541, H.L., distinguishing *Parry* v. *Cleaver* [1970] A.C. 1. Lord Bridge commented, at pp. 546–547, that sick pay is "a partial substitute for earnings and . . . the very antithesis of a pension, which is payable only after employment ceases."

[31] Anderson (1987) 50 M.L.R. 963, 970. This argument is open to the objection that all "benefits" under a contract of employment form part of the wage or salary structure, which the employee "purchases" by working under the terms of the contract.

[32] *Browning* v. *War Office* [1963] 1 Q.B. 750, 759, 770; see also *Dennis* v. *London Passenger Transport Board* [1948] 1 All E.R. 779, where the plaintiff was under a moral but not a legal obligation to repay.

[33] *Hussain* v. *New Taplow Paper Mills Ltd.* [1987] 1 All E.R. 417, 428, *per* Lloyd L.J.; see also *Jenner* v. *Allen West & Co. Ltd.* [1959] 2 All E.R. 115; *cf. McCamley* v. *Cammell Laird Shipbuilders Ltd.* [1990] 1 All E.R. 854, where the Court of Appeal held that the proceeds of an ordinary personal accident policy taken out by an employer for the benefit of employees should not be deducted from the award of damages made against the employer, although the plaintiff made no contribution to the premiums, and, indeed, was unaware of the existence of the policy prior to his accident. The money was payable as a lump sum regardless of fault, with the sum quantified in advance (by reference to a formula in the policy) when it could not have been foreseen what damages might have to be paid if an accident occurred. This was analogous to an act of benevolence by the employer; it was not a method of meeting the employers' liability for sick pay (as in *Hussain* v. *New Taplow Paper Mills Ltd.* [1988] 1 All E.R. 541); nor was it equivalent to an *ex gratia* payment by the tortfeasor where the accident had already occurred.

[34] *Colledge* v. *Bass Mitchells & Butlers Ltd.* [1988] 1 All E.R. 536.

[35] *Ibid.*, p. 540.

disability attributable to the injury. Here restoration of the plaintiff to his pre-accident position is clearly impossible, and the guiding principle is said to be that the award should be fair or reasonable.

1. Pain and suffering

9.51   The plaintiff is entitled to damages for actual and prospective pain and suffering caused by the injury, by a neurosis resulting from the injury, or attributable to any necessary medical treatment for the injury. This includes any discomfort, humiliation, or disfigurement suffered by the plaintiff. A person who suffers mental anguish because he is aware that his life expectancy has been reduced can recover for that anguish.[36] Similarly, a person who is physically or mentally incapacitated by his injuries and is capable of appreciating the condition to which he has been reduced is entitled to be compensated for the anguish that this creates.[37] On the other hand, if the plaintiff is permanently unconscious or for some other reason is incapable of subjectively experiencing pain, there will be no award for pain and suffering.[38] If the plaintiff's marriage prospects have been affected, the award will include an element to compensate for the loss of comfort and companionship which marriage might have brought, although disregarding the economic aspect of loss of marriage prospects.[39]

9.52   A plaintiff who sustains nervous shock in the form of a recognised psychiatric illness is entitled to be compensated for that illness, but not for mere sorrow or grief.[40] If, however, the plaintiff's mental distress or grief at the death of a loved one exacerbates the pain and suffering which the plaintiff sustained in the same incident, preventing the plaintiff from making a recovery as quickly as would otherwise have occurred, this will be reflected in the award of damages for pain and suffering. In *Kralj* v. *McGrath*[41] the plaintiff suffered physical injuries due to the defendant doctor's negligent treatment in the course of delivering a baby. She also suffered shock as a result of being told about the baby's injuries and seeing the child for the eight weeks that it survived. No award was made for the plaintiff's grief at the death of the child, but allowance was made for the fact that her experience of

---

[36] Administration of Justice Act 1982, s.1(1)(*b*). He is not entitled to claim merely for the fact that his life expectancy has been reduced: *ibid.*, s.1(1)(*a*), abolishing the claim for loss of expectation of life.

[37] *H. West & Son Ltd.* v. *Shephard* [1964] A.C. 326.

[38] *Wise* v. *Kay* [1962] 1 Q.B. 638.

[39] *Moriarty* v. *McCarthy* [1978] 2 All E.R. 213; *Hughes* v. *McKeown* [1985] 3 All E.R. 284; *Morgan* v. *Gwent Health Authority, The Independent*, December 14, 1987, C.A.—breakup of the plaintiff's engagement as a result of a negligently administered blood transfusion which would have caused serious complications to a foetus conceived with her fiancé. The chances that the plaintiff would find a husband with whom there would be no complications if she conceived were 17 per cent.

[40] *Hinz* v. *Berry* [1970] 2 Q.B. 40, 42; *McLoughlin* v. *O'Brian* [1982] 2 All E.R. 298, 311, *per* Lord Bridge.

[41] [1986] 1 All E.R. 54; see also *Bagley* v. *North Hertfordshire Health Authority* (1986) 136 New L.J. 1014 on the assessment of damages following a stillbirth. This can include the mother's loss of earnings in having to undergo another pregnancy to complete her planned family: *Kralj* v. *McGrath* [1986] 1 All E.R. 54. For criticism of the principle of compensating for this loss see Burrows, *Remedies for Torts and Breach of Contract*, 1987, pp. 180–181.

her own injuries was more drastic than it would otherwise have been because of the grief which she suffered at the same time in relation to the death of the child. Conversely, if the child had been healthy this would probably have reduced the impact of the plaintiff's injuries, because she would have had the joy of motherhood to console her. In a number of cases awards have included an element for a reactive depression suffered by a patient following negligent medical treatment.[42]

2. Loss of faculty and amenity

The injury itself represents loss of faculty whereas the consequences **9.53** of the injury on the plaintiff's activities represents loss of amenity. This includes *inter alia* loss of job satisfaction,[43] loss of leisure activities and hobbies, and loss of family life. It is rare for the courts to distinguish between these separate heads of damage since normally a single global award is made to cover all the plaintiff's non-pecuniary losses.

The courts operate a "tariff" system with a view to obtaining some **9.54** degree of uniformity between plaintiffs with comparable injuries, and to facilitate the settlement of claims. The tariff is not precisely fixed. There is a band or range of figures for particular injuries which allows the court to take account of subjective factors which may exacerbate, or reduce, the impact of a particular injury on the plaintiff. The tariffs applied should increase over time in order to keep up with inflation.[44] An award of damages will be made for loss of amenity even where the plaintiff is permanently unconscious and is unable to appreciate his

---

[42] *Biles* v. *Barking Health Authority* [1988] C.L.Y. 1103 (discussed by Puxon and Buchan (1988) 138 New L.J. 80)—clinical depression and sexual disfunction following unnecessary sterilisation, probable permanent sterility; *Ackers* v. *Wigan Area Health Authority* [1991] 2 Med. L.R. 232—severe depression after an operation under general anaesthetic where the plaintiff was awake; *Grieve* v. *Salford Health Authority* (1990) 6 P.M.I.L.L. 54, on reactive depression following a stillbirth; *G.* v. *North Tees Health Authority* [1989] F.C.R. 53—general damages of £5,000 each to a 6 year old child and mother, where the child was wrongly identified as a victim of sexual abuse as a result of a mix up with a vaginal swab, and the mother had become depressed and suicidal, until the error was discovered; *Smith* v. *Barking, Havering and Brentwood Health Authority* (1989) 5 P.M.I.L.L. No. 4, where general damages of £3,000 were awarded to a patient for shock and depression caused by discovering, without any prior warning of the risk, that she had been rendered tetraplegic following an operation. The plaintiff would have progressed to this condition within 6–9 months in any event, and the claim in respect an omission to obtain "informed consent" failed on causation.

[43] *Champion* v. *London Fire and Civil Defence Authority*, *The Times*, July 5, 1990.

[44] See, *e.g.*, *Housecroft* v. *Burnett* [1986] 1 All E.R. 332, where the Court of Appeal attempted to set a figure of £75,000 in April 1985 for an average case of tetraplegia with no complications, *i.e.* where the plaintiff is not in pain, is fully aware of the disability, retains the capacity to speak, see and hear, but needs assistance with bodily functions, and has a life expectancy of 25 years or more. Physical pain and any diminution in powers of speech, sight and hearing would justify a higher award, whereas lack of awareness of the condition or a reduced life expectancy would justify a lower award. For awards of general damages in cases of tetraplegia see *Almond* v. *Leeds Western Health Authority* [1990] 1 Med. L.R. 370; *Janardan* v. *East Berkshire Health Authority* [1990] 2 Med.L.R. 1; *Cunningham* v. *Camberwell Health Authority* [1990] 2 Med. L.R. 49. For a table of awards made in cases of anaesthetic error see: (1990) *AVMA Medical & Legal Journal*, No. 1, p. 6.

condition.[45] This treats loss of amenity as an "objective" loss which the fact of unconsciousness does not change.[46]

IV. WRONGFUL BIRTH

9.55 Claims for wrongful birth have given rise to particular difficulties in the assessment of damages, although it now seems to be accepted that the ordinary compensatory principles of assessment should be applied. Wrongful birth involves an action by a parent in respect of the birth of a child which it is claimed should not have occurred, and encompasses failed sterilisation operations,[47] omission to warn about the risks of a sterilisation operation failing to achieve its purpose,[48] failed abortion operations,[49] and a failure to advise a mother of the risk that the foetus may be born with serious disabilities thus depriving her of the opportunity to have an abortion under the Abortion Act 1967.[50]

9.56 Initially there was some hesitation about awarding damages for the financial consequences of a wrongful birth, at least where the child was healthy. In *Udale* v. *Bloomsbury Area Health Authority*[51] Jupp J. held that damages should not be awarded for the cost of bringing up a healthy child following a failed sterilisation operation for reasons of policy. The Court of Appeal rejected this view, however, in *Emeh* v. *Kensington and Chelsea and Westminster Area Health Authority*[52] on the basis that since a sterilisation operation is lawful, and the avoidance of pregnancy and birth was the object of the operation undergone by the plaintiff, the compensatable loss extended to any reasonably foreseeable financial loss directly caused by the unexpected pregnancy. Moreover, there were no good policy reasons for denying a plaintiff's claim for the financial loss, regardless of whether the child was healthy or disabled. The financial loss can include the mother's loss of earnings as a result of having to look after the child, the expense of maintaining the child, the additional expense of maintaining a disabled child, the cost of the child's layette, and in the case of a failed sterilisation the

---

[45] *Wise* v. *Kaye* [1962] 1 Q.B. 638; *H. West & Son Ltd.* v. *Shephard* [1964] A.C. 326; *Lim Poh Choo* v. *Camden and Islington Area Health Authority* [1980] A.C. 174.

[46] In *H. West & Son Ltd.* v. *Shephard* [1964] A.C. 326, 341 Lord Reid, dissenting, commented that: " . . . there is something unreal in saying that a man who knows and feels nothing should get the same as a man who has to live with and put up with his disabilities, merely because they have sustained comparable physical injuries. It is no more possible to compensate an unconscious man than it is to compensate a dead man." The Pearson Commission recommended that damages for non-pecuniary loss should not be recoverable in cases of permanent unconsciousness: *Royal Commission on Civil Liability and Compensation for Personal Injury*, Cmnd. 7054, 1978, Vol. I, paras. 397–398. In *Lim Poh Choo* v. *Camden and Islington Area Health Authority* [1980] A.C. 174, the House of Lords were unwilling to reverse *H. West & Son Ltd.* v. *Shephard*, preferring to leave the issue to legislation.

[47] See § 4.68.

[48] See §§ 6.131 *et seq.*

[49] See § 4.39.

[50] *McKay* v. *Essex Area Health Authority* [1982] Q.B. 1166; § 2.37; *Salih* v. *Enfield Health Authority* [1990] 1 Med. L.R. 333, Q.B.D.

[51] [1983] 2 All E.R. 522; *cf.* the decision of Pain J. in *Thake* v. *Maurice* [1984] 2 All E.R. 513.

[52] [1984] 3 All E.R. 1044, preferring the view of Pain J. in *Thake* v. *Maurice* [1984] 2 All E.R. 513.

cost of a second sterilisation operation.[53] If the parents decide not to have further children because of the problems they face in bringing up a handicapped child, this will produce a saving in expenditure which would otherwise have been incurred and this saving must be brought into account in assessing the cost of providing for the handicapped child.[54]

In the case of a failed sterilisation a plaintiff mother is entitled to an **9.57** award for the pain and suffering involved in the pregnancy and birth, and a second sterilisation operation.[55] There may also be a claim for the parents' loss of amenity for the time and trouble involved in raising the child, but in most cases this will be offset by the parents' happiness and joy in having the child. The set-off only applies, however, to the loss of amenity involved in bringing the child up; there will be no reduction in the award for the pain and distress suffered by the mother during the pregnancy and birth on account of the happiness that a healthy child will bring.[56] Moreover, if the child is handicapped there may be no set-off against the award for loss of amenity for the joys of parenthood.[57]

V. DEATH

At common law a person's death extinguished any cause of action that **9.58** may have existed against him and any cause of action that the deceased may have had against another. Moreover, a person's death did not confer any common law right of action on another person against the person who had caused the death, which meant that the dependants of someone killed by another's negligence had no action in respect of their loss of financial support by the deceased. Both of these rules have been changed by legislation: the Law Reform (Miscellaneous Provisions) Act 1934 and the Fatal Accidents Act 1976 (consolidating previous Fatal Accidents Acts) respectively.

1. Survival of actions

The Law Reform (Miscellaneous Provisions) Act 1934, s.1(1) pro- **9.59** vides that on the death of any person all causes of action (except

---

[53] *Emeh* v. *Kensington and Chelsea Area Health Authority* [1984] 3 All E.R. 1044; *Thake* v. *Maurice* [1986] 1 All E.R. 497; *Scuriaga* v. *Powell* (1979) 123 S.J. 406; aff'd (1980) (unreported), C.A.; *Jones* v. *Berkshire Area Health Authority* (1986) (unreported), Q.B.D.; *Williams* v. *Imrie* (1988) 4 P.M.I.L.L. No. 3; *Salih* v. *Enfield Health Authority* [1990] 1 Med. L.R. 333, Q.B.D. Where the plaintiffs would normally have opted for private education the loss can include the cost of private education for the child: *Bennar* v. *Kettering* [1988] N.L.J. Law Rep. 179.

[54] *Salih* v. *Enfield Health Authority* [1991] 3 All E.R. 400, C.A. Other receipts, such as child benefit must also be deducted from the cost of maintaining the child: *Emeh* v. *Kensington and Chelsea Area Health Authority* [1984] 3 All E.R. 1044. Child benefit is not a "relevant benefit" for the purpose of the recoupment provisions of the Social Security Act 1989: see § 9.43.

[55] In *Scuriaga* v. *Powell* (1979) 123 S.J. 406; aff'd (1980) (unreported), C.A., the award included a sum for diminution of the plaintiff's marriage prospects following a failed abortion operation.

[56] *Thake* v. *Maurice* [1986] 1 All E.R. 497, 508–9.

[57] *Emeh* v. *Kensington and Chelsea Area Health Authority* [1984] 3 All E.R. 1044, 1056.

defamation) subsisting against or vested in him survive against, or, as the case may be, for the benefit of, his estate. The Act does not create a cause of action, it merely allows for the survival of existing actions, except that where, as a result of an act or omission by the deceased, damage has been suffered which would have given rise to a cause of action had he not died before or at the same time as the damage suffered, section 1(4) deems that the cause of action shall subsist as if he had died after the damage was sustained.

9.60   An action brought by the estate of a deceased plaintiff is dealt with on the same basis as for a living plaintiff, and the measure of damages will generally be the same. The estate can recover any expenses incurred or any loss of earnings attributable to the tort up to the date of death, but not after the death.[58] Similarly, pain and suffering and loss of amenity up to the date of death are recoverable.[59] Where the death was caused by the act or omission which gives rise to the cause of action, damages are calculated without reference to any loss or gain consequent upon the death, except that a sum in respect of funeral expenses may be included.[60] Thus, gains to the estate, such as the proceeds of a life insurance policy, and losses, such as the loss of a life interest under a trust, are ignored.

2. Fatal accidents

9.61   The Fatal Accidents Act 1976, s.1(1) confers upon the dependants of a deceased person a cause of action in respect of their loss of financial dependency, provided that the deceased would have had an action in tort in respect of the injuries that caused his death. The dependants have a cause of action in their own right in respect of financial loss (with the exception of damages for bereavement) irrespective of any claim that might be made on behalf of the deceased's estate under the Law Reform (Miscellaneous Provisions) Act 1934. The dependants' action is derivative, in that it can be maintained only if the defendant would have been liable to the deceased, and it is subject to any defences, such as contributory negligence or *volenti non fit injuria*, that the defendant could have raised against the deceased.[61] If for any reason the deceased could not himself have maintained an action at the moment of his death, if, for example, he has sued the defendant to a judgment or settled the claim while still alive, the dependants have no claim.[62]

---

[58] Claims in respect of loss of earnings in the "lost years" do not survive for the benefit of the estate: Law Reform (Miscellaneous Provisions) Act 1934, s.1(2)(a) (as amended by the Administration of Justice Act 1982, s.4(2)), reversing the effect of *Gammell* v. *Wilson* [1982] A.C. 136. Thus, lost years claims are only available to living plaintiffs, or where the death occurred before January 1, 1983.

[59] In *Hicks* v. *Chief Constable of South Yorkshire Police, The Independent*, May 16, 1991, however, the Court of Appeal held that damages for pain and suffering in the few minutes between an injury and death are not recoverable under the Law Reform (Miscellaneous Provisions) Act 1934.

[60] Law Reform (Miscellaneous Provisions) Act 1934, s.1(2)(c).

[61] An apportionment will be made where the death was caused partly by the negligence of the dependent: *Mulholland* v. *McRae* [1961] N.I. 135; but this does not affect the claims of other dependents: *Dodds* v. *Dodds* [1978] Q.B. 543.

[62] The House of Lords assumed that this was the position in *Pickett* v. *British Rail Engineering Ltd.* [1980] A.C. 136. Where the deceased's action was statute-barred under the Limitation Act 1980 the dependants can request the court to exercise its discretion to allow the action to proceed under s.33: see § 10.45.

The class of dependants who can bring a claim under the Fatal **9.62** Accidents Act 1976 is exhaustively defined in section 1 to include: a spouse, former spouse or "cohabitee"[63] of the deceased; any parent or other ascendant, any child or other descendant, or any person treated by the deceased as his parent or as his child; and any person who is, or is the issue of, a brother, sister, uncle or aunt of the deceased. A relationship by marriage is treated as a relationship by blood, and a relationship by half-blood as a relationship of the whole blood. The stepchild of any person is treated as his child, and an illegitimate person is treated as the legitimate child of his mother and reputed father. An action will normally be instituted by the personal representative of the deceased person's estate on behalf of the dependants, but if an action is not commenced within six months any dependant can sue on behalf of all the dependants.[64]

An award of damages under the Fatal Accidents Act may consist of **9.63** either damages for bereavement or damages for the dependant's actual and prospective pecuniary loss. If the dependants have in fact incurred funeral expenses they are entitled to be reimbursed.[65]

Bereavement

Damages for bereavement were introduced by the Administration of **9.64** Justice Act 1982, s.3, creating a new section 1A of the Fatal Accidents Act 1976. This is a fixed sum of £7,500[66] awarded to the spouse of the deceased or the parents of a deceased unmarried minor child (though only the mother in the case of an illegitimate child).[67] Where both parents of a child claim damages for bereavement, the award will be divided equally between them. The award does not require proof of any financial dependancy, and there is no inquiry into the extent of the plaintiff's grief; the award is a conventional sum which may be increased by regulations but not by the courts. A claim for bereavement damages will not survive for the benefit of the spouse's or parent's estate. Where young children are killed damages for bereavement plus funeral expenses will commonly be the only sum payable by the defendant.

Loss of dependency

Damages for loss of financial dependency upon the deceased will be **9.65** awarded in proportion to the injury resulting from the death to the

---

[63] *i.e.*, a person who was living as the husband or wife of the deceased in the same household immediately before the date of the death, and had been so living for at least two years: Fatal Accidents Act 1976, s.1(3)(*b*).

[64] Fatal Accidents Act 1976, s.2.

[65] *Ibid.*, s.3(5).

[66] The award was increased to this figure from £3,500 for causes of action accruing on or after April 1, 1991 by the Damages for Bereavement (Variation of Sum)(England and Wales) Order 1990 (S.I. 1990/2575).

[67] Damages for bereavement will not be awarded to the parents of a stillborn child, although a mother will be entitled to general damages for the loss of satisfaction of bringing her pregnancy to a successful conclusion, and where appropriate, for being unable to complete her planned family: *Bagley* v. *North Hertfordshire Health Authority* (1986) 136 New L.J. 1014. Damages under these heads should be not less than the statutory sum awarded for bereavement.

dependants respectively.[68] This is determined by the multiplier method. The purpose of the award is to provide the dependants with a capital sum which with prudent management will be sufficient to provide material benefits of the same standard and duration as would have been provided for them out of the deceased's earnings had he lived.[69] The starting point is the amount of the deceased's wages, less an amount for his own personal and living expenses. This provides a basic figure for estimating the dependancy.[70] The length of the dependency must then be estimated.[71] This involves consideration of the deceased's pre-accident life expectancy, discounted for the contingency that he might not have lived or continued working for that long in any event. The multiplier must then be modified to take account of the dependant's future prospects. With dependent children the dependency would not normally extend beyond the end of their full time education.[72] A dependent spouse's life expectancy will be taken into account in determining the multiplier, and where the dependant has died before the trial damages will be awarded only for the period of survival after the deceased's death.[73] The multiplier should be calculated from the date of the deceased's death rather than from the date of assessment, as occurs when calculating the prospective pecuniary loss of living plaintiffs, because the multiplier method is appropriate for periods of uncertainty in the assessment and the uncertainty runs from the date of death.[74] This does not mean, however, that where something has happened in the period between the death and the date of assessment which makes the calculation more certain that the event should be ignored. The court will not speculate when it knows. Thus, where there is a long delay between the date of the death and the trial, and it is known that the dependant has survived for that period, this may result in a higher multiplier being applied to the calculation of the dependency because the discount to be applied to allow for the uncertainty of the dependant's survival should be lower.[75]

9.66   In assessing damages payable to a widow in respect of the death of her husband, the prospects of remarriage or, indeed, the fact of remarriage is not taken into account.[76] This rule relieves the court from having to make what were regarded as distasteful assessments of a

---

[68] Fatal Accidents Act 1976, s.3(1).

[69] *Mallett* v. *McMonagle* [1970] A.C. 166, 174, *per* Lord Diplock.

[70] *Davies* v. *Powell Duffryn Associated Collieries Ltd.* [1942] A.C. 601, 617. The multiplicand will be based upon what the deceased would have been earning at the date of assessment not the date of death: *Cookson* v. *Knowles* [1979] A.C. 556, 573, 575.

[71] For discussion of the factors to be taken into account in arriving at an appropriate multiplier see *Corbett* v. *Barking Havering and Brentwood Health Authority* [1991] 1 All E.R. 498, 508–509, *per* Purchas L.J.

[72] Where there is a chance that a child will proceed to higher education, this chance should be reflected in the multiplier and should not be discounted completely: *Corbett* v. *Barking Havering and Brentwood Health Authority* [1991] 1 All E.R. 498, C.A., applying *Davies* v. *Taylor* [1974] A.C. 207.

[73] *Whittome* v. *Coates* [1965] 1 W.L.R. 1285, where the dependant's reduced life expectancy was taken into account; *Williamson* v. *John I. Thornycroft & Co. Ltd.* [1940] 2 K.B. 658, where the dependant died.

[74] *Cookson* v. *Knowles* [1979] A.C. 556; *Graham* v. *Dodds* [1983] 2 All E.R. 953.

[75] *Corbett* v. *Barking Havering and Brentwood Health Authority* [1991] 1 All E.R. 498. This does not put a premium on delay in bringing the claim because the plaintiff may be penalised by the court refusing to award interest on all or part of the award: *ibid.*

[76] Fatal Accidents Act 1976, s.3(3).

widow's prospects of remarriage, although it departs from the compensatory principle of assessing damages, particularly where the widow has in fact remarried and is being supported by her new husband. On the other hand, the prospects of remarriage of a widower, a former spouse and a "cohabitee" are taken into account, and even a widow's prospects of remarriage may have to be considered in relation to her children's claim for loss of dependency.[77] Section 3(4) of the Fatal Accidents Act provides, that when assessing the dependency of a "cohabitee," the fact that the dependant had no enforceable right to financial support by the deceased as a result of their living together should be taken into account. This will be reflected in a lower multiplier.

9.67 The dependant must establish a pecuniary loss resulting from the death, but need not prove that he had received a pecuniary advantage from the deceased before the death. A reasonable expectation of pecuniary benefit had the deceased lived is sufficient.[78] This will usually arise where parents had some expectation of financial support from a child. With young children, however, the prospect of any pecuniary benefit will normally be too speculative.[79] The benefit lost must be the product of the relationship between the dependant and the deceased, not, for example, as a consequence of a contractual obligation.[80]

9.68 The pecuniary advantage lost as a result of the death must be capable of being calculated in monetary terms, but need not be merely financial. It includes gratuitous services rendered by a member of the family, such as a wife or mother.[81] This will be assessed not merely on the basis of the physical tasks that a mother would perform, and so damages are not necessarily limited to the cost of hiring a housekeeper but take into account the whole of a good mother's care of her family.[82] Conversely, where the deceased mother was unreliable and may not have been available to provide steady parental support had she lived, the dependent child's award should be discounted to allow for the real possibility that the mother would not have stayed with her family.[83]

[77] *Thompson* v. *Price* [1973] Q.B. 838.
[78] *Taff Vale Railway Co.* v. *Jenkins* [1913] A.C. 1; *Kandalla* v. *British European Airways* [1981] Q.B. 158. In *Davies* v. *Taylor* [1974] A.C. 207, the plaintiff widow had left her husband 5 weeks before he was killed in a road accident. The House of Lords held that she did not have to prove that it was more probable than not that there would have been a reconciliation, merely that there was a substantial, as opposed to speculative, chance that she would have returned to him and thereby benefited from his survival. Lord Reid said that if the chance was substantial it must be evaluated, but if it was a mere possibility it must be ignored. On the facts the chance of a reconciliation was speculative.
[79] *Barnett* v. *Cohen* [1921] 2 K.B. 461.
[80] *Malyon* v. *Plummer* [1964] 1 Q.B. 330.
[81] *Regan* v. *Williamson* [1976] 1 W.L.R. 305. The fact that those services are now being provided gratuitously by another member of the family does not affect the dependant's claim to compensation: *Hay* v. *Hughes* [1975] 1 All E.R. 257, held that children entitled to the cost of future care following the death of their parents even though they had been, and would continue to be, cared for by their grandmother.
[82] *Hay* v. *Hughes* [1975] 1 All E.R. 257; *Mehmet* v. *Perry* [1977] 2 All E.R. 529, where the father gave up his job to look after the children; damages assessed as his loss of earnings; *Cresswell* v. *Eaton* [1991] 1 All E.R. 484. See also *K.* v. *JMP Co. Ltd.* [1976] Q.B. 85, in relation to claims by 3 illegitimate children in respect of their father's death. Part of the award to the children included an element for their mother's financial loss, because this affected her ability to provide for the children.
[83] *Stanley* v. *Saddique* [1991] 1 All E.R. 529. In these circumstances the multiplier method of assessment will be inappropriate, and damages should be assessed on the basis of a jury award.

Where the court assesses the loss of a mother's services on the basis of the commercial cost of hiring a nanny to look after a child, the award will be reduced to take account of the fact that as the child gets older and becomes more independent he will be less in need of the services of a nanny.[84]

Deductions

9.69   Any benefits which have accrued or will or may accrue to any person from the deceased's estate or otherwise as a result of his death are disregarded.[85] Thus, any insurance money, pension,[86] social security benefits[87] or inheritance from the deceased's estate (including any damages awarded to the estate under a Law Reform (Miscellaneous Provisions) Act 1934 claim[88]) are ignored in calculating the financial loss. "Benefits" are not restricted to direct pecuniary benefits, and so, in assessing a child's loss of dependency following the death of his mother, the fact that he will have a better home and receive a higher standard of motherly services from his stepmother than he would have received from his natural mother, had she lived, is to be disregarded by virtue of section 4.[89]

VI. Damages for Breach of Confidence

9.70 Although there is no doubt that a legal duty of confidence exists between doctor and patient, the remedies available for the enforcement of that duty are somewhat limited in the particular context of the doctor/patient relationship. If the patient becomes aware that a doctor is about to make an unauthorised disclosure of confidential information then he is entitled to an injunction to restrain the disclosure, and in a case such as *W.* v. *Egdell*[90] the return of any medical reports

---

[84] *Spittle* v. *Bunney* [1988] 3 All E.R. 1031; see also *Corbett* v. *Barking Havering and Brentwood Health Authority* [1991] 1 All E.R. 498, 506, where Purchas L.J. said that the method of establishing an infant dependant's loss of its mother's services by taking the net wages of a notional nanny as the basis for the multiplicand was a crude and approximate instrument, acceptable only because there is no better means of approaching this almost unquantifiable aspect of dependency. For the effect of adoption on a child's claim for loss of dependency see *Watson* v. *Willmott* [1991] 1 All E.R. 473.
[85] Fatal Accidents Act 1976, s.4, as substituted by the Administration of Justice Act 1982, s.3.
[86] *Pidduck* v. *Eastern Scottish Omnibuses Ltd.* [1990] 2 All E.R. 69, C.A.—widow's allowance payable to the plaintiff from the deceased's pension scheme on his death to be disregarded by virtue of s.4 in calculating her loss of dependency.
[87] Damages awarded under the Fatal Accidents Act 1976 are also specifically excluded from the rules on recoupment of social security benefits: Social Security Act 1989, s.22(4)(c).
[88] Since a claim for loss of earnings in the lost years does not survive for the benefit of the estate (Law Reform (Miscellaneous Provisions) Act 1934, s.1(2)(a)) the Law Reform Act damages will be limited to any pecuniary loss, including loss of earnings, prior to the death, and an award for pain and suffering and loss of amenity during the period in which the deceased survived. Before the amendment of s.4 of the Fatal Accidents Act 1976 in 1982, Law Reform Act damages passing to a dependant under the estate would have been deducted from the dependency claim.
[89] *Stanley* v. *Saddique* [1991] 1 All E.R. 529.
[90] [1989] 1 All E.R. 1089; see § 2.96.

disclosed to third parties. But if the breach of confidence has already taken place an injunction may be pointless, and the patient may well seek damages for the disclosure itself.

There is considerable doubt, however, about the availability of **9.71** damages as a remedy for a past breach of confidence which is not based on a breach of contract.[91] Claims brought by patients in the N.H.S. would not be founded on contract. Moreover, even where the claim is based in contract it is doubtful that damages would be awarded for the mental distress occasioned by the disclosure of personal information. The general rule is that damages will not be awarded in contract for the mental distress, injury to feelings or annoyance resulting from a breach of contract,[92] unless the contract was itself a contract to provide peace of mind or freedom from distress.[93] This was the view taken by Scott J. in *W.* v. *Egdell*. If W's claim had succeeded he would not have been entitled to damages in contract for shock and distress (except for nominal damages for the breach), and, his Lordship concluded, there was no reason why equity should not follow the law on this point.[94]

The result for the patient is highly unsatisfactory. A past breach of **9.72** confidence will give rise to a claim for damages only if he can establish substantive damage which flowed from the breach, and possibly this would only apply to contractual breaches of confidence.[95] The Law Commission has recommended that the action for breach of confidence should take the form of a statutory tort and that damages for mental distress caused by a past breach should be available,[96] but this recommendation has not been implemented.

---

[91] See the Law Commission Report No. 110 *Breach of Confidence*, 1981, Cmnd. 8388, paras. 4.75–4.77.

[92] *Addis* v. *Gramaphone Co. Ltd.* [1909] A.C. 488; *Bliss* v. *South East Thames Regional Health Authority* [1987] I.C.R. 700, 717–8. Similarly, in the absence of physical injury, there is no liability in tort for mental distress falling short of psychiatric illness: *Hinz* v. *Berry* [1970] 2 Q.B. 40, 42; *McLoughlin* v. *O'Brian* [1982] 2 All E.R. 298, 311; see § 2.44.

[93] *Jarvis* v. *Swan Tours Ltd.* [1973] Q.B. 233; *Heywood* v. *Wellers* [1976] Q.B. 446.

[94] [1989] 1 All E.R. 1089, 1108–9. This point was not considered by the Court of Appeal in *W.* v. *Egdell* [1990] 1 All E.R. 835, in view of the result on liability.

[95] Though if the breach of confidence leads to foreseeable physical harm to the patient this may amount to a breach of the doctor's duty of care to his patient: see *Furniss* v. *Fitchett* [1958] N.Z.L.R. 396, where the facts were somewhat unusual.

[96] *Ante*, n. 91, at §§ 6.5 and 6.114.

CHAPTER 10

PROCEDURE

10.01 Although there are some important practical differences, such as finding suitable expert witnesses and interpreting medical records, in many other respects the conduct of medical negligence claims is no different from any other action in respect of personal injuries, which are generally governed by the procedural Rules of the Supreme Court and the County Court Rules. This chapter deals with some of the most important procedural issues that can arise in the conduct of medical negligence litigation, in particular periods of limitation, and the related question of dismissal for want of prosecution and discovery, including recent changes in the procedure for exchange of expert reports. A section on patients' rights of access to their medical records is included in this chapter because of its relevance to discovery, although the import of these rights is clearly much wider than the conduct of litigation.

I. LIMITATION

10.02 Periods of limitation, within which the plaintiff must commence his action or find it barred, are entirely the creation of statute, now mostly consolidated in the Limitation Act 1980. The basic rule governing an action in tort is that a claim cannot be brought more than six years from the date on which the cause of action accrued.[1] In torts actionable *per se*, such as trespass to the person, the cause of action normally accrues at the date of the defendant's wrong, whereas with torts actionable only on proof of damage, such as negligence, the action accrues when damage occurs. This will usually be at the same time as the defendant's act or omission, but not necessarily so. In contract the limitation period is also six years from the accrual of the action,[2] which normally occurs at the date of the breach of contract.

10.03 The rationale for limitation periods is that they protect defendants from stale claims, they encourage plaintiffs to proceed without unreasonable delay, and they provide finality so that a person can feel

---

[1] Limitation Act 1980, s.2.
[2] *Ibid.*, s.5.

confident after a certain period of time that potential claims against him are closed and he can arrange his affairs accordingly.[3] On the other hand, plaintiffs should not be penalised for failing to institute proceedings at a time when they were unaware that they had sustained any damage or that it was attributable to the defendant, or were simply not in a position to institute proceedings. The difficulty is to reach a reasonable balance between the interests of plaintiffs and those of defendants. This has been achieved by grafting onto the basic limitation periods special rules for cases of personal injuries, plaintiffs under a disability, latent damage, and fraud or concealment of the cause of action by the defendant. In broad terms, the effect of these special statutory provisions is to postpone the operation of the limitation period whilst the plaintiff is unaware of his legal rights. Medical negligence actions are usually, though not exclusively,[4] concerned with claims for personal injuries or death, and this section will concentrate largely on the special rules applying to this form of action.

1. Personal injuries and death

Limitation of action in cases involving personal injuries or death is **10.04** governed, as a general rule,[5] by the provisions of the Limitation Act 1980, ss.11–14 and 33. The basic scheme provides for a three-year limitation period which runs from either: (a) the date on which the cause of action accrued, or (b) if later, the date of knowledge of the existence of a cause of action.[6] This is subject to the court's discretion to allow the action to proceed notwithstanding the expiry of the three-year period.[7]

The three-year period applies to "any action for damage for **10.05** negligence, nuisance or breach of duty . . . where the damages claimed by the plaintiff . . . consist of or include damages in respect of personal injuries to the plaintiff or any other person."[8] Breach of duty is expressly stated to include breach of a contractual duty, and it also covers trespass to the person,[9] even where the trespass is intentional.[10]

---

[3] *Report of the Committee on Limitation of Actions in Cases of Personal Injury* (1962), Cmnd. 1829, para. 17; *Birkett* v. *James* [1978] A.C. 297, 331.

[4] See, *e.g.*, *Pattison* v. *Hobbs, The Times*, November 11, 1985, § 10.06. Any action which gives rise to a claim for pure economic loss will be subject to the ordinary 6 year period of limitation, unless it can be said to cause latent damage; see § 10.54. On the possible claims in respect of economic loss which could be made against a medical practitioner see §§ 2.24–2.25, 2.69.

[5] The Limitation Act 1980 does not apply where a period of limitation is prescribed by other legislation: s.39. Special rules apply to accidents occurring in the course of international travel (Carriage by Air Act 1961, ss.1(1), 5(1), Sched., Art. 29; Carriage by Railway Act 1972, s.1(1), Sched., Art. 17; Carriage of Passengers by Road Act 1974 s.1(1), Art. 22), and nuclear incidents (Nuclear Installations Act 1965, s.15). See also Consumer Protection Act 1987, Schedule 1, in respect of claims under that Act, amending the Limitation Act 1980, *post,* § 10.51.

[6] Limitation Act 1980, s.11(3), (4). The date of accrual will often be the same as the date of the plaintiff's knowledge; see § 10.08. The fact that the Limitation Act 1980 is a consolidating statute means that earlier caselaw on the interpretation of its provisions remains authoritative. The present scheme covering personal injuries was introduced by the Limitation Act 1975, adding new ss.2A–2D to the Limitation Act 1939.

[7] *Ibid.*, s.33; see §§ 10.26 *et seq.*

[8] *Ibid.*, s.11(1).

[9] *Letang* v. *Cooper* [1965] 1 Q.B. 232.

[10] *Long* v. *Hepworth* [1968] 1 W.L.R. 1299.

10.06   "Personal injuries" includes any disease and any impairment of a person's physical or mental condition.[11] Where the breach of duty does not itself cause the personal injuries, but deprives the plaintiff of a chance of receiving compensation for the injuries, the three-year period does not apply. For example, a solicitor's negligence which results in his client's claim for personal injuries becoming statute-barred gives rise to a claim for financial loss which is subject to the ordinary six-year limitation period under section 2 (tort) or section 5 (contract) of the Limitation Act,[12] although this is now subject to specific provisions on latent damage. So where a patient suffers purely financial loss due to a doctor's negligence (*e.g.* giving up work following a negligent misdiagnosis[13]) the six-year period will apply. In *Pattison* v. *Hobbs*[14] the Court of Appeal held that this was the position where the claim was in respect of financial loss resulting from the birth of a healthy child following a negligently performed sterilisation operation. The significance of this is that within the six-year period the plaintiff has an absolute right to bring an action, but if the claim is for personal injuries there is no absolute right after three years, and the plaintiff must rely on the court exercising its discretion to allow his claim to proceed. Thus, in some "wrongful birth" cases, where the action has not been commenced within three years, it might be preferable for the plaintiff to forego the claim for personal injuries (*e.g.* the pain and suffering of pregnancy or of a repeat sterilisation operation), since the bulk of the damages reflect the financial costs of rearing the child.[15] Conversely, if the claim does not include personal injuries there is no discretion to allow the action to continue after the six-year period, unless the damage was latent.[16]

10.07   In computing the three-year period the date on which the accident occurred is ignored.[17] If the court office is closed for the whole of the last day of the period, it is extended until the next day on which the court office is open.[18] As a general rule, once the period has started to run it cannot be suspended; only the issue of the writ stops time running. The parties may agree, expressly or impliedly, to extend the time, but the mere fact that negotiations towards a settlement were in progress when the three-year period expired will not constitute such an agreement, unless the defendant's conduct is such that he is estopped

---

[11] Limitation Act 1980, s.38(1).

[12] See, *e.g.*, *Ackbar* v. *Green & Co. Ltd.* [1975] 1 Q.B. 582, where insurance brokers who failed to obtain insurance against the risk of personal injury were subject to the 6-year period, although the claim materialised when the plaintiff sustained personal injury. Croom-Johnson J. gave the example of a claim against a solicitor; *cf. Paterson* v. *Chadwick* [1974] 1 W.L.R. 890, § 10.84, n. 12, in relation to discovery against third parties under what is now s.34 of the Supreme Court Act 1981.

[13] See *Hedley Byrne & Co. Ltd.* v. *Heller & Partners Ltd.* [1964] A.C. 465, 517, *per* Lord Devlin, § 2.25; see also *Stevens* v. *Bermondsey and Southwark Group Hospital Management Committee* (1963) 107 S.J. 478, § 2.24.

[14] *The Times*, November 11, 1985. See also the comments of Sir John Donaldson M.R. in *Naylor* v. *Preston Area Health Authority* [1987] 2 All E.R. 353, 363, that a claim in respect of a failed vasectomy would not fall within the definition of "personal injuries" under R.S.C., Ord. 1, r. 4.

[15] See § 9.56.

[16] See § 10.54.

[17] *Marren* v. *Dawson Bentley & Co. Ltd.* [1961] 2 Q.B. 135.

[18] *Pritam Kaur* v. *Russell & Sons Ltd.* [1973] Q.B. 336.

from relying on the defence.[19] For these purposes it is only safe to rely on an express admission of liability or an express statement that the defendant will not take the limitation point.

2. Commencement of the three-year period

Time begins to run from either the date on which the cause of action accrued or the date of the plaintiff's knowledge, if later.

Accrual of the cause of action

A cause of action is simply a factual situation entitling a person to a **10.08** remedy.[20] In negligence the action accrues when damage occurs, which is usually but not always at the same time as the defendant's breach of duty. The action will accrue even though the damage is undiscoverable.[21] In the case of minor or trivial harm it will be a question of fact whether the plaintiff has sustained "damage" sufficient for the cause of action to accrue. If it falls within the principle *de minimis non curat lex* it will be ignored, but not otherwise.[22] In cases of progressive damage resulting from a *continuing* breach of duty a fresh cause of action arises so long as the wrongful act continues (as, *e.g.*, in industrial deafness cases). The plaintiff is entitled to claim for so much of the damage as was caused in the three years immediately preceding the issue of the writ. He may be able to claim for earlier damage if the court exercises its discretion under section 33 of the Limitation Act 1980, provided that the earlier damage was attributable to the defendant's breach of duty.[23] If, as a question of fact, the subsequent deterioration of the plaintiff's condition is attributable to events which occurred more than three years before the issue of the writ, the claim is out of time.

In simple contract the cause of action accrues at the date of breach **10.09** of contract, although it is possible that where there is an omission to perform a contractual duty this may constitute a "continuing breach of contract" up to the point at which it is no longer possible to perform the duty, with the cause of action accruing at that date.[24] Thus, an

---

[19] *Deerness* v. *John Keeble & Son Ltd.* [1983] 2 Lloyd's Rep. 260, where the House of Lords declined to infer such an agreement from continuing negotiations and an interim payment; *K. Lokumal & Sons (London) Ltd.* v. *Lotte Shipping Co. Pte. Ltd.* [1985] 2 Lloyd's Rep. 28; *cf. Hare* v. *Personal Representatives of Mohammed Yunis Malik* (1980) 124 S.J. 328, C.A., in the context of a failure to serve the writ within the period allowed by R.S.C., Ord. 6, r. 8(1).

[20] *Letang* v. *Cooper* [1965] 1 Q.B. 232, 242–3, *per* Diplock L.J.

[21] *Cartledge* v. *Jopling & Sons Ltd.* [1963] A.C. 758.

[22] *Ibid.* Asymptomatic, minor physiological damage may be sufficient to give rise to a cause of action: see *Church* v. *Ministry of Defence*, *The Times*, March 7, 1984; *Sykes* v. *Ministry of Defence*, *The Times*, March 23, 1984; *Patterson* v. *Ministry of Defence* [1987] C.L.Y. 1194.

[23] See, *e.g.*, *Thompson* v. *Smiths Shiprepairers (North Shields) Ltd.* [1984] 1 All E.R. 881. If the earlier damage cannot be attributed to the defendant's breach of duty, nonetheless the award of damages for the later, actionable damage may be proportionately greater because additional harm to a person who has an existing disability may have more catastrophic consequences than the initial injury: *Paris* v. *Stepney Borough Council* [1951] A.C. 367; *Berry* v. *Stone Manganese & Marine Ltd.* [1972] 1 Lloyd's Rep. 182, 196.

[24] *Midland Bank Trust Co. Ltd.* v. *Hett, Stubbs & Kemp* [1979] Ch. 384; *cf. Bell* v. *Peter Browne & Co.* [1990] 3 W.L.R. 510, C.A.

omission to give a warning to avoid certain activities which might be dangerous to the patient during the course of treatment could give rise to a continuing duty to give the appropriate advice.

10.10   In practice, the date of accrual of the cause of action is largely irrelevant in actions for personal injuries since time does not run unless and until the plaintiff has the relevant "knowledge," which can occur at the date of accrual or later, but never before the action has accrued.

Date of knowledge

10.11   By section 14(1) references to a person's date of knowledge are references to the date on which he first had knowledge of the following facts:

> "(*a*) that the injury in question was significant; and
> (*b*) that the injury was attributable in whole or in part to the act or omission which is alleged to constitute negligence, nuisance or breach of duty; and
> (*c*) the identity of the defendant; and
> (*d*) if it is alleged that the act or omission was that of a person other than the defendant, the identity of that person and the additional facts supporting the bringing of an action against the defendant . . . "

Where a defendant applies to strike out an action *in limine* on the ground that the date of the plaintiff's knowledge of the relevant facts was more than three years before the issue of the writ, the court should not grant the application unless the issue is clear and obvious and the contrary unarguable.[25]

(a) *Significant injury*

10.12   An injury is significant if the person whose date of knowledge is in question would reasonably have considered it sufficiently serious to justify his instituting proceedings for damages against a defendant who did not dispute liability and was able to satisfy a judgment.[26] This is a combined subjective/objective test:

> "Taking *that* plaintiff, with *that* plaintiff's intelligence, would he have been reasonable in considering the injury not sufficiently serious to justify instituting proceedings for damages?"[27]

It is a question of what a reasonable man of the plaintiff's age, with his background, his intelligence and his disabilities would reasonably have known.[28] However, "significant injury" refers to the gravity of the

---

[25] *Davis* v. *Ministry of Defence, The Times*, August 7, 1985, C.A., *per* May L.J.
[26] Limitation Act 1980, s.14(2).
[27] *McCafferty* v. *Metropolitan Police District Receiver* [1977] 1 W.L.R. 1073, 1081, *per* Geoffrey Lane L.J. See also *Denman* v. *Essex Area Health Authority* (1984) 134 New L.J. 264, where the plaintiff was not aware that his injury (the breakdown of a repair effected by a bone graft operation in 1972, following an accident in 1973, for which the defendants were responsible) was "significant" until he was informed about it by a consultant surgeon in 1979.
[28] *Davis* v. *City and Hackney Health Authority, The Times*, January 27, 1989.

damage and its monetary value. Other personal reasons that the plaintiff may have had for not commencing proceedings are irrelevant, even if they are objectively reasonable.[29] The plaintiff's subjective reasons and beliefs may, however, be relevant to the court's exercise of discretion under section 33.

Where an injury initially appears to be trivial but subsequently turns **10.13** out to be serious, time does not run until the plaintiff knows that the injury is in fact serious. However, section 14(2) appears to make most injuries significant in monetary terms, since it may not take much to justify instituting proceedings against a solvent defendant who admits liability. Thus, where the injury, though minor, is sufficiently serious to institute proceedings, and the plaintiff subsequently discovers a far more serious injury caused by the same accident, time will run from the date of the first injury known to be significant. An action in respect of the second injury commenced more than three years after knowledge of the first injury will be barred.[30] Similarly, if the initial injury is minor but there is a medically recognised risk of deterioration in the future, knowledge of the risk is probably enough to start time running, provided the risk itself is sufficiently serious. The plaintiff should not wait for the risk to materialise.[31]

(b) *Causation*

The plaintiff must have knowledge that the injury was attributable in **10.14** whole or in part to the defendant. This refers to the plaintiff's knowledge of *factual* causation.[32] The plaintiff's ignorance of causation in law is irrelevant. Once the plaintiff has the broad knowledge that his injuries are attributable to the defendant's acts or omissions, he has sufficient knowledge for the purpose of section 14(1)(*b*), even if he does not know the specific acts or omissions and is not in a position to draft a fully particularised statement of claim.[33] Moreover, a plaintiff will be taken to know that his injury was "attributable" to the defendant's act or omission if he knew that it was "capable of being so attributed."[34] Reasonable belief or suspicion, however, are not suffi-

---

[29] *Miller* v. *London Electrical Manufacturing Co. Ltd.* [1976] 2 Lloyd's Rep. 284, where the injury turned out to be more serious than the plaintiff initially thought; *Buck* v. *English Electric Co. Ltd.* [1977] 1 W.L.R. 806, where the plaintiff was still working and did not want to "sponge" on his employer by bringing an action; *McCafferty* v. *Metropolitan Police District Receiver* [1977] 1 W.L.R. 1073, where the plaintiff wanted to preserve good relations with his employer; *Farmer* v. *National Coal Board*, *The Times*, April 27, 1985, C.A., where the plaintiff believed that the only potential defendant was not worth suing because he had no resources.

[30] *Bristow* v. *Grout*, *The Times*, November 3, 1986; see also *Miller* v. *London Electrical Manufacturing Co. Ltd.* [1976] 2 Lloyd's Rep. 284.

[31] Symptomless, minor physiological damage may be actionable, particularly where it carries a slight risk of future damage, and/or gives rise to anxiety in the plaintiff: *Church* v. *Ministry of Defence* (1984) 134 New L.J. 623; *The Times*, March 7, 1984; *Sykes* v. *Ministry of Defence* , *The Times*, March 23, 1984. An award of provisional damages may be appropriate in such a case: see *Patterson* v. *Ministry of Defence* [1987] C.L.Y. 1194.

[32] See, *e.g.*, *Marston* v. *British Railways Board* [1976] I.C.R. 124.

[33] *Wilkinson* v. *Ancliff (BLT) Ltd.* [1986] 3 All E.R. 427, 438, C.A. Knowledge that the injury was caused by an operation is not knowledge that it was attributable to an act or omission which is alleged to constitute negligence, since an injury following an operation may arise without negligence: see *Bentley* v. *Bristol and Western Health Authority*, *The Times*, December 6, 1990, § 10.16.

[34] *Ibid.* "Capable of being so attributed" means attributable as a real, not a fanciful, possibility, but it does not have to be a *probable* cause of the injury. "One is dealing here with knowledge, actual or imputed, and not with proof of liability": *Guidera* v. *NEI Projects (India)* (1990) (unreported), C.A., *per* Sir David Croom–Johnson.

cient to constitute knowledge.[35] In *Stephen* v. *Riverside Health Authority*[36] it was held that even a deep-rooted suspicion or conviction on the part of the plaintiff that an incompetently conducted X-ray had caused her symptoms did not amount to knowledge, when she had been assured by several highly qualified doctors that the dose of radiation she had received was not high and could not have caused the symptoms. It was not until 1985, when she was informed by a medical expert that the symptoms were indicative of a radiation dosage high enough to increase the risk of cancer that the plaintiff acquired knowledge for the purpose of section 14, notwithstanding that an earlier, protective writ had been issued in 1980.

10.15   Similarly, in *Scuriaga* v. *Powell*[37] the defendant performed an unsuccessful abortion on the plaintiff, but the doctor told the plaintiff that the operation had failed because she had a physical defect. She did not know that the failure to terminate the pregnancy was due to the doctor's negligence until she received a consultant's report more than three years after the failed operation. It was held that time did not begin to run until the plaintiff discovered that the failure was due to the doctor's conduct of the operation.

10.16   There has been some difficulty in identifying precisely what a patient must know about his treatment for the purpose of section 14(1)(*b*). Can it be said that a plaintiff's knowledge that his injury was attributable to his "treatment" is knowledge in "broad terms,"[38] where he cannot identify, let alone particularise, the relevant acts or omissions? In *Bentley* v. *Bristol and Western Health Authority*[39] Hirst J. held that a plaintiff's knowledge that an injury which she had suffered was attributable in whole or in part to an operation did not arise until she became aware of some act or omission which could have affected the safety of the operation. Broad knowledge that the injury was caused by the operation *per se* did not set the limitation period running, since the operation is not the act or omission which is itself alleged to constitute negligence. The crucial issue was knowledge of the act or omission alleged to constitute negligence, namely some conduct or failure which could affect the safety of the operation. This would

---

[35] *Ibid.* See also *Davis* v. *Ministry of Defence*, *The Times*, August 7, 1985, C.A., where the plaintiff's strong belief that his dermatitis had been caused by his working conditions and that he had a good claim for damages against the defendants did not amount to "knowledge" since his medical and legal advisers took a different view of the cause of the dermatitis.

[36] [1990] 1 Med. L.R. 261.

[37] (1979) 123 S.J. 406; aff'd 1980 (unreported), C.A.; see also *Bentley* v. *Bristol and Western Health Authority*, *The Times*, December 6, 1990, where the plaintiff had received "universally negative information and advice, both medical and legal" and consequently it could not be said that she knew that her injury was capable of being attributed to the alleged acts of negligence until she received an expert's report to that effect.

[38] Applying *Wilkinson* v. *Ancliff* (*BLT*) *Ltd.* [1986] 3 All E.R. 427, 438, C.A.

[39] *The Times*, December 6, 1990; see also *Driscoll-Varley* v. *Parkside Health Authority* (1990) (unreported), Q.B.D., where Hidden J. held that the test to be applied in s.14(1)(*b*) was not "was there some negligence in the treatment at St. Mary's Hospital which cannot be properly identified but which must have happened?" The Act refers to knowledge that the injury was attributable to "the act or omission which is alleged to constitute negligence" and thus the relevant knowledge was of an act or omission alleged in the plaintiff's statement of claim to constitute negligence, namely premature mobilisation following a fractured leg. An awareness that the leg was not healing properly and a belief that this was attributable to post-operative care was not "knowledge."

frequently depend on information derived by the plaintiff from expert opinion, and the opinion would be relevant in determining the plaintiff's date of knowledge. In *Hendy* v. *Milton Keynes Health Authority*,[40] on the other hand, Blofeld J. concluded that, while a plaintiff's date of knowledge that an injury was attributable in whole or in part to an operation could well have depended on the date when she had received an expert's report, in a less complicated case the date of knowledge arose when she appreciated in general terms that her problems were attributable to the operation, even if the precise terms of what had gone wrong were not known. Eight months after the operation the plaintiff had been told what had happened, and that a second operation had put things right. At that point the doctor, himself an expert, had given the plaintiff sufficient information to set the limitation period running.

In *Nash* v. *Eli Lilly*[41] Hidden J. adopted the approach of Hirst J. in **10.17** *Bentley* v. *Bristol and Western Health Authority*, commenting that there must be a degree of specificity, not a mere global or catch-all character about the act or omission which is alleged to constitute negligence. Attributing the injury to vague and generalised conduct such as "the operation at the hospital" is not enough. The plaintiff must know some specific fact in relation to the conduct of the operation. Moreover, the fact of which the plaintiff must have knowledge is the fact which is the basis of the allegation of negligence upon which the action is founded. That does not mean, however, that the plaintiff must have knowledge of every act or omission set out in the statement of claim, which in *Nash* amounted to 60 pages of pleadings. The crucial issue in that case, which dealt with a number of late claims in the Opren litigation, was the definition of the relevant acts or omissions of the defendants. Hidden J. held that these consisted of (i) exposing the plaintiffs to a drug which was unsafe in that it was capable of causing persistent photosensitivity, and/or (ii) in failing to take reasonable steps to protect the plaintiffs from such a condition.

(c) *Defendant's identity*

This will not normally be a problem in cases of medical negligence, **10.18** although the plaintiff may not know which individual in a team caused the injury.[42]

(d) *Vicarious liability*

Section 14(1)(*d*) refers to the circumstances required to establish an **10.19** employer's vicarious liability for the torts of employees committed in the course of employment, though the wording is wide enough to cover liability for the conduct of independent contractors where the defendant is under a relevant "non-delegable" duty. The precise identity of the employee is irrelevant if the plaintiff is aware that the damage was

---

[40] *The Times*, March 8, 1991.
[41] [1991] 2 Med. L.R. 169.
[42] As, *e.g.*, in *Cassidy* v. *Ministry of Health* [1951] 2 K.B. 343. For the problems a plaintiff may encounter in identifying a corporate defendant see: *Simpson* v. *Norwest Holst (Southern) Ltd.* [1980] 2 All E.R. 471.

caused by one or more of the defendant's employees acting in the course of employment.[43] The plaintiff does not have to know that on the facts the defendant would be held vicariously liable in law.

(e) *Ignorance of the law*

10.20   It is the plaintiff's knowledge of *facts* that governs the commencement date. Section 14(1) specifically provides that the plaintiff's ignorance that, as a matter of law, the facts would give him a cause of action is irrelevant. This is the case even where the plaintiff has received incorrect advice about the legal position, whether from a lawyer or not.[44] Ignorance of the law is relevant, however, to the court's exercise of discretion under section 33.[45]

Constructive knowledge

10.21   A person's knowledge includes constructive knowledge, which by virtue of section 14(3) means:

> "knowledge which he might reasonably have been expected to acquire—
> (a) from facts observable or ascertainable by him; or
> (b) from facts ascertainable by him with the help of medical or other appropriate expert advice which it is reasonable for him to seek;
>
> but a person shall not be fixed under this subsection with knowledge of a fact ascertainable only with the help of expert advice so long as he has taken all reasonable steps to obtain (and, where appropriate, to act on) that advice."

Again, this is a combination of a subjective and an objective test. The plaintiff is fixed with knowledge which *he* might reasonably have been expected to acquire from facts observable or ascertainable by *him*. Mere suspicion does not amount to knowledge.[46] Where the question is whether it was reasonable for the plaintiff to seek expert advice, his personal circumstances should be taken into account.[47]

---

[43] Since, where the defendant is responsible in law for all the staff who played some role in the plaintiff's treatment, it is unnecessary for the plaintiff to identify the particular employee who was at fault in order to establish vicarious liability: *Cassidy* v. *Ministry of Health* [1951] 2 K.B. 343.

[44] See *Farmer* v. *National Coal Board, The Times*, April 27, 1985, C.A., where the erroneous legal advice by a union official that the plaintiff's action had no chance of success did not prevent time running, since from facts ascertainable by her she could reasonably have acquired the necessary knowledge.

[45] Limitation Act 1980, s.33(3)(a) and (e); *Brooks* v. *Coates (U.K.) Ltd.* [1984] 1 All E.R. 702, 713.

[46] *Wilkinson* v. *Ancliff (BLT) Ltd.* [1986] 3 All E.R. 427; *Stephen* v. *Riverside Health Authority* [1990] 1 Med. L.R. 261. Similarly, the plaintiff's "firm belief" that his injury was attributable to the defendant's act or omission is not "knowledge" that it was so attributable where his medical and legal advisers take the view that it could not be so attributed, but rather was constitutional: see *Davis* v. *Ministry of Defence, The Times*, August 7, 1985, C.A.

[47] See *Davis* v. *City and Hackney Health Authority, The Times*, January 27, 1989, on the question of when it is reasonable to consult a solicitor. A failure to seek legal advice will give rise to constructive knowledge of the facts which would have been discovered after the date at which it would have been reasonable to seek such advice: *Hills* v. *Potter* [1983] 3 All E.R. 716, 728; but it may well be reasonable for a plaintiff who is seriously ill or dying not to seek legal advice: *Newton* v. *Cammell Laird & Co. (Shipbuilders and Engineers) Ltd.* [1969] 1 All E.R. 708.

The proviso to section 14(3) prevents a plaintiff from being fixed **10.22** with constructive knowledge where an expert has failed to discover or disclose a relevant fact that ought to have been revealed.[48] It will only apply, however, to facts which are "ascertainable *only* with the help of expert advice." Where the plaintiff himself could have discovered the information, then he is fixed with any knowledge that the expert acting on his behalf ought to have acquired,[49] provided that it was information which the plaintiff could reasonably be expected to acquire.[50]

Particular problems arise when the plaintiff's "expert" is a lawyer. **10.23** First, by virtue of the proviso to section 14(1), where a plaintiff receives erroneous advice about the law (*e.g.* that the facts do not disclose a cause of action) this is irrelevant and does not prevent time running.[51] Secondly, where legal "advice" consists of a failure to discover relevant facts, or a failure to suggest a line of enquiry that would have revealed the facts, then in theory the proviso to section 14(3) applies, and the plaintiff is not fixed with constructive knowledge.[52] But in *Leadbitter* v. *Hodge Finance Ltd.*[53] a very narrow view was taken of the facts which are ascertainable *only* with the help of expert advice. In that case an accident victim was expected to be capable of obtaining a police report, making enquiries of the fire brigade and local residents, and interviewing potential witnesses. This raises a question as to precisely what facts would be treated as ascertainable only with legal assistance. For example, would a patient be expected to seek and obtain his own medical records?

Thirdly, it is possible that section 14(3)(*b*) does not apply to *any* **10.24** form of legal advice. In *Fowell* v. *National Coal Board*[54] the Court of Appeal said, *obiter*, that a party's solicitor was not an "expert" within the meaning of the subsection, which was directed to experts in the sense of expert witnesses.[55] If correct, this would mean that a plaintiff is not constructively fixed with the knowledge of his solicitor *by virtue of section 14(3)*. It would seem, however, that under the general law of agency a plaintiff is fixed with the knowledge that his solicitor actually has, and in *Simpson* v. *Norwest Holst Southern Ltd.*[56] it appears to

---

[48] See, *e.g.*, *Marston* v. *British Railways Board* [1976] I.C.R. 124, where the expert dealt only with the hardness of a metal hammer, not its defective condition; see also *Stephen* v. *Riverside Health Authority* [1990] 1 Med. L.R. 261, where the plaintiff had been assured by a "chorus of highly qualified experts" that her symptoms could not have been caused by the dose of radiation that she had received; *Davis* v. *Ministry of Defence*, *The Times*, August 7, 1985, C.A., § 10.31.

[49] *Leadbitter* v. *Hodge Finance Ltd.* [1982] 2 All E.R. 167, 174–175.

[50] In *Fowell* v. *National Coal Board*, *The Times*, May 28, 1986, Parker L.J. said that the missing facts (namely that workmen were not employed by the defendant but by an independent contractor) were ascertainable by the plaintiff, because he could have simply written to the National Coal Board, but this was knowledge which he could not himself have been reasonably expected to acquire; *cf.* the investigative skills expected of the plaintiff in *Leadbitter* v. *Hodge Finance Ltd.* [1982] 2 All E.R. 167, § 10.23.

[51] *Farmer* v. *National Coal Board*, *The Times*, April 27, 1985, C.A.

[52] See *Central Asbestos Co. Ltd.* v. *Dodd* [1973] A.C. 518, 555–556, *per* Lord Salmon commenting on the effect of the earlier legislation, the Limitation Act 1963, and distinguishing between legal advice which leaves the plaintiff in ignorance of material facts, and legal advice that on the facts he has no remedy in law.

[53] [1982] 2 All E.R. 167, 174–175.

[54] *The Times*, May 28, 1986.

[55] *cf.* s.33(3)(*f*): in exercising its discretion to allow the action to proceed the court will consider the steps taken by the plaintiff to obtain expert advice, including legal advice.

[56] [1980] 2 All E.R. 471, 476.

have been assumed by the Court of Appeal that a plaintiff will also be fixed with knowledge which his solicitor ought reasonably to have acquired.[57] Presumably this would be the position even where the plaintiff could not reasonably have acquired the knowledge himself. Thus, a plaintiff who has no actual or constructive knowledge may be caught by his solicitor's constructive knowledge and will be unable to rely on the proviso to section 14(3)(*b*). In this situation time will run against the plaintiff and he may have to apply to the court to allow the action to proceed under section 33.

10.25   In *Nash* v. *Eli Lilly*,[58] on the other hand, Hidden J. observed that the discussion of this question in *Fowell* was *obiter* and that there was no binding authority as to whether facts ascertainable by a plaintiff with the help of legal advice fall within the terms of section 14(3)(*b*). His Lordship doubted whether ordinarily they do, but could envisage circumstances where they might: if, for example, the identification of a potential defendant turned upon the construction of legislation (*e.g.* the Committee on the Safety of Medicines and the Licensing Authority under the Medicines Act 1968). Moreover, Hidden J. came to the somewhat surprising conclusion that a plaintiff may be fixed with constructive knowledge of facts that his solicitor knows or ought reasonably to have known, because this falls within section 14(3)(*a*) as a fact "ascertainable by him." Thus, "ascertainable" would include facts ascertainable by the plaintiff personally and by others (including lawyers and doctors) ascertaining facts for him. On this interpretation it is not clear why there is any need for subsection 14(3)(*b*), which would appear to be subsumed within subsection 14(3)(*a*). This view would also seem to restore the application of the proviso to legal advice, at least if legal advice can be said to be "expert advice."

3. Court's discretion

10.26   A plaintiff has an indefeasible right to bring an action within the primary three-year limitation period. Where that period has expired the plaintiff may still be able to proceed if he can persuade the court to exercise its discretion under section 33 in his favour.

Availability of the discretion

10.27   In *Firman* v. *Ellis*[59] the Court of Appeal said that the court's discretion under section 33 was unfettered. It was not restricted to a residual category of exceptional cases. This view was approved by the House of Lords in *Thompson* v. *Brown Construction (Ebbw Vale) Ltd.*,[60] subject, however, to the ruling in *Walkley* v. *Precision Forgings Ltd.*[61] In *Walkley* the House of Lords distinguished between a plaintiff

---

[57] See the discussion in *Fowell* v. *National Coal Board*, *The Times*, May 28, 1986, where Parker L.J. specifically left this point open.
[58] [1991] 2 Med. L.R. 169.
[59] [1978] Q.B. 886.
[60] [1981] 2 All E.R. 296; see also *Donovan* v. *Gwentoys Ltd.* [1990] 1 All E.R. 1018, 1023, *per* Lord Griffiths.
[61] [1979] 1 W.L.R. 606.

who had not issued any proceedings within the primary three-year limitation period, who could invoke section 33, and a plaintiff who had issued a writ within the limitation period but who had not proceeded with the action, who could not. A second writ issued out of time would be statute-barred. In *Chappell* v. *Cooper*[62] the Court of Appeal held that *Walkley* would apply, whatever the reason the plaintiff did not proceed with the first action: whether because he or his solicitors failed to serve the writ in time;[63] or because the action was dismissed for want of prosecution; or, for good or bad reasons, the action was discontinued by the plaintiff.[64]

The reasoning behind this distinction is that section 33(1) directs the **10.28** court to have regard to the degree to which the operation of the primary limitation period has prejudiced the plaintiff, but where the plaintiff has issued a writ in time and then for some reason the action has not been pursued he has not been prejudiced by the effect of sections 11 or 12 but by his own dilatoriness. This argument could be applied, however, with as much force to some plaintiffs who have not issued proceedings within the primary limitation period who are prejudiced by their own dilatoriness, but they are at least permitted to argue that the discretion should be exercised. *Walkley* v. *Precision Forgings Ltd.* creates an arbitrary and unjustifiable distinction between categories of plaintiff who are permitted to seek the benefit of section 33.[65]

One exception to the rule in *Walkley* is where the plaintiff has been **10.29** induced to discontinue the action by a misrepresentation or other improper conduct by the defendant. The defendant is then estopped from relying on sections 11 or 12, and it is not a matter of judicial discretion under section 33. However, this exception will be construed narrowly, and does not arise merely from an admission of liability and the making of an interim payment by the defendant.[66] In the absence of an unequivocal agreement by the defendant to waive reliance upon the Limitation Act, it will be difficult to establish that the circumstances are exceptional.[67]

A second exception occurs where the first writ, although issued in **10.30** time, is technically invalid, and a second writ is subsequently issued outside the three-year period. In these circumstances the plaintiff is

---

[62] [1980] 2 All E.R. 463.

[63] See *Deerness* v. *John Keeble & Son Ltd.* [1983] 2 Lloyd's Rep. 260, H.L.

[64] This has implications for negligence claims against solicitors. For example, practitioners who issue the writ in time but carelessly fail to serve it within the 4 months allowed by R.S.C., Ord. 6, r. 8 are in a worse position than those who carelessly allow the primary limitation period to expire, since in the latter, but not the former, case the client has the option of making a section 33 application. If successful, this reduces the chances of the client making a claim in negligence against the solicitor; see Jones (1985) 1 P.N. 159.

[65] See Davies (1982) 98 L.Q.R. 249, 260–265; Morgan (1982) 1 C.J.Q. 109; Jones (1985) 1 P.N. 159, 160.

[66] See *Deerness* v. *John Keeble & Son Ltd.* [1983] 2 Lloyd's Rep. 260, where there had been no dispute on liability and the interim payment had not been made on a "without prejudice" basis. A writ had been issued within the 3-year period but not served, and a second writ issued out of time was held statute-barred by the House of Lords. An interim payment does not constitute an admission of liability, and, moreover, an admission of liability does not reset the "limitation clock."

[67] Note, however, that where the plaintiff's "error" consists of a failure to serve the writ within the period permitted by R.S.C., Ord. 6, r. 8(1) (as amended by S.I. 1989/2427) the court has a discretion to renew the validity of the writ; see § 10.60.

not caught by *Walkley* and can invoke the court's discretion.[68] This only serves to emphasise the completely arbitrary effect of the rule in *Walkley*.

10.31 A third apparent "exception" is where, although earlier proceedings have been commenced and discontinued, it can be said that the plaintiff did not *know* that his injury was capable of being attributed to the defendant's act or omission until much later, notwithstanding his firm belief that it was so attributable. In these circumstances *Walkley* is irrelevant, since the "second" writ will be within the *primary* limitation period. In *Stephen* v. *Riverside Health Authority*[69] a first, protective, writ had been issued in March 1980 (within three years of the incident) and a second writ was issued in February 1988. The plaintiff did not acquire knowledge, within the of meaning section 14, of the causal link between her injury and the defendants' negligence until February 1985, because she had been assured by several experts that her symptoms could not have been caused by the dose of radiation that she had received. Similarly, in *Davis* v. *Ministry of Defence*[70] the plaintiff's first medical and legal advisers had concluded that his dermatitis could not be attributed to the alleged negligence, but was constitutional. The Court of Appeal held that the plaintiff's contrary belief was not the same as knowledge for the purpose of section 14(1)(*b*), and until the plaintiff acquired the relevant knowledge the three-year period did not start to run. Thus, no question of the exercise of the discretion arose; the limitation period had simply not commenced, despite a previous writ.

Exercise of the discretion

10.32 Once it has been determined that the plaintiff is entitled to invoke section 33, it would seem that the court's discretion is completely unfettered.[71] Section 33(1) provides that the court may direct that the three-year period specified by sections 11 and 12 shall not apply if it would be equitable to allow the action to proceed, having regard to the degree to which (a) those sections prejudice the plaintiff, and (b) the decision to allow the action to proceed would prejudice the defendant. The court has to balance the degree of prejudice to the plaintiff caused by the operation of the primary limitation period against the prejudice to the defendant if the action were to be allowed to proceed. The stronger the plaintiff's case is on the merits the greater the prejudice to him, and conversely, the weaker his case the less he is prejudiced. On the other hand, if the defendant has a good case on the merits there is probably less prejudice to him in allowing the action to proceed, although in *Thompson* v. *Brown Construction (Ebbw Vale) Ltd.*[72] Lord

---

[68] *White* v. *Glass, The Times*, February 18, 1989, C.A.; *Wilson* v. *Banner Scaffolding Ltd., The Times*, June 22, 1982.

[69] [1990] 1 Med. L.R. 261.

[70] *The Times*, August 7, 1985; see also *Bentley* v. *Bristol and Western Health Authority, The Times*, December 6, 1990.

[71] *Thompson* v. *Brown Construction (Ebbw Vale) Ltd.* [1981] 2 All E.R. 296; *Donovan* v. *Gwentoys Ltd.* [1990] 1 All E.R. 1018, 1023.

[72] [1981] 2 All E.R. 296 at p. 301.

Diplock said that it was still highly prejudicial to a defendant to allow the action to proceed even where he has a good defence on the merits. It has been argued, and indeed apparently accepted in some cases, that the prejudice to the defendant is at its greatest when he has no defence on the merits since he has been deprived of a cast-iron (limitation) defence. This is not an attractive argument, however, since it undermines the whole rationale of giving the court a discretion to override the primary limitation period.[73] "Prejudice" to the defendant must mean more than simply the removal of the limitation defence.

When considering the degree of prejudice to the parties the court is **10.33** required by section 33(3) to

"have regard to all the circumstances of the case, and in particular to:

(*a*) the length of and reasons for the delay on the part of the plaintiff;

(*b*) the extent to which, having regard to the delay, the evidence . . . is likely to be less cogent . . . ;

(*c*) the conduct of the defendant after the cause of action arose, including the extent (if any) to which he responded to requests reasonably made by the plaintiff for information or inspection for the purpose of ascertaining facts which were or might be relevant to the plaintiff's cause of action against the defendant;

(*d*) the duration of any disability of the plaintiff arising after the date of the accrual of the cause of action;

(*e*) the extent to which the plaintiff acted promptly and reasonably once he knew whether or not the act or omission of the defendant, to which the injury was attributable, might be capable at that time of giving rise to an action for damages;

(*f*) the steps, if any, taken by the plaintiff to obtain medical, legal or other expert advice and the nature of any such advice he may have received."

It has been stressed by both the Court of Appeal and the House of Lords that the court should consider *all* the circumstances of the case, not simply the issues identified by section 33(3).[74] Provided this has been done, the Court of Appeal will be reluctant to interfere with the trial judge's exercise of discretion.[75]

(a) *Length of and reasons for delay*

"Delay" in subsection 33(3)(*a*) and (*b*) refers to the period between **10.34** the expiry of the primary limitation period and the issue of the writ, not the period between the accrual of the action or the plaintiff's "knowledge" and the issue of the writ.[76] However, in *Donovan* v.

---

[73] See Jones (1985) 1 P.N. 159, 162.

[74] *Taylor* v. *Taylor*, *The Times*, April 14, 1984, C.A.; *Donovan* v. *Gwentoys Ltd.* [1990] 1 All E.R. 1018.

[75] *Conry* v. *Simpson* [1983] 3 All E.R. 369; *Bradley* v. *Hanseatic Shipping Co. Ltd.* [1986] 2 Lloyd's Rep. 34. The court will overturn a judge's exercise of discretion only if it can be shown that he has "gone very wrong indeed": *per* Lawton L.J. at p. 38.

[76] *Thompson* v. *Brown Construction (Ebbw Vale) Ltd.* [1981] 2 All E.R. 296, 301; *Eastman* v. *London Country Bus Services Ltd.*, *The Times*, November 23, 1985, C.A.

Gwentoys Ltd.[77] the House of Lords, whilst agreeing with this interpretation of section 33(3), held that in weighing the degree of prejudice to the defendant the court was entitled to take into account the whole period of delay, including that within the primary limitation period, as part of all the circumstances of the case. The delay which their Lordships had in mind appears to be the delay between the commencement of the limitation period and notification to the defendant of the claim, rather than the issue of the writ, the object being to bar "thoroughly stale claims." Lord Griffiths said that:

> " . . . it must always be relevant to consider when the defendant first had notification of the claim and thus the opportunity he will have to meet the claim at the trial if he is not to be permitted to rely on his limitation defence."[78]

Thus, there will be a distinction between cases where the defendant was notified of the claim fairly promptly, and so had an opportunity to give it full consideration, but the limitation period has expired through an oversight by the plaintiff's solicitors,[79] and cases such as *Donovan* v. *Gwentoys Ltd.*, where the defendant first heard of the claim some five years after the accident and was not in a position to investigate it until six years after the events.[80]

10.35   A short delay probably causes little prejudice to the defendant,[81] whereas a delay of five or six years raises a rebuttable presumption of prejudice.[82] The length of the delay is probably of less significance than the reasons for the delay and the effect on the cogency of the evidence. Reasons for the delay will vary considerably, and whereas the plaintiff's subjective beliefs may be irrelevant to the question of his knowledge under section 14 they are relevant to the court's exercise of discretion.[83] The plaintiff may have been unaware of his legal rights[84]; or the injury may not have seemed so serious at first[85]; or he may have

---

[77] [1990] 1 All E.R. 1018.

[78] *Ibid.*, p. 1024. His Lordship added that to the extent that *Eastman* v. *London Country Bus Services Ltd.*, *The Times*, November 23, 1985 appears to cast doubt on this proposition, it should not be followed.

[79] As occurred in *Thompson* v. *Brown Construction (Ebbw Vale) Ltd.* [1981] 2 All E.R. 296; see also *Simpson* v. *Norwest Holst Southern Ltd.* [1980] 2 All E.R. 471, 478, where the claim was only 14 days out of time and the defendants had had an early opportunity of investigating the claim and getting their evidence together.

[80] [1990] 1 All E.R. 1018, 1024, *per* Lord Griffiths; *cf.* the position where the plaintiff is under a disability: the defendant may be seriously prejudiced in his ability to produce evidence, but this is irrelevant: see § 10.48, and *Bull* v. *Devon Area Health Authority* (1989) (unreported), C.A.

[81] *Firman* v. *Ellis* [1978] Q.B. 886; *Simpson* v. *Norwest Holst Southern Ltd.* [1980] 2 All E.R. 471, 478; *Atha* v. *ATV Network* (1983) (unreported), Q.B.D.; *cf. Davis* v. *Soltenpur* (1983) 133 New L.J. 720, where the writ was 24 days late, the defendant's case was "wholly without merit" but the discretion was not exercised in the plaintiff's favour.

[82] *Buck* v. *English Electric Co. Ltd.* [1977] 1 W.L.R. 806, a 9-year delay, but defendants not seriously prejudiced because in that period they had dealt with many similar claims and evidence was available; *Pilmore* v. *Northern Trawlers Ltd.* [1986] 1 Lloyd's Rep. 552 a 9-year delay; *cf. Cornish* v. *Kearley* (1983) 133 New L.J. 870, a 3-year delay, but the reasons for the delay were reasonable, the cogency of the evidence was affected but not greatly, and, in the circumstances, it was not unreasonable for the plaintiff to have delayed taking legal advice.

[83] *Buck* v. *English Electric Co. Ltd.* [1977] 1 W.L.R. 806; *McCafferty* v. *Metropolitan Police District Receiver* [1977] 1 W.L.R. 1073.

[84] *Brooks* v. *Coates (U.K.) Ltd.* [1984] 1 All E.R. 702, 713, where the delay was 15 years, but plaintiff's ignorance was not unreasonable.

[85] *McCafferty* v. *Metropolitan Police District Receiver* [1977] 1 W.L.R. 1073.

felt that he was "sponging" if he sued and may have wanted to maintain good relations with the defendant[86]; or the plaintiff may have been in a debilitated physical and mental state throughout the relevant period.[87] Generally, where the plaintiff's conduct has not been personally blameworthy this will carry considerable weight in persuading the court to exercise the discretion in his favour.[88]

(b) *Cogency of the evidence*

Usually it is the effect of the delay on the cogency of the evidence **10.36** which is most significant. If documents have been destroyed or witnesses have disappeared this is a different situation from cases where there is little real dispute about the facts, since the defendant's ability to defend the case has clearly been prejudiced.[89] Cases which are based on allegations about failures in systems of work are likely to be better documented than "one off" accidents,[90] although cases of medical negligence should, in theory, be reasonably well documented in the medical records.[91] It is not, however, simply a matter of assessing the effect of delay on the cogency of the *defendant's* evidence when assessing prejudice to the defendant. A lack of cogency in the plaintiff's evidence due to delay may be used to the advantage of the plaintiff, for example, in an attempt to explain away or mitigate the effects of omissions or contradictions in that evidence.[92]

(c) *Conduct of the defendant*

Section 33(3)(*c*) refers specifically to the extent to which the **10.37** defendant responded to reasonable requests for information or inspection for the purpose of ascertaining facts which were or might be relevant to the plaintiff's cause of action. A potential defendant does not have a duty to volunteer information but he should not obstruct the plaintiff in obtaining information.[93] This includes the conduct of the

---

[86] *Buck* v. *English Electric Co. Ltd.* [1977] 1 W.L.R. 806; *McCafferty* v. *Metropolitan Police District Receiver* [1977] 1 W.L.R. 1073. A patient's natural reluctance to upset the doctor/patient relationship by engaging in litigation will be relevant here.

[87] *Mills* v. *Dyer-Fare* (1987) (unreported), Q.B.D.; *Birnie* v. *Oxfordshire Health Authority* (1982) 2 *The Lancet* 281, Q.B.D.

[88] *Brooks* v. *Coates (U.K.) Ltd.* [1984] 1 All E.R. 702; *cf. Davies* v. *British Insulated Callender's Cables Ltd.* (1977) 121 S.J. 203, where the plaintiff had no good reason for the delay; discretion was refused.

[89] *Hattam* v. *National Coal Board* (1978) 122 S.J. 777; *cf. Brooks* v. *Coates (U.K.) Ltd.* [1984] 1 All E.R. 702, 713–714.

[90] See, *e.g., Cotton* v. *General Electric Co. Ltd.* (1979) 129 New L.J. 73; *Pilmore* v. *Northern Trawlers Ltd.* [1986] 1 Lloyd's Rep. 552; *Buck* v. *English Electric Co. Ltd.* [1977] 1 W.L.R. 806, where the evidence was no less cogent due to the delay because the defendants had dealt with a number of similar claims.

[91] See, *e.g., Bentley* v. *Bristol and Western Health Authority*, *The Times*, December 6, 1990; *Waghorn* v. *Lewisham and North Southwark Area Health Authority* (1987) (unreported), Q.B.D., where all the hospital records, with the exception of the nursing notes, had been preserved. In *Hills* v. *Potter* [1983] 3 All E.R. 716, 728 Hirst J. said that if the defendant's evidence was accepted then he had suffered no prejudice as a result of the delay. Since the defendant's evidence was accepted, and particularly having regard to the gravity of the plaintiff's injuries, it was proper to disapply the limitation bar.

[92] *Nash* v. *Eli Lilly* [1991] 2 Med. L.R. 169, *per* Hidden J.

[93] *Thompson* v. *Brown Construction (Ebbw Vale) Ltd.* [1981] 2 All E.R. 296, 302. A serious delay in providing the plaintiff's medical records may be a relevant consideration: *Mills* v. *Dyer-Fare* (1987) (unreported), Q.B.D.

defendant's solicitors and his insurers. The defendant's conduct is relevant even where he has made an honest mistake in giving misleading information.[94]

(d) Duration of the disability

10.38   If the plaintiff is under a disability at the date at which the cause of action accrued, the commencement of the limitation period is postponed until he ceases to be under a disability,[95] but supervening disability does not stop time running. It will be taken into account, however, in the exercise of the discretion. Since minority can never supervene, section 33(3)(d) applies only to supervening mental incapacity. Physical disability caused by the accident is not relevant under this heading, though it could be considered under section 33(3)(a) or as part of "all the circumstances of the case."

(e) Extent to which plaintiff acted promptly

10.39   If the plaintiff has acted promptly and reasonably once he became aware of the cause of action, it is not to be counted against him that his lawyers have been dilatory and allowed the primary limitation period to expire.[96] A potential claim against his solicitors, however, may reduce the degree of prejudice suffered by the plaintiff. It is obvious that the date at which the plaintiff became aware of the existence of a cause of action is not necessarily the same as the date of his "knowledge" for the purpose of section 14, and may well be later.[97]

(f) Steps taken to obtain expert advice

10.40   This includes legal advice and whether it was favourable or unfavourable.[98] Thus, while erroneous legal advice will not prevent time running under the three-year limitation period, it is relevant to the exercise of discretion.

(g) Other factors: availability of an alternative remedy

10.41   The availability of an alternative remedy (e.g. against the plaintiff's negligent solicitors) is a "highly relevant consideration," but it is not conclusive against the exercise of the discretion in the plaintiff's favour. Even where the plaintiff would have a cast iron case against his solicitors, he will suffer some prejudice, even if only minor, in having

---

[94] Marston v. British Railways Board [1976] I.C.R. 124; a fortiori where the defendant has deliberately misled the plaintiff: see, e.g., Scuriaga v. Powell (1979) 123 S.J. 406, § 10.15, a case where the defendant's conduct prevented the plaintiff from acquiring knowledge of the relevant facts under s.14.

[95] Limitation Act 1980, s.28, see § 10.48.

[96] Thompson v. Brown Construction (Ebbw Vale) Ltd. [1981] 2 All E.R. 296, 303.

[97] Eastman v. London Country Bus Services Ltd., The Times, November 23, 1985, C.A.

[98] Jones v. G. D. Searle & Co. Ltd. [1978] 3 All E.R. 654. The plaintiff can be required to disclose the nature of the advice he received. See also Halford v. Brookes [1991] 3 All E.R. 559, where the delay was attributable to the plaintiff being advised that her only civil remedy was against the Criminal Injuries Compensation Board. As soon as she was advised that there was another remedy she acted promptly in issuing a writ.

to find and instruct new solicitors, together with additional delay and a possible personal liability for costs up to the date of the court's refusal of the application.[99] Where there is any real dispute about the solicitors' liability in negligence then the chances of the plaintiff having an alternative remedy should be largely disregarded.[1]

Where the plaintiff has already changed solicitors there is less **10.42** prejudice to him if the discretion is not exercised, even in the case of a short delay,[2] and *a fortiori* where the plaintiff has already commenced proceedings against his former solicitors.[3] In *Conry* v. *Simpson*,[4] however, the Court of Appeal refused to interfere with the trial judge's exercise of discretion in favour of the plaintiff, although the writ had been issued three years and 10 months out of time and an action against the former solicitors had been commenced. Stephenson L.J. commented that it is very seldom that a remedy against a solicitor can be as satisfactory as a remedy against the original tortfeasor. On the other hand, in *Donovan* v. *Gwentoys Ltd.*[5] Lord Griffiths said that the plaintiff would suffer "only the slightest prejudice" if she were required to pursue her remedy against her solicitors, although in that case there was severe prejudice to the defendant caused by the delay in notification of a claim.

Other factors may also be relevant to the court's exercise of **10.43** discretion. It is legitimate to take into account the insurance position of both defendant and plaintiff, as part of all the circumstances of the case.[6] The court will not apply different principles to multi-party litigation, however, from the principles applied to ordinary, single plaintiff actions when exercising the discretion. The merits of each case must be considered individually.[7] It has been suggested that the fact that a medical negligence action is a claim for professional negligence may be an additional factor in the defendant's favour when the court considers the exercise of discretion, because such actions have more serious consequences for defendants and should be prosecuted without delay.[8] In *Biss* v. *Lambeth Health Authority*[9] the Court of Appeal held, in the somewhat analogous context of an application to strike out an action for want of prosecution, that there was prejudice to the defendants in the worry that professional staff would suffer with the action hanging over them like the "sword of Damocles," although it would be exceptional to treat the "mere sword of Damocles, hanging for an unnecessary period" as a sufficient reason in itself to strike out.[10]

---

[99] *Thompson* v. *Brown Construction (Ebbw Vale) Ltd.* [1981] 2 All E.R. 296, 301–302. He might prefer to sue the real tortfeasor, said Lord Diplock, rather than his former solicitors. Query, however, why the plaintiff's *preferences* should have any bearing on the balance of prejudice between plaintiff and defendant.

[1] *Firman* v. *Ellis* [1978] Q.B. 886, 916, *per* Geoffrey Lane L.J., who added that it was undesirable that there should be any detailed enquiry into the question of the solicitors' negligence; see generally Jones (1985) 1 P.N. 159.

[2] *Straw* v. *Hicks* (1983) (unreported), C.A.

[3] *Mills* v. *Ritchie* (1984) (unreported), Q.B.D.

[4] [1983] 3 All E.R. 369.

[5] [1990] 1 All E.R. 1018.

[6] *Firman* v. *Ellis* [1978] Q.B. 886, 916; *Liff* v. *Peasley* [1980] 1 W.L.R. 781, 789.

[7] *Nash* v. *Eli Lilly* [1991] 2 Med. L.R. 169.

[8] Jackson and Powell, *Professional Negligence*, 1987, 2nd ed., para. 1.79.

[9] [1978] 1 W.L.R. 382.

[10] *Department of Transport* v. *Chris Smaller (Transport) Ltd.* [1989] 1 All E.R. 897, 905, *per* Lord Griffiths.

4. Death

(i) Fatal Accidents Act 1976

10.44   In an action for loss of dependency under the Fatal Accidents Act 1976 if the death occurred before the expiry of the deceased's three-year limitation period, then a new three-year period commences in favour of the dependants. This period runs from the date of death or the date of the dependants' "knowledge," whichever is later.[11] If there is more than one dependant and their dates of knowledge are different, time runs separately against each of them.[12] If the Fatal Accidents action is not commenced within three years of the death or the date of knowledge of the dependants the action is barred.[13] The court may "disapply" the provisions of section 12, however, by virtue of its discretion under section 33, in which case the guidelines of section 33(3) have effect as if references to the plaintiff (usually the personal representative) included references to the dependants.

10.45   If the deceased's three-year limitation period had expired before he died, then, in theory, he could not have maintained an action at the date of his death and the dependants' action is barred by section 12(1). For this purpose no account is taken of the possibility that the deceased might have made a successful application to override the fixed period under section 33. However, section 33 applies to the Fatal Accidents Act and the court can exercise its discretion and direct that section 12(1) of the Limitation Act 1980 and section 1(1) of the Fatal Accidents Act 1976 shall not apply. In exercising its discretion the court must have regard to the length of and reasons for the delay on the part of the deceased.[14] The court may disapply section 12 only where the reason why the deceased could no longer maintain an action was because of the time limit in section 11.[15] If he could no longer maintain an action for any other reason the court has no discretion to allow the dependants' action to proceed.

(ii) Law Reform (Miscellaneous Provisions) Act 1934

10.46   The position in the case of an action on behalf of the estate of a deceased person under the Law Reform (Miscellaneous Provisions) Act 1934 is similar to that which applies to Fatal Accident Act claims. If the deceased died before the expiry of his three-year limitation period, a new three-year period commences which runs from either the date of death or the date of the personal representative's knowledge, whichever is later.[16] If there is more than one personal representative and their dates of knowledge are different, time runs from the earliest date.[17] If this period expires the personal representative may invoke

---

[11] Limitation Act 1980, s.12. "Knowledge" is defined in s.14; see § 10.11.
[12] *Ibid.*, s.13(1).
[13] *Ibid.*, s.12(2).
[14] Limitation Act 1980, s.33(4).
[15] *Ibid.*, s.33(2).
[16] *Ibid.*, s.11(5).
[17] *Ibid.*, s.11(7); *cf.* the position with dependants under the Fatal Accidents Act, where time runs separately against each dependant: s.13(1).

section 33 requesting the court to exercise its discretion to override the effect of section 11(5).

Where the deceased died after the expiry of his three-year limitation **10.47** period an action by his personal representative is barred by section 11(3), but the court can exercise its discretion under section 33 in favour of the personal representative, again having regard to the length of and the reasons for the delay by the deceased.

5. Persons under a disability

A person is under a disability while he is an infant or of unsound **10.48** mind.[18] An infant is a person under the age of 18,[19] and a person is of unsound mind if, by reason of mental disorder within the meaning of the Mental Health Act 1983, he is incapable of managing and administering his property and affairs.[20] If a person to whom a right of action accrues is under a disability at the date when the action accrued, time does not run until he ceases to be under a disability or dies, whichever occurs first.[21] Thus, an infant has an indefeasible right to bring an action for personal injuries at any time before the age of 21,[22] and a person of unsound mind has three years from the date he becomes sane. There is, of course, nothing to stop a person under a disability bringing an action while still under the disability. If the accident itself caused immediate unsoundness of mind time will not begin to run.[23]

If the plaintiff was not under a disability when the action accrued, **10.49** supervening unsoundness of mind will not prevent time running.[24] This applies even where the supervening disability arose before the plaintiff's date of knowledge under section 14.[25] The apparent harshness of this rule may be mitigated by the court's exercise of discretion under section 33(3)(d).

6. Deliberate concealment

Where any fact relevant to the plaintiff's right of action has been **10.50** deliberately concealed from him by the defendant, the limitation

---

[18] *Ibid.*, s.38(2).

[19] Family Law Reform Act 1969, s.1.

[20] Limitation Act 1980, s.38(3). Under the Mental Health Act 1983, s.1(2) mental disorder is defined as "mental illness, arrested or incomplete development of the mind, psychopathic disorder, and any other disorder or disability of mind." Mental illness does not necessarily mean that the plaintiff was incapable of managing his affairs, and if he is capable of managing his affairs s.28 does not apply: *Dawson* v. *Scott-Brown* (1988) (unreported), C.A.

[21] Limitation Act 1980, s.28(1), (6). This assumes, of course, that the plaintiff has the relevant "knowledge" under s.14. If not, then time will not run until he acquires knowledge. If the person under a disability dies the primary limitation period starts to run, and there can be no further extension under s.28, even if the person to whom the cause of action accrues is himself under a disability: s.28(3).

[22] *Tolley* v. *Morris* [1979] 2 All E.R. 561.

[23] *Kirby* v. *Leather* [1965] 2 Q.B. 367, C.A. This applies if the unsoundness of mind arises at any time before the end of the day on which the accident occurred.

[24] *Purnell* v. *Roche* [1927] 2 Ch. 142.

[25] Except that in a case of latent damage which does not involve a claim for personal injuries, where the plaintiff was under a disability at the "starting date" (as defined in s.14A(5) of the Limitation Act 1980) the limitation period is extended to 3 years from the date when the plaintiff ceased to be under a disability or dies (whichever occurred first), subject to the overall longstop specified in s.14B of 15 years from the date of breach of duty: Limitation Act 1980, s.28A.

period does not begin to run until the plaintiff has discovered the concealment or could with reasonable diligence have discovered it.[26] This provision is not limited to fraud in a technical sense, but includes the deliberate commission of a breach of duty in circumstances in which it is unlikely to be discovered for some time.[27] An assurance to the plaintiff by the defendant that there is "nothing to worry about" when the plaintiff raises a query about facts which might indicate that the defendant has been negligent may constitute deliberate concealment, or, alternatively, the defendant is estopped from raising the limitation defence.[28] In most cases of "deliberate concealment" in personal injuries actions the plaintiff will simply not have the knowledge required under section 14 of the Limitation Act 1980 to start the limitation period running.[29] Deliberate concealment under section 32 might possibly be relevant where the claim is not categorised as an action for personal injuries, since the limitation period runs from the date of accrual of the cause of action not the plaintiff's date of knowledge, unless the damage is latent.

7. Defective products

10.51   Special rules in respect of limitation periods apply to claims brought under the Consumer Protection Act 1987.[30] The plaintiff has three years within which to bring an action, running from either the date on which the action accrued (*i.e.* when the damage occurred) or, if later, the date of his "knowledge."[31] Knowledge is defined in similar terms to that for ordinary personal injuries claims, to include the fact that the damage was significant, that it was caused by the defect and the identity of the defendant.[32] The plaintiff's ignorance that as a matter of law the product was defective is irrelevant and does not prevent time running.

10.52   These rules apply both to personal injuries and property damage claims brought under the Consumer Protection Act 1987. In the case of personal injuries, however, the court has a discretion under the Limitation Act 1980, s.33 to override the three-year limit and allow the action to proceed. But these limitation periods are subject to an overall longstop which expires 10 years after the product was put into circulation by the defendant.[33] The longstop is an absolute bar, even in cases where there has been deliberate concealment or the plaintiff was

---

[26] Limitation Act 1980, s.32(1). "Defendant" includes the defendant's agent and any person through whom the defendant claims and his agent.

[27] *Ibid.*, s.32(2). This includes the commission of a wrong knowingly or recklessly, but negligence is not sufficient. See, however, *Kitchen* v. *Royal Air Force Association* [1958] 1 W.L.R. 563. The non-disclosure to the plaintiff of a medical report prepared by the defendant for the plaintiff's employers does not amount to deliberate concealment: *Dawson* v. *Scott-Brown* (1988) (unreported), C.A.

[28] *Westlake* v. *Bracknell District Council* (1987) 282 E.G. 868.

[29] See *Scuriaga* v. *Powell* (1979) 123 S.J. 406; aff'd 1980 (unreported), C.A., § 10.15. Claims under the Fatal Accidents Act 1976 are specifically excluded from the provisions of s.32: Limitation Act 1980, s.12(3).

[30] Consumer Protection Act 1987, Sched. 1, amending the Limitation Act 1980.

[31] Limitation Act 1980 s.11A(4).

[32] *Ibid.*, s.14(1A); *cf.* s.14(1).

[33] Limitation Act 1980, s.11A(3).

under a disability, and the court has no discretion to override this limit in personal injuries cases, even where the damage had not occurred by the end of the 10-year period. A plaintiff caught by the longstop (a situation which could arise with certain types of drug injury) will have to sue in negligence in order to invoke the court's discretion, since other forms of action are not subject to this longstop.

8. Latent damage

The vast majority of medical negligence actions involve claims in **10.53** respect of personal injuries, but in some circumstances a doctor's negligence may cause purely financial loss.[34] In this situation the ordinary six-year limitation period under section 2 (tort) or section 5 (contract) of the Limitation Act 1980 would normally apply. Where, however, the plaintiff is unaware that he has sustained any damage or loss he may be able to rely on an extended limitation period applicable to cases of latent damage. If, for example, as a result of a negligent diagnosis the doctor wrongly advised the patient that he was medically unfit to carry out a particular type of work and the patient took a lower paid job, he would have suffered a continuing loss of earnings. If more than six years later the patient discovered the error he might be faced with the argument that the six-year limitation period has already expired.[35]

The Latent Damage Act 1986 introduced a special extension of the **10.54** ordinary six-year limitation period in tort[36] in cases of latent damage (other than personal injuries). The plaintiff has three years from the date on which he discovered or ought reasonably to have discovered significant damage, subject to an overall "longstop" which bars all claims brought more than 15 years from the date of the defendant's negligence.[37] The limitation period is six years from the date on which the action accrued or three years from the "starting date," whichever expires later.[38] The starting date is the earliest date on which the plaintiff (or any person in whom the cause of action was vested before him) first had both a right to bring the action, and knowledge of: (a) the material facts about the damage, (b) that the damage was caused by the defendant's negligence, (c) the identity of the defendant, and (d) if the negligence was that of a person other than the defendant, the identity of that person and the facts supporting an action against the

---

[34] See §§ 2.24–2.25, 2.69.

[35] This example could raise problems, however, as to precisely when the cause of action accrued, since it involves a continuing loss. In cases of negligent professional (usually legal) advice the courts have tended to the view that the plaintiff sustains damage when he acts in reliance on the advice by entering into the particular transaction, not when the subsequent financial loss occurs, the damage consisting of a contingent liability to future loss for which the plaintiff could have sued immediately: see *Forster* v. *Oughtred & Co.* [1982] 1 W.L.R. 86; *D. W. Moore & Co. Ltd.* v. *Ferrier* [1988] 1 All E.R. 400; *Bell* v. *Peter Browne & Co.* [1990] 3 All E.R. 124; *cf. Midland Bank Trust Co. Ltd.* v. *Hett, Stubbs & Kemp* [1979] Ch. 384.

[36] The provisions do not apply to claims in contract: *Iron Trade Mutual Insurance Co. Ltd.* v. *J. K. Buckenham Ltd.* [1990] 1 All E.R. 808.

[37] Latent Damage Act 1986, s.1, inserting new ss.14A and 14B into the Limitation Act 1980.

[38] Limitation Act 1980, s.14A(3), (4).

defendant.[39] Material facts are such facts about the damage as would lead a reasonable person who had suffered such damage to consider it sufficiently serious to justify instituting proceedings for damages against a defendant who did not dispute liability and was able to satisfy a judgment.[40] As with the scheme for personal injuries the plaintiff's ignorance that as a matter of law he has a cause of action does not prevent time running,[41] and the plaintiff will be fixed with constructive knowledge, including the knowledge of experts.[42]

10.55　Section 14B provides that an action for damages for negligence (other than for personal injuries) shall not be brought more than 15 years from the date of the act or omission which is alleged to constitute negligence. This overrides section 14A, and it is irrelevant that the cause of action may not yet have accrued (*i.e.* no damage has occurred) or that the starting date has not yet occurred (*i.e.* the damage is still latent).[43]

9. Contribution proceedings

10.56　In contribution proceedings the limitation period is two years from the date of judgment or settlement, even if the plaintiff's claim against the defendant would be statute-barred.[44]

10. New claims in pending actions

10.57　A new claim made in the course of any action is deemed to be a separate action and to have been commenced, in the case of third party proceedings, on the date on which those proceedings were commenced, and in the case of any other new claim, on the same date as the original proceedings.[45] A "new claim" is any claim by way of set-off or counter-claim, any claim involving the addition or substitution of a new cause of action or a new party, and a claim made in or by way of third party proceedings.[46] By section 35(3) of the Limitation Act 1980

---

[39] *Ibid.*, s.14A(5), (6) and (8).

[40] *Ibid.*, s.14A(7).

[41] *Ibid.*, s.14A(9).

[42] *Ibid.*, s.14A(10). The plaintiff will not be fixed with knowledge of a fact ascertainable only with the help of expert advice so long as he has taken all reasonable steps to obtain, and where appropriate act on, that advice: *ibid.*

[43] The provisions in section 32 concerning deliberate concealment are not, however, subject to the longstop: see § 10.50. Sections 14A and 14B do not apply to actions commenced or claims barred before they came into force on September 18, 1986.

[44] Limitation Act 1980, s.10. Where, however, the expiry of the plaintiff's limitation period extinguishes the plaintiff's right of action against the defendant the right to contribution is lost: Civil Liability (Contribution) Act 1978, s.1(3). Most limitation periods do not extinguish the plaintiff's right, but merely bar his remedy. An exception is the 10-year longstop applied to claims for defective products under the Limitation Act 1980, s.11A(3) which does bar the plaintiff's right of action. See further § 7.36.

[45] *Ibid.*, s.35(1).

[46] *Ibid.*, s.35(2) and (1)(*a*). "Third party proceedings" means any proceedings brought in the course of any action by any party to the action against a person not previously a party to the action; other than proceedings brought by joining any such person as a defendant to any claim already made in the original action by the party bringing the action: *ibid.*, s.35(2). Thus, a claim for contribution between existing defendants to an action does not constitute third party proceedings, and they are deemed by s.35(1)(*b*) to have been commenced on the same date as the original action: *Kennett* v. *Brown* [1988] 2 All E.R. 600.

the court cannot allow a new claim, other than an original set-off or counter-claim to be made in a pending action after the expiry of a limitation period which would affect a new action to enforce that claim. The court does not have a discretion to allow amendments to add or substitute a new cause of action or a new party to an existing action, except in three situations: first, where the court exercises its discretion under section 33 to disapply the provisions of sections 12 or 13 in a personal injuries action; secondly, where the claim involves a new cause of action, if the new cause arises out of the same or substantially the same facts as are already in issue on a claim previously made in the original action; and thirdly, in the case of a claim involving a new party, if the addition or substitution of the new party is necessary for the determination of the original action.[47]

11. Burden of proof

The defendant must plead the limitation period in his defence if he **10.58** seeks to rely on it,[48] though he is not obliged to take the point and the court will not do so if the defendant omits it.[49] There is some uncertainty about who has the burden of proof as to whether the action is or is not statute barred. Logically, if limitation is considered to be a defence, the burden of proving that the claim is out of time should rest with the defendant. This view has been adopted on more than one occasion.[50] On the other hand, the Court of Appeal has also stated that the burden of proof lies with the plaintiff.[51] This approach could cause difficulty, since the plaintiff would have to prove a series of negatives in order to show the absence of knowledge.[52] In *Fowell* v. *National Coal Board*,[53] a case involving personal injuries, Parker L.J. said that as limitation is a matter of defence, it must be for the person setting up limitation to assert and prove that the claim is time barred, which, in the first instance, requires no more than proof that the three-year period has elapsed. If this period has elapsed but the plaintiff wishes to argue that the date of knowledge was later, it is for him to assert and give evidence that he first had knowledge of the relevant

---

[47] *Ibid.*, s.35(3)–(6); R.S.C., Ord. 15, r. 6(5), (6); R.S.C., Ord. 20, r. 5(3), (5). On the inter-relationship between s.35(3) and s.33 see *Kennett* v. *Brown* [1988] 2 All E.R. 600.

[48] R.S.C., Ord. 18, r. 8(1). If the defendant considers that he has a good limitation defence his proper course is either to plead the defence and seek a trial of the defence as a preliminary issue, or, in a very clear case, to apply to strike out the claim on the ground that it is frivolous and vexatious and an abuse of the process of the court, but he cannot seek to strike out the claim on the ground that it discloses no reasonable cause of action: *Ronex Properties Ltd.* v. *John Laing Construction Ltd.* [1982] 3 All E.R. 961. Given the availability of the discretion under s.33 of the Limitation Act 1980, it will rarely be possible, in a personal injuries action, to say that the case is "very clear."

[49] See *Kennett* v. *Brown* [1988] 2 All E.R. 600.

[50] *Darley Main Colliery Co.* v. *Mitchell* (1886) 11 App.Cas. 127, 135; *O'Connor* v. *Isaacs* [1956] 2 Q.B. 288, 364; *The Pendrecht* [1980] 2 Lloyd's Rep. 56, 60.

[51] See *Cartledge* v. *Jopling & Sons Ltd.* [1962] 1 Q.B. 189; *London Congregational Union Inc.* v. *Harriss & Harriss* [1988] 1 All E.R. 15; see also *Nash* v. *Eli Lilly* [1991] 2 Med. L.R. 169, Q.B.D., where it was said that the preliminary burden of establishing that a case falls within the limitation period rests with the plaintiff, but thereafter, in relation to the question of a plaintiff's constructive knowledge, the burden falls upon the defendant.

[52] See *Supreme Court Practice* 1988, Vol. 2, para. 6152.

[53] *The Times*, May 28, 1986.

facts under section 14(1) of the Act on a date later than the accrual of the cause of action. If, however, the defendant wishes to displace this by asserting an earlier date of knowledge, it was for him to do so.

10.59   Where the plaintiff makes an application under section 33 to disapply the primary limitation period the burden of proving that it is just and equitable to allow the action to proceed is the plaintiff's.[54]

12. Issuing the writ

10.60   Issuing the writ in effect stops the limitation period from running, but it must be valid, and the plaintiff cannot proceed on an invalid writ. Once the writ has been issued it must normally be served on the defendant within four months, or it ceases to be valid.[55] There is generally no point in delaying service of the writ, particularly since interest on general damages only runs from the date of service.[56] The court has the power to extend the validity of the writ for periods of up to four months at a time,[57] but the court will not normally exercise its discretion to renew if the effect would be to deprive the defendant of the benefit of an accrued limitation period.[58] The fact that in cases of personal injuries the court has a discretion to extend the limitation period under section 33 of the Limitation Act 1980, does not alter the rules on the exercise of discretion to extend the period for service of the writ.[59]

10.61   At one time the view was that the time for service of a writ would be extended only in exceptional circumstances, but it is now clear, following the decision of the House of Lords in *Kleinwort Benson Ltd.* v. *Barbrak Ltd.*,[60] that the power to extend the validity of a writ under R.S.C., Ord. 6, r. 8 is not limited to exceptional circumstances. The test is whether there is a good reason to do so, balancing the hardship to the parties. The plaintiff must first provide an adequate explanation for the failure to serve the writ, and where an application for an extension is made when the writ has ceased to be valid and the relevant limitation period has expired, he must also give a satisfactory explanation of his failure to apply for an extension before the expiry of the validity of the writ. Difficulty in effecting service of the writ is not the only ground upon which the court can exercise its discretion to extend the validity of the writ. A good explanation for omitting to

---

[54] *Thompson* v. *Brown Construction (Ebbw Vale) Ltd.* [1981] 2 All E.R. 296, 303.

[55] R.S.C., Ord. 6, r. 8(1), as amended by S.I. 1989/2427.

[56] See § 9.19.

[57] R.S.C., Ord. 6, r. 8(2), as amended by S.I. 1989/2427. It should not be assumed that an extension will be granted to the maximum period of 4 months. The plaintiff must show that the period of time requested is justified: *Baly* v. *Barrett, The Times*, May 19, 1989, H.L.

[58] *Heaven* v. *Road and Rail Wagons Ltd.* [1965] 2 Q.B. 355; *Austin Rover Group Ltd.* v. *Crouch Butler Savage Associates* [1986] 1 W.L.R. 1102, 1112, C.A. This rule applies even where it cannot be said with certainty that the defendant's limitation defence would succeed. In the absence of special circumstances, if there is a real likelihood or substantial risk that renewal of the writ would deprive the defendant of a good limitation defence the court should not renew the writ: *Wilkinson* v. *Ancliff (BLT) Ltd.* [1986] 3 All E.R. 427, 436.

[59] See *Chappell* v. *Cooper* [1980] 2 All E.R. 463.

[60] [1987] 2 All E.R. 289.

serve the writ could be the saving of unnecessary proceedings and costs, without prejudice to the defendant. If the plaintiff provides an adequate explanation, the court will then weigh the balance of hardship.

The balance of hardship does not in itself constitute good reason for **10.62** extending the validity of a writ, rather where there are matters which could constitute good reason, the balance of hardship may be a relevant consideration in deciding whether an extension should be granted or refused.[61] Moreover, where the court has to exercise its discretion on an application for an extension of the validity of the writ in a personal injury case, there is no obligation to deal with the matter in the same way and by reference to the same principles applied where a plaintiff seeks a discretionary extension of the primary limitation period under section 33 of the Limitation Act 1980.[62]

An express or implied agreement between the parties to defer **10.63** service of the writ is good reason for extending the validity of the writ.[63] The mere fact that negotiations for a settlement are in progress is not necessarily a sufficient reason for failing to serve the writ nor is it a good reason for renewing it,[64] but where there have been co-operative negotiations between plaintiff and defendant conducted on the basis that neither party would take technical objections, then the delay in service of the writ has been contributed to by the defendant and an agreement that service of the writ be deferred may be implied.[65] Similarly, the period for service will be extended where the delay has been contributed to by the defendant because he has given an assurance to the plaintiff that the writ need not be served,[66] or he has evaded service,[67] or the plaintiff has been misled.[68] On the other hand, the fact that the defendant knew that a writ had been issued and that a claim existed, and the fact that he is unable to show any detriment or prejudice in the conduct of his defence,[69] that the failure to serve the writ was an accident or mistake,[70] that the plaintiff was awaiting the outcome of a test case,[71] or that there was delay in obtaining Legal Aid[72] have all been held not to be sufficient grounds for the court to exercise its discretion in the plaintiff's favour.

---

[61] *Waddon* v. *Whitecroft-Scovill* [1988] 1 All E.R. 996, 1003, H.L.
[62] *Ibid.*, p. 1001.
[63] *Heaven* v. *Road and Rail Wagons Ltd.* [1965] 2 Q.B. 355, 365.
[64] *Easy* v. *Universal Anchorage* [1974] 2 All E.R. 1105.
[65] *Hare* v. *Personal Representatives of Mohammed Yunis Malik* (1980) 124 S.J. 328, C.A.
[66] *North* v. *Kirk* (1967) 111 S.J. 793, C.A.
[67] *Heaven* v. *Road and Rail Wagons Ltd.* [1965] 2 Q.B. 355, 365; *Siksnys* v. *Hanley*, *The Times*, May 26, 1982, where the defendant was "elusive."
[68] *Howells* v. *Jones* (1975) 119 S.J. 577, where misleading information as to the defendant's whereabouts was given not by the defendant but by his former employers.
[69] *Heaven* v. *Road and Rail Wagons Ltd.* [1965] 2 Q.B. 355, 365.
[70] *Baker* v. *Bowketts Cakes Ltd.* [1966] 2 All E.R. 290; *Wilkinson* v. *Ancliff (BLT) Ltd.* [1986] 3 All E.R. 427.
[71] *Osborne* v. *Distillers Co. Ltd.* (1967) 112 S.J. 50, C.A.
[72] *Stevens* v. *Services Window and General Cleaning Co. Ltd.* [1967] 1 All E.R. 984. See, however, *Waddon* v. *Whitecroft-Scovill* [1988] 1 All E.R. 996, 1002, H.L., where Lord Brandon rejected the suggestion that, as a matter of law, delays caused by the operation of the Legal Aid system should never be taken into account: "Such delays occur and where they do it would be unrealistic to disregard their effect."

II. DISMISSAL FOR WANT OF PROSECUTION

10.64 Limitation periods are meant to encourage plaintiffs to issue proceed-ings promptly, and in effect they penalise delay prior to the commen-cement of the action. Delay can occur, however, after the action has been started and the court has power under its inherent jurisdiction to dismiss an action for want of prosecution if there has been default in complying with the Rules of the Supreme Court or excessive delay in prosecuting the action.[73] There are two grounds for exercising this power: (i) intentional and contumelious default in complying with a peremptory order of the court, *e.g.*, disobedience to a peremptory order of the court or conduct amounting to an abuse of the process of the court; and (ii) inordinate and inexcusable delay on the part of the plaintiff or his lawyers which gives rise to a substantial risk that a fair trial will not be possible, or is likely to cause or has caused serious prejudice to the defendant or a third party.[74]

10.65 The court will not normally exercise its power to strike out an action for want of prosecution on the ground of inordinate delay while the limitation period is still running, because the plaintiff could simply issue another writ.[75] In *Tolley* v. *Morris*[76] there was a delay of nine years which was "inordinate and inexcusable" but the House of Lords held that as the limitation period did not expire until the plaintiff reached the age of 21 there was no power to strike out. On the other hand, in a personal injuries action the possibility that the plaintiff could invoke section 33 of the Limitation Act 1980, asking the court to exercise its discretion to allow the action to proceed out of time, does not prevent the court striking out for want of prosecution where the primary three-year limitation period has expired.[77] Moreover, where the plaintiff is guilty of a contumelious failure to comply with a peremptory order of the court and the action has been dismissed for want of prosecution, in the absence of some explanation by the plaintiff, the court can exercise its discretion to strike out a second writ issued within the limitation period as an abuse of the process of the court under R.S.C., Ord. 18, r. 9.[78] Furthermore, in *Barclays Bank plc.* v. *Miller*[79] the Court of Appeal considered that, although the court would not normally accede to an application to dismiss for want of prosecution if the limitation period has not expired, where it was open to serious argument whether the claim would be time-barred

---

[73] The court also has express power to dismiss for want of prosecution under R.S.C., Ord. 19, r. 1; Ord. 24, r. 16(1); Ord. 25, r. 1(4); and Ord. 34, r. 2.

[74] *Allen* v. *Sir Alfred McApline & Sons Ltd.* [1968] 2 Q.B. 229; *Birkett* v. *James* [1978] A.C. 297, 318.

[75] *Birkett* v. *James* [1978] A.C. 297, H.L.; *a fortiori* where the defendant joined in continuing the action after notice of intention to proceed and subsequently applied to strike out for want of prosecution within the limitation period: *Simpson* v. *Smith, The Times,* January 19, 1989, C.A.

[76] [1979] 2 All E.R. 561.

[77] *Walkley* v. *Precision Forgings Ltd.* [1979] 1 W.L.R. 606.

[78] *Janov* v. *Morris* [1981] 1 W.L.R. 1389, C.A.; see also *Palmer* v. *Birks* (1985) 135 New L.J. 1256, C.A. Differing views had been expressed in the House of Lords on this point in *Birkett* v. *James* [1978] A.C. 297 and *Tolley* v. *Morris* [1979] 2 All E.R. 561.

[79] [1990] 1 W.L.R. 343; see also *Wright* v. *Morris* (1990) (unreported), C.A., distinguishing *Birkett* v. *James* [1978] A.C. 297 and striking out an action for inordinate and inexcusable delay because it was "clear" that a new action would not be started even though the limitation period had not yet expired.

the court will dismiss the action, leaving the claimant to institute fresh proceedings if he chooses to do so, at which point the limitation issue could be considered.

In considering whether to dismiss for want of prosecution the court **10.66** will consider the prejudice to the defendant caused by the delay, but in assessing prejudice the court should consider only the delay after the issue of the writ, not delay before the start of proceedings.[80] This does not apply, however, in a personal injuries action where the plaintiff has been permitted to continue the action by virtue of the exercise of discretion under section 33 of the Limitation Act 1980. If the writ is issued outside the primary limitation period, and then there is inexcusable delay, the court will consider the totality of the delay, not just the delay after the issue of the writ.[81] Moreover, in any case where the defendant is prejudiced by delay within the limitation period he will only have to show something more than minimal additional prejudice as a result of delay after the issue of the writ.[82] The possibility that the plaintiff might have an alternative remedy against negligent solicitors is not a relevant consideration in an application to strike out for want of prosecution,[83] but it has been held that the worry that professional staff would suffer with an action hanging over them like the "sword of Damocles" can constitute prejudice to the defendant.[84]

III. ACCESS TO HEALTH RECORDS

Although it has long been recognised that a doctor owes a duty of **10.67** confidence with respect to information concerning the patient arising out of the doctor/patient relationship, so that a patient can restrain the unauthorised disclosure of his medical records to third parties, the common law never established a right for the patient to demand access to his own medical records.[85] Patients now have statutory rights of

---

[80] *Birkett* v. *James* [1978] A.C. 297; *Department of Transport* v. *Chris Smaller (Transport) Ltd.* [1989] 1 All E.R. 897, H.L.

[81] *Biss* v. *Lambeth Health Authority* [1978] 1 W.L.R. 382, C.A.

[82] *Department of Transport* v. *Chris Smaller (Transport) Ltd.* [1989] 1 All E.R. 897, H.L.; *Mansouri* v. *Bloomsbury Health Authority*, *The Times*, July 20, 1987, C.A.,— where there is a long delay in issuing the writ within the primary limitation period, subsequent delay in prosecuting the action will more readily be regarded as inordinate on an application to strike out for want of prosecution.

[83] *Birkett* v. *James* [1978] A.C. 297; *cf.* applications under s.33 of the Limitation Act 1980, see §§ 10.41–10.42.

[84] *Biss* v. *Lambeth Health Authority* [1978] 1 W.L.R. 382. This view was regarded as exceptional, however, by the House of Lord in *Department of Transport* v. *Chris Smaller (Transport) Ltd.* [1989] 1 All E.R. 897, 905; see also *Electricity Supply Nominees Ltd.* v. *Longstaff and Shaw Ltd.* (1986) 3 Const. L.J. 183. Dugdale and Stanton, *Professional Negligence*, 1989, 2nd ed., para. 28.06 comment that the Damoclean argument may only be available: "to those whose professional reputation is likely to be seriously damaged by litigation and who may therefore view the proceedings with acute apprehension, or where the worry will impair the professional's ability to provide a proper level of service. Medical professionals are the most likely to fall into this category." See further *Rosen* v. *Marston* (1984) (unreported), C.A., where a delay of 2½ years, in a case where the writ was issued just before the expiry of the limitation period, was held to be excessive; defendant was prejudiced because the claim was a potential threat to his reputation and the anxiety and distress had been hanging over his head for that time.

[85] See, however, *C.* v. *C.* [1946] 1 All E.R. 562, where the patient needed disclosure of the records for the purpose of divorce litigation. See also the comments of Sir John Donaldson M.R. in *Lee* v. *South West Thames Regional Health Authority* [1985] 2 All E.R. 385, 389–390 and *Naylor* v. *Preston Area Health Authority* [1987] 2 All E.R. 353, 360, §§ 10.95–10.96.

access to their records through the Data Protection Act 1984, the Access to Health Records Act 1990 and the Access to Medical Reports Act 1988. This legislation is principally concerned with the right of patients to know what is contained in their medical records and to permit the correction of inaccurate records, but it may also be relevant in the context of litigation as one means of discovering what went wrong with the patient's treatment.

1. Data Protection Act 1984

10.68   The Data Protection Act 1984 gives an individual a right of access to information held about him in computerised form. Under section 21(1) an individual is entitled to be informed by any data user whether the data held by him include personal data of which that individual is the data subject, and to be supplied by any data user with a copy of the information constituting any such personal data held by him.[86] Where the information is expressed in terms which are not intelligible without explanation, the information must be accompanied by an explanation of those terms.

10.69   This right of access to computerised records is limited in the case of health records, however, by the Data Protection (Subject Access Modification) (Health) Order 1987[87] issued under section 29(1) of the Act. The Order applies to personal data consisting of information as to the physical or mental health of the data subject where the data is held by a health professional, or the data is held by a person other than a health professional, but the information constituting the data was first recorded by or on behalf of a health professional.[88] Under regulation 4(2) the access provisions of the Data Protection Act 1984 do not apply where this would either: (a) be likely to cause serious harm to the physical or mental health of the data subject; or (b) be likely to disclose to the data subject the identity of another individual (who has not consented to the disclosure of the information) either as a person to whom the information or part of it relates or as the source of the information or enable that identity to be deduced by the data subject.

10.70   If part of the information can be supplied without causing serious harm to the data subject or in such a way as to prevent the identity of another individual being disclosed or deduced the exemption does not apply, nor where the only individual whose identity is likely to be disclosed or deduced is a health professional who has been involved in the care of the data subject and the information relates to him or he supplied the information in his capacity as a health professional.[89]

---

[86] "Data" means information recorded in a form in which it can be processed by equipment operating automatically in response to instructions given for that purpose: Data Protection Act 1984, s.1(2). "Personal data" means data consisting of information which relates to a living individual, who can be identified from that information (or from that and other information in the possession of the data user), including any expression of opinion about the individual but not any indication of the intentions of the data user in respect of that individual: *ibid.*, s.1(3). "Data subject" means an individual who is the subject of personal data: *ibid.*, s.1(4).
[87] S.I. 1987/1903.
[88] *Ibid.*, reg. 3(1).
[89] *Ibid.*, reg. 4(3).

If the data user is not a health professional he must not supply **10.71**
information to which the Order applies to a data subject under section
21, or withhold information on the basis that the grounds of regulation
4(2) are satisfied, unless he first consults the medical or dental
practitioner responsible for the clinical care of the data subject as to
whether either or both of the grounds are satisfied.[90]

An individual is entitled to compensation for any damage or distress **10.72**
as a result of inaccuracy of data, and data is inaccurate if incorrect or
misleading as to any matter of fact.[91] It is a defence for the defendant
to prove that he took reasonable care to ensure the accuracy of the
data.[92] An individual is also entitled to compensation for any damage
or distress as a result of the loss of or unauthorised disclosure of the
data, subject to the defence of reasonable care, and may apply to a
court for rectification or erasure of inaccurate data, including an
expression of opinion which is based on inaccurate data.[93]

2. Access to Health Records Act 1990

The Access to Health Records Act 1990 confers a right of access on **10.73**
the part of patients or persons acting on their behalf to non-com-
puterised health records.[94] By section 1(1) a "health record" means a
record which, first, consists of information (including an expression of
opinion) relating to the physical or mental health of an individual who
can be identified from that information, or from that and other
information in the possession of the holder of the record; and,
secondly, has been made by or on behalf of a health professional[95] in
connection with the care of that individual. Under section 3(1) an
application for access to a health record may be made to the holder of
the record by: (i) the patient; (ii) a person authorised in writing to
make the application on the patient's behalf; (iii) a person having
parental responsibility for a patient who is a child; (iv) where the
patient is incapable of managing his own affairs, any person appointed
by the court to manage his affairs; and (v) where the patient has died,
the patient's personal representative and any person who may have a
claim arising out of the patient's death.

The holder of the record must give access to the record, within a **10.74**
maximum period of 40 days, by allowing the applicant to inspect the
record (or an extract), or if the applicant so requires by supplying him
with a copy of the record or extract.[96] Where any information is
expressed in terms which are not intelligible without explanation, an
explanation of those terms must be provided.[97]

The right of access is not absolute; there are a number of exceptions. **10.75**
In the case of a child, where the application is made by the patient or a

---

[90] *Ibid.*, reg. 4(5).
[91] Data Protection Act 1984, s.22(1), (4).
[92] *Ibid.*, s.22(3). Special rules apply to data which accurately record information
received or obtained from the data subject or a third party: *ibid.*, s.22(2).
[93] *Ibid.*, ss.23 and 24.
[94] Access to Health Records Act 1990, s.3. The Act excludes information which is
subject to the Data Protection Act 1984: *ibid.*, s.1(1)(*b*).
[95] For the definition of "health professional" see s.2(1).
[96] *Ibid.*, s.3(2), (5).
[97] *Ibid.*, s.3(3).

person authorised in writing to make the application on the patient's behalf, access shall not be given unless the holder of the record is satisfied that the patient is capable of understanding the nature of the application.[98] Where the application is made by a person having parental responsibility for the patient, access shall not be given unless the holder of the record is satisfied either: (a) that the patient has consented to the application or (b) that the patient is incapable of understanding the nature of the application and the giving of access would be in his best interests.[99] On an application, after the patient has died, by the patient's personal representative or any person who may have a claim arising out of the patient's death, access shall not be given if the record includes a note, made at the patient's request, that he did not wish access to be given on such an application.[1] In addition, access does not have to be given to any part of the record which, in the opinion of the holder of the record, would disclose information which is not relevant to any claim which may arise out of the patient's death.[2]

10.76 Section 5(1) contains two significant restrictions on the patient's right of access. Where, in the opinion of the holder of the record, access to any part of a health record would disclose: (i) information likely to cause serious harm to the physical or mental health of the patient or of any other individual; or (ii) information relating to or provided by an individual, other than the patient, who could be identified from that information (unless the individual concerned consents or the individual is a health professional who has been involved in the care of the patient[3]), access shall not be given. Furthermore, section 5(1)(b) excludes any part of a health record which was made before the commencement of the Act, namely November 1, 1991,[4] except, and to the extent that, in the opinion of the holder of the record, the giving of access is necessary in order to make intelligible any part of the record to which access is required to be given.[5]

10.77 A person who considers that any information contained in a health record to which he has been given access is inaccurate may apply to the holder of the record to have the record corrected.[6] The holder of the record must either make the necessary correction, or, if he is not satisfied that the information is inaccurate, make a note in the record of the matters which the applicant considers to be inaccurate, and in either case, supply the applicant with a copy of the correction or note. There is no remedy in damages, however, comparable to that con-

---

[98] *Ibid.*, s.4(1).

[99] *Ibid.*, s.4(2).

[1] *Ibid.*, s.4(3). See also s.5(4) which excludes access in the case of an application made by someone other than the patient (or on the patient's authority) to any part of the record which, in the opinion of the record holder, would disclose information provided by the patient in the expectation that it would not be disclosed to the applicant, or information obtained as a result of any examination or investigation to which the patient consented in the expectation that the information would not be disclosed.

[2] *Ibid.*, s.5(4).

[3] *Ibid.*, s.5(2).

[4] *Ibid.*, s.12(2).

[5] Access to Health Records Act 1990, s.5(2). The Secretary of State has power to make regulations prescribing that access shall not be given under the Act to any part of a health record which satisfies the prescribed conditions: *ibid.*, s.5(5).

[6] *Ibid.*, s.6(1). "Inaccurate" means incorrect, misleading or incomplete: *ibid.*, s.6(3).

tained in the Data Protection Act 1984 in respect of damage or distress suffered as a result of inaccuracy in the health records. The only remedy available under the Act is an application to the High Court for an order requiring the holder of a health record to comply with any requirement of the Act.[7] For the purpose of determining this issue the court may require the record to be available for its own inspection, but shall not require the record to be disclosed to the applicant or his representatives whether by discovery or otherwise.[8]

The Act clearly contemplates patient applications for access to **10.78** health records in advance of litigation, and to this extent it may supplement the provisions of section 33(2) of the Supreme Court Act 1981 for pre-action discovery.[9] It cannot entirely replace this procedure, however, because there are several drawbacks. First, a "health record" is defined as information relating to the physical or mental health of an individual who can be identified from that information, and has been made by or on behalf of a health professional *in connection with the care of that individual*. It is doubtful whether this would apply to all the documents (an accident report, for example) that might be relevant to the conduct of litigation, and which are subject to discovery under the procedure for pre-action discovery. Secondly, the Access to Health Records Act applies only to health records made after November 1, 1991, except to the extent that access is necessary to an earlier record to make intelligible access to a record made after that date. No such restriction applies to the procedure for pre-action discovery. Thirdly, information may be withheld if, in the opinion of the holder of the record, it is likely to cause serious harm to the physical or mental health of the patient or of any other individual, or if the information would, in effect, break another person's confidence. Again, no such restriction applies to discovery under the Supreme Court Act 1981, although an order may direct that disclosure be limited to the applicant's legal advisers or his legal and medical advisers. Finally, it would seem inappropriate to allow the holder of the record, who may be a potential defendant, to determine which information is or is not relevant to any claim which may arise out of the patient's death, as is possible under section 5(4), although, admittedly, under section 33(2) of the Supreme Court Act the documents sought by the applicant must be "relevant to an issue arising or likely to arise out of that claim."

The Access to Health Records Act 1990 may have at least one **10.79** advantage over the Supreme Court Act 1981 in respect of pre-action discovery against a party who is not likely to be a party to the proceedings. It is not possible to obtain an order for pre-action discovery against someone who is not likely to be a party to proceedings, although discovery against third parties is possible once an action has been commenced. Where, however, a third party holds documents which constitute a "health record" within the meaning of section 1(1) the plaintiff will be able to make an application for access to that record under the 1990 Act.

---

[7] *Ibid.*, s.8(1).
[8] *Ibid.*, s.8(4).
[9] See §§ 10.84–10.97.

3. Access to Medical Reports Act 1988

10.80   The Access to Medical Reports Act 1988, s.1, grants an individual a right of access to any medical report relating to the individual which is to be, or in the previous six months has been, supplied by a medical practitioner, who is or has been responsible for the clinical care of the individual, for employment or insurance purposes. The Act does not apply to a report prepared by a doctor who had not previously been responsible for the individual's clinical care, *e.g.*, a doctor instructed by employers or prospective employers on an *ad hoc* basis. The individual must consent to any application to a medical practitioner for a medical report on the individual for employment or insurance purposes, and when giving consent he can state that he wishes to have access to the report before it is supplied. Access means making the report or a copy of it available for the individual's inspection or supplying him with a copy.[10] Where an individual has been given access to a report it should not be supplied to the applicant unless the individual consents, and the individual may request the doctor to amend any part of the report which he considers to be incorrect or misleading.[11]

10.81   Under section 7 there are exceptions to the right of access where disclosure would be likely to cause serious harm to the physical or mental health of the individual or others, or would be likely to reveal information about another person, or to reveal the identity of another person who has supplied information to the practitioner about the individual, (unless that person consents, or the person is a health professional who has been involved in the care of the individual and the information relates to or has been provided by him in that capacity). Where the exceptions apply to a part but not the whole of a medical report the individual's right of access applies to the remainder, and where the exceptions apply to the whole report, the doctor must not supply the report unless the individual consents.

10.82   There is no remedy in damages for a failure to comply with the terms of the Act, but where a person has failed or is likely to fail to comply with any requirement of the Act an individual may apply to the court for an order that he comply with that requirement.

IV. Discovery

10.83 In the past the adversarial nature of civil proceedings was regarded as justification for allowing the parties to a civil action to conceal the nature of their case from each other. This was particularly true of actions for medical negligence. The recent trend, however, has been to move to a more open conduct of litigation, with "cards on the table" so that the parties can assess the relative strengths and weaknesses of their respective cases and where appropriate, settle the action. A more

---

[10] Access to Medical Reports Act 1988, s.4(4). The doctor may charge a reasonable fee for supplying a copy.
[11] *Ibid.*, s.5(1), (2).

open approach also helps the parties narrow the issues in dispute. An initial hurdle that a patient seeking to bring a claim for medical negligence will face is that of obtaining the medical records prior to the issue of proceedings in order to assess the prospects of success in the action. This is not as difficult as it once was, although it can still give rise to some problems.

1. Pre-action discovery

Against a potential defendant

Access to a patient's medical records is essential to enable his legal **10.84** and medical advisers to determine whether an action for negligence has any prospect of success. Section 33(2) of the Supreme Court Act 1981 and R.S.C., Ord. 24, r. 7A provide a procedure by which a potential plaintiff in an action in respect of personal injuries[12] or death may apply for discovery of relevant documents from a potential defendant before commencing an action. As Lord Denning M.R. has observed one of the objects of the provision is to enable the plaintiff to find out whether or not he has a good cause of action before he issues proceedings.[13] It is designed to facilitate settlements and to avoid fruitless actions.[14] The plaintiff should make a written request for voluntary disclosure, however, setting out the nature of his allegations, before making an application under the section. In *Shaw* v. *Vauxhall Motors Ltd.* Lord Denning M.R. said that;

> "All that should be required is that the potential plaintiff should set out in an open letter in general terms his own knowledge, however vague, of how this accident happened. If he does so, and gives information which shows that the reports may well be material, then I think the court may properly order disclosure of them before action [is] brought. That should, I think, be the general practice. It enables each side to know the strength or weakness of the case before embarking on litigation. It is particularly useful in a legal aid case, because it gives solicitors and counsel better material on which to advise."[15]

---

[12] There is no equivalent procedure for actions not involving personal injuries. "Personal injuries" are defined in s.35(5) of the Supreme Court Act 1981 in the same terms as the Limitation Act 1980, s.38, to include any disease and any impairment of a person's physical or mental condition. Thus, some medical negligence claims do not necessarily involve a claim for personal injuries: see, *e.g.*, *Pattison* v. *Hobbs*, *The Times*, November 11, 1985, § 10.06; *Naylor* v. *Preston Area Health Authority* [1987] 2 All E.R. 353, 363, *per* Sir John Donaldson M.R. on failed sterilisation claims. In *Paterson* v. *Chadwick* [1974] 1 W.L.R. 890, however, it was held that the phrase "in respect of" personal injuries or death meant that there must be some connection between the plaintiff's claim and the personal injuries, and that there was such a connection where the plaintiff sought disclosure of her medical records by a hospital authority (under the forerunner to s.34(2) of the Supreme Court Act 1981) in course of a claim against her solicitors for allowing her claim for medical negligence to become statute-barred; *cf.* *Ackbar* v. *Green & Co. Ltd.* [1975] Q.B. 582, § 10.06, n. 12.

[13] *Dunning* v. *Board of Governors of the United Liverpool Hospitals* [1973] 2 All E.R. 454, 457; *Shaw* v. *Vauxhall Motors Ltd.* [1974] 1 W.L.R. 1035, 1039.

[14] *Lee* v. *South West Thames Regional Health Authority* [1985] 2 All E.R. 385, 387.

[15] [1974] 1 W.L.R. 1035, 1039.

Buckley L.J. particularly emphasised the importance of a legally aided plaintiff having information which may affect the prospects of success of the claim as early as possible, since there was a public interest in not continuing a legally aided action if it becomes clear that the plaintiff has no reasonable prospects of success.[16] It is not clear why privately funded plaintiffs should be at any disadvantage in this respect. The public interest in the administration of justice and the interests of all the parties clearly lies in the discontinuance of actions which have no prospects of success.

10.85   Plaintiffs' solicitors should not accept disclosure of the medical records to a nominated medical expert, but should insist on disclosure to themselves in order to organise the records into chronological order, check them against the plaintiff's statement, identify missing documents, and identify the relevant issues for consideration and/or clarification by the medical experts and/or counsel. Disclosure direct to a medical expert can also cause difficulty in obtaining a second opinion if the first report is not as helpful as it might be. First, the plaintiff's solicitors will have to make a further request for voluntary disclosure which the health authority might then resist. Secondly, the defendants will know which experts the plaintiff has obtained a report from and may seek to draw adverse inferences from the fact that a particular report will not be relied on because it has not advanced the plaintiff's case. Orders under section 33(2) of the Supreme Court Act 1981 can exclude production to the patient himself but not to his legal advisers, and if a health authority persists in seeking to limit disclosure to a medical expert an application will have to be made. It is now rarer than it once was for health authorities to refuse voluntary disclosure, provided that it is made clear in the letter of request that there is some basis for the request and that it is not purely speculative.[17]

10.86   The Supreme Court Act 1981[18] permits a person who has not issued a writ to make an application for discovery of documents from a person who is likely to be a party to the proceedings. Section 33(2) provides that:

> "On an application, in accordance with rules of court, of a person who appears to the High Court to be likely to be a party to subsequent proceedings in that court in which a claim in respect of personal injuries to a person, or in respect of a person's death, is likely to be made, the High Court shall, in such circumstances as may be specified in the rules, have power to order a person who appears to the court to be likely to be a party to the proceedings and to be likely to have or to have had in his possession, custody or power any documents which are relevant to an issue arising or likely to arise out of that claim—
>
> (a) to disclose whether those documents are in his possession, custody or power; and

---

[16] *Ibid.*, p. 1040.

[17] The Department of Health has advised health authorities to disclose records without a court order, after consulting the medical staff, unless there is a good reason not to do so: H.C. (82) 16. Note, however, that a patient who makes a request to see his health records under the Access to Health Records Act 1990 does not have to give any reason or justification for the request: see §§ 10.73–10.74.

[18] Equivalent provisions are to be found in the County Courts Act 1984, ss.52–54.

(*b*) to produce such of those documents as are in his possession,
custody or power to the applicant or, on such conditions as
may be specified in the order—

   (i) to the applicant's legal advisers; or

   (ii) to the applicant's legal advisers and any medical or other
professional adviser of the applicant; or

   (iii) if the applicant has no legal adviser, to any medical or
other professional adviser of the applicant."[19]

Applications under section 33(2) of the Supreme Court Act 1981 must
be made by originating summons, and must be supported by an
affidavit stating the grounds on which it is alleged that the parties are
likely to be parties to subsequent proceedings involving a claim for
personal injuries, specifying or describing the documents in respect of
which the order is sought, showing that the documents are relevant to
an issue likely to arise in the proceedings and that the defendant is
likely to have or have had them in his possession, custody or power.[20]
In a medical negligence action there should be little difficulty in
establishing the relevance of the medical records to a potential claim.

In dealing with applications under section 33 the court has to ask **10.87**
itself two questions, the first jurisdictional, the second as to the
exercise of discretion.[21] The jurisdictional question is resolved by
determining the likelihood of participation in proceedings, which
means a reasonable prospect of participation in the proceedings. The
court will not permit "fishing expeditions"[22]; there must be a bona fide
claim. But this does not mean that the applicant has to prove that he
has a good cause of action.[23] In *Dunning* v. *Board of Governors of the
United Liverpool Hospitals* James L.J. said that in order to take
advantage of the section the applicant must:

> "disclose the nature of the claim he intends to make and show
> not only the intention of making it but also that there is a
> reasonable basis for making it. Ill-founded, irresponsible and
> speculative allegations based merely on hope would not provide a
> reasonable basis for an intended claim in subsequent
> proceedings."[24]

The Court of Appeal concluded in *Dunning* v. *Board of Governors* **10.88**
of the United Liverpool Hospitals that an application should not be

---

[19] See also Supreme Court Act 1981, s.33(1), which provides that the court may make
an order providing for the inspection, photographing, preservation, custody and
detention of property, the taking of samples of property and the carrying out of any
experiment on or with any property which may become the subject matter of subsequent
proceedings in the High Court.

[20] R.S.C., Ord. 24, r. 7A. Both privilege and public interest immunity apply to
documents for which an order is sought under ss.33(2) or 34(2) of the Supreme Court
Act 1981: R.S.C., Ord. 24, r. 7A(6) and Supreme Court Act 1981, s.35(1).

[21] *Harris* v. *Newcastle Health Authority* [1989] 2 All E.R. 273, 278, *per* Mann L.J.

[22] *Shaw* v. *Vauxhall Motors Ltd.* [1974] 1 W.L.R. 1035, 1040, *per* Buckley L.J.

[23] "One of the objects of the section is to enable a plaintiff to find out—before he
starts proceedings—whether he has a good cause of action or not. This object would be
defeated if he had to show—in advance—that he had already got a good cause of action
before he saw the documents": *per* Lord Denning M.R. in *Dunning* v. *Board of
Governors of the United Liverpool Hospitals* [1973] 2 All E.R. 454, 457; see also *Shaw* v.
Vauxhall Motors Ltd. [1974] 1 W.L.R. 1035, 1039.

[24] [1973] 2 All E.R. 454, 460. His Lordship added that the word "likely" was to be
construed as meaning a "reasonable prospect."

refused solely on the ground that it was uncertain whether or not there might be a cause of action before the result of the application was known and the plaintiff had had an opportunity to inspect the documents. The word "likely" is satisfied if the action might, or might well, proceed in the unknown circumstances of what discovery might reveal. In *Harris* v. *Newcastle Health Authority*[25] Kerr L.J. said that there is no general rule as to the exercise of the discretion, though if the action is "doomed to failure" then it will be regarded as frivolous, vexatious or otherwise ill-founded, and the application should be refused. It would seem, however, that few cases will meet the "doomed to failure" test in the light of the application of the test in *Harris* itself.[26] Moreover, the procedure is not simply about providing evidence for a plaintiff to bring an action. When the plaintiff obtains discovery this may well indicate that there is truly no basis for an allegation of negligence, and it is in the public interest that litigation which has no prospect of success should not be initiated.

(i) *Relevance of a possible limitation defence*

10.89   In *Harris* v. *Newcastle Health Authority*[27] the defendants declined the plaintiff's request for pre-action discovery on the ground that the action was statute-barred, the events giving rise to the claim having occurred over 20 years before. Both the district registrar and, on appeal, the judge refused the plaintiff's application because the strength of the limitation defence was such that the action was doomed to fail. In the Court of Appeal Kerr L.J. said that if it was plain beyond doubt that a defence of limitation would be raised and would succeed, then the court was entitled to take that matter into account. However, a plaintiff in a personal injuries action can always make an application to override the limitation period under section 33 of the Limitation Act 1980, and that must also be taken into account before it can be said that the action is clearly bound to be defeated by the limitation defence. Kerr L.J. accepted that in the normal run of cases:

" . . . even where a defence of limitation has a strong prospect of success, like here, it is very difficult for a court, on limited material, before pleadings and discovery, to conclude at that stage that the situation is such that the proposed action is bound to fail and therefore frivolous, vexatious or otherwise ill-founded. So in general I would accept . . . that issues relevant to limitation should not enter into consideration on applications for pre-trial discovery."[28]

Accordingly, since it was likely that proceedings would be instituted regardless of the outcome of the application for discovery, and since it could not be said that the proceedings were doomed to failure because pre-trial discovery might reveal facts which would be relevant to the

---

[25] [1989] 2 All E.R. 273, 277.
[26] See § 10.89.
[27] [1989] 2 All E.R. 273.
[28] *Ibid.*, p. 277. Sir John Megaw said, at p. 279, that " . . . it cannot be said with any certainty that on discovery facts would not emerge which would be relevant to the issue of limitation."

success or otherwise of the limitation defence, the court would exercise its discretion to order disclosure of the hospital records.

(ii) *To whom must disclosure be made?*

Under sections 33(2) and 34(2) of the Supreme Court Act 1981 the **10.90** court can order disclosure to the applicant's legal advisers, plus any medical or other professional adviser of the applicant, or if the applicant has no legal adviser, to any medical or other professional adviser. Unlike earlier provisions on pre-trial discovery, this permits the court to order that disclosure exclude the patient himself (though not the patient's legal adviser).[29] In *Davies* v. *Eli Lilly & Co.*[30] the Court of Appeal held that in exceptional circumstances the court will permit a person who is neither a party's legal adviser, nor an employee of a legal adviser, nor a professional expert to undertake the inspection of documents under the provisions of R.S.C., Ord. 24, r. 9, if the person's assistance was essential in the interests of justice and the court was satisfied that there would be no breach of the duty of confidentiality. Accordingly inspection by a "scientific co-ordinator" in the Opren litigation was authorised, even though the defendants objected on the ground that he was a journalist who had been critical of pharmaceutical industry. This decision concerned inspection of documents after an action had been commenced, but there is no reason in principle why it should not also apply to pre-trial discovery provided that the person qualifies as a "professional adviser."

(iii) *Costs*

The person against whom an order is sought is normally entitled to **10.91** his costs of and incidental to the application, and of complying with the order, unless the court otherwise directs.[31] However, where the defendant has no reasonable excuse for failing to comply with a written request for discovery of documents before an application is made, he may be ordered to pay the applicant's costs.[32] In view of the greater emphasis now placed on patients' entitlement to see their medical records,[33] the courts may be more willing to conclude that refusals to

---

[29] Administration of Justice Act 1970, ss.31 and 32(1); *McIvor* v. *Southern Health and Social Services Board* [1978] 2 All E.R. 625, H.L.

[30] [1987] 1 All E.R. 801.

[31] R.S.C., Ord. 62, r. 6(9); Supreme Court Act 1981, s.35(3). An order for disclosure may be made conditional on the applicant giving security for costs: R.S.C., Ord. 24, r. 7A(5).

[32] *Hall* v. *Wandsworth Health Authority* (1985) 129 S.J. 188, where Tudor Price J. remarked that delay should be avoided in personal injury and medical negligence cases; see also *Jacobs* v. *Wessex Regional Health Authority* [1984] C.L.Y. 2618, where the plaintiff's solicitors had pointed out in correspondence with the defendants that an application would result in needless public expense, since the plaintiff was legally aided. The defendants were ordered to pay plaintiff's costs. Note, however, that it is at least arguable that Ord. 62, r. 6(9), does not empower the court to order the defendant to pay the applicant's costs, but merely gives a discretion to refuse to order the applicant to pay the defendant's costs: see Dugdale and Stanton, *Professional Negligence*, 1989, 2nd ed., para. 28.09, n. 10.

[33] See, *e.g*, the Access to Health Records Act 1990, §§ 10.73 *et seq.*, and the remarks of Sir John Donaldson M.R. in *Lee* v. *South West Thames Regional Health Authority* [1985] 2 All E.R. 385, 389–390 and *Naylor* v. *Preston Area Health Authority* [1987] 2 All E.R. 353, 360, §§ 10.95–10.96.

comply with written requests for discovery of medical records are unreasonable, which could lead to more orders for costs against health authorities.[34]

(iv) *Congenital disabilities*

10.92   The Congenital Disabilities (Civil Liability) Act 1976 confers a right of action on a child who is born alive and disabled in respect of the disability, if it is caused by an occurrence which affected either parent's ability to have a normal healthy child, or affected the mother during pregnancy, or affected the mother or child in the course of its birth, causing disabilities which would not otherwise have been present.[35] It is possible for a father, though generally not the mother, to be a defendant to an action brought under the Act by a child. Sections 27–29 of the Human Fertilisation and Embryology Act 1990 deal with the status of the "parents" of children born as a consequence of in vitro fertilisation or artificial insemination, with the consequence that a child's mother or father may, in law, not be the same person as his genetic mother or father. Under section 35(1) of that Act, where, for the purpose of instituting proceedings under the Congenital Disabilities (Civil Liability) Act 1976, it is necessary to identify a person who would or might be the parent of a child but for sections 27–29 of the Human Fertilisation and Embryology Act 1990, the court may on the application of the child make an order requiring the Human Fertilisation and Embryology Authority to disclose any information contained in the register kept in pursuance of section 31 identifying that person. The court must be satisfied that the interests of justice require it to make the order.[36]

Against third parties

10.93   An order for pre-trial discovery can only be made under section 33(2) of the Supreme Court Act 1981 against a person who is "likely to be a party to the proceedings." Thus, if the plaintiff needs discovery of documents from some other person, then, in the absence of voluntary disclosure, he will normally have to issue the writ and apply for discovery against the other person under section 34 of the Supreme Court Act 1981. Voluntary disclosure, however, should be regarded as the norm. In *Walker* v. *Eli Lilly & Co*.[37] Hirst J. stated that health authorities and doctors who are not likely to be defendants should respond readily and promptly to requests for disclosure to avoid unnecessary expense and delay. This point is reinforced by the Access to Health Records Act 1990, which gives patients a right of access to their health records irrespective of the possibility of litigation. The Act

---

[34] Possibly a health authority may be justified in waiting for a court order where it holds confidential information, and would not want to be in breach of a duty of confidence, *e.g.* where relatives have given information about the mental health of the patient: Dugdale and Stanton, *Professional Negligence*, 1989, 2nd ed., para. 28.09, n. 12.
[35] See §§ 2.28 *et seq.*
[36] Human Fertilisation and Embryology Act 1990, ss.35(3) and 34(2).
[37] (1986) 136 New L.J. 608.

may be of some value in seeking discovery against a doctor or health authority who is not a potential defendant, but there are some restrictions on its effectiveness for this purpose.[38]

A further possibility to consider when seeking discovery from a third **10.94** party is the court's inherent power to order a person to disclose information under the principle in *Norwich Pharmacal Co.* v. *Commissioners of Customs and Excise.*[39] Where a person through no fault of his own, and whether voluntarily or not, "has got mixed up in the tortious acts of others so as to facilitate their wrongdoing he may incur no personal liability but he comes under a duty to assist the person who has been wronged by giving him full information and disclosing the identity of the wrongdoers."[40] This allows a potential plaintiff to examine third party documents to identify a wrongdoer and establish a cause of action, including "fishing" for the names of wrongdoers.[41] Discovery under the *Norwich Pharmacal* principle is only available, however, where the third party has been involved in the wrongdoing in some way. It will not be ordered against a "mere witness."[42]

A common law duty of disclosure?

It is possible that the courts could develop a common law duty **10.95** requiring doctors to inform patients about what has happened in the course of a treatment or procedure that has gone wrong. Sir John Donaldson M.R. has expressed strong views on this issue. In *Lee* v. *South West Thames Regional Health Authority*, his Lordship referred to the doctor's duty to answer the patient's questions about proposed treatment following *Sidaway* v. *Bethlem Royal Hospital Governors*,[43] and commented:

> "Why, we ask ourselves, is the position any different if the patient asks what treatment he has in fact had? Let us suppose that a blood transfusion is in contemplation. The patient asks what is involved. He is told that a quantity of blood from a donor will be introduced into his system. He may ask about the risk of AIDS and so forth and will be entitled to straight answers. He consents. Suppose that, by accident, he is given a quantity of air as well as blood and suffers serious ill effects. Is he not entitled to ask what treatment he in fact received, and is the doctor and hospital authority not obliged to tell him, 'in the event you did not only get a blood transfusion. You also got an air transfusion'? Why is the duty different before the treatment from what it is afterwards?
>
> If the duty is the same, then if the patient is refused information to which he is entitled, it must be for consideration whether

---

[38] See § 10.78.
[39] [1974] A.C. 133.
[40] *Ibid.*, p. 175, *per* Lord Reid.
[41] *Loose* v. *Williamson* [1978] 3 All E.R. 89.
[42] *Ricci* v. *Chow* [1987] 3 All E.R. 534. An employee or agent of a corporation which is party to the proceedings is not to be regarded as a mere witness and can be required to give discovery on behalf of the corporation: *Harrington* v. *North London Polytechnic* [1984] 3 All E.R. 666.
[43] [1985] 1 All E.R. 643.

he could not bring an action for breach of contract claiming specific performance of the duty to inform. In other words, whether the patient could not bring an action for discovery, albeit on a novel basis."[44]

10.96   Subsequently, in *Naylor* v. *Preston Area Health Authority*[45] his Lordship returned to this theme, suggesting that in professional negligence cases, and in particular in medical negligence cases, there is a duty of candour resting on the professional man:

> "In this context I was disturbed to be told during the argument of the present appeals that the view was held in some quarters that whilst the duty of candid disclosure, [referred to in *Lee* v. *South West Thames Regional Health Authority*], might give rise to a contractual implied term and so benefit private fee-paying patients, it did not translate into a legal or equitable right for the benefit of national health service patients. This I would entirely repudiate. In my judgment, still admittedly and regretfully *obiter*, it is but one aspect of the general duty of care, arising out of the patient/medical practitioner or hospital authority relationship and gives rise to rights both in contract and in tort. It is also in my judgment, not *obiter*, a factor to be taken into account when exercising the jurisdiction under Order 38 with which we are concerned."

The legal basis for this "duty of candour" remains unclear, particularly since in the tort of negligence, at least, the plaintiff would have to prove that breach of the duty caused him damage, and the circumstances in which non-disclosure will cause further harm to the plaintiff will be rare.[46] A breach of contract, on the other hand, is actionable *per se*, and, indeed, might give rise to a claim for specific performance of the duty. These differences between contract and tort lend some substance to the view that private patients would stand in a better position than N.H.S. patients in this respect.

2. Post-action discovery

Between the parties to the action

10.97   Once an action as been commenced the normal rules on discovery between the parties apply. R.S.C., Ord. 24, r. 1 provides for mutual

---

[44] [1985] 2 All E.R. 385, 389–390. Mustill L.J. agreed with this statement. The difficulty of obtaining information from medical staff when something has gone wrong was illustrated in *Bayliss* v. *Blagg* (1954) 1 B.M.J. 709, in which there had been a long delay by the hospital staff in telling parents about a deterioration in their child's medical condition, and the court concluded that there had been a deliberate attempt by the hospital to conceal and misrepresent to the family the condition of the child. Stable J. observed: "I would like to know if this is the system under our State medical service. The parent has a right to know—this isn't Russia." Counsel for the *defendants* replied: "One can't get facts from hospitals. They are grossly impertinent when you ask."

[45] [1987] 2 All E.R. 353, 360.

[46] See *Stamos* v. *Davies* (1985) 21 D.L.R. (4th) 507, 522, §§ 4.36–4.37. Sir John Donaldson M.R. has said that in *Lee* he was "flying a kite": (1985) 53 Medico-Legal J. 148, 157.

discovery by the parties to the action, after the close of pleadings, of documents[47] which are or have been in the parties' possession, custody or power relating to matters in question in the action. Once the action has been commenced it is inappropriate to seek discovery against other parties to the action under the Supreme Court Act 1981, s.33(2) and R.S.C., Ord. 24, r. 7A. A party to an action can apply at any time for discovery from any other party of particular documents under R.S.C., Ord. 24, r. 7, notwithstanding that he may already have been required to give discovery under rule 2 or 3 of Order 24. The court may refuse to make an order if satisfied that discovery or production of documents for inspection is not necessary either for disposing fairly of the action or for saving costs.[48]

Against third parties

Once an action in respect of personal injuries[49] or death has been **10.98** commenced a person who is not a party to the action may be ordered to disclose documents under section 34 of the Supreme Court Act 1981 and R.S.C., Ord. 24, r. 7A. Section 34(2) is expressed in almost identical terms to section 33(2), except that the court has the power to order disclosure and production of documents by a person who is not a party to the proceedings, where the documents are relevant to an issue arising out of the claim. An application must be made by summons served on the third party personally and on the other parties to the proceedings, and must be supported by an affidavit specifying or describing the documents in respect of which the order is sought, showing that the documents are relevant to an issue likely to arise in the proceedings and that the third party is likely to have or have had them in his possession, custody or power.[50]

A third party cannot be required to produce any documents under **10.99** section 34(2) which he could not be compelled to produce if he had been served with a writ of *subpoena duces tecum* to produce the documents at the trial, nor where discovery is not necessary either for disposing fairly of the action or for saving costs.[51] The applicant does not have to show that without an order it would be impossible to conduct his case, merely that it would help to achieve the proper administration of justice, which is assisted by the promotion of settlements rather than the prolongation of litigation, and by the possibility of early, complete preparation for trial by both parties which the production of documents facilitates.[52]

---

[47] On the meaning of "documents" see *Grant* v. *Southwestern and County Properties Ltd.* [1975] Ch. 185. On the discovery of facts by means of interrogatories see R.S.C., Ord. 26.

[48] R.S.C., Ord. 24, rr. 8 and 13.

[49] "Personal injuries" has the same meaning as under s.33(2): see, in particular, *Paterson* v. *Chadwick* [1974] 1 W.L.R. 890; see further § 10.84, n. 12.

[50] R.S.C., Ord. 24, r. 7A(2), (3). See also County Courts Act 1984, s.53(2).

[51] R.S.C., Ord. 24, rr. 7A(6) and 8. The fact that information was given in confidence to the third party is not a ground for refusing disclosure. Thus, in *Loveday* v. *Renton* [1990] 1 Med. L.R. 117 third party discovery of the raw research data used in the National Childhood Encephalopathy Study was ordered, although steps were taken to preserve the anonymity of patients: see Powers and Harris, *Medical Negligence*, 1990, para. 5.10.

[52] *O'Sullivan* v. *Herdmans Ltd.* [1987] 3 All E.R. 129, 136, H.L.

10.100   There is, of course, nothing to stop voluntary disclosure. In *Walker* v. *Eli Lilly & Co.*[53] the plaintiff applied under section 34(2) for discovery of her hospital medical records from a health authority which was not a party to the proceedings. The authority was reluctant to disclose the records voluntarily. Hirst J. said that where no special consideration of confidentiality is invoked, the court will "almost certainly" order disclosure if a summons should become necessary, and so health authorities and medical practitioners should respond readily and promptly to any requests for disclosure in such cases, so that unnecessary expense and delay can be avoided. The health authority had been anxious that any documents disclosed might subsequently be used against them. His Lordship pointed out, however, that there is an implied undertaking by a party seeking discovery in legal proceedings that documents so obtained will be used only for the purpose of those proceedings and for no other purpose.

3. Privilege

10.101   There is no obligation to produce for inspection a privileged document, although it should be disclosed as in the party's possession if it is relevant to the action. The claim for privilege should be made in the party's list of documents, with a statement of the grounds on which privilege is claimed.[54] The ground of privilege which will most commonly be relevant to medical negligence actions is legal professional privilege, though public interest immunity may, on rare occasions, apply.[55]

Legal professional privilege

10.102   Legal professional privilege can take two forms. First, confidential communications between a solicitor acting in his professional capacity and his client for the purpose of obtaining legal advice and assistance are privileged, whether or not in contemplation of litigation. This will be construed broadly. Where information is passed by the solicitor or client to the other as part of a continuing process aimed at keeping both informed so that advice may be sought and given, privilege will attach.[56] Legal advice is not limited to advice about the law, but can include advice about what should prudently and sensibly be done in the relevant legal context. Privilege does not extend, however, to all communications between solicitor and client on matters within the

---

[53] (1986) 136 New L.J. 608.

[54] R.S.C., Ord. 24, r. 5(2).

[55] Privilege also applies to documents which will expose a party to criminal proceedings or a penalty: Civil Evidence Act 1968, s.14; and to communications conducted on a "without prejudice" basis for the purpose of settling a dispute. "Without prejudice" privilege applies to the substance of the communication rather than the form, so that a document marked "without prejudice" may not be privileged if its purpose is not to reach a compromise, and, conversely privilege may attach even where the words are not used: *Buckinghamshire County Council* v. *Moran* [1989] 2 All E.R. 225; *South Shropshire District Council* v. *Amos* [1987] 1 All E.R. 340.

[56] *Balabel* v. *Air India* [1988] 2 All E.R. 246, C.A.

ordinary business of a solicitor.[57] The privilege is the client's not the solicitor's,[58] and can be waived by the client.

The second form of legal professional privilege applies to communi- **10.103** cations between a solicitor and a third party, either directly or through an agent, which arise after litigation is contemplated or commenced and are made with a view to that litigation. Such communications are privileged if their purpose is to obtain or give advice on the litigation, or obtain evidence to be used in it.[59] Where documents have a dual purpose, the test is whether the dominant purpose of the document was for legal advice in contemplation of litigation. Thus, an accident report will not be privileged unless the sole or dominant purpose for which it was prepared was for submission to a legal adviser for advice in the light of anticipated or existing proceedings.[60] Accident reports are often prepared as a matter of course in order to find out the cause of the accident and avoid future occurrences. In this situation it will be difficult for the report to satisfy the dominant purpose test. The court will look to the substance of the matter. Defendants will be unable to claim privilege by dressing up reports to appear as though the dominant or sole purpose was the collection of evidence in contemplation of litigation, if in reality the report had a dual purpose.[61]

The dominant purpose of a document is not necessarily to be **10.104** determined by the intention of the person who created the document, and so privilege could attach to a letter written by a party to his insurers to inform them about circumstances giving rise to a claim on an indemnity policy which subsequently led to litigation, even though it was the insurers rather than the party who wanted the document for the purpose of obtaining legal advice.[62] It is not necessary for a decision to have been made to instruct solicitors before it can be said that proceedings are contemplated. The test is that if litigation is reasonably in prospect, documents brought into existence for the purpose of enabling solicitors to advise whether a claim should be made or resisted are privileged, provided that this was their dominant purpose when they were created.[63]

---

[57] Ibid.; see, e.g., Conlon v. Conlons Ltd. [1952] 2 All E.R. 462. Privilege applies to communications between an "in-house" salaried lawyer and his employer: Alfred Crompton Amusement Machines Ltd. v. Commissioners of Customs and Excise (No. 2) [1974] A.C. 405; and to communications with counsel: Curtis v. Beaney [1911] P. 181.

[58] Goddard v. Nationwide Building Society [1986] 3 All E.R. 264.

[59] Anderson v. Bank of British Columbia (1876) 2 Ch.D. 644.

[60] Waugh v. British Railways Board [1980] A.C. 521. The time for determining the purpose of a document is when it was brought into being. Thus, the mere fact that litigation was reasonably in prospect and that the documents are subsequently used to obtain legal advice does not necessarily mean that the documents will be privileged where, at the time they were brought into being, there was another dominant purpose: Alfred Crompton Amusement Machines Ltd. v. Commissioners of Customs and Excise (No. 2) [1974] A.C. 405.

[61] Lask v. Gloucester Health Authority (1985) 2 P.N. 92, 100, per O'Connor L.J.: "Once the second purpose is shown to be a purpose of the document, it seems to me that it is impossible to say that the judge was wrong to say that it was an equal purpose because by itself I would have thought that the prevention of similar accidents must be, in a hospital of all places, at least of equal importance as the provision of material for the solicitor." The prevention of future accidents was expressly stated to be a purpose of hospital accident reports in the N.H.S. Circular H.M. (55)66; cf. McAvan v. London Transport Executive (1983) 133 New L.J. 1101.

[62] Guiness Peat Properties v. Fitzroy Robinson Partnership [1987] 2 All E.R. 716.

[63] Ibid.

10.105   Privilege is normally the client's and cannot be relied upon by a third party. In *Lee* v. *South West Thames Regional Health Authority*,[64] however, the Court of Appeal held that a memorandum prepared by a third party, at the request of a potential defendant and for the purpose of enabling the potential defendant to obtain legal advice was privileged. It held that the third party would not be required to disclose the memorandum to the plaintiff on an application for pre-action discovery under section 33(2) of the Supreme Court Act 1981, even though the third party was not at the time that the memorandum was prepared a potential defendant and was in effect sheltering under another potential defendant's privilege. The infant plaintiff was taken to hospital for treatment of burns. He developed respiratory problems and was put on a ventilator, and then he was transferred from a hospital under the responsibility of Hillingdon Area Health Authority to another hospital under North East Thames Area Health Authority. The transfer was carried out by the ambulance service provided by South West Thames Regional Health Authority. The plaintiff sustained brain damage, either in hospital or in transit. Hillingdon, for the purpose of obtaining legal advice, requested and obtained a report by the ambulance crew from South West Thames. Subsequently, South West Thames refused to allow the plaintiff to inspect the memorandum on the ground that it was privileged. It was held that a defendant should be free to seek evidence without being obliged to disclose the results of his researches to his opponent, and that since Hillingdon had not waived their claim to privilege, and it would be impossible in the circumstances for matters to be arranged so that the document could be used against one defendant (South West Thames) and not the other (Hillingdon), inspection should not be ordered.[65]

Public interest immunity

10.106   Documents do not have to be disclosed where disclosure would be injurious to the public interest.[66] This immunity does not depend upon a party objecting to disclosure, but should and can be raised by the court if necessary. The proper approach where there is a question of public interest immunity is to weigh the two public interests, that of the nation or public service in non-disclosure and that of justice in the production of the documents. The court will consider the importance of the documents in the litigation, and whether their absence will result in a denial of justice to one or other of the parties. In *Campell* v. *Tameside Metropolitan Borough Council*[67] Ackner L.J. said that there

---

[64] [1985] 2 All E.R. 385.
[65] Sir John Donaldson M.R. said that the court had reached this conclusion "with undisguised reluctance, because we think that there is something seriously wrong with the law if Marlon's mother cannot find out what exactly caused this brain damage": *ibid.*, p. 389. This prompted his Lordship's comments about a doctor's common law duty to inform patients when something has gone wrong with the treatment: see § 10.95.
[66] R.S.C., Ord. 24, rr. 7A(6) and 15; Supreme Court Act 1981, s.35(1); *Conway* v. *Rimmer* [1968] A.C. 910; *Burmah Oil Co. Ltd.* v. *Bank of England* [1980] A.C. 1090; *D.* v. *N.S.P.C.C.* [1978] A.C. 171; *Air Canada* v. *Secretary of State for Trade* (No. 2) [1983] 1 All E.R. 910.
[67] [1982] 2 All E.R. 791.

is a heavy burden on the party seeking to justify non-disclosure of relevant documents. The confidential nature of the communication is not of itself a sufficient ground if disclosure would assist the court to ascertain facts relevant to the action:

> "The private promise of confidentiality must yield to the general public interest, that in the administration of justice truth will out, unless by reason of the character of the information or the relationship of the recipient of the information to the informant a more important public interest is served by protecting the information or identity of the informant from disclosure in a court of law."[68]

The Court of Appeal held that confidential psychiatric reports which were held, by an education authority on a pupil, were not protected by public interest immunity in an action for negligence against the authority brought by a teacher who had been assaulted by the boy. Lord Denning M.R. commented that he could see no "difference between this case and the ordinary case against a hospital authority for negligence. The reports of nurses and doctors are, of course, confidential; but they must always be disclosed . . . ."[69]

Public interest immunity will rarely be relevant to medical negligence litigation. The issue was raised in *Re HIV Haemophiliac Litigation*[70] in which haemophiliacs and their families who had developed AIDS or been infected with HIV virus as a result of treatment with contaminated blood products imported from the United States were suing, inter alia, the Department of Health, the licensing authority under the Medicines Act 1968, and the national Blood Products Laboratory. The Department of Health claimed public interest immunity in respect of certain documents on the basis that they related to the formulation of policy by ministers or were briefings for ministers about whether a policy of self-sufficiency in blood products should be established, the resources necessary for such a policy, and the role and organisation of the Blood Products Laboratory and the National Blood Transfusion Service. The plaintiffs conceded that public interest immunity arose, but argued that the public interest in the fair trial of the proceedings outweighed the public interest in preserving the immunity. The Court of Appeal accepted the plaintiffs' argument that it was very likely that the documents contained material which would give substantial support to their contentions in the action and that without them the plaintiffs might be deprived of the means of proper presentation of their case.[71] **10.107**

4. Exchange of medical reports

Expert evidence on both liability and causation will normally be crucial to the outcome of a medical negligence action. Under R.S.C., **10.108**

---

[68] *Ibid.*, pp. 796–7, citing Lord Diplock in *D.* v. *N.S.P.C.C.* [1978] A.C. 171, 218.
[69] [1982] 2 All E.R. 791, 796.
[70] (1990) 140 New L.J. 1349.
[71] Applying the test of Lord Fraser in *Air Canada* v. *Secretary of State for Trade* (No. 2) [1983] 1 All E.R. 910, 917. See further Grubb and Pearl (1991) 141 New L.J. 897 and 938. Public interest immunity might also be raised with respect to the disclosure of raw data in research projects, on the ground that patients and doctors might be unwilling to participate in research if they thought that confidential information would have to be disclosed in the course of litigation. On the other hand, confidentiality can be protected by other means: see § 10.99, n. 51.

Ord. 38, r. 36, a party cannot adduce expert evidence at trial without leave of the court or the consent of all the parties unless he has applied to the court under rule 37 or 41 and has complied with any directions given, or he has complied with automatic directions under R.S.C., Ord. 25, r. 8. Automatic directions apply to personal injury actions, but not to actions for medical negligence. Before *Naylor* v. *Preston Area Health Authority*[72] medical negligence actions were considered to be an exception to the normal rule on the disclosure of expert reports when an application for directions was made, in that expert reports on liability and causation were usually not exchanged.[73] The justification for this was said to be that a defendant's expert report in a medical negligence action often commented on the defendant's proofs of evidence, and disclosure of the report would disclose to the plaintiff a summary of the defendant's case. One consequence of this practice was that medical negligence actions were often conducted in the dark, sometimes with unfortunate consequences. This was apparent in *Wilsher* v. *Essex Area Health Authority*, where Mustill L.J. commented that: "practitioners do their clients and the interests of justice no service by continuing to pursue this policy of concealment. . . . To me it seems wrong that in this area of the law, more than in any other, this kind of forensic blind-man's buff should continue to be the norm."[74]

10.109   *Wilsher* proved to be the stimulus to reform. In *Naylor* v. *Preston Area Health Authority*[75] the plaintiffs in a number of medical negligence actions sought orders under R.S.C., Ord. 38, r. 38, for mutual pre-trial disclosure of the substance of the expert evidence to be given at trial. The Court of Appeal held that the court's discretion to order mutual disclosure was wide and unfettered, and applied to medical negligence actions in the same manner as to any other action for professional negligence. In the great majority of cases the interests of justice would be served by full pre-trial disclosure of the substance of the expert evidence, since the issues between the parties would be refined, costs would be saved, and the chances of a pre-trial settlement of the action would be improved. Sir John Donaldson M.R. observed that:

> " . . . nowadays the general rule is that, whilst a party is entitled to privacy in seeking out the 'cards' for his hand, once he has put his hand together, the litigation is to be conducted with all the cards face up on the table. Furthermore, most of the cards have to be put down well before the hearing . . . [This] is the product of a growing appreciation that the public interest demands that justice be provided as swiftly and as economically as possible."[76]

---

[72] [1987] 2 All E.R. 353.
[73] *Rahman* v. *Kirklees Area Health Authority* [1980] 3 All E.R. 610, C.A., applying R.S.C., Ord. 38, r. 37 as it then stood.
[74] [1986] 3 All E.R. 801, 830. There was no exchange of the expert evidence and as a result the parties misunderstood what the case was about, and the trial lasted 4 weeks instead of the anticipated 5 days.
[75] [1987] 2 All E.R. 353.
[76] *Ibid.*, p. 360.

Exchange should normally be accompanied by identification of any medical or scientific literature, published or unpublished, to which the experts intend to refer.[77]

The present rule under R.S.C., Ord. 38, r. 37,[78] is that where an **10.110** application for disclosure is made the court will direct that the substance[79] of the evidence be disclosed in the form of a report, unless there are special reasons for not doing so. Thus, the presumption is in favour of disclosure. In *Naylor* v. *Preston Area Health Authority*[80] it was suggested that disclosure would not be ordered where there is a risk that it would enable the plaintiff or his experts to trim their evidence, or where the defendants had evidence, referred to in their expert reports, that the plaintiff is faking or grossly exaggerating his symptoms. Sir John Donaldson M.R. said that a refusal of disclosure on these grounds should only occur where there is a "solid basis" for thinking that this is the case.

Simultaneous exchange of experts reports should be the normal **10.111** order,[81] although there may be circumstances where sequential disclosure will be appropriate; where, for example, the particulars of negligence are so vague that it would be unfair to the defendants to expect their experts to deal with them until the plaintiff disclosed, either by further particulars or by his own experts' reports, exactly what his case was.[82] Rule 37 applies only to expert evidence that a party wishes to adduce at trial. An unfavourable report that the party does not wish to rely on does not have to be disclosed.[83]

---

[77] *Ibid.*, p. 362, *per* Sir John Donaldson M.R. This does not mean that if an expert is taken by surprise in cross-examination and wishes to rely on other literature he should not be able to do so: *ibid.* On the admissibility of medical literature and summaries of research studies into the effects of a drug, see *H.* v. *Schering Chemicals Ltd.* [1983] 1 All E.R. 849. Where an expert refers in evidence to the results of research published in a reputable journal the court will ordinarily regard the results as supporting inferences fairly to be drawn from them, unless a different approach is shown to be proper, *per* Bingham J. at p. 853.

[78] As amended by S.I. 1989/2427, with effect from June 4, 1990.

[79] On the meaning of "substance" see *Ollett* v. *British Aerojet Ltd.* [1979] 1 W.L.R. 1197.

[80] [1987] 2 All E.R. 353, 360, 365, 367, *per* Sir John Donaldson M.R., Glidewell L.J. and Sir Frederick Lawton respectively. Sir Frederick Lawton suggested that trimming might happen if there is a substantial dispute about primary facts or there is reason to think that the plaintiff's medical experts have mistakenly based their opinions on clinical findings which the defendants can prove were wrong. This would not seem to justify non-disclosure, however, since exchange is intended to narrow the areas of dispute, and if the plaintiff's experts are mistaken it is better for this to be pointed out before the expense of a trial is incurred.

[81] *Naylor* v. *Preston Area Health Authority* [1987] 2 All E.R. 353, 362 and 365, *per* Sir John Donaldson M.R. and Glidewell L.J. respectively. See, however, the new R.S.C., Ord. 18, r. 12 (amended by S.I. 1989/2427) requiring the plaintiff in a personal injuries action to serve, with his statement of claim, a medical report substantiating all the personal injuries alleged in the statement of claim which the plaintiff proposes to adduce in evidence. For discussion of this provision in the context of medical negligence actions see Body and Levy (1990) *A.V.M.A. Medical and Legal Journal*, No. 3, p. 8.

[82] *Ibid.*, p. 367, *per* Sir Frederick Lawton; *Kirkup* v. *British Rail Engineering Ltd.* [1983] 3 All E.R. 147. R.S.C., Ord. 38, r. 38 provides that the court may order a "without prejudice" meeting of the experts for the purpose of identifying those parts of their evidence which are in issue, the purpose being to narrow the matters in dispute and thus save costs.

[83] The report will be privileged: *Causton* v. *Mann Egerton (Johnsons) Ltd.* [1974] 1 All E.R. 453. One consequence of this is that the plaintiff cannot make it a condition of submitting to a medical examination by the defendant's medical expert that the subsequent report be disclosed to him: *Megarity* v. *D. J. Ryan & Sons Ltd.* [1980] 2 All E.R. 832. The plaintiff is protected by the requirement that the defendant disclose the substance of those reports which he intends to rely on at trial.

10.112   It is now possible for the court to order the exchange of non-expert witnesses' written statements of the evidence that they will give in all actions, including medical negligence actions, where the court thinks it fit to do so for the purpose of disposing fairly and expeditiously of the action and to save costs.[84] Either party may apply for a direction, or the court may raise the matter. This is an important provision for the more open conduct of litigation, which is designed to eliminate surprise at the trial and encourage the settlement of actions. It should also help to identify in advance the real issues in dispute and so provide for a more expeditious hearing.

---

[84] R.S.C., Ord. 38, r. 2A, as amended by S.I. 1988/1340.

APPENDIX

CLAIMS OF MEDICAL NEGLIGENCE AGAINST NHS HOSPITAL AND COMMUNITY DOCTORS AND DENTISTS

HC(89)34
HC(FP)(89)22

To: *Regional Health Authorities*
District Health Authorities
Special Health Authorities

Family Practitioner Committees } *For information*
Community Health Councils

Claims of medical negligence against NHS hospital and community doctors and dentists

This circular will be cancelled and deleted from the current communications index on 1 December 1993 unless notified separately.

Summary

This circular describes the arrangements to apply from 1 January 1990 to the handling of claims of negligence against medical and dental staff employed in the hospital and community health services. General practitioners are not directly affected by these new arrangements, unless they have a contract of employment (for example, as a hospital practitioner) with a health authority.

Action required

Health authorities are asked, with effect from 1 January 1990, to:
  (i) assume responsibility for new and existing claims of medical negligence;
  (ii) ensure a named officer has sufficient authority to make decisions on the conduct of cases on the authority's behalf;
  (iii) cease to require their medical and dental staff to subscribe to a recognised professional defence organisation and cease to reimburse two-thirds of medical defence subscriptions;
  (iv) encourage their medical and dental staff to ensure they have adequate defence cover as appropriate;
  (v) distribute urgently to all their medical and dental staff, including those with honorary NHS contracts, copies of a leaflet explaining the new arrangements (which will be sent separately).

Handling claims of medical negligence

Claims lodged on or after 1 January 1990

1. Health authorities, as corporate bodies, are legally liable for the negligent acts of their employees in the course of their NHS employment. From 1 January 1990 health authorities will also be formally responsible for the

407

handling and financing of claims of negligence against their medical and dental staff. With regard to claims lodged on or after 1 January 1990, it is for each health authority to determine how it wishes claims against its medical or dental staff to be handled. Health authorities may wish to make use of the services of the medical defence organisations (at rates to be agreed), but they may also put the work out to other advisers or deal with it in-house, provided they have the necessary expertise.

Claims notified to an MDO before 1 January 1990

2. Subject to final agreement with the medical defence organisations (MDOs) on the detailed financial arrangements, health authorities will take over financial responsibility for cases outstanding at 1 January 1990. The medical defence organisations have been asked to inform health authorities of the cases in which they may have a substantial liability.

3. Health authorities are entitled to take over the management of any cases outstanding, since they will become liable for the costs and damages arising. However, they are strongly advised to employ the MDOs to continue to handle such claims, in consultation with them and on their behalf, until completion. This is essential not only because of the amount of work in progress, but mainly because the re-insurance cover of the MDOs for claims initiated before 1990 would remain valid only if the MDO currently handling the case continued to do so. If required, health authorities should co-operate with an MDO's reinsurers in the conduct of a claim. Since some of the cover is on an aggregate basis the advice in this paragraph applies to both large and small claims. Health authorities are asked to give prior notice to the Department (finance contact point at paragraph 17) where they wish to adopt a different approach in the handling of claims notified before 1 January 1990.

General handling principles

4. Health authorities should take the essential decisions on the handling of claims of medical negligence against their staff, using MDOs or other bodies as their agents and advisers. Authorities should particularly ensure that authority is appropriately delegated to enable decisions to be made promptly, especially where representatives are negotiating a settlement, and are asked to give such authority to a named officer.

5. In deciding how a case should be handled, and in particular whether to resist a claim or seek an out-of-court settlement, health authorities and those advising them should pay particular attention to any view expressed by the practitioner(s) concerned and to any potentially damaging effect on the professional reputation of the practitioner(s) concerned. They should also have clear regard to:

    (i) any point of principle or of wider application raised by the case; and
    (ii) the costs involved.

6. Where a case involves both a health authority and a general medical practitioner (or any other medical or dental practitioner in relation to work for which a health authority is not responsible), the health authority should consult with the practitioner(s) cited or their representative to seek agreement on how the claim should be handled. Where a health authority (or its employees) alone is cited, but there is reason to believe that the action or inaction of a practitioner outside the health authority's responsibility was a material factor in the negligence concerned, the health authority should similarly consult with a view to obtaining a contribution to the eventual costs and damages. Conversely, in cases where such a practitioner alone is cited, there may be circumstances in which an MDO asks the health authority to make a similar contribution, as if it were a defendant. In any such circumstances, health authorities should co-operate fully in the formulation of the

defence and should seek to reach agreement out of court on the proportion in which any costs and damages awarded to the plaintiff should be borne.

7. It is open to the practitioner concerned to employ at his or her expense an expert adviser, but the practitioner can be represented separately in court only with the agreement of the court. The plaintiff and the health authority may agree to separate representation for the practitioner, but under normal circumstances the health authority should not do so if it considers that this would lead to additional costs or damages falling on the health authority.

Coverage of the scheme and practical arrangements

8. The Health Departments' views on some of the questions that have arisen about the coverage and practical operation of the new arrangements are at Annex A. The indemnity scheme applies to all staff in the course of their HCHS employment, including those engaged through private agencies. The Annex is to be reproduced as a leaflet, which the Health Departments will shortly be making available to health authorities who should distribute them to all their medical and dental staff, including those with honorary NHS contracts.

9. Since authorities will be taking financial responsibility in cases of medical negligence it will no longer be necessary for them to require employed staff to subscribe to a recognised professional defence organisation, for example, as in the recommended form of consultant contract at Annex D of PM(79)11. Authorities should inform their medical and dental staff that the provision no longer applies, but they should encourage such staff to ensure that they have adequate defence cover as appropriate.

Financial arrangements

Pooling arrangements for major settlements

10. Where they have not already done so RHAs are strongly recommended to introduce arrangements (for both medical and non-medical negligence) so as to share with Districts the legal costs and damages of individual large settlements or awards, whose incidence can be quite random. The Department will be making arrangements for Authorities without an RHA, for example the London SHAs, to limit the financial effects on them of substantial settlements.

Funding of claims

11. Subject to final agreement with the MDOs, the public sector will have access to a share of the MDOs' reserves in respect of the hospital and community health services. It is expected that the MDOs will each establish a fund to be drawn on according to criteria set by the Health Departments. The Health Departments will be introducing a transitional scheme under which these reserves will be made available to assist health authorities to meet the costs of particularly large settlements. These will usually, but not necessarily, be cases which arose from incidents before 1 January 1990. The Departments propose to set a threshold, initially £300,000 in England and Wales; 80 per cent. of the costs of a settlement above this threshold, including the legal costs, would be met from this source, until the identified funds are exhausted. Detailed information on the means of access to the funds will be given in the December 1989 edition of 'Financial Matters'.

NHS Trusts

12. NHS Trusts will be responsible for claims of negligence against their medical and dental staff. The Departments are considering what arrangements will apply to NHS Trusts and further guidance will be issued in due course.

Monitoring resource consequences

13. To enable the Departments of Health to assess the resource consequences of these changes, health authorities will be required to submit a return (in the form set out at Annex B) shortly after the end of each financial year, starting with the period 1 January—31 March 1990 in order to obtain an early indication of the costs of the scheme.

Review

14. The Health Departments plan to review the operation of these arrangements in 1992, including the effects on individual practitioners.

Cancellation of existing guidance

15. Circulars HM(54)32 and HM(54)43 will be cancelled from 1 January 1990. Paragraph 4(iii) of Annex 1 of EL(89)P/148 (Hospital medical and dental staff: Locum tenens engaged through private agencies) will be cancelled from 1 January 1990.

16. Paragraph 310 of the Terms and Conditions of Service for Hospital Medical and Dental Staff, and paragraph 289 of the Terms and Conditions of Service for Doctors in Community Medicine and the Community Health Service, (the two-thirds reimbursement scheme) shall not have effect after 31 December 1989.

17. Enquiries which cannot be dealt with by RHAs should be addressed as follows:

General	*Finance*
Mr A Doole	Mr M Horah
FPS1A2	FA2
Room 426 Portland Court	Room 629 Friars House
158-176 Great Portland Street	157-168 Blackfriars Road
London WIN 5TB	London SE1 8EU
Tel: 01-872-9302	Tel: 01-972-2000
Ext 48306	Ext 23024

ANNEX A
MEDICAL NEGLIGENCE: NEW NHS ARRANGEMENTS

Introduction

1. New arrangements for dealing with medical negligence claims in the hospital and community health service are being introduced from 1 January 1990. Subject to final agreement with the medical defence organisations on the financial arrangements, health authorities will take direct financial responsibility for cases initiated before that date, as well as for new claims. In future, medical and dental staff employed by health authorities (health boards in Scotland and Northern Ireland) will no longer be required under the terms of their contracts to subscribe to a medical defence organisation. However, the health authority indemnity will cover only health authority responsibilities. The Health Departments advise practitioners to maintain their defence body

membership in order to ensure they are covered for any work which does not fall within the scope of the indemnity scheme.

Set out below are the Health Departments' replies to some of the questions most commonly asked about the operation of the new arrangements.

2. *Why is this change necessary?*

Medical defence subscriptions rose rapidly in the 1980s, because of growth both in the number of medical negligence cases and in the size of the awards made by the courts. Subscriptions tripled between 1986 and 1988, and the Doctors' and Dentists' Review Body concluded that to take account of the increase in subscriptions through practitioners' pay would lead to distortions in pay and pensions. The pressure to relate subscription rates to the practitioner's specialty underlined the difficulty of maintaining the system. The Health Departments issued in March 1989 a proposal for a health authority indemnity. The new arrangements follow discussions with the medical defence organisations, the medical profession, health authority management and other interested bodies.

Coverage

3. *Who is covered by the health authority indemnity scheme?*

Health authorities are liable at law for the negligence (acts or omissions) of their staff in the course of their NHS employment. The legal position is the same for medical and dental staff as for other NHS employees, but for many years doctors and dentists have themselves taken out medical defence cover through the three medical defence organisations (MDOs). Under the indemnity scheme, health authorities will take direct responsibility for costs and damages arising from medical negligence where they (as employers) are vicariously liable for the acts and omissions of their medical and dental staff.

4. *Does this include clinical academics and research workers?*

Health authorities are vicariously liable for the work done by university medical staff and other research workers under their honorary contracts in the course of their NHS duties, but not for pre-clinical or other work in the university.

5. *Is private work in NHS hospitals covered by the indemnity scheme?*

Health authorities will not be responsible for a consultant's private practice, even in an NHS hospital. However, where junior medical staff are involved in the care of private patients in NHS hospitals, they would normally be doing so as part of their contract with the health authority. It remains advisable that any junior doctor who might be involved in any work outside the scope of his or her employment should have medical defence (or insurance) cover.

6. *Is Category 2 work covered?*

Category 2 work (*e.g.* reports for insurance companies) is by definition not undertaken for the employing health authority, and will therefore not be covered by the indemnity scheme; medical defence cover would be appropriate.

7. *Are GMC disciplinary proceedings covered?*

Health authorities should not be financially responsible for the defence of medical staff involved in GMC disciplinary proceedings. It is the responsibility of the practitioner concerned to take out medical defence cover against such an eventuality.

8. *Is a hospital doctor doing a GP locum covered?*

This would not be the responsibility of the health authority, since it would be general practice. The hospital doctor and the general practitioners concerned should ensure that there is appropriate medical defence cover.

9. *Is a GP seeing his own patient in hospital covered?*

A GP providing medical care to patients in hospital under a contractual arrangement, *e.g.* where the GP was employed as a clinical assistant, will be covered by the health authority indemnity. On the other hand, if the health authority is essentially providing only hotel services and the patient(s) remain in the care of the GP, the GP would be responsible and medical defence cover would be appropriate.

10. *Are GP trainees working in general practice covered?*

In general practice the responsibility for training and for paying the salary of a GP trainee rests with the trainer (with funds from the FPC). Where the trainee's medical defence subscription is higher than the subscription of an SHO in the hospital service, he or she may apply through the trainer for the difference in subscription to be reimbursed. While the trainee is receiving a salary in general practice it is advisable that both the trainee and the trainer, and indeed other members of the practice, should have medical defence cover.

11. *Are clinical trials covered?*

The new arrangements do not alter the current legal position. If the health authority was responsible for a clinical trial authorised under the Medicines Act 1968 or its subordinate legislation and that trial was carried out by or on behalf of a doctor involving NHS patients of his, such a doctor would be covered by the indemnity scheme. Similarly, for a trial not involving medicines, the health authority would take financial responsibility unless the trial were covered by such other indemnity as may have been agreed between the health authority and those responsible for the trial. In any case, health authorities should take steps to make sure that they are informed of clinical trials in which their staff are taking part in their NHS employment and that these trials have the required Research Ethics Committee approval.

12. *Would a doctor be covered if he was working other than in accordance with the duties of his post?*

Such a doctor would be covered by the health authority indemnity for actions in the course of NHS employment, and this should be interpreted liberally. For work not covered in this way the doctor may have a civil, or even in extreme circumstances criminal, liability for his actions.

13. *Are doctors attending accident victims ('Good Samaritan' acts) covered?*

By definition, 'Good Samaritan' acts are not part of the doctor's work for the employing authority. Medical defence organisations are willing to provide low-cost cover against the (unusual) event of a doctor performing such an act being sued for negligence.

14. *Are doctors in public health medicine or in community health services doing work for local authorities covered? Are occupational physicians covered?*

Doctors in public health medicine, or clinical medical officers, carrying out local authority functions under their health authority contract would be acting in the course of their NHS employment. They will therefore be covered by the health authority indemnity. The same principle applies to occupational physicians employed by health authorities.

15. *Will NHS hospital doctors working for other agencies, e.g. the Prison Service, be covered?*

In general, health authorities will not be financially responsible for the acts of NHS staff when they are working on a contractual basis for other agencies. (Conversely, they will be responsible where, for example, a Ministry of Defence doctor works in an NHS hospital.) Either the agency commissioning the work would be responsible, or the doctor should have medical defence cover. However, health authorities' indemnity should cover work for which they pay a fee, such as domiciliary visits and family planning services.

16. *Are retired doctors covered?*

The health authority indemnity will apply to acts or omissions in the course of NHS employment, regardless of when the claim was notified. Health authorities will thus cover doctors who have subsequently left the Service, but they may seek their cooperation in statements in the defence of a case.

17. *Are doctors offering services to voluntary bodies such as the Red Cross or hospices covered?*

The health authority would be responsible for the doctor's actions only if the health authority were responsible for the medical staffing of the voluntary body. If not, the doctors concerned may wish to ensure that they have medical defence cover, as they do at present.

18. *Will a health authority provide cover for a locum hospital doctor?*

A health authority will take financial responsibility for the acts and omissions of a locum doctor, whether 'internal' or provided by an external agency.

19. *Are private sector rotations for hospital staff covered?*

The medical staff of independent hospitals are responsible for their own medical defence cover, subject to the requirements of the hospital managers. If NHS staff in the training grades work in independent hospitals as part of their NHS training, they would be covered by the health authority indemnity, provided that such work was covered by an NHS contract.

20. *Will academic General Practice be covered?*

The Health Departments have no plans to extend the health authority indemnity to academic departments of general practice. In respect of general medical services FPCs will be making payments by fees and allowances which include an element for expenses, of which medical defence subscriptions are a part.

Practical arrangements

21. *On what basis will medical defence organisations handle claims for health authorities?*

MDOs, in advising on claims for health authorities, will act as their agents; the charging arrangements for such services are for agreement between the MDO and the authority concerned.

22. *Will doctors be reimbursed by MDOs for the 'unexpired' portion of their subscriptions?*

This is a matter between each MDO and its members.

23. *Will membership of a medical defence organisation continue to be a contractual obligation?*

On an individual basis doctors and dentists may wish to continue their membership in order to receive the cover referred to in paragraphs 5–20 above, as well as the other legal and advisory services provided by the MDOs. The Health Departments are advising health authorities that they should no longer require their medical and dental staff to subscribe to an MDO, but a health authority could require a doctor to be a member of an MDO if the doctor were to be carrying out private work on NHS premises. The two-thirds reimbursement of subscriptions will cease at the end of 1989.

24. *Will medical defence subscriptions be tax-allowable in future?*

The Health Departments understand that medical defence subscriptions will continue to be allowable under income tax rules.

25. *What happens if a doctor wishes to contest a claim which the health authority would prefer to settle out of court, e.g. where a point of principle or a doctor's reputation is at stake?*

While the final decision in a case rests with the health authority since it will bear the financial consequences, it should take careful note of the practitioner's view. Health authorities may seek the advice of the relevant MDO on whether a case should be contested, and they should not settle cases without good cause.

26. *If a doctor wishes to have separate representation in a case, what would be the extent of his liability?*

Since it is the health authority which is sued for the medical negligence of its staff and which will in future be solely financially liable, then it must have the ultimate right to decide how the defence of a case is to be handled. Subject to this, a health authority may welcome a practitioner being separately advised in a case without cost to the health authority. However, if a practitioner claims that his interests in any case are distinct from those of the health authority and wishes to be separately represented in the proceedings, he will need the agreement of the plaintiff, the health authority and the court. If liability is established, he would have to pay not only his own legal expenses but also any further costs incurred as a result of his being separately represented. The health authority would remain liable for the full award of damages to the plaintiff.

27. *Will health authorities put restrictions on the clinical autonomy of doctors?*

Health authorities have a responsibility to organise services in a manner which is in the best interests of patients. In the past, medical defence organisations have advised doctors and dentists on patterns of practice carrying unacceptable dangers to patients. However, there is no question of health authorities barring certain services which carry risks but are a high priority for patients.

28. *Will health authorities be able to secure statements from doctors for the defence of a case of medical negligence?*

Health authorities will need co-operation from medical and dental staff if they are to defend cases. As part of this, practitioners should supply such statements or documents as the health authority or its solicitors may reasonably require in investigating or defending any claim. A doctor's refusal without good reason to provide a statement could result in the health authority being unable to defend itself properly and so incurring additional costs.

29. *Will health authorities be able to trace doctors who formerly worked for them?*

It is accepted that health authorities may have difficulty in tracing the doctors responsible, especially if they were junior medical staff at the time, and in securing statements from them; they may find the MDOs helpful in this respect. Often, however, good medical records kept at the time will be of more value than statements made some years after the event.

30. *Will the new arrangements apply to NHS Trust hospitals (self-governing units)?*

As employers, NHS Trusts will be vicariously liable for the acts of their employed medical and dental staff, and will take the financial responsibility for negligence. Further guidance will be issued in due course.

Financial effects

31. *How can District Health Authorities meet damages which could be as much as £1m for a single case?*

RHAs have been asked to make arrangements under which they will provide an element of cost-sharing with Districts for medical negligence costs above a certain level, as most RHAs do for non-medical negligence actions at present. And for a transitional period health authorities will have access (under certain criteria) to some of the reserves of the MDOs.

32. *The incidence of medical negligence damages may be uneven as between Regions; how will that be met?*

It is quite likely that some Regions will have to pay out more under the new arrangements than they would in reimbursing two-thirds of medical defence subscriptions. The funds from the MDOs will be of some help in the short term, but in the longer run the incidence of medical negligence costs and damages will fall on the Regions where they arise.

UK Health Departments
December 1989

ANNEX B

INFORMATION TO BE RETURNED ANNUALLY, NO LATER THAN 31 MAY (STARTING 31/5/90)

1. The following information should be supplied for the previous financial year:
   i. The number of claims of medical negligence against the health authority and/or its employees, including the number of cases brought forward from an earlier period;
   ii. the number of such cases settled during the period with the health authority's costs, including damages payable, in the following cost bands:

	Number of cases	£	£
(a)			0–100,000
(b)			100,000–200,000
(c)			200,000–300,000
(d)			over £300,000

   iii. The total cost of the settlements reached or awards made; distinguishing
       (a) the Authority's costs from the payment of the plaintiff's costs and damages; and
       (b) an estimate of costs and damages attributable to medical negligence, as distinct from negligence of other staff.
2. Returns to be sent to: FPS1A2
                          Room 426 Portland Court
                          158-176 Great Portland Street
                          London W1N 5TB

GLOSSARY OF MEDICAL TERMS

Abdominoplasty: plastic surgery on the abdomen.

Abduction: movement away from the mid-line.

Acceleration injury: diffuse shearing injury to the brain substance.

Adduction: movement towards the mid-line.

Agnosia: inability to recognise familiar complex auditory, visual or tactile stimuli, despite intact sensory input to the brain.

Agraphia: inability to express thoughts in writing.

AIDS: acquired immune deficiency syndrome; an illness (often if not always fatal) in which opportunistic infections or malignant tumours develop as a result of the severe loss of cellular immunity, which is itself caused by earlier infection with a retrovirus, HIV, transmitted in sexual fluids and blood.

Akinesia: inability to start a movement.

Alexia: loss of power to grasp meaning of written or printed words and sentences.

Amenorrhoea: absence or suppression of menstrual discharge.

Amnesia: disorders of memory, literally without (a) memory (mnesis). May be an imprinting deficit for new material, or a memory retrieval deficit for old material.

Amniocentesis: the process whereby a needle is inserted in the sac which surrounds the fetus in the uterus (the amnion) and some of the contained amniotic fluid is withdrawn. The procedure has a great potential for antenatal diagnosis.

Ankylosis: obliteration of a joint by fusion, either bony or fibrous.

Anosmia: loss of sense of smell. May also affect the perceived taste of liquid and solid foodstuffs.

Anoxia: deficiency in oxygen supply to the brain, if profound, causes permanent brain damage.

Anterograde amnesia: loss of memory for events occurring subsequent to amnesia-causing trauma; patient is unable to acquire or learn new information.

Anticonvulsant: a drug used to reduce the incidence of epileptic fits, for example valproate (Epilim), carbamazepine (Tegretol), phenytoin (Epanutin).

Aorta: the major artery of the body from which all other systemic arteries derive; it originates in the left ventricle of the heart and ends by dividing into the common iliac arteries which are destined to supply blood to the legs.

Aortography: radiographic examination of the aorta, usually by insertion of a catheter into the femoral artery.

Aortoplasty: operation to repair aorta.

Aphasia: absence of the capacity for language comprehension, or expression, in the absence of any defect in the voice, sight or hearing.

Aphonia: inability to make sounds.

Apnoea: suspension or cessation of breathing.

Aplastic anaemia: anaemia (lack of haemoglobin) caused by poor or absent production of blood cells in the bone marrow.

Apraxia: loss of ability to carry out skilled voluntary movements, in the absence of limb paralysis.

Arachnoid mater: a water-tight meningeal membrane forming the outer boundary of the subarachnoid space that contains cerebrospinal fluid.

Arthrodesis: surgical fusion of a joint.

Arthroplasty: surgical reconstitution or replacement of a joint.

Aspiration: sucking out fluid (*e.g.* from a joint or cavity) through a hollow needle.

Astereognosis: inability to recognise objects by touching them alone.

Ataxia: loss of coordination and precision of movement of torso, head or limbs due to a defect in the cerebellum, vestibular or proprioceptive system.

Atrophy: a state of wasting due to some interference with tissue nutrition.

Attention: the active selectiion of information, with concurrent inhibition of other, competing information.

Audiometry: the assessment and quantification of hearing function.

Avascular necrosis: death of tissue through deprivation of blood supply; refers particularly to bones—*e.g.* head of femur following fracture of neck of femur.

Babinski reflex: extension of the great toe on scratching the sole, indicating an upper motor neurone lesion.

Basal ganglia: clusters of nerve cells (grey matter), deep in each cerebral hemisphere, relaying motor and sensory impulses.

Bilateral carotid arteriogram: a picture of the arteries on either side of the neck which supply blood to the head. The examination of the arteries is effected by means of radiology after injection of a radio-opaque material.

Biopsy: sample of tissue taken from the living body for microscopic examination.

Bitemporal hemianopia: loss of the outer halves of both visual fields.

Bi-valve: removal of a plaster cast by cutting along each side of its length, permitting replacement if required.

Bradykinesia: slowness in movement.

Brachial palsy: a condition characterised by a weak, numb or paralysed arm. Often caused by injury to the brachial plexus of nerves which arise from the neck to supply the arm (*e.g.* as a result of a road traffic accident).

Brain stem: posterior part of the brain comprising the midbrain, pons and medulla containing vital centres, ascending and descending tracts, nuclei of cranial nerves and the reticular formation.

Broca's area: an area for speech in the dominant, frontal lobe of the brain.

Bulbar: concerning the medulla.

Burr-hole: hole drilled in the skull.

Bursa: a cyst-like sac between a bony prominence and the skin, *e.g.* pre-patellar bursa, inflammation in which constitutes "housemaid's knee".

Callus: the cement-like new bone formation which produces union of the fragments of a fracture.

Cardiac: pertaining to the heart.

Carotid endarterectomy: operation on the carotid artery (in the neck) to remove debris blocking the artery and hence reduce the risk of a stroke.

Carpal tunnel: the channel in the wrist through which the median nerve passes.

Central nervous system (CNS): comprising the spinal cord and brain, the latter containing the cerebrum, cerebellum, mid-brain, pons and medulla. Excludes peripheral nerves that run outside the spinal cord.

Cephalic: pertaining to the head.

Cerebral: pertaining to the brain.

Cerebral palsy: any of various non-progressive forms of paralysis caused by damage to motor areas of the brain before or during birth, manifested in early childhood by weakness and imperfect control of the affected muscles.

Cervical: pertaining to the neck.

Cervical laminectomy: an operation to remove a prolapsed spinal disc from the neck.

Chondral: pertaining to the cartilage.

Crohn's disease: inflammation of the bowel.

Chronic adhesive arachnoiditis: inflammation of the lining of the brain and spinal cord.

Circumflex artery: an artery of curved or winding form, or which bends around others; example—the circumflex iliac artery.

Claudication: lameness, applied particularly to pain in the calf muscles resulting from defective blood supply owing to arterial disease.

Cognition: mental functions of attention, memory, thinking, perception, and intellectual activity.

Colostomy: the operation of making an artificial opening into the colon (the greater portion of the large intestine) through the abdominal wall.

Coma: absence of awareness of self and environment even when the subject is externally stimulated. Defined on the Glasgow Coma Scale as a score of eight or less.

Comminuted: a type of fracture of a bone in which there are more than two fragments.

Concussion: a reversible disturbance of consciousness following head trauma.

Confabulation: filling in gaps in memory with invented and often improbable stories or facts which the patient accepts as true.

Consciousness: state of awareness of the self and the environment, the opposite of coma.

Contusion: bruising of neural tissue.

Corneal reflex: normal blinking on touching the cornea of the eye.

Corpus callosum: a large bank of nerve fibres connecting the two cerebral hemispheres.

Cortex: the outer layer of a structure, *e.g.* the "shell" of a bone; the surface layer (grey matter) of the cerebral and cerebellar hemispheres of the brain.

Cortical atrophy: thinning of cortical tissue.

Costal: pertaining to the ribs.

Cranial nerves: the nerves of the brain, twelve on each side, arising directly from the brain and the brain stem.

Craniectomy: opening in the skull where the bone is not replaced.

Craniotomy: opening in the skull where the bone is replaced.

Crepitus: a creaking or grating, found in osteo-arthritic joints; also in recent fractures and with inflammation of tendons and their sheaths (tenosynovitis).

CSF: cerebrospinal fluid, which covers the surface of the brain and spinal cord and circulates inside the ventricles of the brain.

CT (Computed Tomography): a scan which uses a finely collimated moving X-ray beam and a computer to construct pictures of a part of the body, which show internal structure as though the organ examined had been sliced open.

Cyanosis: blueness from deficient oxygenation of the blood.

Deceleration injury: *see* Acceleration injury.

Degeneration: death of tissue.

Dementia: deterioration of intellect, involving a diffuse reduction in cognitive functions, and changes in personality.

Demyelination: loss of the myelin that sheathes nerve fibres.

Denial: a defence mechanism whereby unacceptable ideas or facts are not perceived or allowed into full conscious awareness.

Depo-Provera: injectible contraceptive hormone.

Diabetes insipidus: passage of uncontrolled amounts of dilute urine.

Diabetes mellitus: passage of uncontrolled amounts of urine containing too high a concentration of glucose.

Diffuse injury: pattern of brain injury following rapid acceleration or deceleration of the head, as in some falls or road traffic accidents.

Dilatation and Curettage (D and C): scraping the inside of the womb; this procedure is often performed in cases of excessive bleeding.

Diplopia: double vision.

Disarticulation: amputation through a joint.

Disc, intervertebral: fibro-cartilaginous "cushion" between two vertebrae.

Discotomy: surgical incision into a spinal disc.

Disorientation: a state of mental confusion with respect to time, place, identity of self, or other persons or objects.

Distal: farthest point from the centre (opposite to proximal).

Dominant hemisphere: the cerebral hemisphere or side of the brain controlling speech. The left hemisphere in most people.

Dorsal spine: that part of the spine to which the ribs are connected; known also as the "thoracic" spine.

Dorsiflexion: movement of a joint in a backward direction.

Dorsum: back or top, *e.g.* back of hand, top of foot.

Dupuytren's contracture: thickened fibrous tissue in the palm of the hand causing contracture of the fingers.

Dura mater: outer layer of the meninges that are the membranous coverings of the brain. Closely applied to the inner surface of the skull and spinal canal in the vertebrae.

Dys-: prefix meaning difficult, defective, painful, *e.g.* dyspnoea, meaning shortness of breath.

Dyscrasia: an abnormal state of the body or part of the body, especially one due to abnormal development or metabolism.

Dysarthria: disturbance of speech articulation. Pronunciation, intonation and metre of spoken word defective.

Dyslexia: a reading disability.

Dysphagia: disturbance of swallowing.

Dysphasia: disturbance of communication. Receptive component in which the written or spoken word is not perceived correctly. Expressive component in which the patient cannot find the correct word to express themselves.

Dysplasia: malformation, abnormal development of tissue.

-ectomy: suffix meaning surgical excision—*e.g.* patellectomy, removal of the patella.

EEG: (electroencephalography) recording the amplified spontaneous electrical activity of the brain from surface electrodes.

Effusion: extravasation of fluid in a joint (or any cavity), *e.g.* "water on the knee" (*i.e.* synovitis).

Electrocardiogram (ECG): a tracing which represents the passage of the nervous electrical discharge through the muscle of the heart. The technique involves recording from the leads placed on the limbs and on specified parts of the chest wall. Its main use is to follow the progress of a myocardial infarction (ischaemic death of portions of heart muscle) or to assist in the diagnosis in the event of uncertainty: indigestion is, for example, notorious for mimicking cardiac disease.

Electroconvulsive therapy (ECT): an accepted treatment for, particularly, depressive psychosis. It consists of the passage of an electric current through the frontal lobes of the brain.

EMG: (electromyography) recording of muscle and nerve electrical activity.

Embolism: blockage of a blood vessel by a clot which has migrated.

Emphysema, surgical: collection of air in the tissues through puncture of the lung by a fractured rib.

Encephalopathy: brain damage due to various (*e.g.* toxic) causes.

Encephalitis: inflammation of the brain. A potentially fatal viral or bacterial disease that damages the brain and brainstem bilaterally.

ENT: ear, nose and throat.

Enuresis: urinary incontinence during the night.

Epidural: an injection of anaesthetic into the epidural space of the spine, used especially to control pain during childbirth by producing a loss of sensation below the waist without affecting consciousness.

Epilepsy: an episodic disturbance of brain activity following abnormal spontaneous electrical discharges within the brain, leading to a fit.

Epiphyseal line: the cartilaginous plate near the end of a bone at which the bone grows in length.

Epiphysis: the end of a bone during the period of growth.

Erythema: superficial blush or redness of the skin, *e.g.* as from a very slight burn or scald.

Erythrocyte: red blood corpuscle.

Eschar: crust of dead skin.

ESR: erythrocyte sedimentation rate. A laboratory test upon the blood to detect the presence of an inflammatory process in the body.

Evoked response: (or potential) an electrical response recorded in some part of the nervous system (*e.g.* visual cortex), evoked or elicited by stimulation elsewhere (*e.g.* eyes—visual evoked responses).

Extension: moving a joint into the straight position (opposite to flexion).

Extensor plantar response: *see* Babinski.

External: outer side, syn, lateral (opposite to medial).

Fascia: a fibrous membrane.

Flaccidity: loss of normal tone in muscles leaving them abnormally limp.

Flexion: moving a joint into the bent position (opposite to extension).

Flexor plantar response: the normal downward movement of the big toe when the sole is scratched.

Flexor spasm: painful contraction of muscles in spastic limbs.

Focal injury: injury to a circumscribed area of brain.

Fossa: anatomical term for a depression or furrow.

Frontal: at the front of the brain, or the skull.

Frontal lobes: the brain's anterior portions lying above the eyes.

Gangrene: total death of a structure through deprivation of blood supply.

Genu: the knee joint.

Glasgow Coma Scale (GCS): numerical scale from three (total unresponsiveness) to 15 (normal consciousness).

Gliosis: scar tissue replacement of damaged brain tissue.

Gluteal: pertaining to the buttock.

Grand mal epilepsy: epilepsy involving loss of consciousness and generalised convulsions, often associated with urinary incontinence and tongue biting during the fits.

Grey matter: neural tissue largely comprising nerve cell bodies and dendrites constituting the cerebral cortex, the brain nuclei, and central columns of the spinal cord.

Gyri: convolutions on the cortical surface of the brain, representing folds of the cerebral cortex.

Haemarthrosis: effusion of blood in a joint.

Haematoma: clotted blood.

Haemorrhage: blood that has escaped from a blood vessel. An extradural haemorrhage becomes an extradural haematoma when the blood begins to clot.

Hallux: the great toe.

Hemianopia: loss of half of the visual field. If vision is lost on the same side in both eyes, the hemianopia is termed homonymous.

Hemiparesis: unilateral motor weakness, affecting face, arm, and or leg.

Hepatitis: infection of the liver. Hepatitis A, known as infective hepatitis, is spread by ingestion through faecal transmission, and is thus very common in institutions. Hepatitis B, or serum hepatitis, spreads from blood or blood products to blood; it requires either to be injected or to be applied to open breaches in the skin—thus, drug addicts, haemophiliacs and the like are particularly at risk. The third principle variant of the disease is known as hepatitis non-A, non-B and is diagnosed by exclusion of the other recognisable types.

Heterotopic ossification: (calcification) the formation of extraneous bone in muscle tissue, causing painful and often severely restricted movement.

HIV: human Immuno-deficiency virus; this is the virus which causes aids.

Hydrocephalus: accumulation of excessive cerebrospinal fluid in the ventricles of the brain.

Hyper-: prefix meaning increase above the normal.

Hypercarbia: abnormally high concentration of carbon dioxide in the blood.

Hyperphagia: pathological over-eating.

Hypo-: prefix meaning decrease below the normal; anatomical term for below.

Hypotension: low blood pressure.

Hypoxia: the condition of the body when it is supplied with insufficient oxygen for its needs.

Hysterectomy: excision of the uterus.

Iatrogenic: induced unintentionally by a physician through his diagnosis, manner or treatment; of or pertaining to the induction of (mental or bodily) disorders, symptoms, etc., in this way.

Ictal: a symptom or sign during an epileptic fit, causally related to the fit.

Idiopathic: of unknown cause.

Illeum: the lower half of the small intestine.

Illium: the main bone of the pelvis.

Induration: hardening of a tissue.

Infarct: a wedge shaped area of non-viable tissue produced by loss of the blood supply.

Inguinal: pertaining to the groin.

Intelligence: those aspects of cognitive function which are measured by an intelligence test; may reflect the ability to learn from experience, think in abstract terms, and deal effectively with one's environment.

Intercostal: between the ribs.

Intracranial hypertension: high tissue pressure inside the skull, not high blood pressure.

Ipsilateral: on the same side.

IQ (Intelligence Quotient): a statistically derived average of verbal, non-verbal and general ability from one or many test performances which comprise a standardised intelligence test (*e.g. see* WAIS). An individual performance is compared to the average for a particular age group.

Ischaemia: a reduced or insufficient amount of blood being supplied to a region of the brain or body.

-itis: suffix meaning inflammation, *e.g.* osteitis, inflammation of a bone.

Keloid: a scar which is thickened and deep pink in colour.

Kyphosis: posterior convexity of the spine.

Laceration: tearing of tissue.

Laminectomy: excision of one or more of the posterior arches of the vertebrae (each arch being formed by the junction of two laminae), especially as a method of access to the spinal canal.

Laparoscopy: visual examination of the interior of the peritoneal cavity by means of a laparoscope inserted into it through the abdominal wall or vagina.

Laparotomy: a cutting through the abdominal walls into the cavity of the abdomen.

Lateral: outer side, or external (opposite to medial).

Lesion: a structural change in a tissue caused by disease or injury.

Leucocyte: white blood corpuscle.

Lipping: ridge of adventitious bone at joint edges in arthritis (syn. osteophytic formation).

Lobectomy: excision of diseased or traumatised lobe of the brain.

Long term memory: the relatively permanent component of memory, one's previously acquired knowledge, as opposed to the more fluid short term memory.

Lordosis: anterior convexity of spine.

Lumbar: the "small" of the back, *i.e.* situated between the dorsal (thoracic) and sacral levels.

Lumen: the cavity of a tubular structure.

Macro-: prefix meaning abnormally large size.

Malar: pertaining to the cheek.

Mallet finger: inability actively to straighten the terminal joint of a finger.

Mandible: the lower jaw.

Mastoidectomy: an operation to clear out infection in the bony protuberance behind the ear.

Maxilla: the upper jaw and cheek bones.

Medial: inner side, or internal (opposite to lateral).

Mediastinoscopy: procedure to view the organs of the mediastinum. The mediastinum is in the central chest and contains the heart, windpipe (trachea) and gullet (oesophagus).

Medullary cavity: the soft interior of a bone.

Memory: the process through which we retain learned knowledge, in a form that can be recalled later.

Memory span: the number of items (digits, words) that are correctly recalled after a single presentation.

Meningitis: inflammation of the membranes of the brain or spinal cord.

Meniscus: the semilunar cartilage of the knee.

Mesothelioma: a cancer of the pleura (the linings of the inner chest wall and outside surface of the lungs) which is associated with asbestos inhalation.

Micro-: prefix meaning abnormally small size.

Migraine: hemicranial headache due to a disturbance in the normal calibre of the cranial blood vessels. May be precipitated by trauma, and has a number of clinical variants.

Motor: pertaining to movement (applied particularly to muscle action).

MRI: (Magnetic Resonance Image) a scan which uses signals emitted from water in tissue placed in a strong magnetic field and a computer to construct pictures that are presented as apparent slices through the body in any plane. Can detect subtle tissue abnormalities.

Myelination: formation of fatty substance around nerve fibres or axons, important for nerve impulse conduction, the white matter of the brain and spinal cord.

Myelo-: prefix meaning pertaining to the spinal cord.

Myelography: radiography of the spinal cord after injection of a contrast medium (radio opaque liquid) into the subarachnoid space.

Myeloid leukaemia: a virulent species of white cell cancer.

Myo-: prefix meaning pertaining to muscle.

Necrosis: death of tissue, end stage of infarction.

Neural function: the electrical and chemical activity of nerve cells and fibres.

Nystagmus: rhythmic involuntary oscillatory movement of the eyes.

Obtundation: reduction in alertness accompanied by a lowered awareness of the environment, slower psychological responses to stimulation, and increased hours of sleep, often with drowsiness in between.

Occipital lobes: the brain's posterior portions.

Oculo-vestibular reflex: eye movement reflex that is elicited in comatose patients with an intact brain stem, by initiating convection currents in the vestibular apparatus by syringing ice cold water into the external auditory meatus.

Oculomotor: concerned with eye movement.

Oedema: accumulation of fluid in tissues, usually following tissue damage.

Olfactory: pertaining to the sense of smell.

Oligo-: prefix meaning few or lack of.

Orthopaedic: relating to the muscular-skeletal system.

Osteitis: inflammation of bone.

Osteophyte: ridge of adventitious bone at joint edges in arthritis (syn. "lipping").

Osteoporosis: loss of mineral salts from bones, the result of lack of use owing to injury or disease, reducing the mechanical stregnth of the bone.

Osteotomy: dissection of the bones (*anat.*); cutting of a bone in order to correct a deformity (*surg.*).

Outcome: function at a specified interval after an insult or theraputic intervention.

Paget's Disease: a disease which affects chiefly the elderly and is often symptomless, being characterised by the localized alteration of tissue in one or more bones (most often in the spine, skull or pelvis), which becomes thickened and may undergo fracture or bending.

Paired associate learning: the learning of stimulus-response pairs. When the first member of a pair (stimulus) is presented, the patient must give the second member (response).

Palmar flexion: moving the wrist in the direction that the palm faces (syn. flexion).

Para-: prefix meaning by the side of, near, through, abnormality.

Paresis: incomplete paralysis.

Parietal lobes: area of brain midway between the front and back of the head.

Patent ductus arteriosis: the ductus arteriosis is a blood vessel adjacent to the heart which allows blood to bypass the lungs while a foetus is in the womb. At birth it should close. If it remains patent it can result in a "blue baby" and require an operation to tie it off.

Periarthritis: inflammation round a joint, due to infection or injury, causing pain and restricted movement.

Peritoneum: the double serous membrane which lincs the cavity of the abdomen.

Peritonitis: inflammation of the peritoneum, or of some part of it.

Pertussis: whooping-cough.

Petit mal epilepsy: a form of epilepsy involving a momentary alteration in consciousness.

Phenytoin: anticonvulsant drug (trade name: Epanutin).

Pia mater: inner layer of the meninges that are the membranous coverings of the brain. Closely applied to the surface of the brain and the spinal cord.

Pituitary fossa: the bony cavity at the base of the skull where the pituitary gland (which has an important influence on growth and bodily functions) is situated.

423

Plantar flexion: flexing the foot, pointing the toes downwards.

-plegia: suffix meaning paralysis.

Plasticity: the modifiability of a substrate, enabling functional change.

Pneumoconiosis: a disease of the lungs; this condition is often manifested by miners who have been exposed to coal dust.

Pneumothorax: air in the pleural cavity, *e.g.* from puncture of the lung by a fractured rib—and causing collapse of the lung.

Poly-: prefix meaning much or many.

Porencephaly: cavities in the brain substance due to tissue loss after severe brain damage.

Post traumatic amnesia: absence of memory for events surrounding the insult. May occur despite apparently normal levels of arousal.

Prefrontal: the most anterior portion of the frontal lobe.

Primacy effect: (in memory) the tendency for initial words in a list to be recalled more readily than those from the middle or end of the list.

Proactive interference: the interference of earlier learning with the learning and recall of new material.

Prolapse: extrusion or protrusion, of a structure.

Pronation: twisting the forearm, the elbow being fixed, to bring the palm of hand facing downwards (opposite to supination).

Proximal: nearest the centre (opposite to distal).

Psychomotor epilepsy: a form of epileptic seizure in which the individual loses contact with the environment but appears conscious and performs some routine, repetitive act, or engages in more complex activity.

Psychosocial: areas of psychological and social functioning, which may include family status, emotional adjustment, interpersonal skills and adjustment, employment or other activity, financial status, and acceptance of disability.

Ptosis: drooping of the eyelid.

Puerperal Fever: infection of the vagina and uterus consequent on childbirth.

Pulmonary: pertaining to the lung.

Quadriplegia: paralysis of all four limbs.

Reaction time: the time between the presentation of a stimulus and the occurrence of a response.

Recency effect: (in memory) the tendency for the last few words on a list to be recalled more readily than words elsewhere from the list.

Recognition: the correct association of an item with a category.

Reduction: restoration to a normal position, *e.g.* of a fractured bone or a dislocated joint.

Reflex: an automatic response to a stimulus.

Rena: pertaining to the kidney.

Retrieval: locating and reproducing information from memory.

Retro-: prefix meaning behind or backward.

Retroactive interference: the interference in recall of something earlier learned by something subsequently learned.

Retrobulbar bleed: bleeding which occurs behind the eyeball.

Retrograde amnesia: loss of memory for information acquired prior to the event that causes amnesia.

Retrolental fibroplasia: the abnormal proliferation of fibrous tissue immediately behind the lens of the eye, leading to blindness. It was formerly seen in newborn premature infants due to overadministration of oxygen.

Rigidity: increased tone in limb or trunk.

Romberg's sign: pathological increase of body sway when the patient stands erect with toes and heels touching and eyes closed; unsteadiness occurs if test positive. A test of balance and proprioception.

Rotational injury: diffuse shearing injury to brain substance magnified by rotatory forces.

Rubella: german measles.

Sclerosis: increased density, *e.g.* of a bone, owing to disease or injury.

Scoliosis: lateral (*i.e.* sideways) curvature of the spine.

Sensory: pertaining to sensation.

Sequestrum: a fragment of dead bone.

Short term memory: the component of the memory system that has limited capacity and will maintain information for only a brief time.

Sigmoidoscope: a speculum for examining the lower bowel and for assisting in minor operations therein.

Sinus: a track leading from an infected focus, *e.g.* in a bone—to an opening on the surface of the skin.

Slough: tissue, usually skin, dead from infection.

Sodium valproate: anticonvulsant drug (trade name: Epilim).

Somatosensory area: regions in the parietal lobes of the brain which register sensory experiences such as heat, cold, pain and touch.

Spasmodic torticollis: a rheumatic seizure of the muscles of the neck in which it is so twisted as to keep the head turned to one side; also known as wry-neck.

Spondylosis: degenerative changes in the spine.

Status epilepticus: epileptic fits following each other in continuous rapid succession.

Stevens-Johnson syndrome: an illness characterised by a severe widespread rash and mouth ulcers, often caused by an allergic reaction to a drug.

Stupor: unconscious state, but arousable.

Subcortical: beneath the cortex.

Subdural haemorrhage: bleeding, usually due to trauma, between the dura mater and the brain.

Sulci: grooves on the surface of the brain separating cerebral gyri or convolutions.

Supination: twisting the forearm, the elbow being flexed, to bring palm of hand facing upwards (opposite to pronation).

Syndrome: characteristic collection of signs and symptoms.

Synovitis: inflammation of the lining membrane of a joint.

Tachycardia: racing of the heart; increased pulse rate.

Tegretol: anticonvulsant drug.

Temporal lobes: the portions of the brain behind the eyes.

Teratogenic: pertaining to teratogenesis—any substance, agent or process that induces the formation of developmental abnormalities in a foetus.

Test battery: a collection of tests used to appraise individual abilities.

Therapeutia: pertaining to treatment, the application of a remedy.

Thorax, thoracic: the chest, pertaining to the chest.

Thrombosis: clotting (thrombus) in a blood vessel or in the heart.

Tissue: anatomically a complex of similar cells and fibres forming a structure within an organ of the body.

Tracheotomy: operative opening into the trachea (windpipe) to bypass laryngeal or pharyngeal obstruction to the airway.

Traction: method by which fractures are re-aligned by applying linear force at right angles to the displacement of the bone fragments.

Tinnitus: ringing in the ears.

Tone: the tension present in a muscle at rest.

Tubal ligation: the tying off of the fallopian tubes; sterilisation procedure.

Valgus: outward deviation, *e.g.* genu valgum = knock-knee (the tibia deviates outwards from the knee).

Varicosity: dilatation of veins.

Varus: inward deviation, *e.g.* genu varum = bow-leg (the tibia deviates inwards from the knee).

Vasectomy: sterilisation of the male by division of each vas deferens which connects each testis to the urethra; the operation can be carried out under local anaesthesia and on an out-patient basis.

Vegetative state: a condition after severe brain injury, involving a return of wakefulness accompanied by an apparent total lack of cognitive function and awareness of the environment.

Vena Cava: either of the two main veins, conveying venous (blue) blood from the other veins to the heart.

Ventricles: interconnected cavities in the brain containing CSF, comprising the two lateral ventricles, and the third and fourth ventricles.

Ventricular dilatation: an increase in the size of the lateral ventricles of the brain.

Vertigo: unpleasant sensation of abnormal rotation.

Vestibular: concerned with the inner ear labyrinth and its cerebral connections, particularly in the brainstem.

425

Visual fields: area perceived by each eye.

Wechsler Adult Intelligence Scale (WAIS): a set of 11 tests designed to assess general intellectual ability in adults. Latest revision published in 1981, known as the WAIS-R.

Whiplash injury: injury to cervical structures when the head moves violently in one direction and then bounding back in the reverse direction, as when occupants in a vehicle without head restraints are struck from behind.

White matter: the part of the brain and spinal cord that contains myelinated fibres.

Xanth-: prefix meaning yellow.

INDEX

No-fault compensation, 1.10–1.24
accountability, 1.17–1.18
defensive medicine, 1.19
New Zealand, 1.13
Sweden, 1.14

Notes, medical, see **Medical records**

Nurses
carrying out orders, 4.58
employees of hospital, 4.58
operations, swabs, 4.63–4.67
vicarious liability for, 7.10

Obstetrics, 1.08, 3.109, 4.06, 4.11, 4.46, 4.60, 4.61, 4.85, 7.17
emergencies, 4.06
res ipsa loquitur, 3.109, 3.110

Omissions
failure to attend or treat, 4.04–4.08
no duty to act, 2.21, 2.65
sterilisation, no warning of risk of failure, 6.131–6.139

Operations, see also **Negligence, Standard of care**
burns sustained during, 4.62
delay, 4.61
hospital, vicariously liable, 4.57
private treatment, 4.57
resort to surgery, undue haste, 4.61
swabs, left in patient, 4.62–4.67
unfavourable result, 4.60

Pain and suffering, see **Damages**, non-pecuniary loss

Parents, see also **Children**
best interests test, 6.35
consent to treatment for child, 6.35–6.40
emergencies, 6.40
sterilisation of child, 6.37
unreasonable refusal of consent, 6.40

Patients with mental disorder
certification, negligent, 2.56–2.58, 4.103–4.106
consent to treatment, 6.42–6.56
abortion, 6.50
best interests, 6.53
detained patients, 6.49
for mental disorder, 6.42–6.49
necessity, 6.52
procedure, 6.55
sterilisation, 6.50
under Mental Health Act 1983, 6.42–6.49
control of patient, 4.89–4.102
harm to third parties, 2.59–2.68, 4.102
research, 6.114, 6.121
suicide risk, see also **Suicide**
known, 4.90–4.94
undiagnosed, 4.95–4.101
transplantation, 6.128–6.129

Pearson Commission, 1.09, 1.10, 1.11, 1.16, 1.17, 1.24, 2.03, 2.33, 2.36, 3.45, 3.91, 5.10, 8.01, 8.03, 8.52, 8.62, 8.89, 9.03, 9.17, 9.25, 9.29, 9.39, 9.40, 9.42, 9.44, 9.54

Pecuniary loss, see **Damages**

Periodic payments, see **Damages**

Personal injuries, see **Damages, Limitation of action**